学ぶ人は、
変えて
ゆく人だ。

目の前にある問題はもちろん、
人生の問いや、
社会の課題を自ら見つけ、
挑み続けるために、人は学ぶ。
「学び」で、
少しずつ世界は変えてゆける。
いつでも、どこでも、誰でも、
学ぶことができる世の中へ。

旺文社

2021年度第2回　英検1級　解答用紙

【注意事項】
① 解答にはHBの黒鉛筆（シャープペンシルも可）を使用し、解答を訂正する場合には消しゴムで完全に消してください。
② 解答用紙は絶対に汚したり折り曲げたり、所定以外のところへの記入はしないでください。

③ マーク例

良い例	悪い例
●	◐ ✗ ◕

これ以下の濃さのマークは読めません。

1 解答欄

問題番号	1	2	3	4
(1)	①	②	③	④
(2)	①	②	③	④
(3)	①	②	③	④
(4)	①	②	③	④
(5)	①	②	③	④
(6)	①	②	③	④
(7)	①	②	③	④
(8)	①	②	③	④
(9)	①	②	③	④
(10)	①	②	③	④
(11)	①	②	③	④
(12)	①	②	③	④
(13)	①	②	③	④
(14)	①	②	③	④
(15)	①	②	③	④
(16)	①	②	③	④
(17)	①	②	③	④
(18)	①	②	③	④
(19)	①	②	③	④
(20)	①	②	③	④
(21)	①	②	③	④
(22)	①	②	③	④
(23)	①	②	③	④
(24)	①	②	③	④
(25)	①	②	③	④

2 解答欄

問題番号	1	2	3	4
(26)	①	②	③	④
(27)	①	②	③	④
(28)	①	②	③	④
(29)	①	②	③	④
(30)	①	②	③	④
(31)	①	②	③	④

3 解答欄

問題番号	1	2	3	4
(32)	①	②	③	④
(33)	①	②	③	④
(34)	①	②	③	④
(35)	①	②	③	④
(36)	①	②	③	④
(37)	①	②	③	④
(38)	①	②	③	④
(39)	①	②	③	④
(40)	①	②	③	④
(41)	①	②	③	④

※筆記4の解答欄はこの裏にあります。

リスニング解答欄

	問題番号	1	2	3	4
Part 1	No.1	①	②	③	④
	No.2	①	②	③	④
	No.3	①	②	③	④
	No.4	①	②	③	④
	No.5	①	②	③	④
	No.6	①	②	③	④
	No.7	①	②	③	④
	No.8	①	②	③	④
	No.9	①	②	③	④
	No.10	①	②	③	④
Part 2 A	No.11	①	②	③	④
	No.12	①	②	③	④
B	No.13	①	②	③	④
	No.14	①	②	③	④
C	No.15	①	②	③	④
	No.16	①	②	③	④
D	No.17	①	②	③	④
	No.18	①	②	③	④
E	No.19	①	②	③	④
	No.20	①	②	③	④
Part 3 F	No.21	①	②	③	④
G	No.22	①	②	③	④
H	No.23	①	②	③	④
I	No.24	①	②	③	④
J	No.25	①	②	③	④
Part 4	No.26	①	②	③	④
	No.27	①	②	③	④

2021年度第2回
Web特典「自動採点サービス」対応
オンラインマークシート
※検定の回によって2次元コードが違います。
※筆記1～3，リスニングの採点ができます。
※ PCからも利用できます（本書 p.8 参照）。

※実際の解答用紙に似せていますが，デザイン・サイズは異なります。

- 指示事項を守り，文字は，はっきり分かりやすく書いてください。
- 太枠に囲まれた部分のみが採点の対象です。

4 English Composition

Write your English Composition in the space below.

2021年度第1回　英検1級　解答用紙

【注意事項】
① 解答にはHBの黒鉛筆（シャープペンシルも可）を使用し、解答を訂正する場合には消しゴムで完全に消してください。
② 解答用紙は絶対に汚したり折り曲げたり、所定以外のところへの記入はしないでください。
③ マーク例

良い例	悪い例
●	◐ ✕ ◯

 これ以下の濃さのマークは読めません。

1

問題番号	1	2	3	4
(1)	①	②	③	④
(2)	①	②	③	④
(3)	①	②	③	④
(4)	①	②	③	④
(5)	①	②	③	④
(6)	①	②	③	④
(7)	①	②	③	④
(8)	①	②	③	④
(9)	①	②	③	④
(10)	①	②	③	④
(11)	①	②	③	④
(12)	①	②	③	④
(13)	①	②	③	④
(14)	①	②	③	④
(15)	①	②	③	④
(16)	①	②	③	④
(17)	①	②	③	④
(18)	①	②	③	④
(19)	①	②	③	④
(20)	①	②	③	④
(21)	①	②	③	④
(22)	①	②	③	④
(23)	①	②	③	④
(24)	①	②	③	④
(25)	①	②	③	④

2

問題番号	1	2	3	4
(26)	①	②	③	④
(27)	①	②	③	④
(28)	①	②	③	④
(29)	①	②	③	④
(30)	①	②	③	④
(31)	①	②	③	④

3

問題番号	1	2	3	4
(32)	①	②	③	④
(33)	①	②	③	④
(34)	①	②	③	④
(35)	①	②	③	④
(36)	①	②	③	④
(37)	①	②	③	④
(38)	①	②	③	④
(39)	①	②	③	④
(40)	①	②	③	④
(41)	①	②	③	①

※筆記4の解答欄はこの裏にあります。

リスニング解答欄

問題番号	1	2	3	4
Part 1 No.1	①	②	③	④
No.2	①	②	③	④
No.3	①	②	③	④
No.4	①	②	③	④
No.5	①	②	③	④
No.6	①	②	③	④
No.7	①	②	③	④
No.8	①	②	③	④
No.9	①	②	③	④
No.10	①	②	③	④
Part 2 A No.11	①	②	③	④
No.12	①	②	③	④
B No.13	①	②	③	④
No.14	①	②	③	④
C No.15	①	②	③	④
No.16	①	②	③	④
D No.17	①	②	③	④
No.18	①	②	③	④
Part 3 E No.19	①	②	③	④
No.20	①	②	③	④
F No.21	①	②	③	④
G No.22	①	②	③	④
H No.23	①	②	③	④
I No.24	①	②	③	④
J No.25	①	②	③	④
Part 4 No.26	①	②	③	④
No.27	①	②	③	④

2021年度第1回
Web特典「自動採点サービス」対応
オンラインマークシート
※検定の回によって2次元コードが違います。
※筆記1〜3，リスニングの採点ができます。
※ PCからも利用できます（本書 p.8 参照）。

※実際の解答用紙に似せていますが，デザイン・サイズは異なります。

・指示事項を守り，文字は，はっきり分かりやすく書いてください。
・太枠に囲まれた部分のみが採点の対象です。

4 English Composition

Write your English Composition in the space below.

2020年度第3回　英検1級　解答用紙

【注意事項】
①解答にはHBの黒鉛筆（シャープペンシルも可）を使用し、解答を訂正する場合には消しゴムで完全に消してください。
②解答用紙は絶対に汚したり折り曲げたり、所定以外のところへの記入はしないでください。
③マーク例

良い例	悪い例

これ以下の濃さのマークは読めません。

解答欄 1

問題番号	1	2	3	4
(1)	①	②	③	④
(2)	①	②	③	④
(3)	①	②	③	④
(4)	①	②	③	④
(5)	①	②	③	④
(6)	①	②	③	④
(7)	①	②	③	④
(8)	①	②	③	④
(9)	①	②	③	④
(10)	①	②	③	④
(11)	①	②	③	④
(12)	①	②	③	④
(13)	①	②	③	④
(14)	①	②	③	④
(15)	①	②	③	④
(16)	①	②	③	④
(17)	①	②	③	④
(18)	①	②	③	④
(19)	①	②	③	④
(20)	①	②	③	④
(21)	①	②	③	④
(22)	①	②	③	④
(23)	①	②	③	④
(24)	①	②	③	④
(25)	①	②	③	④

解答欄 2

問題番号	1	2	3	4
(26)	①	②	③	④
(27)	①	②	③	④
(28)	①	②	③	④
(29)	①	②	③	④
(30)	①	②	③	④
(31)	①	②	③	④

解答欄 3

問題番号	1	2	3	4
(32)	①	②	③	④
(33)	①	②	③	④
(34)	①	②	③	④
(35)	①	②	③	④
(36)	①	②	③	④
(37)	①	②	③	④
(38)	①	②	③	④
(39)	①	②	③	④
(40)	①	②	③	④
(11)	①	②	③	④

※筆記4の解答欄はこの裏にあります。

リスニング解答欄

問題番号	1	2	3	4
Part 1 No.1	①	②	③	④
No.2	①	②	③	④
No.3	①	②	③	④
No.4	①	②	③	④
No.5	①	②	③	④
No.6	①	②	③	④
No.7	①	②	③	④
No.8	①	②	③	④
No.9	①	②	③	④
No.10	①	②	③	④
Part 2 A No.11	①	②	③	④
No.12	①	②	③	④
B No.13	①	②	③	④
No.14	①	②	③	④
C No.15	①	②	③	④
No.16	①	②	③	④
D No.17	①	②	③	④
No.18	①	②	③	④
E No.19	①	②	③	④
No.20	①	②	③	④
Part 3 F No.21	①	②	③	④
G No.22	①	②	③	④
H No.23	①	②	③	④
I No.24	①	②	③	④
J No.25	①	②	③	④
Part 4 No.26	①	②	③	④
No.27	①	②	③	④

2020年度第3回 Web特典「自動採点サービス」対応 オンラインマークシート
※検定の回によって2次元コードが違います。
※筆記1〜3，リスニングの採点ができます。
※ PCからも利用できます（本書 p.8 参照）。

※実際の解答用紙に似せていますが，デザイン・サイズは異なります。

切り取り線

- 指示事項を守り，文字は，はっきり分かりやすく書いてください。
- 太枠に囲まれた部分のみが採点の対象です。

4 English Composition

Write your English Composition in the space below.

2020年度第2回 英検1級 解答用紙

【注意事項】
① 解答にはHBの黒鉛筆（シャープペンシルも可）を使用し、解答を訂正する場合には消しゴムで完全に消してください。
② 解答用紙は絶対に汚したり折り曲げたり、所定以外のところへの記入はしないでください。
③ マーク例

良い例	悪い例
●	◐ ✖ ◯

これ以下の濃さのマークは読めません。

解答欄 (1)

問題番号	1	2	3	4
(1)	①	②	③	④
(2)	①	②	③	④
(3)	①	②	③	④
(4)	①	②	③	④
(5)	①	②	③	④
(6)	①	②	③	④
(7)	①	②	③	④
(8)	①	②	③	④
(9)	①	②	③	④
(10)	①	②	③	④
(11)	①	②	③	④
(12)	①	②	③	④
(13)	①	②	③	④
(14)	①	②	③	④
(15)	①	②	③	④
(16)	①	②	③	④
(17)	①	②	③	④
(18)	①	②	③	④
(19)	①	②	③	④
(20)	①	②	③	④
(21)	①	②	③	④
(22)	①	②	③	④
(23)	①	②	③	④
(24)	①	②	③	④
(25)	①	②	③	④

解答欄 (2)

問題番号	1	2	3	4
(26)	①	②	③	④
(27)	①	②	③	④
(28)	①	②	③	④
(29)	①	②	③	④
(30)	①	②	③	④
(31)	①	②	③	④

解答欄 (3)

問題番号	1	2	3	4
(32)	①	②	③	④
(33)	①	②	③	④
(34)	①	②	③	④
(35)	①	②	③	④
(36)	①	②	③	④
(37)	①	②	③	④
(38)	①	②	③	④
(39)	①	②	③	④
(40)	①	②	③	④
(41)	①	②	③	④

※筆記4の解答欄はこの裏にあります。

リスニング解答欄

問題番号	1	2	3	4
Part 1 No.1	①	②	③	④
No.2	①	②	③	④
No.3	①	②	③	④
No.4	①	②	③	④
No.5	①	②	③	④
No.6	①	②	③	④
No.7	①	②	③	④
No.8	①	②	③	④
No.9	①	②	③	④
No.10	①	②	③	④
Part 2 A No.11	①	②	③	④
No.12	①	②	③	④
B No.13	①	②	③	④
No.14	①	②	③	④
C No.15	①	②	③	④
No.16	①	②	③	④
D No.17	①	②	③	④
No.18	①	②	③	④
E No.19	①	②	③	④
No.20	①	②	③	④
Part 3 F No.21	①	②	③	④
G No.22	①	②	③	④
H No.23	①	②	③	④
I No.24	①	②	③	④
J No.25	①	②	③	④
Part 4 No.26	①	②	③	④
No.27	①	②	③	④

2020年度第2回　Web特典「自動採点サービス」対応 オンラインマークシート

※検定の回によって2次元コードが違います。
※筆記1〜3，リスニングの採点ができます。
※PCからも利用できます（本書 p.8 参照）。

※実際の解答用紙に似せていますが，デザイン・サイズは異なります。

- 指示事項を守り，文字は，はっきり分かりやすく書いてください。
- 太枠に囲まれた部分のみが採点の対象です。

4 English Composition

Write your English Composition in the space below.

2020年度第1回　英検1級　解答用紙

【注意事項】
① 解答にはHBの黒鉛筆（シャープペンシルも可）を使用し、解答を訂正する場合には消しゴムで完全に消してください。
② 解答用紙は絶対に汚したり折り曲げたり、所定以外のところへの記入はしないでください。

③ マーク例

良い例	悪い例
●	◐ ✗ ◉

 これ以下の濃さのマークは読めません。

1

問題番号	1	2	3	4
(1)	①	②	③	④
(2)	①	②	③	④
(3)	①	②	③	④
(4)	①	②	③	④
(5)	①	②	③	④
(6)	①	②	③	④
(7)	①	②	③	④
(8)	①	②	③	④
(9)	①	②	③	④
(10)	①	②	③	④
(11)	①	②	③	④
(12)	①	②	③	④
(13)	①	②	③	④
(14)	①	②	③	④
(15)	①	②	③	④
(16)	①	②	③	④
(17)	①	②	③	④
(18)	①	②	③	④
(19)	①	②	③	④
(20)	①	②	③	④
(21)	①	②	③	④
(22)	①	②	③	④
(23)	①	②	③	④
(24)	①	②	③	④
(25)	①	②	③	④

2

問題番号	1	2	3	4
(26)	①	②	③	④
(27)	①	②	③	④
(28)	①	②	③	④
(29)	①	②	③	④
(30)	①	②	③	④
(31)	①	②	③	④

3

問題番号	1	2	3	4
(32)	①	②	③	④
(33)	①	②	③	④
(34)	①	②	③	④
(35)	①	②	③	④
(36)	①	②	③	④
(37)	①	②	③	④
(38)	①	②	③	④
(39)	①	②	③	④
(40)	①	②	③	④
(41)	①	②	③	④

※筆記4の解答欄はこの裏にあります。

リスニング解答欄

問題番号		1	2	3	4
Part 1	No.1	①	②	③	④
	No.2	①	②	③	④
	No.3	①	②	③	④
	No.4	①	②	③	④
	No.5	①	②	③	④
	No.6	①	②	③	④
	No.7	①	②	③	④
	No.8	①	②	③	④
	No.9	①	②	③	④
	No.10	①	②	③	④
Part 2 A	No.11	①	②	③	④
	No.12	①	②	③	④
B	No.13	①	②	③	④
	No.14	①	②	③	④
C	No.15	①	②	③	④
	No.16	①	②	③	④
D	No.17	①	②	③	④
	No.18	①	②	③	④
E	No.19	①	②	③	④
	No.20	①	②	③	④
Part 3 F	No.21	①	②	③	④
G	No.22	①	②	③	④
H	No.23	①	②	③	④
I	No.24	①	②	③	④
J	No.25	①	②	③	④
Part 4	No.26	①	②	③	④
	No.27	①	②	③	④

2020年度第1回　Web特典「自動採点サービス」対応
オンラインマークシート

※検定の回によって2次元コードが違います。
※筆記1～3、リスニングの採点ができます。
※PCからも利用できます（本書p.8参照）。

※実際の解答用紙に似ていますが、デザイン・サイズは異なります。

- 指示事項を守り，文字は，はっきり分かりやすく書いてください。
- 太枠に囲まれた部分のみが採点の対象です。

4 English Composition

Write your English Composition in the space below.

2019年度第3回　英検1級　解答用紙

[注意事項]
① 解答にはHBの黒鉛筆（シャープペンシルも可）を使用し、解答を訂正する場合には消しゴムで完全に消してください。
② 解答用紙は絶対に汚したり折り曲げたり、所定以外のところへの記入はしないでください。

③ マーク例

これ以下の濃さのマークは読めません。

1 解答欄

問題番号	1	2	3	4
(1)	①	②	③	④
(2)	①	②	③	④
(3)	①	②	③	④
(4)	①	②	③	④
(5)	①	②	③	④
(6)	①	②	③	④
(7)	①	②	③	④
(8)	①	②	③	④
(9)	①	②	③	④
(10)	①	②	③	④
(11)	①	②	③	④
(12)	①	②	③	④
(13)	①	②	③	④
(14)	①	②	③	④
(15)	①	②	③	④
(16)	①	②	③	④
(17)	①	②	③	④
(18)	①	②	③	④
(19)	①	②	③	④
(20)	①	②	③	④
(21)	①	②	③	④
(22)	①	②	③	④
(23)	①	②	③	④
(24)	①	②	③	④
(25)	①	②	③	④

2 解答欄

問題番号	1	2	3	4
(26)	①	②	③	④
(27)	①	②	③	④
(28)	①	②	③	④
(29)	①	②	③	④
(30)	①	②	③	④
(31)	①	②	③	④

3 解答欄

問題番号	1	2	3	4
(32)	①	②	③	④
(33)	①	②	③	④
(34)	①	②	③	④
(35)	①	②	③	④
(36)	①	②	③	④
(37)	①	②	③	④
(38)	①	②	③	④
(39)	①	②	③	④
(40)	①	②	③	④
(41)	①	②	③	④

※筆記4の解答欄はこの裏にあります。

リスニング解答欄

問題番号	1	2	3	4
Part 1 No.1	①	②	③	④
No.2	①	②	③	④
No.3	①	②	③	④
No.4	①	②	③	④
No.5	①	②	③	④
No.6	①	②	③	④
No.7	①	②	③	④
No.8	①	②	③	④
No.9	①	②	③	④
No.10	①	②	③	④
Part 2 A No.11	①	②	③	④
No.12	①	②	③	④
B No.13	①	②	③	④
No.14	①	②	③	④
C No.15	①	②	③	④
No.16	①	②	③	④
D No.17	①	②	③	④
No.18	①	②	③	④
E No.19	①	②	③	④
No.20	①	②	③	④
Part 3 F No.21	①	②	③	④
G No.22	①	②	③	④
H No.23	①	②	③	④
I No.24	①	②	③	④
J No.25	①	②	③	④
Part 4 No.26	①	②	③	④
No.27	①	②	③	④

2019年度第3回　Web特典「自動採点サービス」対応 オンラインマークシート

※検定の回によって2次元コードが違います。
※筆記1～3、リスニングの採点ができます。
※PCからも利用できます（本書 p.8 参照）。

※実際の解答用紙に似せていますが、デザイン・サイズは異なります。

切り取り線

- 指示事項を守り，文字は，はっきり分かりやすく書いてください。
- 太枠に囲まれた部分のみが採点の対象です。

4 English Composition

Write your English Composition in the space below.

Introduction

はじめに

実用英語技能検定（英検®）は，年間受験者数360万人（英検IBA，英検Jr.との総数）の小学生から社会人まで，幅広い層が受験する国内最大級の資格試験で，1963年の第1回検定からの累計では1億人を超える人々が受験しています。英検®は，コミュニケーションに欠かすことのできない4技能をバランスよく測定することを目的としており，英検®の受験によってご自身の英語力を把握できるだけでなく，進学・就職・留学などの場面で多くのチャンスを手に入れることにつながります。

この『全問題集シリーズ』は，英語を学ぶ皆さまを応援する気持ちを込めて刊行しました。本書は，2021年度第2回検定を含む6回分の過去問を，皆さまの理解が深まるよう，日本語訳や詳しい解説を加えて収録しています。

本書が皆さまの英検合格の足がかりとなり，さらには国際社会で活躍できるような生きた英語を身につけるきっかけとなることを願っています。

最後に，本書を刊行するにあたり多大なご尽力をいただきました松井こずえ先生，鴇﨑敏彦先生，浅場眞紀子先生，Ed Jacob先生に深く感謝の意を表します。

2022年　春

もくじ
Contents

- 本書の使い方 ……………………………………… 3
- 音声について ……………………………………… 4
- Web特典について ………………………………… 7
- 自動採点サービスの利用方法 …………………… 8
- 英検インフォメーション ………………………… 10
  試験内容／英検の種類／合否判定方法／英検（従来型）受験情報―2022年度試験日程・申込方法
- 2021年度の傾向と攻略ポイント ……………… 14
- 二次試験・面接の流れ …………………………… 16

2021年度
- 第2回検定（筆記・リスニング・面接） …… 17
- 第1回検定（筆記・リスニング・面接） …… 41

2020年度
- 第3回検定（筆記・リスニング・面接） …… 65
- 第2回検定（筆記・リスニング・面接） …… 89
- 第1回検定（筆記・リスニング・面接） …… 113

2019年度
- 第3回検定（筆記・リスニング・面接） …… 137

執　筆：松井こずえ（アルカディア・コミュニケーションズ），鴇﨑敏彦（日本獣医生命科学大学），
　　　　浅場眞紀子（Q-Leap），Ed Jacob
編集協力：斉藤 敦，鹿島由紀子，渡邉真理子，Jason A. Chau，株式会社鷗来堂
録　音：ユニバ合同会社
デザイン：林 慎一郎（及川真咲デザイン事務所）
組版・データ作成協力：幸和印刷株式会社

本書の使い方

ここでは，本書の過去問および特典についての活用法の一例を紹介します。

本書の内容

- 過去問 6回分
- 英検インフォメーション (p.10-13)
- 2021年度の傾向と攻略ポイント (p.14-15)
- 二次試験・面接の流れ (p.16)
- Web特典 (p.7-9)

本書の使い方

一次試験対策

情報収集・傾向把握
・英検インフォメーション
・2021年度の傾向と攻略ポイント

過去問にチャレンジ
・2021年度第2回一次試験
・2021年度第1回一次試験
・2020年度第3回一次試験
・2020年度第2回一次試験
・2020年度第1回一次試験
・2019年度第3回一次試験
※【Web特典】自動採点サービスの活用

二次試験対策

情報収集・傾向把握
・二次試験・面接の流れ
・【Web特典】
　面接模範例

過去問にチャレンジ
・2021年度第2回二次試験
・2021年度第1回二次試験
・2020年度第3回二次試験
・2020年度第2回二次試験
・2020年度第1回二次試験
・2019年度第3回二次試験

過去問の取り組み方

1セット目 【本番モード】
本番の試験と同じように，制限時間を設けて取り組みましょう。どの問題形式に時間がかかりすぎているか，正答率が低いかなど，今のあなたの実力を把握しましょう。
「自動採点サービス」を活用して，答え合わせをスムーズに行いましょう。

2〜5セット目 【学習モード】
制限時間をなくし，解けるまで取り組みましょう。
リスニングは音声を繰り返し聞いて解答を導き出してもかまいません。すべての問題に正解できるまで見直します。

6セット目 【仕上げモード】
試験直前の仕上げに利用しましょう。時間を計って本番のつもりで取り組みます。
これまでに取り組んだ6セットの過去問で間違えた問題の解説を本番試験の前にもう一度見直しましょう。

音声について

一次試験・リスニングと二次試験・面接の音声を聞くことができます。本書とともに使い，効果的なリスニング・面接対策をしましょう。

収録内容と特長

一次試験・リスニング

本番の試験の音声を収録	➡	スピードをつかめる！
解答時間は本番通り10秒間	➡	解答時間に慣れる！
収録されている英文は，別冊解答に掲載	➡	聞き取れない箇所を確認できる！

二次試験・面接（スピーキング）

| 独自に制作したモデルスピーチを収録 | ➡ | 模範解答が確認できる！ |
| モデルスピーチは，別冊解答に掲載 | ➡ | 聞き取れない箇所を確認できる！ |

3つの方法で音声が聞けます！

① 公式アプリ「英語の友」(iOS/Android) でお手軽再生

リスニング力を強化する機能満載

- 再生速度変換（0.5～2.0倍速）
- お気に入り機能（絞込み学習）
- オフライン再生
- バックグラウンド再生
- 試験日カウントダウン

※画像はイメージです。

［ご利用方法］

1. 「英語の友」公式サイトより，アプリをインストール
   https://eigonotomo.com/　［英語の友 🔍］
   （右の2次元コードから読み込めます）

2. アプリ内のライブラリよりご購入いただいた書籍を選び，「追加」ボタンを押してください

3. パスワードを入力すると，音声がダウンロードできます
   [パスワード：ebwats] ※すべて半角アルファベット小文字

※本アプリの機能の一部は有料ですが，本書の音声は無料でお聞きいただけます。
※詳しいご利用方法は「英語の友」公式サイト，あるいはアプリ内ヘルプをご参照ください。
※2022年2月24日から2023年8月31日までご利用いただけます。
※本サービスは，上記ご利用期間内でも予告なく終了することがあります。

CDをご希望の方は，別売「2022年度版 英検1級 過去6回全問題集 CD」（本体価格3,300円+税）をご利用ください。

持ち運びに便利な小冊子とCD4枚付き。CDプレーヤーで通して聞くと，本番と同じような環境で練習できます。　※収録箇所は，本書で **CD 1 ①～⑪** のように表示しています。

② パソコンで音声データダウンロード（MP3）

［ご利用方法］

1 Web特典にアクセス　詳細は，p.7をご覧ください。

2 「一次試験［二次試験］音声データダウンロード」から
　聞きたい検定の回を選択してダウンロード

※音声ファイルはzip形式にまとめられた形でダウンロードされます。
※音声の再生にはMP3を再生できる機器などが必要です。ご使用機器，音声再生ソフト等に関する技術的なご質問は，ハードメーカーもしくはソフトメーカーにお願いいたします。

③ スマートフォン・タブレットでストリーミング再生

［ご利用方法］

1 自動採点サービスにアクセス　詳細は，p.8をご覧ください。
　（右の2次元コードから読み込めます）

2 聞きたい検定の回を選び，
　リスニングテストの音声再生ボタンを押す

※自動採点サービスは一次試験に対応していますので，一次試験・リスニングの音声のみお聞きいただけます。（二次試験・面接の音声をお聞きになりたい方は，①リスニングアプリ「英語の友」，②音声データダウンロードをご利用ください）
※音声再生中に音声を止めたい場合は，停止ボタンを押してください。
※個別に問題を再生したい場合は，問題番号を選んでから再生ボタンを押してください。
※音声の再生には多くの通信量が必要となりますので，Wi-Fi環境でのご利用をおすすめいたします。

Web特典について

購入者限定の「Web特典」を，みなさんの英検合格にお役立てください。

ご利用可能期間	2022年2月24日～2023年8月31日 ※本サービスは予告なく変更，終了することがあります。	
アクセス方法	スマートフォン タブレット	右の2次元コードを読み込むと，パスワードなしでアクセスできます！
	PC スマートフォン タブレット 共通	1. Web特典（以下のURL）にアクセスします。 https://eiken.obunsha.co.jp/1q/ 2. 本書を選択し，以下のパスワードを入力します。 **ebwats** ※すべて半角アルファベット小文字

〈特典内容〉

(1) 自動採点サービス
リーディング（筆記1～3），リスニング（Part1～4）の自動採点ができます。詳細はp.8を参照してください。

(2) 解答用紙
本番にそっくりの解答用紙が印刷できるので，何度でも過去問にチャレンジすることができます。

(3) 音声データのダウンロード
一次試験リスニング・二次試験面接の音声データ（MP3）を無料でダウンロードできます。

(4) 1級面接対策
【面接模範例】入室から退室までの模範応答例を見ることができます。各チェックポイントで，受験上の注意点やアドバイスを確認しておきましょう。
【TOPIC CARD】面接模範例で使用しているトピックカードです。印刷して，実際の面接の練習に使ってください。

自動採点サービスの利用方法

正答率や合格ラインとの距離，間違えた問題などの確認ができるサービスです。

ご利用可能期間	2022年2月24日～2023年8月31日 ※本サービスは予告なく変更，終了することがあります。	
アクセス方法	スマートフォンタブレット	右の2次元コードを読み込んでアクセスし，採点する検定の回を選択してください。
	PCスマートフォンタブレット共通	p.7の手順で「Web特典」にアクセスし，「自動採点サービスを使う」を選択してご利用ください。

［ご利用方法］

1 オンラインマークシートにアクセスします

Web特典の「自動採点サービスを使う」から，採点したい検定回を選択するか，各回のマークシートおよび問題編の各回とびらの2次元コードからアクセスします。

2 「問題をはじめる」ボタンを押して筆記試験を始めます

ボタンを押すとタイマーが動き出します。制限時間内に解答できるよう，解答時間を意識して取り組みましょう。

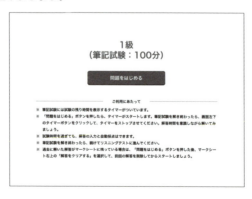

8

3 筆記試験を解答し終わったら、タイマーボタン  を押して
　 タイマーをストップさせます

4 リスニングテストは画面下にある音声再生ボタンを押して
　 音声を再生し、問題に取り組みましょう
　 一度再生ボタンを押したら、最後の問題まで自動的に
　 進んでいきます。

5 リスニングテストが終了したら、
　「答え合わせ」ボタンを押して答え合わせをします

採点結果の見方

タブの選択で【あなたの成績】と【問題ごとの正誤】が切り替えられます。

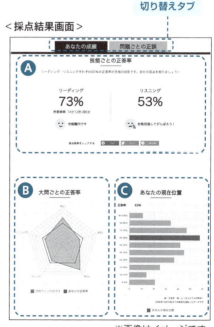

【あなたの成績】
Ⓐ 技能ごとの正答率が表示されます。1級の合格の目安、正答率70％を目指しましょう。
Ⓑ 大問ごとの正答率が表示されます。合格ラインを下回る大問は、対策に力を入れましょう。
Ⓒ 採点サービス利用者の中でのあなたの現在位置が示されます。

【問題ごとの正誤】
各問題のあなたの解答と正解が表示されます。間違っている問題については色で示されますので、別冊解答の解説を見直しましょう。

※画像はイメージです。

9

英検® Information インフォメーション

出典：英検ウェブサイト

英検1級について

1級では，「広く社会生活で求められる英語を十分理解し，また使用できる」ことが求められます。
転職や就職，単位認定，海外留学や入試など，多方面で幅広く活用される資格です。
目安としては「大学上級程度」です。

試験内容

一次試験 筆記・リスニング

主な場面・状況	家庭・学校・職場・地域（各種店舗・公共施設を含む）・電話・アナウンス・講義など
主な話題	社会生活一般・芸術・文化・歴史・教育・科学・自然・環境・医療・テクノロジー・ビジネス・政治など

筆記試験 100分

問題	形式・課題詳細	問題数	満点スコア
1	文脈に合う適切な語句を補う。	25問	850
2	パッセージの空所に文脈に合う適切な語句を補う。	6問	
3	パッセージの内容に関する質問に答える。	10問	
4	指定されたトピックについての英作文を書く。（200〜240語）	1問	850

リスニング 約35分　放送回数/1回

問題	形式・課題詳細	問題数	満点スコア
Part 1	会話の内容に関する質問に答える。	10問	850
Part 2	パッセージの内容に関する質問に答える。	10問	
Part 3	Real-Life形式の放送内容に関する質問に答える。	5問	
Part 4	インタビューの内容に関する質問に答える。	2問	

2021年12月現在の情報を掲載しています。試験に関する情報は変更になる可能性がありますので，受験の際は必ず英検ウェブサイトをご確認ください。

二次試験　面接形式のスピーキングテスト

主な場面・題材	社会性の高い幅広い分野の話題
過去の出題例	科学の発展は常に有益か・芸術への財政的支援増加の是非・世界経済における日本の役割・選挙権の行使を義務化するべきか・遺伝子組み換え食品の安全性・公共の場における治安改善の必要性など

スピーキング　約10分

面接の構成	形式・課題詳細	満点スコア
自由会話	面接委員と簡単な日常会話を行う。	
スピーチ	与えられた5つのトピックの中から1つ選び，スピーチを行う。(2分間)	850
Q&A	スピーチの内容やトピックに関連した質問に答える。	

英検®の種類

英検には，実施方式が異なる複数の試験があります。実施時期や受験上の配慮など，自分に合った方式を選択しましょう。なお，従来型の英検とその他の英検の問題形式，難易度，級認定，合格証明書発行，英検CSEスコア取得等はすべて同じです。

▶英検®(従来型)
紙の問題冊子を見て解答用紙に解答。二次試験を受験するためには，一次試験に合格する必要があります。

▶英検S-CBT
コンピュータを使って受験。1日で4技能を受験することができ，申込時に会場・日程・ライティングの解答方式が選べます。原則，毎週土日に実施されています（級や地域により毎週実施でない場合があります）。ほかの実施方式で取得した一次試験免除の資格も申請可能です。

▶英検S-Interview
点字や吃音等，CBT方式では対応が難しい受験上の配慮が必要な方のみが受験可能。

受験する級によって選択できる方式が異なります。各方式の詳細および最新情報は英検ウェブサイト（https://www.eiken.or.jp/eiken/）をご確認ください。

合否判定方法

統計的に算出される英検CSEスコアに基づいて合否判定されます。Reading, Writing, Listening, Speakingの4技能が均等に評価され、合格基準スコアは固定されています。

▶ 技能別にスコアが算出される！

技能	試験形式	満点スコア	合格基準スコア
Reading（読む）	一次試験（筆記1～3）	850	2028
Writing（書く）	一次試験（筆記4）	850	
Listening（聞く）	一次試験（リスニング）	850	
Speaking（話す）	二次試験（面接）	850	602

- 一次試験の合否は、Reading, Writing, Listeningの技能別にスコアが算出され、それを合算して判定されます。
- 二次試験の合否は、Speakingのみで判定されます。

▶ 合格するためには、技能のバランスが重要！

英検CSEスコアでは、技能ごとに問題数は異なりますが、スコアを均等に配分しているため、各技能のバランスが重要となります。なお、正答数の目安を提示することはできませんが、2016年度第1回一次試験では、1級、準1級は各技能での正答率が7割程度、2級以下は各技能6割程度の正答率の受験者の多くが合格されています。

▶ 英検CSEスコアは国際標準規格CEFRにも対応している！

CEFRとは、Common European Framework of Reference for Languages の略。語学のコミュニケーション能力別のレベルを示す国際標準規格。欧米で幅広く導入され、6つのレベルが設定されています。
4技能の英検CSEスコアの合計「4技能総合スコア」と級ごとのCEFR算出範囲に基づいた「4技能総合CEFR」が成績表に表示されます。

CEFR	英検CSEスコア	実用英語技能検定　各級の合格スコア
C2	4000～3300	1級 満点3400
C1	3299～2600	準1級 満点3000／合格スコア 2630
B2	2599～2300	2級 満点2600／C1扱い
B1	2299～1950	準2級 満点2400／B2扱い／合格スコア 2304
A2	1949～1700	3級 満点2200／B1扱い／合格スコア 1980
A1	1699～1400	A2扱い／合格スコア 1728
	1399～0	A1扱い／合格スコア 1456／CEFR算出範囲外

※ 4級・5級は4技能を測定していないため「4技能総合CEFR」の対象外。
※ 詳しくは英検ウェブサイトをご覧ください。

英検®(従来型)受験情報

※「従来型・本会場」以外の実施方式については，試験日程・申込方法が異なりますので，英検ウェブサイトをご覧ください。
※ 受験情報は変更になる場合があります。

◉ 2022年度 試験日程

第1回
- 申込受付：4月1日 ▶ 5月6日
- 一次試験：6月5日(日)
- 二次試験：A 7月3日(日) / C 7月17日(日)

第2回
- 申込受付：8月1日 ▶ 9月8日
- 一次試験：10月9日(日)
- 二次試験：A 11月6日(日) / C 11月23日(水・祝)

第3回
- 申込受付：11月1日 ▶ 12月15日
- 一次試験：1月22日(日) 2023年
- 二次試験：A 2月19日(日) 2023年 / C 3月5日(日) 2023年

※ 上記以外の日程でも受験できる可能性があります。
※ 二次試験にはA日程，B日程(2〜3級)，C日程(1級，準1級)があり，受験級などの条件により指定されます。
※ 詳しくは英検ウェブサイトをご覧ください。

◉ 申込方法

団体受験	学校や塾などで申し込みをする団体受験もあります。詳しくは先生にお尋ねください。
個人受験	インターネット申込・コンビニ申込・英検特約書店申込のいずれかの方法で申し込みができます。詳しくは英検ウェブサイトをご覧ください。

お問い合わせ先

英検サービスセンター
TEL. 03-3266-8311
(月)〜(金) 9:30〜17:00
(祝日・年末年始を除く)

英検ウェブサイト
www.eiken.or.jp/eiken/
試験についての詳しい情報を見たり，入試等で英検を活用している学校の検索をすることができます。

2021年度の傾向と攻略ポイント

2021年度第1回検定と第2回検定を分析し、出題傾向と攻略ポイントをまとめました。1級の合格に必要な正答率は7割程度と予測されます。正答率が7割を切った大問は苦手な分野だと考えましょう。

一次試験　筆記（100分）

1　短文の語句空所補充
問題数 **25**問　めやす **15**分

傾向　20〜30語程度の短文中の空所に入るべき語句の4択問題が25問。(1)〜(21)が単語、(22)〜(25)が熟語の問題。単語は主に動詞、形容詞、名詞だが、副詞も毎回1問ずつ出題されている。熟語は2〜3語からなる句動詞。

攻略ポイント　素早く状況を理解し、適切な語を選ぶ。高難度の語句が出題されるので、語彙力強化は必須。派生語や類語、語源の知識を利用した学習が効率的だろう。

2　長文の語句空所補充
問題数 **6**問　めやす **15**分

傾向　3段落からなる350語程度の長文2本で、文中の空所に入るべき語句を4つの選択肢から選ぶ問題が各3問（計6問）。

攻略ポイント　全体の構成を考えながら話の流れをしっかり追うことが最重要。特に接続表現が順接か逆接か、代名詞が何を指すか、に注意して読み進め、筋が通る選択肢を選ぼう。

3　長文の内容一致選択
問題数 **10**問　めやす **40**分

傾向　3〜4段落からなる500語程度の長文2本と、7〜8段落の800語程度の長文の計3本で、4つの選択肢から選ぶ内容一致問題が計10問。

攻略ポイント　先に設問を見てその答えを探しながら本文を読み進めたい。正解は本文とは違う表現を使って言い換えられているので、的確な読解力が必要となる。

4　英作文
問題数 **1**問　めやす **25**分

傾向　社会的問題に関する200〜240語の英作文。3つの理由を提示し、「序論」「本論」「結論」で構成することが求められる。出題は、第1回が「経済制裁は役に立つ外交政策ツールか」、第2回が「個人のプライバシーは現代世界において守ることができるか」。

攻略ポイント　明確な論理の展開ができるかを意識して、3つの理由とそれらの補足説明・例示を素早く決めてから、書き始めよう。時間を計って実際に書く練習が非常に有効。

一次試験 リスニング（約35分）

Part 1 Dialogues　　　　問題数 10問

傾向　ダイアログに関する内容一致の4択問題が10問。家庭や職場など，日常のさまざまな場面における男女間の会話が扱われる（(10)のみ3人）。

攻略ポイント　日常会話で使われる句動詞や言い回しが出てくるので慣れておきたい。暗示的な発言の真意を問う設問が多く出題されるので，流れを正確に把握して聞く。

Part 2 Passages　　　　問題数 10問

傾向　短い説明文が5本放送され，それぞれについて内容一致の4択問題が2問ずつ，計10問出題される。内容は学術的なものが多い。

攻略ポイント　最初に読まれるタイトルは内容を予測する上で重要な情報。専門用語や固有名詞が出てきても説明されるか文脈からわかる場合が多いので，慌てずに集中して聞く。

Part 3 Real-Life　　　　問題数 5問

傾向　実生活におけるアナウンスや指示文などが放送され，問題用紙に印刷されている状況（Situation）に合致する内容を選ぶ問題が5問。

攻略ポイント　最初に設けられる10秒間でSituationとQuestionを素早く正確に把握することが最重要。音声が流れたら，状況に合った内容に的を絞って聞き取る。

Part 4 Interview　　　　問題数 2問

傾向　3分〜3分半程度のインタビューが放送され，内容一致の4択問題2問に答える。質問は主にゲストの仕事に関するもの。

攻略ポイント　インタビューの直前にされるゲストの説明を聞き逃さないこと。聞き手からの質問は4つ程度。質問とその応答のポイントを整理して聞く。応答は長めなので適宜メモを取りたい。

 二次試験　面接（約10分）

二次試験では5つのトピックが提示され，1分間で1つを選び準備をして，2分間のスピーチを行う。トピックは社会，政治経済，教育，科学など広い分野にわたる。本年度も，「遺伝子工学の展望」や「国家間の技術格差」など，さまざまな話題が取り上げられた。またどちらの回でも，「インターネット上の情報の量は多いか少ないか」「オンラインメディアは従来の印刷ジャーナリズムを破壊しているか」と情報に関するトピックが出題された。日ごろから問題意識を持ってニュースを読み，国内および国際問題に対して自分の意見をまとめてその根拠となる情報を集め，英語で伝える練習をしておこう。

二次試験・面接の流れ

(1) 入室

係員の指示に従い，面接室に入ります。面接カードを手渡し，指示に従って，着席しましょう。

(2) 氏名の確認と日常会話

面接委員があなたの氏名を確認します。その後，簡単な日常会話をしてから試験開始です。

(3) トピックカードの受け取りとスピーチの考慮

5つのトピックが書かれたトピックカードを受け取ります。1分間でトピックを1つ選び，スピーチの内容を考えます。メモを取ることはできません。

※トピックカードには複数の種類があり，面接委員によっていずれか1枚が手渡されます。本書では英検協会から提供を受けたもののみ掲載しています。

(4) スピーチ (2分間)

面接委員の指示に従い，スピーチをします。スピーチが終わる前に2分が経過してしまった場合は，言いかけていたセンテンスのみ，言い終えることが許可されます。

(5) Q & A (4分間)

スピーチの内容やトピックに関する質疑応答が行われます。質問は，2名の面接委員のそれぞれからされます。

(6) カード返却と退室

試験が終了したら，トピックカードを面接委員に返却し，あいさつをして退室しましょう。

2021-2

Grade 1

一次試験　2021.10.10実施
二次試験　A日程　2021.11.7実施
　　　　　C日程　2021.11.23実施

試験時間

筆記：100分
リスニング：約35分

一次試験・筆記　　　　　p.18〜32
一次試験・リスニング　　p.33〜39
二次試験・面接　　　　　p.40

＊解答・解説は別冊p.5〜56にあります。
＊面接の流れは本書p.16にあります。

2021年度第2回

**Web特典「自動採点サービス」対応
オンラインマークシート**

※検定の回によって2次元コードが違います。
※筆記1〜3，リスニングの採点ができます。
※PCからも利用できます（本書p.8参照）。

一次試験
筆記

1 To complete each item, choose the best word or phrase from among the four choices. Then, on your answer sheet, find the number of the question and mark your answer.

(1) The ancient document was written in a script that for years no one could (   ). Then, finally, a brilliant young scholar worked out its meaning.
1 slander **2** dawdle **3** pledge **4** decipher

(2) After the referee made several serious mistakes during the game, fans showed their (   ) by booing and shouting at him.
1 infamy **2** clatter **3** splendor **4** disdain

(3) Gold is one of the most (   ) metals. This quality allows it to be shaped into many different forms and is one reason it is in such high demand.
1 bombastic **2** malleable **3** parched **4** sordid

(4) The CEO said his company's success throughout the years was a clear (   ) to the wisdom of the policies of the company's past leaders.
1 prospectus **2** abrasion **3** testament **4** reprisal

(5) During his first term, Governor Smith made many (   ). When he tried to get reelected, they supported his opponent, who easily won the election.
1 hermits **2** prodigies **3** adversaries **4** protégés

(6) Aid agencies in the drought-affected region did their best to make sure emergency supplies were distributed (   ) to all citizens in need.
1 spuriously **2** illicitly **3** radiantly **4** equitably

(7) As the coal strike spread and energy shortages became common, a number of industries found themselves in an increasingly (   ) condition.
1 crass **2** acrid **3** dire **4** trite

(8) *A:* Your garden looks (   ). How do you keep it so neat and tidy?
B: To tell the truth, we hired a gardener to look after it.
1 immaculate **2** warped **3** intangible **4** vulgar

(9) In 1993, the entire Internet was made up of just 130 websites. They have continued to (   ), however, and there are said to be over a billion today.
1 pulsate **2** proliferate **3** emancipate **4** enumerate

(10) *A:* Those cakes look really good. Let's have one.
B: You go ahead. I'm on a diet, and I'm determined not to (   ) to temptation.
1 succumb **2** perturb **3** obliterate **4** hassle

(11) In an effort to avoid an oncoming car, the driver (   ) off the side of the road.
1 swaggered **2** cantered **3** careened **4** siphoned

(12) The patient suffers from a (   ) cough. He has been taking medicine for it, but it has continued for over six months.
1 chronic **2** rustic **3** tactful **4** devious

(13) The army patrol encountered an (   ) on the way back to camp. A group of rebel fighters had been waiting for them as they entered a narrow valley.
1 ambush **2** accolade **3** epiphany **4** inception

(14) The politician's popularity has (   ). Two years ago, his approval ratings were high. He then became the target of public criticism last year, but he has since regained support.
1 fluctuated **2** concocted **3** acceded **4** tabulated

(15) Mary has long been a (   ) supporter of the city's plan to build a new highway. She believes it will have a hugely positive effect on the local economy.
1 residual **2** staunch **3** scandalous **4** hereditary

(16) Kyle's back pain was so (   ) that he had a hard time even getting out of bed in the morning.
1 jocular **2** derelict
3 excruciating **4** endearing

(17) Trent caused a small fire in the kitchen when he forgot to turn the stove off. Luckily, he was able to (   ) the flames with a bucket of water before they spread.
1 recant **2** disavow **3** brandish **4** douse

(18) Advancements in surgical techniques have allowed doctors to make smaller (   ) when they perform operations. This

means that scars are much less noticeable.
1 conundrums 2 incisions
3 quagmires   4 caricatures

(19) The president was criticized for giving (   ) answers to questions at the press conference. The journalists who attended had hoped for more-straightforward replies.
1 oblique 2 lucrative 3 rotund 4 exquisite

(20) When Barbara was ill, someone from her family stayed at her side all day and all night. This (   ) continued until she was completely well again.
1 scourge 2 contour 3 cowardice 4 vigil

(21) Although Nina and Judy were twins, they behaved in very different ways at school. Nina was often rude and refused to obey her teachers, while Judy was always (   ).
1 omniscient 2 deferential 3 laborious 4 precipitous

(22) The ambassador decided to (   ) politeness and take a more aggressive stance on the issue after his initial approach failed to have any impact on the negotiations.
1 barge in   2 nibble at
3 pry out   4 dispense with

(23) The marathon runners were (   ) by the cheering crowds along the route. The support encouraged the runners to push hard until the end of the race.
1 spurred on   2 swept aside
3 put out   4 chipped in

(24) In an effort to reduce violent protests, the government has introduced laws to (   ) on large public gatherings.
1 churn out   2 crack down
3 grind up   4 swear in

(25) The soldiers received details of their new posting overseas soon after completing their training. They were ordered to (   ) to a base in West Africa.
1 ship out 2 chime in 3 ebb away 4 nod off

2 Read each passage and choose the best word or phrase from among the four choices for each blank. Then, on your answer sheet, find the number of the question and mark your answer.

Jewel Wasps and Cockroaches

The jewel wasp wields an ability that is vital to its reproduction, and the wasp's prey — the cockroach — plays an essential role. After grasping a cockroach in its jaws, the jewel wasp injects venom into its victim's body, instantly paralyzing the creature's front legs for a brief period. This immobility allows the wasp to deliver its second sting with the precise accuracy required to target specific areas of the cockroach's brain. There, the venom blocks the activity of certain neurons, interfering with the creature's ability to flee from the wasp. The fact that the wasp (**26**) in this way is considered one of the insect's most intriguing aspects.

After the venom takes effect, the cockroach is nearly ready to serve its role as nourishment for the wasp's larva. First, however, the cockroach engages in a prolonged self-grooming ritual while the wasp flies away and locates a hole in which to conceal its victim. Research suggests the cockroach's cleaning behavior is (**27**). It is unknown if the behavior benefits the wasp — for example, by ensuring a clean meal for the wasp's larva — but it was not exhibited when researchers subjected cockroaches to conditions similar to being pierced by a wasp's stinger. The behavior was also absent in cockroaches that simply experienced stress, including being grabbed, but not stung, by jewel wasps.

Upon the wasp's return, the cockroach is fully compliant to the will of its captor. After guiding the cockroach to the hole, the wasp lays an egg on its leg and departs. The wasp larva hatches and takes up residence inside the cockroach's body, using nutrients from the creature to cultivate its own development. But (**28**). Researchers have observed the larva producing a liquid substance that it deploys as a protective shield while in the cockroach's body cavity. The antibiotics within the substance inhibit the growth of bacteria that cockroaches harbor, which can be lethal to the jewel wasp's offspring during its incubation period. After surviving to maturation, the young wasp emerges from the shell of its host, ready to initiate its own search for an unfortunate victim.

(26) 1 risks its own safety
     2 can attract prey to itself
     3 actually protects its victim
     4 can manipulate its victim

(27) 1 essential to its survival
     2 a common response to stress
     3 a specific effect of the venom itself
     4 an attempt to confuse the wasp

(28) 1 the larva must make an important choice
     2 its environment is not without dangers
     3 predators can still locate the hole
     4 the larva's parent still has a role to play

Bertolt Brecht and Epic Theater

    Widely considered one of the greatest directors and playwrights of the twentieth century, Bertolt Brecht was a pioneer of the innovative genre known as "epic theater." Though his work was consistently watchable and humorous, Brecht's plays evolved into acts of rebellion against theatrical conventions of the time. In particular, Brecht sought to overturn the common idea that art should (**29**   ). Productions of the time employed detailed props and scenery, utilized plots centered on contemporary subjects, and featured characters that audiences could easily relate to. Brecht's productions, however, turned traditional scriptwriting and staging on their head, purposely reminding audiences at every turn that they were viewing a heavily dramatized, theatrical interpretation of everyday life rather than a real event occurring before their eyes.

    Brecht particularly despised the principle of catharsis — the release of emotions created when audience members sympathize with characters in ordinary plays. This most harmful of theatrical traditions, he argued, (**30**   ). Brecht therefore employed minimalist scenery and sets, and had his characters address the audience directly or hold up signs expressing their character's traits. By doing so, Brecht intentionally caused his audience to maintain an emotional distance from the characters and events on stage, creating a highly intellectual theater experience. His dramatic devices, Brecht hoped, would provoke the general public into reflecting thoughtfully on the play's themes.

Brecht's plays were almost invariably an expression of his political and philosophical principles, foremost among these being the concept that (　　31　　). One way that he conveyed this was through the use of historical material. Brecht felt such subject matter served to make audiences aware that seemingly momentous and universal events, such as wars, come to an end, and that the way those events were interpreted was often very different after the events themselves had ended. Brecht held the view that human civilization was progressing toward a utopian society and believed that theater could act both as a reminder that life is not static and as a motivator to help people work toward such a goal. While his utopian political views are today sometimes regarded as a weakness, he is revered for his groundbreaking and influential contribution to theater.

---

(29) 1　be a mirror of reality　　　2　unite rather than divide
　　　3　challenge our assumptions　4　always use original ideas

(30) 1　inevitably led to disappointment
　　　2　appealed mainly to playwrights
　　　3　often served to ridicule audiences
　　　4　kept audiences from thinking logically

(31) 1　all individuals are equal
　　　2　nothing is permanent
　　　3　even small acts have consequences
　　　4　history always repeats itself

---

3 *Read each passage and choose the best answer from among the four choices for each question. Then, on your answer sheet, find the number of the question and mark your answer.*

Usury and Sin

Though widely accepted today, charging interest on loaned money, also known as usury, was once considered a major sin. Usury laws were common in the past, and the Roman Catholic Church in particular was known for harshly resisting the practice during the medieval period, expelling those who were guilty of it from the church.

Prohibitions against usury originally arose due to the way that debt and credit were viewed as a system of benevolent aid and trust. People in the poor, rural populations of medieval times formed strong communal ties due to the way that families and friends relied on sharing and lending goods to help one another. Expecting compensation, therefore, for an act that was considered one's social duty was regarded as morally wrong, and this belief persisted following the shift from goods to money as a medium of exchange. Individuals who were destitute or had suffered financial misfortune, however, were forced to turn to the church or the nobility due to their large reserves of capital. And in keeping with the belief at the time regarding the moral nature of debt and credit, lenders who profited from something that was part of one's social and religious responsibility were viewed as sinful.

Some, however, attempted to circumvent church and legal bans on usury in order to profit from moneylending. Various methods emerged to do so, such as complex schemes that involved repaying loans in foreign currencies to use shifting exchange rates as a way to camouflage earned interest. Another method routinely employed by financiers was the "triple contract." This was a combination of contracts that, while separately permissible under laws at the time, together allowed moneylenders to gain interest by becoming business partners with the recipients of their loans. After moneylenders became part of the businesses they had authorized loans to, they were technically earning a profit from their capital rather than illegally gaining interest.

As trade expanded and developed, problems created by usury laws became obvious. Medieval opposition to generating money from money was due to the commonly held view of money as a means of exchange lacking inherent value. Shortages of gold and silver coins and the difficulty of making payments to clients in distant lands, however, led to the development of banks with branches in multiple cities and the emergence of moneychangers who could convert foreign currencies. As wealth spread throughout society, it became clear that moneylenders were not, in fact, receiving "money for nothing." Just as a farmer who lends someone a cow is deprived of the chance to obtain milk and calves from it, the lender of money is deprived of the opportunity to invest in other means of obtaining profits. Along with the changing nature of lending, a greater appreciation arose for the risk that moneylenders were burdened with upon parting with their capital. Over time, the acknowledgment of these factors by the church and scholars helped reframe the debate around usury, prompting the evolution from an outright ban on the charging of interest to the modern usury laws that protect ordinary consumers from excessive charges by loan sharks and credit card companies.

(32) In medieval society, prohibitions surrounding usury

  1 were a manifestation of the belief that it was a sin to request aid from anyone except relatives when one had financial problems.
  2 reflected the idea that people with money should not take unfair advantage of something that was considered a charitable act.
  3 were a demonstration of how the church and the nobility abused their access to large sums of money to exploit the poor.
  4 suggested that people did not have a sufficient understanding of debt and credit to make a lending system work effectively.

(33) According to the passage, what is true about the methods used to profit from moneylending?

  1 They were an example of how views about moneylending were not always the same in different countries and various industries.
  2 They illustrated that the way interest payments were made in medieval times could cause legal disputes between business partners.
  3 They were an indication of how people in medieval times believed that profit and interest were two entirely unconnected concepts.
  4 They showed how some people used indirect ways of earning interest on loans while appearing to obey the law.

(34) Which of the following statements would the author of the passage most likely agree with?

1 Abolishing usury laws in medieval times was only considered after the agricultural industry outgrew the limitations of the financial system.
2 A change in leadership within the church led to a reevaluation of the laws surrounding the borrowing and lending of money.
3 New attitudes toward moneylending were partly a result of increased understanding of the potential losses that could occur from giving out loans.
4 Banks and moneychangers pressured the church to relax its policy on usury as a way to boost profits from international trade.

The Classification Debate

Three varieties of the striolated puffbird in the Brazilian Amazon are virtually identical in appearance, but their songs differ subtly in rhythm and tone. When one scientist approached a committee in charge of bird species classification to advocate for reclassifying the three types into separate species, the committee members faced a dilemma. Were the distinctions sufficient to warrant the creation of two additional species? They eventually added just one. Their decision, however, sparked yet another controversy in the world of taxonomy, the branch of science that deals with identifying and defining the multitude of organisms found in nature.

The number of new species identified worldwide has been increasing as technological advances allow for closer examination of Earth's organisms. The number of bird species in South America alone has grown by over 150 since the year 2000. The vast majority of these, however, were not discovered based on expeditions into the deepest corners of the rain forest. Rather, they were created by reclassifying variants of existing species as a result of breakthroughs in recording technology or genetic classification. And while some argue the nuances detectable in recent years justify such reclassifications, others find the distinctions arbitrary. Bird expert James Remsen sees the current state of bird taxonomy as "trying to make the best of a bad situation," explaining that "we're trying to apply artificial barriers on a continuum."

These disputes have renewed debate over the "species problem," a fundamental issue in taxonomy regarding how to distinguish between species. The problems inherent in the attempts to answer this question underscore Remsen's view. The Biological Species Concept (BSC), for example, has long been a prominent guideline for biologists, defining a species as organisms that can only successfully reproduce with each other and produce healthy, fertile offspring. Using reproduction in this way to draw distinct lines between species causes complications, though. In cases where species have been split into two or more groups for geographical reasons, proponents of the BSC believe that this isolation justifies distinct species classification. It is impossible, they say, to know if these groups would naturally reproduce with each other because they do not meet.

Today, in addition to the BSC, biologists are guided by analysis of both DNA and the evolutionary history of groups of organisms. An example is the taxonomic debate over dingoes in Australia. For centuries, dingoes have been subject to eradication in rural areas due to the threat they pose to livestock. One reason they have not been granted protection is because they are classified as wild dogs, belonging to the same species as domestic dogs. Researchers examined factors including dingoes' bone structure, genetics, and historical lack of domestication, and in 2019, it was determined that a distinct species designation is warranted. This contradicted previous findings that were based on the BSC and which argued that dingoes' interbreeding naturally with domestic dogs shows they are not a distinct species. Considering dingoes' important role in controlling populations of pests such as foxes, the issue shows how taxonomic classification can have major implications both for the management of species and for entire ecosystems.

(35) Why does the author of the passage mention the controversy that arose over the classification of striolated puffbirds?

1 It is an example of the issues related to classifying birds solely based on less-remarkable things like their appearance instead of more-important factors.
2 It shows that the minor distinctions between varieties of animals can make it difficult to be certain if new species classifications are appropriate.
3 It is an example of the problems that occur when scientists

reject existing information about birds in favor of new data gained through fieldwork.

4 It shows that many of the small differences once thought to be significant in classifying species are not actually important at all.

(36) The Biological Species Concept can be problematic because

1 the opportunities that would normally exist for members of the same species to reproduce are sometimes affected by external factors.

2 it was established based on observations of interbreeding between animals kept in captivity rather than observations of animals in their natural habitats.

3 classification factors designed to apply to a specific species are often mistakenly applied to many different organisms.

4 the guidelines it is based on do not attempt to address the basic question of how to assess whether a group of organisms is a distinct species.

(37) What is evident from the situation concerning dingoes?

1 Close analysis of an animal's breeding habits over a long period of time can reveal the importance of that animal to the ecosystems it inhabits.

2 The 2019 research findings will likely result in Australian farmers being given more rights to exterminate dingoes that attack their livestock.

3 Judgments related to the classification of species are likely to be ignored if it is clear that maintaining animal populations leads to economic gain.

4 The decision regarding whether an animal should be considered a distinct species can significantly impact the way it is treated by humans.

The Trail of Tears

Known today as the Trail of Tears, the forcible removal and

migration of approximately 100,000 Native Americans from their ancestral homelands in the southeastern United States during the 1830s marks a dark moment in US history. The route to the new territories extended thousands of kilometers across nine states, and approximately 15,000 men, women, and children are believed to have perished during the removals and subsequent journey.

Prior to the Trail of Tears, a policy of cultural assimilation had been in place. Though Native Americans faced tremendous pressure to embrace Christianity and Western education, their right to retain their ancestral territories was generally acknowledged. In 1830, however, the US Congress passed President Andrew Jackson's Indian Removal Act, a piece of legislation that allowed the government to move tribes from their homelands to new homes in "Indian Territory," located in present-day Oklahoma. The policy faced difficulties, though, when an attempt in 1832 to seize Cherokee-owned land in Georgia was ruled unconstitutional by Chief Justice John Marshall of the Supreme Court. Recognizing the Cherokee tribe as a sovereign nation, the ruling set what appeared to be an important legal precedent. Jackson, though, undeterred and defiant, reportedly reacted to the ruling with the words, "John Marshall has made his decision; now let him enforce it."

Jackson's justifications for Native American removals were almost entirely unfounded. Despite the tribes' efforts to "civilize" themselves, they were criticized for their overreliance on hunting and failure to adopt modern agricultural practices. At the time, James Fenimore Cooper's novel *The Last of the Mohicans* was contributing to the romanticized American myth that Native Americans and their cultures were in the process of vanishing, and Jackson took advantage of this notion, arguing that without relocation, Native Americans and their cultures were doomed. In reality, however, Native American populations were stable and possibly even growing at the time.

According to historian Claudio Saunt, the Native American deportations should be seen in the context of capitalist expansion at the time. White slave owners and investors knew Native American holdings represented some of the most fertile land in the nation, ready to be exploited for farming and construction. Saunt chronicles how banks on the East Coast collaborated with Southern speculators to finance the dispossession of Native American lands, which White men, especially slave owners, saw as a golden opportunity to expand their business enterprises. While the removals were supposedly benign measures carried out to avert Native Americans' extinction, those behind the planning and execution of the removals saw Native American territory in the same way that they viewed slaves — a Godgiven resource to be exploited economically.

Saunt also documents how Southern politicians and Northern allies created a network of offices, soldiers, and administrators to manage the removals. These efforts were incredibly expensive, but the land, when cultivated with the free labor of Black slaves, was seen as worth the costs. East Coast bankers were quickly growing wealthier by financing the dual enterprises of slavery and expulsion, and this, in turn, provided capital for railroads and other large-scale development projects. As horrific as the Trail of Tears was, some argue that it brought technological advancement and infrastructure that were essential for America's emergence as a nation stretching from coast to coast.

The expulsions resulting from the Indian Removal Act provoked different reactions depending on the tribe. Some went voluntarily, while others resisted fiercely. One of the most tragic cases was that of the Cherokees. Faced with enormous pressure, a tiny minority of the tribe's members took it upon themselves to enter into negotiations with the government about moving west, resulting in the Treaty of New Echota. The document was considered invalid by the vast majority of the Cherokees, who argued that the so-called representatives responsible for brokering the terms were not their recognized leaders, and a petition requesting that the treaty be nullified received over 15,000 signatures. Congress, however, passed the treaty legislation, sealing the Cherokees' fate.

Despite a two-year deadline to leave, only about 2,000 Cherokees had set out for Indian Territory by 1838. In an effort to expedite the process, some 7,000 soldiers were ordered into Cherokee territory, where they dragged the Cherokees from their homes at gunpoint and locked them up while looting their homes and belongings. Unsheltered and lacking even basic supplies, the Cherokees were forced to endure long marches in extreme heat and cold. Water scarcity and meager food rations caused them to become malnourished, with many surrendering to deadly diseases. By the time the Cherokees had reached Indian Territory, approximately one-fourth had perished.

By about 1840, most of the tribes had settled on land that the government promised would remain theirs forever. However, they found themselves in a harsh, unfamiliar environment, and suffered appallingly in the coming years. Furthermore, as railroads opened up the American West, large numbers of White settlers flooded Indian Territory, gradually reducing its size until it had completely disappeared by the early twentieth century.

(38) During the 1830s, President Andrew Jackson

    1 began attempting to use the courts to remove Native Americans from their lands after realizing that his assimilation policies were not effective.

    2 was forced to negotiate and alter the way the Indian Removal Act worked after it was rejected by the nation's highest court.

    3 ignored a legal decision which stated that the government did not have the authority to remove Native Americans from their lands without their consent.

    4 was left with no choice but to extend special treatment to the Cherokees that had been denied to people of other tribes.

(39) Which of the following statements would Claudio Saunt most likely agree with?

    1 Though many Native American tribes struggled with poor harvests and decreasing food sources, books often portrayed their lives in a glamorous way.

    2 Though presented as an attempt to aid Native Americans, plans for their removal were actually motivated by the potential for economic gain.

    3 Though many policies were introduced to restrict the influence of Native American cultures, some innovative business ideas helped popularize them.

    4 Though the government was mainly to blame for the removals, Native Americans' cooperation with business leaders created many of their problems.

(40) The Trail of Tears is said to have fueled American expansion

    1 because the rivalry between wealthy businessmen from the

North and the South helped lower the costs of expansion projects and speed up their construction time.
2 because many of the resettled Native Americans were offered jobs in the railroad and construction industries, which proved vital in opening up the country.
3 due to many Native Americans using the money they received from the expulsions and their knowledge of farming to relocate to and cultivate other lands.
4 due to a profitable industry being created around the expulsions, generating wealth that was then used for infrastructure development across the country.

(41) Which of the following statements regarding the Treaty of New Echota is true?

1 The deadline that the Cherokees had been given to sign the treaty did not allow them enough time to make a decision on such an important matter.
2 The petition to have the treaty passed as law was dismissed by officials who felt that there was not enough support from the Cherokees to justify such an action.
3 Many of the Cherokees were upset as they believed that the group responsible for the treaty did not have the authority to enter into negotiations on their behalf.
4 A group of Cherokee leaders felt that the treaty was far less favorable than similar kinds of treaties other tribes had been offered in the past.

4
- *Write an essay on the given TOPIC.*
- *Give THREE reasons to support your answer.*
- *Structure: introduction, main body, and conclusion*
- *Suggested length: 200–240 words*
- *Write your essay in the space provided on Side B of your answer sheet. Any writing outside the space will not be graded.*

TOPIC

Can individual privacy be protected in the modern world?

リスニング

―― Listening Test ――

There are four parts to this listening test.

Part 1	Dialogues: 1 question each	Multiple-choice
Part 2	Passages: 2 questions each	Multiple-choice
Part 3	Real-Life: 1 question each	Multiple-choice
Part 4	Interview: 2 questions	Multiple-choice

※**Listen carefully to the instructions.**

Part 1

No. 1
1 They are made from low-quality materials.
2 They are difficult to adapt for use in Africa.
3 Throwing them away can be dangerous.
4 Donating them is not always a good thing.

No. 2
1 He will succeed in saving the wetlands.
2 He uses his position to do favors for certain people.
3 He works hard to protect the environment.
4 He is popular with his ordinary constituents.

No. 3
1 He worked late the night before.
2 He had an early morning meeting.
3 He has been working alone too often.
4 He did not finish the advertising contract.

No. 4
1 He is not a threat to her.
2 He should be hired as a manager.
3 He seems too confident.
4 He has poor communication skills.

No. 5
1 She has more chores than before.
2 Her exhibition has been successful.
3 She has more time for herself now.
4 Her gallery has closed down.

No. 6
1 He will be angry.
2 He will not notice.
3 He will overreact.
4 He will be understanding.

No. 7
1 The man does not need to repay anything.
2 She will not lend the man money.
3 She is also short of money now.
4 The man misled her on purpose.

No. 8
1 The man is too generous with his time.
2 The vice president does too much overtime.
3 The vice president owes her a favor.
4 The man is not qualified for his position.

No. 9
1 It will affect his work more than it will the woman's.
2 It might help staff expand their professional knowledge.
3 It means he will have to drive more than he currently does.
4 It may help staff strengthen existing client relationships.

No. 10
1 The women's input will be ignored.
2 It will probably be the last one they have to complete.
3 His boss wants to see it before human resources does.
4 It could lead to changes in the workplace.

Part 2

(A)

No. 11
1 It focused only on Internet-based relationships.
2 It was funded by an Internet company.
3 The researchers used outdated technology.
4 The length of the study was inadequate.

No. 12
1 They tend to misuse data from people's profiles.
2 They often ignore factors related to compatibility.
3 They may contribute to creating strong marriages.
4 They have simplified their algorithms recently.

(B)

No. 13
1 They can match the quality of the best natural diamonds.
2 They are unsuitable for use in high-tech tools.
3 They have a different chemical makeup from natural diamonds.
4 They can be more expensive than natural diamonds.

No. 14
1 By operating fewer mines in developing countries.
2 By reducing the size of their workforce.
3 By utilizing environmentally friendly methods.
4 By increasing their production capacity.

(C)

No. 15
1 Improve worker performance through competition.
2 Encourage workers to cooperate with other workers.
3 Teach workers how to cope better with stress.
4 Make it easier to recruit highly skilled workers.

No. 16
1 The true sources of employee motivation.
2 The importance of focusing on success.
3 The skills needed for interacting with customers.
4 The need for companies to minimize costs.

(D)

No. 17
1 The emergence of new marine predators.
2 The development of much stronger fins.
3 The absence of food sources in the ocean.
4 The ability to better detect food sources there.

No. 18
1 The location of their eyes remained unchanged.
2 They likely became able to hunt in a different way.
3 It caused some of them to react faster.
4 It led to harmful effects in the long term.

(E)

No. 19
1 Soldiers had better body armor.
2 More soldiers survived serious wounds.
3 Certain types of weapons were banned.
4 Injuries to soldiers were greatly reduced.

No. 20
1 She made masks using newly discovered materials.
2 She was a plastic surgeon before becoming an artist.
3 She was known for the accuracy of her masks.
4 She was a mental health professional.

Part 3

No. 21

(F)

Situation: You are a Japanese executive arriving at a conference in Australia. You have business cards and an international driver's license, but your passport is at your hotel. You hear the following announcement.

Question: What should you do first?

1 Show your international driver's license at reception.
2 Hand a business card to security as you enter the building.
3 Collect your conference pass at reception.
4 Obtain some forms at the security desk.

No. 22

(G)

Situation: You have brought your car to an automobile repair shop for maintenance before a road trip. Safety is important, but you want to avoid unnecessary repairs. The mechanic tells you the following.

Question: What work should you ask the mechanic to do now?

1 Replace the engine coils.
2 Change the oxygen sensor.
3 Adjust the wheel alignment.
4 Replace the brake pads.

No. 23

(H)

Situation: It is April. You need to take beginner-level German classes before June. You work weekdays until 8 p.m. You call a language school and are told the following.
Question: Which course should you choose?

1 Introduction to German.
2 Basic German for Travel.
3 Intensive German.
4 Private German Online.

No. 24

(I)

Situation: You work at a graphic-design firm and hope to be promoted. Your assistant has not been working on the museum project. Your manager left you the following voice mail.
Question: What should you do?

1 Continue with the museum project as planned.
2 Meet with your assistant to explain his new role.
3 Prepare materials for your performance review.
4 Contact the president with your plan for the client.

No. 25

(J)

Situation: You recently bought a racing bicycle. You want assistance on how to position your feet on the pedals. Your budget is $400. You call the bicycle store and are told the following.
Question: Which option should you choose?

1 The Standard Fit Program.
2 The Dynamic Fit Program.
3 The Biomechanical Tuning Service.
4 The Perfect Fit Tutor.

Part 4

No. 26
1 She is often impressed by the strength of her students' arguments.
2 It can be hard to apply the grading criteria objectively.
3 She sometimes disagrees with the professors' grades.
4 It is the most interesting aspect of being a teaching assistant.

No. 27
1 Make sure that they can explain the material clearly.
2 Try not to be too intimidating toward students.
3 Accept the fact that they will occasionally make mistakes.
4 Allow the students to express themselves during seminars.

二次試験
面 接

A日程 ▶MP3 ▶アプリ ▶CD4 **1**〜**5**

1. Agree or disagree: Urbanization inevitably leads to a lower quality of life
2. Has online media destroyed traditional print journalism?
3. Is a society free of crime an unattainable goal?
4. Has the traditional five-day workweek become outdated in the modern world?
5. Can the technology gap between developed and developing nations ever be eliminated?

C日程

1. Are modern methods of food production sustainable in the long term?
2. Should governments prioritize domestic issues over international issues?
3. Are airline companies doing enough to become more environmentally friendly?
4. Should athletes who take performance-enhancing drugs be banned for life?
5. Agree or disagree: Public surveillance is justified if it helps prevent crimes

（注）モデルスピーチと解説はA日程のみ収録しています。

2021-1

一次試験　2021.5.30実施
二次試験　A日程　2021.6.27実施
　　　　　C日程　2021.7.11実施

Grade 1

試験時間

筆記：100分
リスニング：約35分

一次試験・筆記　　　　　p.42〜56
一次試験・リスニング　　p.57〜63
二次試験・面接　　　　　p.64

＊解答・解説は別冊p.57〜108にあります。
＊面接の流れは本書p.16にあります。

2021年度第1回　**Web特典「自動採点サービス」対応　オンラインマークシート**
※検定の回によって2次元コードが違います。
※筆記1〜3，リスニングの採点ができます。
※ PCからも利用できます（本書 p.8 参照）。

筆記

1 To complete each item, choose the best word or phrase from among the four choices. Then, on your answer sheet, find the number of the question and mark your answer.

(1) Cell phones have become a permanent (   ) in modern society. Most people could not imagine living without one.
1 clasp **2** stint **3** fixture **4** rupture

(2) Colin did not have enough money to pay for the car all at once, so he paid it off in (   ) of $800 a month for two years.
1 dispositions **2** installments
3 enactments **4** speculations

(3) When she asked her boss for a raise, Melanie's (   ) tone of voice made it obvious how nervous she was.
1 garish **2** jovial **3** pompous **4** diffident

(4) The religious sect established a (   ) in a rural area where its followers could live together and share everything. No private property was allowed.
1 dirge **2** prelude **3** repository **4** commune

(5) The famous reporter was fired for (   ) another journalist's work. His article was almost exactly the same as that of the other journalist.
1 alleviating **2** plagiarizing **3** inoculating **4** beleaguering

(6) Now that the local steel factory has closed down, the streets of the once-busy town are lined with (   ) businesses. Most owners have abandoned their stores.
1 rhetorical **2** volatile **3** defunct **4** aspiring

(7) The ambassador's failure to attend the ceremony held in honor of the king was considered an (   ) by his host nation and made already bad relations worse.
1 elucidation **2** affront **3** impasse **4** ultimatum

(8) US border guards managed to (   ) the escaped prisoner as he tried to cross into Canada. He was returned to jail immediately.
1 apprehend **2** pillage **3** exalt **4** acclimate

(9) Anthony enjoyed his first day at his new job. The atmosphere

was ( ), and his colleagues did their best to make him feel welcome.
1 congenial **2** delirious **3** measly **4** implausible

(10) *A:* I just learned I've been ( ) to second violin in the school orchestra. I knew I should've practiced more.
B: Well, if you work hard, I'm sure you can get your previous position back.
1 relegated **2** jeopardized **3** reiterated **4** stowed

(11) After the politician received death threats on social media, many news outlets said that such behavior was ( ) and should be punished.
1 incalculable **2** reprehensible
3 bumbling **4** virtuous

(12) As an increasing number of vehicles are being designed to operate ( ), drivers will be free to relax or get some work done while their cars drive themselves.
1 listlessly **2** forlornly
3 autonomously **4** semantically

(13) The opera singer ( ) in the audience's applause on the final night of the show. She knew she had given the best performance of her life.
1 clamored **2** basked **3** floundered **4** trampled

(14) It is important to check the expiration date of seeds before planting them. If they are too old, there is a strong chance that many of them will not ( ).
1 sprout **2** forestall **3** lunge **4** rescind

(15) *A:* It's such a beautiful night! What's the name of that ( ) over there?
B: That's Orion. You can tell by the row of three stars in the middle.
1 constellation **2** exodus
3 tenet **4** redemption

(16) The official report said that foreign governments were using the Internet to ( ) democracy. It pointed to fake news stories published on various popular websites to influence voters.
1 salivate **2** hoist **3** placate **4** subvert

(17) Roderick was in a car accident last year, but luckily he was not (   ) for any of the damage as it was the other driver's fault.
1 impervious   2 redolent   3 impalpable   4 liable

(18) Guests at the opening of the new national museum had to dress in formal (   ). A few people who wore jeans and T-shirts were turned away at the door.
1 pageant   2 attire   3 parlance   4 attrition

(19) From an early age, the child had an (   ) ability to guess what other people were thinking. His schoolteachers said they had never seen anything like it before.
1 impetuous   2 idyllic   3 uncanny   4 odious

(20) The actor is now at the (   ) of his career, having recently received universal praise and numerous awards for his latest film role.
1 pinnacle   2 figment   3 relapse   4 vortex

(21) Reza thinks his boss is too (   ). He finds it frustrating because she always wants to discuss small, unimportant details.
1 unseemly   2 indignant   3 apolitical   4 pedantic

(22) The meeting was supposed to (   ) by noon, but it was still going on at 1:30 p.m. By then, most of the people were very hungry.
1 wind up   2 shell out   3 wear in   4 spill over

(23) The new prime minister's economic policy focuses on (   ) inflation. He has promised to get prices under control as quickly as possible.
1 sounding out   2 stitching up
3 reining in   4 locking away

(24) The detective spent several months (   ) the circumstances surrounding the murder before he was able to discover who had done it.
1 tilting at   2 swinging around
3 digging into   4 bracing for

(25) *A:* Carlos, did you (   ) the dates for your time off this summer? I was hoping we could make our vacation plans soon.
B: Not yet, honey. I'll talk to the boss about it tomorrow and then make a decision.
1 shy away   2 settle on   3 strip out   4 hang back

2 *Read each passage and choose the best word or phrase from among the four choices for each blank. Then, on your answer sheet, find the number of the question and mark your answer.*

Jediism

Based on the *Star Wars* science fiction movies, Jediism is a pop-culture philosophy with a substantial worldwide following. Its practitioners seek to emulate a group of spiritual warriors from the movies who are masters of a phenomenon called "the Force," an energy that underlies all creation and gives the warriors supernatural abilities. Followers see Jediism as a legitimate religion, but as a spiritual practice anchored in fiction it is the focus of frequent ridicule. In response, however, believers point out that many members of other religions (**26**). Major religions commonly use stories to communicate moral or spiritual lessons, and these often contain fantastical elements — talking animals, for example — which strongly suggest that they do not describe actual historical events. Yet just as this does not necessarily discredit such faiths, so practitioners of Jediism feel its origin in fiction should not affect its validity.

Following a movie-based philosophy can, however, (**27**). In the case of Jediism, followers are well known for enthusiastically investing substantial amounts of money in costumes, imitation weapons, and other paraphernalia. While it can be argued that many elements in the movies are purposely designed to facilitate the purchase of related merchandise, such behavior appears contrary to the prohibition against excessive ownership of material goods expounded in the movies. Most followers simply ignore the inconsistency, though some do attempt to recycle or take other measures to reduce their possessions.

Gaining official recognition has presented difficulties for Jediism. In the United Kingdom, an application for tax-exempt status was rejected on the basis of Jediism's lack of both structure and a unifying system of belief. Yet despite its failure to attain official designation, Jediism is evidence of (**28**) in the West. As Western culture has been influenced by Eastern religions such as Buddhism, which may not have concepts of God that are recognizable to many Westerners or which lack the type of worship found in Christianity, clear lines that could be used to characterize

45

and legitimize religious practices have become difficult to draw. Commentators frequently depict Jediism as exemplifying both the decline in authoritarian, highly structured organizations and the rise of groups focused on their members' personal fulfillment.

---

(26)   1 often claim religious ignorance
        2 are not supportive of wild beliefs
        3 have been persecuted in the past
        4 do not take all their sources literally

(27)   1 cause many to reject the movies
        2 give rise to ironic situations
        3 place excessive hardship on followers
        4 lead to antisocial attitudes

(28)   1 new governmental approaches toward religion
        2 a surge in general religious sentiment
        3 a shift in the way religion itself is perceived
        4 society's influence on older religions

Webster's Third

When the most prominent dictionary maker in the United States, Merriam-Webster, published its *Webster's Third New International Dictionary* in 1961, it expected the dictionary to be received as a groundbreaking reference tool for the modern era. Influenced by recent trends in linguistics, *Webster's Third* took an innovative "descriptivist" approach, focusing on how English is actually written and spoken by ordinary people in everyday life. Critics, however, charged that the dictionary's authors had (**29**). They argued that dictionaries are meant to be "prescriptive"; that is, their role is to make authoritative pronouncements on correct usage and pronunciation. Some even complained that the abandonment of prescriptivism was sending the English language down a slippery slope into linguistic chaos. They were particularly irate about the alleged endorsement of slang terms like "ain't," which *Webster's Third* asserted was "used orally . . . by many cultivated speakers."

It can be said, however, that *Webster's Third* was rooted in (**30**). From the late 1700s, dictionaries had been embraced just as fully by the lower classes as by the highly educated elite. Marginalized and oppressed minorities used them as a path to attain the literacy forbidden to them, and immigrants to the country viewed dictionaries as indispensable learning tools to aid linguistic and cultural assimilation. *Webster's Third* epitomized this egalitarian mentality, utilizing, for example, sentences not just from Shakespeare and the Bible but from Hollywood actors and other nontraditional sources as well, further reinforcing its accessibility and inclusivity.

Superficially, the uproar *Webster's Third* created among the elite and academics was a conflict about whether words like "ain't" should be labeled with disparaging terms such as "incorrect" and "illiterate," or with more diplomatic ones such as "nonstandard." On a deeper level, though, it reflected a radical cultural shift in which absolute ideas about right and wrong were fading and pressures to conform were declining, as exemplified by the growing feminist movement and the rejection of authority by young people that occurred in the 1960s. Therefore, when considered in the context of such movements, *Webster's Third* is a pioneering work in the field of linguistics as well as (**31**).

---

(29) 1 acted in an irresponsible way
    2 misunderstood descriptivism
    3 made things needlessly complicated
    4 fallen behind the times

(30) 1 a disturbing American tendency
    2 incorrect assumptions about American society
    3 the influence of the American upper class
    4 the American attitude toward dictionaries

(31) 1 a result of extreme compromise
    2 a reflection of social change
    3 an attempt to profit from a trend
    4 an extension of academic biases

Conspicuous Consumption

According to the economic law of demand, there is a negative correlation between the price of an item and the demand for it. Significant price increases of a product by a company, therefore, should motivate consumers to switch to a competitor that provides an equivalent product at a more reasonable price. In 1899, however, economist Thorstein Veblen coined the term "conspicuous consumption," arguing that specific segments of society were unconcerned with the market value of certain products and would spend lavishly on anything that provided opportunities to display their wealth and prominence. These goods — items such as rare and fine wines and handcrafted watches — have subsequently become known as "Veblen goods." Unlike ordinary consumer goods, the price increase — even a substantial one — of Veblen goods will not have an adverse effect on the volume of their sales to wealthy consumers and may even add to their appeal. Veblen based his theory on observations of American millionaires, such as William Randolph Hearst and Andrew Carnegie, whose opulent concert halls, mansions, and museums appeared to have been built as much to reflect the owners' affluence as for any practical purpose. Veblen saw such displays as the manifestation of an innate desire that "prompts us to outdo those with whom we are in the habit of classing ourselves."

Conspicuous consumption, however, has also been observed in other segments of society where visible displays of opulence imply wealth beyond that of the purchaser's actual status. For such individuals, purchasing luxury goods is seen more as a tool by which they might appear to be a member of a higher social class. Economists point out that to avoid the stigma associated with poverty, people tend to splurge on visible indicators of affluence, regardless of price changes. A case in point is the role emerging economies play in driving the luxury goods market. Consumers in growing markets such as Russia, China, and Saudi Arabia, economists note, have become essential drivers of growth in luxury goods sales in recent decades, despite the fact that average incomes are significantly lower than they are in developed nations, such as the United States or Japan. In fact, it is common, economists say, for less-affluent consumers to spend beyond their means and purchase status symbols in order to emulate wealthy individuals.

Veblen's theory paints an incomplete picture, however. Recent research shows that wealthy people flaunting their money signifies a phase of economic maturity, and that this visibly extravagant spending tends to fade as the wealth gap narrows. As individuals, classes, or countries begin to enjoy higher levels of affluence, patterns of "inconspicuous consumption" begin to emerge, and access to exclusive services becomes increasingly sought-after and valuable. Luxury goods still retain some semblance of importance as status symbols, but these services begin to account for an increasing proportion of expenditure and prioritize self-improvement and exclusivity. As such, experiences such as having a life coach, joining a boutique health clinic, or attending an invitation-only event become better demonstrators of the economic class to which an individual belongs than simply owning a designer watch.

(32) What is one thing that we learn about "Veblen goods"?

1 Their popularity among some consumers is defined more by the degree of wealth they signify than by the price of the goods themselves.
2 Because they are subject to frequent shifts in demand, manufacturers that produce them often do so at a considerable risk.
3 Consumers looking for bargains are often drawn to them as the goods frequently experience periods where they are lower in price.
4 They are more likely to follow the law of demand than ordinary consumer goods due to their superior quality.

(33) According to the passage, which of the following statements would economists most likely agree with?

1 The trend of purchasing luxury goods is strongest among those who have just recently advanced to a higher social class.
2 Luxury goods are more accessible to wealthy people in developing nations than they are to people with similar levels of wealth in developed ones.

3 Despite being unable to afford luxury goods, some people buy them to avoid appearing as though they are from a low-income background.
4 While luxury goods are highly popular among the wealthy at first, they lose their luxury status as they begin to be purchased by poor people.

(34) The author of the passage suggests that Thorstein Veblen's theory does not account for

1 recent cycles of economic downturn, which prohibit people from all segments of society from accumulating greater levels of wealth.
2 the increase of financial prosperity as a result of economic growth, which leads to a decline in the use of luxury goods to represent status.
3 a proportion of people across all wealth groups who are rejecting luxury goods as a means of displaying their wealth and status in society.
4 the promotion of inconspicuous luxury goods affordable to members of lower economic classes becoming a more common occurrence.

Fossil-Fuel Subsidies

A report by the International Monetary Fund (IMF) revealed that governments provided $5.2 trillion in subsidies to fossil-fuel companies in 2017. In light of evidence that fossil-fuel-related pollution causes millions of deaths each year, supporting the use of fossil fuels appears both morally questionable and in direct opposition to government pledges to reduce carbon emissions. However, the subsidy total is misleading in that it includes both pretax and posttax subsidies. The former are what most people associate with the word "subsidy"—things like cash handouts and tax breaks for oil companies that are designed to lower the cost of production, resulting in lower prices for consumers. The vast majority of the subsidies in the report, however, are of the posttax variety. These represent the additional burden on taxpayers that is the consequence of our dependence on fossil fuels—everything from oil-spill cleanup bills to increased traffic congestion and road accidents. Numerous critics contest the IMF's definition of subsidies, pointing out that there is obviously a high degree of subjectivity with regard to whether such costs should be included in these calculations. When posttax subsidies are excluded, the amount decreases to $424 billion, a fraction of the original sum.

While the inclusion of posttax subsidies may have been deceptive, a closer look at their societal costs is troubling. Many in society indeed gain an advantage from the economic and lifestyle benefits afforded from consumption of fossil-fuel-based energy, but the approximately 200,000 air-pollution-related deaths recorded annually in the United States reflect the unfortunate price that some are forced to pay. Furthermore, research indicates that there are racial and socioeconomic disparities in the extent to which the consequences of fossil-fuel use have a positive or negative impact on individuals' lives. Studies show, for example, that White Americans are responsible for 17 percent more air pollution than they are subjected to, while Black and Hispanic Americans are exposed to well over 50 percent more than they cause.

The indirect nature of posttax subsidies, however, makes them much harder to deal with than pretax subsidies. And while pretax subsidies are declining worldwide, their removal could be a double-edged sword. Since they do decrease the direct financial burden on consumers, removing them would add stress to low-income households, and in some cases drive very poor individuals to use cheaper fuels that release even greater amounts of pollutants than fossil fuels do. At the same time, these very households experience a disproportionate amount of suffering and hardship as a result of the activity the subsidies encourage. Experts say a more effective strategy for governments is to focus on the broader societal costs. There can be initiatives, for example, to tax companies that extract and produce fossil fuels on the emissions they release and redistribute the money to those their activities affect the most. This would impose a degree of accountability on the fossil-fuel industry while easing the impacts on low-income households. It would also, and perhaps more importantly, result in higher prices for fossil fuels, mitigating the degree of damage they cause by incentivizing the research and development of energy from cleaner sources.

(**35**)　According to the author of the passage, the subsidy total reported by the International Monetary Fund is misleading because

1 the organization calculates the amounts of pretax subsidies directly based on an estimation of what it believes posttax subsidies should be.
2 the subsidy total does not take into account the future costs of commitments by governments to reduce emissions of harmful greenhouse gases.
3 the organization ignores the fact that pretax subsidies often do not help lower production costs or pass on cheaper fuel costs to the general public.
4 the subsidy total includes a large portion of various costs paid by taxpayers that do not fit the conventional idea of what makes up a subsidy.

(36) In the second paragraph, what does the author of the passage reveal about fossil fuels?

1 If current trends in fossil-fuel use continue, the people who consume more of them will suffer the most severe health consequences.
2 The worst of the negative effects on the public that result from the burning of fossil fuels have been discovered to be unrelated to air pollution.
3 There is an imbalance between the benefits minorities receive from fossil-fuel subsidies and the negative effects they suffer from fossil-fuel use.
4 The specific ways in which fossil fuels are consumed by some minorities have little effect on the amount of pollution fossil fuels ultimately cause.

(37) Which of the following would likely be part of the strategy that experts recommend?

1 Removing posttax subsidies paid to fossil-fuel companies and redirecting the money to industries that work to improve air quality.
2 Introducing policies that hold fossil-fuel companies directly responsible for the pollution they cause while ensuring low-

income households benefit financially.
3 Providing pretax subsidies to companies in clean-energy industries and rewarding them for making clean energy more accessible to low-income households.
4 Ensuring that any cuts to pretax subsidies are carried out at the same rate as reductions in posttax subsidies are.

Plant Intelligence

Taking it for granted that a central nervous system — and a brain in particular — is a prerequisite for intelligence, scientists have long asserted that only humans and animals are capable of thinking. Based on this view, research into intelligence has been defined by IQ tests and other objective measurements of the ability to do things like answering written questions, solving physical puzzles, and demonstrating memory skills through actions.

Proponents of an emerging field known as plant neurobiology, however, have disputed the scientific consensus, arguing that the lack of a central nervous system does not necessarily preclude plants from possessing some form of intelligence. They contend that ordinary biological, chemical, and genetic mechanisms in plants do not adequately explain the wide array of highly sophisticated behaviors that they exhibit. Advocates claim, therefore, that plants are not simply passive elements in their environment, but are, in fact, capable of sensing and assessing stimuli from multiple environmental factors in order to coordinate appropriate responses. Such assertions, however, have been met with skepticism and even outright hostility in the scientific community.

Research by Monica Gagliano of the University of Western Australia attempted to validate some of plant neurobiology's controversial claims using the mimosa plant, which is known for defensively curling its leaves in reaction to being touched or disturbed. Gagliano's experiment involved exposing over 50 mimosa plants to weekly sessions of controlled, harmless dropping motions. She observed that, over time, some of the plants stopped reacting defensively, indicating they had learned that danger was not imminent. To discount the possibility that the plants' lack of reaction to being dropped could be attributed to fatigue or something similar, Gagliano exposed some of the plants to a sudden shaking motion.

Though the process of adapting to being dropped had been gradual, the shaking motion instantly returned the plants to their normal defensive behavior. When she exposed them to the dropping motions again, the plants "remembered" what they had previously learned, suggesting that they were purposely altering their response to being dropped based on experience.

Research like this supports the growing argument that while plants may not have brains, their behavior in reaction to environmental stimuli is evidence of a brainlike information-processing system. Scientists who support this theory have also noted that, on a biological level, the chemical signaling systems found in the nervous systems of animals have been identified in plants, too.

Despite the mounting research lending support to the concept of plant intelligence, Gagliano and others who advocate for further studies into this field have come under fire from those who doubt the validity of such research. In direct response to Gagliano's experiment, some argue that dropping a plant is not a common occurrence in nature, and thus cannot be considered a reliable trigger for the type of learning Gagliano ascribes to her plants. Instead, they describe the behavior of Gagliano's plants as the result of evolutionary adaptation, an automatic reaction programmed by nature over many generations. In response, Gagliano points out that the stimulus in her experiment was artificial, so it does not make sense that plants could have undergone an evolutionary adaptation to something that does not occur in their natural environment. Her argument that the plants' response could not be innate is further supported by the fact that some of her plants learned faster than others.

Stefano Mancuso, the director of the International Laboratory of Plant Neurobiology in Florence, Italy, approaches the controversy in a different way. His research has revealed unusual levels of electrical activity and oxygen consumption in the roots of plants, possibly hinting at a "root brain." A firm advocate of plant neurobiology, Mancuso believes that plant intelligence is analogous to the distributed intelligence observed in swarm behavior. In bird flocks, for example, birds follow rules for the collective good of the group, such as maintaining appropriate distances between each other when flying. This type of collective behavior, he suggests, is not unlike the manner in which individual roots of a plant act in a coordinated manner to benefit the entire organism.

The contention surrounding plant neurobiology has reignited a broader debate about intelligence. According to Mancuso, our reluctance to apply intelligence to other organisms may be due to psychologically based biases. In his opinion, we are able to accept the concept of artificial intelligence in the machines we build, for example, because they serve us and are our own creations. On the other hand, our hostility to plant intelligence, he believes, could be a manifestation of the somber realization that while a world without plants would be disastrous for humans, the opposite would likely not be an issue for plants. Considering Mancuso's perspective, perhaps the simplification of plant intelligence as just a consequence of electrical signals exchanged between cells could be deemed unfairly dismissive.

(38) Why is plant neurobiology controversial in the scientific community?

1 It argues that the very same methods used by scientists to determine a human subject's level of intelligence should also be applied to other organisms.
2 It proposes that the biological, chemical, and genetic processes observed in plant behavior operate differently from those in humans and animals.
3 It implies that mechanisms previously thought to underlie the human central nervous system do not function as scientists have always believed.
4 It makes claims regarding the fundamental mechanisms behind intelligence that are in opposition to the ideas held by a majority of scientists.

(39) Monica Gagliano's experiment on the mimosa plant suggests that

1 since the plant displayed delayed defensive behavior when presented with threats, it is unable to react quickly to danger.
2 the plant's ability to act upon what it has remembered is greatly affected by the degree of fatigue that it is experiencing at any one time.
3 the plant demonstrates the capacity to distinguish between various types of sensory input as well as exhibit different reactions to them.
4 since there were inconsistencies in the ways the plant reacted to being shaken, learning speed is not the same between species.

(40) According to the passage, which of the following statements would Gagliano most likely agree with?

  1 Testing plants with a stimulus they do not experience in nature helps to show that their response is actually based on learning.
  2 The way plants adapt over generations is actually more similar to the way humans learn than most researchers believe.
  3 The consensus among scientists that plants are in possession of a nervous system provides enough justification to compare plant behavior with that of animals.
  4 Though plants' information-processing systems work much more slowly than those of humans, it does not mean they are necessarily inferior.

(41) What does Stefano Mancuso imply regarding plant intelligence?

  1 If researchers chose to compare plants to animals other than humans, the field of plant neurobiology would advance far more quickly.
  2 Despite some similarity between how humans and plants formulate various behaviors, it is irresponsible to assume that this relates to intelligence in the same way.
  3 Human attitudes toward the concept of intelligence in plants may be related to how we understand and rationalize our relationship with them.
  4 The fact that electrical-activity levels are similar in plant roots and the brains of birds suggests that they may operate similarly.

4
- *Write an essay on the given TOPIC.*
- *Give THREE reasons to support your answer.*
- *Structure: introduction, main body, and conclusion*
- *Suggested length: 200–240 words*
- *Write your essay in the space provided on Side B of your answer sheet. Any writing outside the space will not be graded.*

TOPIC

Are economic sanctions a useful foreign-policy tool?

リスニング

―――――― Listening Test ――――――

There are four parts to this listening test.

Part 1	Dialogues: 1 question each	Multiple-choice
Part 2	Passages: 2 questions each	Multiple-choice
Part 3	Real-Life: 1 question each	Multiple-choice
Part 4	Interview: 2 questions	Multiple-choice

※**Listen carefully to the instructions.**

Part 1

No. 1
1 Her back pain became less severe.
2 She was worried about side effects.
3 Her doctor suggested it might not be safe.
4 She heard it was ineffective against back pain.

No. 2
1 He did not get along with the staff.
2 Employee turnover was high.
3 He had to deal with many complaints.
4 Product quality was better.

No. 3
1 The declining quality of school meals.
2 The proposal to open a snack shop.
3 The lack of convenient restaurants in the area.
4 The increasing cost of school meals.

No. 4
1 He is planning to leave the company.
2 He is away on business for much of the year.
3 His current project has become complicated.
4 His boss will not extend the deadline.

No. 5		1 It is not being advertised well. 2 The location of the house might put buyers off. 3 There are better houses available in the area. 4 The asking price for the house may be too high.
No. 6		1 She may stop buying organic food. 2 She has reduced her shopping budget. 3 She is committed to helping the environment. 4 She has found a cheaper organic-food store.
No. 7		1 Contact the insurance company. 2 Renegotiate the payments on the car. 3 Purchase a more fuel-efficient vehicle. 4 Spend less money on other things.
No. 8		1 The job's salary is not as high as he expected. 2 His wife places too much emphasis on money. 3 The job would force him to change his lifestyle. 4 His family may go further into debt.
No. 9		1 Replace her car's brake drums. 2 Go to a cheaper garage. 3 Get her car repaired as soon as possible. 4 Pay for the repairs in advance.
No. 10		1 The agencies have found some ideal candidates. 2 Dan should lower his expectations. 3 Philip Johnson's sales record is not outstanding. 4 Dan should make the final hiring decision.

Part 2

(A)

No. 11
1 Our brains do not age in the same way as our bodies do.
2 Electrical stimulation may cause serious mental issues.
3 Learning is not connected to other brain functions.
4 Synchronizing brain waves improves memory function.

No. 12
1 It has potential uses beyond improving memory and learning.
2 It has helped to identify previously unknown conditions.
3 It has demonstrated long-term effectiveness.
4 It has proved unsuitable for treating brain disorders.

(B)

No. 13
1 It was once covered in dense rain forest.
2 It has several distinct ecological environments.
3 It attracted many species from other landmasses.
4 It remains isolated from modern civilization.

No. 14
1 By comparing it to wildlife on other islands.
2 By recruiting local people as guides.
3 By examining past changes in the climate.
4 By copying methods used in other countries.

No. 15		**(C)** 1 Germany's nuclear program depended on it. 2 It prevents atoms from splitting. 3 German scientists thought it was unsafe. 4 No neutrons can pass through it.
No. 16		1 Germany had stolen nuclear technology from the US. 2 Britain had not developed a nuclear program. 3 An air attack on Vemork would not have succeeded. 4 The US needed Vemork to produce heavy water.
No. 17		**(D)** 1 They would have been more conclusive using x-rays. 2 The imaging technology he used limited their accuracy. 3 They revealed it was made of wood rather than bronze. 4 His analysis differed from that of Roman scientists.
No. 18		1 It is older than similar ancient devices that have been found. 2 Some of the information it revealed was incorrect. 3 It may not have been the first of its kind. 4 The way it was originally used was not efficient.
No. 19		**(E)** 1 It was started by homeless people living in the city. 2 Environmental conditions helped it to spread quickly. 3 It did not affect buildings in the business district. 4 Firefighters thought they had brought it under control.
No. 20		1 The height of new buildings was restricted. 2 Reconstruction resulted in population growth. 3 Famous architects overcharged for their services. 4 Officials ignored fire codes to speed up reconstruction.

Part 3

(F)

No. 21

Situation: You have recently started an entry-level job at an automobile parts manufacturer. You work in the legal department. At a staff meeting, the company president says the following.

Question: What do you need to do first?

1 Review the standards for manufacturing goods.
2 Create a summary of legal requirements for recalls.
3 Check the procedures for amending existing contracts.
4 Investigate lawsuits the company might face.

(G)

No. 22

Situation: You live in the US and need to fly to Canada in one week due to a family emergency. Your Japanese passport expires in two months. A travel agent tells you the following.

Question: What should you do?

1 Consult with officials at the airport in Canada.
2 Apply for a temporary passport online.
3 Go downtown to get a new passport.
4 Visit a Japanese consulate after arriving in Canada.

No. 23

(H)

Situation: You and your family recently moved abroad. You are enrolling your daughter in a primary school. She completed her vaccinations in Japan. A school administrator tells you the following.

Question: What should you do before the first day of school?

1 Submit the signed permission forms.
2 Have a doctor give your daughter a checkup.
3 Submit proof of immunization.
4 Get a letter from your employer.

No. 24

(I)

Situation: Your Gold membership with E-Zonia Travel will expire soon, and you would like to renew it. Your total budget for the year is $3,000. An agency representative gives you the following advice.

Question: What should you do?

1 Raise your spending to the E-Zonia minimum.
2 Apply for an E-Zonia credit card.
3 Book a flight through E-Zonia before the year's end.
4 Reserve four nights at an E-Zonia partner hotel.

(J)

No. 25

Situation: You are an American citizen living overseas. You want to transfer money from your US bank account to your daughter's account. You call your bank, and a representative tells you the following.

Question: What should you do first to obtain an access code?

1 Change your account password.
2 Reconfirm your e-mail address.
3 Visit a bank branch in person.
4 Answer two security questions.

Part 4

No. 26

1 They do not fully understand the value of their jewelry.
2 They are overly attached to worthless sentimental pieces.
3 They rely too much on market prices for gold and silver.
4 They often neglect to check the reputation of the jeweler.

No. 27

1 It has led to some jewelry makers leaving the profession.
2 It has reduced his profits, despite the high price of gold.
3 It is similar to destroying a valuable work of art.
4 It is occurring less frequently than it did in the past.

二次試験
面　接

[A日程]　▶MP3　▶アプリ　▶CD 4 ⑥〜⑩

1. Should democratic nations try to force democracy on other nations?
2. Information in the Internet age — too much or not enough?
3. Could genetic engineering be the solution to human health problems?
4. Is there too much emphasis on technology in professional sports today?
5. Agree or disagree: A single world government would benefit the planet

[C日程]

1. Agree or disagree: Business monopolies can be beneficial to society
2. Should the decentralization of power be a key goal of the government?
3. Is more regulation the answer to cybercrime?
4. Has news objectivity become impossible in the age of social media?
5. Should more be done to promote awareness of mental health issues?

（注）モデルスピーチと解説はA日程のみ収録しています。

2020-3

一次試験　2021.1.24実施
二次試験　A日程　2021.2.21実施
　　　　　B日程　2021.2.28実施

Grade 1

試験時間
筆記：100分
リスニング：約35分

一次試験・筆記　　　　　p.66〜80
一次試験・リスニング　　p.81〜87
二次試験・面接　　　　　　　p.88

＊解答・解説は別冊p.109〜160にあります。
＊面接の流れは本書p.16にあります。

2020年度第3回

Web特典「自動採点サービス」対応
オンラインマークシート

※検定の回によって2次元コードが違います。
※筆記1〜3，リスニングの採点ができます。
※PCからも利用できます（本書p.8参照）。

一次試験
筆 記

1 To complete each item, choose the best word or phrase from among the four choices. Then, on your answer sheet, find the number of the question and mark your answer.

(1) The new president of RC Computers (　　) several decisions made by the previous president. He believed that they had been mistakes and were hurting the company's sales.
1 perpetuated　**2** prefaced　**3** overrode　**4** satiated

(2) Brendan has been an (　　) supporter of the Greenville Wolves basketball team since he was a child. Every season, he goes to as many of their games as he can.
1 elusive　**2** ardent　**3** ornate　**4** apathetic

(3) After the church began offering weekend religious education programs for children, its (　　) grew steadily, with new families joining every month.
1 partition　**2** compilation　**3** inhibition　**4** congregation

(4) Owing to the sudden (　　) in the value of the currency this year, the prices of imported goods have risen sharply.
1 depreciation　　　　　**2** rendition
3 demarcation　　　　　**4** extraction

(5) The new tax was highly unpopular, so the finance minister decided to wait until public criticism had (　　) before introducing any further taxes.
1 abated　**2** permeated　**3** corroded　**4** instigated

(6) *A:* Honey, I want this new house, but what if we can't sell the one we live in now?
B: We'll make the purchase agreement (　　) on the sale of our current house. So if we can't sell it, we won't have to buy the new one.
1 plenary　**2** appalling　**3** filial　**4** contingent

(7) Lucy sustained a mild (　　) in the car accident and was treated at a local hospital. The doctor said her head would hurt for the next couple of weeks.
1 conciliation　**2** conurbation　**3** contraption　**4** concussion

(8) The climb to the top of the tower turned out to be more

( ) than the tourists had expected. By the time they reached the top, most of them felt exhausted.
1 arduous **2** shattered **3** barbarous **4** decrepit

(9) When Tim moved to the city, he could only afford to rent an old, run-down apartment. When his mother visited, she was shocked at the ( ) conditions he lived in.
1 colossal **2** auxiliary **3** squalid **4** inadvertent

(10) Many people were shocked by the new biography of the wartime leader. They accused the author of ( ) a great man by reporting unproven rumors.
1 deviating **2** soliciting **3** denigrating **4** incubating

(11) The president was concerned about the sudden increase of enemy troops on the border. He feared his country could be invaded and ( ) by its powerful neighbor.
1 annexed **2** yielded **3** vacillated **4** proffered

(12) People tend to judge an academic institution by the success of its graduates, but that is not the only ( ) for determining how good a school is.
1 allegory **2** yardstick **3** exponent **4** blurb

(13) As a young politician, Ramesh had been widely ( ) as a future leader. After falling seriously ill, however, he was forced to give up his political career.
1 touted **2** pulverized **3** fermented **4** pared

(14) Many cheeses from Europe are well known for having ( ) aromas, but those who love eating them do not mind their smell at all.
1 pungent **2** truculent **3** dreary **4** murky

(15) *A:* Gina, you look ( ). What's wrong?
B: I spent the whole day taking care of my sister's three kids. I was totally exhausted after just a couple of hours.
1 frazzled **2** awry **3** insufferable **4** overt

(16) The criminal's detailed knowledge of the bank's security led the police to believe that he must have had an ( ) inside the organization.
1 electorate **2** autocrat **3** extrovert **4** accomplice

(17) *A:* Have you seen the latest opinion polls on the prime minister?

67

B: Yes, he's doing terribly. After that last public debate, his approval ratings have dropped to a (   ) 10 percent.
1 candid   **2** virulent   **3** petulant   **4** paltry

(18) When Roland learned his business partner had been overcharging clients, he quit and (   ) all ties with the company. He did not want to be associated with such activity.
1 presaged   **2** instilled   **3** repatriated   **4** severed

(19) The police concluded that the murder was (   ). It was clear from the evidence that the killer had planned every last detail of the crime.
1 premeditated   **2** embittered
3 threaded   **4** gleaned

(20) Mr. Garcia was shocked when one of his staff members had the (   ) to ask for a pay raise on the same day that she overslept and arrived late for work.
1 sham   **2** wrath   **3** gall   **4** piety

(21) Initial attempts to market the new product in creative ways were only (   ) successful, so the company decided to rethink its sales strategy.
1 heartily   **2** marginally   **3** vehemently   **4** intently

(22) When the school administrators found out that some students had cheated on their final exams, they were quick to (   ) punishments to everyone involved.
1 dish out   **2** tear off   **3** wire up   **4** dive into

(23) Franklin was (   ) by the news that his sister had won $50 million in the lottery. He never thought that anyone he knew would become so rich overnight.
1 blasted off   **2** blown away   **3** bashed in   **4** boiled over

(24) Although young tigers can (   ) themselves by the age of 18 months, they usually stay with their mother until they are around two-and-a-half years old.
1 skirt around   **2** lag behind   **3** fend for   **4** tangle with

(25) The news photographer was (   ) by a hotel worker that a film star was vacationing there, so he rushed to the hotel to try to get a picture.
1 tipped off   **2** scrimped on
3 worked over   **4** clogged up

2
Read each passage and choose the best word or phrase from among the four choices for each blank. Then, on your answer sheet, find the number of the question and mark your answer.

The Mitchell Map

In 1750, John Mitchell, an American doctor living in England, was tasked with creating a map of North America by the Earl of Halifax, a high-ranking British official. Britain's relations with France were tense at the time, with ongoing disputes over control of North American colonial territories, where France was constructing military fortifications. Halifax, in charge of managing these colonies, was determined to rally government support for a campaign to resist the intrusions. The map he commissioned Mitchell to make (　26　). Mitchell was a supporter of Britain's claims over North America, and this bias was noticeable in the borders he drew and the numerous annotations regarding British territorial claims in early versions of his map. That sentiment was further apparent in subsequent publications of the map, with even less land being recognized as belonging to France. This helped sway public and political opinion, hastening a series of events that led to the two nations competing fiercely over colonial interests.

While France's defeat in the ensuing conflict resulted in a massive territorial acquisition for Britain, the vast amounts of money it had poured into the war caused British national debt to soar. In an attempt to offset this loss, Britain passed the Stamp Act in 1765, which exacted the first direct tax on the American colonies. Protests erupted throughout the colonies in retaliation, culminating in the American Revolution. With another military conflict so soon after its previous one, Britain's victory against France had clearly (　27　).

The Revolutionary War, fought between Britain and its American colonies over eight years, concluded in 1783. It was an auspicious ending for the Americans, who not only broke free from Britain's grasp but also gained possession of a generous amount of land, thanks to the British and American negotiators using Mitchell's map to draw up the new territorial boundaries. Given the contrast between the original intention behind the map's creation and its eventual role in the aftermath of the war, there is little doubt that Mitchell himself — had he been alive to witness the signing — would have disapproved of (28   ). Mitchell's map, by playing a key role in helping encourage conflict with the French, ultimately paved the way for American independence from the British.

---

(26) 1 led him to change his mind
     2 had been created far too late
     3 succeeded in this objective
     4 helped the opposite to occur

(27) 1 reduced its appetite for war
     2 threatened other nations
     3 come at a high price
     4 helped it gain new allies

(28) 1 the benefits afforded to Britain
     2 how American requests were denied
     3 the simplifications made to his map
     4 how his map had been put to use

Acting and the Brain

An actor's role is to inhabit a variety of different characters with mind-sets that can differ substantially from their own. It has been suggested, however, that (29   ). Crucial to the success of an actor's performance is a phenomenon known as "suspension of disbelief," which involves convincing audiences to cast aside critical thinking and disregard the knowledge that the actor is not, in reality, the character being portrayed. Yet it is the ability of actors to lose themselves in the characters they play that makes suspension of disbelief possible, and many actors claim that the lengths they go to in their attempts to immerse themselves in characters' emotions take a psychological toll. This is said to be particularly true when actors portray individuals in stories dealing with domestic violence or sexual assault.

It now appears that (30   ). A research team at a Canadian university monitored actors as they responded to a series of questions under different conditions, including responding as themselves and also "in character" after preparing for a role in a Shakespeare play. The researchers found that when subjects had "become" the character in the play, they experienced a large decrease in activity in areas of the brain associated with the processing of self-related information. This suggests actors do, in fact, run the risk of compromising their own identity when they transform into a character.

The Canadian researchers tested their ideas about self even further by instructing the actors to respond to questions using a foreign accent but without "becoming" someone who would naturally speak in that accent. The brain activity monitored during this experiment suggested that simply talking in an uncommon way could facilitate the weakening of the self. This is supported by another study involving ordinary people, in which subjects were asked questions about their own personality and that of a friend. Later, when asked about their own personality again, the subjects responded in a manner that suggested they had subconsciously shifted perception of their own personality closer to that of their friend's, highlighting how even ordinary people's brains experience a degree of instability when processing identity. The findings, it seems, underline a fragility to people's sense of self that (**31**   ).

---

(29) 1 only certain types of actors can do this
　　 2 this can sometimes be harmful to actors
　　 3 an actor's true purpose is different
　　 4 this is actually impossible for an actor

(30) 1 this applies more to the least-skilled actors
　　 2 the mind is not that easily influenced
　　 3 this concern should be taken seriously
　　 4 performing strengthens relationships among actors

(31) 1 can only be understood by some
　　 2 is not simply limited to actors
　　 3 may damage relationships
　　 4 many actors refuse to accept

3 *Read each passage and choose the best answer from among the four choices for each question. Then, on your answer sheet, find the number of the question and mark your answer.*

Business and Sustainability

In 2015, the United Nations unanimously adopted the Sustainable Development Goals (SDGs)—an initiative calling on governments, businesses, and ordinary citizens alike to help realize a more prosperous and sustainable global future by tackling poverty and protecting the environment. While many businesses have seemed to enthusiastically embrace the SDGs, there appears to be a worrying disconnect between what these companies say and what they actually do. According to one study conducted by the global investment management firm PIMCO, the fact that a large number of firms reference the SDGs in corporate reporting indicates a widespread awareness regarding their existence and importance. Fewer than one in ten firms, however, provided figures indicating quantifiable progress toward targets, and the report's authors concluded that "most companies still lack the expertise to identify activity and targets that can add business value."

While it is true that the disparity could be the result of the relative newness and unfamiliarity of the SDGs, others have taken a more cynical view. Numerous corporations have been accused of "greenwashing," a term referring to attempts to deceive the general public into thinking that firms care more about the environment than they really do. A significant number of the 17 SDGs directly address issues like clean energy and the protection and restoration of ecosystems, and critics point out that it is all too easy to take existing practices, as well as projects already in the pipeline, and manipulate them into a form resembling an SDG target, with the ambiguous wording of the SDGs making them highly susceptible to this practice. In addition, some firms have also been accused of double-dealing in the name of SDG compliance by, for example, attempting to beef up their public image with substantial contributions to environmental groups but failing to pay living wages to their employees. Since the SDGs were intended to be catalysts for innovation and transformation that are universally beneficial, these practices are clearly missing the mark.

Accusations against companies suspected of greenwashing often portray SDG reporting in an unflattering light, but there may be a silver lining to the controversy surrounding the practice. Any degree of SDG reporting opens a company up to increased scrutiny of its sustainability practices. In recent years, it has become extremely common for public opinion to spur even the most uncompromising corporation to expand sustainability efforts, yet this inevitably leads to an avalanche of greenwashing accusations. Erica Charles, lecturer at Glasgow Caledonian University London, however, suggests that just a miniscule, public-relations-inspired shift in practices at a multinational corporation can have a significant "impact and ripple effect on the rest of the industry to review their approach to business." Some would argue that for this reason it is essential that critics exercise a degree of restraint in their accusations against what they perceive as insufficient reporting, since an excessively harsh media backlash could deter corporations from doing anything at all. Even a failed or insincere corporate effort made under the guise of environmental sustainability, it appears, may not be an entirely wasted endeavor after all.

(32) According to the study conducted by PIMCO,

　1 the slowdown in progress toward SDG targets set by companies since 2015 indicates that firms fear the targets will negatively affect profits.
　2 distrust of the United Nations' motives is the main reason that many companies have been slow to acknowledge the importance of the SDGs.
　3 companies appear to be attempting to hide their violations of the SDGs by falsifying the numbers in the reports that they provide.
　4 many corporations approve of the SDGs but have been unable to determine how to implement them in a way that is beneficial to their business.

(33) What is one reason that firms get accused of "greenwashing"?

　1 The unclear wording of some of the SDGs has caused so much confusion that misunderstandings about their policies are almost certain to arise.
　2 Some have been attempting to make it appear that things they were already doing are part of their efforts to comply with the SDGs.

3 The unrealistic targets set in many of the SDGs have forced some companies to pretend that they are meeting every single one of the goals.
4 Companies know that since many of the SDGs are unrelated to the environment, it is easier to focus on those and neglect the environment-related ones.

(34) How can Erica Charles's comment best be interpreted in the context of the passage?

1 Large companies are trying to undermine SDG reporting by influencing other firms in their industry to resist environmental regulation.
2 Rather than focusing on the largest corporations in an industry, it is important for critics to look at all businesses responsible for greenwashing.
3 When large companies implement minor changes that do not appear significant, it may be unwise to be overly critical of them.
4 The majority of SDG reporting at large companies is so poorly conducted that an entirely new system needs to be developed.

Rent Control

In the face of skyrocketing housing costs in major metropolises throughout the United States, numerous municipalities have imposed rent-control legislation designed to ensure stable access to housing for low-income residents. These laws are generally set by a city-run committee and ensure that housing costs will not rise by more than a very small percentage annually. While on the surface rent control can be seen as shielding vulnerable citizens from economic hardship, these restrictions are almost universally condemned by economists. They argue that since rent control has the effect of limiting landlord income, the laws reduce incentives to construct new properties. Available rental units inevitably become scarcer, and in accordance with the principles of supply and demand, rents for the housing that is exempt from rent control are driven up. In addition, tenants fortunate enough to occupy rent-controlled units tend to stay in them even when their economic circumstances improve, greatly amplifying the negative effect on the housing supply available to people with lower incomes. It is apparent then, economists argue, that rent-control laws aggravate the very issue they are intended to remedy.

On the other hand, rent-control advocates point out that recently constructed housing is generally exempt from rent-control legislation. Studies have, in fact, indicated that most rent-control regulation does not adversely affect new housing construction in cities where it is imposed on preexisting properties in the market. Economists argue, though, that rent control instead pushes landlords to take steps such as converting rental properties into for-sale units, or even selling them to their longtime occupants, further contributing to shortfalls in the rental-housing supply.

Both economists and proponents of rent-control measures agree on one thing: limiting rents lowers the risk of financially disadvantaged people being displaced from their homes. What is more, researchers who examined the addresses and migration histories of residents in San Francisco found that low-income people, and especially minorities, who had lived in a rent-controlled unit were more likely to continue residing in the city even after vacating the rent-controlled unit. While this is a positive finding for a subset of low-income people, economists say the measures do not address the problem of others unable to find housing because of the lack of affordable options resulting from the short supply of rental units.

Often overlooked by economists, however, is the issue of housing stability. US tax laws grant homeowners significant benefits in the form of tax breaks; people lacking sufficient funds to purchase a home are unable to take advantage of these. Without rent controls, low-income renters are therefore at especially high risk of being evicted because of financial hardship. The damaging effect of forced moves on mental and physical health is well documented, and it has been shown to impact women more severely than men. This is particularly concerning given that children of women who experience stress during pregnancy suffer long-term psychological consequences, and children with little residential stability are also less likely to graduate from high school. While the quantitative arguments economists make when decrying rent control do have some validity, city officials must not overlook its broader, more positive implications.

(35) One common criticism made by economists about rent control is that

1 it has been unable to compensate for the sharp rise in rents resulting from building booms in recent years.
2 the city committees that regulate rental apartments can be easily influenced by landlords to force people to leave rent-controlled units.
3 it actually limits the living choices that are available to residents who may not be as economically advantaged as others.
4 although it helps increase the supply of available apartments in a city, it also contributes to reduced demand for them.

(36) Which of the following statements would supporters of rent control most likely agree with?

1 While rent control may be a result of temporary housing shortages, these are balanced out in the long run by an increase in construction.
2 Since many older buildings are not subject to rent control, rental-housing shortages are actually the result of a lack of new construction projects.
3 The measures taken by landlords in response to rent-control laws actually tend to lead to an increase in the availability of housing.
4 Rent control affects the housing market less than economists claim because the laws usually only affect rental properties already available.

(37) What does the author of the passage imply about rent control in the last paragraph?

1 While economists' warnings about rent-control laws make little sense at present, the issue will need to be reconsidered by future generations.
2 Despite any drawbacks of rent-control laws, they play an important role in society that cannot be measured by economic analysis alone.
3 The negative consequences that rent-control laws have on the housing market outweigh the social benefits they can lead to.
4 The benefits that rent-control laws provide for wealthier

populations eventually end up being available to society as a whole.

Nasser and Pan-Arabism

In 1952, a group of army officers seized power from the British-backed monarchy in Egypt, forcing the nation's king, Farouk I, into exile. The rebels were part of a nationalist movement within the military forces of Egypt, known as the Free Officers, which had formed around the anticolonialist ideology of its leader, a young Egyptian officer named Gamal Abdel Nasser. Its official head at the time of the coup was Mohammed Naguib, a senior army officer and war hero, whom Nasser installed as a figurehead. Nasser was taking advantage of Naguib's tremendous renown among the general public to legitimize the new regime since he himself lacked the prestige necessary for the role at the time. When Naguib overstepped his bounds by attempting to defy Nasser, however, he was removed from power and Nasser emerged from the shadows, assuming the country's leadership in 1954.

During his long years in power, Nasser remade Egypt. He instituted a far-reaching modernization program that included free education and medical care, improved housing, and labor reforms. A feudal system of land ownership during the monarchy had created an unequal distribution of wealth, which Nasser addressed with reforms that improved conditions for farmers and limited the amount of land individuals could own. Nasser came from humble beginnings and presented himself as a man of the people. "Nasserism," as his ideology became known, was rooted in socialism and wealth redistribution, and unlike previous rulers, Nasser remained free of corruption.

This is not to say, however, that his rule was benign. Dissent was mercilessly crushed, and Nasser expressed open contempt for democracy. He saw both his egalitarian social programs and harsh enforcement tactics as essential for attaining his vision of Arab unity, or pan-Arabism, across the Middle East. If Egypt were to take the dominant role in a unified Arab world, it would first have to bolster its economy and improve social welfare domestically while ensuring that any opponents who might undermine Nasser's policies were kept off the political stage.

Anticolonialism was the foundation of Nasser's foreign policy, and he supported liberation movements throughout Africa. Aided by his charisma and public-speaking talents, Nasser not only transformed Egyptian society but also provided a model to which other Arab nations could aspire. Nasser stepped into the international spotlight in 1956, when he nationalized the strategically and economically important Suez Canal. Despite its location within Egyptian territory, it had been jointly owned and operated by Britain and France, but Egyptian soldiers seized control of the canal. Israeli, French, and British forces invaded the country, quickly defeating Egyptian forces in the Suez region and precipitating what became known as the "Suez Crisis." Egypt enjoyed greater success on the diplomatic front, however. The Soviet Union was courting Egyptian favor at the time with a view to greater influence in the region in the future, and condemned what it saw as an example of Western imperialism. The Soviets even went so far as to threaten a nuclear strike against Western Europe if the invaders failed to withdraw. A horrified United States intervened behind the scenes to avert a confrontation with the Soviets, resulting in a humiliating withdrawal by the European and Israeli invaders. Nasser emerged from the Suez Crisis having not only defied the West but triumphed against long odds, albeit due in part to the fortuitous intercession of the Americans and Soviets. Nasser's actions nonetheless resulted in mass displays of public adulation throughout the Middle East and the consolidation of his leadership role within it.

At the height of Nasser's power, Arab unity seemed a genuine possibility. Having shaken off colonial rule, nations in the Middle East stood together in solidarity and identified as an independent geopolitical bloc. Yet the 1958 formation of the United Arab Republic, a union between Egypt and Syria, was short-lived owing to Syrian dissatisfaction with Nasser-imposed centralization policies. The notion that Arab nations could unify was smashed in 1967, when Egypt led surrounding Arab countries into a disastrous war with Israel, the result of which was not only a significant loss of territory but also a deep, abiding wound inflicted upon the Arab psyche.

Nasser's popularity waned in the years before his death in 1970, but he remains an icon to many throughout the Middle East, even though disunity and conflict today have lessened the prospect of pan-Arabism. In post-Nasser Egypt, the gulf between rich and poor continues to fluctuate, and Nasser's goal of social equality appears unlikely to come to fruition. Despite the nostalgia for Nasser's rule, however, some commentators insist his charisma made Egyptians blind to his failings, such as the fact that his wealth-redistribution policies encouraged an economic overreliance on the state by the work force which continues to this day. While there is truth in such accusations, in the end, since Nasser's popularity has always been primarily a product of his ideology rather than his accomplishments, the nostalgia will likely endure for years to come.

(38) What can be inferred about the Free Officers?

1 Gamal Abdel Nasser believed it would be necessary to break up the group after Mohammed Naguib attempted to alter its leadership structure.
2 Though the group's actions received widespread support due to Naguib's reputation, the loss of his position showed he was not an essential figure.
3 There was conflict between Nasser and Naguib over the degree of democracy the group would allow after it took power.
4 While its principles were based on Naguib's ideas, Nasser felt he himself had to be in control to ensure the coup was peaceful rather than violent.

(39) According to the author of the passage, what was the primary reason for Nasser's harsh political policies?

1 His ultimate objective of uniting the Arab world under Egyptian leadership required that domestic policies be introduced without obstacles.
2 He feared the increased wealth and education of ordinary people could lead to the rise of political opponents who favored socialism.
3 He feared his humble origins and lack of wealth would lead both the Egyptian public and other politicians to view him as a weak leader.
4 His opposition to the monarchy was not shared by most people, who believed their quality of life had been better under the previous government.

(40) Which of the following statements best describes the outcome of the "Suez Crisis"?

1 What at first appeared as a victory turned out to have done irreparable damage to Egypt's relationship with crucial Western allies.
2 Although Nasser gained a slight advantage near the end of the crisis, Egypt's military losses demonstrated that long-term success was impossible.
3 While Nasser initially appeared to side with the Soviets, his policy change at the end of the crisis demonstrated he was actually allied with the United States.
4 Nasser was able to win a significant political victory against Western powers, although it was partly due to factors beyond his control.

(41) What explanation does the author of the passage give for the way that many modern Egyptians feel about Nasser and his rule?

1 The working class in Egypt has not forgiven Nasser for damage resulting from the war with Israel despite its admiration for him as a person.
2 It is influenced more by the philosophy and vision that Nasser represented for Egypt than by the changes that arose from his policies.
3 The changes in social welfare and education for all Egyptians that Nasser introduced have had long-term benefits despite subsequent leaders' failings.
4 It has been shaped by people who fail to understand how much Nasser's personality and charisma inspired Egyptians during his rule.

4
- *Write an essay on the given TOPIC.*
- *Give THREE reasons to support your answer.*
- *Structure: introduction, main body, and conclusion*
- *Suggested length: 200–240 words*
- *Write your essay in the space provided on Side B of your answer sheet. Any writing outside the space will not be graded.*

TOPIC
Agree or disagree: Globalization is a positive force in today's world

リスニング

―――― Listening Test ――――

There are four parts to this listening test.

Part 1	Dialogues: 1 question each	Multiple-choice
Part 2	Passages: 2 questions each	Multiple-choice
Part 3	Real-Life: 1 question each	Multiple-choice
Part 4	Interview: 2 questions	Multiple-choice

※Listen carefully to the instructions.

Part 1

No. 1
1 The woman should consider improving her skill set.
2 The woman has set her standards too high.
3 He deserves to be considered for the position.
4 He can cover until they find the right person.

No. 2
1 Consult with his sales staff.
2 Reschedule the feedback meeting.
3 Cut the salaries of his staff.
4 Request additional staff.

No. 3
1 She plays for the New York symphony orchestra.
2 She just started teaching the violin.
3 She demands a lot from her students.
4 She prefers to work with beginners.

No. 4
1 He missed an appointment with his boss.
2 He forgot to make copies for his boss.
3 He broke the copier by accident.
4 He failed to get the copier fixed.

| No. 5 | 1 Change their advertising strategy.
2 Wait for the results of the TV ads.
3 Carry out more marketing polls.
4 Cancel the direct-mail campaign. |

| No. 6 | 1 He does not feel competent yet.
2 His clients at RCB are dissatisfied.
3 He is not used to having tight deadlines.
4 He does not think RCB's products will sell. |

| No. 7 | 1 The man should keep calling the number.
2 The man should use this experience to become a salesman.
3 The man should make use of the filing system.
4 The man should give up hope of getting his money back. |

| No. 8 | 1 Search for a more convenient location.
2 Decide to rent the office space.
3 Look for something smaller elsewhere.
4 Move again within a few years. |

| No. 9 | 1 It is not close enough to public transportation.
2 It would cost them too much to repair themselves.
3 It could be dangerous for elderly visitors.
4 It does not have space outside to build a ramp. |

| No. 10 | 1 The curriculum is the wrong level for students.
2 Helen is not fulfilling her responsibilities.
3 Margaret is too strong and overly bossy.
4 The teachers are creating too many materials. |

Part 2

No. 11

(A)
1 Children of strict parents are more likely to rebel.
2 Family values have little to do with political beliefs.
3 The way people are raised affects their political views.
4 People try to take different viewpoints from their parents.

No. 12
1 It seems to be caused by biological factors.
2 It makes people ignore negative stimuli.
3 It only develops in the brain during adulthood.
4 It affects liberals more than conservatives.

No. 13

(B)
1 The decreasing proportion of young adults.
2 Senior citizens living alone after a spouse dies.
3 Fewer divorced people remarrying.
4 Greater wealth leading to a higher divorce rate.

No. 14
1 They struggle to provide for their families.
2 They tend to seek educated spouses.
3 They often have children immediately after marriage.
4 They now get married later in life.

No. 15

(C)
1 Mental illness must be treated immediately.
2 External factors are not what make people happy.
3 People should be less individualistic.
4 Mental illness is more common than people think.

No. 16
1 It is more expensive than traditional therapies.
2 It takes a long time to be effective.
3 It could affect treatment for mentally ill patients.
4 It has no effect in preventing mental illness.

(D)

No. 17
1 They were given health tonics that contained it.
2 They were required to apply it to their fingers.
3 They put radium-covered brushes into their mouths.
4 They used it to clean their brushes.

No. 18
1 It proved that radium in paint was not dangerous.
2 It showed the women's exposure levels were low.
3 It successfully avoided lawsuits.
4 It used biased research results.

(E)

No. 19
1 They will improve the utilization of robots.
2 They greatly improve security in companies.
3 They are essential for human survival.
4 They are unavoidable in future workplaces.

No. 20
1 The technology could easily be stolen.
2 The safety of such devices is still uncertain.
3 The microchips may produce inaccurate data.
4 The implants are known to cause health issues.

Part 3

No. 21

(F)
Situation: You are purchasing a diving watch, and the store clerk is telling you about maintenance. You usually go scuba diving five times a year.
Question: What should you do?

1 Have the watch serviced every three years.
2 Purchase the recommended cleaner and brush.
3 Keep some replacement parts handy.
4 Replace the battery every five years.

No. 22

(G)
Situation: An airline lost your baggage several weeks ago, and you want to be compensated in some way. You fly on a regular basis. A lawyer gives you the following advice.
Question: What should you do?

1 Call the airline for a cash settlement.
2 Have a lawyer represent you in court.
3 Submit a claim form with receipts.
4 Wait for an offer of travel vouchers.

No. 23

(H)

Situation: You are on a business trip. You listen to a voice mail that a coworker left you over three hours ago. You will be in a conference meeting tomorrow morning until noon.

Question: What should you do?

1 Send the client a revised contract.
2 Answer the client's questions by e-mail.
3 Wait for the client to call.
4 Contact the client after he returns from Brazil.

No. 24

(I)

Situation: You are discussing your investments with your financial adviser. You want to earn at least 3 percent interest on your holdings, but you also want to minimize your risk.

Question: What should you do with your money?

1 Keep it in the American money-market account.
2 Invest it in the American real-estate investment trust.
3 Shift it to the Australian money-market account.
4 Move it to a Japanese bond-investment fund.

No. 25

(J)

Situation: You are buying lottery tickets for the first time. You want to increase your chances of winning. The clerk gives you the following advice.

Question: What should you do if you do not win on the first drawing?

1 Open an online account and submit your ticket numbers.
2 Download a claim form from the lottery's website.
3 Send your tickets to the state lottery office.
4 Take losing tickets to any lottery retailer.

Part 4

No. 26
1. People have free time in summer because the financial year ends in March.
2. Excellent teamwork means people change jobs less often than in other industries.
3. Those who can handle the pressures of the job usually become reliable coworkers.
4. New recruits need three years of experience before they work with clients.

No. 27
1. The United Nations must do more to help companies protect the environment.
2. The majority of companies now feel that it is important to their business.
3. Investors should fund efforts by companies to do work in the community.
4. Many companies ignore it to focus on charity events and art projects.

二次試験
面　接

A日程　🔊　▶MP3　▶アプリ　▶CD 4 [11]〜[15]

1. Would the global economy benefit from a single world currency?
2. Can labor unions effectively support workers in the modern business world?
3. Agree or disagree: The traditional family unit has lost its central role in modern society
4. Do the advantages of jury trials outweigh the disadvantages?
5. Will the human race one day be the cause of its own downfall?

B日程

1. Can Japan ever repeat the successful economic performance it enjoyed in the past?
2. Should essential workers such as doctors and firefighters be allowed to strike?
3. Can political violence ever be justified?
4. Agree or disagree: Interpersonal communication skills are becoming less important in the digital age
5. Should companies abandon the concept of lifetime employment for their employees?

（注）モデルスピーチと解説はA日程のみ収録しています。

2020-2

一次試験　2020.10.11実施
二次試験　A日程　2020.11.8実施
　　　　　B日程　2020.11.15実施

Grade 1

試験時間

筆記：100分
リスニング：約35分

一次試験・筆記　　　　　p.90〜104
一次試験・リスニングp.105〜111
二次試験・面接　　　　　　p.112

＊解答・解説は別冊p.161〜212にあります。
＊面接の流れは本書p.16にあります。

2020年度第2回　**Web特典「自動採点サービス」対応 オンラインマークシート**
※検定の回によって2次元コードが違います。
※筆記1〜3，リスニングの採点ができます。
※PCからも利用できます（本書p.8参照）。

一次試験
筆 記

1 To complete each item, choose the best word or phrase from among the four choices. Then, on your answer sheet, find the number of the question and mark your answer.

(1) The (　　) between the neighbors over property lines grew more intense each day. Eventually, they stopped talking to each other, and the matter had to be settled in court.
1 patronage　**2** gadget　**3** dexterity　**4** feud

(2) Coach Lawson warned her team not to become (　　). She told them that even though they were in first place in the league, they still had to train just as hard as always.
1 ostensible　**2** complacent　**3** exemplary　**4** intrinsic

(3) When Nigel left the restaurant, he was shocked to be (　　) by an aggressive drunken man who demanded money from him.
1 accosted　**2** implicated　**3** alienated　**4** insinuated

(4) *A:* If Joe wants to give up studying Spanish, let him.
B: Honestly, I think you give him too much (　　). He's not old enough to decide that kind of thing himself.
1 cavern　**2** latitude　**3** derision　**4** arrogance

(5) In order to (　　) the success of its antismoking campaign, the government hired researchers to find out how many people had really quit smoking.
1 upend　**2** span　**3** gauge　**4** slouch

(6) Some scientists believe it may one day be possible to turn the (　　) surface of Mars into a green environment that is livable for human beings.
1 flagrant　**2** succinct　**3** desolate　**4** discrete

(7) Joanne's new boss is the (　　) of her old one. Her previous boss used to constantly make rude demands, but her new boss is always polite and respectful.
1 antithesis　**2** prophet　**3** protagonist　**4** interlude

(8) Duncan's antique pocket watch means everything to him. It was (　　) to him by his grandfather when he passed away five years ago.
1 garnished　**2** chastised　**3** bequeathed　**4** precipitated

(9) In court, the bank robber's sister was sentenced for (　　) him in the crime by helping him hide after the robbery.
1 agonizing　　2 remonstrating
3 abetting　　4 disseminating

(10) *A:* As soon as we walked into the store, the staff started trying to convince us to buy things. They wouldn't leave us alone!
B: That type of (　　) sales pressure is the reason I hate going shopping.
1 relentless　2 incumbent　3 morose　4 auspicious

(11) The teacher introduced a reward system in her classroom. She hoped that it would serve as a (　　) that would motivate her students to learn.
1 precept　2 catalyst　3 pallor　4 crux

(12) *A:* Everything on the menu is so expensive, Ben. Are you sure we can afford this?
B: We have to (　　) ourselves now and then, Jane. Let's enjoy dinner tonight and worry about money another time.
1 abstain　2 indulge　3 exasperate　4 deluge

(13) Rongal was tired of the (　　) tasks he was doing, so he asked his boss if he could do some work that required more thought and skill.
1 subliminal　2 cerebral　3 menial　4 genial

(14) The detective (　　) pursued her cases until she solved them. She would not give up until she found the criminals responsible.
1 brusquely　2 sheepishly　3 daintily　4 tenaciously

(15) Although he did not make any direct criticisms, Mayor Chapman's speech contained a considerable amount of (　　) about the previous mayor's policies.
1 cove　2 innuendo　3 placebo　4 allegiance

(16) In an effort to promote child welfare, medical experts advise parents who smoke not to do so in the (　　) of their children.
1 shackle　2 vicinity　3 morsel　4 rubble

(17) *A:* Were you upset when your husband forgot your wedding anniversary?
B: Yes, I was (　　). I didn't talk to him for three days.
1 livid　2 anecdotal　3 fervent　4 putrid

(18) After Wesley used his laptop for 10 hours straight, his eyesight began to (   ). He decided to take a break and finish his work the next day.
1 drool   **2** coalesce   **3** blur   **4** chip

(19) In (   ) for the missile attacks on his country last week, the president ordered the air force to bomb selected military targets in the enemy's capital city.
1 retaliation   **2** adulation   **3** combustion   **4** modulation

(20) The author's latest book (   ) deep into the origins of the industrial revolution. It contains an astonishing amount of research.
1 blurts   **2** parries   **3** jiggles   **4** delves

(21) Sajid is well known in the office for his (   ) manner. He is always the first to welcome new staff, show them around, and help them relax.
1 abominable   **2** dank   **3** affable   **4** bereft

(22) The champion wrestler has never been defeated, so most experts think it is unlikely the challenger can (   ) a victory in the final.
1 pull off   **2** burn out   **3** ease off   **4** shoot back

(23) *A:* Mom, I'm going to ask Dad to let me go to the concert on Sunday.
B: You should wait until he has (   ) a bit. He's still furious about your brother's poor grades.
1 simmered down   **2** tapered off
3 boxed up   **4** cranked out

(24) The painters made good progress on the building at first, but then a bad storm (   ) the work by several days. They were not able to finish on schedule.
1 hinged on   **2** cleaned out   **3** set back   **4** pulled away

(25) Sylvia used to play a lot of video games, but her interest in them has been (   ). Now, she only plays them occasionally.
1 blowing up   **2** harping on
3 brimming over   **4** petering out

2 *Read each passage and choose the best word or phrase from among the four choices for each blank. Then, on your answer sheet, find the number of the question and mark your answer.*

Reforming Prisons

Recidivism rates in the United States are staggeringly high, with approximately 68 percent of ex-convicts facing rearrest within three years of being released. The huge number of repeat offenders not only reflects poorly on the nation's penal system but also causes significant concerns for the communities former prisoners are being released back into.

Sociologist William R. Kelly believes the recidivism crisis is a consequence of the mistaken assumption that (26). Logically, of course, incarceration, or the threat of it, should reduce the likelihood that an individual will offend again. However, Kelly argues that criminals tend to be individuals whose "circumstances and experiences typically differ in fundamental ways from the non-offending population." He points out that the majority suffer from mental illness or substance-abuse disorders, and are therefore unlikely, and often unable, to weigh the consequences of their actions.

What is more, critics argue that programs to treat mental health and addiction issues at prison facilities have (27). Inflicting punishment, it often seems, has become a fundamental part of the criminal justice system, and critics claim that even when reform opportunities exist, they tend to be viewed as an exception rather than the norm. Given this situation, the gap between inmates' rehabilitative needs and the harsh reality of the US penal system's response is hardly surprising.

This is particularly apparent in a widespread, but controversial, form of behavioral correction utilized in many US prisons: solitary confinement. This nearly unbearable isolation in a small, cramped cell for up to 23 hours a day can go on for months or even years. The practice was first advocated in the United States in the eighteenth century by religious groups with the well-intentioned view that inmates should be given time to reflect on and repent for their crimes. Studies have shown, however, that inmates subjected to such conditions are, conversely, more likely to return to criminality after their release from prison. In light of both this and the psychological harm these conditions can inflict, the practice is undoubtedly (28).

Recidivism seems to be fueled not only by the lack of appropriate resources in prisons but also by the means employed inside them.

---

(26) 1 law enforcement unfairly targets ex-convicts
　　　2 prison is effective for preventing crime
　　　3 most criminals have psychological problems
　　　4 everyone in prison is actually guilty

(27) 1 not been sufficiently implemented
　　　2 brought unreasonable financial burdens
　　　3 created a new set of problems
　　　4 been unpopular with prisoners

(28) 1 punishing the wrong people
　　　2 effective only for repeat offenders
　　　3 contrary to the original intention behind it
　　　4 dependent upon prisoners' cooperation

The Surveillance Economy

　　Digital technology is often considered the modern equivalent of Gutenberg's printing press, yet people today seem as blind to the ramifications of the current upheavals in society and economics as those in the 1400s were. Some consequences are already emerging, though, and one highly concerning aspect of the digital revolution is the tendency of tech companies to (　29　). A new style of capitalism is arising wherein the raw material that generates revenues takes the form of behavioral data based on the analysis of billions of actions occurring on free digital services, such as posts on social media sites. The monetization of this digital gold mine begins with data gathering, which is generally conducted without users' awareness or consent. Algorithms are then employed to analyze the data and generate behavioral predictions about shopping habits, for example, which are eventually traded on new types of digital marketplaces.

　　This economic model is called "surveillance capitalism," and the strategies employed by the tech firms involved are often said to be based on the idea that it is more effective to (　30　). For example, technology firms have been known to scan millions of copyrighted materials and make profits from them. Should a scandal over their unauthorized use of the data threaten to damage their reputation, the firms will attempt to smooth things over with the general public while paying off any fines with their enormous profits.

Experts such as Harvard University's Shoshana Zuboff see the attitudes of tech firms toward behavioral data as unreasonable. In Zuboff's view, they consider data to be (31   ). Even in cases in which companies have been explicitly denied permission to use certain data, it is common for them to extract or infer what they want through the use of sophisticated algorithms and other analysis techniques. And it is this same sense of extreme entitlement that, ironically, often leads them to patent the very data extraction and analysis techniques that they utilize. Every product branded as "smart," "personalized," or a "digital assistant," warns Zuboff, has the sinister potential to be used as a tool in the surveillance economy.

(29) 1 merge with other firms
2 overprice their services
3 steal other firms' technologies
4 profit from people's ignorance

(30) 1 confuse than to clarify
2 ignore facts than to deny them
3 ask for forgiveness than permission
4 avoid than confront

(31) 1 a resource free for the taking
2 something that never contains errors
3 an extremely heavy burden
4 less valuable than it once was

3 Read each passage and choose the best answer from among the four choices for each question. Then, on your answer sheet, find the number of the question and mark your answer.

Psychology's Replication Crisis

Reproducibility is a cornerstone of science, yet a growing chorus of researchers have claimed that numerous experiments, even ones carried out by esteemed psychologists and reported in prestigious journals, cannot be successfully replicated. One notable example is a widely cited piece of psychological research claiming that completing word puzzles designed to evoke images associated with old age caused the experiment's subjects to walk more slowly afterward. However, it has never been successfully confirmed by other researchers. Defenders of studies that came under fire when they could not be replicated, however, presented a host of possible explanations for the inconsistencies, alleging that the researchers who attempted the replications lacked the necessary competence, or claiming that sample sizes in the follow-ups had been insufficient. In response, a project was undertaken under the direction of University of Virginia researcher Brian Nosek in the 2010s that put nearly 100 celebrated psychology studies to the test by attempting to reproduce them. Every effort was made to ensure the experiments were as reliable as possible, including increasing the number of subjects from that of the original sample sizes. The results were startling: only about half the studies investigated made the grade, highlighting what has been dubbed psychology's "replication crisis."

While there have been cases of outright fraud and complaints that journals tend to favor studies that confirm the researchers' hypothesis, perhaps the most disturbing trend revealed in the wake of Nosek's study is what is known as "p-hacking." This is coined from the statistical term "p-value," which is calculated by researchers to show the probability that their experimental results are actually being produced by the effect they are studying rather than by random chance or some other factor. In their quest to obtain an acceptable p-value, researchers have been accused of omitting undesirable data, choosing statistical tests that are more likely to confirm their desired results, and being selective about which observations are compared with each other. In one survey, over 40 percent of psychology researchers admitted to some form of p-hacking, and, astonishingly, the majority felt their research methods were defensible because they were carrying out practices that are well established, and even taught, in the profession. This is what makes p-hacking so insidious. The combined effect of fraud, publication bias, and p-hacking has caused many to question the validity of psychology studies appearing in well-known textbooks and journals.

While some researchers worry the crisis will reduce their field to the status of pseudoscientific nonsense, others have noted that it could be beneficial. The follow-up testing conducted in Nosek's study that brought the validity of psychological research into question actually demonstrates that lab experiments, when conducted to the highest standards of practice, are a valid method of studying human behavior. In addition, the reproduction of some original findings helps validate the theories behind them. Nosek says studies like the ones in his project are usually overlooked because "the incentives for individual scientists prioritize novelty over replication." He suggests that enticements such as publication and funding should be geared equally toward rewarding both new discoveries and the substantiation of previous ones.

(32) One feature of the project coordinated by Brian Nosek was that

1 the replication studies were carried out by researchers with better academic reputations than the researchers who had published the original studies.
2 it attempted to address accusations that had been made by people who believed that earlier replication studies had not been conducted properly.
3 around half of the original experiments that were chosen to be performed again had not been the subject of any previous replication studies.
4 it focused only on replicating the results of studies that the original researchers had expressed uncertainty about when they were first conducted.

(33) What does the author of the passage say about "p-hacking"?

1 Although more attention is paid to the practice, it is actually much less serious than more common problems, such as fraud and bias in journals.
2 Since it is so hard to be certain whether a "p-value" is accurate, it is almost impossible to prove that a researcher is guilty of p-hacking.
3 Although the practice is harmful to the validity of research, manipulating data is considered by many in the field of psychology to be acceptable.
4 Since journals have actually been proven to encourage the

practice, they should not pretend that it is not extremely common in the field of psychology.

(34) According to the passage, how could the replication crisis actually be beneficial?

1 By increasing awareness of the need for novel ideas in psychology, the crisis is likely to lead to the development of various new theories.
2 The studies that cause doubt about the original psychology experiments are themselves an indicator that psychology experiments can be reliable.
3 By casting doubt on famous researchers' work, it could create opportunities for lesser-known researchers to get unusual findings published.
4 The results of many studies that were once discredited have since been shown to be among the most reliable in the field of psychology.

The Treaty of Versailles

The Treaty of Versailles officially ended World War I in 1919, after more than four years of bloodshed between the Triple Entente of France, Russia, and Britain, and the Central Powers, made up of Germany and its allies. The actual fighting, however, had ceased with an armistice agreement signed in 1918. This came about when German leaders recognized that enemy offensives had brought the German military to its knees, leading them to make massive concessions to halt the fighting and prevent an invasion of their borders. Nevertheless, the success of Germany's wartime propaganda campaign, including reports of fictional victories on the front lines, meant civilians were unaware German forces were being crushed. When the fighting ended, German chancellor Friedrich Ebert made the deceptive declaration that German troops had returned "unconquered from the field of battle." Though intended to maintain national pride, this statement contributed significantly to the widespread delusions about the result of the war, and these helped give rise to a betrayal myth known as the "stab in the back." According to this notion, since Germany had not been defeated militarily, it must have been betrayed from within. As a result, nationalists were able to blame labor organizations, socialists, and the country's Jewish population for the seemingly disadvantageous terms the Treaty of Versailles imposed on Germany.

The most infamous section of the treaty was Article 231, commonly known as the "war guilt clause." It established Germany's responsibility for its actions as a basis for surrendering territory and making financial reparations. Nationalists, bitter from the German defeat, however, condemned it and claimed the reparation costs demanded by the Triple Entente were so excessive that they impoverished the nation. When read in context, though, it becomes evident that, rather than condemning Germany for the outbreak of hostilities, Article 231 primarily served to establish that Germany was legally obligated to abide by the demands for reparations laid out in other articles of the treaty, one of which actually limited Germany's responsibility mainly to paying for damage incurred by civilians. The clause is therefore more accurately viewed as part of a concession to Germany by the victors.

When Adolf Hitler's Nazi Party took power in the 1930s, it claimed Germany, as a victim of the terms imposed by the Treaty of Versailles, had become an international outcast. Playing on the notion of Article 231 as a war guilt clause, the Nazis fanned the flames of German resentment. Their claim was adopted in many historical narratives and taken as fact by influential individuals, like Britain's wartime prime minister David Lloyd George, who joined in laying much of the blame for Germany's renewed postwar militarism on the legacy of the Treaty of Versailles. In fact, this interpretation is still commonly cited as a key cause of World War II. It can be argued, however, that the Nazis had it entirely backwards. Their illegal rearmament and seizure of territory, which violated the Treaty of Versailles, were the true impetus for Germany's exclusion from the international community. Perhaps it is time to relegate Article 231's label as the "war guilt clause" to simply a footnote of history.

(35) The "stab in the back" myth originated because

   1 the actions of Germany's chancellor immediately following the signing of the armistice caused his relationship with the army to worsen greatly.

   2 German leaders misled the public about the war's outcome, causing misunderstandings about why the country had accepted the Treaty of Versailles.

3 errors made by German commanders in the war's early days weakened the country's bargaining position when the Treaty of Versailles was proposed.

4 enemy propaganda that had been intended to influence German civilians instead caused the military to turn against the country's government.

(36) In what way was Article 231 misinterpreted?

1 Despite many people thinking it did not mean Germany had to pay for damage caused during the war, it had other economic effects that were even more serious.

2 Despite its language being thought of as similar to that used in other treaties, its penalties were actually more severe than even nationalists claimed.

3 Although it was seen as giving in to the demands of German leaders, it contained wording that accused Germany of committing various war crimes.

4 Although it was seen as severely punishing Germany for starting the war, it mostly gave a legal basis for terms that were relatively favorable for the country.

(37) What was one effect of the Nazis' interpretation of the Treaty of Versailles?

1 By arguing that the treaty was intended to encourage Germany to expand its military and increase its territory, the Nazis were able to gain more power.

2 Partially admitting that Germany was guilty of starting the war helped the Nazis to improve their image in the international community.

3 Causing people to ignore Article 231 and focus on other parts of the treaty helped the Nazis negotiate the return of territory that had been lost in the war.

4 Though the treaty came to be blamed for Germany's problems, it was really the Nazis themselves who were causing them.

Peru's Guano Boom

When Peru achieved its independence from Spain in the 1820s, it was beset by economic woes. The hard-fought war for freedom had damaged the trade in silver between the two countries, leading to the collapse of the silver mines that had been the backbone of Peru's economy. The conflict had also put the country in massive debt to British bankers, from whom the Peruvian government had borrowed heavily to fund its war effort. Struggling unsuccessfully to develop its economy for two decades following independence, Peru was eventually handed a glimmer of hope in the form of an unlikely resource: seabird manure.

This waste product, known as guano, had accumulated in enormous mounds on the Chincha Islands off the country's coast. Its shores, drenched in nourishing waters flowing from the Pacific Ocean and teeming with various marine species, attracted a large predatory bird population. The combination of cool ocean currents and warm tropical air created an exceedingly arid environment, ensuring that the abundant nutrients naturally present in the guano were not dispersed by precipitation. The particularly high nitrogen content in guano, in fact, is what made the waste material an ideal fertilizer. Indigenous peoples had been using the guano sustainably as such for centuries, carefully timing its extraction from the islands so as not to disturb the seabird populations and penalizing anyone who harmed the birds during mating season with death.

Guano was not widely appreciated in Europe, however, until 1838, when two businessmen in Peru sent samples to Britain, where farmers soon noted its effect on depleted soil. The surge in demand for food caused by an enormous population boom had led to unsustainable farming practices, while the population shift from rural to urban areas driven by industrialization meant human waste wound up in cities rather than being returned to farmland to be used as fertilizer, as had previously been the case. Guano proved a magic bullet to invigorate the degraded soil. By 1841, trade in the product between Peru and Britain was well underway, ushering in the Guano Age.

The Peruvian government enjoyed a monopoly over the Chincha Islands' guano, but the country lacked both the capital and the expertise to effectively manage international shipping and sales. Consequently, these were consigned to British merchants, who received a substantial commission for their efforts. Furthermore, payment was not rendered to the Peruvian government until transactions were finalized — a rather lengthy process considering that loading one ship could take well over a month. This drove Peru to borrow further from British creditors — who, in many cases, were the very same companies entrusted to ship the product — and pay them back with interest using money earned from the sales. The benefits of drawing out this process were not lost on the merchants, who were soon profiting more from granting advances to the Peruvian government than from their commission on guano sales.

Nevertheless, the partnership bolstered Peru's standing with international creditors. Its record of defaulting on its payments had made potential lenders hesitant to risk their capital on loans to the government. The control over Peru's guano revenue exercised by the wealthy, reputable British merchants, however, instilled confidence that the country could be trusted to make good on its debts, opening up Peru's access to capital markets abroad.

By the late 1850s, the export of hundreds of thousands of tons of guano annually to foreign countries was contributing over three-quarters of Peru's national revenue, yet the country remained in perpetual debt. In order to gain better loan terms and to stem outflows of revenue from the country, the Peruvian government encouraged domestic companies to compete in the guano market by granting them special business concessions. British companies maintained their large degree of control, however, by simply entering into partnerships with Peruvian firms, resulting in the continued flow of capital out of Peru.

Spurred on by the access to loans afforded the country on the basis of the seemingly constant stream of guano revenue, the Peruvian government fell into a ruinous habit of unrestrained borrowing. Rampant corruption among the ruling class only made matters worse, and although much money had been poured into various public projects, little had been spent on efforts to diversify and stabilize the economy in the long term.

The guano-driven "prosperity" Peru enjoyed eventually proved painfully finite. Ravaged by the guano trade, the Chincha Islands' once-gigantic mounds of manure that had formed over thousands of years were almost depleted by the 1870s, and the seabirds relied on for replenishing the supply had been largely driven away or killed after decades of incessant extraction. The shortage spelled economic disaster for Peru, whose lack of economic prudence left it no better off after the guano boom than it had been before it. Swedish historian

Magnus Mörner, echoing the opinion of many scholars, stated that, for Peru, "guano wealth was, on the whole, a developmental opportunity missed."

(38) What was true of the guano on the Chincha Islands?

1 The ocean current in the area of the islands carried large amounts of nitrates to the guano mounds, making them resistant to the effects of the islands' arid air.
2 The guano that was richest in nitrates was difficult to access because it was trapped in the inner sections of the huge mounds that had been formed.
3 Its effectiveness as a fertilizer was due to the particular climatic conditions on the islands, which enabled the preservation of its key component.
4 Indigenous peoples who inhabited the area did not realize guano had potential as a fertilizer until the seabirds that produced it had already disappeared.

(39) The demand for guano in Britain in the mid-1800s was the result of

1 Peruvian businesses spreading false rumors about guano's benefits and taking advantage of British farmers' desperation to boost their failing crops.
2 a desire to revitalize farmland damaged by excessive amounts of human waste accumulating in rural areas that lacked the resources to manage it.
3 trends toward urban farming that had developed due to the highly wasteful farming practices carried out in rural areas.
4 a serious agricultural problem that had developed due to the drastic change in waste-usage practices that had accompanied urbanization.

(40) Why did British merchants delay the sale of guano?

1 Negotiations with Peru for financial assistance to deal with shipping and marketing problems were taking longer than they had initially expected.

2 The longer the Peruvian government had to wait for the money earned from guano sales, the more the merchants could earn from the interest on loans.
   3 The merchants were upset because the Peruvian government would only pay them their commission at times that coincided with the receipt of loans from abroad.
   4 Taking the time to negotiate guano sale prices with overseas buyers was essential for the merchants, allowing them to maximize their profits.

(41) What is one reason Peru did not benefit economically from its guano industry in the long term?

   1 The high cost of extracting guano from the Chincha Islands caused the government to mismanage its budget in ways that hurt domestic industries.
   2 The boost in its ability to obtain credit that had resulted from its foreign partnerships caused it to take on an excessive amount of debt.
   3 The end of regulation on guano extraction in the 1870s led wealthy Peruvians to remove much of it for private gain without regard for the seabirds' welfare.
   4 The inefficiency of forcing Peruvian and British firms to cooperate with each other caused a significant decline in the industry's profits.

4
- *Write an essay on the given TOPIC.*
- *Give THREE reasons to support your answer.*
- *Structure: introduction, main body, and conclusion*
- *Suggested length: 200–240 words*
- *Write your essay in the space provided on Side B of your answer sheet. <u>Any writing outside the space will not be graded.</u>*

TOPIC

Agree or disagree: Global overpopulation is a serious threat to the future of humankind

一次試験
リスニング

―― Listening Test ――

There are four parts to this listening test.

Part 1	Dialogues: 1 question each	Multiple-choice
Part 2	Passages: 2 questions each	Multiple-choice
Part 3	Real-Life: 1 question each	Multiple-choice
Part 4	Interview: 2 questions	Multiple-choice

※Listen carefully to the instructions.

Part 1　　　　　　　　　🔊　▶MP3 ▶アプリ ▶CD 2 26〜36

No. 1
1 By transferring the woman to a regional office.
2 By reducing the woman's need to travel.
3 By getting someone to help with the woman's children.
4 By offering the woman a different position.

No. 2
1 Leave the office early to get Clive.
2 Drive her mother to the airport.
3 Pick Clive up after work.
4 Buy dinner on her way home.

No. 3
1 Threaten to resign from the board.
2 Advise the president to step down.
3 Gather the support of others.
4 Talk with Margaret about her attitude.

No. 4
1 He has little experience directing movies.
2 He got poor reviews for his latest movie.
3 He has never directed for TV before.
4 He could not get good actors for his TV show.

No. 5	1 The man will not let the woman buy the product. 2 The man is doubtful of the advertisement's claims. 3 The woman's father has the same product. 4 The woman prefers to shop at regular stores.
No. 6	1 The equipment is outdated. 2 The man needs to save more money. 3 The man should not exercise so much. 4 The man paid too much for his membership.
No. 7	1 She always wanted to design furniture. 2 Design offers greater earning potential. 3 She is no longer interested in sculpture. 4 Fine art was more challenging than she thought.
No. 8	1 The woman should have done her paper sooner. 2 He does not have time to go to lunch. 3 The woman should not go to Jim's party. 4 He cannot meet the woman later.
No. 9	1 His wife's sister expects too much. 2 His wife should make the trip alone. 3 His wife's sister sometimes tells lies. 4 His wife may hurt Judy's feelings.
No. 10	1 Preventing the Japanese staff from quitting. 2 Preventing employees from suing the company. 3 Finding a local company to take over current clients. 4 Protecting the company's image as a good employer.

Part 2

(A)

No. 11
1 They are only available to a few students.
2 They focus primarily on the highest-paying jobs.
3 They do not affect employment rates.
4 They have helped students avoid high debt.

No. 12
1 They may limit participants' job options.
2 Employers take unfair advantage of participants.
3 They make it harder for high school students to graduate.
4 High school students are too young to decide on a career.

(B)

No. 13
1 They are not harmful to the ozone layer.
2 They are made by recycling old petroleum-based products.
3 They are less reliant on fossil fuels.
4 They are easier to turn into useful products.

No. 14
1 They can only be reused once.
2 They require special processing to be recycled.
3 The methane they produce harms recycling systems.
4 The plants used to make them are disappearing.

(C)

No. 15
1. She would quit the US Navy in protest.
2. She would not be able to complete the assigned task.
3. She would damage the computer system.
4. She would not need to ask for a later deadline.

No. 16
1. Convincing the US government it needed fewer warships.
2. Ensuring that submarines would be safer to operate.
3. Discovering a new way to fight sea battles.
4. Changing how modern naval vessels are designed.

(D)

No. 17
1. They lay more eggs than any other marine species.
2. The females are larger than the males.
3. They change sex to aid reproduction.
4. The females are sometimes eaten by the males.

No. 18
1. By converting carbon into waste matter.
2. By absorbing CO_2 directly from the air.
3. By helping algae reproduce more quickly.
4. By keeping algae from sinking.

(E)

No. 19
1. Their lungs were larger than previously believed.
2. They had developed rare types of cancer.
3. Their lungs had been affected by air pollution.
4. They had been treated for diseases that are common today.

No. 20
1. They especially affected wealthy Egyptians.
2. They played an important role in preserving mummies.
3. They were first identified by ancient Egyptians.
4. They affected a wide range of people in ancient Egypt.

Part 3

(F)

No. 21

Situation: You live in Japan. You plan to study full-time at a university abroad for three years. You call the university's foreign-student adviser to ask about healthcare coverage.

Question: What should you do to secure the least expensive healthcare option?

1 Apply for free coverage using your student visa.
2 Pay a fee when applying for your student visa.
3 Obtain travel health insurance for your full stay.
4 Apply only for private medical services for the first year.

(G)

No. 22

Situation: You want to get a bank loan to buy an apartment. You are still paying your student loan. A friend who works at a bank gives you some advice.

Question: Which kind of loan should you choose?

1 A 30-year fixed-rate loan.
2 A 20-year fixed-rate loan.
3 A 30-year adjustable-rate loan.
4 A 20-year adjustable-rate loan.

	(H)
No. 23	*Situation:* You are a customer marketing manager at a health-food company. You are listening to your boss talk about the company's new products at a staff meeting. *Question:* What should you do first? 1 Promote the 20% discount to customers. 2 Prepare a digital campaign. 3 Identify events with promotional potential. 4 Recruit people to help during the marathon.
	(I)
No. 24	*Situation:* You are moving out of a 100-square-meter, two-bedroom apartment. You would prefer not to move your belongings yourself. Your budget is $900. A truck-rental representative tells you the following. *Question:* Which truck should you choose? 1 The 3-meter truck without movers. 2 The 4.5-meter truck with movers. 3 The 6-meter truck with movers. 4 The 7-meter truck without movers.
	(J)
No. 25	*Situation:* You are returning home after a two-year working holiday abroad. You ask an adviser about getting back the pension payments you have made, which total $6,000. *Question:* What should you do first to claim back your pension payments? 1 Complete the online application immediately. 2 Complete the online application after your visa expires. 3 Submit a paper application after leaving the country. 4 Submit a paper application before returning home.

Part 4

No. 26
1. Growth in the German solar power market helped China become the industry leader.
2. Chinese demand for solar power has helped boost Japan's exports.
3. Japanese technology has been copied by Chinese and European rivals.
4. China now supports Japanese companies wishing to do business in Germany.

No. 27
1. Companies that build power plants are reluctant to stop using fossil fuels.
2. Demand for ecofriendly energy is forcing companies to change their policies.
3. Renewable energy is set to surpass fossil fuels in terms of cost efficiency.
4. Companies are not able to supply enough solar panels in the long term.

二次試験 面接

[A日程] ▶MP3 ▶アプリ ▶CD 4 16〜20

1. Should the government ultimately be responsible for the health of its citizens?
2. Agree or disagree: The militarization of space is a threat to future generations
3. Will there ever be a need for Japan to revise its firearms laws?
4. Are concerns about the safety of genetically modified food warranted?
5. Have humans done irreversible damage to the planet?

[B日程]

1. Will humans always have a negative impact on biodiversity?
2. Has the rise of social media affected people's morals?
3. Do people in democratic societies take their rights for granted?
4. Agree or disagree: It is wrong to treat drug addicts as criminals
5. Will there always be conflict between nations?

(注) モデルスピーチと解説はA日程のみ収録しています。

2020-1

一次試験　2020.6.28実施
二次試験　A日程　2020.8.22実施
　　　　　B日程　2020.8.23実施

Grade 1

試験時間
筆記：100分
リスニング：約35分

一次試験・筆記　　　　　p.114〜128
一次試験・リスニングp.129〜135
二次試験・面接　　　　　　p.136

＊解答・解説は別冊p.213〜264にあります。
＊面接の流れは本書p.16にあります。

2020年度第1回　Web特典「自動採点サービス」対応
オンラインマークシート
※検定の回によって2次元コードが違います。
※筆記1〜3，リスニングの採点ができます。
※PCからも利用できます（本書p.8参照）。

筆 記

> **1** To complete each item, choose the best word or phrase from among the four choices. Then, on your answer sheet, find the number of the question and mark your answer.

(1) The man's long-term illness was causing him to look (   ). Despite eating regularly, he could not seem to put on any weight.
1 condescending 2 raucous
3 emaciated   4 fanatical

(2) Although career opportunities for women have improved in recent years, (   ) still exists in the workplace. Some male bosses believe women are less capable than men.
1 chauvinism 2 connotation 3 decorum 4 profanity

(3) Following its election (   ), in which it lost every seat it had in the parliament, the party decided to break up.
1 debacle   2 submersion
3 impeachment   4 respite

(4) Kevin is very shy, so his friend Susan had to (   ) him into asking Miranda for a date. "Kevin, if you don't ask her soon, someone else will," she said.
1 regale   2 flunk   3 goad   4 pilfer

(5) *A:* Did you persuade your parents to let you go abroad by yourself?
B: No. I did my best to (   ) their fears, but they still insist it's too dangerous.
1 forfeit   2 allay   3 infer   4 muddle

(6) The exterior of the home was extremely beautiful. In (   ) contrast, however, the inside was a complete mess.
1 flimsy   2 uptight   3 furtive   4 stark

(7) The champion ice skater had little time to (   ) her victory at the tournament. Within days, she was already training for the next competition.
1 savor   2 thwart   3 clobber   4 distort

(8) After a lengthy period of (   ), the criminal was allowed to enter society again.

1 initiation　　　　　　2 incarceration
3 amplification　　　　4 summation

(9) The government was (　　) in the newspapers for its slow response after the natural disaster. All of the criticism has hurt the president's chances for reelection.
1 caressed　2 tantalized　3 elongated　4 lambasted

(10) After Christine's husband failed to notice her hints about her weight gain, she decided to tell him (　　) that he needed to go on a diet.
1 evasively　　　　2 stupendously
3 explicitly　　　　4 abysmally

(11) The CEO thought the investment would be a good idea, but in (　　), it turned out to have been a huge mistake that cost the company millions of dollars.
1 solace　2 hindsight　3 disclaimer　4 regression

(12) Firefighters believed the forest fire was caused by (　　) from a nearby campfire that had not been fully extinguished.
1 felonies　2 incisions　3 allusions　4 embers

(13) The young boy ate messily in front of the houseguests. Later, his mother scolded him for his (　　) behavior during dinner.
1 somber　2 colloquial　3 comatose　4 uncouth

(14) After the scandal, journalists (　　) the star's home for over a week, but she refused to give any interviews.
1 squabbled　2 jostled　3 besieged　4 deformed

(15) Frustrated with his low salary, Ethan decided to quit his job and look for something more (　　).
1 macabre　2 vexing　3 requisite　4 lucrative

(16) According to the government spokesperson, (　　) would be granted to political refugees. However, immigrants who were in the country illegally would be sent home.
1 bigotry　2 asylum　3 foyer　4 mirage

(17) Because there is no minimum wage in the country, many workers are living in (　　) poverty, unable to pay for even daily necessities.
1 resplendent　　　　2 tacit
3 scrumptious　　　　4 abject

(18) The terrorist group is now (   ) all of the e-mails that are sent within its organization so that government agencies will be unable to access the contents.
1 encrypting   2 usurping
3 vanquishing   4 coveting

(19) The nail was so firmly (   ) in the wood that it was almost impossible to remove.
1 embedded   2 scrawled   3 tarnished   4 polarized

(20) As the manager of a consumer call center, Kim is an expert at dealing with (   ) customers. No matter how upset they are, she is always able to calm them down.
1 irate   2 translucent   3 tepid   4 debonair

(21) The sculpture was praised for its beautifully (   ) details and perfect proportions.
1 sedated   2 wanton   3 chiseled   4 sporadic

(22) The reporter thought the politician's support for the new law (   ) corruption, so he began an investigation. Sure enough, the politician was found to have accepted bribes.
1 pined for   2 smacked of
3 railed against   4 snuffed out

(23) The company (   ) a great deal of criticism when it was discovered that it was paying workers in its overseas factories just a few dollars a day.
1 snapped out of   2 picked up on
3 came in for   4 boiled down to

(24) The police were asked to (   ) security at the politician's residence after she received death threats.
1 beef up   2 gloss over   3 reel in   4 sift through

(25) Brian constantly (   ) his wife, buying her expensive jewelry and taking her on luxurious vacations.
1 passes over   2 pieces together
3 ramps up   4 dotes on

2
Read each passage and choose the best word or phrase from among the four choices for each blank. Then, on your answer sheet, find the number of the question and mark your answer.

The Evolution of Awe

While it is easy to imagine that an emotion such as fear might have evolved to help humans avoid physical danger, or that love fosters interdependent relationships that increase one's chances of survival, emotions like awe can leave evolutionary scientists scratching their heads. In recent decades, however, researchers, such as the University of Pennsylvania's David Yaden, have come up with potential explanations for why awe developed. Awe can be evoked by positive or negative experiences — a magnificent landscape, for example, or a scene of immense destruction. According to Yaden, this (**26**). Yaden's research has supported this claim by providing evidence of a correlation between awe and things like social bonding. He therefore suggests that the emotion must be linked to human survival, possibly having evolved to facilitate group cohesion.

Yaden speculates that in our primitive past, awe may also have (**27**). Our fondness for magnificent views is obvious in our attraction to landscapes such as elevated plateaus or towering cliffs, but our primitive ancestors may have sought them out for other reasons too. The ability to spot approaching predators or adversaries, and the defensive potential offered by elevated positions, could have contributed to human beings' attraction to spectacular scenery.

Alternatively, researcher Michelle Shiota of Arizona State University suggests that awe could have evolved for a different reason. In a study led by Shiota, researchers asked participants to describe memories of times when they had experienced awe or some positive emotion like happiness. The study tasked them with reading argumentative essays in favor of an unpopular opinion, and the researchers assumed that participants who agreed with the essays must have been successfully persuaded by the arguments. Some of the essays contained feeble arguments, while others were meant to be highly convincing. It was found that those participants who had described awe were much better able to see problems with the feeble arguments than those who described other emotions. Shiota therefore concluded that awe aids people in (**28**). If this research is correct, then it appears that developing our sense of awe may have demonstrable benefits in everyday life.

---

(26) 1 increases individual ambition
 2 provides an escape from reality
 3 creates feelings of connectedness
 4 reduces motivation to take action

(27) 1 demonstrated a negative human bias
 2 encouraged humans to take risks
 3 increased humans' fear of high places
 4 reflected humans' desire for safety

(28) 1 remembering crucial information
 2 processing information critically
 3 convincing others to believe them
 4 improving their self-confidence

The New Atheism

Atheism, or disbelief in the existence of God, has grown more common in Western societies during the past hundred years. In the early 2000s, however, an intellectual, largely science-based "New Atheist" movement became increasingly prominent in the West. The New Atheists were mainly made up of scientists and intellectuals, and they (29   ). Atheists of the past had tended to believe that science was incapable of addressing the concept of God and generally accepted that science and religion should be treated as two distinct, nonoverlapping domains. The New Atheists, though, argued strenuously that the existence of God should be subject to the same scientific tests for validity as anything else within the natural world. Moreover, trends like rising religious extremism caused the New Atheists to view organized religion as an obstacle to world peace and scientific advancement, so they actively sought to reduce its international influence.

To this end, the New Atheists took an inflexible approach, and critics even characterized the movement as "militant atheism." In fact, it was sometimes pointed out that it (**30**) religious extremism. Prominent New Atheists, like Sam Harris, for example, made statements such as "ideas which divide one group of human beings from another, only to unite them in slaughter, generally have their roots in religion." Such uncompromising condemnation of those they disagreed with struck critics as reminiscent of those with radical religious views.

Due in part to the debate over religious extremism that followed the terrorist attacks on September 11, 2001, prominent New Atheists were seemingly everywhere in the media and their books topped various bestseller lists. Yet in the broader view, the influence of the New Atheists (**31**). According to demographer Eric Kaufmann, the younger generation in the developing world is rejecting the trend away from religion that has been occurring in Western nations under the influence of the New Atheists and the other forces that have shaped it. Kaufmann suggests that even the least religious societies will likely be affected by a rise in immigrants from religious regions, meaning that the New Atheists' efforts may be negated by other factors, despite their successes in converting people to atheism.

---

(29) 1 pretended to believe religious teachings
    2 adopted a more confrontational position
    3 supported some aspects of religion
    4 attempted to be more respectful

(30) 1 was strikingly similar to
    2 intentionally deceived people about
    3 denied the existence of
    4 actually drove people to accept

(31) 1 reflected their noble intentions
    2 may grow even stronger
    3 harmed other atheists
    4 should not be overstated

3 *Read each passage and choose the best answer from among the four choices for each question. Then, on your answer sheet, find the number of the question and mark your answer.*

Harold Pinter

Harold Pinter rose to prominence in the 1960s and 1970s as one of the most important British playwrights of the twentieth century. His scriptwriting is notable for the air of mystery and menace he conveys by casting doubt upon what appear to be the facts of stories taking place in everyday settings. In his first full-length play, *The Birthday Party*, for example, two strangers enter a boarding house and proceed to terrorize Stanley, one of the guests. Who the strangers are, what their purpose is, and how they are connected to their victim are never explained. Plays utilizing such dramatic devices, however, initially frustrated both critics and audiences alike, since exposition that would allow them to grasp a play's meaning and the motivations behind the characters' actions was considered an indispensable part of scriptwriting. Though *The Birthday Party* was initially a commercial failure, Pinter's unconventional style became renowned in his subsequent plays.

Using psychological manipulation, Pinter's characters play elaborate power games with one another, struggle for dominance, and employ language as a weapon to gain control. As opposed to straightforward questions and answers, their conversations tend to sound more like private monologues with occasional interruptions by the listener, and rarely serve the purpose of clearly conveying information. Indeed, their dialogue frequently contradicts their thoughts, which are sometimes only hinted at by their silences. They are often confused about their identity and live in a world governed by dread and uncertainty. Typically, a dominant intruder will arrive without warning and upset the status quo by seeking to impose his or her will upon those present. What follows is a negotiation for some sort of advantage, whether that be between two strangers, a husband and wife, or a torturer and his or her victim. With what his biographer, Michael Billington, calls his "ability to create dramatic poetry out of everyday speech," Pinter builds a tension which rarely explodes but nevertheless produces a dramatic, compelling, and, at times, darkly humorous effect.

Though widely praised for his revolutionary storytelling and dialogue, Pinter failed to attain the widespread adoration that some other playwrights have achieved. One reason is that his works were often met with confusion, followed by irritation, and they were dismissed by many as both pretentious and obscure. Journalist Paul Vallely, however, sees such reactions as being the result of Pinter's brilliance in creating a "blank screen on which it is possible for everyone to project their own incarnations of reality." In contrast to past writers like Charles Dickens, in whose works characters were clearly on the side of either good or evil, Pinter's main subject matter was the moral ambiguities of modern existence. Vallely argues that Pinter's "strength lies in the immediacy with which he conveys that sense, even to those who could not begin to articulate it." Despite Pinter's somewhat divisive reputation, his work continues to be performed regularly, and it is unlikely that it will ever fall into obscurity, which is the common fate of the majority of playwrights.

(32) Why did Harold Pinter's plays cause negative reactions at first?

1 They were considered to represent a blend of theatrical genres that were generally viewed as being incompatible with one another.
2 Their ordinary settings and apparently purposeless characters were seen as critical of the very people who were viewing them.
3 They failed to deliver information and context that were generally regarded as dramatically necessary for the comprehension of such material.
4 Their thematic nature forced audiences to more actively interpret the work by themselves, thus devaluing the opinions of professional theater critics.

(33) What is one thing we learn about the characters in Pinter's plays?

1 Rather than attempting to attain a better understanding of a given situation, they tend to be motivated by a desire to know themselves more fully.
2 Rather than building greater understanding, their conversations frequently conceal what they are actually thinking about.
3 They reflect Pinter's belief that once intruders gain dominance

in a situation, victims can do little to resist their aggression.
4 They tend to misunderstand things about other characters that have been written in a way that is obvious to the audience, but not to them.

(34) Which of the following statements would Paul Vallely most likely agree with?

1 Pinter had a talent for portraying the uncertainty about right and wrong in society, but it caused him to be less popular than he might have been.
2 Although Pinter's writing style made many people angry, authors like Charles Dickens were also highly controversial while they were alive.
3 Because Pinter's plays were so immoral, they cannot be considered as being on the same level with other great theatrical productions.
4 Pinter's talent for dialogue and storytelling caused many people to think his plays were better than they really were.

Finding Memories

Modern investigations into the mechanisms underlying human memory became possible with the invention of the microscope in the sixteenth century and led to the eventual discovery and classification of neurons. Further advancement was made through Spanish neuroscientist Santiago Ramón y Cajal's neuron-staining technique, which provided images of these specialized cells that make up the human nervous system. His work helped establish the dominance of the so-called neuron doctrine, which held that rather than being fused together into a seamless network, neurons were actually distinct units. This in turn led to the discovery that neurons communicate with each other through the transfer of electrical signals facilitated via knoblike structures called synapses. This work became the foundation of the now generally accepted idea that memory formation depends on the enhancement of synaptic connections between neurons.

Recent research led by neurobiologist David Glanzman at the University of California, Los Angeles, however, has cast doubt on the prevailing theory with an experiment involving snails. Mild electric shocks were administered to a group of snails, provoking them to recoil for extended periods of time. When touched again softly without receiving an electric shock, the snails still pulled in some of their body parts for up to a minute, demonstrating a learned defensive behavior against the shocks. A molecule called ribonucleic acid (RNA), which is responsible for carrying instructions for the synthesis of proteins, was then extracted from these snails and injected into a second group of snails that had not received any electric shocks. The snails from the second group then began retracting their bodies for extended periods, similar to snails from the first group, in response to soft, nonelectrical touches. Glanzman claims this response suggests that although synaptic strengthening does occur during the brain's neural response to a stimulus, experiences are actually recorded within neurons where RNA molecules are produced. "If memories were stored at synapses, there is no way our experiment would have worked," he says.

Scientists in the traditionalist camp, however, are not convinced. Pointing out that RNA-based biological changes happen on a timescale of minutes or hours, they question how it could be part of the mechanism for something like memory recall, which is nearly instantaneous. Further complicating the matter is James V. McConnell's infamous attempt in the 1950s to prove the existence of what he referred to as "memory RNA." McConnell trained flatworms to navigate mazes and then fed their bodies to untrained worms that suddenly appeared to become able to emulate the trained worms' maze-running skills. The research and the numerous attempts to reproduce it have been ridiculed and served up as a cautionary tale about scientists seeking publicity through sensational yet scientifically questionable research. This has added a stigma to any theory associating memory formation with RNA. In recent years, however, some aspects of McConnell's research appear to have been reproduced successfully. Consequently, members of the scientific community who support Glanzman suggest that his work has now added convincing evidence to the notion that RNA may be the key to furthering our understanding of the formation of memories.

(35) What contribution did Santiago Ramón y Cajal make to the understanding of memory?

   1 His staining technique allowed later scientists to discover

which types of neurons were able to transmit electrical signals.
2 He disproved the neuron doctrine by demonstrating how networks of neurons use electrical signals to communicate with one another.
3 His images representing the electrical signals sent out by neurons proved that the nervous system was made up of uninterrupted networks of neurons.
4 He provided evidence that neurons were actually separate, individual cells, laying the groundwork for the discovery of synapses.

(36) The results of the snail experiment indicate that

1 rather than being stored in synaptic connections, memories appear to be stored within the brain's neurons themselves.
2 synapse enhancement is a temporary reaction to information left there due to the flow of RNA molecules between neurons.
3 memory formation depends less on the stimuli that the brain is exposed to than on the way that it reacts to them chemically.
4 memory accuracy can be directly correlated to the amount of RNA molecules that the brain is capable of producing.

(37) What is one possible explanation for the criticism that David Glanzman's research has received?

1 The differences between snails and flatworms are so significant that Glanzman's experiment's results are unlikely to apply to both.
2 Glanzman's ideas remind members of the scientific community of research that had been looked down on in the past.
3 There is a strong possibility that Glanzman has borrowed ideas from another researcher without giving him sufficient credit.
4 Glanzman seems unlikely to be correct because James V. McConnell demonstrated that RNA takes a long time to produce an effect.

The Falklands War

The sovereignty of the Falkland Islands, which lie 480 kilometers east of Argentina's coast, became an ongoing source of dispute between Argentina and the United Kingdom following their forcible seizure by the British in 1833. The British government, however, eventually concluded that the remote colony was becoming a burden and became increasingly hesitant to invest in its security.

In 1982, Argentina's dictator, General Leopoldo Galtieri, made the decision to abandon diplomatic negotiations and reclaim the islands by force. This was chiefly to diminish popular discontent: economic mismanagement and human rights abuses had caused his dictatorship to be highly despised, and Galtieri hoped to spark a patriotic fever that would divert the public eye from his regime's shortcomings. On April 2, Argentine troops landed on the islands and overwhelmed the small British military force there, leading to widespread jubilation in Argentina and a surge in support for the Galtieri regime. The invasion caught the British government completely unprepared. Indeed, immediately prior to it, Prime Minister Margaret Thatcher had, for budgetary reasons, withdrawn Britain's only warship from the Falklands' vicinity.

Given Argentina's geographic advantage and relatively sophisticated armed forces, many British commanders doubted the islands could be forcibly retaken. Despite this, a naval task force was swiftly assembled, and the British government declared a 370-kilometer war zone around the islands. Their initial assumption was that this would intimidate Galtieri into accepting a diplomatic settlement, which they made more palatable with substantial concessions.

As the task force sailed south, intense diplomatic activity to obtain a peaceful resolution was undertaken by both the United States and the United Nations, but Galtieri insisted on nothing less than complete sovereignty for Argentina. Most European countries expressed support for Britain, while the majority of Latin American countries supported Argentina. Having counted on US neutrality from the outset, it was a significant blow to Argentina when the United States supported Britain, as Argentina was left at a distinct strategic disadvantage: its opponent now had access to sophisticated US communications technology and crucial military intelligence data.

On May 2, a British nuclear submarine was issued controversial orders to sink an Argentine warship—the ARA *General Belgrano*—

which was outside the official war zone. While the British justified the attack on the grounds that the *Belgrano* had been sailing toward their task force, Argentina claimed it had been heading in the opposite direction. The action resulted in 323 deaths — the conflict's single greatest loss of life. Thatcher was accused by political opponents of ordering the attack to deliberately provoke an escalation in the conflict and curtail hopes of a diplomatic resolution. Yet it was later admitted by Argentine naval chiefs that the *Belgrano*, which had been weaving in and out of the war zone, had indeed been an active threat to the British task force. Furthermore, both sides at that point regarded the South Atlantic, in general, as a legitimate theater of war.

Sinking the *Belgrano* demonstrated Britain's resolution to retake the islands by force, and sent a clear message to Argentina, which, realizing that its ships were vulnerable to torpedo attacks, confined most of them to port. Its navy was effectively sidelined for the rest of the war, which undoubtedly helped to limit subsequent casualties at sea, on both sides.

Despite Argentina's air force being outclassed, its pilots demonstrated both skill and motivation in their operations against the British. Yet their planes could only perform single strikes on the task force, as the Falklands were at the extreme edge of their combat range. Argentina was unable to prevent the British from making a landing from sea on the islands on May 21, but the effectiveness of their inland defense led to several intense battles. Although their regular soldiers proved to be formidable opponents, the bulk of Argentina's troops had been conscripted into the army against their will and were poorly trained, inadequately prepared, and ill-equipped. "We were cannon fodder in a war we couldn't win," one veteran later claimed.

The British took approximately 11,400 Argentine prisoners, and Argentina's forces formally surrendered on June 14. Defeat meant the end for the country's military government: thoroughly discredited, it was replaced by a civilian administration in 1983. Conversely, that the British had won back the islands with minimal casualties — 255 British lives were lost — meant a huge boost to Thatcher's popularity and helped her to win the next election. The war did not, however, settle the dispute: Argentina maintains its claim to the Falklands. Ironically, had Argentina not embarked on its ill-advised military endeavor, it may well have gained possession of them because the declining population would have eventually meant that British governance was no longer viable. Instead, post-1982, Britain has strengthened both its military and economic commitment to the islands, and the status quo remains unchanged.

(38) General Leopoldo Galtieri decided to invade the Falkland Islands in 1982 because

  1 the British refusal to engage in a formal discussion regarding their future left him with no other option than to resort to military force.
  2 he correctly calculated that it would boost morale in his country, thereby distracting citizens from the domestic situation in Argentina.
  3 his commanders had convinced him that, due to Britain's growing military presence, Argentina needed to attack quickly if it was to achieve victory.
  4 demand for an invasion by the general public overcame his reluctance to take the risk of invading them.

(39) Why did diplomatic efforts to avoid war fail?

  1 Despite the British offering a degree of flexibility concerning an eventual settlement, Argentina adopted an inflexible stance regarding ownership.
  2 The sudden loss of support from trusted allies like the United States made Britain feel it was left with no choice but to use military force.
  3 Division within the international community meant that the United Nations was unable to lay sufficient groundwork to negotiate a peace agreement.
  4 Once UN support had tipped the balance in their favor, the British refused to pursue their objective by means of negotiation.

(40) How did the sinking of the ARA *General Belgrano* alter the circumstances surrounding the conflict?

  1 Argentina's commanders revised their naval tactics, resulting in their warships preventing British reinforcements from

approaching the war zone.
2 Prime Minister Margaret Thatcher's unwillingness to listen to her military commanders led to an escalation in the seriousness of the overall situation.
3 Argentina's original intention of gaining a diplomatic advantage through a show of force was transformed into a serious effort to win military victory.
4 Little further naval engagement occurred, due to the fact that the British navy obviously posed too great a threat to Argentina's surface vessels.

(41) What conclusion does the author of the passage draw about the Falklands War?

1 Argentina had little chance of permanently taking the Falklands by force, but would likely have obtained them if it had waited for Britain to leave.
2 Had Argentina's air force been more committed to preventing a British landing, the outcome of the conflict could well have been different.
3 Although Britain was able to overthrow the military government in Argentina, the new civilian one is in many ways even worse.
4 Had Thatcher not ordered that the Falklands be retaken, it is likely that the people living there would be much better off today.

4
- Write an essay on the given TOPIC.
- Give THREE reasons to support your answer.
- Structure: introduction, main body, and conclusion
- Suggested length: 200–240 words
- Write your essay in the space provided on Side B of your answer sheet. Any writing outside the space will not be graded.

TOPIC

Agree or disagree: Improving relations with other Asian nations should be a priority for the Japanese government

リスニング

―――――― **Listening Test** ――――――

There are four parts to this listening test.

Part 1	Dialogues: 1 question each	Multiple-choice
Part 2	Passages: 2 questions each	Multiple-choice
Part 3	Real-Life: 1 question each	Multiple-choice
Part 4	Interview: 2 questions	Multiple-choice

※**Listen carefully to the instructions.**

Part 1 ▶MP3 ▶アプリ ▶CD3 **1**～**11**

No. 1
1 The characters were boring.
2 The clues were too obvious.
3 The plot was not complex enough.
4 The ending was not appealing.

No. 2
1 The man's explanations were easy to follow.
2 The man should have used more examples.
3 The topic was too difficult for the audience.
4 The first part was the most interesting.

No. 3
1 The chairman asked Jane to visit L.A.
2 Peter's boss decided to cancel the contract.
3 The client changed its decision.
4 Jane made some changes to the contract.

No. 4
1 Think about spending more on traveling.
2 Be more cautious with their investments.
3 Consider the idea of buying a second home.
4 Ask the Dawsons for advice about second homes.

No. 5	1 Complain to the town office about his neighbor. 2 Keep his fence inside the property line. 3 Discuss the problem with her husband. 4 Get advice about the fence from his neighbor.
No. 6	1 She postponed finishing her doctoral degree. 2 She was highly qualified for her new job. 3 She has applied for a new position. 4 She declined the job offer from the university.
No. 7	1 They sell the glasses he wants. 2 They will accept his insurance. 3 They have cheaper medicine than clinics. 4 They offer low-cost eye exams.
No. 8	1 Wait before taking action. 2 Talk to her manager now. 3 Look for another position. 4 Become a contract worker.
No. 9	1 Teachers should not have to clean classrooms. 2 Canceling school buses could affect students' safety. 3 Taxes should be raised to pay for school costs. 4 More money should be spent on maintaining facilities.
No. 10	1 Taking the position could help Sarah's career. 2 Sarah does not need to learn about software applications. 3 It would be better for Sarah to focus on hardware skills. 4 Sarah is not performing well on her current project.

Part 2

(A)

No. 11
1. Copper and tin slowly ran out.
2. Miners' salary demands were too high.
3. American mines began using superior mining technology.
4. Copper and tin became easier to obtain elsewhere.

No. 12
1. It would be less damaging to the environment.
2. It would use existing storage facilities.
3. It would cut costs by using natural heat.
4. It would use surface water to purify lithium.

(B)

No. 13
1. It tends to target specific types of customers.
2. It is less costly than other types of advertising.
3. It is often ignored by consumers nowadays.
4. It gets better results than TV or print advertisements.

No. 14
1. It avoids the use of social media sites.
2. It relies on the results of consumer surveys.
3. It uses much longer advertising campaigns.
4. It relies on people looking for what they already want.

(C)

No. 15
1. He demanded to be worshiped as a god.
2. It is said he released people who were slaves.
3. He divided his empire among other rulers.
4. It is said he created a new religion.

No. 16
1. It influenced modern ideas about human rights.
2. It made translation of an ancient language possible.
3. It led to the fall of a powerful empire.
4. It inspired the creation of the United Nations.

(D)

No. 17
1 Their economic status.
2 The political ideas they have.
3 Their level of education.
4 The views of those around them.

No. 18
1 Scientific experiments are becoming harder to perform.
2 Some people misunderstand how science works.
3 More children are being vaccinated than ever before.
4 Scientific research is sometimes biased.

(E)

No. 19
1 It is particularly common in the retina.
2 It is reduced when the retina receives light.
3 It helps to prevent people from going blind.
4 It is a process that begins in the brain.

No. 20
1 Coffee increases oxidative stress in the retina.
2 Chlorogenic acid can damage certain types of cells.
3 Drinking coffee makes the retina more sensitive.
4 Chlorogenic acid can protect the retina from damage.

Part 3

(F)

No. 21

Situation: You go to a cell-phone store to talk about reducing your bill. You currently pay $80 per month. You often call clients, so the number of minutes is most important to you.

Question: Which plan should you choose?

1 The Plus Pack with your current plan.
2 The Value Extra Plan.
3 The Mega Mobile Plan.
4 The Free Together Service.

(G)

No. 22

Situation: You are representing your company at a job fair. You have already checked in. You paid for two tables but only found one at your booth. You hear the following announcement.

Question: What should you do first?

1 Talk to the staff in the inventory room.
2 Inquire at the welcome desk.
3 Present your receipt at the information table.
4 Go to the corporate services booth.

(H)

No. 23

Situation: You are studying in the US for a year. You want to spend your weekends volunteering, so you attend an orientation session at a youth center. You enjoy physical activities.

Question: Which volunteer group should you join?

1 The Palz Program.
2 The LifeTrip Program.
3 The Playground Associates.
4 The Handy Helpers.

No. 24

(I)

Situation: Your landlord claims you caused damage to the apartment you are moving out of. He is refusing to return your deposit. The Tenant Information Bureau tells you the following.

Question: What should you do first to try to get some money back?

1 Take the case to court.
2 Make the repairs yourself.
3 Speak directly to previous tenants.
4 Ask professionals for repair estimates.

No. 25

(J)

Situation: You teach journalism at a university and want your students to meet a TV news host. You cannot visit the TV station before 1 p.m. A representative tells you the following.

Question: Which broadcaster should you arrange to meet?

1 Brad Quentin.
2 Katie Ferris.
3 Valerie Ortiz.
4 Lance Bridges.

Part 4

No. 26
1 The musicians he has worked with understand the challenges he faces.
2 Companies often take advantage of people who work alone.
3 Musicians rarely pay as much as companies for the same work.
4 He has had to adapt his style to match Japanese tastes.

No. 27
1 He is usually able to guide them in the way he feels is appropriate.
2 He prefers working with other creators as it gives him inspiration.
3 He often has no choice but to accommodate requests from clients.
4 He prides himself on completing them within the budget.

二次試験
面 接

A日程 🔊 ▶MP3 ▶アプリ ▶CD 4 **21**〜**25**

1. Should foreign policy be based on moral principles or national interest?
2. Have modern societies become too focused on consumerism?
3. Should international child adoption be more strictly regulated?
4. Agree or disagree: The work ethic of Japanese people has changed in recent years
5. Is capital punishment an effective deterrent to crime?

B日程

1. Agree or disagree: Art is losing its relevance
2. Can political activism really make a difference?
3. Should factory farming be banned?
4. Do multinational corporations take their social responsibilities seriously enough?
5. Do humans rule technology or does it rule us?

（注）モデルスピーチと解説はA日程のみ収録しています。

2019-3

一次試験　2020.1.26実施
二次試験　A日程　2020.2.23実施
　　　　　B日程　2020.3.1実施

Grade 1

試験時間

筆記：100分
リスニング：約35分

一次試験・筆記　　　　　p.138〜152
一次試験・リスニング p.153〜159
二次試験・面接　　　　　　p.160

＊解答・解説は別冊p.265〜316にあります。
＊面接の流れは本書p.16にあります。

2019年度第3回

Web特典「自動採点サービス」対応
オンラインマークシート

※検定の回によって2次元コードが違います。
※筆記1〜3，リスニングの採点ができます。
※ PC からも利用できます (本書 p.8 参照)。

一次試験
筆 記

1 To complete each item, choose the best word or phrase from among the four choices. Then, on your answer sheet, find the number of the question and mark your answer.

(1) When Beth was given the assignment, it seemed like an (   ) task. To her surprise, though, she finished on time.
1 ineligible　　　　　**2** inanimate
3 insurmountable　　**4** inebriated

(2) *A:* Did you understand yesterday's economics lecture?
B: No, I was completely (   ) by it. It was as though the teacher was speaking a foreign language!
1 tethered　　**2** lathered　　**3** whittled　　**4** baffled

(3) Although Trevor's disease is a serious one, he has an excellent (   ) for recovery because he is young and the condition was discovered early.
1 prognosis　**2** coercion　**3** pinnacle　**4** gradation

(4) Eastford University was once in the very top (   ) of the nation's schools. Today, however, it is considered to be just average.
1 unison　　**2** echelon　　**3** paradigm　　**4** tundra

(5) The novel was fiercely criticized by reviewers, with one even saying the author was completely (   ) of literary talent.
1 pliant　　**2** audacious　　**3** effusive　　**4** devoid

(6) Last week, a member of the purchasing department staff was fired for taking (   ). He was receiving money for ordering parts from a supplier whose goods were of poor quality.
1 backdrops　　　　**2** kickbacks
3 shortcomings　　**4** loopholes

(7) Margaret tried to (   ) her cat down from the tree with a bowl of milk, but it refused to move.
1 fling　　**2** coax　　**3** smear　　**4** glide

(8) The salesman (   ) the virtues of the sports car at length, but the customer was not convinced it was worth its high price.
1 inscribed　　**2** enthralled　　**3** extolled　　**4** abridged

(9) *A:* The boss refused my request for leave to go to my sister's

wedding in Canada.
B: You should ask Tim for help. He has a lot of (   ) with the boss. I'm sure he could get permission for you.
1 cohort   **2** clash   **3** cavity   **4** clout

(10) To avoid confusing customers by suddenly putting a completely new version of its software on the market, the company introduced (   ) changes over a two-year period.
1 incremental **2** parenthetical **3** opulent **4** buoyant

(11) Amanda tried to get the project's due date changed, but her supervisor refused to (   ). "The deadline must be met," he said.
1 emulate   **2** leer   **3** pervade   **4** budge

(12) Despite being accused of serious crimes, the defendant looked on (   ) throughout her trial. Many people were disturbed by her lack of emotion.
1 ruefully   **2** exquisitely   **3** nominally   **4** impassively

(13) After his vacation, the man wrote to the travel agency with a (   ) of complaints about everything from the rude hotel staff to the poor meals.
1 litany   **2** renunciation   **3** melancholy   **4** remittance

(14) When he lost his job, Dylan became (   ). After a couple of weeks, though, he began to feel more positive and decided to start looking for work.
1 cumbersome **2** despondent **3** poised **4** magnanimous

(15) When the bus driver suddenly braked hard, all the passengers (   ) forward. Luckily, no one was seriously injured.
1 ambushed   **2** rebuked   **3** lurched   **4** bellowed

(16) The dentist waited until the (   ) took effect before beginning the work. He did not want the patient to feel any pain.
1 anesthetic **2** remuneration **3** scourge **4** tycoon

(17) Good writers often have the ability to create (   ) stories. They can move us to tears with a few well-chosen words.
1 gullible   **2** fastidious   **3** poignant   **4** nebulous

(18) Eva hoped to (   ) her children's interest in music by taking them to concerts and buying them musical instruments.
1 oust   **2** irk   **3** spurn   **4** pique

(19) Jonathan has a (   ) attitude to work. He often comes in late, rarely meets his deadlines, and never shows respect to his superiors.
1 cavalier   **2** beguiling   **3** deferential   **4** savvy

(20) *A:* Bill, I'm sorry, but I won't be able to lend you that $100 after all.
B: Oh no! You can't (   ) on your promise now. I need that money to pay my rent.
1 placate   **2** renege   **3** faze   **4** appease

(21) One of the tent ropes was (   ), so Paula moved the tent peg to tighten it up.
1 idyllic   **2** deceased   **3** slack   **4** specious

(22) *A:* Have you decided what to do during the Christmas holidays?
B: Not yet, but I'm (   ) the idea of visiting my brother in Paris.
1 jockeying for   **2** meting out
3 mulling over   **4** lousing up

(23) Brenda had always wanted to live abroad, so when her company announced it would be opening a branch in Istanbul, she immediately (   ) a transfer.
1 squared off against   **2** put in for
3 loaded up on   **4** picked up after

(24) Reggie does not have any ambitious plans for the future. He is happy to just (   ), enjoying each day as it comes.
1 coast along   **2** creep in   **3** bunch up   **4** fire away

(25) The principal said if the student did not (   ) to having cheated on the test, he would be suspended. After admitting to it, he was made to write a letter of apology.
1 pan out   **2** nail down   **3** mill around   **4** own up

---

2 *Read each passage and choose the best word or phrase from among the four choices for each blank. Then, on your answer sheet, find the number of the question and mark your answer.*

An Ancient Work Force

While many archaeologists seek mummies and golden treasures beneath Egypt's sands, Mark Lehner is on a quest to investigate a more mundane subject: the lives of the laborers who constructed the pyramids. Though Lehner's research is not glamorous, he contends that his archaeological finds are beginning to reveal, in his words, "(26)." During his long career, Lehner's discoveries have shed light on the logistics of feeding, organizing, and providing accommodation for the thousands of laborers needed for the massive construction projects. He has unearthed not one but two lost cities which housed workers in the vicinity of the pyramids. Lehner argues the epic scale of the undertaking was integral to the development of national unity because it brought together laborers from throughout the enormous kingdom, which, as Lehner notes, effectively "bound all these disparate areas . . . into a whole."

Lehner's findings contradict the common belief that the construction of the pyramids (27). This idea originates in the writing of the Greek historian Herodotus, who made the claim in his *Histories* many centuries after the pyramids' completion. However, Lehner's excavations of the food preparation facilities and the massive barracks in which workers were housed have turned up evidence of slaughtered cattle and numerous religious inscriptions. These indicate that the builders who worked on the pyramids were not being forced to labor under the threat of whips but rather were motivated by feasts of prime beef and increased odds of obtaining an eternal afterlife.

While the skilled main work force was permanent, a rotating system of manual laborers was also utilized. Though service was mandatory, the duration appears to have been temporary, and these laborers would have had a strong (28). Lehner explains this attitude, saying, "People were not atomized, separate individuals with the political and economic freedom that we take for granted." In Egypt's hierarchical civilization, every single individual had a duty to provide service to someone else — even the most elite officials in the kingdom. As Lehner's work continues, evidence is accumulating that the Egyptian pharaohs presided over a civilization even more complex and cohesive than had been previously imagined.

---

(26) **1** what is really contained in the pyramids
    2 the degree of conflict in the region

    3 how the pyramids helped to build Egypt
    4 the world's oldest construction techniques

(27) 1 stimulated the economy
       2 occurred over multiple generations
       3 was carried out using slave labor
       4 led to Egypt's decline

(28) 1 fear of the skilled builders
       2 sense of social obligation
       3 desire for job security
       4 motivation to finish the project quickly

Language Diversity

    The human race exhibits an incredible degree of linguistic diversity, with more than 7,500 documented languages in existence today. Researchers have long been puzzled, however, by the question of why languages (　　29　　). The South Pacific nation of Papua New Guinea, for example, covers less than 0.5 percent of Earth's land area yet is home to about 10 percent of the planet's languages. Russia, for all its immensity — it covers a whopping 11 percent of Earth's land area — is home to a mere 1.5 percent of the planet's languages. A global-scale analysis performed by biologist Xia Hua of the Australian National University has recently offered some insight into the phenomenon, examining the two predominant theories: isolation and ecological risk.

    Hua concluded that the isolation theory (　　30　　). Landscape features such as rivers have long been regarded as barriers, and the resulting isolation was believed to lead to distinctions in languages among various groups. Hua's research did confirm a direct link between the presence of rivers and the number of languages in a region. However, further analysis indicated that rivers were only contributing to diversity because they facilitated the survival of smaller populations. Hua writes that rivers "seem to act more as an ecological resource than a barrier to interaction."

    The ecological risk hypothesis holds that factors such as climate and resource availability are prime determiners of language diversity, and Hua found that harsher climatic conditions in a region result in fewer languages being spoken. Her research indicated that language diversity correlates strongly to latitude, with vastly more languages being spoken in equatorial regions and fewer in northern and southern regions. In regions near the equator, which boast consistently warm temperatures and plentiful rainfall, growing seasons are much longer. It seems logical, therefore, that (**31**). This allowed a diverse range of languages to develop among independent, smaller cultural groups. In contrast, regions with cold, barren winters made communication among groups of people over distances essential for obtaining resources and maximizing productivity, so the development of disparate languages was not favored. The ecological risk hypothesis is supported by the latitudinal patterns of language diversity observed worldwide.

---

(29) 1 evolve so quickly
2 are gradually disappearing
3 have tended to become more similar
4 are spread across the world so unevenly

(30) 1 ignores a crucial part of human nature
2 confuses diversity with change
3 only applies in the absence of natural barriers
4 is not fully supported by her data

(31) 1 there would be an emphasis on travel
2 less cooperation would be required
3 certain types of crops would be desirable
4 language would take on greater importance

---

3 *Read each passage and choose the best answer from among the four choices for each question. Then, on your answer sheet, find the number of the question and mark your answer.*

Chile under Pinochet

In Chile's 1970 presidential race, voters elected Salvador Allende, a Marxist who ran on a socialist platform of nationalizing

143

the mineral industry and redistributing land and income. Just three years later, the Chilean army, led by General Augusto Pinochet, overthrew Allende and installed a military dictatorship. Pinochet and his supporters were convinced the previous regime had led the nation to the brink of civil war. Although Allende had been legitimately elected, his socialist government's policies and actions caused turmoil among the people and threatened commerce, creating an unbridgeable gulf that divided the country. These divisions were encouraged by the US government, which drastically reduced aid to Chile as a means of political opposition, and by foreign corporations with interests in valuable minerals such as copper. In any case, Pinochet's coup d'état ended Chilean democracy, which dated back to the 1930s, and ushered in an era of repression and brutality unparalleled in the nation's history. Pinochet banned opposition parties, suspended the constitution, and cracked down on political dissent. His regime had more than 100,000 citizens arrested, tortured tens of thousands, and murdered some 3,000 "enemies of the state." For many Chileans, the next 17 years were a nightmare of fear and repression.

Following the takeover, Pinochet appointed a group of US-educated Chilean economists who, in stark contrast to Allende's nationalization and central planning, instituted a radical free-market economic policy that led to high levels of unemployment and bankruptcies within the financial sector. Wages decreased and welfare spending was slashed, hitting the lowest segment of society the hardest. Still, after an economic crisis in 1982, Chile's GDP began to grow at a steady average rate of 5.9 percent, the fastest in Latin America. Foreign companies whose assets had been seized by the Allende government were invited back, and state-owned companies were privatized, although the copper industry — by far the biggest earner of foreign currency — remained under direct state control. The export sector flourished, and poverty levels fell from 50 percent in 1984 to 34 percent in 1989. Although some world leaders credited Pinochet for these achievements, the crucial role of the country's vast mineral wealth cannot be underestimated.

During the second half of his dictatorship, Pinochet's iron grip relaxed slightly. A new constitution in 1980 opened the way to a plebiscite, in which the people could give an up-or-down vote on his continued rule. Pinochet hoped his economic success would enable him to remain in power, but in 1988, Chileans voted for a restoration of democracy with 56 percent in favor and 44 percent opposed. Stepping down in 1990, Pinochet nevertheless retained command of the armed forces and laid claim to a lifelong Senate seat. Chile continued to prosper as a result of successive administrations building upon the economic foundations he had put in place, and the country is widely considered a Latin American success story. Yet it was only when the shackles of dictatorship were removed that an investment-led boom would improve overall living standards. While his supporters believe he saved the country from becoming a communist state in the mold of Cuba, for many Chileans, Pinochet's economic successes will always be overshadowed by the oppression they endured under him.

(32) What does the author of the passage imply in the first paragraph?

1 Doubts about whether Salvador Allende's government had been democratically elected caused suspicions about its political goals.
2 Allende's removal was believed to be necessary to reverse political decisions that were threatening Chile's social and financial stability.
3 Augusto Pinochet mistakenly believed the United States would support him if he attempted to remove Allende from power.
4 Military leaders sympathetic to the United States hoped Allende's removal would allow the Americans to control Chile's mineral resources.

(33) What conclusion can be drawn about the economic achievements of Pinochet's regime?

1 Although Pinochet claimed his policies were more successful than those of Allende, many actually had very similar results in the long term.
2 Forcing weakly performing finance companies out of business was a key factor in allowing the economy to recover in the early 1980s.
3 Despite the growth in Chile's economy, foreign countries

were reluctant to invest there because of its overreliance on its mineral wealth.
4 Had the government not maintained control of the copper industry, Pinochet's economic policies might not have been as successful as they were.

(34) What does the author of the passage believe is true of Chile's return to democracy?

1 Pinochet's insistence on retaining a position within the government regardless of the result of the plebiscite ultimately led to him losing power.
2 Despite voting against Pinochet, the majority of Chileans believed long-term improvements to the economy would be more likely if he could stay in power.
3 The country's increased prosperity was only made possible by ensuring that Pinochet maintained control of the military and kept his political influence.
4 Pinochet provided the basis for economic prosperity, but major economic growth would not have been possible without political freedom.

The Positive Side of Psychopaths

Psychopaths — who are, incidentally, most often men — constitute roughly 1 percent of the population. What sets psychopaths apart is their inability to empathize with the emotions of other people. Self-centered, superficially charming, and persuasive, they pursue their goals with cold detachment, using whatever means they consider necessary. Moreover, they have little consideration for the social consequences of their actions. Taken at face value, these traits would appear to be highly dangerous and toxic, as reinforced by the popular Hollywood conception of the psychopathic killer. But the notion of the "successful psychopath" has existed for a long time. In the 1940s, American psychologist Hervey M. Cleckley articulated this apparent contradiction, postulating that many psychopaths are able to assume a veneer of normalcy which enables them to play a legitimate role within society.

In his 2012 book, *The Wisdom of Psychopaths*, psychologist

Kevin Dutton expanded on Cleckley's thesis. Dutton controversially asserted that in certain professions and high-pressure situations, the attributes of psychopaths not only help them function but also position them to excel. Emotional detachment and fearlessness help them advance in business and earn them distinction in military service. Dutton posits a spectrum of psychopathy, with violent criminals at one end and elite soldiers and CEOs at the other. The crucial distinction, he says, is how psychopaths choose to channel their unique personality traits, none of which are "inherently bad in themselves" but are detrimental "when they are deployed inflexibly." In other words, if psychopaths apply their ruthlessness too strongly or inappropriately, it transforms into callousness. Are psychopaths able to modulate their own behavior? Dutton believes so: "The key is having the right combination of traits at the right levels and in the right context." He believes the contributions of psychopaths tend to be short term rather than long term, but concludes that the small number of them occupying key positions represents a net gain for society overall.

Psychologist Martha Stout, author of *The Sociopath Next Door*, is working to alert people to the dangers of psychopathy and disputes Dutton's claim. Countering his idea that psychopathy is present in degrees, she points out that so-called moderate psychopaths would be more accurately characterized as narcissists — people who are egotistical and lack empathy, but who "nonetheless, in their own way, can love." By definition, psychopaths are without a conscience, and are thus incapable of caring or exhibiting the "wisdom" Dutton optimistically ascribes to them. Stout also holds that the grounds on which Dutton bases his arguments are shaky "Most of the science that he cites possesses a relationship to his thesis that is equivocal at best, and at worst downright misleading," she writes. Evidence from recent studies supports Stout's position. Researchers have found that, despite their charm, psychopaths in management positions often create counterproductive, chaotic work environments marred by bullying, conflict, and a lack of well-being among employees. Moreover, a study of hedge fund managers conducted by the University of Denver found that those with psychopathic tendencies produced lower returns over time. They may be effective at gaining power, but when it comes to using that authority constructively, psychopaths seem to fall short.

(35) What best characterizes Hervey M. Cleckley's position regarding the "successful psychopath"?

   1 As most psychopaths are men, gender bias in society results in the dangerous negative traits they possess being overlooked or excused.
   2 A large number of psychopaths are able to adapt to conventional expectations and therefore function as apparently normal members of society.
   3 No long-term progress in treating psychopaths can be made until the public's tendency to associate psychopathy with criminality is challenged.
   4 Addressing the negative emotions psychopaths feel about their condition is the first step in helping them to interact constructively with others.

(36) How does Kevin Dutton justify his theory that psychopaths have a role to play in society?

   1 Applied correctly and in the proper proportions, the characteristics that define them can be utilized to enable them to outperform their peers.
   2 The short-term results they obtain are more beneficial and far-reaching than the small, steady gains made during the career spans of normal people.
   3 Psychopaths whose activities harm society are outnumbered by those whose specific attributes will help them rise to the top of their profession.
   4 Since no person is fundamentally bad, society does not need to change the behavior of psychopaths, even when it is extreme.

(37) What does the author of the passage suggest about Dutton's argument?

   1 Dutton's lack of experience working directly with victims of psychopathic behavior makes his argument less convincing than Martha Stout's.
   2 Dutton's argument cannot be considered credible because he seems to have purposely altered evidence and data.

3 Despite flaws in Dutton's thesis, he is correct in his belief that psychopaths tend to function well in the workplace for only a short time.
4 Dutton's thesis is likely incorrect given that psychopaths in leadership positions usually produce negative overall outcomes in the long term.

CRISPR Gene Editing

Gregor Mendel's discovery of the principles of genetic inheritance in the 1860s opened the way for scientists to manipulate plant and animal genes. In the early years of genetic manipulation, however, the rate of mutagenesis, or genetic change, could not be controlled directly through selective breeding, so results were often unpredictable and required generations of trial and error. Later developments, such as employing radiation and chemical treatments, succeeded in accelerating mutagenesis, but produced results just as random as breeding did.

It finally became possible to directly manipulate an organism's genome through the insertion of foreign DNA in the 1970s, but the first techniques developed were not suitable for targeting a specific location on the genome. Even when the targeting of specific genes through the synthesis of artificial proteins became a reality, an elaborate and time-consuming process was necessary to adapt the delivery system for each individual gene. This severely restricted the techniques' potential applications.

It was not until 2012 that scientists developed a technology commonly referred to as CRISPR, which has tremendous potential as a superior method for manipulating genes. CRISPR stands for Clustered Regularly Interspaced Short Palindromic Repeats. In nature, CRISPRs are used by bacteria to defend themselves from viruses and consist of repeating sequences of DNA building blocks, or nucleotides, within the bacteria's DNA which are able to store segments of DNA from viruses. When a bacterium is attacked by a virus and is successful in exterminating it, the bacterium sends out enzymes which collect the virus's DNA. They then cut it into smaller sections and store it between the bacterium's CRISPRs as a reference to be used in case of future attacks. If the bacterium is attacked by the same virus again, the stored DNA from the previously defeated virus is copied into molecules, which then assist a predatory enzyme in navigating to a specific site in the virus's genome. The enzyme then chops a section out of the virus's DNA, thereby making it harmless.

The discovery of a preexisting, natural mechanism capable of altering specific DNA sequences to remove, add, or alter genetic material turned out to be a godsend to geneticists. In the years since, scientists have figured out not only how to trick CRISPRs into hunting for and cutting non-viral DNA, but also how to insert desired DNA sequences into the spaces between the CRISPRs and use the natural cellular repair mechanisms of DNA to patch up where cuts have been made. CRISPR can be utilized to target and remove or replace any segment of any organism's DNA. Additionally, because it is self-contained and self-directed, CRISPR can achieve, in a few hours and at a negligible price, what previous techniques took weeks or months to accomplish.

While numerous industries are interested in CRISPR, the immediate beneficiaries are the medical and agricultural sectors. The technology offers the possibility of not only eliminating diseases that stem from gene defects but also potentially changing the face of medicine by expanding the roles of beneficial genes. Imagine directing immune cells to fight cancerous tumors or growing transplantable human organs in pigs — to name just two projects that researchers are optimistic about. Agricultural scientists envision attaining long-cherished goals such as creating crops resistant to insect pests and disease or developing new crop varieties packed with nutrition. Since CRISPR edits DNA so precisely and allows for genetic editing instead of including alien genes in the target organism, its proponents in the agricultural sector believe it can allay the fears of genetic contamination that are associated with genetically modified (GM) products, allowing CRISPR-created crops to circumvent the criticism and strict regulations GM crops are subject to.

The principles of genetic inheritance predict individual genes have a 50 percent chance of being inherited by the next generation during sexual reproduction. In theory, CRISPR can increase that probability to nearly 100 percent, which would empower scientists to spread a modified gene throughout an entire species to effect a desired change. Scientists envision changing the rules of inheritance to eradicate mankind's worst afflictions by engineering their extinction — or that of the species that spread them. Malaria, Lyme disease, and invasive species are already being targeted for eradication with this technology, despite the potential for unintended consequences.

Those consequences, however, are one reason critics say CRISPR gene editing is no magic bullet. The knock-on effects of destroying, say, every *Anopheles* mosquito on Earth in order to eliminate malaria are almost certainly greater than anyone can anticipate. Furthermore, there have been instances in lab experiments in which CRISPR has targeted a DNA sequence at locations other than where scientists expected the DNA cut to occur. Additionally, recent studies have shown CRISPR-edited cells can trigger cancer. At this point, the risks and uncertainty surrounding how CRISPR works and how inheritance of its genetic changes will affect subsequent generations are too great to take anything but a cautious approach.

(38) What was true of genetic manipulation before CRISPR?

1 It was not until it became possible to insert DNA into organisms that mutagenesis could be sped up enough to be widely practical.
2 Although the desired changes to genes might be achieved, scientists found they would be reversed within a few generations.
3 Radiation and chemical treatments enabled changes to be made accurately but turned out to be no faster than manipulating genes through breeding.
4 The techniques that were available to scientists were either lacking in precision or could not be applied in an efficient manner.

(39) In bacteria, the DNA stored between CRISPRs

1 causes enzymes to mistakenly attack healthy DNA that has been altered by the activity of an attacking virus.
2 is used in molecules that guide enzymes which are capable of cutting apart the DNA of a virus.
3 helps to ensure that the molecules containing healthy DNA are able to repair the enzymes that have been infected by a virus.
4 can transform enzymes into spaces that are ideal for storing molecules containing the bacteria's DNA.

(40) What do people in the agricultural industry see as a key benefit of performing gene editing with CRISPR?

1 Crops can be modified without taking the risk of inserting genes from foreign organisms into them.
2 Gene editing of agricultural crops with CRISPR will become accessible and efficient once appropriate regulations are implemented.
3 By transferring genes from harmful organisms into crops, it will be possible to make them immune to disease and insect-related damage.
4 CRISPR could enable scientists to enhance immunity to diseases in pigs and other livestock, thereby reducing dependence on medication.

(41) One reason some people urge caution when dealing with CRISPR is that

1 its promotion as a possible cure for cancer is exaggerated, as research into agricultural applications has revealed substantial drawbacks to its use.
2 the genetic changes that it causes in organisms may not be passed down in the long term, despite its benefits in the short term.
3 it is unrealistic to think the complete elimination of diseases like malaria can be accomplished using just one technology.
4 scientists' knowledge of the way it works is too limited for them to foresee all the potential effects of editing species' DNA.

4
- *Write an essay on the given TOPIC.*
- *Give THREE reasons to support your answer.*
- *Structure: introduction, main body, and conclusion*
- *Suggested length: 200–240 words*
- *Write your essay in the space provided on Side B of your answer sheet. Any writing outside the space will not be graded.*

TOPIC
Can renewable energy sources replace fossil fuels?

リスニング

―――― Listening Test ――――

There are four parts to this listening test.

Part 1	Dialogues: 1 question each	Multiple-choice
Part 2	Passages: 2 questions each	Multiple-choice
Part 3	Real-Life: 1 question each	Multiple-choice
Part 4	Interview: 2 questions	Multiple-choice

※**Listen carefully to the instructions.**

Part 1

No. 1
1 He is still considering his options.
2 He agrees with the woman's choice.
3 He prefers a candidate with experience.
4 He thinks it is time for someone new.

No. 2
1 He thinks his wife will be upset about the cost.
2 He thinks the accident was not his fault.
3 His insurance will not cover the repairs.
4 His insurance fees will increase.

No. 3
1 A price reduction might be possible.
2 She cannot give an answer today.
3 Longer stays require earlier reservations.
4 October is a rather busy time.

No. 4
1 The seminar she attended was a waste of time.
2 She could not complete the business deal.
3 The electronics firm will not negotiate the price.
4 Her ability to negotiate has improved recently.

No. 5	1 Terry should discuss his problems with his teacher. 2 Terry should spend less time studying vocabulary. 3 Terry should use a different method to learn words. 4 Terry should let her help him study for the test.
No. 6	1 Improve her job performance. 2 Ask her colleagues for advice. 3 Begin looking for a new job. 4 Make her work ambitions clearer.
No. 7	1 Having a meeting this afternoon. 2 Picking Mr. Li up for dinner at 7. 3 Giving Mr. Li time to rest. 4 Discussing business over dinner.
No. 8	1 He was recently promoted at work. 2 He has turned his life around. 3 He has decided to return to college. 4 He had an argument with his boss.
No. 9	1 A dog breeder is the safest option. 2 They should not take in any more dogs. 3 Shelter dogs are fine if you choose carefully. 4 It is easier to train younger dogs.
No. 10	1 His emphasis on productivity has been beneficial. 2 His lack of supervision gives his staff freedom. 3 His excessive spending strains their budget. 4 His hiring practices are better than the previous boss's.

Part 2

(A)

No. 11
1. It can kill harmful plants.
2. It helps soil produce more oxygen.
3. It can prevent the release of carbon into the air.
4. It releases carbon faster than regular fertilizers do.

No. 12
1. Its potential effect on soil may be exaggerated.
2. Its use can improve crop quality and quantity.
3. It is most suitable for modern agriculture.
4. It might cause long-term environmental damage.

(B)

No. 13
1. It prevents blood clot formation near an injury.
2. It reduces patients' blood pressure.
3. It changes the composition of blood.
4. It boosts the body's ability to close a wound.

No. 14
1. It can be reused a number of times.
2. It removes harmful bacteria from wounds.
3. It can be made more cheaply than ordinary bandages.
4. It does not have to be removed.

(C)

No. 15
1. Sell products that are not designed to last long.
2. Label older products as new products.
3. Make repair manuals difficult to understand.
4. Hire too few workers with technical skills.

No. 16
1. By suing manufacturers.
2. By reselling used parts and products.
3. By encouraging the sharing of information.
4. By purchasing goods online.

(D)

No. 17
1 It does not include some types of income.
2 It does not measure wealth distribution in a country.
3 The way it is measured has changed over time.
4 Economists disagree on how to calculate it.

No. 18
1 Their people suffer from high levels of crime.
2 Their people do not enjoy gender equality.
3 Their people should be taxed more.
4 Their people are more likely to be content.

(E)

No. 19
1 The clothes people wear can affect their performance.
2 Dressing similarly improves people's relationships.
3 People's clothes rarely affect how others judge them.
4 Clothing color has little effect on cognitive performance.

No. 20
1 Inmate numbers declined rapidly.
2 Inmates' behavioral problems were reduced.
3 Inmates were punished more frequently.
4 Inmates refused to wear the new uniforms.

Part 3

No. 21

(F)

Situation: You plan to enter a doctoral program in engineering and need a research grant. You have not yet decided on your research focus. A recent graduate offers the following advice.

Question: What should you do first?

1 Ask a professor who has taught you before.
2 Make inquiries about engineering professors.
3 Read some journal articles on your general research field.
4 Contact the local government about the grant application.

No. 22

(G)

Situation: Your doctor is explaining your options for giving birth. You do not want to be separated from your baby at any time. You have $1,500 to pay any costs not covered by insurance.

Question: Where should you give birth?

1 In the hospital's maternity ward.
2 In the in-hospital birth center.
3 In a private birthing center.
4 In your home.

No. 23

(H)

Situation: You are a department manager at a company in Canada. You are being transferred to Japan in eight weeks. Your boss tells you the following.

Question: What should you do first?

1 Reach out to the sales department manager.
2 Start training Alberto for the position.
3 Consult with a recruitment agency.
4 Contact the personnel department about Evelyn.

No. 24

(I)

Situation: An assistant at the dentist's office is explaining how to use a kit to whiten your teeth at home. Two of your teeth were replaced by implants last year.

Question: What should you do to get the best results?

1 Schedule an earlier follow-up appointment.
2 Start with longer whitening sessions.
3 Monitor changes in the color of your teeth.
4 Use desensitizing cream before each session.

No. 25

(J)

Situation: You are a Japanese citizen living in Japan. You would like to buy a house in Australia as an investment. A real estate agent tells you the following.

Question: What should you do first?

1 Apply to become a resident of Australia.
2 Find a property to purchase.
3 Submit an approval document.
4 Obtain an Australian tax file number.

Part 4

No. 26
1 They should not be made to feel that they have failed.
2 They should do physical exercise to help them become mentally stronger.
3 They should spend time with people who have similar conditions.
4 They should get more support from their families.

No. 27
1 It is important for them to monitor their own stress levels.
2 The good ones have usually faced emotional challenges themselves.
3 It helps if they have had experience working in the business world.
4 The work can seriously affect their own personal relationships.

二次試験 面接

A日程

1. Will artificial intelligence transform the world economy for the better?
2. Is it ever acceptable for companies to monitor employees' social media use?
3. Is reducing poverty the key to reducing crime?
4. Should violent sports, such as boxing, be banned from the Olympics?
5. Agree or disagree: More resources should be spent on pushing the frontiers of science

B日程

1. Does social media put too much pressure on people to conform to certain ways of living?
2. Will virtual currencies ever be the norm?
3. Agree or disagree: Technology is having a negative effect on the evolution of education
4. Should vaccinations for infectious diseases be mandatory?
5. Should advertising aimed at young people be more strictly regulated?

（注）モデルスピーチと解説はA日程のみ収録しています。

2022年度版

文部科学省後援

英検®1級
過去6回全問題集

別冊解答

英検®は、公益財団法人 日本英語検定協会の登録商標です。

旺文社

文部科学省後援

英検®1級
過去6回全問題集

別冊解答

2022年度版

英検®は、公益財団法人 日本英語検定協会の登録商標です。

旺文社

もくじ

Contents

2021年度　第2回検定　解答・解説 ………………………… 5

　　　　　　第1回検定　解答・解説 ………………………… 57

2020年度　第3回検定　解答・解説 ………………………… 109

　　　　　　第2回検定　解答・解説 ………………………… 161

　　　　　　第1回検定　解答・解説 ………………………… 213

2019年度　第3回検定　解答・解説 ………………………… 265

2021-2

一次試験
筆記解答・解説　　p.6〜24

一次試験
リスニング解答・解説　　p.25〜52

二次試験
面接解答・解説　　p.53〜56

解 答 一 覧

一次試験・筆記

1
(1)	4	(10)	1	(19)	1
(2)	4	(11)	3	(20)	4
(3)	2	(12)	1	(21)	2
(4)	3	(13)	1	(22)	4
(5)	3	(14)	1	(23)	1
(6)	4	(15)	2	(24)	2
(7)	3	(16)	3	(25)	1
(8)	1	(17)	4		
(9)	2	(18)	2		

2
(26)	4	(29)	1	
(27)	3	(30)	4	
(28)	2	(31)	2	

3
(32)	2	(35)	2	(38)	3
(33)	4	(36)	1	(39)	2
(34)	3	(37)	4	(40)	4
				(41)	3

4　解答例は本文参照

一次試験・リスニング

Part 1
No. 1	3	No. 5	3	No. 9	2
No. 2	2	No. 6	4	No.10	4
No. 3	1	No. 7	3		
No. 4	1	No. 8	1		

Part 2
No.11	4	No.15	1	No.19	2
No.12	3	No.16	1	No.20	3
No.13	1	No.17	4		
No.14	3	No.18	2		

Part 3
No.21	4	No.23	4	No.25	3
No.22	1	No.24	1		

Part 4
No.26	2	No.27	1

一次試験・筆記 1　問題編 p.18〜20

(1) ― 解答 4

訳　その古文書は，長年にわたって誰も解読できない手書き文字で書かれていた。その後，ついに優秀な若い学者がその意味を解明した。

語句　1「〜を中傷する」　2「(時)をぶらぶらして過ごす」
3「〜を固く約束する」　4「〜を解読する」

解説　ついに意味を解明したのだから，それまでは誰も decipher「解読する」ことができなかったのだ。work out「(問題など)を苦労して解く」。

(2) ― 解答 4

訳　審判員が試合中にいくつか大きなミスをした後，ファンたちはブーイングや彼に向かって怒鳴ることで侮蔑の態度を示した。

語句　1「悪名，不名誉」　2「カタカタいう音」
3「豪華さ，輝き」　4「軽蔑」

解説　何度も重大ミスをした審判。ファンがブーイングと怒鳴ることで何を表すのか，を考えると disdain「軽蔑」だ。類義語は scorn, contempt。

(3) ― 解答 2

訳　金は最も可鍛性のある金属の1つだ。この性質が金をさまざまな形に成形することができるようにし，金がとても需要の高い1つの理由だ。

語句　1「大言壮語の」　2「可鍛性の」
3「干上がった」　4「汚い」

解説　さまざまな形にすることができる性質を持つのだから，金は malleable (= easy to press into different shapes)「可鍛性の」金属だ。

(4) ― 解答 3

訳　CEOは，ここ何年にもわたる会社の成功は，会社の過去のリーダーたちが取った方針の知恵の明白な証だと言った。

語句　1「(事業などの)説明書」　2「摩滅，皮膚のすりむけ」
3「証明するもの」　4「報復」

解説　長年の会社の成功は先人たちの知恵の何か，を考えて選択肢を見ると testament「証明するもの」が適切。a testament to 〜「〜の証し」。

(5) ― 解答 3

訳　最初の任期中にスミス知事は多くの敵を作った。彼が再選を目指したとき，彼らは対立候補を支持し，対立候補はやすやすと選挙に勝った。

語句　1「隠遁者(いんとん)」　2「神童」　3「敵」　4「被保護者」

解説　2文目の they が指す対象が文中にないので，they に当たる語が空所に入る。they は対立候補を支持したのだから，知事が作ったのは adversaries「敵」だ。

(6) ― 解答 ④

訳 干ばつに襲われた地域の援助機関は，緊急救援物資が援助を必要としているすべての市民に公平に分配されることを確実にするため，ベストを尽くした。

語句 1「偽って」 2「不法に」 3「光り輝いて」 4「公平に」

解説 救援物資は困っている全市民にどのように分配されるべきか，を考えると副詞 equitably「公平に」が適切。名詞形は equity「公平」。

(7) ― 解答 ③

訳 炭鉱でのストライキが広がりエネルギー不足がよく起こるにつれ，いくつかの業界は自分たちがますます悲惨な状況に陥っているのに気付いた。

語句 1「愚かな，粗野な」 2「(味などが) ぴりっとする」
3「悲惨な，ひどい」 4「使い古された，陳腐な」

解説 エネルギー不足がよくあるのだから，いくつかの産業界の状態は dire「悲惨な」のだ。類義語は terrible, dreadful。

(8) ― 解答 ①

訳 A：あなたの庭は非の打ち所がないようね。どうやって，きちんと整えておくの？
B：実を言うと，手入れをしてくれる庭師を雇ったんだ。

語句 1「汚れ〔欠点〕のない」 2「ゆがんだ」
3「触れることができない」 4「下品な，低俗な」

解説 庭師が手入れをした，とても neat and tidy「きちんと整って」いる庭なのだから，immaculate「欠点のない」庭なのだ。

(9) ― 解答 ②

訳 1993年にインターネット全体はたった130のウェブサイトでできていた。しかし，それらは急増し続け，今日では10億を超えると言われている。

語句 1「脈打つ」
2「急増する」
3「～を（束縛などから）解放する」
4「～を列挙する」

解説 たった130だったのが今では10億を超えているのだから，ウェブサイトは proliferate「急増する」ことを続けているのだ。類義語は multiply。

(10) ― 解答 ①

訳 A：あれらのケーキ，本当においしそうだ。1つ食べようよ。
B：どうぞ。私はダイエット中で，誘惑に負けないと決心しているの。

語句 1「負ける，屈する」 2「～の心をかき乱す」
3「～を（完全に）消す」 4「口論する」

解説 ダイエット中なのだから，Bがしないと決めているのは succumb to

temptation「誘惑に負ける」だ。succumb to ~「~に負ける，屈する」。

(11)−解答 ③

訳 対向車を避けようとして，運転手は路肩を外れて揺れながら突っ走った。

語句 1「いばって歩いた」
2「(馬が) 緩い駆け足で行った」
3「(車などが) 揺れながら疾走した」
4「(液体が) サイフォンを通った」

解説 対向車を避けるためなのだから，車は路肩を離れて careened「(制御が困難で左右に) 揺れながら疾走した」のだ。

(12)−解答 ①

訳 その患者は慢性のせきで苦しんでいる。彼はそのための薬を服用してきたが，せきは6カ月以上も続いている。

語句 1「慢性の」　2「田舎の」　3「如才ない」　4「狡猾な」

解説 患者のせきは薬を服用しながらも半年以上続いているのだから，chronic「慢性の」なのだ。反意語は acute「(病気が) 急性の」。

(13)−解答 ①

訳 陸軍巡察隊は駐屯地に戻る途中で待ち伏せ攻撃に遭った。彼らが狭い谷間に入ると，反乱兵のグループが彼らを待っていた。

語句 1「待ち伏せ (攻撃)」　2「称賛」
3「直観的把握」　4「初め，始まり」

解説 反乱兵たちは巡察隊が来るのを狭い谷間で待ち構えていたのだから，巡察隊が出くわしたのは ambush「待ち伏せ攻撃」だ。

(14)−解答 ①

訳 その政治家の人気は変動した。2年前は彼の支持率は高かった。その後，彼は昨年国民の批判の標的となったが，それ以来支持を取り戻してきた。

語句 1「変動した」　2「混ぜ合わせて作った」
3「同意した，継承した」　4「表にまとめた」

解説 時系列では「高い支持率→国民の批判の的→支持を取り戻す」となっているのだから，政治家の人気は fluctuated「変動した」のだ。

(15)−解答 ②

訳 メアリーは長いこと新しい幹線道路を建設する市の計画の忠実な支持者だ。それは地元の経済に大きなプラスの影響を与えると，彼女は信じている。

語句 1「残りの」　2「忠実な」　3「恥ずべき」　4「遺伝(性)の」

解説 新しい幹線道路は地元経済に大きなプラス効果があると信じているメアリーは，計画の staunch「忠実な，断固たる」支持者だ。

(16)−解答 ③

訳 カイルの背中の痛みはとてもひどかったので，朝ベッドから出るのさえ

8

大変だった。

- 語句 **1**「おどけた」　**2**「（家屋などが）見捨てられた」
  3「ひどく痛い，苦しめる」　**4**「人に好かれる」
- 解説 ベッドから出るのにさえ苦労するのだから，背中の痛みは excruciating「ひどく痛い」のだ。excruciating pain「耐え難いほどの痛み，激痛」。

(17) – 解答 **4**

- 訳 トレントはこんろを止めるのを忘れて台所で小さな火事を起こした。幸いにも，彼は炎が広がる前にバケツ1杯の水をぶっかけて炎を消すことができた。
- 語句 **1**「～を取り消す」　**2**「～を否認する」
  3「（武器など）を振り回す」　**4**「～に（水などを）ぶっかける」
- 解説 Luckily があるので，消火できたのだ。バケツの水を炎に…とくれば douse「～に（水などを）ぶっかける，（火など）を（水をかけて）消す」だ。

(18) – 解答 **2**

- 訳 外科技術の進歩で，手術を行うときに医者はより小さな切開ができるようになった。これは傷がずっと目立たなくなることを意味する。
- 語句 **1**「なぞなぞ，難問」　**2**「切開，切り込み」
  3「沼地」　**4**「風刺画」
- 解説 傷が目立たなくなるのだから，医者は手術時にもっと小さな incision「切開」をすることができるようになったのだ。

(19) – 解答 **1**

- 訳 社長は記者会見で質問に対して遠回しの回答をしたことを批判された。参加したジャーナリストたちはもっと明快な返答を望んでいた。
- 語句 **1**「遠回しの」　**2**「もうかる」
  3「丸い」　**4**「この上なく優れた」
- 解説 もっと明快な返答が望まれていたのだから，批判された社長がしたのは oblique「遠回しの」回答だ。

(20) – 解答 **4**

- 訳 バーバラが病気だったとき，家族の誰かが昼も夜もずっと彼女のそばにいた。この寝ずの番は，彼女が全快するまで続いた。
- 語句 **1**「難儀，厄難」　**2**「輪郭（線）」
  3「臆病」　**4**「寝ずの番」
- 解説 昼夜を問わず誰かが病気のバーバラのそばにいたのだから，彼女が全快するまで続いたのは vigil「寝ずの番」だ。

(21) – 解答 **2**

- 訳 ニーナとジュディーは双子だったが，学校ではまったく違った態度を取った。ニーナはしばしば失礼で教師の指示に従うのを拒み，一方ジュデ

ィーはいつも敬意を表した。

- **語句** 1「全知の」 2「敬意を表する」
  3「（仕事などが）骨の折れる」 4「絶壁の（ような）」
- **解説** 態度がまったく違う2人なのだから，失礼で教師に従わないニーナと違って，ジュディーの態度は deferential「敬意を表する」だったのだ。

(22) – 解答 4

- **訳** 大使は最初の取り組み方が何ら交渉に影響を与えられなかった後，礼儀正しさをなしにしてその問題についてもっと積極的な態度を取ることを決めた。
- **語句** 1「（部屋などに）どかどか入り込む」
  2「～を少しずつかじる」
  3「（情報など）を探り出す」
  4「～なしで済ます」
- **解説** 最初のやり方が失敗した後なので，最初のやり方が空所直後の politeness で，これをやめて aggressive にすると決めたと考えると理にかなう。

(23) – 解答 1

- **訳** マラソン走者たちは，沿道で声援を送る観衆によって鼓舞された。そのサポートが走者たちをレースの最後までがんばるように励ました。
- **語句** 1「鼓舞された」 2「掃いて脇へどけられた」
  3「外に出された」 4「（金銭）出し合われた」
- **解説** 観衆の声援で走者は spurred on「鼓舞された」と考えられる。2文目「そのサポート（声援）が走者のがんばりを促した」が裏付けとなる。

(24) – 解答 2

- **訳** 暴力的な抗議行動を減らそうとして，政府は街頭での大人数の集会を厳しく取り締まる法律を制定した。
- **語句** 1「～を大量生産する」 2「厳しく取り締まる」
  3「ひいて粉にする」 4「～を宣誓就任させる」
- **解説** 暴力的抗議行動を減らすために導入した法律なのだから，大人数の集会について crack down「断固たる処置を取る，厳しく取り締まる」ものだ。

(25) – 解答 1

- **訳** 兵士たちは訓練の完了後すぐに，海外の新しい配属の詳細を受け取った。彼らは西アフリカの基地へ出発するように命じられた。
- **語句** 1「（別の任地へ）出発する」 2「（話に）加わる」
  3「衰える，弱る」 4「居眠りをする」
- **解説** 兵士は新しい配属の詳細を受け取ったのだから，命じられたのは西アフリカの基地へ ship out「出発する」ことだ。ship out は軍務で別の場所に出発するときに使われることが多い。

| 一次試験・筆記 | **2** | 問題編 p.21〜23 |

全文訳　宝石バチとゴキブリ

　宝石バチは生殖に欠かせないある能力を使う。そして，このハチの獲物であるゴキブリが極めて重要な役割を果たす。宝石バチは，顎でゴキブリをつかんだ後，獲物の体内に毒を注入し，瞬時にその生き物の前脚を短時間まひさせる。こうして動かなくなることで，ハチは，ゴキブリの脳の特定部位を狙うために必要となる確かな精度で2回目の針を刺すことができる。そこで毒液が特定の神経細胞の活動を遮断し，その生き物がハチから逃げる能力を妨げる。このハチがこのように獲物を操ることができるという事実は，この昆虫の最も興味深い特徴の1つだと考えられている。

　毒が効くと，ゴキブリがハチの幼虫の栄養物としての役割を果たす準備がほとんど整う。しかしまず，ハチが飛び去って獲物を隠す穴を決めている間に，ゴキブリは長い身づくろいの儀式を行う。研究によると，ゴキブリの清浄行動は毒自体の特定の効果である。この行動が，例えばハチの幼虫にきれいな食事を確保することでハチに利益をもたらしているかどうかはわかっていないが，研究者たちがゴキブリをハチの針で刺されたのと同じような状態にしたときには，この行動は見られなかった。この行動はまた，宝石バチに捕えられても刺されていない状態など，単にストレスを経験しただけのゴキブリにもなかった。

　ハチが戻ると，ゴキブリは完全に捕獲者の意のままだ。ハチは，ゴキブリを穴に誘導すると，その脚に卵を1つ産んで去る。ハチの幼虫がふ化し，ゴキブリの体内に居を定め，自分自身の成長を養うために，その生き物からの栄養を利用する。しかし，その環境に危険がないわけではない。研究者たちは，ゴキブリの体腔内にいる間に防御用の盾として配備する液状物を，幼虫が出すのを観察している。この液状物に含まれる抗生物質は，（ゴキブリの体内での）潜伏期に宝石バチの子孫を死に至らせる可能性がある，ゴキブリが体内に持つ細菌の増殖を抑える。成熟するまで生き延びると，若いハチは宿主の外皮から出てきて，不運な獲物を自ら探し始める準備が整う。

> 語句　venom「（蛇・クモ・ハチなどの）毒液，毒」，paralyze「〜をまひさせる」，neuron「ニューロン，神経単位」，flee「逃げる」，intriguing「興味をそそる」，larva「幼虫」，prolonged「長引く」，self-grooming「独り身づくろい」，subject *A* to *B*「AにBを受けさせる」，pierce「〜を刺す」，compliant「従順な」，captor「捕獲者」，cavity「空洞，穴」，inhibit「〜を抑制する」，harbor「〜を住まわせる」，incubation「潜伏」，maturation「成熟」

(26) – 解答

> 解説　ハチはこの方法で何をするのか，が空所に入る。この段落の説明によると，宝石バチは捕まえたゴキブリに毒を注入して前脚が動かない状態にした上で，再度脳の特定部位に毒を注入して逃げる能力を奪う。これが

in this way に相当するので，ハチはゴキブリを「操ることができる」と考えるのが自然。また，ゴキブリが行う清浄行動（第2段落）やハチの意のままになること（第3段落冒頭）が補強となっている。

(27) – 解答 ③

解説 ゴキブリの清浄行動は何であるか，が空所に入る。第2段落後半で「ハチに刺されたのと同様の状態にしても，捕まえられても刺されないなどストレスを経験させても清浄行動は見られなかった」と述べられているので，この行動は **3**「毒自体の特定の効果」だと考えられる。空所文の直後で「この行動が……ハチに利益を与えているかどうかはわかっていない」と述べられているので **1** は誤りである。

(28) – 解答 ②

解説 第3段落後半で，幼虫は（ゴキブリの体内での）潜伏期に，ゴキブリが体内に持つ細菌の増殖によって死ぬ可能性があるという危険が述べられている。このことを「環境に危険がないわけではない」と言い換えた **2** が正解。

全文訳 ベルトルト・ブレヒトと叙事演劇

20世紀の偉大な演出家・劇作家の1人と広く認められているベルトルト・ブレヒトは，「叙事演劇」として知られる革新的なジャンルの先駆者であった。彼の作品は常に見て楽しくユーモアがあったが，ブレヒトの演劇は，当時の演劇の慣習に反抗する行為へと発展した。特に，ブレヒトは，芸術は現実を映し出す鏡であるべきという一般的な考えを覆そうとした。当時の作品は細かく作り込んだ小道具と舞台装置を使い，今日的な問題を中心とする筋書きを利用し，観客が簡単に共感できる登場人物を主役にしていた。しかし，ブレヒトの作品は従来の脚本術と演出法を覆し，観客に，自分たちが見ているのは目の前で起こっている実際の出来事ではなく，大幅に脚色され芝居じみた日常生活の解釈であることを，至る所で意図的に思い出させた。

ブレヒトは特に，普通の演劇において観客が登場人物に共感するときに生み出される感情の放出である，カタルシスの原理をひどく嫌った。これは演劇の伝統の中で最も有害で，観客を論理的に考えないようにさせる，と彼は主張した。それ故にブレヒトは必要最低限の舞台装置とセットを使って，登場人物に直接観客に話しかけさせたり，自分の特徴を表すプラカードを掲げさせたりした。そうすることで，ブレヒトは意図的に，観客に舞台の登場人物と出来事から心理的距離を保たせ，非常に知的な劇場体験を作り出したのだ。ブレヒトは，自分の劇の工夫が一般大衆を刺激してその戯曲の主題をじっくりと考えさせることを願った。

ブレヒトの戯曲は，ほとんど常に彼の政治的・哲学的な信念の表現で，その中で真っ先に挙げられるのは，永遠のものはない，という観念だった。彼がこれを伝えた1つの方法は，歴史的題材の使用を通してだ。戦争のように見たところ重大で普遍的な出来事には終わりが来ること，そして，そうした出来事がどのように解釈されるかは出来事そ

のものが終わった後ではたいてい非常に異なることを，観客に気付かせるのに，そのような題材は役立つとブレヒトは感じていた。ブレヒトは，人類の文明はユートピア的社会に向かって進んでいるという考えを抱いており，演劇は，人生は静的ではないことを思い出させるものとして，また，人々がそのような目標を目指して励むのを助けるための意欲を与えるものとしての両方の役割を果たし得ると信じていた。彼のユートピア的な政治観は，今日では弱さと見なされることもあるが，演劇に与えた革新的で多大な貢献のために，彼はあがめられている。

> 語句 watchable「見て楽しい」，rebellion「反乱，反逆」，theatrical「劇の，芝居じみた」，prop「小道具」，scenery「(背景を含む) 舞台装置」，turn ~ on its head「~をひっくり返す」，at every turn「至る所で」，dramatize「~を脚色する」，despise「~を軽蔑する，嫌悪する」，employ「~を使用する」，trait「特徴」，device「工夫，方策」，reflect on ~「~を熟考する」，invariably「常に，いつも」，convey「~を伝える」，momentous「重大な」，universal「全世界の，普遍的な」，static「静的な，固定的な」，revere「~をあがめる，崇敬する」

(29) – 解答 ①

解説 ブレヒトが覆そうとした一般的な考えとは何かを，空所以降の記述から読み取る。ブレヒト以前の演劇が重視したのは，作り込んだ小道具と舞台装置，今日的な筋書き，観客が共感できる登場人物，つまり実際の出来事 (a real event) が舞台で起きているかのように見せることだった。それに合うのは，**1**「現実を映し出す鏡」である。

(30) – 解答 ④

解説 ブレヒトが最も有害な伝統だと嫌悪するカタルシスは何をするのか，が空所に入る。ブレヒトは，観客に登場人物などから心理的距離を取らせて知的な劇場体験を作り出し，観客が演劇の主題をじっくり考える (reflecting thoughtfully on the play's themes) ことを望んだ (第2段落後半) のだから，彼が嫌うのはそれとは逆のことなので，**4**「観客を論理的に考えないようにさせる」が適切。

(31) – 解答 ②

解説 空所に入るのは，ブレヒトの信念の中で先頭に来る観念 (concept) の内容。彼はこの観念を伝えるのに歴史的題材を使ったが，それは「見たところ重大で普遍的な出来事には終わりが来る」こと，また，同じ出来事の解釈が出来事の後では大きく変わることを観客に気付かせるのに役立つから (第3段落第3文)。これらのことで伝えられるのは**2**「永遠のものはない」という観念だ。

全文訳　高利貸しと罪

　貸した金に対して利息を請求することは高利貸しとしても知られ，今日では広く受け入れられているが，かつては大きな罪と見なされていた。昔は，高利貸し規制法は普通のことで，特にローマカトリック教会は，中世の時代にこの行いに厳しく反対することで知られており，その罪を犯した者を教会から追放した。

　元々高利貸しが禁止されるようになったのは，借金と信用貸しが，善意による援助と信頼のシステムと考えられていたことによる。中世の貧しい農村部の人々は，家族と友人が助け合うために物を共有し貸すことに頼ることによって，強い共同社会のつながりを形成した。それ故，人の社会的義務と考えられている行為に対して報酬を期待するのは，道徳的に間違っていると見なされ，そしてこの考えは，交換の媒体が物からお金へと変化した後もずっと続いた。しかし，貧窮していたり金銭上の不運に苦しんでいたりした人たちは，教会や貴族が資本を多量に蓄えていたので，彼らに頼らざるを得なかった。そして，借金と信用貸しの道徳的な本質に関する当時の考えに沿って，人の社会的・宗教的責任の一部であるものから利益を得る金貸しは，罪深いと見なされた。

　しかし，貸金業から利益を得るために，教会と高利貸しの法的禁止の抜け道を見つけようとする者もいた。そうするために多様な方法が出現した。例えば，稼いだ利息を隠す方法として変動する為替レートを利用しようと，外貨で借金を返済することを伴う複雑な策略などである。ほかの方法で貸金業者が日常的に用いたのは「3つ組み契約」だ。これは複数の契約を組み合わせたもので，契約が個別なら当時の法律で許可されていたが，合わせると，貸金業者は貸し付ける金の受取人の共同経営者となることで利息を得ることができた。貸金業者は自分が貸し付けを認めた先である企業の一部となった後，違法に利息を得るのではなく，厳密に言えば自分の資本から利益を得ていたのだ。

　取引が拡大し成長するにつれ，高利貸し規制法によって引き起こされる問題が明らかになった。お金からお金を生み出すことに対する中世の反発は，交換手段としてのお金には内在的価値が欠けているという一般的な考え方のせいだった。しかし，金貨と銀貨の不足と遠方にいる顧客への支払いの困難さが，多数の都市に支店を持つ銀行の発展と，外貨を両替できる両替商の出現につながった。富が社会の隅々にまで行き渡ると，実のところ貸金業者は「何もしないでお金」を受け取っているわけではないことが明らかになった。誰かに雌牛を貸す農夫がその牛から乳と子牛を得る機会を奪われているのとまったく同じように，貸金業者は利益を得るほかの方法に投資する機会を奪われている。貸し付けの性質が変化するとともに，貸金業者が資金を手放すときに負うリスクがより深く理解されるようになった。時がたつにつれ，これらの要因は教会や学者によって認められて高利貸しに関する議論を組み立て直すのに役立ち，利息請求の全面的禁止から，一般消費者を高利貸し業者とクレジットカード会社が課す法外な料金から守る現代的な高利貸し規制法への進化を促した。

語句　usury「高利貸し」, benevolent「善意の, 優しい」, communal「共同社会の」, destitute「極貧の」, misfortune「不運」, nobility「貴族（階級）」, sinful「罪深い」, circumvent「（法律など）の抜け道を見つける」, camouflage「～を偽装する, 隠す」, financier「金融業者, 貸金業者」, permissible「許される」, technically「正式には, 厳密には」, moneychanger「両替商」, be deprived of ～「～を奪われている」, reframe「～を作り直す, 再構成する」, loan shark「高利貸し（業者）」

(32) －解答　②

問題文の訳　中世の社会で, 高利貸しを取り巻く禁止事項は,

選択肢の訳
1　人が金銭的問題を抱えたときに親族以外の誰かに援助を求めるのは罪である, という信念の現れだった。
2　お金がある人々は慈善行為と見なされることを不当に利用するべきではない, という考えを反映していた。
3　教会と貴族が, 貧民を搾取するために, 大金を使える機会をどのように悪用したか, の実証であった。
4　人々が, 貸付制度を効果的に機能させるのに十分な借金と信用貸しの理解を持っていなかったことを示唆した。

解説　第2段落に高利貸し禁止の経緯がある。中世の貧しい相互扶助社会で, 物の貸し借りは「善意による援助と信頼のシステム」であり「人の社会的義務」と見なされ「故に報酬を得るのは道徳的に間違っている」という考えが発生し, これに沿って「義務である行為で利益を得る貸金は罪」となった。このことをまとめた 2 が正解。2 の charitable act は本文の benevolent aid の言い換え。

(33) －解答　④

問題文の訳　この文章によると, 貸金業から利益を得るために使われた方法についてどれが正しいか。

選択肢の訳
1　それらは, 貸金業についての考えが, さまざまな国といろいろな産業によって必ずしも同じとは限らないことの例だった。
2　それらは, 中世で利息が支払われた方法が, 共同経営者たちの間に法的な争いを起こし得ることの例証だった。
3　それらは, 中世の人々が利益と利息は2つのまったく無関係な概念だと信じていたことを示すものだった。
4　それらは, 一部の人々が法に従うように見えながらも, 貸付で利息を稼ぐ間接的な方法を使ったことを示した。

解説　第3段落冒頭に, 貸金業から利益を得るために法的禁止を回避しようとした者もいたとあり, 以下でその方法が説明されている。変動する為替レートを利用して利息を隠す, 法的に許される別々の契約を組み合わせ

て「違法に利息を得る（illegally gaining interest）のではなく」資本から利益を得る方法など。これらを「法に従う（obey the law）ように見える間接的な（indirect）方法」と述べた **4** が正解。

(34) - 解答 **3**

問題文の訳 この文章の筆者は，以下の記述のどれと意見が一致する可能性が最も高いだろうか。

選択肢の訳
1 中世に高利貸し規制法を廃止することは，農業が金融システムの限界より大きくなった後にやっと検討された。
2 教会内部での指導者層の交代が，お金の貸し借りを取り巻く法律の見直しにつながった。
3 貸金業に対する新たな姿勢は，部分的には，貸付金を与えることによって起こり得る潜在的損失に対する理解が深まったことの結果だった。
4 銀行と両替商が，国際貿易からの利益を押し上げる方法として，高利貸しに関する方針を緩和するよう教会に圧力をかけた。

解説 第4段落で，貸金業者が負う①利益を得るほかの方法に投資する機会を奪われるリスクが「より深く理解されて（a greater appreciation arose）」，②高利貸しの議論の見直しに役立ったことが述べられている。このことをまとめた **3** が正解。**3** では，①は potential losses，②は New attitudes toward moneylending に言い換えられている。

全文訳 **分類論争**

　ブラジルのアマゾンに生息する3つの変種のタテフオオガシラは，見た目はほぼ同一だが，鳴き声はリズムと音色が微妙に違う。1人の科学者が，この3つの変種を別々の種に分類し直すことを提唱するために，鳥の種の分類を担当する委員会に話を持ちかけたとき，委員たちはジレンマに陥った。その違いは，追加で2つの種を作る正当な理由となるのに十分だったのか？ 結局，彼らは1つだけ追加した。しかし彼らの決定は，自然界に見られる多くの生物の特定と定義を扱う科学分野である分類学の世界で，さらにもう1つの論争を巻き起こした。

　技術の進歩によって地球の生物をより詳しく調べることが可能となるにつれて，世界中で特定される新種の数は増えてきている。南米だけで，鳥の種の数は2000年以来150以上増えた。しかし，これらの大部分は，熱帯雨林の奥深い隅々に遠征して発見されたのではなかった。むしろ，記録技術や遺伝的分類における飛躍的進歩の結果として，既存の種の変種を分類し直すことで作り出されたのだった。そして，近年検知可能となった微妙な差異はそのような再分類を正当化すると主張する者がいる一方で，その区別を恣意的だと考える者もいる。鳥類専門家のジェイムズ・レムセンは，鳥の分類学の現状を「悪い状況で最善を尽くそうとしている」と見ており，「私たちは1つの連続するものに人為的な境界をつけようとしているのです」と説明する。

これらの議論により，種の区別方法に関する分類学における根本的な問題である「種の問題」を巡る論争が再び始まった。この問いに答えようとする試みに固有の問題は，レムセンの見解を際立たせる。例えば，生物学的種の概念（BSC）は生物学者にとって長い間有名な指針で，相互間でのみうまく生殖できて健康で繁殖力のある子孫を産むことができる生物，として種を定義する。しかし，種の間に明確な線引きをするためにこのように生殖を使うとややこしい問題が起こる。地理的な理由で種が2つ以上のグループに分かれた場合，BSCの支持者は，この分離が別個の種の分類を正当化すると考える。これらのグループは出会わないのだから，相互間で自然生殖するであろうかどうかを知るのは不可能だ，と彼らは言う。

今日では，BSCに加えて，生物学者は，生物のグループのDNAと進化の歴史の両方の分析によって手引きされる。1つの例は，オーストラリアに生息するディンゴを巡る分類上の論争だ。ディンゴは家畜に及ぼす脅威のため，何世紀にもわたって農村部で駆除の対象になってきた。それらが保護されてこなかった1つの理由は，野生の犬で，家畜犬と同じ種に属すると分類されているからである。研究者たちがディンゴの骨格，遺伝的特徴および歴史的に家畜化されていないことなどの要因を調べ，2019年に，別個の種の指定が正当だと決定された。これは，BSCに基づいて，ディンゴが自然に家畜犬と行う交配は彼らが別個の種ではないことを表す，と主張する以前の結論を否定した。キツネなど有害生物の個体数を抑制するのにディンゴが果たす重要な役割を考えると，この問題は，分類学的な分類が種の管理にも生態系全体にも重大な影響を及ぼし得ることを表している。

語句　subtly「微妙に」，reclassify「～を再分類する」，taxonomy「分類学」，multitude「大勢，多数」，nuance「微妙な差異」，detectable「探知できる」，continuum「連続（体）」，underscore「～を強調する」，fertile「繁殖力のある」，proponent「支持者」，eradication「根絶，撲滅」，genetics「遺伝的特徴［構成］」，domestication「家畜化」，interbreeding「交配」

(35) – 解答 ②

問題文の訳　なぜこの文章の筆者はタテフオオガシラの分類に関して起こった論争に言及しているのか。

選択肢の訳
1 もっと重要な要因ではなく，見た目のようなあまり注目に値しないことだけに基づく鳥の分類に関連する問題の例である。
2 動物の変種間のささいな違いが，新しい種の分類が適切かどうかを確かにするのを困難にし得ることを示している。
3 科学者たちが，実地調査を通して得られた新しいデータを支持し，鳥についての既存の情報を退けるときに起こる問題の例である。
4 種の分類でかつては重要だと考えられたわずかな違いの多くは，実はまったく重要ではないことを示している。

解説　第1段落に，外見は同じだが鳴き声が微妙に違うタテフオオガシラの3

つの変種を別々の種に分類することを提案されたとき，鳴き声の微妙な違いは2つの新種を作るほどのものか，というジレンマに委員会に陥ったことが述べられており，**2**の内容の具体的な例示となっている。

(36) - 解答 ①

問題文の訳 生物学的種の概念に問題があり得る理由は，

選択肢の訳
1 同じ種のメンバーが生殖するために通常あるであろう機会は，時に外的要因に影響されることだ。
2 それが，自然生息地での動物の観察ではなく，飼育された動物間の交配の観察に基づいて制定されたことだ。
3 特定の種に適用するように作られた分類の要因が，しばしば誤って多くの異なる生物に適用されることだ。
4 基にしている指針が，ある生物のグループが別の種であるかどうかを評価する方法という根本的な問題に対処しようとしていないことだ。

解説 生物学的種の概念（BSC）の問題は第3段落後半にある。同じ種が地理的な理由で複数のグループに分かれた場合にほかのグループと出会わないために，相互間で自然生殖するかがわからず，BSCの考えでは別個の種になること。ほかのグループとの出会いを「生殖のために通常ある機会」，地理的な理由を「外的要因」と言い換えた**1**が正解。

(37) - 解答 ④

問題文の訳 ディンゴに関する状況から明らかなのはどれか。

選択肢の訳
1 長期にわたる動物の繁殖習性の緻密な分析が，それが生息する生態系に対するその動物の重要性を明らかにし得る。
2 2019年の調査結果により，家畜を襲うディンゴを駆除するより多くの権利がオーストラリアの農民に与えられることになりそうだ。
3 動物の個体数を維持することが経済的利益につながることが明確なら，種の分類に関連する判断はおそらく無視される。
4 ある動物が別個の種と見なされるべきかどうかについての決定は，人間によるその動物の扱われ方に大きな影響を及ぼし得る。

解説 第4段落に，「有害生物の抑制で重要な役割を果たすにもかかわらず，野生の犬と分類されていたので長年駆除の対象であり保護されなかった」というディンゴの状況が，「分類が種の管理に重大な影響を及ぼし得ることを表す（最終文）」と述べられている。この最終文の部分を言い換えた**4**が正解。本文の major implications は**4**では significantly impact に，management of species は way it is treated by humans に言い換えられている。

全文訳 涙の道

今日では涙の道として知られているが，約10万人のアメリカ先住民が，1830年代

の間に米国南東部にある先祖代々の居住地から強制的にさせられた移動および移住は，アメリカ史における暗い時期を表す。新たな土地へ行くルートは9つの州を横断して数千キロメートルにわたり，およそ1万5千人の男性，女性，子供が立退きとそれに続く旅の間に亡くなったと考えられている。

　涙の道に先立って，文化的な同化政策が実施されていた。アメリカ先住民はキリスト教と西洋教育を受け入れるように求める非常に大きな圧力に直面したが，彼らが先祖代々の土地を保有する権利は，たいてい認められた。しかし，1830年にアメリカ議会はアンドリュー・ジャクソン大統領の政権下でインディアン移住法を可決したが，これは部族を彼らの居住地から現在のオクラホマ州に位置する「インディアン居留地」にある新たな生活の地へと移動させることを，政府ができるようにする法律だった。しかし，1832年にチェロキー族が所有するジョージア州の土地を没収しようとしたことについて，最高裁判所のジョン・マーシャル長官が違憲判決を下したとき，この政策は困難に直面した。この判決は，チェロキー族を主権国家として認め，重要な判例のようなものを作った。しかし，ジャクソンはくじけることなく反抗的で，伝えられるところによれば，「ジョン・マーシャルが判決を下したのだ。さあ，彼にそれを実行させろ」という言葉で判決に応じた。

　ジャクソンがアメリカ先住民の強制移住を正当化した理由は，ほぼ全面的に事実無根だった。部族は自らを「文明化」しようと努力したにもかかわらず，狩猟への過度の依存と近代的な農業方式を導入しないことで非難された。当時ジェイムズ・フェニモア・クーパーの小説『モヒカン族の最後』が一因で，アメリカ先住民と彼らの文化は消滅しつつある，というロマンチックに描かれたアメリカの神話があり，ジャクソンはこの考えをうまく利用して，移住しないとアメリカ先住民と彼らの文化は滅びる運命にあると主張した。しかし実際には，当時アメリカ先住民の人口は安定しており，おそらく増えてさえいた。

　歴史学者のクローディオ・ソーントは，アメリカ先住民の強制移住は当時の資本主義の拡大という文脈で捉えるべきだ，と言う。白人の奴隷所有者と投資家は，アメリカ先住民の保有地が全国で最も肥沃な土地のいくつかであり，農業経営と建設のためにすぐに利用できることを知っていた。アメリカ先住民の土地の所有権奪取を白人，特に奴隷所有者が事業を拡大する絶好の機会と見て，これに出資するためにどのように東海岸の銀行が南部の投機家と協力したのかを，ソーントは年代記として描いている。強制移住は，アメリカ先住民の絶滅を防ぐために行われる親切な対策だとされていたが，強制移住の立案と実行の背後にいた人々は，奴隷を経済的に利用されるために神から与えられた資源だと考えていたのと同じように，アメリカ先住民の土地を見ていた。

　ソーントはまた，南部の政治家たちと北部の協力者たちが強制移住を何とかやり遂げるために，どのように役所・軍人・行政官のネットワークを作り上げたのかも記録している。これらの取り組みには信じられないほど費用がかかったが，その土地は，黒人奴隷の無料の労働者を使って耕せばコストに見合うと見なされた。東海岸の銀行家たちは，奴隷所有と強制移住の二重の事業に出資することで急速に裕福になっており，そしてこ

のことが次に，鉄道やほかの大規模開発事業の資金を提供した。涙の道は恐ろしかったけれども，太平洋岸から大西洋岸まで広がる国としてのアメリカの出現に不可欠であった技術的進歩とインフラをもたらした，と主張する者もいる。

インディアン移住法から生じた強制移住は，部族によって異なる反応を引き起こした。自発的に行く者がいる一方で，激しく抵抗する者もいた。最も悲劇的な事例の1つは，チェロキー族であった。非常に大きな圧力にさらされて，部族のごく少数の人々が西への移動について政府と交渉を始めることを独断で決め，ニューエコタ条約を結んだ。チェロキー族の大多数がその文書を無効と見なし，条件の仲介に関与した代表者とやらは自分たちが認めたリーダーではないと主張し，この条約を無効にするよう求める請願書には1万5千を超える署名が集まった。しかし，議会はその条約を可決して法律と認め，チェロキー族の運命は決まった。

退去の期限は2年であったが，1838年までにインディアン居留地に向かったチェロキー族は約2千人だけであった。その進行をはかどらせるため，約7千人の兵士がチェロキー族の土地へ行くように命じられ，そこで銃を突き付けてチェロキー族を家から引きずり出して閉じ込め，その間に彼らの家と持ち物を略奪した。保護施設をあてがわれず基本的な物資さえもなかったので，チェロキー族は極度の暑さと寒さの中で長距離の行進に耐えなければならなかった。水不足とわずかな食料の配給のせいで彼らは栄養失調になり，多くの者が死に至る病に屈した。チェロキー族がインディアン居留地に到着するころには，およそ4分の1が亡くなっていた。

1840年ごろまでに，ほとんどの部族は，永久に彼らのものであり続けると政府が約束した土地に定住していた。しかし，彼らは自分たちが厳しく不慣れな環境にいることがわかり，それから何年間もひどく苦しんだ。さらに，鉄道がアメリカ西部を開くにつれて多くの白人移住者がインディアン居留地に押し寄せたので，その規模は徐々に縮小し，20世紀初頭には完全に消滅していた。

語句　forcible「強制的な」, ancestral「祖先の」, perish「死ぬ」, assimilation「同化」, unconstitutional「違憲の」, sovereign nation「主権国家」, undeterred「くじけない」, defiant「反抗的な」, unfounded「根拠のない」, civilize「〜を文明化する」, overreliance「過度の依存」, romanticize「〜をロマンチックに描く」, doomed「破滅する運命にある」, deportation「強制退去」, holdings「保有財産」, fertile「(土地が)肥えた」, chronicle「〜を年代記に載せる」, speculator「投機家」, dispossession「(不動産の)所有権奪取」, golden opportunity「絶好の機会」, benign「優しい, 慈悲深い」, avert「〜を避ける，防ぐ」, slavery「奴隷所有」, expulsion「排除すること，追放」, horrific「恐ろしい」, take it upon *oneself* to *do*「〜することを独断で決める」, invalid「無効の」, broker「〜の仲介をする」, nullify「〜を無効にする」, seal「(運命・死など)を決める」, expedite「〜を促進する」, loot「〜を略奪する」, unsheltered「保護

されていない」，scarcity「欠乏，不足」，meager「わずかな」，malnourished「栄養失調の」，appallingly「ぞっとするほど」

(38) －解答 ③

問題文の訳 1830年代の間，アンドリュー・ジャクソン大統領は，

選択肢の訳
1 彼の同化政策は効果がないとわかった後，アメリカ先住民を彼らの土地から追い出すために，裁判所を利用しようとし始めた。
2 インディアン移住法が国の最高裁で却下された後，その法律が機能する方法を協議して変えるよう強いられた。
3 政府はアメリカ先住民を彼らの土地から本人の同意なしに追い出す権力を持たない，と述べる法的判断を無視した。
4 ほかの部族の人々には与えなかった特別待遇をチェロキー族に与える以外選択肢がなかった。

解説 チェロキー族所有のジョージア州の土地を政府が没収することは違憲だと最高裁で判決が下されたが，ジャクソンはくじけず反抗的だった（第2段落後半）のだから，彼はこの法的判断を無視したのだ。3で述べている法的判断（legal decision）の内容はこの言い換え。彼は裁判所を利用しようとしておらず，移住法は最高裁で却下されていないので1，2は誤りである。

(39) －解答 ②

問題文の訳 クローディオ・ソーントは以下の記述のどれと意見が一致する可能性が最も高いだろうか。

選択肢の訳
1 多くのアメリカ先住民の部族が不作と食料源の減少に苦労したが，書物はたいてい彼らの生活を華やかに描いた。
2 アメリカ先住民を支援するための試みとして提示されたが，彼らの強制移住は実は経済的利益の可能性によって動機付けられていた。
3 アメリカ先住民の文化の影響を規制するために多くの政策が導入されたが，いくつかの革新的なビジネスアイデアがそれらを世に広める助けとなった。
4 政府が強制移住の主な責めを負うべきだが，アメリカ先住民が実業界のリーダーたちと協力したことが先住民の多くの問題を引き起こした。

解説 第4段落の冒頭で，強制移住は資本主義の拡大の一環だというソーントの立場が明示されている。具体的な記述が続いた後，最終文に「強制移住の建前はアメリカ先住民の絶滅防止のためだが，その立案・実行をした人々は先住民の土地を経済的に利用できる資源と見ていた」ことが示されている。このことを言い換えた**2**が正解。

(40) －解答 ④

問題文の訳 涙の道がアメリカの拡大に勢いをつけたと言われているのは，

選択肢の訳　1　北部と南部の裕福な実業家たちの間の競争が，拡大事業のコストを減らし建設のピッチを上げる助けになったからだ。
2　別の場所に定住させられた多くのアメリカ先住民には鉄道業と建設業の仕事が与えられたが，そのことが国を開拓するのに不可欠だったと判明したからだ。
3　多くのアメリカ先住民が強制移住で受け取ったお金と農業の知識を，ほかの土地に引っ越して耕作するために使ったからだ。
4　強制移住を巡ってもうかる産業が作り出され，その後全国でインフラ開発に使われた富を生んだからだ。

解説　涙の道とはアメリカ先住民の強制移住のこと（第1段落冒頭）。第5段落で，先住民の土地を耕作させるための奴隷所有と強制移住への事業出資で裕福になった銀行家が，次に鉄道など大規模開発事業に資金提供したので，広いアメリカに必要なインフラができたことが述べられている。このことを「強制移住を巡って産業が作られ」と言い換えた**4**が正解。

(41) – 解答　**3**

問題文の訳　ニューエコタ条約に関する以下の記述のどれが正しいか。

選択肢の訳　1　チェロキー族が条約に署名するために与えられた期限は，そのような重要な事柄について決定を下す余裕を彼らに与えなかった。
2　条約を法律として通過させてほしいという請願書は，そのような活動を正当化するのに十分な支持がチェロキー族からはない，と感じた役人たちによって退けられた。
3　その条約に関与したグループには自分たちを代表して交渉を始める権限がないと信じていたので，チェロキー族の多くが動揺した。
4　チェロキー族のリーダーたちのグループが，その条約は過去にほかの部族が提示された同じような種類の条約よりもずっと好ましくないと感じた。

解説　ニューエコタ条約については第6段落にある。この条約は部族のごく少数が独断で政府と交渉してまとめたが，彼らは自分たちが認めたリーダーではないと大多数のチェロキーが主張してこの条約を無効と見なし，条約破棄を求めたことが述べられている。このことを言い換えた**3**が正解。3では自分たちが認めたリーダーではないことを「自分たちを代表して交渉する権限がない」と言い換えている。

一次試験・筆記 **4** 問題編 p.32

解答例

Technological advancements have undoubtedly brought convenience to our lives. However, the commodification of personal data, digitization of society, and scarcity of laws have eroded our ability to protect individual privacy in the modern world.

The Internet has paved the way for the accumulation and trading of data regarding users' online habits. Scandals involving the sale of users' social media data, for example, are proof that our digital footprints are now lucrative commodities. Moreover, penalties for selling this data are a fraction of the revenues gained from the activity, which may incentivize corporations to continue violating people's privacy.

Additionally, as society becomes ever more digitized, individuals are being compelled to disclose more personal data. Registering private information on governmental sites, for example, may afford citizens access to vital public services such as healthcare. Once registered, however, it may not be possible for citizens to control how their data is used, thereby making the safeguarding of their personal details unfeasible.

The struggle to maintain individual privacy is further exemplified by a conspicuous lack of legislation. Devising and authorizing laws is a protracted process, requiring meticulous consideration. The massive effort required to safeguard the huge amounts of data generated by our daily activities has left lawmakers struggling to keep up.

Thus, in the face of capitalist greed and intrusive governance, both of which are escaping the reach of overwhelmed judicial systems, protecting individual privacy has become an impossible task.

トピックの訳　「個人のプライバシーは現代世界において守ることができるか」

解説　解答例はトピックに対してNoで「個人のプライバシーは守れない」との立場。導入部で述べる3つの理由とその根拠は、①個人データの商品化 (commodification of personal data)：データの売買がもうかるので、罰金を払っても売買を続ける企業がある、②社会のデジタル化 (digitization of society)：ネットのサービス利用時に登録が必要とな

る個人データが，どう使われるかわからない，③法律の不足 (scarcity of laws)：法不足のため個人情報保持に苦労しているが，法制定にかかる作業は長く膨大で追い付かない，である。

　3つの理由はどれも技術的進歩に関連するもの。導入部でこれらの理由を列挙することによって予想される内容の範囲を冒頭で絞り込めるため，読み手が理解しやすいエッセーとなっている。

　難しい単語を多く使っているので，全体が引き締まっている。日ごろからエッセーに使えそうな単語，この例では commodification「商品化」，digitization「デジタル化」，scarcity「不足，欠乏」，feasible「実行可能な」などは，スペルを間違えずに書けて使えるようにしておきたい。

　また，導入部分（第1段落）で示した理由①②③を，結論部分（第5段落）で，①を資本家の欲 (capitalist greed)，②を押し付けがましい管理 (intrusive governance)，③を司法制度の力の及ぶ範囲から逃れる (escaping the reach of ... judicial systems)，と言い換えているのは見事だ。なお，解答例は236語で理想的な長さだ。

一次試験・リスニング Part 1　問題編 p.33～34

No.1 - 解答　3

スクリプト
☆：Is that a new cell phone, Martin?
★：Yeah, I got it yesterday.
☆：What about your old one?
★：Donated it. A friend works for an organization that sends used phones to people in Africa who can't afford new ones.
☆：That's great.
★：Yeah, and it reduces the garbage created by discarded cell phones. Did you know they contain hazardous chemicals?
☆：No, I didn't. Actually, I've been thinking about getting a new phone. Can I pass on my old one when I do?
★：Sure.

Question: What does the man imply about cell phones?

全文訳
☆：それって新しい携帯電話かしら、マーティン？
★：そうだよ、昨日買ったんだ。
☆：古いのはどうしたの？
★：寄付したよ。新しい携帯電話を買う余裕がないアフリカの人たちに中古のものを送っている団体で、友達が働いているんだ。
☆：それは素晴らしいわね。
★：そうだね、それにそうすることで、携帯電話を捨てることによって生じるごみが減少するんだ。携帯電話には危険な化学物質が含まれているって知っていたかい？
☆：いいえ、知らなかったわ。実は、ずっと新しい携帯電話を買おうと思っていたの。買ったら古いのを預けてもいいかしら？
★：もちろん。

質問：携帯電話について男性は暗に何と言っているか。

選択肢の訳
1　低品質の素材で作られている。
2　アフリカで使えるように改造するのは難しい。
3　捨てると危険な場合がある。
4　寄付することは必ずしもよいことではない。

解説　男性は3つ目の発言で、携帯電話を寄付すればごみになる携帯電話が減ることと、携帯電話には hazardous chemicals が含まれていることを指摘している。つまり、携帯電話を throw away「捨てる」ことは危険を伴う場合があると暗に言っていることになる。

No.2 − 解答 ②

スクリプト
★: Patricia, I heard you sent a letter to Congressman Taylor. What's he up to this time?
☆: He's pushing this stupid industrial development near the Fairfield Wetlands.
★: Unbelievable!
☆: Some friends and I are campaigning to get protected status for the wetlands. It's just like when he tried to turn the old Weller Farmstead into a golf course.
★: I'm sure you'll get a lot of support. It's about time Taylor started helping his ordinary constituents, not just his rich friends in business.

Question: What does the man imply about Congressman Taylor?

全文訳
★: パトリシア，テイラー議員に手紙を送ったって聞いたけど。彼は今度は何をしようとしているんだい？
☆: フェアフィールド湿地帯の近くで工業開発なんていうばかげたことを推し進めているのよ。
★: 信じられない！
☆: 友人数人と私で湿地の保護指定を獲得するために運動しているの。テイラー議員が昔のウェラー農園をゴルフ場にしようとしたときとまったく同じよ。
★: きっと支持をたくさん得られるよ。もういいかげん，テイラーは仕事上の金持ちの友達だけじゃなくて，普通の有権者を助け始めるべきだよ。

質問: テイラー議員について男性は暗に何と言っているか。

選択肢の訳
1 湿地を救うのに成功するだろう。
2 ある特定の人たちに特別な計らいをするために地位を利用している。
3 環境を保護するために尽力している。
4 普通の有権者に人気がある。

解説 開発推進派のテイラー議員に対して女性は環境保護派で，男性は女性に全面的に賛同しているという構図は明快である。正解 **2** の certain people は，最後の男性の発言の his rich friends in business を指している。

No.3 − 解答 ①

スクリプト
☆: Richard, you look really beat. What's going on?
★: I was here most of the night finishing that new advertising contract. The sales department said that they need it by nine this morning.
☆: You finished it by yourself?
★: Yes, unfortunately.
☆: That's rough. Can I get you a cup of coffee or something?

★： That sounds like just what the doctor ordered.

Question: What's the matter with Richard?

全文訳
☆： リチャード，疲れ切っているわね。どうしたっていうの？
★： ほとんど一晩中ここにいて，例の新しい広告契約書を仕上げていたんだ。今朝9時までに必要だと営業部に言われてさ。
☆： 1人で仕上げたの？
★： ああ，残念ながら。
☆： ひどい話ね。コーヒーか何か持って来てあげようか。
★： それは願ったりかなったりだ。
質問：リチャードはどうしたのか。

選択肢の訳
1 昨夜遅くまで働いた。
2 早朝会議があった。
3 1人で働くことが多過ぎる。
4 広告契約書を仕上げられなかった。

解説　男性の最初の発言の I was here most of the night finishing that new advertising contract. から，ほぼ徹夜で仕事をしていたことがわかるので正解は **1**。昨夜は1人で働いたが，**3** のように too often という内容は会話にない。just what the doctor ordered「まさに必要なもの」。

No.4 - 解答 ①

スクリプト
★： Well, we've interviewed all the candidates, and now it's decision time.
☆： Hmm . . . I was impressed with the last applicant. He was well qualified and very articulate. And he has copywriting experience.
★： That's true. He also seemed ambitious. Are you sure you can stand the competition, Ruth?
☆： Come off it. He wasn't that good.
★： Actually, I think he could be future management material.
☆： In that case, maybe you should watch your own back, Bob!

Question: What does the woman imply about the applicant?

全文訳
★： さて，候補者全員の面接が終わりましたから，結論を出す時間です。
☆： うーん……私は最後の志願者が印象に残りました。資格も十分にあり，発言もとてもはっきりしていました。それに，コピーライターの経験もあります。
★： そうですね。それに意欲的にも見えました。彼との競争に耐えられると思いますか，ルース。
☆： ばかなことを言わないでくださいよ。彼はそんな大したことなかったです。
★： いや，彼は将来の管理職になるだけの人材じゃないかと思いますよ。

☆：もしそうなら，追い上げられないように注意した方がいいかもしれませんね，ボブ！

質問：この志願者について女性は暗に何と言っているか。

選択肢の訳
1 彼女にとっての脅威ではない。
2 管理職として採用されるべきだ。
3 自信があり過ぎるように見える。
4 コミュニケーション能力が弱い。

解説　Are you sure you can stand the competition, Ruth?「彼との競争に耐えられると思いますか，ルース」と聞かれた女性は，2つ目の発言で Come off it.「ばかなことを言わないで」(= Stop joking!) と答えているので，**1** が正解。

No.5 - 解答 ③

スクリプト
★：Judy, I guess you have a lot of free time now that both your kids have gone away to college.
☆：Well, definitely more. But I still manage to fill the time doing things around the house.
★：Don't you ever find yourself getting bored?
☆：Not at all! There are so many things I want to do. I haven't mentioned this before, but . . . I'm going to exhibit some of my paintings at a small gallery downtown.
★：That's great! Congratulations. You know, I always thought you had some hidden talent. I guess it was just a matter of getting your foot in the door.
☆：Having my own exhibition's been something I've always dreamed about, but I never imagined it would actually happen.
★：Good for you. Definitely send me an invitation.

Question: What do we learn about the woman?

全文訳
★：ジュディー，子供が2人とも大学に入って家を出たんだから，今は自由な時間がたくさんあるんじゃないのかい。
☆：そうね，確かに増えたわ。でも家のことをやっていればまだ何とか時間をつぶせるわね。
★：飽きてくることはないの？
☆：全然！　やりたいことが山ほどあるのよ。このことは今まで言っていなかったけど……街中の小さなギャラリーで私の描いた絵をいくつか展示してくれることになったの。
★：すごいね！　おめでとう。まあ，君には隠れた才能があると常々思っていたよ。あとは始めの一歩を踏み出すかどうかだけだったと思うよ。
☆：自分の展覧会を開くのは昔からの夢だったんだけど，それが実現するな

んて想像もしなかったわ。
★：よかったね。必ず招待状を送ってよ。
質問：女性についてわかることは何か。

<選択肢の訳>
1　彼女は前よりも家事が増えた。
2　彼女の展覧会は成功だった。
3　彼女は今の方が自分のための時間が増えた。
4　彼女のギャラリーは閉鎖された。

<解説> 1つずつ確認しよう。「増えた」のは家事ではなく自由時間なので1は誤り。展覧会はまだ開かれていないので2も誤り。自分のギャラリーを持っているわけではないので4も誤り。女性は最初の発言で「(自由な時間が)増えた」と述べているので，3が正解。絵画や展覧会の話もこれにまつわることである。

No.6 - 解答 ④

<スクリプト>
★：Mr. Lang isn't going to be happy when he finds this mistake in our data.
☆：Yeah, but I don't think he'll overreact. He's usually pretty considerate.
★：Sure, but remember the last time we messed things up?
☆：Yeah, but this time it's nothing major. I'm sure he'll cut us some slack.
★：I sure hope so. We were up all night on this.

Question: How does the woman predict the boss will react?

<全文訳>
★：僕たちのデータのこの間違いを見つけたら，ラングさんは不満に思うだろうね。
☆：ええ，だけど過剰に反応することはないと思うわ。普段はかなり思いやりがある人だもの。
★：確かにそうだけど，前回僕たちが大失敗したときのことを覚えている？
☆：ええ，だけど今回のは大したことないわ。きっと大目に見てくれるわよ。
★：本当にそうだといいんだけど。僕たちは徹夜でこれに取り組んだんだから。

質問：上司がどう反応すると女性は予測しているか。

<選択肢の訳>
1　怒る。
2　気付かない。
3　過剰に反応する。
4　理解を示す。

<解説> 会話中で Mr. Lang や he と呼ばれているのが2人の上司。仕事でミスをした2人だが，女性の方は一貫して楽観的で，上司は considerate だし今回のミスは nothing major だから，大事にはならないと考えてい

る。したがって **4** が正解。cut ~ some slack「~を大目に見る」。

No.7 −解答 ③

スクリプト
☆：Hey, Francis. I'm glad I caught you. Do you happen to have that money I lent you?
★：Sorry. I've been meaning to talk to you about that. Is it OK if I give you half now and the rest after my next payday?
☆：Seriously? You promised it wouldn't be a problem to repay me this month.
★：I know, but I've had a couple of unexpected expenses.
☆：It'll put me in a bit of a bind. We all have bills to pay, you know. Still, I guess half is better than nothing.
★：Thanks. I really appreciate it.

Question: What does the woman imply?

全文訳
☆：こんにちは、フランシス。捕まってよかったわ。私が貸したあのお金だけど、持ち合わせているかしら。
★：ごめんよ。そのことについてずっと君と話すつもりでいたんだ。今半分を返して、残りは次の給料日の後でも構わないかな？
☆：本気なの？ 今月に返済するということで問題ないって約束したわよね。
★：わかっているけど、予定外の出費がいくつかあったんだ。
☆：それはちょっと困るわ。私たちの誰もが、支払わなければならない請求書を抱えているんだから。それでも、ゼロよりは半分の方がましかもしれないわね。
★：ありがとう。本当に感謝するよ。

質問：女性は暗に何と言っているか。

選択肢の訳
1 男性は何も返済する必要はない。
2 彼女は男性に金を貸さないだろう。
3 彼女も今、金が不足している。
4 男性は故意に女性を欺いた。

解説　金を貸した男性から、約束の全額ではなく、取りあえず半額の返済を提案された女性は、3つ目の発言で、It'll put me in a bit of a bind. We all have bills to pay と言っている。つまり、女性も支払いを抱えて金が不足していることがわかる。put ~ in a bind「~を困らせる」。

No.8 −解答 ①

スクリプト
☆：Steve, were you making photocopies for the board meeting again this morning?
★：Yeah, the vice president asked me to lend him a hand because his assistant's off sick.
☆：Maybe it's none of my business, but aren't you too busy for that

30

sort of thing? You're a section manager, not an assistant.
★： Maybe, but you never know when the shoe will be on the other foot.
☆： I doubt the vice president would return the favor.
★： Not him necessarily, but we're all in this together, right? And taking an extra 15 minutes to make copies isn't the end of the world.
☆： Suit yourself.

Question: What does the woman imply?

全文訳
☆： スティーブ，今朝また取締役会用にコピーを取っていたわよね。
★： ああ，アシスタントが病気で休みだから手を貸してくれないかと副社長が頼んできたんだ。
☆： 私には関係ないことかもしれないけど，そんなことをしている暇はないんじゃない？ あなたは課長であって，アシスタントではないのよ。
★： そうかもしれないけど，いつ逆の立場になるかわからないからね。
☆： 副社長が恩返しをするとは思えないけど。
★： 彼がそうするとは限らないけど，僕たちは一心同体だよね？ それに，コピーを取るのに15分余分な時間がかかっても大したことじゃないよ。
☆： 好きにすればいいわ。

質問：女性は暗に何と言っているか。

選択肢の訳
1　男性はあまりに惜しげもなく自分の時間を割く。
2　副社長はあまりにも残業が多い。
3　副社長は彼女に借りがある。
4　男性は現在の地位にふさわしくない。

解説　本来の仕事ではないことまで引き受けてしまう男性を女性は心配しているが，男性はいつ the shoe will be on the other foot「立場が逆転する」かわからないし，自分たちは一心同体であり，コピーを取ることくらい the end of the world「大変なこと」ではない，と答えている。そして，女性は最後の発言で Suit yourself.「お好きなように」と述べているので，正解は **1**。

No.9 – 解答 ②

スクリプト
★： Man, I'm glad that meeting is over. What do you think of the proposed change for the sales department, Bev?
☆： Honestly, I'm in shock. Each of us has spent all this time developing proficiency in a specific field to better serve clients, and now they want to assign us to customers simply based on location!
★： I mean, I know we sometimes have to travel a long way to get to a

☆ : client, but I thought giving them the expertise they needed and building up a relationship was worth the time and mileage.

☆ : Right. Being restricted to a certain geographic area could cost us dozens of our existing client relationships. And building new ones will take time, too.

★ : Well, it's done now. I guess we'll just have to share as much information about existing customers as we can with the guys in the other regions. I see one upside, though: instead of just working in one specialist area, we'll get a chance to learn new things.

☆ : I suppose. But I still think we risk losing some of our big accounts if we make this switch.

★ : Seems like management thinks the long-term savings in time and money will be worthwhile.

☆ : Well, we'll just have to wait and see, but I won't be holding my breath.

Question: What is one thing the man says about the proposed change?

全文訳 ★ : やれやれ，あの会議が終わってうれしいよ。営業部の改革案をどう思う，ベブ？

☆ : 正直言って，ショックを受けているわ。顧客によりよいサービスを提供しようと，私たち一人一人が特定の分野での熟練度を高めることにずっと時間を費やしてきたのに，今度は，場所だけを基に私たちを顧客に割り当てたいと言うんだもの！

★ : つまりさ，確かに顧客のところに行くのに長い距離を移動しなければならないことも時にはあるけど，顧客が必要とする専門知識を提供して関係を構築することには，その時間と移動距離をかける価値があると僕は思っていたよ。

☆ : そうよね。特定の地理的エリアに限定されれば，私たちが今持っている顧客との関係を何十も失うかもしれないわ。それに，新しい関係を築くのに時間もかかるだろうし。

★ : まあ，もう決まったことだ。現在の顧客情報をできるだけ多く，ほかの地域の連中と共有しなければならないだろうね。だけど，1ついい点があることも認めるよ。1つの専門的分野だけで働く代わりに，新しいことを学ぶ機会を得ることになるね。

☆ : そうでしょうね。だけど，やっぱり，この変更をすると大きな得意先をいくつか失う危険があると思うわ。

★ : 時間とお金の長期的節約はやってみる価値がある，と経営陣は思ってい

るようだね。
☆：まあ，成り行きを見守るしかないでしょうけど，期待はしないわね。
質問：改革案について男性が言っていることの1つは何か。
選択肢の訳　1　女性の仕事よりも男性の仕事の方に大きな影響を与える。
　　　　　　2　スタッフが専門的知識を広げるのに役立つかもしれない。
　　　　　　3　今よりも長距離を運転しなければならなくなることを意味する。
　　　　　　4　スタッフが現在の顧客との関係を強化するのに役立つかもしれない。
解説　質問の the proposed change とは，営業部員がエリアに関係なく得意分野に応じて顧客を担当していたこれまでのやり方を変えて，エリアごとに営業部員を配置すること。一貫して懐疑的な女性に男性はおおむね同調しているが，3つ目の発言の後半で I see one upside と言って，we'll get a chance to learn new things という利点を挙げている。**2** がこの利点を言い換えている。account「得意先」。not hold *one's* breath「期待を持たない」。

No.10 解答

スクリプト
★：Hey, did you guys fill out the year-end review yet?
☆：The one we use to evaluate last year's projects?
★：Yeah. We're supposed to turn it in by the end of this week.
○：I hate doing that. It's always about 10 pages long.
☆：Me, too. The instructions are so complicated.
★：I've already spent two hours on it, and I'm not even halfway through.
☆：Well, I'm not going to spend so much time on it. It's just going to end up in a pile on our boss's desk like it always does.
○：I agree. I've never gotten any feedback regarding anything I've submitted.
★：Actually, our boss is not going to see it. It's going straight to human resources. New policy.
○：You mean there's a chance our suggestions about how to improve some processes might actually get heard?
★：Could be. They're specifically asking for feedback about project management.
☆：In that case, it might be worth taking seriously. There's no way I'll get to it today, though.
★：Let's go through some of the key points over lunch tomorrow. If we present a united front, they might actually listen.
☆：OK.
○：I guess it couldn't hurt.

Question: What does the man imply about this year's review?

全文訳
- ★： ねえ、君たちは年末評価書にもう記入した？
- ☆： 去年の企画を評価するために使うやつ？
- ★： うん。今週末までに提出することになっているよ。
- ○： 私、あれをするのは嫌い。いつも10ページくらいあるんだもの。
- ☆： 私も。指示がすごく複雑なのよね。
- ★： 僕はもう2時間かけてやっているけど、半分も終わっていないよ。
- ☆： うーん、私はあれにそんなに時間はかけないわ。毎度そうだけど、結局上司の机に山積みになるだけじゃない。
- ○： 本当よね。提出したものに関して何ひとつ反応が返ってきたためしがないんだもの。
- ★： 実はね、上司が見ることはないんだ。人事部へ直行するんだよ。新しい方針なんだ。
- ○： いくつかの工程をどう改善するかについての私たちの提案が、実際に聞いてもらえるかもしれないチャンスがあるっていうこと？
- ★： かもね。特に企画管理についての意見を求めているよ。
- ☆： そういうことなら、真剣に取り組む価値があるかもしれないわね。今日取りかかるのは絶対無理だけど。
- ★： 明日ランチを食べながら、大事なポイントをいくつか検討しようよ。共同戦線を張れば、実際に耳を傾けてくれるかもしれないよ。
- ☆： わかったわ。
- ○： やって損になることはないわね。

質問：今年の評価書について男性は暗に何と言っているか。

選択肢の訳
1. 女性たちの意見は無視される。
2. おそらく彼らが記入しなければならない最後の評価書になる。
3. 人事部が見る前に上司が見たがっている。
4. 職場の変化につながるかもしれない。

解説 同僚3人の会話。これまで評価書は放置されていたが、男性は4つ目の発言で、評価書は人事部に直行すると言っている。新しい方針なので、今年からそうなることを意味する。そして、それを知った女性の1人が、our suggestions about how to improve some processes を聞いてもらえるかもしれないと言い、男性も肯定している。つまり、今年の評価書は、社員の声が職場に反映される可能性を与えるものということになる。present a united front「共同戦線を張る」。

A

(スクリプト) **Digital Relationships**

There has been considerable concern about the effects of the Internet on people's social well-being. An influential study at one university found that subjects felt increasingly socially isolated the more time they spent online. This confirmed a common belief that the Internet weakens personal bonds by emphasizing the quantity of one's so-called friends over the quality of relationships. Superficial interactions are encouraged, leaving people feeling lonelier and less connected to one another. However, the university study has been the subject of some criticism. Among other problems, it focused on novice Internet users over a short duration. Many of the same subjects, when contacted years after the study ended, stated that continued Internet use had actually had a positive effect on their social well-being.

More-recent research suggests that Internet use may have other benefits. For example, searching for romantic partners online can lead to successful relationships. Some dating sites utilize complicated algorithms to match people with each other. This may help people find their ideal partner and form long-term romantic partnerships. Moreover, in some studies, spouses who had met online reported increased marital satisfaction and may therefore face a lower risk of divorce than those who met offline.

Questions
No.11 What is one criticism that has been raised about the university study?
No.12 What is one thing the speaker suggests about dating sites?

(全文訳) **デジタルな人間関係**

インターネットが人々の社会生活の充足感に与える影響に関しては相当な懸念が持たれてきた。ある大学の有力な研究で、被験者がオンラインで費やす時間が長いほど、彼らはますます社会的な孤立感を深めるようになることがわかった。このことにより、インターネットは人間関係の質よりもいわゆる友達の数の多さを重要視することで個人的な結び付きを弱める、という通説が正しいと確認された。表面的な交流が促されて、人々はより孤独感を深め、お互いのつながりが薄くなっていると感じてしまうのだ。しかしながら、その大学の研究は一部で批判の対象となっている。ほかにも問題はあるが、その研究は短期間の間に初心者のインターネットユーザーに焦点を当てた。研究が終了した数年後に連絡を取ってみたところ、同じ被験者の多くは、継続してインターネットを利用したことが実際に自身の社会生活の充足感にプラスの影響を与えたと明言した。

さらに最近の調査では、インターネットの利用にはほかにも利点があるかもしれない

ことが示唆されている。例えば，オンラインで恋人を探すと良好な関係につながる可能性があるのだ。一部の出会い系サイトは，人同士を引き合わせるために複雑なアルゴリズムを活用している。このことが人々にとって理想の相手を見つけ，長期的な恋愛関係を形成するための手助けとなるかもしれない。さらに，一部の研究では，オンラインで出会った配偶者たちは結婚満足度が高まったと報告しており，それ故，オフラインで出会った人たちよりも離婚のリスクが低くなるかもしれない。

語句 subject「被験者，対象」，spouse「配偶者」

No.11 解答 ④

質問の訳 その大学の研究について唱えられている批判の1つは何か。
選択肢の訳
1 インターネットに基づいた人間関係にのみ焦点を当てた。
2 インターネット会社から資金提供を受けた。
3 研究員たちが時代遅れの技術を利用した。
4 研究の期間が不十分であった。

解説 第1段落後半に，novice Internet users を対象とした短期間の研究であることが問題点の1つだとあり，続く最終文で，数年後には同じ被験者の多くが continued Internet use にプラスの側面があったと明言したと述べられている。このことを研究期間が inadequate「不十分だ」と表現した4が正解。

No.12 解答 ③

質問の訳 話者が出会い系サイトについて示唆していることの1つは何か。
選択肢の訳
1 人々のプロフィールから得たデータを悪用する傾向がある。
2 相性に関連する要因をしばしば無視する。
3 強い夫婦関係を築くのに貢献するかもしれない。
4 最近になってアルゴリズムを単純化した。

解説 第2段落最終文で，オンラインで出会った配偶者たちが increased marital satisfaction を報告している研究があり，オフラインで出会った人たちよりも離婚のリスクが低下する可能性があると述べられている。このことを creating strong marriages に貢献する可能性があると言い換えた3が正解。

B

スクリプト **Synthetic Diamonds**

Although laboratory-made diamonds have been used in machinery and cutting tools for decades, they have rarely been used for jewelry. That may be changing, however. Some laboratories have even succeeded in producing Type IIa diamonds, the purest category. This is significant, as only a very small percentage of all naturally mined diamonds are Type IIa. The new, high-quality synthetic diamonds are chemically identical to their natural counterparts, and they are now challenging natural diamonds for a share of the consumer jewelry market.

Quality, though, is not the only factor attracting consumers to synthetic diamonds. Mining for natural diamonds has a reputation for oppressive working conditions and environmental unsustainability. Synthetic-diamond manufacturers claim their production methods avoid labor concerns and result in fewer carbon dioxide emissions than mining. However, closing diamond mines could have detrimental effects on local communities. In some developing nations, diamond mines are one of the few means of employment. Therefore, some people argue that it is better to improve pay and conditions for miners than to take away their jobs. Efforts have been made by diamond-mining companies to address environmental concerns. In response to pressure from environmental groups, some diamond-mining companies have adopted carbon-capture technology, with the aim of becoming carbon neutral.

Questions

No.13 What do we learn about synthetic diamonds?

No.14 What is one way some diamond-mining companies are trying to improve their practices?

全文訳　**合成ダイヤモンド**

　実験室で作られたダイヤモンドは，何十年もの間機械や切削工具に使用されてきたが，宝飾品のために使用されることはめったになかった。ところが，このことが変わりつつあるようだ。最高純度に分類されるタイプⅡaダイヤモンドの製造に成功した実験室すらある。これは大きな意義のあることだ。というのも，すべての天然採掘のダイヤモンドの中でタイプⅡaダイヤモンドはほんのわずかな割合しかないからだ。その新しい高品質の合成ダイヤモンドは，天然のものと化学的に同一で，現在，宝飾品の消費者市場のシェアをかけて天然ダイヤモンドに挑んでいるところである。

　だが，品質が消費者を合成ダイヤモンドに引き付けている唯一の要因ではない。天然ダイヤモンドの採掘には，過酷な労働条件と環境の非持続可能性という評判があるのだ。合成ダイヤモンドの製造業者は，自分たちの製造方法は労働問題を回避しており，結果的に二酸化炭素の排出量が採掘よりも少なくなると主張している。しかしながら，ダイヤモンド鉱山を閉鎖することは地元の地域社会に悪影響を及ぼす可能性がある。一部の発展途上国では，ダイヤモンド鉱山が数少ない雇用手段の1つになっている。それ故，鉱山労働者の給料と条件を改善する方が，彼らの職を奪うよりも望ましいと主張する人もいる。環境問題に対処するために，ダイヤモンド採掘企業によって努力がなされてきた。環境保護団体からの圧力に応え，一部のダイヤモンド採掘企業は，カーボンニュートラルになることを目指して，炭素回収技術を採用している。

　語句　synthetic「合成の」，unsustainability「非持続可能性」，detrimental「有害な」

No.13 解答 ①

質問の訳　合成ダイヤモンドについて何がわかるか。

選択肢の訳
1 最高の天然ダイヤモンドの品質に匹敵する。
2 ハイテク機器への使用には適さない。
3 天然ダイヤモンドとは化学組成が異なっている。
4 天然ダイヤモンドよりも高額な場合がある。

解説　第1段落前半で，天然でもごくわずかしかない最高純度の合成ダイヤモンドの製造に成功したこと，また，後半で，新たな高品質の合成ダイヤモンドは their natural counterparts，つまり天然ダイヤモンドと化学的に同一であることが述べられている。これらを品質の点で can match「匹敵する」と言い換えた **1** が正解。

No.14 解答 ③

質問の訳　一部のダイヤモンド採掘企業が慣行の改善を試みている方法の1つは何か。

選択肢の訳
1 発展途上国で運営する鉱山の数を減らすことによって。
2 従業員の規模を縮小することによって。
3 環境に優しい方法を利用することによって。
4 生産能力を高めることによって。

解説　第2段落後半で，ダイヤモンド採掘業者は environmental concerns に対処するために努力を続けていると述べられた後，続く最終文に，一部の業者は carbon neutral になることを目指して carbon-capture technology「炭素回収技術」を採用している，とある。よって，正解は **3**。

スクリプト **Gamification**

These days, many businesses are incorporating features common to games through a practice known as gamification. Customer-support centers, for instance, may allow customers to award points to customer-service agents based on the quality of the service they provide. The agents get rewards, such as additional pay, based on the number of points they receive. Their scores are also displayed to other agents, and some managers believe this can create an atmosphere where employees try to compete with one another to satisfy customers. Some managers also believe this element of competition can make the work more enjoyable, which could prove especially useful in jobs where wages are low and employee turnover is high.

Critics of gamification argue that it reduces employee morale in the long term. Research has demonstrated that the most powerful motivators for employees are independence, skill development, and the satisfaction that comes from being engaged in meaningful work. External rewards may fail to satisfy these needs. Furthermore, it could be argued that such reward systems focus too much on success. According to one expert on game design, including more possibilities for failure would encourage workers to stay more committed to their work.

Questions
No.15 What do some managers believe gamification can do?
No.16 According to critics, what does gamification fail to address?

全文訳 ゲーミフィケーション

最近では，多くの企業がゲーミフィケーションとして知られる手法を通じて，ゲームと共通の特徴を取り入れている。例えば，顧客サポートセンターが顧客に対して，顧客サービス担当者が提供するサービスの質に基づいてその担当者にポイントを付与することを認めることもある。受け取ったポイント数に基づいて，担当者は割増賃金などの報酬を手にする。彼らの得点はほかの担当者にも開示されており，このことにより従業員たちがお互いに競い合って顧客を満足させようとする雰囲気を作り出すことができると考えている経営者もいる。また，一部の経営者は，この競争の要素によって仕事がより楽しめるものとなり，そのことが，賃金が低く従業員の離職率が高い仕事では，結果的に特に役に立つかもしれないと考えている。

ゲーミフィケーションに批判的な人たちは，長期的に見るとそれが従業員の士気を低下させると主張している。調査によって，従業員にとっての最強の動機付け要因は，自立，能力開発，そして，有意義な仕事に従事することから得られる満足感であることが証明されている。外的報酬ではこれらの要求を満たすことができないかもしれない。さらに，そういった報酬制度は成功に重点を置き過ぎていると論じることもできる。あるゲーム設計の専門家によると，失敗の可能性をより多く含めておくことで，労働者はより熱心に仕事に取り組み続ける気になるようだ。

語句 gamification「ゲーミフィケーション（ゲームの要素をゲーム以外の活動に応用すること）」，turnover「離職率」

No.15 解答

質問の訳 一部の経営者はゲーミフィケーションに何ができると考えているか。
選択肢の訳
1 競争を通じて労働者の業績を向上させる。
2 労働者にほかの労働者と協力するよう促す。
3 労働者により優れたストレスの対処法を教える。
4 高度な技術を持った労働者を採用しやすくする。

解説 一部の経営者の考えは第1段落後半で語られている。そこには，ポイント制の導入で従業員が顧客の満足を得るために競い合うようになり，その競争の要素によって仕事が more enjoyable になる，とある。つまり，競争によって従業員の performance が向上すると考えていることにな

るので，**1** が正解。

No.16 解答

質問の訳 批判的な人たちによると，ゲーミフィケーションは何に対処できないか。
選択肢の訳
1　従業員の動機付けの真の源。
2　成功に重点を置くことの重要性。
3　顧客との交流に必要とされる技能。
4　企業がコストを最小限に抑える必要性。

解説 第2段落で批判的な人たちの主張が述べられており，中ほどに External rewards may fail to satisfy these needs. とある。この these needs はその前の文で挙げられた3つの the most powerful motivators for employees のことを指しているので，正解は **1**。external rewards は成功に対して与えられる昇進や昇給のことだが，そのための競争をあおるより，失敗を許容するなどして従業員のやる気や満足感を引き出す方が結果的に有益だというのが批判派の考えということになる。

 Land-Based Vertebrates

All land-based vertebrates — animals with a spine — are believed to have evolved from sea creatures. Scientists had long speculated that the move onto land occurred when some sea creatures' fins became stronger. Having stronger fins would have allowed creatures to move onto land to escape predators that could only swim. Recent research, however, indicates that sea creatures began to leave the ocean because they experienced a dramatic increase in eye size. This development meant that they were better equipped to spot potential food sources, like insects, on land, and it triggered a transition to searching out such prey.

Another evolutionary adaptation involving vision coincided with the move to land. The eyes of some creatures began moving toward the tops of their heads. This would not have benefited creatures when looking through water, as water restricts visual range, but the change would have allowed them to see more clearly when above the surface. These developments in visual ability may also have contributed to a change in neural circuitry. Such a change may have helped land-based vertebrates to develop skills such as planning when they hunted, rather than relying solely on quick reaction times.

Questions
No.17 According to recent research, what caused sea creatures to move onto land?
No.18 What does the speaker say about the development of land-based vertebrates?

全文訳　陸生の脊椎動物

すべての陸生の脊椎動物，つまり背骨を持つ動物は，海洋生物から進化したと考えられている。科学者たちは長らく，陸上への移動が起こったのは一部の海洋生物のひれがより強くなったときだと推測してきた。より強いひれを持つことで，生物は陸上に移動し，泳ぐことしかできない捕食者から逃れることが可能になったのであろう。ところが，最近の研究では，海洋生物が海を離れ始めたのは，目の大きさの劇的な拡大を経験したためであることが示されている。この発達が意味したのは，これらの海洋生物に備わる，陸上にいる昆虫のような潜在的な食糧源を見つける能力が以前よりも高まったということであり，そのことが，そういった獲物の探索への移行を引き起こした。

視覚に関連したもう1つの進化的適応が，陸への移動と同時に発生した。一部の生物の目が頭頂部に向かって移動し始めたのだ。水は視界を制限するので，このことは水中で見る際には生物に恩恵をもたらさなかったであろうが，その変化によって，水面から出たときによりはっきりと見ることができるようになったであろう。また，これらの視覚能力の発達は，神経回路に変化をもたらす一因になったかもしれない。そういった変化のおかげで，陸生の脊椎動物は，狩りをする際に，単に素早い反応時間に頼るのではなく，計画を立てるといった能力を伸ばすことができたかもしれないのだ。

語句　land-based「陸生の」, vertebrate「脊椎動物」, neural circuitry「神経回路」

No.17 解答 ④

質問の訳　最近の研究によると，何が原因で海洋生物は陸上に移動したのか。

選択肢の訳
1 新たな海洋捕食者の出現。
2 はるかに強いひれの発達。
3 海中における食糧源の欠乏。
4 そこで食糧源を発見する能力の向上。

解説　最近の研究成果は第1段落後半で語られている。そこには，海洋生物が陸上に移動したのは a dramatic increase in eye size を経験したからで，この発達は to spot potential food sources, like insects, on land の能力が向上したことを意味した，とある。よって，正解は **4**。強いひれの発達が原因というのは従来の考え方なので，**2** は不適。

No.18 解答 ②

質問の訳　陸生の脊椎動物の発達について話者は何と言っているか。

選択肢の訳
1 目の位置は変化しないままだった。
2 異なる方法で狩りをすることができるようになったようだ。
3 一部の脊椎動物の反応がより速くなる原因となった。
4 長期的に見ると悪影響をもたらした。

解説　第2段落後半で，視覚能力の発達は neural circuitry「神経回路」の変化をもたらし，そういった変化が，狩りをする際に計画を立てるといっ

た能力の発達に役立った可能性があると述べられている。つまり，狩りの方法に変化が生じた可能性があると指摘しているので，正解は **2**。

スクリプト **Masking War Injuries**

World War I was brutal in many ways. The use of machine guns and other powerful weapons caused terrible destruction. In addition, much of the fighting took place in long, deep ditches known as trenches. Although trenches protected soldiers' bodies, their heads were often exposed, leaving them vulnerable to machine gun and sniper fire. As a result, many soldiers suffered injuries to their faces. In contrast to previous wars, however, advancements in surgical techniques allowed increased survival rates for those with serious wounds. Still, many soldiers were left with facial injuries for life, and some felt ashamed of their injuries.

Around the same time, the field of cosmetic surgery was emerging. Artists began helping injured soldiers by creating facial parts made from metal, including complete masks made from thin sheets of copper. Sculptor Anna Coleman Ladd became famous for her mask-making skills. She took great care to ensure that the features on her masks were accurate and that the color matched the patient's skin color exactly. She was able to create a new face that was amazingly similar to the original by using photos of the victims before they were injured. These developments gave many soldiers the confidence to resume productive lives.

Questions
No.19 What is one way that World War I was different from previous conflicts?
No.20 What is true of Anna Coleman Ladd?

全文訳 **戦傷を仮面で隠す**

第1次世界大戦は多くの点で残酷だった。機関銃をはじめとする強力な武器を使用したことでひどい破壊が引き起こされた。さらに，戦闘の多くは，塹壕として知られる長く深い溝の中で行われた。塹壕は兵士たちの体を守ったが，彼らの頭部は露出していることが多く，機関銃や狙撃手の射撃を受けやすい状態にあった。その結果，多くの兵士が顔に傷を負った。しかしながら，それまでの戦争と比べて，外科技術の進歩によって，重傷を負った人たちの生存率を上げることができた。それでも，多くの兵士は生涯顔に傷を負ったままであり，その傷を恥ずかしく思う者もいた。

同じ時期に，美容整形という分野が生まれつつあった。芸術家たちが，薄い銅板でできた完全な仮面を含め，金属でできた顔のパーツを作り出すことによって，負傷した兵士たちを助け始めた。彫刻家のアンナ・コールマン・ラッドは仮面制作の技術で有名になった。彼女は細心の注意を払って，仮面の顔立ちが正確であるように，そして，色が患者の皮膚の色と正確に一致するように努めた。負傷する前の被害者の写真を使うこと

で，彼女は元の顔に驚くほど似た新たな顔を作り出すことができた。これらの進歩が多くの兵士に，有意義な人生を取り戻す自信を与えたのだ。

語句 trench「塹壕」，vulnerable「攻撃されやすい」

No.19 解答 ②

質問の訳 第1次世界大戦がそれまでの紛争と異なっていた点の1つは何か。
選択肢の訳
1 兵士たちがより優れた防弾服を持っていた。
2 より多くの兵士が重傷を乗り切った。
3 特定の種類の武器が禁止された。
4 兵士たちの負傷が大幅に減少した。

解説 第1段落後半で，これまでの戦争と比べて，外科技術の進歩によってthose with serious wounds の生存率の上昇が可能になったと述べられている。この点を survived serious wounds という表現を使って言い換えた **2** が正解。防弾服と武器の禁止に関しては触れられていないので，**1** と **3** は不適。多くの兵士が顔を負傷したので，**4** も不適。

No.20 解答 ③

質問の訳 アンナ・コールマン・ラッドについて当てはまることは何か。
選択肢の訳
1 新たに発見された素材を用いて仮面を作った。
2 芸術家になる前は形成外科医だった。
3 仮面の正確さで知られていた。
4 精神衛生の専門家だった。

解説 第2段落中ほどで her mask-making skills で有名になったと述べられた後，続く文に，細心の注意で仮面の顔立ちの正確さと皮膚の色の正確な一致を目指した，とある。**3** がこの彼女の技術の特徴を，accuracy という語を使って「仮面の正確さ」と簡潔にまとめている。

一次試験・リスニング **Part 3** 問題編 p.37～38

F

スクリプト

You have 10 seconds to read the situation and Question No. 21.

Welcome to the conference. Due to increased security, we ask that you keep your conference pass with you at all times. If you are just arriving, please proceed directly to reception to check in and receive your pass. Valid ID will be required. Australian nationals may present any government-issued ID, such as a driver's license. For international attendees, a valid passport will be required. If you do not have your passport with you, an international driver's license is acceptable, but you will first need to fill in some additional forms to confirm your personal details. These are available at the security desk. Please note that a company business card will not be accepted as a valid ID. We ask for your patience while these security checks are being completed. Thank you for your cooperation and understanding.

Now mark your answer on your answer sheet.

全文訳

　会議にようこそいらっしゃいました。セキュリティー強化のため，会議の入場許可証を常に携帯いただきますようお願い申し上げます。到着されたばかりの方は，そのまま受付にお進みいただき，お手続きをして入場許可証をお受け取りください。有効な身分証明書が必要になります。オーストラリア国籍の方は，例えば運転免許証など，政府発行の身分証明書でしたら，どれをご提示いただいても構いません。外国人の出席者の方は，有効なパスポートが必要になります。パスポートがお手元にない場合は，国際運転免許証でも受け付けておりますが，まず追加の用紙数枚に必要事項を記入していただいて，詳細な個人情報を確認させていただかなければなりません。この用紙は警備デスクにてご用意しております。会社の名刺は有効な身分証明書として受け付けておりませんのでご注意ください。これらのセキュリティーチェックが完了するまでの間，しばらくお待ちいただきますようお願い申し上げます。ご協力とご理解に感謝申し上げます。

No.21 解答 ④

状況の訳　あなたは日本人の重役で，オーストラリアで開かれる会議に到着したところである。あなたは名刺と国際運転免許証を持っているが，パスポートはホテルにある。あなたは次のアナウンスを聞く。

質問の訳　あなたはまず何をすべきか。

選択肢の訳
1 受付で国際運転免許証を提示する。
2 建物に入る際に警備員に名刺を渡す。
3 受付で会議の入場許可証を受け取る。
4 警備デスクで数枚の用紙を入手する。

語句　attendee「出席者」

解説　名刺と国際運転免許証は所持しているが，パスポートはホテルに置いてきたあなたは，国際運転免許証で受け付けてもらうことになる。その場合は，まず some additional forms を完成させる必要があると告げられた後，その用紙は警備デスクで入手可能との説明を受ける。よって，正解は 4。1 と 3 は追加の用紙を完成させた後ですべきことなので不適。

G

スクリプト

You have 10 seconds to read the situation and Question No. 22.

We've checked your vehicle. You said a warning light sometimes tells you to check the engine. The problem seems to be aging engine coils. If they're faulty, the engine will sometimes misfire or stall. I'd recommend getting those changed now. They could be a safety hazard, especially if you'll be on the road for long periods. We also checked your oxygen sensor, which could fail to detect toxic emissions if it's worn out, but it's working. We also noticed that your wheel alignment was off. This could have been very dangerous, so we went ahead and adjusted that for you. Your brake cables are in good shape and shouldn't need any repairs for the time being. It's been a while since you replaced the brake pads, though, so next time you bring the car in, you might want to consider getting that done.

Now mark your answer on your answer sheet.

全文訳

お客さまのお車を点検しました。時々警告灯がついて，エンジンを点検するようにとの指示が出るとおっしゃっていましたね。問題はエンジンの点火コイルが古くなっていることのようです。点火コイルに不具合がありますと，エンジンが点火しなかったり，止まったりすることが時々あります。今交換されることをお勧めします。特に長期間車でお出かけになる場合は，安全上問題となるかもしれません。酸素センサーも点検しまして，劣化すると有害排出物を検知できなくなることもあるのですが，作動しています。ホイールアライメントが狂っていることもわかりました。このままではとても危険だったかもしれないので，お客さまのために先に調整しておきました。ブレーキケーブルはよい状態ですので，当分の間何も修理する必要はないでしょう。ですが，ブレーキパッドは取り換えてからしばらくたっていますので，次にお車を持ち込まれたときに，お取り換えをご検討なさるとよろしいかもしれません。

No.22 解答 ①

状況の訳 あなたは車で旅行する前に整備をしてもらうため，自動車修理工場に車を持ち込んだ。安全は重要だが，必要のない修理は避けたいと思っている。整備士はあなたに次のことを告げる。

質問の訳 あなたは今整備士にどの作業をするように頼むべきか。

選択肢の訳
1 エンジンの点火コイルを取り換える。
2 酸素センサーを交換する。
3 ホイールアライメントを調整する。
4 ブレーキパッドを取り換える。

語句 coil「（エンジンの）点火コイル」，misfire「点火しない」，wheel alignment「ホイールアライメント（自動車の車輪の整列具合）」

解説 整備士は問題となっている aging engine coils の交換を勧めており，特に長期間の旅行では a safety hazard になる可能性があると告げている。よって，現時点で頼むべき作業は **1**。**2** の the oxygen sensor は作

45

動していて、**3** の the wheel alignment は調整済みであり、**4** の the brake pads の交換は次回の点検時に検討すればよいことなので不適。

H

(スクリプト)

You have 10 seconds to read the situation and Question No. 23.

We offer several options. Introduction to German is held on Mondays from 8 p.m. to 9 p.m. and runs from June 1st to July 15th. We also offer Basic German for Travel on Wednesdays and Saturdays from 5 p.m. to 7 p.m. This is a one-month course and begins from the first of each month. You'd need to attend both sessions each week. Of course, the fastest way to learn a language is through immersion, and our three-week Intensive German course beginning this month will get you speaking the language in no time, with a class every weekday from 7 p.m. to 9 p.m. Finally, there's our Private German Online course. This beginners' course costs more than group classes, but lessons can be arranged to fit your schedule. And no matter which course you choose, you are welcome to attend our open conversation sessions on Saturday afternoons from noon to 4 p.m.

Now mark your answer on your answer sheet.

(全文訳)

当校では複数の選択肢を提供しております。「ドイツ語入門」は毎週月曜日午後8時から午後9時の間に開講され、6月1日から7月15日まで続きます。毎週水曜日と土曜日の午後5時から午後7時の間に「旅行のための基礎ドイツ語」も提供しております。こちらは1カ月間の講座で、毎月初めから始まります。毎週両方の授業に出席していただくことになります。もちろん、言語を学ぶ一番の近道は没入法でして、今月始まる3週間の「集中ドイツ語」講座ですと、平日毎日午後7時から午後9時までの授業を受ければ、あっという間にドイツ語を話し始めているでしょう。最後に、「オンライン個別ドイツ語」講座がございます。この初級者向けの講座は集団の授業よりも費用はかかりますが、個人の予定に合うようにレッスンを調整することができます。そして、どの講座をお選びになったとしても、毎週土曜日の午後、正午から午後4時まで行われている参加自由の会話セッションにいつでもご参加いただけます。

No.23 解答 ④

(状況の訳) 今は4月である。あなたは6月になる前に初級者レベルのドイツ語の授業を受ける必要がある。あなたは平日午後8時まで働いている。あなたは語学学校に電話をして、次のことを告げられる。

(質問の訳) あなたはどの講座を選ぶべきか。

(選択肢の訳)
1 ドイツ語入門。
2 旅行のための基礎ドイツ語。
3 集中ドイツ語。
4 オンライン個別ドイツ語。

> 語句　immersion「没入法，イマージョン（外国語だけで授業を行う教育法）」
> 解説　状況で述べられている条件から，あなたが選ぶことができるのは，初級者向けの講座であり，自身の予定に合わせてレッスンの調整が可能と紹介された **4** の「オンライン個別ドイツ語」のみである。**1** は 6 月 1 日から始まり，**2** は水曜午後 5 時開始の授業に参加できず，**3** は平日午後 7 時開始なので不適。

> スクリプト

You have 10 seconds to read the situation and Question No. 24.

Hi. Great news. G-P Industries wants us to come up with a whole new image for them, and you're my first choice to head the project. I know you're currently committed to the museum project, so it's up to you whether to stay on that or take this on. The president will keep a close eye on this new project, so it would be a good opportunity to get her attention, especially with performance reviews coming up in a couple of months. Maybe your assistant could step up and replace you on the museum project if he's already involved? If not, the museum director wouldn't be happy about any staff changes this late in the game, so I'd recommend playing it safe. We don't want to jeopardize the chances of future work with the museum, and I'm sure you'll have other opportunities to impress the president.

Now mark your answer on your answer sheet.

> 全文訳

もしもし。とてもいい知らせです。G-P インダストリーズが私たちに自社のまったく新しいイメージを考案してほしいとのことで，あなたがそのプロジェクトを指揮してほしいと私が最初に選んだ人です。あなたが現在，博物館のプロジェクトに全力を注いでいることはわかっていますので，それをそのまま続けるか，これを引き受けるかどうかはあなた次第です。社長はこの新たなプロジェクトを注視するでしょうから，特に業績評価が数カ月後に迫っているので，彼女に注目されるいい機会になるでしょう。あなたのアシスタントが博物館のプロジェクトに既に携わっていたら，おそらく昇進してあなたの後任になることができるのではないでしょうか？ もし携わっていなかったら，博物館の館長はこんな遅過ぎるタイミングではいかなるスタッフの変更も不満に思うでしょうから，安全策を取ることをお勧めします。博物館との今後の仕事の機会を危うくすることを私たちは望んでいないし，あなたが社長に好印象を与える機会はきっとまたあると思います。

No.24 解答

> 状況の訳　あなたはグラフィックデザイン会社に勤務しており，昇進を望んでいる。あなたのアシスタントは博物館のプロジェクトに取り組んできていな

い。あなたの部の部長はあなたに次のボイスメールを残した。

質問の訳 あなたは何をすべきか。
選択肢の訳
1 予定どおり博物館のプロジェクトを続ける。
2 新たな役割を説明するためにアシスタントと打ち合わせをする。
3 自身の業績評価のための資料を準備する。
4 クライアント向けのプランを携えて社長と連絡を取る。

語句 step up「昇進する」, late in the game「タイミングが遅過ぎて」, jeopardize「～を危うくする」

解説 新たなプロジェクトを引き受けるかどうかはあなた次第。社長も注視するはずなので，昇進を望むあなたには絶好の機会だが，現在注力している博物館のプロジェクトにアシスタントが携わっておらず，後任の適任者が不在なので，部長の忠告どおり play it safe「安全策を取る」，つまり今回の昇進は諦めて博物館のプロジェクトを続ける方が無難である。

J

スクリプト

You have 10 seconds to read the situation and Question No. 25.

OK, our Standard Fit Program, priced at $200, uses precise measurements to make sure your bike's geometry and setup are appropriate for standard use. The Dynamic Fit Program, which is $250, measures your power output on a test bike with high precision. We work from those results to make adjustments that will give you maximum power. The Biomechanical Tuning Service, for $350, includes the key features of those two programs and adds data capture and video analysis to fine-tune your ride. This really helps with the positioning of the seat and your shoes, so your feet lock into your pedals at the optimal angle. Finally, the Perfect Fit Tutor also offers a premium tuning service performed by our trained physiotherapist. She'll analyze your movements to spot physical problems affecting your riding technique and give you exercises to address them. That option's normally $550 but is discounted by $50 right now.

Now mark your answer on your answer sheet.

全文訳

わかりました，当店のスタンダード・フィット・プログラムは，料金は200ドルとなっていまして，正確な測定法を用いて，お客さまの自転車のジオメトリーとセッティングが標準的な使用に適しているかどうかを確認します。ダイナミック・フィット・プログラムですが，250ドルでして，試乗自転車を使ってお客さまの出力を高い精度で測定します。その結果を基に作業して，お客さまが最大限の力を発揮できるように調整します。バイオメカニカル・チューニング・サービスは，350ドルとなっていますが，それら2つのプログラムの主要な特徴が含まれていまして，乗り心地を微調整するためにデータ収集とビデオ分析が加わります。これはサドルと靴の位置を調整するのに本当に

役に立つので，お客さまの足は最適な角度でペダルに固定されます。最後に，パーフェクト・フィット・チューターも，当店の熟練した理学療法士が実施する質の高い調整サービスを提供します。彼女がお客さまの動きを分析して，乗車技術に影響を与えている身体的な諸問題を発見し，それらに対処するための運動をお伝えします。そちらをお選びになると，通常は550ドルですが，今ですと50ドル割引いたします。

No.25 解答 ③

状況の訳 あなたは最近，レース用自転車を購入した。あなたは足をペダルのどの位置に乗せるかについて助力がほしいと思っている。あなたの予算は400ドルである。あなたは自転車店に電話をして，次のことを告げられる。

質問の訳 あなたはどの選択肢を選ぶべきか。

選択肢の訳
1 スタンダード・フィット・プログラム。
2 ダイナミック・フィット・プログラム。
3 バイオメカニカル・チューニング・サービス。
4 パーフェクト・フィット・チューター。

語句 geometry「ジオメトリー，幾何学的配置」，setup「セッティング（サドルの高さやハンドルまでの距離などの調整）」，fine-tune「〜を微調整する」，optimal「最適な」，physiotherapist「理学療法士」

解説 ペダルに置く足の位置を決める方法を教えてもらえて，予算は400ドルまでという条件を満たすのは，the positioning of the seat and your shoes に本当に役立つものであり，価格は350ドルだと紹介された3のバイオメカニカル・チューニング・サービスのみである。4も a premium tuning service を提供するが，割引後の価格でも500ドルと予算オーバーなので不適。

スクリプト

This is an interview with Christine Baker, a graduate student and teaching assistant at a university.

Interviewer (I): Welcome to *Voices on Campus*. Christine, thanks for joining us today.

Christine Baker (C): Thanks for having me.

I: So, could you tell us a little about what you do as a teaching assistant?

C: Well, I help teach small seminar classes focusing on specific areas the students are working on.

I: What do you enjoy most about it?

C: Well, the students come from diverse ethnic, cultural, and religious backgrounds, so there are a lot of interesting and sometimes heated debates in the seminars. Plus, I feel like a sort of minor celebrity. I teach about 80 students over the course of each semester, and now everywhere I go on campus somebody recognizes me. I've met all kinds of people I wouldn't have gotten to know otherwise.

I: That's great. And what would you say are the biggest challenges you face in your job?

C: Well, to be honest, it's taken a while to get used to evaluating the students' writing assignments. Fortunately, the professors have helped me get a good handle on grading procedures. Sometimes, though, students question their grades. Usually, I can defend the scores I give, but at first, I found myself changing grades more often than I would've liked. So, a skill I had to work on was applying each professor's grading criteria consistently and not being influenced by other factors. Things like whether I agreed with the argument the student was making in the paper. I have to put my feelings about the content aside and focus on whether the paper meets the criteria for the assignment. That's made things a lot easier.

I: Interesting. So, what advice would you give to new teaching assistants?

C: Well, when I started teaching, I was intimidated by the things people told me. Stuff like, "Never let the students know you're nervous," and "Never apologize." I second-guessed myself sometimes because I really wanted to measure up to what I imagined their standards for a teacher were. But, quite often, the students would say they were really getting a lot out of my seminars. So, I gradually learned that for the students, the seminars are more about the material they're there to learn and less about the person that's helping them to learn it. I would say that the key is to be thoroughly familiar with the material beforehand. Not just having a firm grasp on it yourself but making sure you can convey what's in your head to a group of students, some of whom will be very quick on the uptake. Anyway, when I began focusing on the students' needs rather than my own worries, things started going a lot better.

I: That sounds like good advice. Thanks for sharing your experiences with us today, Christine.

C: It was my pleasure.

Questions

No.26 What does Christine say about grading students' writing assignments?

No.27 What does Christine say is one important thing for teaching assistants to do?

> [!NOTE] 全文訳

これは大学院生で,大学で教育助手をしているクリスティーン・ベーカーとのインタビューです。

聞き手(以下「聞」):「キャンパスの声」にようこそ。クリスティーン,今日はご参加いただきありがとうございます。

クリスティーン・ベーカー(以下「ク」): お招きいただきありがとうございます。

聞: では,教育助手としてどんなことをされているのか,少しお話しいただけますか。

ク: えー,学生たちが取り組んでいる特定の分野に焦点を合わせた少人数のゼミクラスを教えるのを手助けしています。

聞: それをしていて一番楽しいと感じることは何ですか。

ク: そうですね,学生たちはさまざまな民族的,文化的,そして宗教的背景を持っていますので,ゼミでは多くの興味深い,そして時には白熱した議論が行われます。それに,私はまるでちょっとした有名人のような感じがしています。私は各学期を通じて約80人の学生を教えていて,今ではキャンパスのどこへ行っても,誰かが私に気が付きます。教育助手をしていなかったらおそらく知り合いになることはなかったさまざまな人たちと私は出会いました。

聞: それは素晴らしいですね。では,仕事をする上で直面する最大の課題は何だとお考えですか。

ク: うーん,正直に言いますと,学生たちのレポート課題の評価に慣れるのに少し時間がかかりました。ありがたいことに,教授たちが手助けをしてくれて,採点の手順をしっかりと理解することができました。ですが,学生たちが自身の評点に疑問を抱くことが時々あります。たいていは,自分がつける点数の正当性を主張することができるのですが,最初のうちは,気が付くと,思っていた以上に頻繁に評点を変えていました。ですから,私が磨かなければならなかった技能は,各教授の採点基準を一貫して適用して,その他の要因には影響を受けないことでした。学生がレポートで論じている主張に私が賛同したかどうか,といったようなことです。内容についての私の感想は脇に置いておいて,レポートがその課題の基準を満たしているかどうかに重点を置かなければなりません。そうすることで物事がずっと進めやすくなりました。

聞: 興味深いですね。それでは,新人の教育助手に向けてどのようなアドバイスを送りますか。

ク: そうですね,私が教え始めたときは,人から言われたことで臆病になっていました。「絶対に学生たちに緊張していることを知られてはいけない」とか「絶対に謝ってはいけない」といったようなことです。私はあれでよかったのだろうかと後で思うことが時々あったのですが,それは,そういう人たちが教師に求める基準だと私が想像したものに本当に到達したいと思っていたからなのです。ですが,学生たちは,かなりの頻度で,私のゼミから本当に多くのことを学んでいると言ってくれました。それで,徐々にわかってきたのが,学生たちにとってゼミは,そこで学ぶ題材の方がより重要

であって，それを学ぶ手助けをする人はそれほど重要ではないということです。鍵となるのは，前もって題材に完全に精通しておくことだと言えるでしょう。自分自身がしっかりと題材を理解するだけではなく，自分が考えていることを学生グループに確実に伝えることができるようにしておくと，理解がとても早くなる学生が出てくるでしょう。とにかく，私自身の心配よりも学生たちのニーズの方に重点を置き始めてから，はるかに順調に物事が進み始めました。

聞：よいアドバイスになりそうですね。今日はご自身の経験を私たちにお話しいただきありがとうございました，クリスティーン。

ク：どういたしまして。

> 語句　get a handle on ~「~を理解する」，defend「~の正当性を主張する」，intimidate「~を臆病にする」，second-guess「~に後でとやかく言う」，measure up to ~「~に達する」，be quick on the uptake「理解が早い」

No.26 解答 ②

質問の訳　学生たちのレポート課題を採点することについてクリスティーンは何と言っているか。

選択肢の訳
1　学生たちの主張の力強さにたびたび感銘を受けている。
2　客観的に採点基準を適用することが難しい場合がある。
3　教授たちの評点に賛同できないときがある。
4　教育助手としての最も興味深い側面である。

解説　クリスティーンは4つ目の発言で，evaluating the students' writing assignments に慣れるのに少し時間がかかり，各教授の採点基準の一貫した適用と，自分の意見など，その他の要因の影響の除外に取り組む必要があったと述べている。このことを objectively「客観的に」採点基準を適用するのが難しい場合があると言い換えた 2 が正解。

No.27 解答 ①

質問の訳　教育助手がするべき重要なことの1つは何であるとクリスティーンは言っているか。

選択肢の訳
1　確実に題材の明快な説明ができるようにしておく。
2　学生たちに対して威圧的になり過ぎないように心がける。
3　時には間違えることがあるという事実を受け入れる。
4　学生たちがゼミの最中に自分の考えを述べるのを許可する。

解説　新人の教育助手へのアドバイスを求められたクリスティーンは，5つ目の発言で，前もって the material に精通しておくことが鍵であり，自分自身がしっかり理解するだけではなく，what's in your head を確実に伝えられるようにしておくことで，学生の早い理解に結び付くと述べている。このアドバイスを explain the material clearly という表現を使って言い換えた 1 が正解。

ここでは，A日程の5つのトピックをモデルスピーチとしました。

A日程

1. Agree or disagree: Urbanization inevitably leads to a lower quality of life

I disagree with the idea that urbanization has led to a lower quality of life. Not only has the spread of cities helped make people better off economically, but it has also provided better access to various services and benefited the environment. Firstly, cities are the backbone of economic growth. With large populations living in dense areas, they provide large workforces for factories and corporations. As companies grow, they pay workers' salaries and give out benefits, leading to a higher standard of living. Another advantage is the ease of access to a multitude of services that improve our daily lives. Everything from medical care to education to food shopping is much more widely available in urban areas. This improved access to so many different kinds of services has led to better health, increased literacy, and improved nutrition. Finally, by concentrating populations, cities greatly reduce people's environmental impact. They allow for efficient public transportation, and apartment living greatly reduces the amount of building materials and energy needed for housing. This means cities produce far less carbon per person than rural areas do. Without urbanization, I think it's clear that society would not be nearly as advanced, and billions of people would not enjoy the quality of life that they have today.

> **解説** 「賛成か反対か：都市化による生活の質の低下は避けられない」
>
> トピックに対して反対の立場から，その理由として①労働力が集中することで企業が発展する，②医療から教育まであらゆるサービスが提供されている，③資源の効率化により1人当たりの二酸化炭素の排出量が減る，という3点を挙げ，都市化により逆に生活の質は上がると主張している。賛成意見を述べたい場合は，人口が集中することによる競争の激化，生活費の高騰，精神的ストレス，などを理由にできるだろう。重複しない理由を3つ言えればベストだが，2つしか思い付かない場合は丁寧に具体例を入れよう。

2. Has online media destroyed traditional print journalism?

I think it would be an exaggeration to say that online media has destroyed print journalism. I'd like to discuss magazines' and newspapers' circulation, prestige, and quality to explain why. Firstly, while magazine and newspaper circulations have definitely declined, they are still read by hundreds of millions of people every single day. Reading on paper is easier on your eyes and makes it easier to concentrate, so there are still a huge number of people who prefer reading news and articles in this way. Furthermore, print publications still have a huge amount of prestige. Names like the New York Times and Time are far more trusted and respected than most online news sources. In fact, much of the news that you read online is actually based on reporting by journalists working for print publications. Perhaps the biggest reason is that the quality of most print publications still surpasses that of online sources. Readers of print publications tend to be more demanding of careful fact-checking and high-quality reporting. There will always be readers who are willing to pay for quality print journalism. As a result of its still-substantial circulation, prestige and quality, I think that traditional print journalism will be around for a long time.

> **解説** 「インターネットメディアは伝統的な紙媒体のジャーナリズムを破壊したか」
>
> 冒頭の10秒ほどで自分の意見とその理由を含むスピーチ構成を無駄なく伝え，聞き手の気をそらさない工夫がある。トピックに対して反対の立場から，紙媒体のメディアについて①必要とする人は多く発行部数もまだ多い，②知名度も高くネットを含む多くのニュースの発信源である，③信頼度と質で他に勝っている，という3点からその優位性を主張している。冒頭で I think it would be an exaggeration ... としているように，新しいメディアによる影響は認めつつも「破壊」は言い過ぎではないか，という一貫した立場を取っている。

3. Is a society free of crime an unattainable goal?

Crime has been around as long as human civilization, and I think that, unfortunately, while it can be reduced and controlled, it can never be eliminated. The most important reason is that science has shown that criminal behavior is built into some people's brains. Many people may hope, for example, that social programs can reform criminals. However, due to people having a fixed nature, it is actually impossible to manipulate people into acting in ways that coincide with society's idealized behavior. Secondly, there is a huge amount of conflict between people with different politics, religions, and cultures these days. Because of this, there will always be some people who feel the only solution to their problems is violence, and that explains the constant threat of terrorism. Since ideological and cultural conflict has existed throughout all of human history, the crimes that stem from this will never disappear. Lastly, I'd like to discuss inequality in modern society. Poverty has always been a major cause of crime. As the gap between rich and poor increases, it seems certain that not having enough income will cause people to commit more crimes. When you look at all of these factors together, eliminating crime completely cannot ever be achieved.

解説 「無犯罪社会は達成不可能な目標か」

自分の意見を表明する前に人類史における犯罪について言及したことで視野の広さを感じさせる。このようにスピーチの最初で聞き手の心をぐっとつかめると効果的だ。トピックを肯定する立場から「犯罪は減らせても完璧になくすことは不可能」を前提に，以下の3点を理由としている：①科学的見地から犯罪性は一部の人間の本質である，②複雑化する社会の中で思想や文化の衝突は避けられず暴力が解決策となってしまう場合も多い，③貧富の差が広がる中で貧困層による犯罪は避けられない。客観的で論理性の高い優れたスピーチなのでお手本にしたい。

4. Has the traditional five-day workweek become outdated in the modern world?

These days, there are a lot of reports in the media about four-day workweeks, and I think they're very likely to become a reality in the near future. In this speech, I'd like to share my thoughts about why five-day workweeks are outdated. One very important reason is technology. Thanks to AI and robots, many things that once had to be done by humans can now be done by technology. This means that workers can maintain their productivity without working as many hours. Next, reducing energy consumption is imperative in modern society, and four-day workweeks can contribute to this. When workers don't have to commute as often, fossil fuel use is reduced. Additionally, if companies can close down one extra day per week, it reduces electricity use as well. Finally, society is placing much more importance on work-life balance these days. Five-day workweeks make it harder for people to spend time with their friends or family, so more workers are demanding an increase in their leisure time. Furthermore, many studies have shown that work-life balance is important for workers' physical and mental health. Based on technological advances, the environmental benefits, and the advantages in terms of work-life balance, I feel that four-day workweeks are definitely going to replace five-day ones.

解説 「伝統的な週5日勤務は現代社会では時代遅れか」

トピックに対して賛成の立場から挙げている3つの理由は，①テクノロジーによる効率性の向上，②通勤を減らすことによる省エネへの貢献，そして③ワークライフバランスの重要性，である。このスピーチの冒頭部分で使っている I'd like to share my thoughts about why ～「自分がなぜ～と思うのかをお伝えしたい」という表現は，押し付けがましくなく洗練された言い回しなので覚えておくことをお勧めする。また，最後の結論部分で簡潔に3つの理由をまとめているところも，基本のテクニックとはいえ忘れがちなことなのでぜひ参考にしたい。

5. Can the technology gap between developed and developing nations ever be eliminated?

The technology gap between developed and developing nations is a serious problem, but, fortunately, I think it is solvable due to globalization, climate change awareness, and the portability of technology. The main reason is globalization. In the past, when nations created new technologies, governments and businesses were able to control their spread. Now, however, science and the economy have become globally connected, so there is much more transfer of technologies internationally. Second, increased awareness of the climate change crisis has made technology-sharing a top priority for many developed countries. It has been recognized that all nations require advanced technologies to work together in keeping global warming under control. To this end, many governmental, technological and non-profit organizations are working hard to ensure that technologies are spread where they are needed the most. A third reason is that technology itself is becoming much more portable. Devices like smartphones and laptop computers can easily be carried anywhere in the world, no matter how isolated an area is. This miniaturization has helped billions of people get their hands on various technologies, and they will be able to use them to develop new technologies of their own. As you can see, I'm very optimistic about closing the technology gap due to globalization, climate change awareness, and the portability of technology.

解説 「先進国と発展途上国の間のテクノロジー格差は埋められるか」

トピックに対し，①グローバリゼーションによる技術移転，②地球温暖化に対応するための地球規模の技術共有の必要性，③デバイスの携帯化による技術の拡散，の3点から，格差解消は可能であるとしている。3つに共通するのは「グローバル化による技術の透明化と普遍化」だが，それをさらに具体的に落とし込むことで独立した理由にして発話を充実させている。選んだトピックに対し，1つの大きな理由しか思い付かない場合，できるだけ具体的なものに分けてみるとこのスピーチのように発話量をぐっと伸ばせるので試してみよう。

2021-1

一次試験
筆記解答・解説　　p.58〜76

一次試験
リスニング解答・解説　　p.77〜104

二次試験
面接解答・解説　　p.105〜108

解 答 一 覧

一次試験・筆記

1
(1)	3	(10)	1	(19)	3
(2)	2	(11)	2	(20)	1
(3)	4	(12)	3	(21)	4
(4)	4	(13)	2	(22)	1
(5)	2	(14)	1	(23)	3
(6)	3	(15)	1	(24)	3
(7)	2	(16)	4	(25)	2
(8)	1	(17)	4		
(9)	1	(18)	2		

2
(26)	4	(29)	1
(27)	2	(30)	4
(28)	3	(31)	2

3
(32)	1	(35)	4	(38)	4
(33)	3	(36)	3	(39)	3
(34)	2	(37)	2	(40)	1
				(41)	3

4　解答例は本文参照

一次試験・リスニング

Part 1
No. 1	2	No. 5	4	No. 9	3
No. 2	3	No. 6	1	No.10	3
No. 3	2	No. 7	4		
No. 4	3	No. 8	3		

Part 2
No.11	4	No.15	1	No.19	2
No.12	1	No.16	3	No.20	2
No.13	2	No.17	2		
No.14	3	No.18	3		

Part 3
No.21	2	No.23	3	No.25	4
No.22	3	No.24	4		

Part 4　No.26　1　│　No.27　3

一次試験・筆記 1　問題編 p.42〜44

(1) ─ **解答 3**

[訳] 携帯電話は現代社会において常に身近にある存在になった。ほとんどの人は，携帯電話のない暮らしを想像できないかもしれない。

[語句] 1「留め金」　2「(就労などの) 期間」
3「定着したもの」　4「破裂」

[解説] 動詞 fix「〜を固定する」から連想されるように，本来 fixture は流し台や便器など「建物内に固定された備品」を意味するが，問題文のように，ある状況や時代などに「定着したもの［人］，いつもそこにある存在」の意味でも用いられる。

(2) ─ **解答 2**

[訳] コリンには車の代金を一括で支払うだけのお金がなかったので，2年間月々800ドルの分割払いで完済した。

[語句] 1「性質，気質」　2「分割払いの1回分」
3「(法律の) 制定」　4「思案，熟考」

[解説] 名詞 installment は動詞 install とは意味上のつながりがないので，単独で覚えておく必要がある。「(連続小説・連続番組などの) 1回分」という意味もある。

(3) ─ **解答 4**

[訳] メラニーが上司に賃上げを求めたとき，自信なさげな口調から，彼女がいかに緊張しているか明らかだった。

[語句] 1「けばけばしい」　2「陽気な」
3「尊大な」　4「自信のない」

[解説] nervous だったということは，自分の要求が受け入れられるかどうか不安で，diffident「自信のない，おずおずした」話し方だったと考えられる。

(4) ─ **解答 4**

[訳] その教派は，信者が一緒に住みすべてを共有することのできる農村地域に生活共同体を設立した。私的所有は一切認められなかった。

[語句] 1「挽歌(ばんか)」　2「前兆」　3「貯蔵所」　4「生活共同体」

[解説] 第1文の where 以下と第2文がそのまま commune「生活共同体，コミューン」の定義になっている。動詞 commune「親しく語らう」とは発音が違うので確認しておこう。

(5) ─ **解答 2**

[訳] その有名な記者は，別のジャーナリストの仕事を剽窃(ひょうせつ)したことで首になった。彼の記事は，その別のジャーナリストの記事とほとんどまったく

58

同じだった。
- 語句 1「〜を和らげる」 2「〜を剽窃する」
  3「〜に予防接種をする」 4「(困難などが)〜につきまとう」
- 解説 他人の文章やアイデアなどを盗んで自分のものとして発表することをplagiarize「〜を剽窃する，盗用する」と言う。名詞 plagiarism「剽窃，盗用」も覚えておきたい。

(6) — 解答 **3**
- 訳 地元の鉄鋼工場が閉鎖されてしまったので，かつてにぎわった町の市街地には営業していない商店が立ち並んでいる。ほとんどの店主は店を放棄した。
- 語句 1「修辞学の」 2「不安定な」 3「廃れた」 4「大望を抱く」
- 解説 工場が閉鎖して寂れた商店街の様子。defunct は，接頭辞 de-「反対，逆の」と function「機能」から，「機能していない」といった意味だと推測できる。

(7) — 解答 **2**
- 訳 国王をたたえて催された式典にその大使が出席しなかったことは，接受国から侮辱と見なされ，既に悪くなっていた関係をさらに悪化させた。
- 語句 1「解明」 2「侮辱」 3「袋小路」 4「最後通告」
- 解説 国と国の関係を悪化させたのだから，大使の行為は affront「侮辱」と見なされたことになる。affront には「〜を侮辱する」という動詞の意味もある。

(8) — 解答 **1**
- 訳 米国国境警備隊は，その脱獄囚がカナダへの国境を越えようとするところを何とか逮捕した。彼は直ちに刑務所に戻された。
- 語句 1「〜を逮捕する」 2「〜を略奪する」
  3「〜の地位を高める」 4「〜を順応させる」
- 解説 apprehend は catch，arrest「〜を逮捕する」の堅い語。なお，名詞 apprehension には「逮捕」の意味もあるが，むしろ「不安，心配」の意味で覚えておきたい。

(9) — 解答 **1**
- 訳 アンソニーは新しい仕事の初日を楽しんだ。雰囲気は和やかだったし，彼を温かく迎え入れるよう同僚たちは精一杯のことをした。
- 語句 1「和やかな，快適な」 2「錯乱した」
  3「ほんのわずかの」 4「本当とは思えない」
- 解説 genial は人や振る舞いが「親切な，愛想のいい」という意味だが，接頭辞 con-「共に」が付くと，「人を幸せな気分にさせる，一緒にいて楽しい」というニュアンスが加わり，人だけでなく場所・環境・仕事などについても用いられる。

(10) – 解答 ①

訳 A：さっき知ったんだけど，学校のオーケストラで第二バイオリンに降格されたよ。もっと練習しなきゃとはわかっていたんだけど。
B：うーん，がんばればきっと前のポジションを取り戻せるよ。

語句 1「格下げされる」 2「危うくされる」
3「反復される」 4「きちんとしまわれる」

解説 relegate A to B は「A を B (低い地位など) に降格する，格下げする」という意味。previous position は第一バイオリンだったことになる。

(11) – 解答 ②

訳 その政治家がソーシャルメディアで殺人脅迫を受けた後，そうした行為は非難に値し罰せられるべきだと多くの報道機関が述べた。

語句 1「数え切れない」 2「非難されるべき」
3「ぎこちない」 4「徳のある」

解説 reprehensible は，動詞 reprehend「〜を叱責する，非難する」の形容詞形。道徳的・倫理的に問題のあることについて多く用いられる。

(12) – 解答 ③

訳 自動で動くよう作られている車両の数が増加するにつれ，ドライバーは，車が自分で運転する間，自由にくつろいだり仕事を片付けたりできるようになる。

語句 1「無気力に」 2「わびしげに」 3「自律的に」 4「意味論的に」

解説 autonomously は国・組織・人などについて「自律的に，自立して」という意味で用いられることが多いが，機械にも使われる。「自動運転車」は autonomous vehicle [car] と言う。

(13) – 解答 ②

訳 公演の最後の夜，そのオペラ歌手は観客の喝采に酔いしれた。生涯最高のパフォーマンスをしたと彼女にはわかっていた。

語句 1「大声で叫んだ」 2「(称賛などに) 浸った」
3「まごついた」 4「踏みつけた」

解説 bask は bask in the sun「日光浴をする」といった使い方が基本だが，問題文のようにも用いられる。太陽の心地よいぬくもりを全身に受けるように，称賛を浴びて喜びを味わっているという意味合いである。

(14) – 解答 ①

訳 種を植える前には，有効期限を確認することが大切だ。種が古過ぎれば，その多くが発芽しない可能性が高い。

語句 1「芽を出す」 2「〜を未然に防ぐ」
3「(剣などで) 突く」 4「(法律など) を廃止する」

解説 種が古ければ，芽が出ないかもしれない。sprout は，「大量に出現する，急速に成長する」という意味も重要。その意味ではしばしば up を伴う。

(15) – 解答 ①

訳 A：とても美しい夜ね！　あそこにあるあの星座の名前は何？
B：あれはオリオン座。中央に並んでいる3つ星でわかるよ。

語句 1「星座」　2「大量出国」　3「教義」　4「救済」

解説 語幹 stella は「星」の意味で，stellar「星の」という形容詞もある。constellation は，「（有名人などの）一団，（関連あるものの）集まり」という意味も覚えておきたい。

(16) – 解答 ④

訳 公式報告書によると，いくつかの外国政府が民主主義を転覆させるためにインターネットを利用していた。報告書は，有権者に影響を与えようとさまざまな人気のあるウェブサイトに掲載されたフェイクニュース記事を示した。

語句 1「唾液を（過度に）分泌する」　2「（重い物）を持ち上げる」
3「～をなだめる」　4「（政府など）を打倒する」

解説 subvert は，革命やクーデターのように暴力・武力を用いるのではなく，秘密活動を通じて，あるいは問題文のように情報を操作するなどして，間接的に既成の体制を転覆させることを言う。

(17) – 解答 ④

訳 ロデリックは去年自動車事故に遭ったが，相手の運転手の過失だったので，幸い損害に対する責任は一切なかった。

語句 1「影響されない」　2「暗示する」
3「触知できない」　4「責任がある」

解説 liable for ～ は「～に対して（法的に）責任がある」という意味。名詞は liability「（法的）責任」だが，それぞれ多義語なのでほかの意味も確認しておこう。

(18) – 解答 ②

訳 新しい国立博物館の開会式の来賓は，フォーマルな服装を着用しなければならなかった。ジーンズとTシャツ姿の少数の人たちは，入り口で入館を拒否された。

語句 1「美人コンテスト」　2「服装」
3「話し方」　4「摩滅」

解説 attire は clothes, clothing「服装」の堅い語で，改まった服装に用いることが多い。動詞を使った be attired in ～「～に身を包んでいる」も覚えておきたい。

(19) – 解答 ③

訳 その子供には年少のころから，他人が考えていることを言い当てる不思議な能力があった。そのようなものはそれまで見たことがないと教師たちは言った。

語句 1「衝動的な」　2「牧歌的な」　3「奇怪な」　4「非常に不快な」
解説 uncanny は, 理屈では説明できない信じ難いことについて用いる形容詞。ややニュアンスは違うが, unearthly, preternatural などの類義語も確認しておこう。

(20) - 解答 ①

訳 その俳優は最近, 最新映画で演じた役で万人の称賛と数々の賞を受け, 今やキャリアの絶頂にある。

語句 1「頂点」　2「想像の産物」　3「逆戻り」　4「渦」
解説 pinnacle は「(教会の) 小尖塔, (山の) 尖峰」から転じて, 比喩的に「(成功・人生などの) 頂点, 絶頂」の意味でも用いられる。

(21) - 解答 ④

訳 上司は枝葉末節にこだわり過ぎだ, とレザは思っている。いつも上司がささいで取るに足りない細部について話し合いたがるので, 彼はフラストレーションを感じている。

語句 1「見苦しい」　2「憤った」
3「政治に無関心な」　4「枝葉末節を気にかける」
解説 pedantic は日本語の「ペダンティックな, 学問や知識をひけらかす」と違い,「枝葉末節にこだわる」が最も一般的な意味。

(22) - 解答 ①

訳 会議は正午までには終わるはずだったが, 午後1時半になってもまだ続いていた。そのころには, ほとんどの人はとてもおなかがすいていた。

語句 1「終わる」　2「大金をしぶしぶ払う」
3「(靴など) を履き慣らす」　4「あふれ出る」
解説 文脈から, 空所には「終わる」という意味の句動詞が入るとわかる。wind up は, 特に会議・演説・協議などが「終わる」場合に用いられる。

(23) - 解答 ③

訳 新総理大臣の経済政策は, インフレを抑え込むことに重点を置いている。可及的速やかに物価を制御すると彼は約束した。

語句 1「〜を打診する」　2「〜を縫い合わせる」
3「〜を厳しく抑制する」　4「〜をしまい込む」
解説 名詞 rein「(馬を御する) 手綱」から, 句動詞 rein in は「(人・事) を厳しく抑える」という意味になる。名詞を用いた keep a tight rein on 〜 も同じ意味。

(24) - 解答 ③

訳 刑事は殺人の実行犯が誰かわかるまで, 数カ月を費やして事件を巡る状況を掘り下げた。

語句 1「(文章・言葉で)〜を攻撃する」　2「〜の向きを変える」
3「〜を探る」　4「〜に備える」

> **解説** dig は「掘る」が基本の意味。dig into ～ は比喩的に，情報をつかんだり秘密を暴いたりするために「～を探る，探求する」という意味で用いられる。

(25) – 解答

> **訳** A：カーロス，今年の夏，休みを取る日にちは決めた？ そろそろ私たちの休暇の予定を立てられたらと思うんだけど。
> B：まだなんだよね。明日上司と話して，それから決めるよ。

> **語句** 1「尻込みする」
> 2「～を決定する」
> 3「(部屋など) から家具などを取り去る」
> 4「尻込みする」

> **解説** settle on ～ は，選択肢の中から「～を [に] 決める，選ぶ」こと。settle on a date「日にちを決定する」のように選択のテーマを提示する使い方と，settle on April 1st「4月1日に決定する」のように具体的な選択肢を示す使い方がある。

一次試験・筆記 2 問題編 p.45～47

全文訳 **ジェダイ教**

　SF映画『スター・ウォーズ』シリーズに基づくジェダイ教は，世界中に相当数の信奉者を持つポップカルチャー哲学である。その実践者が手本にしようとするのは，この映画に登場する一団の魂の戦士，すべての創造物の基礎を成し自分たちに超自然的能力を与えてくれるエネルギーである「フォース」という現象を自在に操る者たちだ。信奉者たちはジェダイ教を正当な宗教と見なしているが，ジェダイ教はフィクションに根ざす精神的実践としてしばしば嘲笑の的となる。しかし，信者たちはそれに応えて，ほかの宗教の多くの信者がそれらの宗教の起源すべてを文字どおりに受け取っているわけではない，と指摘する。主要な宗教は道徳的教訓や精神的教訓を伝えるために一般的に物語を用いるが，こうした物語には，例えば言葉を話す動物といった空想的な要素がしばしば含まれており，実際の歴史上の出来事を述べたものではないことを強く示唆している。だがこのことがそうした宗教にとって必ずしも不名誉とはならないのと同じように，フィクションに出自を持つことがジェダイ教の正当性を左右すべきではない，とジェダイ教の実践者たちは感じている。

　しかし，映画に基づく哲学を信奉することは，皮肉な状況を引き起こすこともある。ジェダイ教の場合，信奉者たちは，衣装や模造武器といった装備類に相当な金額を熱心に投資することでよく知られている。映画の多くの要素は関連商品の購入を促すよう意図的に作られていると論じることもできるが，そうした振る舞いは，映画で詳述されている物質的財産の過剰な所有の禁止に反するように見える。ほとんどの信奉者はこの矛

盾をあっさり無視している。リサイクルなどの対策を取って所有物を減らそうと試みる人も確かにいるのだが。

　公的な認知を得ることは，ジェダイ教に困難をもたらしている。英国では，免税資格の申請が，ジェダイ教はまとまりも信仰の統一的体系も持たないという根拠で却下された。だが公的に（宗教としての）指定を獲得することがかなわずとも，ジェダイ教は，西洋において宗教それ自体の受け取られ方が変化していることの証左である。西洋文化は，例えば仏教のように，多くの西洋人には容易にそれとわかる神という概念を持たないかもしれない，あるいはキリスト教に見られるタイプの崇拝を持たない東洋の宗教の影響を受けてきているので，宗教的慣行を特徴付けて正当とするのに用いられるような明確な境界線を引くのは困難になっている。評論家はしばしば，ジェダイ教は，権威主義的で高度に体系化された組織の衰退と，信者の個人的充足感に焦点を当てる集団の台頭の双方を例証するものだと説明する。

　　語句　emulate「～を見習う」，underlie「～の基礎を成す」，anchored in ～「～にしっかり根を下ろした」，ridicule「あざけり，嘲笑」，discredit「～の信用を傷つける」，paraphernalia「装備，道具」，purposely「故意に」，expound「～を詳細に説明する」，inconsistency「矛盾，不一致」，tax-exempt「免税の」，designation「指定，選定」，legitimize「～を正当とする」，exemplify「～を例証する」，authoritarian「権威主義の」，fulfillment「充足感」

(26)　解答　**4**

解説　空所文の however から，以下ではジェダイ教への嘲笑に対する反論が書かれていると考えられる。空所の次の文では，信奉者がジェダイ教の正当性を主張する根拠として，主要な宗教の教えに空想的な要素が含まれている事実が挙げられている。つまり，**4** のように，宗教の起源は文字どおりに受け取られるべきものではなく，フィクションが含まれる点において多くの宗教とジェダイ教は同列だ，とジェダイ教の信者は指摘していることになる。

(27)　解答　**2**

解説　第2段落で述べられているのは，映画は過度の物質的所有を戒める内容なのに，ジェダイ教信者が映画の関連グッズを大量に購入している矛盾した現状である。**2** がこれを ironic situations「皮肉な状況」とまとめている。

(28)　解答　**3**

解説　西洋における何の証拠なのかを考える。続く文では，東洋の宗教の影響を受けた西洋文化において宗教の正当性が揺らいでいることが述べられ，最後の文では，権威主義から個人主義への移行が取り上げられている。つまり，**3** のように，西洋では宗教観それ自体が変化していることになる。

> 全文訳　ウェブスター第3版

　米国で最も著名な辞書制作会社メリアム・ウェブスター社が1961年に『ウェブスター新国際辞典第3版』を出版したとき，この辞書が現代にとって画期的な参照ツールとして迎えられることを同社は期待した。言語学の当時新しいトレンドに影響された『ウェブスター第3版』は，英語が日常生活において普通の人々によって実際にどのように書かれ話されているかに焦点を当てる，革新的な「記述主義的」アプローチを採用した。しかし批判的な人たちは，この辞書の著者たちは無責任な振る舞いをしたと非難した。辞書は「規範的」でなければならないと彼らは主張した。規範的とは，辞書の役割は正しい用法と発音に関して権威を持って判断することだ，ということである。規範主義の放棄により英語は転落の一途をたどり言語学的無秩序状態に陥りつつある，と苦情を言う人すらいた。彼らが特に激怒したのは，ain'tのような俗語が是認されるとされたことで，『ウェブスター第3版』は，ain'tは「多くの教養ある話し手によって……口語で用いら」れていると主張した。

　しかし，『ウェブスター第3版』は辞書に対するアメリカ人の姿勢に起因していたとも言える。辞書は1700年代の終盤から，高等教育を受けたエリートからと同じように，下層階級の人々からも十分に受け入れられていた。社会の周縁に追いやられ抑圧されたマイノリティーは，自分たちに禁じられた読み書きの力を獲得する道として辞書を用い，この国への移民は，辞書を言語的同化と文化的同化を補助する不可欠な学習ツールと見なしていた。『ウェブスター第3版』はこの平等主義的考え方を体現するもので，例えば，シェークスピアと聖書からだけでなくハリウッドの俳優などの非伝統的な出典からの文も活用し，利用しやすさと包摂性を一層強化した。

　表面的には，『ウェブスター第3版』がエリートと学者の間に引き起こした騒ぎは，ain'tのような語に「不正確」「語法に反する」といった見下した用語でラベルを付けるべきなのか，それとも「非標準」といったもっと当たり障りのない用語でラベルを付けるべきなのかに関する争いだった。だがもっと深いレベルでは，1960年代に起きたフェミニズム運動の拡大と若者による権威の拒否が例証するように，善悪に関する絶対的理念が徐々に消失し順応への圧力が衰えつつあった根源的な文化的転換を反映していた。したがって，そうした運動の文脈で考えれば，『ウェブスター第3版』は言語学の分野における先駆的な仕事であるだけでなく，社会的変化を反映したものでもある。

> 語句　groundbreaking「草分け的な」, descriptivist「記述主義的な」, prescriptive「規範的な」, authoritative「権威のある」, pronouncement「宣告, 判断」, abandonment「放棄」, prescriptivism「規範主義」, slippery slope「先行き不安な状態」, irate「激怒した」, endorsement「承認, 是認」, cultivated「教養のある」, marginalize「〜を主流から外す」, oppress「〜を抑圧する」, epitomize「〜の典型である」, egalitarian「平等主義の」, nontraditional「非伝統的な」, inclusivity「包摂性, 誰にでも開かれていること」, disparaging「軽蔑する」, nonstandard「非標準的な」

(29) – 解答 ①

解説 空所には,『ウェブスター第3版』を批判する内容が入る。空所前後の記述によると, 辞書は本来規範的でなければならないのに『ウェブスター第3版』は記述主義的アプローチを採用し, 英語を無秩序状態に陥れている, というのが批判者の主張。それを irresponsible「無責任な」という語でまとめた **1** が正解である。

(30) – 解答 ④

解説 空所後を読むと, 当時米国ではエリートだけでなく下層階級の人々も平等に辞書を利用するようになっており,『ウェブスター第3版』の大衆的路線はその状況に対応するものだったことがわかる。それに合致する選択肢は **4** のみ。

(31) – 解答 ②

解説 空所文の such movements は, 前の文の the growing feminist movement and the rejection of authority by young people を指す。その文によると,『ウェブスター第3版』を巡る騒動はそうした運動が例証する根源的な社会的転換を反映していたのだから, この辞書は「社会的変化の反映」だとすると文脈に合う。

一次試験・筆記 3　問題編 p.48～56

全文訳　顕示的消費

　需要に関する経済法則によると, 物品の価格とその需要には負の相関関係がある。したがって, 企業が製品を大幅に値上げすれば, もっと手ごろな価格で同等の製品を供給する競合他社に切り替える動機を消費者に与えるはずである。しかし1899年に, 経済学者ソースティン・ヴェブレンは「顕示的消費」という用語を作り, 社会の特定の層はある一定の製品の市場価値には無関心で, 自らの富と卓越を誇示する機会を与えてくれる物なら何にでも惜しみなくお金を使うものだと論じた。これらの商品──希少な高級ワインや手作りの腕時計といった物品──は, 以後「ヴェブレン財」として知られるようになった。普通の消費財と違い, ヴェブレン財の値上げは, かなりの値上げであっても, 富裕な消費者への販売量には悪影響を与えないし, かえって訴求力を増すこともあるかもしれない。ヴェブレンはウィリアム・ランドルフ・ハーストやアンドリュー・カーネギーといったアメリカの大富豪を観察して理論の基礎としたのだが, 彼らの豪勢なコンサートホールと大邸宅と博物館は, いかなる実用的目的で建てられたにせよ, それと同じくらい所有者の富を反映させるために建てられたように見えた。そうした誇示は「常日ごろから自分と同類だと見なしている人たちより勝るよう促す」生得の欲望の表出だ, とヴェブレンは考えた。

　しかし, 顕示的消費は社会のほかの層でも観察されており, その層では, 豪勢さの明

らかな誇示は，購入者の実際の地位が持つ富を超えた富を暗に示している。そうした人たちにとって，ぜいたく品の購入は，自分がより高い社会階級の一員に見えるかもしれないように用いるツールと考えられている。経済学者の指摘によると，貧困から連想される恥辱を避けるため，人々は価格の変化などお構いなしに，明らかに富の指標となる物に散財する傾向がある。好例は，新興経済国がぜいたく品市場を動かす上で果たす役割である。ロシアや中国やサウジアラビアなどの成長市場の消費者は，米国や日本などの先進国より平均収入がかなり低いにもかかわらず，最近数十年で，ぜいたく品の売り上げを伸ばす必須の原動力になった，と経済学者は述べる。実際，経済学者が言うには，さほど裕福ではない消費者が富裕な人たちを手本にしようと，収入に見合わない支出をしてステータスシンボルを購入するのは普通のことである。

しかし，ヴェブレンの理論が描くイメージは不完全である。最近の研究によると，資産をひけらかす富裕な人々は経済的成熟の1つの段階を意味するもので，この明らかに節度を欠いた出費は，富の格差が縮小するにつれて徐々に消える傾向がある。個人や階級や国がより高いレベルの富を享受し出すと，多くのパターンの「非顕示的消費」が現れ始め，専用のサービスを利用できる権利がますます珍重され貴重になる。ぜいたく品はステータスシンボルとしてなお重要性らしきものをいくぶん保持するが，これらのサービスが支出に占める割合は次第に増えるようになり，自分磨きと排他性を優先するようになる。そういう事情なので，ライフコーチを雇ったり，高級ヘルスクリニックの会員になったり，完全招待制のイベントに参加したりといった経験の方が，単にデザイナーウォッチを所有することより，個人が所属する経済的階級をよく実証するものになるのである。

> 語句　coin「（新語）を作り出す」，unconcerned「無関心な」，lavishly「気前よく」，handcrafted「手作りの」，opulent「豪勢な」，affluence「富，裕福」，innate「生得の」，outdo「～に勝る」，opulence「豪勢さ」，stigma「汚名，恥辱」，splurge on ～「～に湯水のようにお金を使う」，case in point「適例」，emerging「新興の」，affluent「裕福な」，emulate「～を見習う」，flaunt「～をひけらかす」，sought-after「需要が多い」，semblance「見かけ，～らしさ」，prioritize「～を優先する」，exclusivity「排他性」

(32) – 解答　**1**

問題文の訳　「ヴェブレン財」についてわかることの1つは何か。

選択肢の訳
1　ヴェブレン財が一部の消費者に持つ人気は，商品それ自体の価格より，それらが意味する富の度合いによって定められる。
2　ヴェブレン財は頻繁に需要の変化を被るので，それらを生産する製造業者はしばしばかなりのリスクを冒して生産する。
3　それらの商品は価格が下がる時期を頻繁に経るので，格安品を探す消費者がしばしば引き寄せられる。
4　ヴェブレン財は品質が優れているので，普通の消費財よりも需要の法

21年度第1回　筆記

67

則に従う可能性が高い。

> 解説　第1段落第3文に，anything that provided opportunities to display their wealth and prominence というヴェブレン財の定義が書かれている。そして第5文から，富裕層は価格に関係なくヴェブレン財を買い続けることがわかる。これらの特徴に合致するのは **1**。**4** の「需要の法則に従う可能性が高い」が当てはまるのは普通の消費財の方である。

(33) – 解答 **3**

> 問題文の訳　この文章の記述によると，経済学者は以下の記述のどれと意見が一致する可能性が最も高いだろうか。

> 選択肢の訳
> 1　ぜいたく品を購入する傾向は，より高い社会階級につい最近上がった人たちの間で最も強い。
> 2　発展途上国の富裕な人々の方が，同じようなレベルの富を持つ先進国の人々より，ぜいたく品を手に入れやすい。
> 3　ぜいたく品を買う余裕がないにもかかわらず，低所得層の出身であるように見えるのを避けるためにぜいたく品を買う人たちがいる。
> 4　ぜいたく品は最初富裕層に非常に人気があっても，貧しい人々が購入し始めるとぜいたく品としての地位を失う。

> 解説　第2段落に，裕福ではない人たちの購買行動についての経済学者の考えが書かれている。第3文 Economists point out ... が **3** の内容とほぼ同じ。本文の avoid the stigma associated with poverty を選択肢では avoid appearing as though they are from a low-income background と言い換えている。

(34) – 解答 **2**

> 問題文の訳　この文章の筆者は，ソースティン・ヴェブレンの理論は以下のことを説明していないと示唆している。

> 選択肢の訳
> 1　社会のすべての層の人々がさらに高いレベルの富を蓄積するのを妨げる，最近の景気下降の循環。
> 2　地位を象徴するものとしてのぜいたく品の使用の衰退につながる，経済成長の結果としての金銭的繁栄の増大。
> 3　社会で富と地位を誇示する手段としてのぜいたく品を拒否する，すべての資産集団にわたりある割合で存在する人々。
> 4　より低い経済的階級の構成員が手に入れられる非顕示的ぜいたく品の販売促進がより普通の出来事になること。

> 解説　第3段落ではヴェブレンの理論が incomplete である理由が説明されている。社会がより豊かになると，富裕層でなくても買えるぜいたく品より，exclusive や exclusivity という語が示すように，利用者が限定された排他的なサービスが経済的階級を証明するものになる。これに合致するのは **2** である。

全文訳　化石燃料補助金

　2017年に各国政府が化石燃料企業に対し5.2兆ドルの補助金を交付したことを，国際通貨基金（IMF）の報告書が明らかにした。化石燃料関連の汚染が毎年数百万人の死の原因となっている証拠に照らして考えると，化石燃料の利用を支援することは倫理的に問題があるように思えるし，二酸化炭素排出量を減らすという各国政府の誓約に完全に反するようにも思える。しかし，補助金の総計が税前の補助金と税後の補助金両方を含む点において，この総計は誤解を招くものだ。前者はほとんどの人が「補助金」という語を聞いて思い浮かべるもの——生産コストを下げ，その結果消費者価格を引き下げることを目的に石油会社に支給される現金や，税の軽減措置といったものである。しかし，報告書に書かれた補助金の大半はさまざまな税後のタイプだ。これらは，私たちの化石燃料への依存の結果，納税者にとってさらなる重荷となるもので，石油流出事故の後始末の費用から交通渋滞と交通事故の増加に至るあらゆるものである。多数の批判的な人がIMFによる補助金の定義に異議を申し立て，そうしたコストをこの計算に含めるべきかどうかに関しては明らかに主観が大きく関与していると指摘する。税後の補助金を除外すれば金額は4,240億ドルとなり，最初の合計のほんの一部に減少する。

　税後の補助金を含めることは人を惑わすものだったかもしれないが，その社会的コストをより注意深く見ると不安になる。社会の多数の人は，化石燃料に基づくエネルギー消費がもたらす経済的恩恵と生活様式の恩恵から実際にメリットを得ているのだが，米国で毎年記録される約20万の大気汚染関連死者は，一部の人が払わざるを得ない不幸な代償を反映している。さらに，調査が示すところによると，化石燃料使用が結果的に個人の生活にどの程度プラスあるいはマイナスの影響をもたらすかには，人種的不均衡と社会経済的不均衡がある。例えば，研究によると，白人アメリカ人は自分たちが被るより17%多くの大気汚染の原因を作り出すが，一方黒人アメリカ人とヒスパニック系アメリカ人は，自分たちが原因となるより優に50%を超える大気汚染にさらされている。

　しかし，税後の補助金は間接的な性質であるが故に，税前の補助金より対処するのがずっと難しい。そして税前の補助金は世界中で減ってはいるのだが，撤廃はもろ刃の剣かもしれない。税前の補助金が消費者への直接の金銭的負担を減らすのは確かだから，撤廃すれば低所得世帯への圧迫が大きくなるだろうし，化石燃料よりさらに大量の汚染物質を放出するもっと安価な燃料を用いるよう，非常に貧しい人たちを追い込む場合もあるだろう。同時に，この補助金が奨励する活動の結果として，不釣り合いに多い苦悩と苦難を経験するのはまさにこれらの世帯なのである。各国政府にとってのより効果的な戦略は，より幅広い社会的コストに重点を置くことだ，と専門家は言う。例えば，化石燃料を採掘して生産する企業に，放出する排出物に対して課税し，そのお金を，それらの企業の活動から最も多くの影響を受ける人たちに再分配する新規構想があってもよい。そうすれば，低所得世帯への影響を軽減すると同時に，化石燃料産業にある程度の説明責任を課すことになるだろう。また，もっと重要なことかもしれないが，結果的に化石燃料の価格が上昇し，よりクリーンなエネルギー源の研究と開発に報奨金を出すことによって，化石燃料がもたらす被害の程度を軽減することになるだろう。

語句 pretax「税引き前の」, posttax「税引き後の」, handout「補助金」, tax break「税の軽減措置」, oil spill「石油流出（事故）」, subjectivity「主観（性）」, societal「社会の」, socioeconomic「社会経済的な」, disparity「不均衡」, double-edged sword「もろ刃の剣」, pollutant「汚染物質」, disproportionate「不釣り合いな」, redistribute「～を再分配する」, accountability「説明責任」, mitigate「～を軽減する, 和らげる」, incentivize「～に報奨金を出す」

(35) – 解答 ④

問題文の訳 この文章の筆者によると, 国際通貨基金が報告した補助金の総計は誤解を招くものである。なぜなら,

選択肢の訳
1 この組織が, 税後の補助金はそうあるべきだと自らが考える推計に直接基づいて税前の補助金の額を計算しているからである。
2 この補助金の総計が, 有害な温室効果ガスの排出量を削減するという各国政府の約束の将来的コストを考慮に入れていないからである。
3 税前の補助金は, 生産コストを下げたり, より安価な燃料コストを一般大衆に渡したりする上でしばしば有用ではないことを, この組織が無視しているからである。
4 この補助金の総計は, 何をもって補助金とするのかという通念に合致しない, 納税者が払うさまざまなコストの大きな部分を含んでいるからである。

解説 第1段落では補助金を pretax と posttax に分けているが, 語の意味にとらわれて考え過ぎることがないようにしたい。pretax は第4文に書かれているように, 一般にイメージされる補助金のこと。posttax は第6文で the consequence of our dependence on fossil fuels と説明され具体例が2つ挙げられていることから, 化石燃料を使用することで納税者が間接的に負担しなければならない環境的・社会的コストだと考えられる。したがって **4** が正解。

(36) – 解答 ③

問題文の訳 第2段落で, この文章の筆者は化石燃料について何を明らかにしているか。

選択肢の訳
1 化石燃料使用の現在の流れが続けば, より多くの化石燃料を消費する人たちが最も深刻な健康への影響を受けることになる。
2 化石燃料を燃やすことから帰結する大衆へのマイナスの影響の最悪のものは, 大気汚染とは無関係であることがわかっている。
3 マイノリティーが化石燃料補助金から受ける恩恵と, 彼らが化石燃料使用から被るマイナスの影響の間には, 不均衡が存在する。
4 一部のマイノリティーが化石燃料を消費する特定のやり方は, 化石燃料が最終的にもたらす汚染の量にほとんど影響しない。

解説 第2段落では, 化石燃料について2つのことが述べられている。1つは,

化石燃料は恩恵ももたらすが，大気汚染により多くの人が亡くなっていること。もう1つは，人種や社会経済的背景によって，化石燃料が与える影響に不均衡があること。後者が**3**の内容と一致する。本文で例として挙げている Black and Hispanic Americans を選択肢では minorities とまとめ，disparities を imbalance と言い換えている。

(37) – 解答 ②

問題文の訳 以下のどれが，専門家が推薦する戦略の一部である可能性が高いか。

選択肢の訳
1 化石燃料企業に払う税後の補助金を撤廃し，空気の質の改善に取り組む産業にそのお金を向け直すこと。
2 低所得世帯が確実に金銭的な利益を得られるようにすると同時に，化石燃料企業が，自分たちが引き起こす汚染の責任を直接負うようにさせる政策を導入すること。
3 クリーンエネルギー産業の企業に税前の補助金を交付し，低所得世帯がクリーンエネルギーをより手に入れやすくすることに対してそれらの企業に褒賞を与えること。
4 税前の補助金のいかなる削減も，税後の補助金の減額が実行されるのと同じ割合で確実に実行されるようにすること。

解説 第3段落半ばの Experts say ... 以下に，専門家の意見が書かれている。具体的な提案は，化石燃料企業の排出物に課税して汚染に対する責任を負わせ，そのお金を低所得世帯に分配すること。本文の impose ... industry を hold ... responsible と言い換え，低所得世帯へのお金の分配を benefit financially と表した **2** が正解である。

全文訳 **植物の知性**

　中枢神経系——それもとりわけ脳——が知性の必要条件であることを科学者は当然視し，思考することができるのは人間と動物だけだと昔から主張してきた。この見解に基づき，知性の研究は，IQテストなど，筆記問題に答えたり物理パズルを解いたり行動によって記憶術を実証したりといったことをする能力の客観的測定に枠組みが限定されてきた。

　しかし，植物神経生物学として知られる新興分野の支持者は，中枢神経系の欠如は必ずしも植物が何らかの形態の知性を持つ妨げにはならないと論じて，この科学的総意に異を唱えてきた。植物にある通常の生物学的・化学的・遺伝的メカニズムでは，植物が示す非常に高度な幅広い行動の数々を十分に説明できない，と彼らは主張する。したがって，植物は単に置かれた環境における受動的要素なのではなく，実際は，適切な反応を組織的に導き出すために，多様な環境要因からの刺激を感知し評価することができるのだ，と唱道者たちは主張する。しかし，そうした主張は科学界から懐疑で，それどころかあからさまな敵意で迎えられてきた。

　西オーストラリア大学のモニカ・ガグリアーノの研究は，触れられたり邪魔されたり

すると防御するように葉をくるりと丸めることで知られる植物オジギソウを用いて，植物神経生物学の物議をかもす主張の一部が正しいことを証明しようと試みた。ガグリアーノの実験の内容は，毎週何度か，50以上のオジギソウを制御された無害な落下する動きにさらすことだった。時がたつと，植物の一部が防御する反応をしなくなったことに彼女は気付いた。これは，危険が差し迫ったものではないと植物が学習したことを示していた。落とされることに植物が反応しなかったことの原因が疲労かそれに類することにあるかもしれない可能性を排除するため，ガグリアーノは植物の一部を突然揺さぶる動きにさらした。落とされることへの順応は緩やかだったのに，揺さぶる動きは直ちに植物を通常の防御行動へと戻した。再び落下する動きにさらすと，植物は以前学習したことを「思い出した」。これは，植物が経験に基づいて，落とされることへの反応を意図的に変えていることを示唆していた。

　こうした研究は，植物は脳を持たないかもしれないが，環境的刺激に対する反応における植物の行動は脳のような情報処理システムの証拠だ，という主張の高まりを裏付けるものである。この説を支持する科学者たちは，生物学的レベルでは，動物の神経系に見られる化学信号伝達システムは植物にも確認されているとも述べている。

　植物の知性という考えに裏付けを与える研究が増えているにもかかわらず，この分野の一層の調査を提唱するガグリアーノなどの人たちは，そうした研究の妥当性を疑う人たちから批判を浴びている。ガグリアーノの実験に直接反応する一部の人たちは，植物を落下させることは自然界の普通の出来事ではなく，したがって，実験で用いた植物が行ったとガグリアーノが言う種類の学習の確かな誘因と考えることはできない，と論じる。そうではなく，ガグリアーノの植物の行動は進化的適応の帰結，つまり多くの世代にわたって自然がプログラムした自動的反応なのだ，と彼らは説明する。それに応えてガグリアーノは，自分が実験で用いた刺激は人工的なものだったのだから，置かれた自然環境では生じないことに植物が進化的適応を経ることができたなどということは理にかなわない，と指摘する。植物の反応が生得のものだったはずがないという彼女の主張は，彼女が用いた植物の中に，ほかより速く学習したものがあったことからもさらに裏付けられる。

　イタリアのフィレンツェにある国際植物ニューロバイオロジー研究所の所長ステファノ・マンクーゾは，この論争に別の方法で取り組んでいる。彼の研究は植物の根の異常な電気的活動量と酸素消費量を明らかにしたが，これはもしかすると「根脳」の存在を暗に示しているのかもしれない。植物神経生物学の強固な主張者であるマンクーゾは，植物の知性は群れ行動に観察される分散型知性に似ていると考えている。例えば鳥の群れでは，鳥は，飛ぶときは互いに適度な距離を保つといった，集団の集合的利益にかなうルールに従う。このタイプの集合的行動は，植物の個々の根がその生物全体のためになるよう協調して振る舞うやり方と似ていなくもないのではないか，と彼は言う。

　植物神経生物学を巡る論戦は，知性に関するより広範な論争を再び活発化させている。マンクーゾによると，私たちが知性をほかの生物に適用したがらないのは，心理的根拠によるバイアスのせいかもしれない。彼の意見では，例えば私たちは，自分たちが作る

機械の人工知能という考えを受け入れることができるが，それは，機械が私たちに奉仕するものであり，私たちの手に成る創造物だからである。それに引き換え，私たちが植物の知性に対して抱く敵意は，植物のない世界は人間にとって破滅的なものになるだろうが，一方その逆は植物にとっておそらく問題にならないだろう，という暗たんたる認識の現れなのかもしれない，と彼は考えている。マンクーゾの視点を考慮すると，植物の知性は細胞間で交換される電気信号の結果でしかないと単純化することは，不当に尊大だと考えられるかもしれない。

> 語句　prerequisite「必要条件」, proponent「支持者」, emerging「新興の」, neurobiology「神経生物学」, preclude *A* from *do*ing「A が〜するのを阻む」, skepticism「懐疑心」, validate「〜の正しさを立証する」, mimosa「オジギソウ」, discount「〜を軽視する，勘定に入れない」, mounting「増えている」, ascribe *A* to *B*「A を B に帰する」, innate「生得の」, analogous to 〜「〜に似た」, reignite「〜に再び火をつける」, somber「暗い，暗たんとした」, simplification「単純化」, dismissive「尊大な，軽蔑的な」

(38) – 解答 ④

問題文の訳　なぜ植物神経生物学は科学界で物議をかもしているのか。

選択肢の訳
1 植物神経生物学は，人間の被験者の知性レベルを確定するために科学者が用いるのとまさに同じ手法をほかの生物にも応用すべきだと主張している。
2 植物神経生物学は，植物の行動に観察される生物学的・化学的・遺伝的プロセスは人間と動物のプロセスとは作用の仕方が異なると提唱している。
3 植物神経生物学は，人間の中枢神経系の基礎となっていると以前は思われていたメカニズムが，科学者がずっと考えてきたようには機能しないと暗に示している。
4 植物神経生物学は，知性の背後にある根本的メカニズムに関して，大多数の科学者が抱いている考えに反対する主張を行っている。

解説　知性を持つのは人間と動物だけというのが従来からの説（第 1 段落）だが，植物神経生物学は植物にも何らかの知性があると唱えて科学界から疑問視されている（第 2 段落）という大まかな流れが理解できれば，**4** が正解だとわかる。植物神経生物学は，生物学的・化学的・遺伝的メカニズムだけでは植物の行動を説明できないと言っているだけであり，**2** のように植物は人間と動物とは異なると主張しているわけではない。

(39) – 解答 ③

問題文の訳　モニカ・ガグリアーノがオジギソウで行った実験が示唆するのは，

選択肢の訳
1 この植物は脅威を突き付けられたときに遅れた防御行動を示したのだから，危険に素早く反応することはできない，ということである。

2 記憶したことに基づいて行動できるこの植物の能力は，いかなる時においてもこの植物が感じている疲労の程度に大きく左右される，ということである。
3 この植物は，さまざまなタイプの感覚入力に対して異なる反応を示すのみならず，それらを区別する能力を証明している，ということである。
4 揺さぶられることに対するこの植物の反応の仕方は一貫していなかったのだから，学習速度は種の間で同じではない，ということである。

解説 ガグリアーノの実験は第3段落で詳述されている。オジギソウを上から落とす実験を繰り返すと，次第に葉を丸める防御行動を取らないものが現れた。次に揺さぶるという別の動きには直ちに防御行動を示したが，再び落とすと，学習したことを思い出し，防御行動を取らなかった。落とす・揺さぶるという動きを sensory input と表した **3** が正解。ガグリアーノはオジギソウの反応に fatigue が関与しないことを証明しようとしたのだから，**2** は誤りである。

(40) – 解答 ①

問題文の訳 この文章によると，ガグリアーノは以下の記述のどれと意見が一致する可能性が最も高いだろうか。

選択肢の訳
1 自然界では経験しない刺激を用いて植物をテストすることは，植物の反応が実際に学習に基づいていることを証明する助けとなる。
2 植物が何世代もかけて適応するやり方は，ほとんどの研究者が考えているよりも，人間が学習するやり方に実は似ている。
3 植物は神経系を有しているという科学者間の総意は，植物の行動を動物の行動と比較することを十分に正当化する。
4 植物の情報処理システムは人間のものよりずっとゆっくりと働くが，だからと言って必ずしも劣っているわけではない。

解説 第5段落に，ガグリアーノへの批判とガグリアーノの反論が書かれている。批判者は，自然界では生じない手法を用いて得た植物の反応は学習ではなく進化的適応だと言うが，それに対しガグリアーノは，人工的な刺激に進化的に適応することはあり得ないし，植物の学習速度に違いがあったことからも，生得の反応とは言えないと主張する。**1** がガグリアーノの反論と一致する。

(41) – 解答 ③

問題文の訳 ステファノ・マンクーゾは植物の知性に関して暗に何と言っているか。

選択肢の訳
1 もし研究者が人間以外の動物を植物と比較することにすれば，植物神経生物学分野ははるかに急速に進歩するだろう。
2 人間と植物がさまざまな行動を練り上げるやり方は多少類似しているとはいえ，そのことが同じように知性に関連すると推定するのは無責任である。

3 植物における知性という考えに対する人間の態度は，私たちが植物と自分たちとの関係をどのように理解し合理化するかに関連するかもしれない。
4 植物の根と鳥の脳の電気的活動量が似ていることは，それらの作用の仕方も似ているかもしれないことを示唆する。

解説 最終段落のマンクーゾの主張によると，人間以外の生物に知性を認めたがらない考え方は心理的バイアスに基づく。それは，人間は植物なしでは生存できないが植物は人間なしでも構わないという認識が，人間が創造物の頂点に立つという考えと相いれないことから来る敵意である。それに合致するのは **3**。選択肢の rationalize は理屈を用いてそうした不都合な真実を隠そうとすることで，この文章では植物の知性を電気信号で説明しようとする尊大な態度を指す。

一次試験・筆記 4 問題編 p.56

解答例

Of the numerous foreign-policy tools used by governments to navigate globally contentious situations, economic sanctions are extremely effective for upholding laws and treaties, settling disagreements in an indirect manner, and even forging international support.

In cases where a country's actions violate international law, economic sanctions can yield effective results. Dictatorships, for example, typically rely on imported resources for their militaries and illegal activities. When these nations refuse calls to engage in diplomatic discussions, economic sanctions can be used to restrict the flow of specific resources and curb the proliferation of the offending activities.

Economic sanctions are also a nonconfrontational approach to resolving international disputes. Some foreign-policy tools, such as military intervention or diplomatic sanctions, can exacerbate tensions by elevating the risk of armed warfare or shutting down crucial avenues of negotiation. Economic sanctions, however, avoid the use of force while still effecting a positive outcome.

Furthermore, economic sanctions can be instrumental in garnering multilateral support. The decision to levy economic sanctions is commonly regarded as a way for a country to reinforce its commitment to issues such as human rights. Such stances are often universally praised and can encourage other nations to follow suit.

　Strengthening solidarity on the international stage is no doubt a welcome benefit of economic sanctions, but in times when there is a need to enforce international law or foster peaceful resolutions, the true usefulness of such sanctions in foreign policy becomes particularly apparent.

トピックの訳　「経済制裁は役に立つ外交政策ツールか」

解説　全体の構成は，自分の立場を明示する導入の段落，3つの理由について論じる3つの段落，自分の立場を再確認する結論の段落の5段落という基本に則ったものである。経済制裁は extremely effective だとして，トピックに対する全面的な Yes. の立場を表明している。3つの理由としては，「法律と条約を守ること」「不和を間接的に解決すること」「国際的支持を築くこと」を挙げている。それぞれやや抽象的な言い回しだが，続く段落で具体的に論じられている。

　最初の理由については，独裁国家を例に挙げ，国際法を破るそうした国は輸入した資源を用いて軍事活動や違法活動をしているのだから，経済制裁を科すことでそうした資源の流入を止められるとしている。最初の段落で述べている laws and treaties を，ここでは international law とまとめている。2つ目の理由については，軍事的干渉や外交裁はむしろ緊張を悪化させる恐れがあり，経済制裁のように正面からの対決を避けるやり方の方が国際紛争の解決策として有効だとしている。nonconfrontational「対決姿勢ではない」という語が，「間接的に解決する」ことに相当する。そして3つ目の理由については，例えば人権問題への取り組みは普遍的に称賛される姿勢なので，そのような問題を理由とした経済制裁は国際的な支持を得やすいと述べている。

　結論の段落では，3つ目の理由を Strengthening solidarity on the international stage と言い換え，それが経済制裁の有効性それ自体を論じたものというより経済制裁によるメリットの考察である点を考慮して，ほかの2つの理由とは区別し，その2つの理由を言い換えた enforce international law と foster peaceful resolutions が経済制裁の有用性を真に示すものだと締めくくっている。

　反対の立場なら，食糧や医薬品など必需品の禁輸は相手国の国民を苦しめることになり人道主義的に問題がある，国連が経済制裁を決議したとしても抜け駆けをする国が出てくれば実効性が担保されない，経済制裁は対象国からの敵意や憎悪をあおる可能性があるのだから話し合いによる問題解決に勝るものはない，などの理由が考えられるだろう。

一次試験・リスニング Part 1 問題編 p.57〜58

No.1 - 解答 ②

スクリプト
★: So, Mrs. Rowlands, has the medicine I prescribed for your back pain last month made a difference?
☆: Honestly, Doctor, I've been reluctant to even try it.
★: Why?
☆: I read online that it can cause sleeplessness and irritability. I have so much trouble with insomnia that I'd rather put up with back pain than risk aggravating the problem.
★: Well, I've prescribed that medication to many patients, and none of them has ever experienced problems.
☆: I'd still feel better if you could give me something else.
Question: Why did Mrs. Rowlands not take the medicine?

全文訳
★: さて、ローランズさん、先月処方した腰痛の薬で少しはよくなりましたか?
☆: 本当のことを言うと、先生、使ってみたいという気持ちすら起きないんです。
★: どうしてですか?
☆: ネットで読んだんですが、不眠といらいらの原因になることがあるそうです。私は不眠症でとても苦労しているので、問題を悪化させるリスクを冒すくらいなら、腰痛は我慢しようと思うんです。
★: うーん、あの薬はたくさんの患者さんに処方してきましたが、問題があった人は1人もいませんよ。
☆: それでも、別の薬を出していただいた方がありがたいです。
質問: なぜローランズさんはその薬を服用しなかったのか。

選択肢の訳
1 腰痛が前よりひどくなくなった。
2 副作用が心配だった。
3 その薬は安全ではないかもしれないと医師がそれとなく言った。
4 その薬は腰痛に効かないと耳にした。

解説 女性の2つ目の発言の sleeplessness と irritability は薬の side effects「副作用」。続けて言っている insomnia が「不眠症」の意味だとわかれば、女性が副作用である sleeplessness を心配していると判断できる。

No.2 - 解答 ③

スクリプト
☆: Hi, Al. I haven't seen you for... well, since you left the company. Have you found another job yet?
★: Yes, I work for Plexar now. I miss you guys, but I'm much

　　　　happier there.
☆： Good for you. What makes Plexar so much better, besides the products?
★： That's just it. All my clients know we sell high-quality products, so they trust me. I get far fewer complaints than I did with MediaSavvy, and my sales volume's through the roof.
☆： I'll bet. Let me know if they have any openings in marketing, would you?
★： Sure, Linda. I will.

Question: What can be inferred about the man's previous job?

【全文訳】
☆： こんにちは，アル。久しぶり……えーと，あなたが会社を辞めて以来ね。もう別の仕事は見つかった？
★： うん，今はプレクサーで働いている。君たちに会えなくて寂しいけど，プレクサーにいる方がずっと幸せだよ。
☆： よかったわね。プレクサーの方がずっといいというのはどうしてなの，製品のほかに。
★： それが決め手なんだよ。うちが高品質の製品を売っていると僕の顧客はみんな知っているので，僕を信頼してくれる。苦情はメディアサビーのころよりはるかに少なくなったし，僕の売上額はうなぎ上りさ。
☆： そうでしょうね。マーケティングで求人があったら教えてもらえるかな。
★： いいよ，リンダ。そうするよ。

質問： 男性の前の仕事について何を推測できるか。

【選択肢の訳】
1　彼はスタッフとうまくいっていなかった。
2　社員の入れ替わりが激しかった。
3　彼は多くの苦情に対応しなければならなかった。
4　製品の品質がもっとよかった。

【解説】男性の発言の I miss you guys から，人間関係は良好だったと考えられるので，**1** は誤り。**2** についての話はない。新しい職場では I get far fewer complaints ... と言っているので，**3** が正解。品質がいいのは Plexar の方なので，**4** は誤りである。

No.3 — 解答 ②

【スクリプト】
☆： Mike, have you read this newsletter from Kate's school?
★： Not yet. Is there anything interesting?
☆： Well, it appears there's a proposal to open a snack shop on the school grounds. I don't like the sound of that.
★： Sounds convenient. But I know what you're getting at. It's related to the meeting last semester about healthier school meals, right?
☆： Exactly. What's the point of encouraging healthy eating habits if

there's a shop selling junk food at school?
- ★: Well, we don't know yet what control the school will have over it.
- ☆: True, but I'm not convinced it'll be much.

Question: What is the woman concerned about?

全文訳
- ☆: マイク，ケイトの学校からのこの学校便りは読んだ？
- ★: まだだけど，何か興味深いことが載っている？
- ☆: えー，学校の構内に軽食の店を開く提案があるみたい。なんだか気に入らないわ。
- ★: 便利そうじゃないか。だけど言いたいことはわかるよ。もっと健康にいい給食についての先学期の会議に関係があるんだよね？
- ☆: そのとおりよ。ジャンクフードを売る店が学校にあったら，健康的な食習慣を奨励する意味がどこにあるっていうの。
- ★: うーん，学校がその店をどれだけ管理できるかは，まだわからない。
- ☆: そうだけど，大して管理できるとは決して思わないわ。

質問：女性は何を心配しているか。

選択肢の訳
1　給食の質の低下。
2　軽食の店を開くという提案。
3　地域に手近な飲食店がないこと。
4　給食の費用の上昇。

解説　女性の2つ目の発言にある proposal to open a snack shop と同じ **2** が正解。続く会話から，女性は給食の改善を求めているのに，snack shop ができるとその努力が無意味になると思っていることがわかる。snack shop のせいで給食の質が下がるとは言っていないので，**1** は誤り。

No.4 - 解答 **3**

スクリプト
- ☆: I'm surprised to see you eating lunch in the cafeteria, Tatsuo.
- ★: Yeah, I usually prefer to get away from the office, but I'm preparing for the company's stock exchange listing.
- ☆: Oh right, that's pretty exciting. It's going to mean big things for the company. It's scheduled for next year, right?
- ★: That was the plan, but listing requirements have become stricter of late. With the global slowdown, it's more difficult to list. I've gotten even busier.
- ☆: Well, I hope it doesn't take too much out of you.

Question: What does the man say?

全文訳
- ☆: あなたがカフェテリアで昼ご飯を食べているなんて，驚いたわ，タツオ。
- ★: うん，普通は会社の外に行く方が好きなんだけど，会社の証券取引所上場の準備をしているんだよ。

☆：ああ，そうだったわね。結構わくわくする。会社にとってとても大事なことになるもの。来年の予定よね？

★：計画ではそうだったんだけど，最近は上場の要件が厳しくなっているんだ。世界的に景気が減速しているから，上場は前より難しい。僕は一層忙しくなったよ。

☆：まあ，負担になり過ぎないといいけどね。

質問：男性は何と言っているか。

選択肢の訳
1　会社を辞めるつもりでいる。
2　その年の多くは出張で不在である。
3　現在抱えているプロジェクトが複雑になった。
4　上司が締め切りを延ばさない。

解説　男性が外出せずに社員食堂でランチを食べているのは，listing「上場」の準備のため。男性は2つ目の発言で，上場の要件が stricter になったので忙しくなったと言っている。stricter を complicated と言い換えた **3** が正解。

No.5 − 解答 ④

スクリプト
★：I see the "For Sale" sign on the Wilsons' house is still there.
☆：That's strange. I thought that place would sell in a flash. It's in a lovely spot.
★：Well, it's a buyer's market at the moment.
☆：Now you mention it, they said something about that on the news last night.
★：If the Wilsons are in a hurry, they'll have to rethink their asking price.
☆：That's a shame, though. It looks like pretty good value to me.

Question: Why does the man think the house is still for sale?

全文訳
★：ウィルソンさんの家の「売り出し中」の看板はまだそのままだね。
☆：おかしいわ。あの家はあっという間に売れると思ったのに。すごくいい場所にあるから。
★：まあ，今は買い手市場だし。
☆：そう言えば，昨日の夜のニュースでそんなような話をしていたわ。
★：ウィルソンさんたちが急いでいるなら，希望価格を考え直さなければならなくなるね。
☆：でも，それは気の毒だわ。私にはかなりお値打ちに思えるけど。

質問：その家がまだ売り出し中なのはなぜだと男性は思っているか。

選択肢の訳
1　宣伝が十分にされていない。
2　家の立地のせいで買い手に敬遠されるのかもしれない。
3　その地域ではもっといい家が手に入る。

4　家の売却希望価格が高過ぎるのかもしれない。

解説　男性が2つ目の発言で言っている buyer's market は，需要より供給が多いため価格が下がっている状態のこと。つまり，男性の次の発言の rethink their asking price は「今の希望価格は高過ぎるので考え直して値下げする」ことを意味する。したがって **4** が正解。

No.6 - 解答 ①

スクリプト
★：Lesley, how nice to see you. I didn't know you shopped here.
☆：I just started recently. I'm trying to be more careful about what I eat. The prices are a little steep, though.
★：True, but you have to be prepared to fork out a bit extra for organic food.
☆：I guess so.
★：And you get the satisfaction of knowing you're making a contribution to the environment.
☆：It's a tough choice, though. If I don't notice any improvements in my health, I may switch back to my regular place.

Question: What do we learn about the woman?

全文訳
★：レズリー，奇遇だね。君がここで買い物をしているとは知らなかったよ。
☆：最近来るようになったばかり。食べる物に前より気を使うようにしているの。価格はちょっと高いけどね。
★：そうだけど，オーガニック食品にはちょっと余分に払う覚悟がなきゃね。
☆：そうみたいね。
★：それに，環境に貢献していると知る満足感を得られるし。
☆：難しい選択だけどね。健康にまったく改善が見られなければ，いつもの店に戻るかもしれない。

質問：女性について何がわかるか。

選択肢の訳
1　オーガニック食品を買うのをやめるかもしれない。
2　買い物の予算を減らした。
3　環境を助けることに熱心である。
4　もっと安いオーガニック食品店を見つけた。

解説　オーガニック食品に熱心な男性に対し女性は現実的で，効果がなければ I may switch back to my regular place と最後に言っている。いつも買い物をしている店に戻るということは，**1** のようにオーガニック食品をやめると示唆していることになる。**3** が当てはまるのは男性である。fork out「（大金）を払う」。

No.7 - 解答 ④

スクリプト
☆：You're looking kind of stressed, honey. Everything OK?
★：Yeah. I'm just trying to figure out how to adjust our budget to

accommodate the new car expenses.
☆： I thought we'd worked out manageable payments.
★： For the car itself, we did, but insurance costs quite a bit more for a sports car. And it really goes through gas.
☆： It's fun to drive, but if it doesn't make economic sense, we can do without it.
★： It hasn't come to that just yet. I'm sure we can figure out a way to cut corners elsewhere.

Question: What will the couple probably do?

全文訳
☆： 何だかストレスがたまっているみたいね，あなた。大丈夫？
★： うん。予算をどうやりくりして新車の出費を工面するか，解決策を考えているんだ。
☆： 無理なく支払えるよう計算したと思ったけど。
★： 車それ自体の計算はしたけど，スポーツカーは保険が少しばかり高くつくんだよ。それにガソリンをすごく食うし。
☆： 車を運転するのは楽しいけど，経済的に割に合わないなら，なしで済ませてもいいわよ。
★： まだそこまでの話ではないね。ほかのところで費用を削れる方法がきっと見つかるよ。

質問： この夫婦はおそらくどうするか。

選択肢の訳
1　保険会社に連絡する。
2　車の支払いについて再交渉する。
3　もっと燃費のいい車両を購入する。
4　ほかのことに支出するお金を減らす。

解説　夫は新車の保険やガソリン代をどう捻出するか頭を悩ませている。妻は we can do without it と言って車を手放すことを提案しているが，夫は最後に cut corners elsewhere の方法を考え出すと言っている。これは車以外の出費を減らすという意味なので，**4** が正解となる。

No.8 – 解答 ③

スクリプト
☆： Hi, Sam. How's the job search going?
★： I got an offer that I'm considering from a firm in the city. Great salary, but a lot of business trips, and a two-hour-a-day commute, which I'm not sure I can handle.
☆： What does your wife think?
★： She understands my reluctance. But she'd like to put a dent in our debt and start a college fund for the kids.
☆： The commute sounds tough, but she does have a point.
★： She sure does. The question is whether it's worth the extra stress

and time away.

Question: What is the man's main concern?

全文訳
☆：こんにちは、サム。職探しの調子はどう？
★：市内の会社からオファーをもらって検討中。給料はすごくいいんだけど、出張が多いし、通勤に1日2時間かかるんで、うまくこなせるかどうか自信がないんだ。
☆：奥さんはどう思っているの？
★：僕が乗り気じゃないのをわかってくれている。だけど彼女は、借金を減らして、子供たちの大学進学資金を準備し始めたいと思っている。
☆：通勤は大変そうだけど、奥さんの言うこともっともね。
★：そうなんだよ。問題は、ストレスと家から離れる時間が増えるだけの価値があるかどうかだね。

質問：男性の主な懸念は何か。

選択肢の訳
1 その仕事の給料が思ったほど高くない。
2 妻がお金を重視し過ぎる。
3 その仕事は生活様式の変化を彼に強いるだろう。
4 家族がさらに借金を抱えるかもしれない。

解説 新しい仕事のオファーを受けるべきか男性は悩んでいるが、その理由は、出張が多く通勤時間が長いこと。それを change his lifestyle とまとめた **3** が正解。男性の妻がお金を重視しているのは確かだが、女性の she does have a point という指摘に男性は She sure does. と答えているので、**2** のように too much とまでは考えていない。put a dent in ~「~を減らす」。

No.9 - 解答 ③

スクリプト
★：OK, ma'am. You're all set with new tires, but when I was changing them I found a problem with the brakes.
☆：Really? I haven't noticed anything unusual.
★：Well, your front brakes are fine, but the problem is with your rear ones. The pads are worn and need to be replaced.
☆：I hadn't planned on that expense. Will they last a couple more months?
★：Possibly, but you risk causing damage to the brake drums and may end up having to replace them as well.
☆：Well, I certainly don't want to pay even more. If I leave it here today, would you be able to replace the pads?
★：Unfortunately, I'll have to order the parts.
☆：How soon can you get it done, then?
★：Let's see. The earliest would be next Monday morning. Will that

work for you?
☆: Yes, that's fine. How much can I expect all this to cost?
★: About $300, including labor.
☆: Wow, that's a lot.
★: We do offer a payment plan, so you can break up the cost into four monthly payments.
☆: That would really help me out. Thanks.

Question: What does the woman decide to do?

全文訳
★: さあ，お客さま。新しいタイヤの取り付けはこれで完了ですが，交換しているときブレーキに問題を見つけました。
☆: 本当？ 特に異常には気付かなかったけど。
★: えー，前ブレーキは大丈夫なんですが，問題があるのは後ろブレーキですね。パッドがすり減っていて，交換が必要です。
☆: その出費は予定外だわ。あと2，3カ月もたないかしら。
★: もつかもしれませんが，ブレーキドラムの損傷の原因になるリスクがありますし，結局ブレーキドラムも交換する羽目になるかもしれませんよ。
☆: うーん，それ以上払うことになるのは絶対に嫌だわ。今日こちらに置いていったら，パッドを交換していただけますか。
★: 残念ですが，部品を注文しなければなりません。
☆: それじゃ，いつごろまでにやってもらえますか。
★: えっと，一番早くて来週月曜日の午前中ですね。それで問題ありませんか。
☆: ええ，それで結構です。全部まとめていくらかかると思えばいいでしょう。
★: 工賃を入れて300ドルくらいです。
☆: まあ，大金ね。
★: 支払いのプランをご用意していますから，費用は4回の月賦に分けていただくこともできます。
☆: そうしてもらえると本当に助かるわ。ありがとう。

質問：女性はどうすることに決めているか。

選択肢の訳
1　車のブレーキドラムを交換する。
2　もっと安い修理工場に行く。
3　できるだけ早く車を修理してもらう。
4　修理代金を前払いする。

解説
タイヤ交換の際にブレーキに異常が見つかったことから会話が進んでいく。女性の3つ目の発言の I certainly don't want to pay even more は，パッド交換ならまだしも，ブレーキドラム交換にはお金を使いたくないという意味なので，**1**は誤り。続けて日程の話になり，早くて月曜

日の午前中と言う男性に対し女性は that's fine と答えているので，**3** が正解となる。最後に分割払いで話がまとまっているので，**4** は誤りである。

No.10 解答 ③

スクリプト
☆： So, Dan, what do you think of the candidates we've interviewed so far?
★： I think Philip Johnson could be a good addition to our team.
☆： Mary?
○： Hmm . . . I'm not sure. Philip's still young, which is a plus, I guess, since he can grow with the job . . .
★： He also graduated from a good university, and he has some sales experience in our industry. Hopefully, that means he'd require less training.
☆： I guess so, but Philip seems too quiet and shy. I have to say, none of the interviewees seemed really outstanding. There's no one who's really "wowed" me.
○： I agree. We haven't seen a candidate with a proven track record of boosting sales. We're looking for someone who's proactive, someone who can expand our customer base.
☆： I know it's a lot of work, but personally I'd rather continue this process in the hopes of finding a candidate who meets all our criteria.
★： I still think someone like Philip is worth considering.
☆： Look, why don't we keep him as a backup for now? Meanwhile, Dan, can you let our recruiting agencies know the position is still open?
★： OK, if you're sure. I'll also let them know that the rest didn't make the grade.

Question: What do the two women think?

全文訳
☆： では，ダン，これまで面接してきた候補者たちのことをどう思う？
★： フィリップ・ジョンソンは僕たちのチームのいい戦力になるかもしれないと思う。
☆： メアリーは？
○： うーん……よくわからない。フィリップはまだ若いから，その点はプラス材料じゃないかな，仕事とともに成長できるんだから……
★： それに彼はいい大学を卒業しているし，僕たちの業界で少し営業の経験がある。ということは，きっと研修が少なくて済むんじゃないかな。
☆： そうかもしれないけど，フィリップはあまりに物静かで内気な感じね。

はっきり言って，面接を受けた人の中で特にずば抜けた人はいないと思えた。私を本当に「あっと言わせた」人はいないわね。
○：同感だわ。売り上げを伸ばしたという確かな実績を持った候補者には出会えていない。私たちが探しているのは，先を読んで行動する人，私たちの顧客基盤を広げることができる人よ。
☆：とても大変なのはわかっているけど，個人的には，私たちの基準をすべて満たす候補者が見つかることを期待して，できればこの作業を続けたいわ。
★：それでも，フィリップのような人は検討に値すると思うけど。
☆：ねえ，取りあえず彼を補欠としてキープしたらどうかしら。それと同時に，ダン，人材紹介会社にポストはまだ空いていると伝えてもらえる？
★：わかった，君が本当にそれでいいなら。残りの人たちは基準に達しなかったとも伝えておくよ。

質問：2人の女性はどう思っているか。

選択肢の訳
1　紹介会社は理想的な候補者を数人見つけた。
2　ダンは期待値を下げるべきだ。
3　フィリップ・ジョンソンの営業記録はずば抜けていない。
4　ダンが最終的な採用の判断を下すべきだ。

解説　社員の採用に関する男女3人の会話。男性はフィリップ・ジョンソンを推す理由の1つに営業経験を挙げているが，それに対して女性の1人はnone of the interviewees seemed really outstandingと述べ，もう1人の女性も，確かな営業実績のある候補者はいなかったと言っている。つまり2人とも，フィリップの営業実績がoutstanding「ずば抜けた」ものではないと考えていることがわかるので，3が正解。期待値が高いのはダンではなく女性たちなので，2は誤り。make the grade「要求された水準に達する」。

A

スクリプト **Electricity and the Brain**

As we age, our bodies become less nimble. The same thing can also happen to our brains. While occasional bouts of forgetfulness may not be serious, mental decline can be a sign of more-severe conditions like dementia or Alzheimer's disease. However, neuroscientist Robert Reinhart believes electrical stimulation can help. In a controlled study, Reinhart applied electrical currents to parts of the brain involved in short-term memory, also known as working memory. He found that by using electricity to synchronize brain waves in certain areas, working memory could be significantly improved, and learning ability could also be enhanced.

Such results seem promising. Furthermore, using electrical stimulation therapy may not be confined to improving working memory or helping us to become better learners. It is hoped it can also be used to help treat brain disorders including autism, schizophrenia, and Parkinson's disease. Poor synchronization of brain waves in different areas of the brain is believed to be a factor in such conditions. However, while electrical stimulation to synchronize brain waves proved effective in Reinhart's study, its viability as a long-term treatment has yet to be determined.

Questions

No.11 What is one thing Robert Reinhart's research illustrates?

No.12 What does the speaker suggest about electrical stimulation therapy?

全文訳　**電気と脳**

年を取ると，私たちの体の敏しょう性は低下する。同じことが私たちの脳にも起こり得る。時折短期的に忘れっぽくなっても深刻ではないかもしれないが，知能の衰えは，認知症やアルツハイマー病といったより重度の疾患の兆候のこともある。しかし，神経科学者ロバート・ラインハートは，電気刺激が助けになり得ると考えている。対照研究で，ラインハートは，短期記憶に関与する脳の部位に電流を流した。短期記憶は作業記憶としても知られる。電気を用いてある領域の脳波を同期させると，作業記憶を著しく改善することができ，学習能力も強化され得ることを彼は発見した。

こうした結果は期待できるように思える。さらに，電気刺激療法を用いることは，作業記憶を改善したり，私たちがよりよい学習者になる助けになったりすることにとどまらないかもしれない。電気刺激療法は，自閉症と統合失調症とパーキンソン病を含む脳の病気の治療を助けることにも使えると期待されている。そうした疾患では，脳の異なる領域で脳波がうまく同期しないことが１つの要因だと考えられている。しかし，脳波

を同期させる電気刺激はラインハートの研究では有効だとわかったものの，長期的治療として実現できるかどうかはまだ確定していない。

語句 nimble「敏しょうな」，bout「(病気などの) 短い期間」，dementia「認知症」，neuroscientist「神経科学者」，synchronize「〜を同期させる」，autism「自閉症」，schizophrenia「統合失調症」，viability「実現可能なこと」

No.11 解答 ④

質問の訳 ロバート・ラインハートの研究が例示する1つのことは何か。
選択肢の訳
1 私たちの脳は，体が年を取るのと同じようには年を取らない。
2 電気刺激は精神に重大な問題を引き起こすかもしれない。
3 学習は脳のほかの機能と関係がない。
4 脳波を同期させると記憶機能が改善する。

解説 第1段落後半でラインハートの研究が手短に述べられている。by using electricity to synchronize brain waves ... working memory could be significantly improved を 4 が簡潔にまとめている。中ほどの electrical stimulation can help の help は精神疾患を助けるという意味なので，2 は誤り。

No.12 解答 ①

質問の訳 電気刺激療法について話者は何を示唆しているか。
選択肢の訳
1 記憶の改善と学習を超えた潜在的利用法がある。
2 これまで知られていなかった疾患を特定するのに役立ってきた。
3 長期的効果を証明した。
4 脳の病気の治療には適さないとわかった。

解説 第2段落冒頭の may not be confined to ... を has potential uses beyond ... と言い換えた 1 が正解。3 の長期的効果については，最後の文で has yet to be determined と言っているので，まだ証明されていないことになる。

B

スクリプト **Madagascar's Biodiversity**

Madagascar has one of the highest levels of biodiversity on Earth, with up to 90 percent of its plants and animals found nowhere else. The island split from other landmasses about 80 million years ago, which allowed the flora and fauna there to evolve in isolation. Scientists also believe that significant variations in its landscape contribute to biodiversity. The mountain range running down the middle of the island separates a rain forest on one side from desert-like plains on the other. This combination allowed the development of unique habitats that have encouraged a variety of plant and animal adaptations.

Unfortunately, Madagascar's biodiversity is threatened by human activities that are causing climate change. The island's isolation as well as its terrain, rainfall, and other variables make it difficult for researchers to predict how different species will respond to alterations in their environment. One method being used by researchers is to study how species on the island reacted to past environmental changes. This could help identify which plants and animals are vulnerable today. A concern with this model, however, is that it involves examining environmental fluctuations which occurred over tens of thousands of years. The human causes of climate change, in contrast, have been occurring for a far shorter period of time.

Questions
No.13 What is one reason given for Madagascar's biodiversity?
No.14 How are researchers trying to identify Madagascar's vulnerable wildlife?

全文訳　マダガスカルの生物多様性

　マダガスカルの生物多様性は地球でも最高レベルの1つで，その動植物の最大90％はほかのどこにも見られない。この島はおよそ8千万年前にほかの大陸塊から分離し，そのため島の動植物相は孤立して進化することができた。科学者は，島の風景が変化に富んでいることが生物多様性に寄与しているとも考えている。島の中央を走る山脈が，片方の熱帯雨林をもう一方の砂漠のような平原から切り離している。この組み合わせが，多様な動植物の適応を促してきた特異な生息環境の発達を可能にしたのである。

　残念なことに，気候変動の原因となっている人間の活動によって，マダガスカルの生物多様性は脅かされている。島の孤立だけでなく地形や降雨量などの変動要因が，置かれた環境の変化にさまざまな種がどう対応するか，研究者が予測することを困難にしている。研究者が用いている1つの手法は，島の生物種が過去の環境変化にどう反応したかを調査することである。これは，今日どの動植物が変化に弱いかを特定する上で役立つかもしれない。しかし，このモデルに関する1つの懸念は，数万年にわたって生じた環境変動の検証が必要なことである。それに比べて，気候変動の人為的原因が生じているのははるかに短い期間である。

　　　語句　landmass「大陸塊」，flora and fauna「動植物相」，terrain「地形」

No.13 解答

質問の訳　マダガスカルの生物多様性の1つの理由として挙げられているのは何か。
選択肢の訳
1　かつてうっそうとした熱帯雨林に覆われていた。
2　いくつかのまったく異なる生態学的環境がある。
3　ほかの大陸塊から多くの種を引き付けた。
4　現代文明から孤立したままである。

解説　第1段落で，マダガスカルの生物多様性の理由が2つ挙げられている。1つは，大昔から大陸から切り離されていること。もう1つは，中ほど

で significant variations in its landscape contribute to biodiversity と言っているように，熱帯雨林と砂漠に似た平原といった多様な環境があること。**2** が2つ目の理由に合致する。

No.14 解答

- 質問の訳　研究者はマダガスカルの変化に弱い野生生物をどのように特定しようとしているか。
- 選択肢の訳
  1. ほかの島の野生生物と比較することによって。
  2. 地元の人たちをガイドとして募集することによって。
  3. 過去の気候の変化を検証することによって。
  4. ほかの国で用いられている手法を模倣することによって。
- 解説　第2段落の冒頭で climate change というキーワードが提示されている。中ほどに出てくる environmental changes と後半に出てくる environmental fluctuations は，climate change を言い換えたものと考えられる。研究者はこれらと生物種との関係を調べているのだから，**3** のように気候変動を調べていることになる。

C

スクリプト　**Operation Gunnerside**

During World War II, Germany initiated a secret nuclear program with the goal of building an atomic bomb. German scientists, however, faced an obstacle: their production strategy involved an extremely rare substance known as heavy water, which contains a different form of hydrogen to that of regular water. This difference allows heavy water to slow the movement of neutrons, which is essential for the correct chain reaction required for an atomic explosion to take place. Heavy water was therefore key to the German program's success. Only one facility produced heavy water at the time: a hydroelectric power plant in Norway called Vemork.

After Germany occupied Norway, the US and Britain decided to attack Vemork to halt Germany's nuclear progress. However, as the heavy-water reactor was in the basement of the building, air strikes would have failed. Therefore, in a mission known as Operation Gunnerside, a small unit of British-trained Norwegian soldiers was sent to destroy the reactor with explosives. The soldiers obtained detailed information about the building's layout, enabling them to sneak in, set the explosives, and escape. Operation Gunnerside was one of the most important steps toward stopping Germany's wartime nuclear program.

Questions
No.15 What is one thing we learn about heavy water?
No.16 Why was Operation Gunnerside necessary?

> 全文訳　**ガンナーサイド作戦**

　第2次世界大戦中，ドイツは原子爆弾の製造を目標に，秘密の核プログラムに着手した。しかし，ドイツの科学者たちはある障害に直面した。彼らの生産戦略には，通常の水とは違う形態の水素を含む，重水として知られる極めて珍しい物質が必須だった。重水はこの違いにより中性子の動きを遅くすることができるのだが，この中性子の動きは核爆発が起きるのに必要な正しい連鎖反応に欠かせない。したがって，重水はドイツのプログラムが成功するための鍵だった。当時重水を生産する施設は1つしかなかった。ノルウェーのベモルクという水力発電所である。

　ドイツがノルウェーを占領した後，米国と英国はドイツの核開発の進展を止めるためにベモルクを攻撃する決断を下した。しかし，重水炉は建物の地下にあったので，空爆をしたとしても失敗しただろう。それ故，ガンナーサイド作戦として知られるミッションで，英国で訓練を受けたノルウェー兵の小部隊が爆薬で炉を破壊すべく送り込まれた。兵士たちは建物の設計図の詳細な情報を手に入れ，そのおかげで彼らは忍び込んで爆薬を仕掛け，脱出することができた。ガンナーサイド作戦は，ドイツの戦時核プログラムを止めるための最も重要なステップの1つだった。

> 語句　neutron「中性子」，hydroelectric power plant「水力発電所」

No.15 解答　①

> 質問の訳　重水についてわかる1つのことは何か。
> 選択肢の訳　**1** ドイツの核プログラムは重水に頼っていた。
> 　　　　　**2** 重水は原子が分裂するのを防ぐ。
> 　　　　　**3** ドイツの科学者たちは重水が危険だと思った。
> 　　　　　**4** どんな中性子も重水を通り抜けられない。
> 解説　重水については第1段落で説明されている。極めて珍しい物質であること，通常の水とは水素の形態が違うこと，中性子の動きを遅くすること，ドイツの核開発の鍵だったがノルウェーの水力発電所でしか生産されていなかったことである。**1** が，ドイツの核開発に欠かせなかったことを depended on it と表している。

No.16 解答　③

> 質問の訳　なぜガンナーサイド作戦が必要だったか。
> 選択肢の訳　**1** ドイツは米国から核技術を盗んでいた。
> 　　　　　**2** 英国は核プログラムを開発していなかった。
> 　　　　　**3** ベモルクに空襲しても成功しなかっただろう。
> 　　　　　**4** 米国はベモルクに重水を生産してもらう必要があった。
> 解説　ガンナーサイド作戦は，ベモルク発電所を攻撃してドイツの核開発を止めることが目的だった。第2段落の前半で，重水炉が地下にあったので air strikes would have failed と言っており，**3** が failed を not ... succeeded と言い換えている。空爆で重水炉を破壊するのは無理なの

で，小部隊による潜入作戦が行われた，というのが話の展開である。

スクリプト **The World's First Computer?**

In 1901, divers near the Greek island of Antikythera discovered an ancient Roman shipwreck full of artifacts, including a shoebox-sized bronze mechanism in a wooden case. The mechanism was largely ignored until the mid-twentieth century, when science historian Derek de Solla Price began to study it. In the early 1970s, he had x-ray and gamma-ray images of the mechanism taken. After analyzing the results, Price theorized the device was an "ancient analog computer," constructed around 87 BC. The technology available to him at the time was limited, and the images he took were difficult to interpret conclusively. However, Price believed the mechanism's inscriptions and gear system were designed to track the movements of planets and stars.

In the following decades, a mechanical engineer analyzed the inner workings of the mechanism using more-advanced imaging technology. According to the engineer, dials on the front and back would have conveyed information about the movements of the sun, the moon, and individual stars. Although no other such ancient device has ever been found, many historians believe the mechanism's complexity means it must have had a predecessor. This theory is supported by first-century-BC writings of the Roman statesman Cicero, which describe similar types of astronomical-calculator devices.

Questions

No.17 What is true of Derek de Solla Price's observations of the mechanism?
No.18 What do Cicero's writings suggest about the mechanism?

全文訳 **世界初のコンピューター？**

　1901年に，ギリシャのアンティキテラ島の近くにいたダイバーたちが，工芸品でいっぱいの古代ローマの沈没船を発見したが，工芸品の中には木箱に入った靴箱大の青銅の機械装置があった。この機械装置は，科学史家デレク・デ・ソーラ・プライスがその調査を始めた20世紀半ばまでおおむね無視されていた。1970年代初頭に，彼は機械装置のエックス線画像とガンマ線画像を撮ってもらった。結果を分析した後，プライスは，この装置は「古代のアナログコンピューター」で，紀元前87年前後に組み立てられたという説を立てた。当時彼が利用できた科学技術は限られており，彼が撮った画像からは決定的な解釈が困難だった。しかしプライスは，機械装置に刻まれた文字と歯車装置は惑星と星の動きを追うためのものだと考えていた。

　続く数十年の間に，ある機械工学者が，より進んだ画像処理技術を用いて機械装置内部の仕組みを分析した。その工学者によると，表と裏の目盛りは，太陽と月と個々の星の動きに関する情報を伝えたのだと思われる。そうした古代の装置はほかに見つかったことがないが，この機械装置の複雑さからすると，先行するものがあったに違いないと

多くの歴史家は考えている。この説は，同様のタイプの天文計算機装置を記述している，ローマの政治家キケロの紀元前1世紀の著作に裏付けられる。

> 語句 shipwreck「難破船，沈没船」，artifact「工芸品」，theorize「〜という学説を立てる」，conclusively「決定的に」，inscription「碑文，銘」，imaging「画像処理」

No.17 解答 ②

質問の訳　デレク・デ・ソーラ・プライスのこの機械装置の観察について正しいのは何か。

選択肢の訳
1　エックス線を使えば観察はもっと決定的なものになっただろう。
2　彼が用いた画像処理技術が観察の正確さを制限した。
3　機械装置が青銅製でなく木製であることが観察で明らかになった。
4　彼の分析はローマの科学者たちの分析と違っていた。

解説　プライスの観察はエックス線画像とガンマ線画像によるものだが，この技術は limited だったので画像は difficult to interpret conclusively だったと第1段落の後半で言っている。これを全体的に言い換えた **2** が正解。imaging technology はエックス線とガンマ線のこと。

No.18 解答 ③

質問の訳　キケロの著作はこの機械装置について何を示唆しているか。

選択肢の訳
1　機械装置はこれまで見つかっている同様の古代の装置より古い。
2　機械装置が明らかにした情報には不正確なものもあった。
3　機械装置はその種のもののうち最初のものではなかったかもしれない。
4　機械装置の当初の用いられ方は効率的ではなかった。

解説　キケロの名前は最後に出てくるが，その文は This theory is supported by ... で始まる。This theory がその前の the mechanism's complexity means it must have had a predecessor を指すと理解できれば，この機械装置が最初に作られたものではないという内容の **3** を選ぶことができる。

E

スクリプト **The Chicago Fire**

The Chicago Fire of 1871 is one of the most infamous disasters in US history, killing nearly 300 people and leaving one in three residents homeless. The fire's exact cause is still unknown, but it is believed to have started in a barn in the southwest of the city. Firefighters responded immediately, but they accidentally went to the wrong location. As a result, the fire rapidly spread out of control, intensified by a severe regional drought and the proximity of wooden structures in the city. Thousands of buildings, including the entire downtown business district, were destroyed. Among them was the facility that controlled the city's water supply. This left Chicago helpless, and the blaze burned unchecked for two days.

　Despite the widespread devastation, reconstruction began immediately. Officials introduced stricter fire and building codes, and great progress was made in public health thanks to new infrastructure that reduced water pollution. The reconstruction effort attracted prominent architects, resulting not only in careful replanning of the city center but also the erection of the world's first skyscraper. The rebuilding also attracted many new residents. The pre-fire population had been approximately 300,000, but by 1890, the city's population had increased to over 1 million.

Questions
No.19 What is one thing we learn about the Chicago Fire of 1871?
No.20 What is one thing that happened following the fire?

全文訳　**シカゴ大火**

　1871年のシカゴ大火は米国の歴史で最も悪名高い大惨事の1つで，300人近い人が亡くなり，3人に1人の住民が住む家をなくした。火災の正確な原因は今でも不明だが，市の南西部の納屋が火元だと考えられている。消防士は直ちに反応したが，誤って違う場所に行ってしまった。その結果，深刻な地域的干ばつと市内の木造建造物が近接していたことで勢いを増した火災は，急速に広がって手が付けられなくなった。中心部のビジネス地区全体を含む数千もの建物が全焼した。その中には，市の水道を制御する施設もあった。これでシカゴはお手上げ状態になり，炎は歯止めなく2日間燃えた。

　広範囲に荒廃したにもかかわらず，直ちに復興が始まった。役人はより厳格な火災基準と建築基準を導入し，水質汚染を減らした新たなインフラのおかげで公衆衛生は大きく進歩した。復興の取り組みは有力な建築家を引き付け，その結果都心部が入念に再設計されただけでなく，世界初の超高層ビルが建設されることとなった。建物の再建は多くの新住民を引き付けもした。火災以前の人口は約30万だったが，1890年には市の人口は100万以上に増えていた。

語句　proximity「近いこと，近接」，unchecked「抑制されない」，devastation「破壊，荒廃」，replanning「再計画，再設計」，erection「建設」，rebuilding「再建」

No.19 解答 ②

質問の訳　1871年のシカゴ大火についてわかる1つのことは何か。
選択肢の訳　1　市内に住むホームレスの人たちが火元だった。
　　　　　2　環境状態が火災の急速な拡大の手助けをした。
　　　　　3　ビジネス地区の建物には影響がなかった。
　　　　　4　消防士たちは火災を抑え込んだと思った。
解説　第1段落中ほどで火災が拡大した理由について intensified by a severe

regional drought and the proximity of wooden structures in the city と言っているが，この２つの理由を Environmental conditions とまとめた **2** が正解。**1** は放送文に出てくる homeless という語を使った引っかけ，ビジネス地区は全部焼けたのだから **3** は誤り，火災は under control ではなく out of control だったのだから **4** も誤りである。

No.20 解答 ②

質問の訳　火災に続いて起きた１つのことは何か。
選択肢の訳
1　新しい建築物の高さが制限された。
2　復興の結果人口が増加した。
3　有名な建築家たちが功労に対して法外な請求をした。
4　役人たちは復興を加速するため火災基準を無視した。

解説　第２段落は火災後の復興について述べている。最後に人口の変化に触れて，新住民の流入により火災前の 30 万から 1890 年には 100 万以上に増えたと言っているので **2** が正解。stricter ... building codes が導入されたとは言っているが，skyscraper が建設されたことから，**1** のように高さを制限する基準ではなかったことがわかる。

一次試験・リスニング　Part 3　問題編 p.61〜63

F

スクリプト

You have 10 seconds to read the situation and Question No. 21.

Despite our commitment to the highest manufacturing standards, we are now looking at undertaking a product recall, which is needed to prevent any possible injuries. I've drawn up a plan to assign roles and spell out exactly what steps are required to carry out such a recall. The priority for senior members of the legal team is to explore any possible lawsuits we could be facing. For junior legal staff, I want you to look into any legal procedures we need to follow for this kind of recall, then write up your findings so all of us can quickly and easily understand and review them. You will also all need to thoroughly review the guidelines for making changes to our current contracts, including supplier contracts, but that can come later. As we make progress on these steps, the manufacturing department will need to conduct a thorough review of production standards.

Now mark your answer on your answer sheet.

全文訳

　わが社は最高の製造基準を守ると約束していますが，製品のリコールをすることについて今検討しています。これは，どんなけがの可能性も防ぐために必要なことです。役割の分担と，そうしたリコールを実行するにはいったいどのような段階が必要かを明確に説明した計画書を作成しました。法務チームの上級メンバーの優先課題は，わが社が受けるかもしれない可能性のあるどんな訴訟についても調査することです。下級法務スタッフの皆さんにしてほしいのは，この種のリコールで従う必要のあるどんな法的手続きについても調べ，それから調査結果を書類にまとめて，私たち全員が手早く簡単に理解し見直しができるようにすることです。また皆さん全員が，供給業者の契約を含むわが社の現在の契約に変更を加えるためのガイドラインを徹底的に見直す必要がありますが，それは後で構いません。これらのステップが進展すれば，製造部は生産基準の徹底的な見直しを行うことが必要になります。

No.21 解答　❷

状況の訳　あなたは最近，自動車部品製造会社で未経験者向けの仕事を始めたところである。法務部で働いている。スタッフ会議で社長が次のことを言う。
質問の訳　あなたはまず何をする必要があるか。
選択肢の訳
1　製品の製造基準を見直す。
2　リコールの法的要件の要約をつくる。
3　既存の契約を修正する手続きを確認する。
4　会社が受けるかもしれない訴訟を調査する。

語句　spell out「〜を明確に説明する」

解説　状況でポイントになるのは entry-level job と legal department だと思われる。リコール対策の進め方について話す社長は，まず senior members に訴訟の調査をするよう言うが，これは entry-level ではないので **4** は外れる。続けて junior legal staff にしてほしいこととして，リコールに必要な法的手続きを調べて書類にまとめるよう言っている。あなたは junior だと考えられるので，**2** が正解となる。**1** は製造部がすること，**3** は that can come later なので，まずするべきことではない。

スクリプト

You have 10 seconds to read the situation and Question No. 22.

　It's a good thing you asked about your passport. A lot of travelers assume they can go abroad on any valid passport, but that's not always true. Canada is more lenient than other countries about allowing foreigners in with only a few months remaining on their passport, but I'd still advise you to renew it to be on the safe side. The Japanese consulate downtown is helpful in these situations. You don't have much time, so you should go tomorrow and have your passport renewed right away. Take all necessary documents, a photo, and anything else listed on their website. It usually takes five days, but it might be quicker, considering the circumstances. I wouldn't advise purchasing a ticket until you've done that, as you might not be able to reschedule, and you won't get a refund if you cancel.

Now mark your answer on your answer sheet.

全文訳

パスポートのことをお尋ねいただいてよかったです。有効なパスポートならどんなものでも外国に行けると思い込んでいる旅行者が多いですが，必ずしもそうではありません。パスポートの期限が数カ月しか残っていない外国人を入国させることについては，カナダはほかの国より寛大ですが，それでも安全策を取ってパスポートを更新するようお勧めします。中心街にある日本領事館がこうした状況では役立ちます。あまり時間がありませんから，明日行ってすぐにパスポートを更新してもらうのがいいでしょう。必要な書類全部と写真，あと領事館のサイトに載っているものがほかにあれば持って行ってください。普通5日かかりますが，状況を考えればもっと早いかもしれません。それが片付くまでは，チケットは購入しないようお勧めします。予定を変更できないかもしれませんし，キャンセルしても払い戻しを受けられませんから。

No.22 解答 ③

状況の訳 あなたは米国に住んでいて，家族の急な用件で1週間後に飛行機でカナダに行く必要がある。日本のパスポートは2カ月後に失効する。旅行代理店の人が次の話をする。

質問の訳 あなたは何をすべきか。

選択肢の訳
1 カナダの空港で係員に相談する。
2 一時パスポートをネットで申請する。
3 新しいパスポートをもらいに中心街に行く。
4 カナダに着いた後で日本領事館を訪ねる。

語句 lenient「寛大な」, consulate「領事館」

解説 旅行代理店の人のアドバイスは明快で，有効期限が数カ月あるパスポートでも入国できないことがあるので，念のためすぐにパスポートを更新するのがいい，というもの。更新できる場所については The Japanese consulate downtown と言っており，それを単に downtown と表した **3** が正解である。

H

スクリプト

You have 10 seconds to read the situation and Question No. 23.

Welcome to Brookton Primary School. On the morning your daughter starts school, you'll receive some permission forms for school outings. You'll be asked to sign and return those within a day or two. We require all students to be fully vaccinated before the first day of the term, and any family doctor can provide the immunizations if they haven't been completed. If they have been completed, written proof of immunization should be submitted. School starts next month, so time is of the essence for those. I understand you're also requesting after-school care. For this, we'll need a letter from your employer stating your work hours and commuting time. We can provide temporary care until 6 p.m. for two weeks to give you time to get that letter. Finally, here is a list of our uniform requirements. We have a grace period of one week before the uniform is required.

Now mark your answer on your answer sheet.

全文訳

ブルックトン小学校にようこそ。娘さんの学校初日の午前中に，学校の遠足の承諾書を何枚かお受け取りいただきます。署名して1日か2日以内に戻していただくようお願いします。学期初日の前にワクチン接種が完了していることを生徒全員に義務付けており，済んでいなければ，どこのかかりつけ医でも接種を受けられます。接種済みの場合は，書面のワクチン接種済み証明書を提出していただくことになります。学校は来月始まりますから，済んでいない生徒には時間がとにかく重要です。確か放課後の保育もご要望でしたね。これについては，勤務時間と通勤時間を明記したあなたの雇用主からの手紙が必要になります。その手紙をもらう時間を差し上げるため，2週間，午後6時まで一時的保育を提供できます。最後ですが，こちらが当校で必要な制服のリストです。制服が必須になるまで1週間の猶予期間があります。

No.23 解答 ③

状況の訳 あなたと家族は最近外国に引っ越した。あなたは娘を小学校に入学させるところである。娘は日本でワクチン接種を済ませた。学校の事務職員が次の話をする。

質問の訳 学校初日の前にあなたは何をすべきか。

選択肢の訳
1 署名した承諾書を提出する。
2 医師に娘の健康診断をしてもらう。
3 ワクチン接種済み証明書を提出する。
4 あなたの雇用主から手紙をもらう。

語句 outing「遠足」，of the essence「極めて重要な」，grace period「猶予期間」

解説 選択肢にはする必要があることとないことが混在しているので，学校が始まる前にしなければならないことに集中して聞く。1の承諾書は学校初日の後に提出することになる。ワクチンは接種済みなので2の必要はない。3は来月学校が始まるまでに提出しなければならないので，これ

が正解である。**4**は学校が始まってから2週間の余裕があるので，必ず初日の前にする必要はない。

(スクリプト)

You have 10 seconds to read the situation and Question No. 24.

Unfortunately, you don't currently qualify for Gold membership renewal next year. It is still possible to meet the criteria, however. As a rule, you need to spend a minimum of $4,000 a year on travel through E-Zonia, or book at least two weeks' accommodation at qualifying hotels. You've spent about $2,000 in total so far but trying to reach the minimum would take you beyond the budget you mentioned. Still, I see you've stayed for 10 days at our partner hotels. You've already mentioned you plan to travel during the Christmas holidays, so we can book you something for then if you'd like. Just four more nights would do the trick, and that can be done within your budget. For future reference, you might also want to consider obtaining an E-Zonia credit card, as you'll save an additional 5 percent on all flight bookings made through our website.

Now mark your answer on your answer sheet.

(全文訳)

残念ですが，現在は来年のゴールド会員更新の資格をお持ちではありません。ですが，基準を満たすことはまだ可能です。原則として，Eゾニアを介した旅行に1年で最低4千ドル使っていただくか，資格を満たすホテルで少なくとも2週間の宿泊を予約していただく必要があります。今のところ総額で2千ドルほどお使いですが，最低額に届くようにしようとすると，先ほどおっしゃった予算を超えることになります。それでも，当社のパートナーホテルに10日間宿泊されています。クリスマス休暇中に旅行するご予定だと既に伺いましたので，よろしければその時のためにこちらで何か予約をお取りすることもできます。あとたった4泊で目的達成ですし，それならご予算内で収まります。今後のご参考までに，Eゾニアのクレジットカードを作ることを検討された方がいいかもしれません。当社のサイト経由で予約するすべての航空便がさらに5%お得になりますから。

No.24 解答 ④

状況の訳 Eゾニア・トラベルのゴールド会員資格が間もなく切れるので，あなたは更新したいと思っている。あなたの年間総予算は3千ドルである。代理店の係員が次のアドバイスをする。

質問の訳 あなたは何をすべきか。

選択肢の訳 1 支出をEゾニアの最低額まで引き上げる。
2 Eゾニアのクレジットカードを申し込む。

3　年末までにEゾニアを介して航空便を予約する。
　　　4　Eゾニアのパートナーホテルで4泊予約する。

（語句）do the trick「目的を達する」

（解説）係員が最初に提示している更新の条件は，1年で最低4千ドル使うことか，指定のホテルで少なくとも2週間の宿泊を予約すること。前者は係員も言っているように予算オーバーなので，必然的に後者を選ぶことになる。Just four more nights would do the trick が，あと4泊予約すれば更新条件をクリアするという意味だと理解できれば，迷わず**4**を選ぶことができる。

（スクリプト）

　You have 10 seconds to read the situation and Question No. 25.

　Government regulations have become stricter, and staff at any branch can explain the new procedures. If you're unable to visit a bank branch here in the US personally, you'll need to do everything online. Access your account online and click on the "Make a Payment" option. Then, click on "Wire Transfer." To complete the wire transfer form, you'll need a single-use security access code. To get that, you'll need to complete a two-stage authentication process, so the first thing you have to do is complete the two security questions you set up when you originally opened your account. Once you've done that, you need to enter your account password. After those steps are done, you can request the code to be sent to your preregistered e-mail address. You can then complete the transfer online, but you'll have to reenter your password for any subsequent transfers.

　Now mark your answer on your answer sheet.

（全文訳）

　政府の規制が以前より厳しくなり，どの支店のスタッフも新しい手続きの説明ができます。こちらのアメリカの銀行支店にご自分で行くことができないのなら，全部ネットでする必要があります。ネットでアカウントにアクセスし，「支払いをする」というオプションをクリックしてください。次に「電信送金」をクリックします。電信送金の書式に記入するには，使い捨てのセキュリティーアクセスコードが必要になります。それを手に入れるには2段階の認証プロセスを完了する必要があるので，まずしなければならないのは，最初に口座を作ったときに設定した2つのセキュリティー質問に対し答えを記入することです。それが終わると，口座のパスワードを入力する必要があります。これらのステップが終わった後で，あらかじめ登録したメールアドレスにコードを送ってもらうよう要請できます。そうするとネット送金を完了することができますが，ほかに続けて送金する場合はパスワードを再入力しなければなりません。

No.25 解答 ④

状況の訳 あなたは海外に住むアメリカ市民である。アメリカの銀行口座から娘の口座に送金したい。銀行に電話すると,係員が次の話をする。

質問の訳 アクセスコードを入手するには,あなたはまず何をすべきか。

選択肢の訳
1 アカウントのパスワードを変更する。
2 メールアドレスを再確認する。
3 自ら銀行の支店を訪ねる。
4 2つのセキュリティー質問に答える。

語句 single-use「1度だけ使用する,使い捨ての」,authentication「認証」

解説 to obtain an access code のようなポイントとなる要素が状況ではなく質問に含まれている場合もあるので,先読みでは注意したい。中ほどの you'll need a single-use security access code. To get that が聞き取れたら,次にアクセスコードの入手方法に関する情報が話されるはずなので,聞き逃さないこと。2段階の認証プロセスがあり,1つ目は complete the two security questions なので **4** が正解となる。

一次試験・リスニング Part4 問題編 p.63 ▶MP3 ▶アプリ ▶CD 1 49〜50

スクリプト

This is an interview with Gary Stevens, a jewelry seller in New York.

I (Interviewer): We have Gary Stevens with us today. Welcome, Gary.

G (Gary Stevens): Thank you for having me.

I: Could you tell us a little bit about what you do?

G: Well, I run my own business buying and selling jewelry in New York. I sell to private customers as well as other jewelers in the trade. I can help customers order what they like through a catalog, or I can have something custom-made for them.

I: I see. What are some of the issues that customers often face?

G: When buying something, customers are often tempted by the biggest stones, but this isn't always indicative of the quality of the jewelry as a whole. Likewise, customers are not aware of how valuable a piece of jewelry might be before they attempt to sell it to us. Something that they think is cheap costume jewelry might have diamonds in it, whereas an impressive-looking piece might not be worth much. Sometimes, customers return to my store asking to buy back a sentimental piece that they've already sold me. This is possible when I still have the item in question, but in a situation where a gold ring is scrapped, for example, you cannot simply put it back together. Especially in the case of family heirlooms, it's often better to just keep it in the family. As a word of advice to customers, I'll say, "Before you sell us your jewelry, it's important that you think about this decision carefully."

I: Is there a benefit to working in a place like New York City?

G: New York has a large jewelry district, and while this does mean competition for customers, it also allows jewelers to help one another. Someone who, for example, is skilled at resetting stones can do repairs for someone else without that expertise. There are many different companies that work in a wide variety of styles using different metals, and sometimes if we know someone who can meet a customer's needs, we can refer the customer to that person.

I: Could you tell us about some recent trends in the industry?

G: Due to the sharp increase in the price of gold and silver, people are increasingly selling their jewelry just for the value of the metal. While this can be an attractive option at first, to me it seems like a shortsighted decision. Fine jewelry is a work of art just like an expensive painting or a sculpture, but the work of talented jewelers is disappearing forever because people are more interested in making a quick profit. Before someone decides to scrap something, I always ask them to consider it carefully.

I: Lastly, do you have any words of wisdom for new jewelers or people interested in becoming one?

G: First of all, it's important to have a lot of background knowledge. By studying gemology or something similar, one can identify the cut and quality of stones used, and can tell genuine items from, for example, cut glass made to look like a stone. Precision and attention to detail are also necessary when making jewelry. If you happen to ruin a diamond or expensive stone while cutting and sculpting it, it can be difficult to fix your mistake.

I: Gary, thank you very much for your time.

G: It was my pleasure.

Questions

No.26 What is an issue Gary says many people face when selling their jewelry?

No.27 What does Gary say about selling jewelry for the price of the metal?

全文訳

これはニューヨークの宝飾商であるギャリー・スティーブンズとのインタビューです。

聞き手（以下「聞」）：今日はギャリー・スティーブンズをお招きしています。ようこそ，

ギャリー。

ギャリー・スティーブンズ（以下「ギ」）：呼んでいただきありがとうございます。

聞：お仕事について少し教えていただけますか。

ギ：えー，宝飾品の売買をする自分の店をニューヨークで経営しています。個人のお客さんにも，業界のほかの宝飾店にも販売しています。お客さんが気に入ったものをカタログで注文するお手伝いもできますし，オーダーメイドでお客さんに何かお作りすることもできます。

聞：なるほど。客が直面する問題にはどういったものがありますか。

ギ：何か買うとき，お客さんは一番大きな宝石に引き付けられることが多いですが，これは必ずしも宝飾品全体としての品質を示すものではありません。同様に，1点の宝飾品を私たちに売ろうとする前は，お客さんはそれがどれだけ価値があるかもしれないのかを知りません。安物のコスチュームジュエリーだと思ったものにダイヤモンドが使われているかもしれませんし，一方，見た目は見事なものが，それほど価値がないかもしれません。時々お客さんが私の店に戻ってきて，既に私に売ってしまった思い入れのあるものを買い戻したいと言うことがあります。問題の品物を私がまだ持っていれば可能ですが，例えば金の指輪がスクラップにされてしまった状況では，元の形に戻すことはできっこありません。特に家族の家宝の場合は，とにかく家族で取っておく方がいいことが多いです。お客さんへの忠告の言葉として，「当店に宝飾品を売る前に，その決断についてよく考えることが重要です」と言っておきたいです。

聞：ニューヨーク市のような場所で働くことにメリットはありますか。

ギ：ニューヨークには大きな宝飾店街があり，これは確かにお客さんの獲得競争を意味しますが，宝飾店が助け合うことも可能になります。例えば，宝石をはめ直す技術に優れている人は，その専門技術がない別の人の代わりに修理をすることができます。さまざまな金属を用いてバラエティーに富んだスタイルで仕事をするさまざまな会社がたくさんあり，時には，お客さんのニーズを満たすことのできる知り合いがいれば，そのお客さんをその人に回すことができます。

聞：業界の最近の動向について少し教えていただけますか。

ギ：金と銀の価格が急速に上がっているので，金属の価値だけで宝飾品を売る人が増えています。これは最初は魅力的な選択のこともありますが，私には近視眼的な決断のように思えます。ファインジュエリーは高価な絵画や彫刻のような芸術作品ですが，才能のある宝石職人の作品は永遠に姿を消しつつあります。それは，手っ取り早くもうけることへの関心が強くなっているからです。何かをスクラップにすると決める前に，よく考えてほしいと私はいつも言います。

聞：最後に，新米宝石職人や，宝石職人になることに興味がある人に，何か先人のお言葉を頂けますか。

ギ：まず何よりも，背景知識をたくさん持っていることが大切です。宝石学や同様のことを学べば，使われている宝石のカットと品質を特定できますし，本物と，例えば宝石に似せて作られたカットガラスを区別できます。正確さと細部への注意も，宝飾品

を作る際には必要です。ダイヤモンドや高価な宝石をカットして彫刻している間に偶然駄目にしてしまうと，間違いを修正するのは難しいことがあります。
聞：ギャリー，お時間を頂きありがとうございました。
ギ：どういたしまして。

> 語句　indicative of ～「～を示す」，costume jewelry「コスチュームジュエリー（ファッション性を優先して人工の宝石などを用いた宝飾品）」，heirloom「先祖代々伝えられた家財」，shortsighted「近視眼的な」，fine jewelry「ファインジュエリー（天然の宝石や貴金属を用いた高級宝飾品）」，gemology「宝石学」

No.26 解答 ①

> 質問の訳　宝飾品を売るときに多くの人が直面する問題は何だとギャリーは言っているか。

> 選択肢の訳
> 1　彼らは自分の宝飾品の価値を十分には理解していない。
> 2　彼らは思い入れのある無価値な品物に過度に愛着を持っている。
> 3　彼らは金と銀の市場価格に依存し過ぎである。
> 4　彼らはその宝飾店の評判を調べるのをしばしば怠る。

> 解説　客が直面する問題について聞かれたギャリーは，3つ目の発言で，客が目を奪われる大きな宝石が宝飾品の品質を表すとは限らないと言い，続けて，宝飾品を売ろうとしている客について，customers are not aware of how valuable a piece of jewelry might be と述べている。1がこれと同じ内容である。2の sentimental pieces への愛着についても発言しているが，worthless だとは言っていない。

No.27 解答 ③

> 質問の訳　宝飾品を金属の値段で売ることについてギャリーは何と言っているか。

> 選択肢の訳
> 1　一部の宝飾品製造者が職を去る結果になっている。
> 2　金の高価格にもかかわらず，彼の利益を減らした。
> 3　貴重な芸術作品を破壊することに似ている。
> 4　昔よりも行われる頻度が減っている。

> 解説　質問の selling jewelry for the price of the metal に対応するのは，ギャリーの5つ目の発言中の selling their jewelry just for the value of the metal である。metal，つまり金と銀の高騰に目がくらんで宝飾品を手放すことを shortsighted だと批判するギャリーは，Fine jewelry is a work of art just like an expensive painting or a sculpture と宝飾品を芸術作品にたとえ，スクラップにされることを憂えている。それに合致するのは 3 である。

二次試験・面接 　トピックカード A 日程 　問題編 p.64

ここでは，A日程の5つのトピックをモデルスピーチとしました。

A日程

1. Should democratic nations try to force democracy on other nations?

I strongly disagree that democratic nations should try to force their system of government on other countries. First of all, the whole concept of democracy is based on freedom. Democracy requires willing participation and must be the decision of the country's own citizens in order to be successful. Therefore, democratic nations should give aid and provide education to encourage the natural evolution of democracy instead of using force. Another reason is based on history. There are many examples of unsuccessful attempts to use military action to bring about democratic changes. For example, in recent decades in Afghanistan, the attempt to introduce democratic changes by entering the country and occupying it cost many thousands of lives and the endeavor was largely unsuccessful. Finally, efforts to impose democracy can harm a country's reputation. Many places around the world resent the actions that America has taken by invading, imposing economic sanctions, and manipulating politics around the world. Trying to impose democracy while ignoring any oppositions from the international community only does more harm than good. When you consider the basic democratic principle of freedom, the examples of history, and the harm to countries' reputations, it seems clear that attempting to force democracy on other countries is a mistake.

> 解説 「民主主義国家は他国に民主主義を強要すべきか」
>
> 強く反対する立場からのスピーチなので，冒頭で明瞭にその立場を述べている。①民主主義の根幹は自由意思なので強要するべきではない，②歴史的にも民主主義を強要して失敗した例には大きな犠牲が伴った，③民主主義を強要した側の評判が落ちるリスクがある，という3つの理由に対して具体例を加えて議論を展開している。②と③はアメリカを例に取っており，②をさらに展開したものが③となっている。このように先に話したものを利用して論点を深めるアプローチを用いるのもよい。

2. Information in the Internet age — too much or not enough?

In my opinion, there is no such thing as "too much information" as long as you can make a distinction between what is real and what is fake. Firstly, the spread of information in the Internet age has brought incredible technological changes. For example, medical science is helping people to live longer, healthier lives. Also, new technologies like smartphones and AI are driving economic growth and making people's lives more convenient. Secondly, greater access to information is bringing peace to the world. The spread of information through things like social media, news programming, and even movies and music is creating a new world culture that is helping to overcome old problems like racism and national rivalries. The better people understand each other, the less likely they are to come into conflict. Lastly, greater access to information is helping people to make better decisions if they have enough literacy. In the past, checking facts was difficult, but now, when politicians make claims or when people get medical advice, it's possible to check whether the information is true on the Internet. This is leading to a better-informed, better-educated general public. Based on the reasons I've given, I think it's obvious that increasing the availability of information on the Internet makes the world a much better place.

> **解説**　「インターネット時代の情報——情報過多か情報不足か」
> 正面から答えるのではなく，条件付きながらも「情報過多ということはあり得ない」と聞き手の興味を引く切り出し方になっている。そこから，情報が多いことの利点を①インターネットによる情報の拡散は多くの技術的発展に寄与してきた，②人々が正しい情報を得やすいほど世界平和が実現しやすくなる，③正しい情報が伝わることで人々はよりよい判断ができる，という3つにまとめている。技術革新，世界平和，個人の生活の向上，と重複しない観点から，正しい情報が広く十分に与えられることの重要性を強調している。

3. Could genetic engineering be the solution to human health problems?

Although many people fear the idea of genetic engineering, I think it could be a solution to human health problems because it could cure diseases, increase human lifespans, and help people to overcome disabilities. Recently, a technology called CRISPR has been invented, which allows scientists to alter people's genes. Using CRISPR, it will someday be possible to prevent inherited illnesses, such as Huntington's disease. CRISPR also has the potential to lead to treatments for cancer and other deadly illnesses that kill millions of people. I've read that scientists also believe it may be possible to prevent cells from aging through genetic engineering. There are some plants and animals that live for hundreds or even thousands of years, and by combining their DNA with ours, it may be possible for humans to live much longer than they do now. Finally, genetic engineering offers hope to people with disabilities, such as people who are paralyzed or visually impaired. If cells, tissue, and bones can be regrown through genetic engineering, people who thought they would never walk or see again may someday regain these abilities. In conclusion, I believe that scientists should make every effort to pursue genetic engineering in order to improve human health.

> **解説** 「遺伝子工学は人類の健康問題の解決策となるか」
>
> 冒頭で「自分とは異なる立場」,「自分の意見」そして「3つの理由」のすべてを網羅する計画性の高いスピーチ。準備時間内にきれいに構成を決められればぜひトライしてみたいスタイルだ。ここでは遺伝子工学が多くの健康問題を解決できるはずだ,という立場から,以下の3点を強調している。①CRISPR（ゲノム編集技術の1つ）が深刻な病を治療できる可能性,②遺伝子操作によって実現される長寿,③身体の障害の克服,である。科学関連のトピックは知識がないと話せないので,常に情報をアップデートしておこう。

4. Is there too much emphasis on technology in professional sports today?

While some people may say there is too much emphasis on technology in professional sports today, I think that the changes have mainly been beneficial. One important reason is that technology has greatly improved the performance of professional athletes. These days, athletes and coaches are able to analyze athletes' technique using slow-motion cameras and sophisticated computer systems. By seeing their mistakes and improving their efficiency, many athletes have been able to break world records. This also makes watching sports more exciting for spectators. Next, thanks to advances in sports medicine, injuries now heal faster, and even serious injuries that previously forced athletes to retire can now be healed. Health management using medical data has extended the lifespan of athletes as well. Finally, instant replays have made sporting events fairer. In the past, biased referees often affected the outcome of games. Now, though, officials and fans can see exactly what happened, so there are fewer bad calls because referees know their decisions will be reviewed. Furthermore, if bad calls are made, instant replays make it easier to correct them. As I've discussed, technology is improving athletic performance, making sports safer, and improving referees' decisions. For these reasons, I think there should be more, not less, emphasis on technology in sports.

> **解説** 「今日のプロスポーツにおいてテクノロジーは重視され過ぎているか」
>
> 冒頭部分では While some people may say ～, I think ～「一部の人

は〜という意見かもしれないが，私は〜と思う」という発話の定型パターンを使っている。定型パターンをいくつか持つと労せずに聞き手に正確な意図を伝えられるので，ぜひ覚えておきたい。ここでは反対の立場から，プロスポーツにおけるテクノロジーの重要性を強調している。理由として，①データ分析によるパフォーマンスの向上，②スポーツ医学の発展，③試合における審判の公平性の向上，の３点にテクノロジーが寄与したとしている。

5. Agree or disagree: A single world government would benefit the planet

I'm opposed to the idea of a single world government. Please allow me to explain why I believe it would be bad for the human race as a whole. First, a world government would threaten human advancement. Currently, all countries are in serious economic competition with each other. But without borders, there would likely be fewer large companies that control their industries and put effort into developing science or technology. This could greatly slow down the progress of humankind. Another problem is that a world government would likely be dominated by just a few powerful countries. Politicians would tend to favor their own regions, giving them economic benefits and working for their own interests rather than the good of all the people in the world. Finally, it would be dangerous if there was that much power in a single organization. Today, if one government is taken over by a dictator, other countries and military alliances are able to act together to weaken, contain, or overthrow the government that is causing problems. This would be impossible, however, if one government controlled the entire world. For these reasons, I think that the current system in which each country has its own government is more beneficial to humankind.

解説　「賛成か反対か：単一世界政府は地球のためになる」
　反対の立場から３つの考え得る理由．①競争がなくなることで人類の進歩が停滞する可能性があること，②単一世界政府の下では一部の強国だけが恩恵を受ける可能性があること，③１つの組織に強大な力を与えるのは相互監視が効かなくなるので危険であること，を示している。このような「もし〜だったら」タイプのトピックの場合，１級レベルの話者であれば，仮定の話と現実の話をきちんと分けて話せることが重要だ。もしあなたが自信をもって仮定法を使えなければ，今日から練習を始めよう。

2020-3

一次試験
筆記解答・解説　p.110〜128

一次試験
リスニング解答・解説　p.129〜156

二次試験
面接解答・解説　p.157〜160

解答一覧

一次試験・筆記

1

(1)	3	(10)	3	(19)	1
(2)	2	(11)	1	(20)	3
(3)	4	(12)	2	(21)	2
(4)	1	(13)	1	(22)	1
(5)	1	(14)	1	(23)	2
(6)	4	(15)	1	(24)	3
(7)	4	(16)	4	(25)	1
(8)	1	(17)	4		
(9)	3	(18)	4		

2

(26)	3	(29)	2
(27)	3	(30)	3
(28)	4	(31)	2

3

(32)	4	(35)	3	(38)	2
(33)	2	(36)	4	(39)	1
(34)	3	(37)	2	(40)	4
				(41)	2

4 解答例は本文参照

一次試験・リスニング

Part 1
No. 1	2	No. 5	1	No. 9	3
No. 2	4	No. 6	1	No.10	2
No. 3	3	No. 7	4		
No. 4	4	No. 8	2		

Part 2
No.11	3	No.15	2	No.19	4
No.12	1	No.16	3	No.20	2
No.13	2	No.17	3		
No.14	4	No.18	4		

Part 3
No.21	1	No.23	2	No.25	1
No.22	4	No.24	3		

Part 4　No.26　3　｜　No.27　2

一次試験・筆記 1 　問題編 p.66〜68

(1) ― 解答 ③
- 訳　RC コンピューターズの新社長は，前社長が下したいくつかの決定を覆した。それらの決定は誤りで，会社の売り上げを損なっていると彼は考えていた。
- 語句　1「〜を永続させた」　2「〜に序文を付けた」
3「〜を覆した」　4「〜を十分に満足させた」
- 解説　前任者の決定が誤りで不利益を与えると新任者が考えるなら，その決定を「覆す」のが普通だと考えられる。override の類義語に overrule, overturn があるが，overturn は「(判決)を覆す」という意味で用いられることが多い。

(2) ― 解答 ②
- 訳　ブレンダンは子供のころから，バスケットボールチームのグリーンビル・ウルブズの熱烈なサポーターだ。毎シーズン，彼はできるだけ多く彼らの試合を見に行く。
- 語句　1「捕まえにくい」　2「熱烈な」
3「飾り立てた」　4「無感動な」
- 解説　第2文から，ブレンダンがウルブズの大ファンだとわかる。ardent の類義語は avid, fervent, passionate など。

(3) ― 解答 ④
- 訳　その教会が子供向けに週末の宗教教育プログラムを提供し始めてから，毎月新しい家族が加わり，会衆の数が着実に増えた。
- 語句　1「仕切り」　2「編集」　3「抑制」　4「会衆」
- 解説　congregation は，礼拝のため教会に集まる信徒たち，つまり「会衆」を表す集合名詞。動詞 congregate は一般的に「集まる」という意味で用いられるが，名詞になると宗教的な意味を帯びる。

(4) ― 解答 ①
- 訳　通貨の価値が今年突然下落したため，輸入品の価格が急上昇した。
- 語句　1「価値の低下」　2「翻訳，演奏」　3「境界，区別」　4「摘出，抽出」
- 解説　輸入品の値上がりは，例えば円安のように自国の通貨価値が「下落」した場合に起こる。depreciation の反意語は appreciation「価値の上昇」。

(5) ― 解答 ①
- 訳　新税が非常に不評だったので，財務大臣は，世間の批判が弱まるまで待ってから何かそれ以上の税金を導入することにした。
- 語句　1「弱まった」　2「染み込んだ」
3「腐食した」　4「〜をそそのかした」

解説 新税が不評な間に別の税金を導入するとさらに大きな反発を招く恐れがあるので，大臣は批判が「弱まる」のを待つことにしたのだと考えられる。abate は，強風や激しい感情などが「衰える，弱まる」という意味。

(6) ― 解答 ④

訳 A：あなた，私はこの新しい家がいいと思うけど，今住んでいる家が売れなかったらどうなるかしら。
B：今の家が売れた場合に購入する契約をするよ。だから，今の家が売れなかったら，新しい家は買わなくてもいいんだ。

語句 1「全員出席の」 2「恐ろしい」 3「子の」 4「依存する」

解説 contingent on [upon] 〜 は「〜に依存する，左右される」という意味。今の家が売れたら新しい家を買うが，売れなかったら買わない，という契約を結ぶことになる。

(7) ― 解答 ④

訳 ルーシーはその自動車事故で軽い脳振とうを起こし，地元の病院で手当てを受けた。今後2，3週間は頭が痛むでしょう，と医師は言った。

語句 1「慰撫」 2「大都市圏」 3「妙な仕掛け」 4「脳振とう」

解説 日本語では日常的に使われる病名や医学用語，例えば脳に関する語であれば stroke「脳卒中」, infarction「梗塞」, dementia「認知症」, blood clot「血栓」などは英語でも覚えておきたい。

(8) ― 解答 ①

訳 塔のてっぺんまで上るのは，観光客たちが予想していたより骨が折れるとわかった。上り切ったころには，彼らのほとんどは疲れ果てていた。

語句 1「骨の折れる」 2「動揺した」 3「残虐な」 4「老いぼれた」

解説 てっぺんに着いたらほとんどの人は疲れ果てていたのだから，塔を上るのは身体的に相当きつかったのだ。arduous は「骨の折れる，難儀な」という意味。

(9) ― 解答 ③

訳 その市に引っ越したとき，ティムには古くて荒れ果てたアパートを借りるお金しかなかった。訪ねて来た母親は，彼が暮らす汚らしい状況にショックを受けた。

語句 1「巨大な」 2「補助の」 3「汚い」 4「不注意による」

解説 第1文から，ティムの住環境はかなりひどいとわかる。squalid は「汚い，むさくるしい」という意味。名詞 squalor「不潔，むさくるしさ」も覚えておきたい。

(10) ― 解答 ③

訳 その戦時指導者の新しい伝記に多くの人が憤慨した。彼らは著者を，証明されていないうわさを伝えて偉人をおとしめたと非難した。

語句 1「逸脱している」 2「〜を懇願している」

111

3「~を中傷している」　　　　4「(卵) を抱いている」

解説 多くの人は「証明されていないうわさを伝えて」いると非難しているのだから，その伝記は戦時指導者（＝偉人）をネガティブに描いていると考えられる。

(11) - 解答 ①

訳 敵国が突然国境の部隊を増員したことを大統領は懸念していた。自国が強大な隣国に侵略され併合されるかもしれない，と彼は危惧した。

語句 1「併合された」　　　　2「産出された」
3「ためらった」　　　　4「提供された」

解説「アネックス」は「別館」の意味で日本語になっているが，動詞 annex は「~を（武力で）併合する」という意味。その名詞「併合」は annexation。

(12) - 解答 ②

訳 人は教育機関を卒業生の成功で判断する傾向があるが，学校がどれだけ優れているかを決める基準はそれだけではない。

語句 1「寓話(ぐうわ)」　2「基準」　3「主唱者」　4「宣伝文」

解説 yardstick は「1ヤードの物差し」が原義で，そこから比喩的に「（評価・判断などの）基準，尺度」という意味で用いられるようになった語。

(13) - 解答 ①

訳 若手政治家のころ，ラメシュは将来のリーダーだと広くもてはやされた。しかし，重い病にかかった後，彼は政治家としてのキャリアを諦めざるを得なかった。

語句 1「褒めそやされた」　　　2「砕かれた」
3「発酵された」　　　　　4「皮をむかれた」

解説 praise, laud, commend は実績に基づいて「~を称賛する」という意味だが，tout は，実績の有無にかかわらず世間にアピールするために「~を褒めそやす」というニュアンスで用いられる。

(14) - 解答 ①

訳 ヨーロッパの多くのチーズは鼻につんとくる香りを持つことでよく知られているが，そうしたチーズを食べるのが好きな人たちはその匂いをまったく気にしない。

語句 1「鼻につんとくる」　　　2「攻撃的な」
3「物寂しい」　　　　　　4「暗い，濁った」

解説 文の後半を裏返せば，好きではない人には匂いが気になるということになる。pungent は，快・不快を問わず味や匂いが舌や鼻を強く刺激するさまを表す。

(15) - 解答 ①

訳 A：ジーナ，疲れ切った顔ね。どうしたの？
B：1日ずっと，姉の3人の子供の世話をしていたの。たった2，3時

間ですっかり疲れ果てたわ。

語句　1「くたくたに疲れた」　　2「曲がって」
　　　3「耐え難い」　　　　　　4「公然の」

解説　frazzled は，身体的にも精神的にも疲れ切ったというニュアンスの語。名詞 frazzle を用いた be worn to a frazzle「くたくたに疲れる」という表現もある。

(16) – 解答　4

訳　犯人が銀行のセキュリティーについて熟知していたことから，犯人には銀行組織内部に共犯者がいたはずだと警察は考えた。

語句　1「有権者」　2「専制君主」　3「社交的な人」　4「共犯者」

解説　セキュリティーに関する情報を漏らす「共犯者」が銀行内部にいた，と考えると文脈に合う。accomplice の類義語は confederate。また，complicit「共謀した」，complicity「共犯，共謀」といった関連語もまとめて覚えておきたい。

(17) – 解答　4

訳　A：総理大臣についての最新の世論調査は見た？
　　B：うん，ぼろぼろだね。前回の公開討論会の後，彼の支持率はたったの 10%に下がったよ。

語句　1「率直な」　2「毒性の強い」　3「怒りっぽい」　4「ごくわずかの」

解説　paltry は主に数量について「ごくわずかの，たったの」という意味。類義語は meager, measly など。反対に数量の大きさを強調する形容詞には staggering, whopping などがある。

(18) – 解答　4

訳　ビジネスパートナーが顧客に過剰請求をしていると知ったローランドは，辞職してその会社とのあらゆる関係を断った。彼はそうした行為にかかわりたくなかった。

語句　1「～の前兆となった」　　2「～を徐々に教え込んだ」
　　　3「～を本国に送還した」　4「～を断った」

解説　sever は，「（物）を切断する，切り離す」ことにも，「（関係・連絡など）を断つ」ことにも用いられる。名詞は severance。

(19) – 解答　1

訳　その殺人は計画的なものだったと警察は結論付けた。殺人犯が犯罪を一から十まで詳細に計画していたことは証拠から明らかだった。

語句　1「前もって計画された」　2「つらい思いをした」
　　　3「糸を通された」　　　　4「少しずつ集められた」

解説　pre（前もって）+ meditated（熟考された）と分解すると，語の意味を類推できる。premeditated は，犯罪や攻撃など他者に害を及ぼす行為について用いられる。

(20)－解答 **3**

訳　ガルシア氏は，部下の1人が寝坊して仕事に遅刻したその日に図々しく昇給を願い出たことにあきれ返った。

語句　1「偽物」　2「憤怒」　3「図々しさ」　4「敬虔(けいけん)」

解説　遅刻したその日に昇給を求める振る舞いは「図々しさ」以外の何物でもない。gall は have the gall to *do*「図々しくも～する，厚かましくも～する」というフレーズで用いられることが多い。

(21)－解答 **2**

訳　新製品を独創的な方法で売り出す当初の試みはほんの少ししか成功しなかったので，その会社は販売戦略を考え直すことにした。

語句　1「心から」　2「わずかに」　3「猛烈に」　4「熱心に」

解説　販売戦略を考え直すということは，当初の試みはうまくいかなかったことになる。marginally は (very) slightly と同義で，「わずかに，ほんの少し」という意味。

(22)－解答 **1**

訳　一部の生徒が最終試験で不正をしたことを知った学校管理者たちは，関与した全員にすぐさま罰を与えた。

語句　1「(罰) を与える」　2「～を引きはがす」
3「～に配線工事をする」　4「～に没頭する」

解説　dish out には「～を（気前よく）配る，与える」という意味があり，目的語は money や advice のように人が喜ぶものもあれば，punishment や criticism のように人に嫌がられるものもある。

(23)－解答 **2**

訳　フランクリンは，妹が宝くじで5千万ドル当てたという知らせに驚嘆した。知っている人が突然そんな金持ちになるなどと思ったこともなかった。

語句　1「吹き飛ばされた」　2「驚嘆した」
3「たたき壊された」　4「煮こぼれさせた」

解説　句動詞 blow away には，「～を撃ち殺す；～に大勝する」などのほかに，「～を驚嘆させる，感動させる」という意味がある。

(24)－解答 **3**

訳　若いトラは生後18カ月になるころには自力で生きていくことができるのだが，2歳半くらいまでは母親と一緒にいるのが普通だ。

語句　1「～のへりに沿って進む」　2「～より遅れる」
3「～をやりくりする」　4「～とけんかをする」

解説　fend for *oneself* は「自分で自分の面倒を見る，独力でやっていく」という意味。動詞 fend には fend off「（攻撃・批判など）から身を守る，～をかわす」という句動詞もあり，こちらも覚えておきたい。

(25)−解答 ①

訳 その報道カメラマンはホテルの従業員から，映画スターがそのホテルで休暇を過ごしているという裏情報を聞いたので，写真を撮ろうと急いでホテルに行った。

語句 1「内報を受けた」　2「倹約された」
3「よく検査された」　4「詰まった」

解説 tip off は多くの場合「（警察）に内報する，密告する」という意味だが，問題文のように「（人）に秘密の情報を教える」という意味でも用いられる。

一次試験・筆記 2　問題編 p.69〜71

全文訳　ミッチェル地図

1750年，イングランドに住むアメリカの医師ジョン・ミッチェルは，英国の高官ハリファックス伯爵から，北アメリカの地図を作製する任務を与えられた。当時，英国とフランスの関係は緊張しており，フランスが軍事的防御施設を建設していた北アメリカ植民地領土の支配権を巡る論争が続いていた。これらの植民地の経営責任者だったハリファックスは，こうした侵犯に抵抗する活動への政府の支持を結集しようと決意していた。彼がミッチェルに作るよう委託した地図は，この目的を達した。ミッチェルは北アメリカに対する英国の権利の主張の支持者で，この偏向は，地図の初期の版に彼が引いた境界と，英国の領土権の主張に関する多数の注釈に顕著に表れていた。その心情は，引き続き出版された地図ではさらに明白で，フランス領と認められる土地はもっと減っていた。これは世論と政界の意見を動かす力となり，植民地の利害を巡って両国が激しく競い合うこととなった一連の出来事を促進した。

続いて起きた紛争でフランスが敗れた結果，英国は大量の領土を獲得したものの，戦争に注ぎ込んだ莫大な金額のせいで英国の国家債務は急増した。この損失を埋め合わせようと英国は1765年に印紙法を成立させたが，これはアメリカ植民地に最初の直接税を課すものだった。報復として植民地全域で抗議が噴出し，最終的にアメリカ独立戦争を招いた。1つ軍事紛争が終わった後にこれほど早く別の紛争が起きたのだから，フランスに対する英国の勝利は明らかに高い代償を伴っていた。

英国とそのアメリカ植民地の間で8年にわたって戦われた独立戦争は，1783年に終結した。これはアメリカ人にとって明るい前途を予感させる結末であり，アメリカ人は英国の支配から自由になっただけでなく，領土の新境界線を画定するために英国とアメリカの交渉者がミッチェルの地図を用いたおかげで，土地をたんまり手に入れたのである。地図作製の裏にあった当初の意図と，戦争の余波が残る中で地図が最終的に果たした役割との対照を考えると，ミッチェル自身は――もし存命で調印を見届けていれば――まず間違いなく，自分の地図がそのように利用されたことを認めなかっただろう。

ミッチェルの地図は，フランスとの争いを鼓舞する助けとなる上で重要な役割を果たすことによって，究極的には，アメリカの英国からの独立への道を開いたのである。

> 語句 high-ranking「高位の」，ongoing「進行中の」，fortification「防備用施設」，annotation「注釈」，sway「(意見など)に影響を与える」，ensuing「続いて起こる」，exact「(税金など)を課す」，erupt「(暴力などが)発生する」，retaliation「報復」，culminate in ～「～で頂点に達する」，auspicious「縁起のよい，幸先のよい」，grasp「掌握，支配」，aftermath「結果，余波」，disapprove of ～「～を非とする」

(26) – 解答 **3**

> 解説 空所の前の文の intrusions は，フランスがアメリカ植民地に軍事拠点を築いていたこと。政府の支持を得てこれに対抗することがハリファックスの意図だったのだから，ミッチェルの地図が世論と政界の意見を動かしてフランスとの競争が激化した，という空所後の内容から考えると，地図はハリファックスの思惑どおりの成果を上げた，つまり「目的を達した」ことになる。

(27) – 解答 **3**

> 解説 空所文の前半は，フランスとの戦いが終わったら独立戦争が起きるという，紛争が相次いだ状況を指す。第2段落によると，対フランス戦で抱えた債務を埋め合わせるために英国が導入した印紙税への反発が引き金となって独立戦争が起きたのだから，フランスに対する勝利は，アメリカを失うという「高い代償を伴っていた」と考えると筋が通る。

(28) – 解答 **4**

> 解説 第1段落によると，ミッチェルは英国のアメリカ植民地政策の支持者で，地図では英国の領土が広くなるように境界を引いた。そして第3段落では，アメリカの領土を画定する際にその境界線が用いられ，アメリカは a generous amount of land を手に入れたと書かれている。自分の地図が英国に不利になるよう利用されたのだから，ミッチェルが生きていれば反対していただろうと考えられる。

全文訳 **演技と脳**

　俳優の役目は，考え方が自分とは大きく違うこともあるさまざまな異なる登場人物になり切ることである。しかし，これは時に俳優に害を及ぼすこともあるのではないかと言われてきた。俳優の演技の成功に決定的に重要なのは「不信の停止」として知られる現象で，何かと言うと，批判的思考を捨て，俳優は実際には演じられている登場人物ではないとわかっていても無視するよう，観客を納得させることである。だが，不信の停止が可能になるのは，演じる登場人物に俳優が没入できるからであり，多くの俳優は，登場人物の感情に浸り切ろうとしゃにむに努力することは心理的に悪影響を及ぼすと主張する。これが特に当てはまると言われるのは，家庭内暴力や性的暴行を題材とする物

語で俳優が人物を演じる場合である。

　この懸念は真剣に受け止められるべきだと今では思われる。カナダの大学の研究チームが，俳優がいろいろな条件下で一連の質問に回答する様子を観察した。条件の1つは，自分自身として，そしてまたシェークスピア劇の役の準備をした後で「登場人物として」回答することだった。被験者が劇の登場人物に「なって」いたときに，自己関連情報の処理に関連する脳の領域の活動が大きく減少したことを研究者たちは発見した。これが示唆するのは，俳優は登場人物に変容するとき，自らのアイデンティティーを危うくするリスクを実際に冒しているということである。

　カナダの研究者たちは，質問には外国のアクセントを使って回答し，しかしそのアクセントで自然に話すだろう人に「なる」ことなく回答するよう俳優たちに指示することによって，自己に関する自分たちの考えをさらに深く検証した。この実験中に観察された脳の活動は，単に普通でない話し方をするだけで自己の弱体化が助長され得ることを示唆した。これは，一般人が参加した別の研究によって裏付けられる。その研究では，被験者は自分の性格と友人の性格について質問された。その後，自分の性格について再度質問されると，被験者は，自分の性格についての認識を友人の性格についての認識に近づくよう無意識のうちに変化させていたことを示唆するようなやり方で回答し，一般人の脳ですらアイデンティティーを処理する際はある程度の不安定さを経ることを物語っていた。この研究結果は，単に俳優には限られない人々の自己感覚のもろさを強調しているように思われる。

> 語句　inhabit「〜に宿る，存する」，mind-set「考え方，意見」，disbelief「不信」，cast aside「〜を捨てる」，take a toll「悪影響を及ぼす」，compromise「〜を危うくする」，subconsciously「無意識に」，fragility「もろさ」

(29) — 解答 ②

解説　空所前の however から，俳優の役目は登場人物になり切ることだという前の文に対する異論，あるいはその否定的側面に関する記述が続くと予想される。段落後半にあるように，観客を納得させるために役になり切ろうとすることは「心理的に悪影響を及ぼす」と多くの俳優は言うのだから，「俳優に害を及ぼすこともある」ことになる。

(30) — 解答 ③

解説　空所が段落冒頭の文にあるので，この段落をまとめるような内容が入ると考えられる。素の自分としての回答と役になり切ったときの回答を比較した研究で，後者では「自らのアイデンティティーを危うくするリスク」があることがわかった。これは，第1段落では仮説として扱われていた「俳優に害を及ぼす」という懸念が研究で裏付けられたことを意味する。したがって，「この懸念は真剣に受け止められるべき」が文脈に合う。

(31) ─ 解答 ②

解説 第3段落では，俳優に外国のアクセントで回答させた研究と，一般人に自分と友人の性格について答えさせた後で自分の性格だけについて答えさせた研究について書かれている。いずれも，外国のアクセントまたは友人の性格に引きずられる回答だったのだから，「単に俳優には限られない」という研究結果が得られたことになる。

一次試験・筆記 3　問題編 p.72〜80

全文訳 ビジネスと持続可能性

　2015年に国際連合は持続可能な開発目標（SDGs）を全会一致で採択したが，これは，貧困への取り組みと環境保護によって，より繁栄した持続可能な地球の未来を実現する力となることを各国政府と事業者と一般市民に等しく求める構想である。多くの事業者がSDGsを熱心に受け入れているように思える一方で，これらの企業が言うことと実際にすることの間には気がかりな断絶があるように見える。世界的な投資運用会社PIMCOが行ったある調査によると，多数の会社が企業報告でSDGsに言及していることは，SDGsの存在と重要性に関する意識の広がりを示している。しかし，目標に向けた数値化可能な進展を示す数字を挙げた会社は10分の1に満たず，この調査報告書の執筆者たちは，「ほとんどの企業は，事業価値を付加できる活動と目標を特定するための専門的知識をいまだに持っていない」と結論付けた。

　この落差が，SDGsが比較的新しくなじみのないことの結果かもしれないのは確かだが，もっとシニカルな見方をしている人たちもいる。数多くの企業が，企業が実際よりも環境に関心を寄せていると一般大衆を欺いて思わせる試みを指す用語である「グリーンウォッシング」をしていると非難されているのである。17のSDGsのうち相当数は，クリーンエネルギーや生態系の保護・回復といった課題を直接扱うもので，批判者たちの指摘によると，既に進行中のプロジェクトだけでなく既存の実践を取り上げ，それらをSDGs目標に似た形に仕立て上げることはいとも簡単であり，SDGsは曖昧な言葉遣いのせいでこうした行いには非常に弱い。加えて，一部の企業は，SDGsコンプライアンスの名の下に二枚舌を使っているという非難も受けている。環境保護団体に多額の寄付をして世間のイメージをよくしようとしながら従業員には生活賃金を払わない，というのがその一例である。SDGsの意図は普遍的に有益な革新と変容への触媒になることだったのだから，こうした行いは明らかに誤りである。

　グリーンウォッシングを疑われる企業に対する非難はSDGs報告をしばしば好意的でない見方で描くが，この慣行を巡る論争には希望を持てる側面があるかもしれない。いかなる程度のSDGs報告であっても，持続可能性の実践について，企業をそれまで以上の精査にさらす。近年では，最も腰の重い企業ですら持続可能性の取り組みを拡大するよう世論が駆り立てるのが極めて一般的になっているが，それにもかかわらず，こ

のことがグリーンウォッシングをしているという非難の殺到を招くのは避けられない。しかし，グラスゴー・カレドニアン大学ロンドン校の講師エリカ・チャールズは，多国籍企業の実践におけるほんのわずかな，広報活動に触発された変化でも，重大な「影響と波及効果を同業他社に与え，事業への取り組み方法を見直すようにさせる」こともあるのではないかと言う。こういった理由から，批判者は不十分な報告だと理解したものに対する非難を多少自制することが肝要だ，と主張する人もいるだろう。メディアからの過度に厳しい反発に思いとどまって，企業がまったく何もしなくなるかもしれないからである。環境の持続可能性を装って行われる企業の取り組みが失敗したり不誠実なものだったりしても，結局のところまったく無駄な努力ではないのかもしれないと思える。

> 語句　unanimously「全員一致で」，disconnect「断絶」，reference「〜に言及する」，quantifiable「数量化できる」，disparity「相違，不均衡」，in the pipeline「進行中で」，wording「言葉遣い，言い回し」，double-dealing「二枚舌，言行不一致」，beef up「〜を増強する」，living wage「生活賃金（最低限の生活を維持するために必要な賃金）」，catalyst「触媒，触発するもの」，transformation「変化，変容」，miss the mark「的を外す，失敗する」，unflattering「好意的でない」，silver lining「明るい希望」，uncompromising「妥協しない，頑固な」，avalanche「殺到」，miniscule「微小な」，ripple effect「波状効果」，backlash「(社会的な) 反発」，insincere「誠意のない」，wasted「無駄な」

(32) – 解答　4

問題文の訳　PIMCO が行った調査によると，

選択肢の訳
1　企業が設定した SDGs 目標に向けた進展の 2015 年以来の減速は，目標が利益に悪影響を与えると企業が恐れていることを示している。
2　国際連合の動機に対する不信感が，多くの企業が SDGs の重要性をなかなか認めようとしていない主な理由である。
3　企業は発表する報告書の数字を改ざんすることで，SDGs に違反していることを隠そうとしているように見える。
4　多くの企業は SDGs に賛同しているが，事業に有益な方法でどのようにそれらを実行するかを決められないでいる。

解説　第 1 段落からわかるのは，多くの企業が SDGs の理念を受け入れながら，どのように企業活動に組み込めばいいのか戸惑っている現状である。それに合致するのは **4**。本文の many businesses ... embrace the SDGs を many corporations approve of the SDGs と，add business value を beneficial to their business と言い換えている。

(33) – 解答　2

問題文の訳　企業が「グリーンウォッシング」をしていると非難される 1 つの理由は何か。

選択肢の訳　1　SDGs のいくつかの不明瞭な言葉遣いが大きな混乱を招いているので，企業の方針に関する誤解がほぼ確実に生じる。
2　一部の企業は，自分たちが既にしていたことを SDGs に沿って行動する取り組みの一部に見せかけようと試みている。
3　SDGs の多くに設定されている非現実的な目標が，個々の目標すべてを満たしているふりをするよう一部の企業に強いている。
4　SDGs の多くは環境とは無関係なのだから，それらに重点を置き，環境関連の目標はないがしろにした方が楽だということを企業は知っている。

解説　第 2 段落では，企業への批判が 2 つ取り上げられている。1 つは，SDGs 以前からしていることを SDGs への取り組みに見せかけ，「やっている感」を演出すること。もう 1 つは，多額の寄付と低賃金のように表の顔と裏の顔を使い分けていること。2 が前者と一致する。1 の「SDGs のいくつかの不明瞭な言葉遣い」は本文にあるが，企業が都合のいいように利用しているだけで，企業についての誤解を招く原因になっているわけではない。

(34) – 解答　3

問題文の訳　エリカ・チャールズの論評は，この文章の文脈ではどう解釈するのが最適か。

選択肢の訳　1　大企業は，同業他社に影響を与えて環境規制に抵抗させることによって，SDGs 報告を骨抜きにしようとしている。
2　批判者は 1 つの産業の最大手企業に重点を置くのではなく，グリーンウォッシングの責任を問われる全事業者に目を向けることが重要である。
3　重要とは思えない小さな変化を大企業が実行するときは，過度に批判的になるのは賢明ではないかもしれない。
4　大企業の SDGs 報告の大半は非常にいい加減に行われているので，全面的に新しいシステムを開発する必要がある。

解説　第 3 段落第 1 文の the practice は greenwashing を指す。これに silver lining「希望を持てる側面」があるということは，この段落では greenwashing のポジティブな面を扱うと予想される。わずかな変化が一石を投じて業界全体を変えることもあり得る，というチャールズのコメントと，何もしないよりはグリーンウォッシングの方がましなのだから厳し過ぎる非難で企業を委縮させるべきではない，という続く内容から，3 が正解。

全文訳　**家賃統制**

米国全域の主要な大都市での住居費急騰に直面し，多数の自治体は，低所得住民が安

定した住宅利用機会を確保できることを目的とする家賃統制法を課している。一般にこれらの法律は市が運営する委員会によって定められ，住居費が毎年ごくわずかな率以上に上昇しないことを保証する。表面上は，家賃統制は弱い市民を経済的苦境から保護するものと見なすことができるものの，これらの制限は経済学者からほぼ一様に糾弾されている。彼らの主張によると，家賃統制には家主の収入を制限する効果があるのだから，法律は新規の不動産物件を建てるインセンティブを減少させる。利用できる賃貸物件が乏しくなるのは避けられず，需要と供給の原理に従って，家賃統制を免除された住宅の家賃は急激に押し上げられる。加えて，家賃統制された物件に居住する幸運に恵まれた借家人は，自分の経済状況がよくなってもその物件にとどまり続ける傾向があり，より所得の低い人たちが利用できる住宅供給に与える悪影響を大きく拡大させる。そうであるなら，家賃統制法が改善しようとするまさにその問題を法自体が悪化させるのは明白だ，と経済学者は主張する。

一方，家賃統制支持派は，建設されて間もない住宅は一般に家賃統制法を免除されていると指摘する。実際，これまでの研究が示すところでは，市場に以前から存在する不動産物件に家賃統制規制が課せられている都市では，ほとんどの規制は新規の住宅建設に悪影響を与えない。しかし経済学者の主張では，その代わり家主は家賃統制によって，賃貸不動産を販売用物件に変えたり，さらには長期居住者に売ったりといった手段を講じることを余儀なくされ，賃貸住宅の供給不足をさらに助長する。

経済学者と家賃統制支持派両者が一致している点が1つある。家賃を制限すれば，金銭的に恵まれない人々が自宅から強制退去させられるリスクが下がることである。さらに，サンフランシスコ住民の住所と移住の履歴を調べた研究者の調査では，家賃統制された物件に住んでいた低所得層，特にマイノリティーは，家賃統制された物件から退去した後も市内に居住し続ける可能性がより高かった。これは低所得層の一部には明るい調査結果だが，賃貸物件の供給不足に由来する安価な選択肢の欠如のために住宅を見つけることのできないほかの人々の問題にこの対策は対処していない，と経済学者は言う。

しかし，経済学者がしばしば見逃すのは，住宅の安定性の問題である。米国の税法は，税の減免という形で，持ち家の所有者にかなりの給付金を与えている。つまり，家を購入するのに十分な資金を持たない人は，これらの給付金を利用できないのである。したがって家賃統制がなければ，低所得の借家人は金銭的苦境のために立ち退かされるリスクが特に高くなる。強制的な引っ越しが心身の健康に与える有害な影響は多くの文書で裏付けられており，男性より女性への影響の方が深刻だと証明されている。妊娠中にストレスを受ける女性の子供が長期的な心理的影響を被ることを考えれば，これは特に気がかりであり，また，住居がほとんど安定しない子供の方が，高校を卒業する確率も低い。家賃統制を公然と非難する際に経済学者が挙げる量的な論拠に幾分かの妥当性があるのは確かだが，家賃統制のより広くより有益な意味合いを市の職員たちは見逃してはならない。

語句　skyrocket「急騰する」，municipality「自治体」，drive up「（価格など）を急速に上昇させる」，amplify「～を増強する，拡大する」，

aggravate「～を悪化させる」，preexisting「以前から存在する」，for-sale「販売用の」，shortfall「不足」，displace「～を強制退去させる」，vacate「～を立ち退く」，subset「部分集合」，tax break「税の軽減措置」，evict「～を立ち退かせる」，decry「～を公然と非難する」

(35) – 解答 ③

問題文の訳 家賃統制について経済学者が共通して批判していることの1つは，

選択肢の訳
1. 近年の建設ブームに起因する家賃の急上昇を家賃統制が補えていないことである。
2. 賃貸アパートを規制する市の委員会が，家賃統制されている物件から人々を強制的に出て行かせるよう，家主から容易に影響され得ることである。
3. ほかの人たちほど経済的に恵まれていないかもしれない住民が利用できる住居の選択肢を，家賃統制が実際には制限していることである。
4. 家賃統制は市内で利用できるアパートの供給を増やす助けとなるが，アパートの需要を減らす一因にもなることである。

解説 問題文の common criticism made by economists は，第1段落第3文の universally condemned by economists に対応している。同段落の続く記述によると，家賃収入が低いと新しい物件が建たない→家賃統制されていない物件の家賃が上がる→家賃統制されている物件を借りている人たちが出て行かない→さらに所得の低い人たちが借りる物件が不足する，という結果を招く。これに合致するのは **3** である。

(36) – 解答 ④

問題文の訳 家賃統制支持派は以下の記述のどれに最も賛同する可能性が高いか。

選択肢の訳
1. 家賃統制は一時的な住宅不足の結果かもしれないが，不足は長期的には建設の増加によって相殺される。
2. 築年数がたった多くの建物は家賃統制の適用を受けないのだから，賃貸住宅不足は実際には新規建設事業の欠如の結果である。
3. 家賃統制法に対応して家主が取る対策は，実際には住宅を利用できる可能性が増える結果になる傾向がある。
4. 家賃統制法は通例既に利用可能な賃貸不動産にしか影響しないので，家賃統制は経済学者が主張するほど住宅市場に影響しない。

解説 第2段落前半に家賃統制支持派の主張が書かれている。新規に建設される住宅には家賃統制が適用されないのだからさして悪影響は受けない，というのが彼らの考えで，家賃統制が新規住宅建設へのインセンティブをそぐという経済学者たちの主張と対立する。したがって **4** が正解である。

(37) – 解答 ②

問題文の訳 この文章の筆者は最終段落で家賃統制について暗に何と言っているか。

選択肢の訳　1　家賃統制法に関する経済学者の警告は現時点ではほとんど意味を成さないが，この問題は将来の世代によって再考される必要がある。
2　家賃統制法にいかなる欠点があろうと，経済学的分析だけでは測れない重要な役割を社会で果たしている。
3　家賃統制法が住宅市場に与える悪影響は，家賃統制法がもたらし得る社会的恩恵より大きい。
4　家賃統制法がより豊かな人々に与える恩恵は，最終的には社会全体が利用できるようになる。

解説　最終段落では，housing stability の問題を取り上げている。住まいが安定しなければ心身の健康が侵され，子供の将来にも悪影響を与える。家賃統制にはこうしたマイナス面を防ぐ役割もあるというのが筆者の考えで，経済学者の主張に一理あることは認めながらも，家賃統制を肯定的に捉えている。経済学者による批判を drawbacks とまとめ，本文の the quantitative arguments economists make を economic analysis と短く言い換えた **2** が正解。

全文訳　**ナセルと汎アラブ主義**

　1952年，陸軍将校のグループが，英国の支援を受けるエジプトの君主制から権力を奪い，国王ファルーク1世を国外に追放した。反乱軍は自由将校団として知られるエジプト軍隊内部の民族主義運動の一部で，このグループは，指導者であるガマル・アブデル・ナセルという若いエジプト人将校の反植民地イデオロギーを中心に結成されていた。クーデター時の公式のトップは陸軍上級将校である戦争の英雄ムハンマド・ナギーブで，ナセルは彼を名目だけの長に据えた。ナセル自身はその役回りに必要な威信を当時は欠いていたので，彼は新政権に正統性を与えるため，ナギーブが一般大衆から集めるとてつもない声望を利用していたのである。しかし，身の程をわきまえずナセルに反旗を翻そうとしたナギーブは権力の座から排除され，黒子から表舞台に立ったナセルが1954年に国の指導者の地位に就いた。

　政権を担っていた長い年月の間に，ナセルはエジプトを作り変えた。彼は，無償の教育と医療，住宅供給の改善，労働改革を含む遠大な近代化プログラムを策定した。君主制の間の土地所有の封建制度によって富の不平等な配分が生まれていたが，ナセルは，農民に有利なように条件を改善し，個人が所有できる土地の量を制限する改革でこれに対処した。ナセルは庶民の出であり，人民の味方を自任していた。彼のイデオロギーは「ナセル主義」として知られるようになったが，社会主義と富の再配分に根ざすものであり，また彼以前の支配者と違い，ナセルは汚職と無縁だった。

　しかし，だからと言って彼の統治が温情的だったわけではない。異論は容赦なく弾圧され，ナセルは民主主義へのあからさまな軽蔑を表明した。彼は，中東全域におけるアラブ統一，すなわち汎アラブ主義というビジョンを達成するには，自身の平等主義的社会プログラムと苛烈な施行戦術はどちらも欠かせないと考えていた。統一されたアラブ

世界でエジプトが盟主としての役割を担うことになるとすれば，まずエジプトは，ナセルの政策に害を及ぼす可能性のある敵は誰であっても確実に政治の舞台から遠ざけながら，国内的に経済を強化し社会福祉を改善しなければならなかった。
　反植民地主義がナセルの外交政策の基本であり，彼はアフリカ全土の解放運動を支援した。自身のカリスマと演説の才に助けられたナセルは，エジプト社会を変容させたのみならず，ほかのアラブ諸国の熱望の対象となり得るモデルも示した。ナセルが国際的に注目を浴びるようになったのは，1956年，戦略的かつ経済的に重要なスエズ運河を国有化したときのことである。スエズ運河はエジプト領土内に位置するにもかかわらず，英国とフランスが共同で所有し運用していたのだが，エジプト兵たちが運河の支配権を奪った。イスラエルとフランスと英国の三軍がエジプトに侵攻し，スエズ地域のエジプト軍を直ちに打ち負かして「スエズ危機」として知られるようになったものを突然引き起こした。しかし，エジプトは外交分野でもっと大きな成功を収めた。ソビエト連邦は，その地域での将来的な影響力拡大をもくろんで当時エジプトの歓心を買おうとしており，西側帝国主義の事例と見なすものを激しく非難した。ソ連政府は，侵攻者が撤退しなければ西側ヨーロッパへの核攻撃も辞さない構えすら見せた。恐れおののいた米国はソ連政府との対立を回避するため舞台裏で介入し，結果的にヨーロッパとイスラエルの侵攻者は屈辱的な撤退をした。ナセルは西側に公然と逆らってスエズ危機を切り抜けたのみならず，見込みの低い賭けに勝利したのだが，しかしその幾分かは米ソ政府の思いがけない仲裁によるものだった。それにもかかわらず，ナセルの行動の結果，中東全域で大衆から賛美の声が湧き上がり，中東内で彼の指導者としての役割が強化された。
　ナセルが権力の絶頂にあったとき，アラブ統一は真に実現可能に思われた。植民地支配を脱した中東諸国は連帯して共に立ち上がり，独立した地政学的ブロックとしての自己同一性を獲得した。だが，1958年に成立した，エジプトとシリアの連合国であるアラブ連合共和国は，ナセルが課した中央集権化政策にシリアが不満だったせいで短命に終わった。アラブ諸国の統一が可能だという考えは，エジプトが周辺アラブ国家を率いてイスラエルとの破滅的な戦争を行った1967年に打ち砕かれた。この戦争の結果，相当な領土が失われただけでなく，また，アラブ人の魂は消えることのない深い傷を負ったのである。
　ナセルの人気は1970年に亡くなる前の年月で衰えたが，たとえ今日の不和と争いが汎アラブ主義の見通しを暗くしているとしても，中東の至る所で彼は相変わらず多くの人から偶像視されている。ナセル後のエジプトでは貧富の隔たりが変動し続け，社会的平等というナセルの目標が成就する可能性は低そうである。しかし，ナセルの統治への郷愁にもかかわらず，エジプト人は彼のカリスマに目がくらみ欠点が見えなかったのだ，と主張する評論家もいる。欠点とは例えば，彼の富の再分配政策が，今日まで続く労働人口の国家への過度の経済的依存を助長したことである。そうした非難は確かにもっともだが，結局のところ，常にナセルの人気は業績というより主として彼のイデオロギーの産物だったのだから，この郷愁はおそらくこの先も長く存続することだろう。

　語句　anticolonialist「反植民地の」，coup「クーデター」，figurehead「名

目だけの長」，legitimize「～を合法と認める」，overstep「～を（踏み）越える」，defy「～に（公然と）反抗する」，remake「～を作り直す」，far-reaching「遠大な」，feudal「封建制度の」，benign「慈悲深い，優しい」，dissent「不賛成，異議」，egalitarian「平等主義の」，bolster「～を強化する」，precipitate「～を突然引き起こす」，court「（好意など）を得ようと努める」，avert「～を回避する」，humiliating「屈辱的な」，long odds「あまり見込みのないこと」，fortuitous「偶然の，思いがけない」，intercession「仲裁，とりなし」，adulation「賛美」，consolidation「強化」，geopolitical「地政学的な」，centralization「中央集権化」，abiding「持続する」，psyche「魂，精神」，icon「偶像」，disunity「不和」，fluctuate「変動する」，fruition「達成，実現」，failing「欠点」，overreliance「過度の依存」

(38) – 解答 **2**

問題文の訳 自由将校団について何が推測されるか。

選択肢の訳
1 ムハンマド・ナギーブがグループの指揮権構造を変えようと試みた後，ガマル・アブデル・ナセルはグループを解散する必要があるだろうと考えた。
2 ナギーブの名声のためグループの行動は広範な支持を受けたが，彼が地位を失ったことは，彼が必要不可欠な人物ではなかったことを示していた。
3 グループが権力を握った後どの程度の民主主義を認めるかについて，ナセルとナギーブの間に対立があった。
4 その主義主張はナギーブの考えに基づいていたが，ナセルは，クーデターが暴力的でなく確実に平和的に行われるようにするには自分が統御しなければならないと感じた。

解説 第1段落が自由将校団によるクーデターを簡潔にまとめている。ナセルはナギーブの名声を利用してクーデターを実行したが，結局ナギーブを排除して自ら権力の座に就いた。つまり，**2**のように，ナギーブはお飾りにすぎなかったことになる。**1**と**3**に関する記述はない。自由将校団はナセルの反植民地イデオロギーの下に結集したのだから，**4**は前半を読んだだけで誤りだとわかる。

(39) – 解答 **1**

問題文の訳 この文章の筆者によると，ナセルの苛烈な政治的政策の主たる理由は何だったか。

選択肢の訳
1 エジプトが主導してアラブ世界を統一するという彼の究極の目標は，国内政策が障害なく導入されることを必要とした。
2 普通の人々の富の増加と教育向上は，社会主義を支持する政敵の台頭を招くかもしれない，と彼は恐れていた。

3　自身が庶民の出であり富を持たないことで，エジプト人大衆もほかの政治家たちも彼を弱い指導者と見なすようになるだろう，と彼は恐れていた。
　　　4　君主制への彼の反対はほとんどの人に共有されておらず，ほとんどの人は，前の政権下の方が生活の質はよかったと考えていた。
　解説　第3段落前半に，問題文と同じ harsh という語がある。この段落によると，ナセルは，アラブ統一を主導するには国内基盤の安定が必須と考え，苛烈な政治を行った。異論を弾圧し敵を政治の舞台から遠ざけるという本文の内容を without obstacles とまとめた **1** が正解である。

(40) – 解答 ④

　問題文の訳　以下の記述の中で「スエズ危機」の帰結を最もよく表しているのはどれか。
　選択肢の訳
　　　1　最初は勝利に思えたものが，エジプトと非常に重要な西側同盟国との関係に修復不能なダメージを与えたことがわかった。
　　　2　危機が終わりに近づくとナセルはわずかに優勢になったが，エジプトの軍事的敗北は長期的成功が不可能なことを証明した。
　　　3　当初ナセルはソ連政府の側についているように見えたが，危機の終わりに際しての彼の政策変更は，彼が実際は米国と同盟を結んだことを証明した。
　　　4　ナセルは西側列強に対して大きな政治的勝利を勝ち取ることができたが，とはいえその一部は彼の力が及ばない要因によるものだった。
　解説　第4段落中ほど以降がスエズ危機の記述に充てられている。軍事的には敗北したエジプトだったが，ソ連と米国の外交的介入によって最終的には勝利を得た。段落後半で the fortuitous intercession「思いがけない仲裁」と書かれているように，核攻撃をちらつかせて影響力拡大を狙うソ連と，ソ連との対決を恐れる米国という，ナセルの思惑を超えた国際政治事情を **4** が factors beyond his control と表している。

(41) – 解答 ②

　問題文の訳　この文章の筆者は，多くの現代エジプト人がナセルと彼の統治についてどう感じているかをどのように説明しているか。
　選択肢の訳
　　　1　エジプトの労働者階級は，ナセルを個人としては尊敬しているものの，イスラエルとの戦争がもたらしたダメージについては彼を許していない。
　　　2　ナセルの政策に起因する変化による影響よりも，ナセルがエジプトのために示した哲学とビジョンによる影響を多く受けている。
　　　3　ナセルが導入した全エジプト人のための社会福祉と教育における変化は，彼に続く指導者たちの欠点にもかかわらず，長期的利益をもたらしている。

4 ナセルの個性とカリスマが彼の統治中にエジプト人をどれだけ鼓舞したかを理解できない人々によって形作られている。

解説 ナセル時代への郷愁が今も根強く残ることについて，最終段落に説明がある。ナセル人気は彼の accomplishments ではなく ideology によるものだ，という最終文がポイント。**2** が accomplishments を the changes that arose from his policies と言い換え，ideology を the philosophy and vision と言い換えている。ideology とは，エジプトの指導下によるアラブ統一という理想のことである。

一次試験・筆記 4　問題編 p.80

解答例　Beneath globalization's seemingly positive effects of international trade and integrated markets lie worrying issues. Centralized authoritative bodies, suppression of local economies, and the exploitation of foreign labor are just some of the problems accompanying a more globalized world.

As economies grow more interconnected, further regulation of trade and business becomes necessary. More powerful nations, however, are often quick to seize upon this by establishing central trade commissions and all-encompassing laws, leading to smaller countries having less autonomy to make their own decisions regarding how money, labor, and products flow through their economies.

In addition to drawing power away from developing countries, globalization also stifles their local economies. The rising desirability of certain products grants corporations that create them greater financial leverage to purchase land and materials in poorer countries. By doing so, corporations appropriate valuable local resources for foreign markets that could be better used for local consumption.

Even more concerning is the treatment of foreign labor. Manufacturing is often outsourced to poorer countries to slash costs, which, some argue, provides jobs for low-income communities. In reality, this fosters an unhealthy reliance on large companies, which are then free to exploit local labor—including children—with low wages and poor conditions.

From the perspective of developing countries, it is clear the problems arising from one-sided regulatory pressure, monopolization of smaller economies, and the abuse of poor, vulnerable workers are aspects of globalization that, if ignored, will only continue to worsen.

トピックの訳　「賛成か反対か：グローバリゼーションは今日の世界においてプラスに働く力である」

解説　グローバリゼーションは，経済・政治・文化・情報・テクノロジーなど多方面から論じることができるトピックである。この解答例は論点を経済に絞り，disagree の立場からグローバリゼーションを批判している。第1段落でポイントとして挙げているのは「中央集権化した権威機関」「地域経済の抑圧」「海外労働力の搾取」の3つ。第2段落以降でそれぞれのポイントを1つずつ詳述し，最終段落で3つのポイントを再確認して結論とする，基本的な5段落構成のエッセイである。

　最初のポイントについては，貿易とビジネスの規制は大国の主導下で作られる委員会や法により決定されるので，小国が自律的に意思決定することができなくなるとしている。2つ目のポイントについては，地域経済を潤すべき特産品や資源が企業に吸い上げられて海外に流出し，地域経済を圧迫すると論じている。そして最後のポイントについては，海外の安価な労働力を求める大企業によって，子供を含む労働者が搾取されていると指摘している。いずれも，グローバリゼーションは先進国と発展途上国の格差を埋めるものではなく，むしろ拡大させるものだという視点で貫かれており，非常に説得力のある内容になっている。

　トピックに agree の立場を取るなら，第1段落冒頭に書かれているように，国際貿易と統合市場のメリットについて述べることができる。例えば，貿易の自由化は世界的な経済成長を促す，市場が統合され関税が撤廃されれば消費者はより安価で質の高い製品やサービスを利用することができる，発展途上国は先進国の技術を取り入れることで自国の発展につなげることができる，など，一般的にグローバリゼーションの恩恵と考えられるポイントは数多い。

　この解答例の表面面で注目したいのは，第1段落と最終段落でのポイントの大胆な言い換えに加え，第3段落冒頭で In addition to drawing power away from developing countries，第4段落冒頭で Even more concerning is と，長いつなぎ言葉を用いていることである。例えば Secondly，In addition，Furthermore などの簡単な副詞（句）で済ますのではなく，このように前の段落の内容を受ける形で次の段落につなぐことで，全体の流れが非常にスムーズになっている。

一次試験・リスニング Part 1 問題編 p.81〜82

No.1 — 解答 2

スクリプト
★: That was the last interviewee. Looks like we have some decent candidates for the manager position.
☆: I'm not convinced we should stop looking yet.
★: But the position has been open for over a month. I've been covering as best I can, but it's a struggle.
☆: I know, but the job requires a very specific skill set.
★: Several applicants seem to meet most of our requirements. Perhaps you should adjust your expectations a little. I mean, we could wait forever for the perfect person.
☆: I'm not so sure. I don't want to jump the gun.
Question: What does the man imply?

全文訳
★: 面接を受けるのはあの人が最後だったね。マネージャーのポジションにふさわしい候補者が何人かいるようだ。
☆: 探すのをやめた方がいいとはまだ確信できないわ。
★: だけどこのポジションは1カ月以上空席のままだよ。僕ができる限りカバーしているけど，四苦八苦している。
☆: そうだけど，この仕事にはとても特別なスキルセットが必要よ。
★: 何人かの応募者は僕たちの条件のほとんどを満たしているように思える。君の期待は少し修正が必要なんじゃないかな。つまり，完璧な人を待っていても切りがないかもしれない。
☆: それはどうかしら。私は早まったことはしたくない。
質問: 男性は暗に何と言っているか。

選択肢の訳
1 女性は自分のスキルセットを向上させることを考えるべきだ。
2 女性が設定している基準は高過ぎる。
3 彼はそのポジションの候補者として考慮に値する。
4 適任者が見つかるまで彼がカバーすることができる。

解説 今回の応募者に適任者が数名いると考える男性は，意見を異にする女性に対して，3つ目の発言で Perhaps you should adjust your expectations a little. と言っている。つまり，女性の期待（=基準）は高過ぎると思っていることになる。jump the gun「早まったことをする」。

No.2 — 解答 4

スクリプト
☆: Frank, will you be available on Friday for a feedback session about last month's sales figures?
★: Friday? I've got two meetings in the morning, and I promised a

　　　　　client I'd visit their office that afternoon.
☆： Frank, you know I've been telling you to delegate more.
★： Believe it or not, I took your advice to heart. But my whole staff is working overtime now, so I can't ask them to do more.
☆： Then you have to ask your boss to bring additional sales staff on board.
★： I wish it were that easy. As you know, the president wants to cut costs.
☆： Yeah, but without a properly functioning sales team, the company's future would be pretty hopeless. I think you have a strong case, so don't give up so easily.

Question: What does the woman suggest that the man do?

全文訳
☆： フランク，金曜日に，先月の売上高に関するフィードバックセッションに出る時間はある？
★： 金曜日？　午前中に会議が2つあって，その日の午後はクライアントのオフィスを訪問する約束がある。
☆： フランク，ほかの人にもっと仕事を振るよう，ずっと言い続けているじゃない。
★： まさかと思うかもしれないけど，ご忠告は心に染みたよ。でも，今は部下全員が残業をしているから，もっとやってくれとは頼めないんだ。
☆： じゃあ，追加の営業スタッフを入れてくれるよう，上司に頼まないと。
★： そう簡単だといいんだけど。知ってのとおり，社長はコストを削減したがっているから。
☆： そうね，だけど，きちんと機能する営業チームがなければ，会社の将来に希望があまり持てなくなる。あなたには十分な論拠があると思うから，そんなに簡単に諦めちゃ駄目よ。

質問：女性は男性が何をすることを提案しているか。

選択肢の訳
1　営業スタッフに相談する。
2　フィードバック会議の日時を変更する。
3　部下の給料を削減する。
4　追加のスタッフを頼む。

解説　部下も忙しいので自分で仕事をたくさん抱え込んでいる男性に，女性が改善策を述べている。女性は3つ目の発言で ask your boss to bring additional sales staff on board と提案し，男性が否定的な答えをすると，最後の発言で，営業チームの重要性を力説している。つまり，スタッフの増員を頼むべきだという提案は一貫していることになる。

No.3 - 解答　③

スクリプト　★： Hi, Lisa. How are you enjoying your violin classes?

☆： They're good but very demanding.
★： Yeah, I studied with Mrs. Jackson for years.
☆： I've been playing since I was a kid, but she has me working on the basics.
★： It's just to perfect your technique.
☆： I know, but she's such a slave driver!
★： You do know that she's the most sought-after teacher in New York, and a virtuoso herself.
☆： That's true.
★： It'll be tough, but if you stick with Mrs. Jackson, you won't regret it.

Question: What do we learn about Mrs. Jackson?

全文訳
★： やあ，リサ。バイオリンの授業は楽しい？
☆： いい授業だけど，とてもきついわね。
★： そうだよね，僕は何年もジャクソン先生の下で学んだから。
☆： 私は子供のころからずっと弾いているのに，先生は基礎をやらせるのよ。
★： それは君の技術を完璧にするためだよ。
☆： わかるけど，先生はすごいスパルタ教師だわ！
★： 先生がニューヨークで最も引っ張りだこの教師で，彼女自身が名演奏家だと，君も知っているだろう。
☆： そのとおりね。
★： 大変だけど，ジャクソン先生についていけば後悔することはないよ。

質問：ジャクソン先生について何がわかるか。

選択肢の訳
1　ニューヨークの交響楽団で演奏している。
2　バイオリンを教え始めたばかりだ。
3　生徒に多くを要求する。
4　初心者を担当する方が好きだ。

解説　女性は最初の発言で授業は very demanding だと言い，3つ目の発言で先生は slave driver「厳しい教師，人使いの荒い人」だと述べている。したがって **3** が正解。ジャクソン先生の活動拠点はニューヨークだが，交響楽団に所属しているとは言っていない。virtuoso「名演奏家」。

No.4 - 解答 ④

スクリプト
☆： Hey, Patrick, you better watch out for the boss today.
★： Why? What's up?
☆： She needed to make a bunch of copies this morning, but the copy machine was still broken.
★： Oh no. I was supposed to call and get the maintenance company to come. It totally slipped my mind.

☆：Don't worry too much. She tends to blow things out of proportion, but she usually forgives and forgets pretty quickly.
★：Well, I'll get on it now and stay under her radar for the rest of the day.

Question: Why is the man worried?

全文訳
☆：ねえパトリック，今日は上司に気を付けた方がいいわよ。
★：どうして？　何があったの？
☆：今朝彼女はコピーを大量に取る必要があったんだけど，コピー機が壊れたままだったの。
★：しまった。僕がメンテナンス会社に電話して，来てもらうことになっていたんだ。すっかり忘れていたよ。
☆：心配し過ぎることはないわ。彼女は何でも大げさに騒ぎがちだけど，たいてい結構早く許してくれるし，忘れるから。
★：うーん，コピー機の件はすぐに何とかして，後は今日1日彼女の目を逃れることにするよ。

質問：男性はなぜ心配しているのか。

選択肢の訳
1　彼は上司と会う約束を守らなかった。
2　彼は上司の代わりにコピーを取るのを忘れた。
3　彼はうっかりコピー機を壊した。
4　彼はコピー機を修理してもらわなかった。

解説　女性は2つ目の発言で，今朝上司が使おうとしたらコピー機が壊れたままだったと話し，男性はそれに対してI was supposed to call and get the maintenance company to come. と言っている。コピー機の修理依頼は男性の担当だったことがわかるので，**4**が正解。get on ～「～に取りかかる」，stay under *A's* radar「Aの目を逃れる」。

No.5 – 解答 ①

スクリプト
★：So, Janet, did the boss like our ideas for the new TV ad campaign?
☆：Actually, he said our budget is going to be halved.
★：That's insane. That won't be nearly enough.
☆：Tell me about it. He wants to put more ads on the radio. Thinks it's a more cost-efficient way to reach our target market.
★：Not according to our marketing polls.
☆：He also suggested we try another direct-mail campaign and see how that pans out.
★：Well, I guess we'll just have to do what he wants.

Question: What does the boss want these people to do?

全文訳
★：それで，ジャネット，新しいテレビ広告キャンペーンの僕たちのアイデアを上司は気に入ってくれた？

☆: 実はね，私たちの予算は半分になると言われたわ。
★: むちゃくちゃだ。それじゃ到底足りないよ。
☆: 本当よね。彼はラジオでもっと広告を流したいの。うちのターゲット市場に届くには，その方がコスト効率がいいと思っているのよ。
★: 僕たちのマーケティング調査によるとそうじゃない。
☆: ダイレクトメールキャンペーンをまたやってみて，どんな結果になるか様子を見てはどうかとも言われたわ。
★: うーん，彼が望むようにするしかなさそうだね。

質問：上司はこの人たちにどうしてほしいのか。

選択肢の訳
1 広告戦略を変更する。
2 テレビ広告の結果を待つ。
3 もっとマーケティング調査を行う。
4 ダイレクトメールキャンペーンを中止する。

解説 女性が上司の意向を男性に伝えている。上司の希望は put more ads on the radio と try another direct-mail campaign なので，2人が最初に提案したテレビ広告という戦略は却下されたことになる。したがって正解は **1**。pan out 「（結局〜に）終わる」。

No.6 — 解答

スクリプト
☆: Tom, long time no see. How's everything with your new job at the ad company?
★: In one word, stressful. The majority of ads I create are for engineers, so I have to get all the technical details right, and that's not easy.
☆: And I guess you have a lot of tight deadlines.
★: Yes, but that's nothing new. The problem is I have to do a lot more research now, too.
☆: You always did great work at RCB Graphics, so I'm sure you'll get used to it soon.
★: Thanks. I hope you're right.

Question: What is the man's concern?

全文訳
☆: トム，久しぶり。広告会社での新しい仕事はうまくいっているの？
★: 一言で言うと，ストレスがたまるね。僕が作る広告の大半はエンジニア向けだから，技術的な詳細を全部正確に理解しなければならなくて，それが楽じゃないんだ。
☆: それに厳しい締め切りをたくさん抱えているんでしょうね。
★: うん，でもそれは今に始まったことじゃない。問題は，今では前よりずっと多くの調査をしなければならないことなんだ。
☆: あなたは RCB グラフィックス社ではいつも立派な仕事をしていたんだ

から，きっとすぐに慣れるわよ。
★：ありがとう。そうだといいんだけど。
質問：男性の懸念は何か。

選択肢の訳
1　彼はまだ十分な能力があると感じていない。
2　RCB 社での彼の顧客は不満を抱いている。
3　彼は厳しい締め切りを抱えることに慣れていない。
4　彼は RCB 社の製品は売れないだろうと思っている。

解説　男性は，新しい仕事はストレスがたまると述べ，技術的詳細の正確な理解の必要性と調査量の増加をその理由に挙げている。そして，すぐに慣れると励ます女性に対しても I hope you're right. と控えめに答えていることから，自分が今の仕事に competent「十分な能力がある」とは思っていないことがわかる。厳しい締め切りは nothing new だと言っているので 3 は誤り。

No.7 – 解答　④

スクリプト
★：I think I've been tricked!
☆：Tricked? By whom?
★：A salesman came to my door. He was so persuasive I didn't know how to say no.
☆：Oh no, you didn't buy something, did you?
★：Well, he said it was a revolutionary new filing system. But when the package arrived this morning, it was just a plastic box. For $100!
☆：Have you tried to contact him?
★：I rang the number he gave straightaway, but it turns out there's no such number.
☆：I think you're going to have to chalk this one up to experience.

Question: What does the woman think?

全文訳
★：だまされたみたいだ！
☆：だまされた？　誰に？
★：セールスマンが訪ねてきたんだ。すごく説得力があったから，断りようがなくて。
☆：あらまあ，何か買わなかったでしょうね。
★：うーん，革命的な新型ファイリングシステムだと言っていた。だけど今朝荷物が届いたら，ただのプラスチックの箱だった。100 ドルしたんだよ！
☆：連絡してみた？
★：教えてもらった番号にすぐ電話したんだけど，結局そんな番号はないんだよ。

☆：この件をいい経験としなければならないでしょうね。

質問：女性はどう思っているか。

選択肢の訳
1 男性はその番号に電話し続けるべきだ。
2 男性はこの経験を使ってセールスマンになるべきだ。
3 男性はファイリングシステムを利用するべきだ。
4 男性はお金を取り戻す望みを捨てるべきだ。

解説 女性の1つ目と2つ目の発言は男性に話を促すための発話で，女性の考えは最後の発言にある。chalk ～ up to experience は「（失敗など）を貴重な経験として覚えておく，教訓とする」という意味なので，今回の件については諦めた方がいいと思っていることになる。したがって**4**が正解。

No.8 - 解答 ②

スクリプト
★：So, what do you think of the office space, Ms. Kato?
☆：The location is outstanding, but it's quite a bit more spacious than what we were originally looking for.
★：I understand that, but given the way your firm has been expanding over the past two years, it might make sense to allow yourself some flexibility.
☆：Good point. On a square-meter basis the price is certainly reasonable. And I'd hate to have to think about relocating again, at least not for several years.

Question: What will the woman probably do?

全文訳
★：それで，このオフィス物件はどう思われますか，カトーさま。
☆：立地は素晴らしいけれど，私たちが最初探していたより少し広々としていますね。
★：それはわかりますが，そちらの会社がこの2年でどれだけ成長してきたかを考えると，多少は柔軟性を持たせておくのが賢明かもしれませんよ。
☆：確かにそうね。平米当たりだと賃料は確かにお手ごろです。それに，少なくとも数年は，また移転しなければならないなんて考えるのも嫌だし。

質問：女性はおそらくどうするか。

選択肢の訳
1 もっと便利な場所を探す。
2 このオフィス物件を借りることに決める。
3 よそでもっと狭いところを探す。
4 数年以内にまた引っ越す。

解説 不動産屋と客の会話。女性の a bit more spacious という発言を受けて，男性は allow yourself some flexibility と提案しているが，これは，会社のさらなる成長を見越してこの広いオフィスを借りておくということ。女性の最後の発言から，提案に対して前向きな気持ちになっている

ことがわかる。

No.9 - 解答 ③

スクリプト

★: This is a great apartment. I think it would suit your parents well.

☆: Yeah, the location is great, and it's in the vicinity of the train station. It might need a few modifications for them, though.

★: Well, let's think about what they'll need. Your dad's still fairly strong, so the outside steps shouldn't be a problem for him.

☆: Yeah, but I think a ramp would be better, especially if Mom needs a wheelchair, which is looking increasingly likely.

★: I'm sure a ramp could be added. Maybe even a wheelchair lift, if it comes to that.

☆: There's also no handrail to support them if they were to slip. Mom's going to want to bring her friends over, and they're all in their 70s or 80s.

★: Safety's definitely a concern. And since we're on the subject, there's no outdoor light by the walkway leading to the steps.

☆: I'm thinking we could probably take care of what we've discussed, which would keep costs down.

★: Maybe, but let's ask the agent if the building's owner could do them first, or even if they're possible. If not, we can look at some other places before we decide.

Question: What is one thing these people say about the apartment?

全文訳

★: 素晴らしいマンションだね。ご両親にぴったりだろうと思う。

☆: ええ、立地が素晴らしいし、駅にも近い。両親のために少しリフォームする必要があるかもしれないけど。

★: じゃあ、ご両親が必要になるものを考えてみよう。お父さんはまだまあまあ達者だから、外の階段は問題にならないはずだ。

☆: ええ、だけどスロープの方がいいだろうと思う。特にママが車椅子が必要になったらね。そうなりそうな感じがどんどん強くなっているし。

★: スロープはきっと足せるよ。ことによると車椅子用の昇降機も。必要になればだけど。

☆: 足を滑らせでもしたときに体を支える手すりもないわ。ママは友達を連れて来たがるだろうし、みんな70代か80代だもの。

★: 安全性は確かに懸念材料だ。その話になったついでだけど、階段につながる通路に外灯がないね。

☆: 今話し合ったことはたぶん自分たちで何とかできるんじゃないかしら。そうすれば費用を安く抑えられるだろうし。

★: そうかもしれないけど、ビルのオーナーがそうしたことを最初にやって

くれるかどうか，あるいはそもそもそうしたことが可能かどうか，業者に聞いてみよう。無理なら，決める前にほかの物件を当たってみてもいいんだし。

質問：この人たちがこのマンションについて言っていることの1つは何か。

選択肢の訳 1 公共交通機関に十分近くない。
2 自分で修理するとお金がかかり過ぎるだろう。
3 高齢の訪問客には危険かもしれない。
4 外にスロープを作るスペースがない。

解説 女性の高齢の両親にマンションを探している夫婦の会話。女性の最初の発言の it's in the vicinity of the train station から，**1** は誤り。また女性は最後の発言で，それまで話していたリフォームを自分ですれば which would keep costs down と言っているので，**2** も誤り。男性の3つ目の発言の I'm sure a ramp could be added. から，**4** も誤り。女性が3つ目の発言で，母親が招くであろう高齢の友人たちにからめて，手すりがないので危ないといったことを述べているが，それが **3** と合致する。

No.10 解答

スクリプト ☆：Thanks for coming to this meeting. I wanted to catch up on progress with the English program at our affiliated elementary school. Did you get everything sorted out?

★：Quite the opposite. We observed classes and talked with teachers, and it's the same old story. The two part-timers are doing great in the circumstances, though.

○：Yes, but one of them told me she may give notice if things continue as they are.

☆：You're kidding. Give me some specifics.

★：Well, curriculum development is so far behind schedule that teachers often have no materials for classes.

☆：But that's Helen's job, not theirs. That's the whole reason we sent her out from the university.

★：Exactly. And that seems to be the heart of the problem. Helen seems to be leaving work early and isn't getting the curriculum done.

○：I also hear that some of the teachers are afraid to confront her, too, since they think she's their boss.

☆：But she's not. Margaret is.

★：That's not how they see it.

○：So, what can we do? Are you considering pulling Helen out of the elementary school?

★: We're not there yet. I suggest we sit down with her and have a frank discussion. We need to set clear goals and then monitor things more carefully.

☆: OK, and we also need to make clear that Margaret's in overall charge of the English program and make sure that she's being more proactive.

Question: What is one of the problems at the elementary school?

全文訳 ☆: 今日は集まってくれてありがとう。うちの付属小学校の英語プログラムの進捗状況を教えてもらいたかったの。万事うまく処理できた？

★: 正反対です。授業を視察して教師たちと話したんですが、よくある話ですよ。この状況で、2人の非常勤教師はとてもよくやっていますけどね。

○: ええ、だけどそのうち1人に、このままこんなふうに続くのなら辞表を出すかもしれないと言われました。

☆: そんなばかな。詳しいことを教えて。

★: えー、カリキュラム開発が予定よりずっと遅れていて、教師に授業の教材がないこともしばしばなんです。

☆: だけどそれはヘレンの仕事で、教師たちの仕事じゃないわ。そのためだけに大学から彼女を派遣したのよ。

★: そのとおりです。そしてそれが問題の核心のようです。ヘレンは仕事を早退して、カリキュラムを終わらせていないようなんです。

○: 教師たちは彼女を上司だと思っているので、直談判するのを怖がっている人もいると聞いています。

☆: だけど彼女は上司じゃない。上司はマーガレットよ。

★: 彼らはそういう見方はしていないんです。

○: じゃあ、どうすればいいでしょう。小学校からヘレンを外すことを検討しますか？

★: それはまだ早いでしょう。彼女と膝を交えて率直に話し合うことを提案します。明確な目標を定めて、もっと慎重にいろいろ見極める必要があります。

☆: わかった、それに、マーガレットが英語プログラムの全体責任者であることをはっきりさせて、彼女がもっと能動的に動くようきっちりさせる必要もあるわね。

質問: 小学校の問題の1つは何か。

選択肢の訳　1　カリキュラムのレベルが生徒に合っていない。
2　ヘレンが責任を果たしていない。
3　マーガレットが強過ぎて過度に威張り散らしている。
4　教師たちが教材を作り過ぎている。

> **解説** 小学校で起きている問題の内容は，男性の２つ目の発言以降で述べられている。カリキュラム開発が遅れていて教材が足りない→それはヘレンの仕事だ→ヘレンがサボってカリキュラムを終わらせていない，と続く会話の流れから，**2** が正解。本当はマーガレットが boss なのに教師たちはヘレンを boss と見なしているのだから，**3** は誤り。

A

スクリプト **Political Beliefs**

Many people assume that people's political beliefs are the result of choices made based on logical thinking and the observation of reality. Recent research, however, has questioned this assumption. A study by researcher Chris Fraley, for example, has suggested that children raised by strict, authoritarian parents often have conservative views as adults. On the other hand, children who grow up in households where they are given more freedom and allowed to express their opinions tend to identify themselves as liberal when they reach adulthood.

Other researchers have found evidence that the reasons for one's political beliefs are at least partially biological. For instance, a study by two political scientists demonstrated that conservatives tend to react faster and more intensely than liberals to negative stimuli such as shocking photos. This "negativity bias," the scientists say, appears to be hard-wired into the brain. Moreover, DNA comparisons in another study also indicated that liberals and conservatives have differences in certain genes that affect how the brain reacts to threats or how open it is to new ideas. It is therefore possible that nature, as well as nurture, shapes our political beliefs.

Questions
No.11 What did Chris Fraley's research suggest?
No.12 What do the two political scientists believe about "negativity bias"?

全文訳 **政治的信念**

人々の政治的信念は論理的思考と現実の観察に基づいて行われる選択の結果だ，と多くの人は想定する。しかし，最近の研究が，この想定に異議を唱えている。例えば，研究者クリス・フレイリーによる研究は，厳格で権威主義的な親に育てられた子供は大人になるとしばしば保守的な考えを持つことを示唆している。一方，より多くの自由を与えられ，意見を述べることを許される家庭で育つ子供は，成人に達すると自らをリベラルだと認識する傾向がある。

人の政治的信念の理由が少なくとも部分的には生物学的なものである証拠を発見した研究者もいる。例えば，保守的な人の方がリベラルな人より，ショッキングな写真などのネガティブな刺激に対してより速くより激しく反応する傾向があることを，2人の政治学者による研究が証明した。この「ネガティビティバイアス」は脳のシステムに組み込まれているように思える，とこの学者たちは言う。さらに，別の研究におけるDNAの比較も，脅威に対する脳の反応の仕方や脳が新しい考えにどのくらい開かれているかに影響するある特定の遺伝子が，保守的な人とリベラルな人では違うことを示した。したがって，育ちだけでなく生まれも，私たちの政治的信念を形成することがあり得るのである。

> 語句　authoritarian「権威主義の」，hard-wired「(脳などに) 深く刻み込まれた」，nurture「養育，育ち」

No.11 解答 ③

> 質問の訳　クリス・フレイリーの研究は何を示唆したか。
> 選択肢の訳
> 1　厳格な親の子供の方が反抗する可能性が高い。
> 2　家族の価値観は政治的信念とほとんど関係がない。
> 3　どのように育てられるかが人の政治的考えに影響する。
> 4　人は親とは違う視点を取ろうとする。

> 解説　第1段落で述べられているフレイリーの研究によると，厳格で権威主義的な親の子供はしばしば conservative に育ち，自由に意見を述べられる家庭の子供は liberal に育つ傾向がある，という違いがある。つまり，3のように，育つ環境が political views に影響を与えることになる。

No.12 解答 ①

> 質問の訳　2人の政治学者は「ネガティビティバイアス」についてどう考えているか。
> 選択肢の訳
> 1　生物学的要因が原因に思える。
> 2　人にネガティブな刺激を無視させる。
> 3　成人の間の脳でだけ発達する。
> 4　保守的な人よりリベラルな人の方に多く影響する。

> 解説　第2段落によると，政治学者が言っているのは，negativity bias は be hard-wired into the brain に思えるということ。これは「脳に生得的に備わっている」という意味で，政治的信念の理由の一部は biological なものだという段落冒頭の記述に対応している。したがって 1 が正解。

B

> スクリプト　**Households and Marriage**

　According to the US Census Bureau, people living in married households in the US are now outnumbered by those living in other types of household arrangements. Various factors are responsible for this change, including the tendency of younger adults to live together before getting married. The senior-citizen demographic is another factor behind the change, because when one spouse dies, a "single-person household" is created. For a number of reasons, including greater wealth, elderly people who lose a spouse are tending to live on their own rather than move in with their families as they may have in the past. What is more, elderly people are less likely to remarry than younger adults are.

Another notable fact is that college graduates tend to postpone marriage until they have greater financial stability. Reduced job opportunities and lower salaries also seem to be making it harder for some people with less education to get married and start a family. Both factors may be contributing to the lower number of married households. Interestingly, however, when college graduates eventually do get married, they are now less likely to divorce, resulting in lower divorce rates overall.

Questions
No.13 What is one cause of the declining number of married households?
No.14 What has been observed among college graduates?

全文訳　**世帯と結婚**

　米国国勢調査局によると，米国では既婚世帯に住む人より，ほかのタイプの世帯構成に住む人の方が今では数が多い。この変化を引き起こしている要因はさまざまだが，若年層の人たちが結婚前に一緒に住む傾向はその1つである。一方の配偶者が死ぬと「単身世帯」ができるから，高齢者の世代人口もこの変化の背後にある別の要因である。資産の増大などいくつかの理由で，配偶者を亡くした高齢者は，昔なら家族と同居を始めたかもしれないが，むしろ1人暮らしをする傾向にある。さらに，高齢者は若年層より再婚する可能性が低い。

　もう1つの注目すべき要因は，経済的により安定するまで大卒者が結婚を遅らせる傾向があることである。雇用機会の減少と給料の減少も，学歴の低い一部の人が結婚し家族を持つことをより困難にしているように思える。両方の要因が，既婚世帯数の減少の一因なのかもしれない。しかし，興味深いことに，大卒者が最終的にいざ結婚してみると，離婚する可能性は低く，その結果離婚率が全体的に低下している。

　　語句　outnumber「～より数で勝る」，demographic「世代人口」

No.13 解答　2

質問の訳　既婚世帯数が減少している原因の1つは何か。
選択肢の訳　1　若い大人の比率の低下。
　　　　　　2　配偶者が死んだ後1人で暮らす高齢者。
　　　　　　3　再婚する離婚者の減少。
　　　　　　4　離婚率の上昇につながる資産の増大。

解説 第1段落で、既婚世帯数減少の理由を2つの年齢層に関して述べている。1つは、若年層が結婚前に一緒に住むこと。もう1つは、elderly people who lose a spouse are tending to live on their own であること。後者を言い換えた **2** が正解である。

No.14 解答 ④

質問の訳 大卒者の間に何が観察されているか。
選択肢の訳
1 家族を養おうと苦労している。
2 学歴の高い配偶者を見つけようとする傾向がある。
3 しばしば結婚してすぐに子供を持つ。
4 今ではもっと年齢を重ねてから結婚する。

解説 第2段落では college graduates について、経済的に安定するまで結婚を遅らせること、実際に結婚したら離婚する可能性が低いことの2点が述べられている。結婚を遅らせることを **4** が get married later in life と言い換えている。

スクリプト **Positive Psychology**

　Psychology has traditionally focused on classifying and treating mental illness. In recent years, however, a movement known as positive psychology has been attempting to revolutionize the profession. Rather than focusing on the treatment of mental illness, positive psychology seeks to actively prevent it by helping people build feelings of fulfillment and self-worth. One of its central principles is that one's circumstances in life play a much smaller role in determining happiness than most people imagine. Accordingly, people who win the lottery, or even suddenly suffer a serious physical injury, will frequently return to their previous level of contentment within a matter of months. Positive psychology therefore seeks to help individuals find peace of mind through altering their attitudes and ways of looking at the world.

　Positive psychology, however, is not without its critics. According to noted psychologist Paul Wong, since there are limitations on time and financial resources, changing the focus of psychology to individuals who are currently free of mental dysfunction could have serious consequences. Logically, if more resources are devoted to that group, people with existing mental issues are more likely to be neglected.

Questions
No.15 What is one of the main ideas behind positive psychology?
No.16 What is one criticism Paul Wong makes of positive psychology?

全文訳 **ポジティブ心理学**
　心理学は伝統的に、精神病を分類し治療することに重点を置いてきた。しかし近年、

ポジティブ心理学として知られる運動が，この専門職に革命を起こそうと試みている。ポジティブ心理学は精神病の治療に重点を置くのではなく，人が充足感と自己価値感を築くのを助けることによって，積極的に精神病を予防しようと努める。その中心原則の1つは，幸福を決定する上で人生の境遇が果たす役割はほとんどの人が思うよりずっと小さい，ということである。したがって，宝くじを当てた人は，あるいは突然体に重傷を負った人ですら，しばしばほんの数カ月のうちに以前の満足度に戻ることになる。それ故，ポジティブ心理学は，個人の考え方と世界の見方を変えることを通して個人が心の平静を見つける手助けをしようと努める。

しかし，ポジティブ心理学を批判する人がいないわけではない。著名な心理学者ポール・ワンによると，時間と金銭的資源には限りがあるのだから，心理学の重点を現時点で精神的機能障害を持たない個人に変えると，重大な結果を招くかもしれない。論理的には，その集団により多くの資源を割けば，現に精神的問題を抱える人たちがないがしろにされる可能性が増すことになる。

語句　self-worth「自尊心」，contentment「満足」，dysfunction「機能障害」

No.15 解答　2

質問の訳　ポジティブ心理学を支える主な理念の1つは何か。
選択肢の訳　1　精神病は直ちに治療されなければならない。
2　外的要因は人を幸福にするものではない。
3　人はもっと個人主義でなくなるべきだ。
4　精神病は人が思うよりもありふれている。

解説　質問のone of the main ideasは，第1段落中ほどのOne of its central principlesに対応している。その文のone's circumstances in lifeをExternal factorsと，determining happinessをwhat make people happyと言い換えた2が正解。

No.16 解答　3

質問の訳　ポール・ワンのポジティブ心理学に対する1つの批判は何か。
選択肢の訳　1　伝統的療法より高額である。
2　効果が出るまで長時間かかる。
3　精神病患者の治療に影響を与えるかもしれない。
4　精神病の予防に何の効果もない。

解説　第1段落によると，ポジティブ心理学は精神病をprevent「予防する」ことを重視する。それに対する批判者として第2段落で登場するポール・ワンは，限られた時間と金銭的資源を予防に回すことに疑義を呈している。3が，最後の文のpeople with existing mental issues are more likely to be neglectedを全体的に言い換えている。

D

スクリプト **Radium Poisoning**

　Radium is now known to be an extremely hazardous substance, but when first discovered, it was actually used as a health tonic. Radium glows in the dark, so it was also used to paint the faces of clocks and dials used by the US military during World War I. The company that made them employed women as they were considered better suited to the delicate work of painting because of their slender fingers. The women would paint with radium all day, frequently inserting the brushes between their lips to ensure they had very fine points.

　Eventually, however, the women began dying of radium poisoning. Their employer denied responsibility, claiming that radium was harmless. However, the research that the employer relied on was conducted by the radium industry, whose scientists had a clear interest in claiming that radium was safe. In the years that followed, lawsuits were brought against the company. Eventually, the courts ruled against the company. It was one of the first cases in the US in which an employer was held accountable for its employees' health issues.

Questions

No.17 What is one way the women were exposed to radium?
No.18 What does the speaker say about the women's employer?

全文訳 **ラジウム中毒**

　ラジウムは極度に危険な物質だと今ではわかっているが，発見された当初は，強壮剤として実際に用いられた。ラジウムは暗闇で発光するので，第1次世界大戦中に米軍が用いた時計の文字盤と目盛りに塗装するためにも用いられた。それらを製造した会社は女性を雇用したが，それは，女性の方が指がほっそりしているので塗装という繊細な作業に向いていると考えられたからだった。女性たちは一日中ラジウムで塗装し，ブラシの先端がきちんととがっているよう，ブラシを唇の間に挟むこともしばしばだった。

　しかし，最終的に女性たちはラジウム中毒で死に始めた。雇用主は，ラジウムは無害だと主張して責任を否定した。しかし，雇用主が依拠した研究はラジウム産業が行ったもので，産業の科学者たちには，ラジウムが安全だと主張することに明白な利害関係があった。続く年月の間に，その会社に対する訴訟が相次いだ。最終的に，法廷は会社を有罪とする判決を下した。これは，雇用主は従業員の健康問題に対して責任があるとされた，米国で最初の裁判の1つだった。

　　語句 poisoning「中毒」, health tonic「強壮剤」

No.17 解答 ③

　質問の訳 女性たちは1つにはどのようにしてラジウムに被ばくしたか。
　選択肢の訳 **1** ラジウムを含む強壮剤を与えられた。

- **2** 指にラジウムを塗る必要があった。
- **3** ラジウムで覆われたブラシを口の中に入れた。
- **4** ラジウムを用いて自分が使うブラシをきれいにした。

解説 第1段落の最後で述べられている the brushes は，ラジウムを塗るために使ったブラシだと考えられる。それを唇に挟んだということは，**3**のように，口の中に入れたことになる。強壮剤はラジウムが用いられた一例，指は女性がラジウム塗装の仕事に雇われた理由として挙げられているだけである。

No.18 解答

質問の訳 女性たちの雇用主について話者は何と言っているか。
選択肢の訳
1 塗料の中のラジウムは危険ではないと証明した。
2 女性たちの被ばく量が低いことを示した。
3 訴訟を避けることに成功した。
4 偏った研究結果を用いた。

解説 第2段落の However, the research ... の文がポイント。雇用主はラジウム産業が行った研究に依拠したと述べた後の whose scientists had a clear interest in claiming that radium was safe から，研究に携わった科学者が研究結果をゆがめた可能性があることを話者は示唆している。それを biased を用いて表した **4** が正解である。

E

(スクリプト) **Technology in Our Bodies**

A technology company in the state of Wisconsin was recently the first in the United States to implant microchips into the hands of some of its workers. Now those employees can unlock doors, operate office equipment, log into computers, and buy items from vending machines at the company with a simple wave of the hand. Supporters of this technology view such implanted devices as cutting-edge, efficient, and inevitable. Some people insist that enhancing human bodies with technology will be necessary for them to be able to compete against machines, robots, and artificial intelligence in the workplaces of the future.

Among critics, the biggest issues are security and privacy. Such technology could eventually contain tracking devices that would allow managers to monitor their workers' movements even outside the workplace. Another concern is that outside parties could access private data. Although the manufacturer maintains the implanted devices are secure, they cannot rule out hacking entirely. Health concerns are another issue. Any device implanted into the body carries the potential for infection or migration away from the implant site. Furthermore, although such devices have been approved by the US Food and Drug Administration, the long-term health effects of implanted devices are unknown.

Questions

No.19 What do supporters say about implanted microchips?

No.20 Why are some people against placing microchips into people's bodies?

全文訳 体内のテクノロジー

　ウィスコンシン州のテクノロジー企業が，最近，米国で初めて一部の労働者の手にマイクロチップを埋め込んだ。今ではそれらの従業員は，単に手を振るだけでドアのロックを解除し，オフィス機器を操作し，コンピューターにログインし，会社の自動販売機で品物を買うことができる。このテクノロジーを支持する人たちは，そうした埋め込まれた装置は最先端で効率的で不可避だと考える。人体をテクノロジーで向上させることは，将来の職場で人体が機械，ロボット，人工知能と渡り合うために必要となるだろうと主張する人たちもいる。

　批判的な人たちの間で最大の争点は，安全とプライバシーである。そうしたテクノロジーは，最終的に，管理者が労働者の動きを職場外でも監視することを可能にする追跡装置を含むようになるかもしれない。もう１つの懸念は，外部の第三者が個人データにアクセスするかもしれないことである。埋め込まれた装置は安全だと製造者が主張しても，製造者はハッキングの可能性を完全に排除することはできない。健康に関する懸念も，もう１つの争点である。体に埋め込まれたどんな装置も，感染の可能性や埋め込んだ場所から移動する可能性を秘めている。さらに，そうした装置が米国食品医薬品局の認可を得ているとはいえ，埋め込まれた装置が健康に与える長期的影響は未知である。

　語句 cutting-edge「最先端の」

No.19 解答 ④

質問の訳 支持する人たちは埋め込まれたマイクロチップについて何と言っているか。

選択肢の訳
1　ロボットの利用を進歩させる。
2　会社のセキュリティーを大きく向上させる。
3　人間が生き残るために必須である。
4　将来の職場では避けられない。

解説 第１段落半ばの Supporters of this technology ... 以下の２文が支持者の主張。まず，cutting-edge, efficient, and inevitable とこのテクノロジーの特徴を挙げ，続いて，将来の職場でロボットなどと渡り合うために必要だと具体的に述べている。inevitable を unavoidable と言い換えた **4** が正解である。

No.20 解答 ②

質問の訳 なぜ一部の人は人の体にマイクロチップを入れることに反対なのか。

選択肢の訳
1　このテクノロジーは簡単に盗まれるかもしれない。

2 そうした装置の安全性はまだ定かでない。
3 マイクロチップは不正確なデータを作成するかもしれない。
4 埋め込まれた物は健康問題を引き起こすことが知られている。

解説　批判者の意見は第2段落でいくつか挙げられている。労働者が職場の外でも監視される可能性，ハッキングにより個人データが盗まれる危険性，装置が人体に及ぼし得る健康被害。最後の文で言っている the long-term health effects of implanted devices are unknown を **2** が短くまとめている。

  問題編 p.85～86　

F

You have 10 seconds to read the situation and Question No. 21.

The watch you've chosen is high quality, and with the right care it could last for generations. As a mechanical watch, it doesn't have a battery; a similar quartz diving watch would need a new battery every few years. Since it's automatic, it will remain accurate if you wear it a couple of times a week, as the movement of your arm will wind it. To make sure the parts stay in working order, I recommend having it serviced by a professional. Once every five years is standard, but once every three years is recommended if you go scuba diving four or more times a year. Also, after using this watch while diving, remember to clean it with a soft toothbrush and fresh water. Avoid using any detergents or other cleaners, as they may destroy the waterproofing.

Now mark your answer on your answer sheet.

全文訳
　お選びいただいた腕時計は高品質で，正しく手入れすれば何世代ももちます。機械式時計なので，電池はありません。似たようなクオーツ式のダイバーズウォッチなら，数年おきに新しい電池が必要になります。自動巻きですから，週に2，3回着ければ腕の動きで巻いてくれるので，常に時間が正確です。間違いなく部品が正常に作動しているようにするには，専門家に点検修理してもらうことをお勧めします。5年おきに1回が標準ですが，年4回以上スキューバダイビングに行かれるのでしたら，3年おきに1回がお勧めです。また，ダイビング中にこの時計を使った後は，柔らかい歯ブラシと真水で必ず洗ってください。合成洗剤などの洗浄剤は防水を駄目にするかもしれないので，一切使わないようにしてください。

No.21 解答 ①

状況の訳 あなたはダイバーズウォッチを買うところで，店員がメンテナンスについて説明している。あなたはたいてい年に5回スキューバダイビングに行く。

質問の訳 あなたは何をすべきか。

選択肢の訳
1 腕時計を3年おきに点検修理してもらう。
2 推薦された洗浄剤とブラシを買う。
3 交換部品を少し手元に用意しておく。
4 電池を5年おきに交換する。

語句 detergent「合成洗剤」

解説 it doesn't have a battery と言っているので4は誤り。partsに関しては専門家に点検修理してもらうよう言っているので3も誤り。点検修理は5年に1回が標準だが年4回以上スキューバダイビングに行くなら3年に1回がいいと言っているので，年に5回という状況の条件から，1が正解。洗浄剤は使わず歯ブラシと真水で洗うよう言っているので，2は誤りである。

スクリプト

You have 10 seconds to read the situation and Question No. 22.

I know you've called the airline without satisfaction, so hold off on that route. International law requires airlines to provide compensation for the value of your bags and contents up to $3,400, so they have to do something eventually. You've already submitted an itemized list of the contents and value of your baggage with your claim form. It's a shame you don't have any receipts for the items because that would strengthen your case. It's likely you'll get offered travel vouchers for the airline as compensation instead of cash. You said you want to avoid a lengthy legal battle, so waiting to see if their voucher offer is acceptable makes sense. Otherwise, taking the airline to court is an option. I can file the claim for you, but my fees are likely to exceed the amount of damages you will be awarded.

Now mark your answer on your answer sheet.

全文訳

航空会社に電話しても満足のいく結果は得られなかったわけですから，そっち方面は取りあえずやめておきましょう。国際法は航空会社に対して，あなたのかばんと中身の価値に対して最大3,400ドルの補償をするよう定めていますから，航空会社は最終的に何かしなければなりません。あなたは既に，荷物の中身と価値を箇条書きしたリストを請求書と一緒に提出しています。品目の領収書があれば立場が強くなりますから，1枚もお持ちでないのは残念です。現金の代わりに，補償としてその航空会社で使える旅

行クーポンの申し出がある可能性が高いです。長く続く法廷闘争は避けたいというお話でしたから，あちらのクーポンの申し出が受け入れられるものかどうか様子見をするのが妥当です。そうでなければ，裁判で航空会社を訴えるのも選択肢です。私が代わりに請求を申し立ててもいいですが，私の報酬は，受け取れる補償金の額を上回る可能性が高いです。

No.22 解答 ④

状況の訳 航空会社が数週間前にあなたの荷物を紛失し，あなたは何らかの補償をしてほしいと思っている。あなたは定期的に飛行機に乗る。弁護士が次のアドバイスをする。

質問の訳 あなたは何をすべきか。

選択肢の訳
1 現金で解決するよう航空会社に電話をする。
2 弁護士に法廷で代理人を務めてもらう。
3 領収書付きの請求書を提出する。
4 旅行クーポンの申し出を待つ。

語句 hold off on ～「～を先に延ばす」，itemize「～を箇条書きにする」

解説 電話は既に試みてうまくいかなかったので hold off on that route と弁護士が冒頭で言っていることから，1 は誤り。claim form は提出済みで，なおかつ you don't have any receipts なので 3 も誤り。waiting to see if their voucher offer is acceptable makes sense と弁護士はアドバイスし，定期的に飛行機に乗るのならクーポンは有用なので，4 が正解。弁護士料金が補償金を上回るだろうと最後に言っているので，2 は現実的な選択肢ではない。

H

スクリプト

You have 10 seconds to read the situation and Question No. 23.

Hi, this is Keith from the head office. It's 5:30 p.m. now. Our new client, Bill Fleischman, just called me to discuss the contract we sent him last week. He wants to ask you some questions before he'll agree to sign it. He said he'd be in his office for another two hours. If you can call him before he leaves, that would be great. If not, he'd like you to call him in the morning as he has to head to Brazil on business in the afternoon. If you're not free to talk in the morning, maybe you should e-mail him a response to his questions. He wants to know if he'll be allowed to sell competing products from other manufacturers and if we can revise the contract to specify that.

Now mark your answer on your answer sheet.

全文訳
やあ，本社のキースです。今，午後 5 時半です。うちの新規の顧客のビル・フライシ

ュマンさんからさっき電話があって，先週こちらから送った契約書について話し合いたいということでした。契約書へのサインに同意する前に，あなたにいくつか質問したいそうです。あと 2 時間オフィスにいるという話でした。彼が退社する前に電話できれば一番いいです。無理なら，彼は午後出張でブラジルに向かわなければならないので，午前中に電話してほしいとのことです。午前中に話す余裕がなければ，質問への回答をメールするのがいいかもしれません。彼が知りたいのは，ほかの製造会社の競合商品を売っても構わないか，それを明記するよううちが契約書を修正できるか，ということです。

No.23 解答

状況の訳 あなたは出張中である。3 時間以上前に同僚があなたに残したボイスメールを聞く。あなたは明日の午前中，正午まで会議に出る。

質問の訳 あなたは何をすべきか。

選択肢の訳
1 顧客に修正した契約書を送る。
2 顧客の質問にメールで回答する。
3 顧客から電話が来るのを待つ。
4 ブラジルから戻った後で顧客に連絡する。

語句 specify「～を明確に記す」

解説 顧客が今日オフィスにいるのはあと 2 時間と話者は言っており，3 時間以上過ぎているので顧客は既に退社している。明日の午前中は正午まで会議なので電話できない。話者のもう 1 つの提案は maybe you should e-mail him a response to his questions で，それに従うことになる。したがって **2** が正解。

スクリプト

You have 10 seconds to read the situation and Question No. 24.

The American money-market account you're in has been earning 4 percent interest, but that'll fall to 2 percent at the end of the month. You've got several options for your holdings. Our top earner is an American real-estate investment trust that delivered 5 percent growth last year. Real estate is cyclical, though, so it's not the safest choice. Another possibility is transferring your money to our Australian money-market account. This guarantees 4 percent interest for six months. Foreign exchange rates do fluctuate, but the Australian dollar is also predicted to remain stable after that guarantee period, too. Or you could shift your money to a Japanese bond-investment fund. That's a low-risk option, but it also means it won't deliver more than 2 percent interest. Anyway, I think those are your best options at present.

Now mark your answer on your answer sheet.

全文訳

　お持ちのアメリカのマネーマーケット口座はずっと4％の利回りを出していますが，今月末に2％に下がります。運用資金に対する選択肢はいくつかあります。当社の稼ぎ頭は，昨年5％の成長を達成したアメリカの不動産投資トラストです。ですが不動産には周期がありますから，最も安全な選択肢ではありません。別の可能性は，当社のオーストラリアのマネーマーケット口座にお金を移すことです。これは，半年間4％の利回りを保証します。外国為替レートは必ず変動しますが，オーストラリアドルはその保証期間の後もずっと安定しているとも予測されています。あるいは，日本の債券投資ファンドにお金を移してもいいかもしれません。そちらは低リスクの選択肢ですが，つまり，2％を超える利回りは達成しないということでもあります。ともかく，今のところ以上が最善の選択肢だと思います。

No.24 解答 ③

状況の訳　あなたはファイナンシャルアドバイザーと投資について話し合っている。運用資金に対し最低3％の利回りは稼ぎたいが，リスクを最小限にもしたい。

質問の訳　あなたはお金をどうすべきか。

選択肢の訳
1　アメリカのマネーマーケット口座に置いておく。
2　アメリカの不動産投資トラストに投資する。
3　オーストラリアのマネーマーケット口座に移す。
4　日本の債券投資ファンドに移す。

語句　cyclical「周期的な」，fluctuate「変動する」

解説　耳慣れない金融用語に惑わされず，at least 3 percent interest と minimize your risk という2つの条件に関する内容に集中して聴く。アメリカのマネーマーケット口座は利回りが2％に下がる。アメリカの不動産投資トラストは5％だが，最も安全な選択肢ではない。オーストラリアのマネーマーケット口座は半年間4％が保証され，その後も安定が見込まれる。日本の債券投資ファンドは低リスクだが2％。条件に合うのは3のオーストラリアのマネーマーケット口座である。

スクリプト

You have 10 seconds to read the situation and Question No. 25.

The main drawing is held on Saturday, so check the results online or in the newspaper. The process for collecting your winnings varies. If you win under $600, just take your winning ticket to any lottery retailer and collect the cash. If you win $600 or more, download a claim form and take your winning ticket and a valid photo ID to a lottery district office. And don't throw your tickets away if you don't win on Saturday, as our state has a second-chance lottery.

To enter, create an account on the state lottery website. Some states require you to mail in your tickets, but here you just submit lottery ticket numbers through your account. Your chances on the second drawing actually increase, since a lot of people don't know about it or don't bother to enter.

Now mark your answer on your answer sheet.

全文訳

　主な抽選は土曜日に行われるので，結果はオンラインか新聞で確認してください。当選金を受け取る手順はさまざまです。当選金額が 600 ドル未満なら，どこでもいいので宝くじ売り場に当たり券を持って行き，現金を受け取るだけです。当選金額が 600 ドル以上なら，請求用紙をダウンロードし，当たり券と有効な写真付き身分証明書を持って宝くじの地区事務所に行ってください。それから，土曜日に当たらなくても券を捨てないでください。私たちの州では外れくじの再抽選がありますから。登録するには，州の宝くじサイトでアカウントを作ってください。券を郵送するよう求める州もありますが，こちらでは，アカウント経由で宝くじ券の番号を送信するだけで済みます。多くの人はこのことを知らないか，わざわざ登録したりしませんから，再抽選で当たる確率は実際上がります。

No.25 解答 ①

状況の訳　あなたは初めて宝くじ券を買っている。当たる確率を上げたい。販売員が次のアドバイスをする。

質問の訳　最初の抽選で当たらなかったらあなたはどうすべきか。

選択肢の訳　1　オンラインアカウントを開設し券の番号を送信する。
　　　　　2　宝くじのサイトから請求用紙をダウンロードする。
　　　　　3　州の宝くじ事務所に券を送る。
　　　　　4　どこでもいいので宝くじ売り場に外れ券を持って行く。

語句　winnings「賞金，当選金」

解説　質問の if you do not win on the first drawing に該当するのは，中ほどの if you don't win on Saturday である。最初の抽選で外れても second-chance lottery があり，参加する人が多くないので Your chances on the second drawing actually increase だと言っている。登録に必要なのは create an account on the state lottery website と submit lottery ticket numbers だから，1 が正解となる。

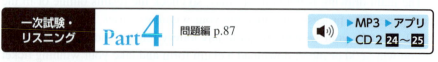

スクリプト

This is an interview with Emily Lee, who works in investor relations.

I (Interviewer): Thanks for tuning in, everyone. Today, we're talking with Emily Lee. Welcome.

EL (Emily Lee): Nice to be here.

I: So, what is investor relations?

EL: Well, many Japanese companies have international investors, and my company makes reports and communicates all the financial and nonfinancial information to these investors so they can decide how they would like to continue investing in the future.

I: And what sort of challenges do you face in your job?

EL: There are many, many challenges in this job, but one of the main ones is scheduling. So, in Japan, the fiscal year ends in March, which means everything piles up in the summer. When that happens, I sometimes have five or six reports going simultaneously, and that can be a lot of pressure, because you don't want there to be any mistakes. I have seen colleagues stay overnight, through weekends, not sleep, in order to meet deadlines from clients. Because of this, there can be quite high turnover in the IR field. So, many people only last between two to three years before they think they'll move on to a different job, in a different industry altogether, or stay in the IR industry, but not be client-facing. Morale can be a little bit low when you lose some of your favorite, or most competent, coworkers over time, but I feel that it makes the people who stay gel together all the better. And when you have people who are experienced and know what they're doing, it makes the workflow much easier as well.

I: So, what are the annual reports aimed at?

EL: Their main purpose is to explain the financial situation of a company, because these investors are abroad. They're not on the ground to see what the actual circumstances are, so the report explains to them how a company has done over the past year, and what they're planning to do in the future. That includes midterm management plans, and what their nonfinancial goals are. So, things relating to charity work, or anything that could relate to corporate social responsibility.

I: Could you tell us briefly what corporate social responsibility is?

EL: Corporate social responsibility is how a company addresses their social responsibility to the planet and to the communities it operates in. So, for example, the social side can be organizing charity events, or art events, in the community for people to participate in for free. Another example is the environmental side, where a company will try to lower its emissions volumes in order to hit certain goals put out by the United Nations.

I: And do you think that most companies take CSR seriously?

EL: I think most companies do, if only because they must. Certain things have come into law, due to the environmental impact of how companies operate on the planet. There is also something called the SDGs, which is the sustainable development goals put out by the United Nations in 2015. For example, how to promote clean water, how to promote less inequality in the world — and companies will use these goals as guidelines for how they can operate.

I: Well, Emily, thanks so much for coming in today. That was very interesting.

EL: Thanks for having me.

Questions

No.26 What is one thing Emily implies about working in the investor relations industry?

No.27 What does Emily think about corporate social responsibility?

全文訳

これはインベスター・リレーションズの仕事をしているエミリー・リーとのインタビューです。

聞き手（以下「聞」）： 皆さん，お聴きいただきありがとうございます。今日は，エミリー・リーとトークします。ようこそ。

エミリー・リー（以下「エ」）： よろしくお願いします。

聞： さて，インベスター・リレーションズとは何ですか。

エ： えー，多くの日本企業には国際投資家がいて，私の会社は，それらの投資家が将来的に投資し続けたいと思うかどうかを決められるよう，報告書を作り，あらゆる財務情報と非財務情報を彼らに伝えています。

聞： それで，お仕事ではどういった難題に直面しますか。

エ： この仕事には実にたくさんの難題がありますが，主なものの1つはスケジュール管理です。つまり，日本では会計年度が終わるのは3月で，ということは，何やかやと夏にどんどんたまるわけです。そうなると，時に5つか6つの報告書を同時に動かすことになり，間違いは1つもないようにしたいですから，すごくプレッシャーになることがあります。顧客の締め切りに間に合わせるため，同僚が週末ずっと眠らずに泊まりがけで居残りしているのを目にしてきました。このため，IR分野では離職率がかなり高いことがあります。つまり，まったく違う業界の違う仕事に転職しよう，あるいはIR業界に残っても顧客と対面はしないと思うようになるまで，多くの人は2年から3年しか続かないんです。時がたつうちに一番好きな同僚やとても有能な同僚の何人かを失うと士気が少し下がることもありますが，そうしたことは，残った人たちの結束をかえって強くすると感じます。そして，経験を積んで万事のみ込んでいる人たちがいると，業務の流れがずっと容易にもなります。

聞： では，年間報告書は何を目標にしているのですか。

エ：主な目的は企業の財務状況を説明することですね，これらの投資家は外国にいますから。彼らは実際の状況がどうなのかを現場で見ることはできませんから，企業が過去1年間どんな具合だったか，今後何をする計画なのかを，報告書が投資家に説明するんです。それには，中期経営計画と，企業の非財務目標が何なのかが含まれます。つまり，慈善事業に関する事柄や，企業の社会的責任に関連するかもしれないものは何でもです。

聞：企業の社会的責任とは何なのか，簡潔に教えてもらえますか。

エ：企業の社会的責任とは，事業を行う場である地球と地域社会に対する社会的責任に，企業がどのように取り組んでいるかということです。つまり，例えば社会的側面としては，人々が無料で参加できるようなチャリティーイベントやアートイベントを地域社会で組織することがあり得るでしょう。別の例は環境的側面で，その場合企業は，国際連合が発表する一定の目標を達成するために排出物の量を減らそうとします。

聞：それで，ほとんどの企業は CSR を真剣に受け止めていると思いますか。

エ：そうせざるを得ないからだとしても，ほとんどの企業はそうしていると思います。企業の地球での事業運営が環境に与える影響のため，一定の事柄は法制化されています。SDGs というものもあり，これは，2015年に国際連合が発表した持続可能な開発目標です。例えば，きれいな水をどのように広めるか，世界の不平等の縮小をどのように進めるかといったことですが——企業はこれらの目標を，どのように事業を行えるかの指針として用いることになります。

聞：さて，エミリー，今日はお越しいただきどうもありがとうございました。とても興味深いお話でした。

エ：お招きいただきありがとうございました。

語句 turnover「離職率，転職率」，gel together「結束する」，workflow「仕事の流れ」，on the ground「現場で」，midterm「中間の」

No.26 解答 ③

質問の訳 インベスター・リレーションズ業界で働くことについて，エミリーが暗に言っていることの1つは何か。

選択肢の訳
1 会計年度が3月に終わるので，人々は夏に自由な時間がある。
2 卓越したチームワークは，ほかの業界よりも転職する人が少ないことを意味する。
3 仕事のプレッシャーに対応できる人たちは，たいてい信頼できる同僚になる。
4 新人は顧客と仕事をする前に3年の経験が必要だ。

解説 エミリーは3つ目の発言で，インベスター・リレーションズ（IR）業界の難題の1つとして，スケジュール管理の難しさを挙げている。そして，そのプレッシャーのせいで離職率が高いが，やめずに残った人たちの結束が強くなり，経験を積んだ人が残れば業務がはかどるといったこ

とを言っている。やめずに残ることを「プレッシャーに対応できる」，結束が強くなることを「信頼できる」と表した 3 が正解。

No.27 解答 ②

質問の訳　企業の社会的責任についてエミリーはどう思っているか。

選択肢の訳
1 企業の環境保護を支援するため，国際連合はもっと多くのことをしなければならない。
2 企業の大多数は，企業の社会的責任が事業にとって重要だと今では感じている。
3 投資家は，地域社会で仕事をしようとする企業の取り組みに資金を出すべきだ。
4 多くの企業は，チャリティーイベントとアートプロジェクトに集中するため，企業の社会的責任を無視している。

解説　エミリーは5つ目と6つ目の発言で企業の社会的責任について話している。聞き手が言っている CSR が唐突な印象を与えるが，話の流れから，corporate social responsibility の頭文字だと見当がつく。ほとんどの企業は CSR を真剣に受け止めているか，という聞き手の質問に I think most companies do と答えていること，また，企業は SDGs（持続可能な開発目標）を指針とするだろう，という発言から，エミリーは 2 のように思っているとわかる。

ここでは，A日程の5つのトピックをモデルスピーチとしました。

A日程

1. Would the global economy benefit from a single world currency?

　A single currency would definitely benefit the global economy. It would boost global trade, make investing easier, and encourage tourism. First, let's consider global trade. Today, when businesses import or export goods, there are usually additional costs because their money may need to be converted to a foreign currency. If we adopted a global currency, this additional cost would vanish, making trade between foreign countries more accessible. Investors would also benefit. Whenever people invest abroad, they have to worry not only about whether the investment itself will rise in value, but about the price of the foreign currency. If everyone used the same currency, this risk would be eliminated, making investing simpler and more profitable. Finally, it could be good for the tourism industry. It would save people the trouble of exchanging currencies, so they'd be more likely to go abroad. Furthermore, it would be easier to understand prices, encouraging people to spend more. Since tourism is an important part of the world economy, this could have a significant economic impact. In conclusion, we are currently living in an era of globalization, so the potential advantages related to global trade, investment, and travel make it clear that we should have a single world currency.

> 解説　「単一の国際通貨によって世界経済は恩恵を受けるか」
>
> 　賛成の立場を取る根拠は3つ，①貿易におけるコストの削減，②投資の際のリスクの軽減，③海外旅行での利便性，である。重複しない理由を出すことで広い視野から単一国際通貨が世界経済にもたらす利点を説明できている。さらに，自分が仮定していることは仮定法，事実は現在形，と明確に分けて話し，聞き手に誤解を与えない発話となっている。最後のまとめも既出の表現の繰り返しではなく，言い換え表現を使って同じ主張を述べることで発話レベルの高さをアピールできている。

2. Can labor unions effectively support workers in the modern business world?

　In my opinion, labor unions are gradually losing their ability to support workers in the modern business world. Union membership is decreasing, corporations are becoming more powerful, and labor laws are weakening. In the years after World War II, the majority of Japanese workers were union members, but now only certain occupations, like teachers and government workers, tend to have strong unions. While unions are helping to maintain wages and benefits in some workplaces, the majority of workers have no organization to protect them. Another problem is that companies are becoming much more powerful these days. In today's world, companies can easily use outsourced or temporary workers instead of regular full-time employees. Workers know that if they strike or try to form unions, they can easily be replaced, and this puts them in a weak position when negotiating with companies. Finally, labor laws are becoming weaker around the world and this reduces the power of labor unions. Such laws usually make it difficult for unions to encourage workers to become members. Without a high number of members, unions cannot help workers effectively. Although there are a few jobs where unions are still important, in general, they have lost most of their power to protect workers.

> **解説**　「現代のビジネス環境において労働組合は効果的に労働者をサポートできているか」
>
> 否定の立場から3つの理由として①労働組合の組合員が減少している，②労働者より企業が強い立場になっている，③労働法の力が弱まっている，と述べている。理由のそれぞれに事実に基づいた具体例を挙げていることで，主張の信頼性を高く維持することができている。労働組合の問題は考えたことがないという人もいるだろう。本番のスピーチで，挙げた理由のすべてに具体例を思い付けなかったとしても焦らずに，出せる具体例を丁寧に，わかりやすく説明するようにするとよいだろう。

3. Agree or disagree: The traditional family unit has lost its central role in modern society

　I think traditional families are still extremely common in modern society. I'd like to talk about mainstream values, finances, and government policies to explain my opinion. First of all, although I am personally supportive of the rise of non-traditional family units, I accept the fact that the majority of people around the world value the idea of having a nuclear family. TV programs and movies still largely reinforce society's ideal of two-parent households. Traditional families also have an advantage when it comes to their personal finances. Many housing or car loan institutions still generally give the best rates to married couples, with or without children. Also, it is well known that many companies give better healthcare, pension, and paid leave benefits to employees who are married and have children. Lastly, government policies are mainly based on the idea that people will live in traditional families. Married couples receive various tax benefits, and welfare and educational services are also based on the assumption that people will be living in traditional family units. Based on things like values, finances, and government policies, it seems clear that traditional family units still have a central role in modern Japanese society.

> **解説**　「賛成か反対か：伝統的な家族単位は現代社会においてその重要な役割を失った」
>
> 反対の立場から3つの理由として①伝統的な家族単位の価値観は社会に根付いている，②融資や年金など経済面で有利である，③国の政策は家族単位を標準に作られるので税制や教育などにおいても恩恵を受けやすい，を挙げ，根拠としている。このスピーチのように，設問にあるtraditional family unitとは何か（ここでは核家族），という定義を先に示しておくと論理を展開しやすい。賛成の立場を取る場合，シングルペアレントや同性婚などが世間で認知を得つつあることを中心に意見を展開するとよいだろう。

4. Do the advantages of jury trials outweigh the disadvantages?

I believe jury trials have many benefits. They create less bias, make the legal system more open, and offer hope of making trials fairer. First, without jury trials, cases would be decided by highly educated elites who may have biases against the underprivileged. However, since juries are made up of people from all walks of life, they give accused criminals an opportunity to be judged by their peers. Another important reason for having jury trials is that ordinary people get to participate in the justice system. Most people know little about what happens in courts except for what they see on TV shows. However, when ordinary people experience being in juries themselves, they learn more about the justice system and there is increased public awareness of what is happening in court. Last but not least, they may help to lower Japan's extremely high conviction rate. Critics often say that people have very little chance of being found not guilty in Japanese criminal trials. However, having larger groups of diverse people could lower the odds that an innocent person will be found guilty. Although jury trials may not be perfect, I believe their advantages far outweigh the disadvantages.

> **解説**　「陪審裁判制度の利点は欠点を上回るか」
>
> 陪審裁判制度を積極的に肯定するスピーチ。3つの根拠として，①裁判官などエリートだけによる判断ではなくさまざまな経験を経た人に判断

してもらえる，②一般の人が裁判にかかわることによって司法への理解を深められる，③さまざまな人々がかかわることによって有罪判決の率を下げられるのではないか，を挙げている。裁判に関するトピックは知識がないと対応が難しいのももちろんだが，法律関連の正確な英語表現を最低限知っている必要がある。海外の司法ドラマや映画なども参考にして，日ごろから発話練習しておこう。

5. Will the human race one day be the cause of its own downfall?

I think that it is unlikely for humanity to one day cause its own downfall. Technology, environmentalism, and space exploration are factors that will help us to survive. Although some people worry that there are problems which may bring down human civilization, technology is often the solution. For example, as the world faces overpopulation, food insecurity will likely become a major issue. Scientists are working on methods to create sustainable food sources in non-traditional ways, such as growing plants in closed spaces using artificial sunlight. Next, humans will find a way to overcome the climate change crisis. Many citizens, especially from the younger generation, are pressuring their governments to take the issue very seriously, and things like investment in renewable fuels and pollution regulations will be able to save the climate in time. Finally, exploring space will ensure the survival of humans. There are currently many efforts to explore whether humans may be able to live on Mars someday. Once humans have colonized Mars, we have two planets to live on, so even if there were a global catastrophe on one planet, the people on the other would survive. I know some people are afraid humans will destroy themselves, but when you consider technology, the environmental movement, and space exploration, extinction seems unlikely.

解説　「人類はいつか自分たち自身を破滅に追い込むだろうか」

否定の立場の意見を，主にテクノロジーを理由に絞って展開している例。このようにテクノロジーという枠の中でさらに細分化した3点をサポートとして使うことでスピーチの具体性を上げることができる。ここでは，①食料危機に対応するためのさまざまな技術的解決，②気候変動に関しての若い世代からの圧力と再生可能燃料への投資，③宇宙開発を通しての火星移住などの可能性，というテクノロジーによる解決方法を紹介し，人類はさまざまな危機に直面してはいるが絶滅はしないだろうと結論付けている。

2020-2

- **一次試験**
  筆記解答・解説　p.162〜180
- **一次試験**
  リスニング解答・解説　p.181〜208
- **二次試験**
  面接解答・解説　p.209〜212

解答一覧

一次試験・筆記

1
(1)	4	(10)	1	(19)	1
(2)	2	(11)	2	(20)	4
(3)	1	(12)	2	(21)	3
(4)	2	(13)	3	(22)	1
(5)	3	(14)	4	(23)	1
(6)	3	(15)	2	(24)	3
(7)	1	(16)	2	(25)	4
(8)	3	(17)	1		
(9)	3	(18)	3		

2
(26)	2	(29)	4
(27)	1	(30)	3
(28)	3	(31)	1

3
(32)	2	(35)	2	(38)	3
(33)	3	(36)	4	(39)	4
(34)	2	(37)	4	(40)	2
				(41)	2

4　解答例は本文参照

一次試験・リスニング

Part 1
No. 1	2	No. 5	2	No. 9	1
No. 2	3	No. 6	4	No.10	4
No. 3	3	No. 7	2		
No. 4	3	No. 8	1		

Part 2
No.11	4	No.15	2	No.19	3
No.12	1	No.16	4	No.20	4
No.13	3	No.17	3		
No.14	2	No.18	1		

Part 3
No.21	2	No.23	4	No.25	4
No.22	1	No.24	2		

Part 4
No.26	1	No.27	3

一次試験・筆記 1　問題編 p.90〜92

(1) ― 解答 ④

訳　その隣人間の土地の境界線を巡る**争い**は，日ごとに激しくなった。結局は互いに口を利かなくなり，その件は裁判でけりを付けねばならなかった。

語句　1「後援」　2「ちょっとした機械装置」　3「器用さ」　4「争い，確執」

解説　土地の境界線を巡る隣人間の何が激しくなったのか，を考えると feud「争い，確執」が適切。第2文「裁判で決着を付ける」が裏付けとなる。

(2) ― 解答 ②

訳　コーチのローソンは，自分のチームに**自己満足し**ないように警告した。彼らはリーグで首位であるけれどもいつもと同じように一生懸命にトレーニングをしなければならない，と彼女は彼らに言った。

語句　1「見せかけの」　2「自己満足した」　3「模範的な」　4「本来備わっている」

解説　リーグで首位でも懸命に練習するように言ったのだから，コーチは complacent「自己満足した」にならないように注意したのだ。

(3) ― 解答 ①

訳　ナイジェルがレストランを出たとき，彼に金を要求する攻撃的な酔った男に**声をかけ**られて衝撃を受けた。

語句　1「近寄って声をかけられる」　2「巻き込まれる」　3「疎外される」　4「(不愉快なことを) ほのめかされる」

解説　金銭を求める攻撃的な酔っぱらいに何をされるとショックを受けるか，を考えて選択肢を見ると，accost「(知らない人) に近寄ってぶしつけに声をかける」を使った 1 が正解。

(4) ― 解答 ②

訳　A：もしジョーがスペイン語の勉強をやめたいのなら，そうさせてやりなさい。
B：正直に言って，あなたは彼に**自由**を与え過ぎだと思う。彼はそういったことを自分で決められる年じゃないわ。

語句　1「大洞窟」　2「自由（度）；緯度」　3「あざけり」　4「傲慢さ」

解説　ジョーがしたいならそうさせろ，と言う A はジョーに何を与え過ぎか。「(行動・思考などの) 自由」を意味する latitude が適切。

(5) ― 解答 ③

訳　禁煙運動の成功を**評価する**目的で，何人が実際に禁煙したのかを知るた

めに政府は調査員を雇った。

- 語句　1「～を逆さまにする」　2「～に及ぶ」
- 　　　3「～を測る」　　　　　4「前かがみになる」
- 解説　実際に禁煙した人数を知るのは，禁煙運動の成功をどうするためか，を考えると gauge「～を（正確に）測る」が正解。gauge は発音に注意。

(6) — 解答 3

訳　いつか火星の荒涼とした表面を人間が住める緑の多い環境に変えられるかもしれない，と信じる科学者もいる。

- 語句　1「（行為や状況が）目に余る」　2「簡潔な」
- 　　　3「荒れ果てた」　　　　　　　4「別々の」
- 解説　人が住める緑の多い環境へと変えるのだから，実際の火星の表面はそれとは逆の状態である。よって desolate「荒れ果てた，住む人もない」が正解。

(7) — 解答 1

訳　ジョアンの新しい上司は以前の上司と正反対だ。前の上司は常に無礼な要求をしたものだが，新しい上司はいつも丁寧で礼儀正しい。

- 語句　1「正反対（のもの）」　　2「予言者」
- 　　　3「主人公，主唱者」　　　4「幕あい」
- 解説　前の上司は無礼（rude）だったのだから，丁寧で礼儀正しい（polite and respectful）新しい上司は，以前の上司とは antithesis「正反対」だ。

(8) — 解答 3

訳　ダンカンの骨董の懐中時計は，彼にとってかけがえのないものだ。それは5年前に祖父が亡くなったときに祖父から彼に遺言で譲られたのだ。

- 語句　1「（料理に）添えられた」　2「厳しく非難された」
- 　　　3「遺言で譲られた」　　　　4「真っ逆さまに落とされた」
- 解説　時計は祖父によってダンカンにどうされたのか。祖父が亡くなったときのことなので，bequeathed「遺言で譲られた」が適切。

(9) — 解答 3

訳　法廷で銀行強盗犯の姉は，強盗後に彼が身を隠すのを手伝ったことにより，犯罪で彼をほう助した罪で刑を宣告された。

- 語句　1「ひどく苦しむこと」　　　2「抗議すること」
- 　　　3「～をほう助［教唆］すること」　4「（情報・知識など）を広めること」
- 解説　姉は強盗犯が犯行後に隠れるのを助けたのだから，犯人を「ほう助した」ことで判決を受けた。abet は犯人を help or encourage することで，前者がほう助，後者が教唆。

(10) — 解答 1

訳　A：私たちが店に入るとすぐに，スタッフたちが私たちを説得して物を買わせようとし始めたの。彼らはちっとも私たちを放っておいてく

れなかったわ！
B：あの手の容赦のない販売圧力が，私が買い物に行くのが嫌な理由だよ。

語句　1「情け容赦のない」　2「現職の」
3「むっつりした」　4「幸先のよい」

解説　入店するなり物を買わせようと店員が客から離れない販売圧力を何と形容するか。relentless「情け容赦のない」が適切。

(11) – 解答 2

訳　先生は教室に報賞制度を導入した。彼女は，それが生徒たちを勉強する気にさせる触媒として役立つことを望んだ。

語句　1「(行動・考え方の) 指針，教訓」　2「触媒」
3「(顔などの) 青白さ」　4「要点，難問」

解説　報賞制度は生徒をやる気にさせる何としての役割を果たす（serve as）のか，を考えると catalyst「触媒」だ。

(12) – 解答 2

訳　A：メニューのすべてがとても高いわ，ベン。本当に私たちにこのような余裕があるの？
B：私たちは時々ぜいたくをしなきゃ，ジェーン。今夜は夕飯を楽しんで，お金の心配は別の時にしよう。

語句　1「(差し) 控える」　2「～をほしいままにさせる」
3「～を憤慨させる」　4「～を水浸しにする」

解説　お金の心配をせず食事を楽しもうと言う B は，時々は自分たちを indulge「ほしいままにさせる，甘やかす」必要があると思っているのだ。

(13) – 解答 3

訳　ロンガルは自分がしているつまらない仕事にうんざりしたので，もっと思考力と熟練を必要とする仕事ができるかどうか上司に尋ねた。

語句　1「潜在意識の」　2「(大) 脳の」
3「(仕事などが) つまらない」　4「親切で付き合いやすい」

解説　ロンガルはもっと思考力とスキルがいる仕事をしたいのだから，彼が今しているのは menial「つまらない」仕事なのだ。

(14) – 解答 4

訳　その刑事は解決するまで粘り強く事件を追いかけた。彼女は責任を負うべき犯人を見つけるまで諦めようとはしなかった。

語句　1「ぶっきらぼうに」　2「おどおどして」
3「優美に」　4「粘り強く」

解説　犯人を見つけるまで諦めなかったのだから，刑事は事件を tenaciously「粘り強く」追ったのだ。the criminals responsible「責任がある犯罪者」は the criminals who were responsible の省略と考えればよい。

(15) 解答 ②

訳 直接的な批判はまったくしなかったが，チャップマン市長の演説は前市長の政策について相当な量の当てこすりを含んでいた。

語句 1「(湾内の) 入り江」　2「当てこすり」
3「偽薬」　4「忠誠」

解説 直接的な批判がない市長の演説は何を含むのか，を考えて選択肢を見ると innuendo「当てこすり」が適切。

(16) 解答 ②

訳 児童福祉を増進するために，医療専門家たちは喫煙する親に子供の近くでそうしないように勧めた。

語句 1「手かせ，足かせ」　2「近いこと」
3「少量」　4「がれき」

解説 専門家は喫煙する親に対して，子供の「近く」で喫煙しないように勧めると考えるのが自然。in the vicinity of ～「～の近くに」。

(17) 解答 ①

訳 A：あなたの夫が結婚記念日を忘れたときに動揺した？
B：ええ，激怒したわ。3日間彼と話をしなかった。

語句 1「激怒した」　2「逸話の」　3「熱心な」　4「腐敗した」

解説 記念日を忘れた夫と3日も話さなかったのだから，Bは非常に怒ったのだ。livid (= extremely angry) が正解。類義語は furious。

(18) 解答 ③

訳 ウェズリーはノートパソコンを10時間連続で使った後，目がかすみ始めた。彼は休憩を取って翌日仕事を終わらせることを決めた。

語句 1「よだれを垂らす」　2「合体する」
3「ぼやける」　4「(陶器などが) 欠ける」

解説 パソコンを10時間続けて使ったのだから，視界は blur「ぼやける」と考えられる。副詞 straight は「続けて，途切れずに」。

(19) 解答 ①

訳 先週の自国へのミサイル攻撃に対する報復として，大統領は敵の首都にある選ばれた軍事目標を爆撃するように空軍に命じた。

語句 1「仕返し」　2「(極端な) お世辞」
3「燃焼」　4「調節」

解説 自国が攻撃されてから敵地への爆撃を命じたのだから，この命令は retaliation「仕返し」だ。in retaliation for ～「～に対する報復として」。

(20) 解答 ④

訳 その作家の最新本は，産業革命の起源を深く掘り下げている。その本は驚くべき量の調査を含んでいる。

語句 1「～をうっかりしゃべる」　2「(攻撃を) 受け流す」

165

3「左右［上下］に急速に動く」　4「（問題などを）掘り下げる」

解説 本は多量の調査を含むのだから，革命の起源を深く delve「掘り下げ」ているのだ。delve into ～「～を掘り下げる，堀り下げて調べる」。

(21) 解答 ③

訳 サジドは愛想のよい態度でオフィスでよく知られている。彼はいつも一番乗りで新しいスタッフを歓迎し，案内をし，彼らがくつろぐのを助ける。

語句 1「嫌悪感を引き起こす」　2「湿っぽくてうすら寒い」
3「愛想のよい」　4「失って」

解説 サジドは常に新人を歓迎・案内してくつろがせる最初の人（the first）なのだから，彼の態度は affable「愛想のよい，親しみやすい」のだ。

(22) 解答 ①

訳 そのレスリングのチャンピオンは負けたことがないので，ほとんどの専門家は挑戦者が決勝戦で勝利を収めることはできそうにないと思っている。

語句 1「～をうまくやり遂げる」　2「～を焼き尽くす」
3「～を緩める」　4「すぐに言い返す」

解説 そのチャンピオンは不敗なのだから，挑戦者は勝てそうもないと考えられる。pull off「（難しいこと）をうまくやり遂げる」。

(23) 解答 ①

訳 A：お母さん，私は日曜日にコンサートに行かせてくれるようお父さんに頼むつもり。
B：彼が少し落ち着くまで待つべきよ。彼はあなたのお兄さんの悪い成績についてまだ激怒しているわ。

語句 1「（怒りなどが）静まる」　2「次第に減る」
3「～を箱詰めにする」　4「～を機械的に作り出す」

解説 父は激怒して（furious）いるのだから，頼み事をするのは simmer down「（怒りが）静まる」まで待つべきだ。calm [cool] down もほぼ同じ意味。

(24) 解答 ③

訳 塗装工たちはその建物に関して当初は順調に進んだが，それからひどい嵐が作業を数日遅らせた。彼らは予定どおりに終えることができなかった。

語句 1「～にかかっていた」　2「（引き出しなど）の内部を掃除した」
3「～を遅らせた」　4「～を引き離した」

解説 ひどい嵐なのだから，作業を数日「遅らせた」と考えられる。set back は「（物事（の進行））を遅らせる」という意味。

(25) 解答 ④

訳 シルビアはたくさんのテレビゲームをしていたが，それらへの彼女の興

味は**次第になくなって**きた。今はたまにしかゲームをしない。

- 語句
  1 「～を爆破している；～を膨らませている」
  2 「～をくどくどと繰り返し話している」
  3 「あふれている」
  4 「次第になくなっている」
- 解説　前は多くのゲームをしたが今はたまにしかしないのだから、ゲームへの興味がなくなってきたのだ。peter out「次第に減少してなくなる」。

一次試験・筆記 2　問題編 p.93～95

全文訳　刑務所を改革する

　米国での再犯率は信じ難いほど高く、釈放されてから3年以内に再逮捕される前科者は約68%だ。再犯者の極めて高い数は、この国の刑法制度にとって不名誉となるばかりでなく、かつての受刑者が釈放されて戻って行く地域社会にも重大な懸念を生じさせる。

　社会学者のウィリアム・R・ケリーは、再犯の危機は刑務所が犯罪を防ぐのに効果的だという誤った想定の結果だと信じる。論理的には、もちろん、投獄や投獄の脅威は、個人が再び罪を犯す可能性を減らすはずだ。しかしケリーは、犯罪者は「環境と経験が罪を犯さない人々と根本的な点で概して異なる」個人でありがちだ、と主張する。大多数が精神病や薬物乱用障害で苦しみ、それ故に自らの行動が招く結果を慎重に考えそうもないし、たいていは考えることができない、と彼は指摘する。

　その上、批判家たちは、刑務所で心の健康と中毒問題を治療するプログラムが十分に実施されてこなかったと主張する。罰を加えることが刑事司法制度の基本部分になったと思えることがしばしばあるし、矯正の機会があるときでさえ、それらの機会は普通のことではなく例外だと見なされがちだ、と批判家たちは主張する。この状況を考えると、受刑者の社会復帰のためのニーズと米国刑法制度の対応の厳しい現実との間にある隔たりはまったく驚くに当たらない。

　このことは、多くの米国の刑務所で利用されている、普及しているが異論のある行動矯正の形式、すなわち独房監禁において特に明白だ。小さくて狭苦しい独房で1日最大23時間過ごすというこのほぼ耐えられない孤立状態が何カ月、ことによると何年もの間続く可能性があるのだ。この慣行は、受刑者は犯した罪を反省し悔いる時間を与えられるべきだという善意の考えを持つ宗教団体によって、18世紀に初めて米国で提唱された。しかし、研究によれば、そのような状況にさらされた受刑者は刑務所から釈放された後、逆により犯罪に戻りやすいことがわかった。このこととそのような状況が与え得る心理的危害の両方を鑑みると、この慣行は疑いもなく、その裏にあった当初の意図に反している。再犯は、刑務所における適切な資源の不足によってだけではなく、刑務所内で用いられる方法によってもあおられるようだ。

- 語句　recidivism rate「再犯率，累犯率」, staggeringly「びっくりさせるほ

どに」，ex-convict「前科者」，rearrest「再逮捕」，repeat offender「再犯者」，penal system「刑法制度」，incarceration「投獄」，non-offending「罪を犯していない」，weigh「～をよく考える」，inflict「～を科す」，inmate「受刑者，服役囚」，rehabilitative「社会復帰のための」，cramped「窮屈な」，well-intentioned「善意の」，repent「悔やむ」，conversely「逆に」

(26) - 解答 ②

解説 空所文でケリーは「高い再犯率は誤った想定の結果だ」と考えており，同格 that に続く空所に入るのは，その想定の内容。続けて「論理的には投獄が再犯を減らすはずだが，実際は多くの犯罪者が自分の行動の結果を考えない」ことを述べて，投獄が抑止力にならないことを示している。よって，誤った想定とは，**2** の「刑務所が犯罪を防ぐのに効果的だ」ということになる。

(27) - 解答 ①

解説 刑務所での心の健康と中毒を治療するプログラムはどうであるのか，が空所に入る。空所後を読むと，刑務所で矯正の機会があっても例外と見なされ，受刑者の社会復帰のためのニーズと現実には隔たりがあることがわかる。つまり，**1** のように，プログラムは十分には実施されていないことになる。

(28) - 解答 ③

解説 第 4 段落では独房監禁（solitary confinement）について述べており，空所文の主語 the practice はこれを指す。独房監禁は，最初は受刑者に悔恨の時間を与えるべきとの善意で提唱されたが，逆により再犯しやすくなると研究でわかった（第 3，4 文）。このことを「当初の意図に反する」とまとめた **3** が正解。

全文訳 **監視経済**

　デジタル技術はグーテンベルクの印刷機の現代版だとしばしば見なされるが，現代の人々は 1400 年代の人々がそうだったように，社会と経済における進行中の大変動から派生的に起こる結果がわからないようだ。いくつかの結果は既に現れているが，デジタル革命の 1 つの非常に心配な側面は，人々の無知から利益を得るテクノロジー企業の傾向だ。新型の資本主義が起こっており，そこでは，収益を生む原料は，ソーシャルメディアサイト上の投稿のような無料のデジタルサービスで発生する数十億の行動の分析に基づく行動データの形を取る。このデジタルの宝の山の収益化はデータ収集で始まるが，これは一般に利用者が知らないうちに，または利用者の同意なしに行われる。その後，アルゴリズムを用いてデータを解析し，例えば買い物習慣についての行動予測を生成して，それらが最終的には新型のデジタル市場で売買される。

　この経済モデルは「監視資本主義」と呼ばれ，関連するテクノロジー企業が用いる戦

略は，許可を求めるより許しを求める方が効果的だという考えに基づくとしばしば言われている。例えば，テクノロジー企業は何百万もの著作物をスキャンしてそれらから利益を得ていることが知られている。万一彼らのデータ無断使用を巡るスキャンダルが彼らの評判を傷つける恐れがあれば，企業は自己の莫大(ばくだい)な利益でどんな罰金でも支払って一般大衆を相手に事を丸く収めようとするだろう。

　ハーバード大学のショシャナ・ズボフのような専門家たちは，テクノロジー企業の行動データに対する態度を理不尽だと見る。ズボフの考えでは，彼らはデータを自由に取れる資源であると考えている。企業が特定のデータを利用するのをはっきりと拒否された場合でさえ，非常に高度なアルゴリズムやほかの分析技術を使って彼らが欲しいものを抽出したり推測したりするのは普通のことだ。そして，この同じ極端な権利意識が，皮肉にも，彼らが使うまさにそのデータ抽出と分析技術の特許を彼らにしばしば取らせるのだ。「スマート」「パーソナライズド」や「デジタル・アシスタント」と銘打ったあらゆる製品には，監視経済における道具として使われる不吉な潜在力がある，とズボフは警告する。

> [語句] ramification「(派生的に起こる) 結果」，upheaval「大変動」，monetization「収益化」，algorithm「アルゴリズム」，unauthorized「認可されていない」，smooth over「(問題など) を和らげる」，explicitly「明白に」，infer「～を推測する」，entitlement「権利 [資格] (の付与)」，patent「～の特許権を取る」，sinister「邪悪な，不吉な」

(29) －解答 **4**
　[解説] デジタル革命の心配な面はテクノロジー企業が何をする傾向か，が空所に入る。第1段落後半に「利用者が知らないか同意なしに (without users' awareness or consent) 行動データを収集し，それを解析した行動予測を売買する」という企業の収益化 (monetization) の方法が示されている。これを「人々の無知から利益を得る」と言い換えた **4** が正解。

(30) －解答 **3**
　[解説] 「監視資本主義」で企業が使う戦略では何がより効果的か，が空所に入る。空所文に続く例は「企業が既に行っている著作物のスキャンが無断使用として自社の評判を傷つけるなら，どんな罰金でも払って丸く収めようとする」というもの。よって，企業は **3** の「許可を求めるより (後から) 許しを求める」ことが効果的と考えていることになる。

(31) －解答 **1**
　[解説] ズボフの考えでは，テクノロジー企業 (they = tech firms) はデータを何だと見なしているか。空所文の後に「データ使用を拒否されても，(データから) 欲しいものを抽出・推測するのが普通」とある。また第1，2段落で述べられている「利用者の同意なしにデータを収集」や

20年度第2回　筆記

169

「(許可を得ずに) 著作物をスキャンする」からも，企業がデータを自由に取れる資源と見ていることがわかる。

一次試験・筆記 3 　問題編 p.95 〜 104

全文訳　心理学の再現性の危機

　再現性は科学の要であるが，数多くの実験は，立派な心理学者によって行われ権威あるジャーナルで発表された実験でさえも，うまく再現することができない，と異口同音に主張する研究者たちの声が高まっている。1つの有名な例は，広く引用される心理学的研究で，老齢と関連するイメージを思い起こさせるように作られたワード・パズルを完成することが原因で後に被験者の歩く速度が遅くなった，と主張した。しかし，ほかの研究者によるその確認が成功したためしはない。しかし，再現できなかったときに非難を浴びた研究の擁護者たちは，再現を試みた研究者たちに必要な能力が欠けていたと言い立てたり，追跡調査でのサンプルサイズが不十分だったと主張したりして，一貫性のなさについて多くの考えられる説明を提示した。これに応じて，2010年代にバージニア大学の研究者ブライアン・ノセクの指導の下で，100近くの有名な心理学の研究の再現を試みてテストするプロジェクトが始まった。元のサンプルサイズの被験者数から数を増やすことを含め，実験が可能な限り信頼できるものであることを保証するためにあらゆる努力がなされた。結果は衝撃的で，調べた研究のたったの半分ほどしか及第点に達せず，心理学の「再現性の危機」と呼ばれてきたものを浮き彫りにした。

　あからさまな不正の場合と，ジャーナルは研究者の仮説を確認する研究を好む傾向があるという不満がある一方，ノセクの研究の結果として明らかになったおそらく最も憂慮すべき傾向は，「p値ハッキング」として知られるものだ。これは統計学用語の「p値」から作られた語で，p値は，実験結果が偶然や何かほかの要因によってではなく自分が研究している効果で実際に引き起こされている確率を表すために，研究者によって計算される。研究者たちは許容できるp値を得ようとして，望ましくないデータを除外し，彼らが望む結果を裏付けする可能性のより高い統計的テストを選び，そしてどの観察記録を互いに比較するかについて選択的であることを非難されてきた。ある調査では，40%を超える心理学研究者が何らかの形でのp値ハッキングを認め，そして驚いたことには，彼らはその専門職で十分に確立し，教えられさえもしたやり方を行っていたので，大多数が自己の研究方法は正当と認められると思っていた。p値ハッキングが知られずに拡大するのはそのせいである。不正と公表の偏りとp値ハッキングの複合効果のせいで，多くの人は有名な教科書とジャーナルに出ている心理学研究の妥当性を疑問に思ってきた。

　この危機は自分たちの分野を疑似科学的なナンセンスに格下げするであろうと心配する研究者がいる一方で，利益をもたらし得ると言う研究者もいる。心理学的研究の妥当性に疑問を投げかけたノセクの研究で行われた追跡調査は，実は研究所の実験は最高の

実施基準で行われる場合，人間行動を研究する有効な方法であることをはっきり示している。加えて，いくつかの元の研究結果の再現は，その背後にある理論が正しいことを証明するのに役立つ。「個々の科学者に対する報奨は再現性よりも目新しさを優先する」ため，彼のプロジェクトで行ったような研究はたいてい見過ごされる，とノセクは言う。発表や資金提供のような魅力になるものは，新発見と以前の発見の実証の両方に報いるように同等に調整されるべきだ，と彼は提案する。

> 語句　replication「再現」，reproducibility「再現性」，subject「対象者，被験者」，come under fire「非難〔批判〕を浴びる」，inconsistency「不一致，矛盾」，follow-up「追跡調査」，startling「驚くべき」，make the grade「基準に達する，合格する」，dub *A B*「AをBと呼ぶ」，defensible「擁護できる」，insidious「知らないうちに進行する」，pseudoscientific「疑似科学的な」，validate「〜が正しいことを証明する」，prioritize「〜を優先する」，novelty「目新しさ」，enticement「誘惑，魅力」，be geared toward 〜「〜に（合わせて）調整する」，substantiation「実証」

(32) – 解答　2

> 問題文の訳　ブライアン・ノセクによって組織されたプロジェクトの1つの特徴は，
>
> 選択肢の訳
> 1　再現研究が，元の研究を発表した研究者よりも学問的な評判が高い研究者によって行われたことである。
> 2　以前の再現研究は適切に行われていなかったと信じる人々がしてきた非難に取り組もうとしたことである。
> 3　再度行うために選ばれた元の実験のうち約半分は，以前に再現研究の対象になったことがなかったことである。
> 4　最初に行われたとき，元の研究者が確信がないと述べた研究結果を再現することにのみ焦点を当てたことである。
>
> 解説　ノセクのプロジェクトについては第1段落後半にある。再現できなかった研究の擁護者たちが，再現研究での研究者の力量や追跡調査のサンプルサイズの不足を言い立てた（第4文）が，それに応えて（In response）彼のプロジェクトは始められた。このことを，「適切に行われなかった」と言い換えてまとめた 2 が正解。

(33) – 解答　3

> 問題文の訳　この文章の筆者は「p値ハッキング」について何と言っているか。
>
> 選択肢の訳
> 1　その行為にはより多くの注意が払われているが，不正とジャーナルでの偏りのようなもっとよくある問題よりも実際はずっと深刻度は低い。
> 2　「p値」が正確かどうかを確信するのはとても困難なので，研究者にp値ハッキングの罪があることを証明するのはほぼ不可能だ。
> 3　その行為は研究の妥当性に悪影響を及ぼすが，データ操作は心理学の

分野にいる多数の人々から許容できると見なされている。

4 ジャーナルは実はその行為を奨励してきたとわかっているのだから，それは心理学分野では極めて一般的というわけではない，というふりをすべきでない。

解説 p 値ハッキングについては第 2 段落にある。大多数の研究者が，望ましくないデータを除外するといった p 値ハッキングは自分の職で十分に確立した（well established ... in the profession）行為であり擁護できる（defensible）と考えている。また，心理学研究の妥当性に疑問を持たせる原因の 1 つが p 値ハッキングだ（同最終文）。これらをまとめた **3** が正解。

(34) – 解答 ②

問題文の訳 この文章によると，再現性の危機はどのように実際に有益であり得るのか。

選択肢の訳
1 心理学において新しい考えが必要であるという認識を高めることで，その危機はさまざまな新しい理論の発展につながりそうだ。
2 元々の心理学実験に疑念を抱かせる研究は，それ自体が心理学実験は信頼でき得ることを示す指標だ。
3 有名な研究者たちの研究を疑うことで，あまり知られていない研究者たちが独特な発見を発表する機会を作るかもしれない。
4 かつて信頼できないものとされた多くの研究結果は，その後，心理学分野で最も信頼できる結果に含まれることが示されてきた。

解説 有益であり得ることは第 3 段落第 2，3 文にある。第 2 文を言い換えてまとめたのが **2**。本文の The follow-up testing conducted in Nosek's study that brought the validity of psychological research into question を The studies that cause doubt about the original psychology experiments と言い換え，valid を reliable と言い換えている。

全文訳 ベルサイユ条約

　フランス・ロシア・英国の三国協商と，ドイツとその同盟国から成る中央同盟国の間の 4 年を超える血で血を洗う戦いの後，1919 年にベルサイユ条約が正式に第 1 次世界大戦を終わらせた。しかし，実際の戦いは 1918 年に調印された休戦協定で終わっていた。そうなったのは，敵の攻撃がドイツ軍を屈服させたとドイツの指導者たちが認めたときであり，その結果彼らは，戦闘を中止させ国境への侵攻を防ぐために大幅な譲歩をすることになった。それにもかかわらず，前線での架空の勝利報告を含むドイツの戦時政治宣伝活動の成功によって，民間人はドイツ軍が総崩れになっていたことを知らなかった。戦闘が終わると，ドイツ首相フリードリヒ・エーベルトは，ドイツ軍は「戦場から征服されずに」帰還した，と偽りの宣言を行った。この発言の意図は国家の威信を維

持することだったが，戦争の結果について広く誤った思い込みを招く大きな一因となり，その思い込みが，「背後の一突き」と言われる裏切りの神話を生じさせる一助となった。この考えによると，ドイツは軍事的に敗北したわけではないのだから，内部から裏切りに遭ったに違いない。その結果国家主義者は，ベルサイユ条約がドイツに課した見たところ不利な条項を，労働者団体と社会主義者と国内のユダヤ人のせいにすることができた。

　条約の最も悪名高い部分は231条で，一般に「戦争責任条項」という名で知られている。これは，自らの行動に対するドイツの責任を，領土を割譲し金銭的賠償を行う根拠として確定させた。しかし，ドイツの敗北に憤っていた国家主義者はこの条項を激しく非難し，三国協商が要求した賠償費用があまりに過大だったので国は貧困に陥ったと主張した。だが，文脈の中で読むと，231条は，戦争の勃発を招いたことでドイツを厳しく責めるものというより，ドイツには条約のほかの条項で詳しく定められた賠償金の要求に従う法的義務があると規定することが主な役目だったことが明らかになる。実際，条項の1つは，ドイツの責任を主に民間人が被った損害の支払いに限定していた。したがって，より正確には，この条項は戦勝国によるドイツへの譲歩の一部と見なされるものだ。

　アドルフ・ヒトラーのナチ党は1930年代に政権に就くと，ベルサイユ条約が課した条件の犠牲者であるドイツは国際的なのけ者になった，と主張した。231条は戦争責任条項だとする考え方を巧みに利用して，ナチスはドイツ人の憤りをあおった。彼らの主張は多くの歴史物語に採用され，英国の戦時中の首相デイビッド・ロイド・ジョージのような有力者はそれを事実と受け止めた。ロイド・ジョージは，ドイツが戦後に復活させた軍国主義の責任の多くをベルサイユ条約の遺産に負わせる人々の列に加わったのである。事実，この解釈は第2次世界大戦の主要な原因として今もなお広く言及される。しかし，ナチスはまったく逆の考え方をしていたと論じることもできる。ベルサイユ条約に違反した彼らの違法な再軍備と領土の奪取が，国際社会からドイツが排除された本当の動因だったのだ。231条の「戦争責任条項」というレッテルを，単なる歴史の補足説明に降格させる頃合いなのかもしれない。

> [語句] bloodshed「流血（の惨事）」, armistice「休戦（協定）」, offensive「攻撃（態度）」, bring *a person* to *a person's* knees「（人）をひざまずかせる，屈服させる」, deceptive「人を欺く」, unconquered「征服されていない」, delusion「誤った思い込み，妄想」, surrender「～を引き渡す」, reparations「賠償金」, impoverish「～を貧乏にする」, outbreak「突然の発生，勃発」, hostilities「戦争［戦闘］（行為）」, abide by ～「（規則など）に従う」, lay out「～を詳しく述べる」, incur「（損害など）を被る」, take power「権力［政権］を握る」, outcast「（社会の）のけ者」, play on ～「（人の感情など）をかき立てる，～につけ込む」, fan the flames「あおり立てる」, resentment「憤り，敵意」, militarism「軍国主義（体制）」, rearmament「再軍備」, impetus

「起動力，推進力」，exclusion「除外」，relegate *A* to *B*「A を B に格下げする」，footnote「脚注，補足説明」

(35) – 解答 ②

問題文の訳 「背後の一突き」という神話が起こった理由は，

選択肢の訳
1 休戦協定に署名した直後のドイツ首相の行動が，彼と軍の関係をひどく悪化させたことである。
2 ドイツの指導者たちが戦争の帰結について国民を欺いたので，国がベルサイユ条約を受け入れた理由について誤解を招いたことである。
3 戦争初期にドイツの司令官たちが犯したミスが，ベルサイユ条約が提案されたときに国の交渉上の立場を弱めたことである。
4 ドイツの民間人に影響を与えることを意図していた敵の政治宣伝活動が，その代わりに軍が政府の敵に回る原因になったことである。

解説 第 1 段落後半に，首相の偽りの宣言（deceptive declaration）のせいで民間人が戦争の結果について誤った思い込み（delusions）をして「ドイツ軍は敗北しなかったのに過酷なベルサイユ条約を受け入れたのは内部の裏切りがあったからに違いない」と考える「背後の一突き」の神話が生じたことが示されている。このことをまとめた **2** が正解。

(36) – 解答 ④

問題文の訳 231 条はどのように誤って解釈されたか。

選択肢の訳
1 それは戦時中にもたらされた被害の支払いをドイツがしなければならないことを意味するのではないと多くの人々が思っていたが，さらにいっそう深刻なほかの経済的影響があった。
2 それの文言はほかの条約で使われた文言と似ていると思われていたにもかかわらず，それの刑罰は実は国家主義者でさえもが主張したより厳しかった。
3 それはドイツの指導者たちの要求に屈したものと見られたが，ドイツがさまざまな戦争犯罪を行ったと非難する表現を含んでいた。
4 それは戦争を始めたことでドイツを厳しく罰するものと見られたが，主にドイツにとって比較的好ましい条件の法的根拠を与えていた。

解説 231 条は，戦争の勃発を招いたとドイツを厳しく責めるのではなく，ドイツの賠償責任を民間の損害に限定した（ドイツには好都合な）条項などに従う法的義務を規定するものだった（第 2 段落第 4 文）。このことを，outbreak of hostilities → starting the war, primarily → mostly, was legally obligated → gave a legal basis とそれぞれ本文を言い換えてまとめた **4** が正解。

(37) – 解答 ④

問題文の訳 何がベルサイユ条約のナチスの解釈の 1 つの結果だったか。

選択肢の訳
1 その条約はドイツが軍事拡大をして領土を増やすのを促すことを意図

していたと主張することで，ナチスはより大きな権力を得ることができた。
　2　ドイツが戦争を始めた罪を部分的に認めたことが，ナチスが国際社会での印象をよくするのに役立った。
　3　人々に231条を無視させて条約のほかの部分に注目させたことが，ナチスが戦争で失った領土の返還を交渉するのに役立った。
　4　ドイツの諸問題の責任はその条約にあるとされるようになったが，実は問題を引き起こしていたのはナチス自身だった。

【解説】第3段落第4文の this interpretation は，ドイツはベルサイユ条約のせいで国際的に排斥された犠牲者だというナチスの解釈を指す。この解釈は英国の政治家などにも受け入れられ，ドイツが再び軍国主義の道を歩んだのはベルサイユ条約の責任だとする考えが定説になっている。これが **4** の前半に合致する。しかし実際は，ドイツが国際的に孤立したのはドイツの条約違反が原因だった（第6文）。これが **4** の後半に合致する。

【全文訳】　**ペルーのグアノにわか景気**
　ペルーが1820年代にスペインからの独立を果たしたとき，経済的苦境に悩まされた。自由を求める熾烈（しれつ）な戦いは，両国間の銀の取引に損害を与えており，ペルー経済の主力であった銀山の衰退をもたらした。また，ペルー政府は戦費を出すために英国の銀行家たちから大金を借りたため，この紛争は国に巨額の負債を負わせていた。独立後の20年間ペルーは経済を発展させようと奮闘したがうまくいかず，ついに思いも寄らない資源である海鳥のふん，という形でいちるの希望を手にした。
　この老廃物はグアノ（鳥糞石（ちょうふん））として知られており，ペルーの海岸沖にあるチンチャ諸島で巨大な山となって堆積していた。その海岸は，太平洋から注ぐ栄養分の多い水に浸され，種々の海洋生物でいっぱいで，捕食鳥の大きな個体群を引き寄せた。冷たい海流と暖かい熱帯地方の空気の組み合わせが非常に乾燥した環境をつくり，天然でグアノに存在する豊富な栄養分が降水で分散されないことを確かにした。実際，グアノの特に高い窒素含有量が，この老廃物を理想的な肥料にするのだ。先住民は何世紀もの間そういうもの（肥料）としてグアノを持続可能な方法で利用してきた。海鳥の個体数を乱さないように島々から採取するのにふさわしい時期を注意深く選び，交尾期の間に鳥に危害を加えた者は誰でも死をもって罰した。
　しかし，ペルーの2人の実業家がサンプルを英国に送った1838年まで，グアノはヨーロッパで広く価値を認められていなかった。英国では農業経営者たちが痩せた土壌に対するグアノの効果にすぐに気付いた。ものすごい人口急増に起因する食糧需要の急上昇が持続不可能な農法をもたらしていたが，一方では，産業化によって農村地域から都市部へ人口が移動し，人間の排せつ物は以前そうであったように肥料として利用されるために農地に戻されるのではなく，都市で終わることになった。グアノは痩せた土壌に

活力を与える特効薬であるとわかった。1841年までには，ペルーと英国との間のその産出物（グアノ）の取引は軌道に乗り，グアノ時代の到来を告げた。

　ペルー政府はチンチャ諸島のグアノの独占を享受したが，この国は海外に向けた発送と販売を効果的に運営する資本と専門的知識の両方を欠いていた。その結果として，それらは英国の商人たちに委託され，商人たちはそれらの仕事に対してかなりの手数料を受け取った。その上，支払いは取引が完了するまでペルー政府にされなかった——船1隻の荷積みに優に1カ月以上かかり得ることを考えればかなり長いプロセスだ。このためペルーは英国の債権者から——多くの場合，産出物（グアノ）の発送を任されたまさに同じ会社だったのだが——さらに借金をして，販売で稼いだ金を使って利子とともに彼らに返済した。このプロセスを長引かせる利得は商人たちにもわかり，商人たちは間もなくグアノ販売の手数料よりもペルー政府に前借りを認めることからより利益を得ていた。

　それにもかかわらず，この協力関係は海外の債権者とのペルーの立ち位置を強化した。ペルーが債務不履行となった経歴が，潜在的な貸し手に自己の資本金をペルー政府に貸し付けて危険にさらすことをためらわせていた。しかし，ペルーのグアノの収入は裕福で評判のよい英国の商人たちに管理されていたことが，この国なら借金を返すと当てにしていいだろうという信頼を植え付け，ペルーが海外の資本市場を利用する道を切り開いた。

　1850年代末期までには，外国に向けた年間何十万トンというグアノの輸出は，ペルーの国家歳入の4分の3以上に寄与していたが，この国には終わりのない借金があるままだった。よりよい融資条件を得て国から歳入が流出するのを止めるために，ペルー政府は特別な事業特権を与えることによって国内企業がグアノ市場で競争することを奨励した。しかし，英国企業はペルー企業とただ協力関係を結ぶだけで大きな支配力を維持したので，ペルーから資本が流出し続ける結果になった。

　見たところグアノからの収入が絶えないことに基づいて国が融資を受けられるようになったことに駆り立てられ，ペルー政府は無制限に借り入れるという破滅を招く習慣に陥った。まん延した支配階級の汚職は事態をさらに悪化させるばかりで，さまざまな公共事業に大金がつぎ込まれたが，長期的に経済を多様化して安定させる取り組みにはほとんど費やされなかった。

　ペルーが享受したグアノ主導の「繁栄」は，痛ましくなるほどに限りがあることが結局はわかった。チンチャ諸島の何千年にもわたって形作られたかつて巨大だったふんの山は，グアノの取引で破壊されて1870年代までにはほぼ枯渇し，供給を補充すると当てにされていた海鳥たちは，何十年の絶え間ない採取の後には大部分が追い払われていたか殺されていた。その欠乏はペルーに経済的な災いを招き，経済的な思慮分別を欠いていたせいで，ペルーはグアノのにわか景気の後はその前よりも裕福にはなっていなかった。スウェーデンの歴史家マグヌス・メルネルは多くの学者の意見を繰り返して，ペルーにとって「グアノの富は，全体的に見ると，逃した発展の好機であった」と述べた。

　　語句　be beset by ～「～に悩まされる」，woe「災い，悩みの種」，hard-fought「激戦の」, backbone「中軸, 根幹」, glimmer of hope「かすかな望み」, manure「肥料, 肥やし」, nourishing「栄養のある」, teem with ~「~に富む」, predatory「捕食性の」, arid「乾燥した」, nutrient「栄養分」, precipitation「降水」, sustainably「持続可能なように」, extraction「抽出, 採取」, penalize「~を罰する」, deplete「~を枯渇させる」, surge「急増, 急上昇」, unsustainable「持続できない」, wind up in ~「最終的に~に行き着く」, magic bullet「妙案, 特効薬」, invigorate「~を元気[活気]付ける」, degrade「~の質を低下させる」, usher in「~の到来を告げる」, consign「~を委託する」, finalize「~を完結させる」, entrust A to do「Aに~することを委ねる」, draw out「~を長引かせる」, be lost on ~「(人)に理解されない」, bolster「~を支える, 強固にする」, default on ~「(債務など)を履行しない」, instill「(思想・感情など)を徐々に注ぎ込む」, make good on ~「(負債など)を返済する」, perpetual「永久の, 永続する」, stem「~を止める」, outflow「流出」, concession「特権, 免許」, ruinous「破壊的な, 破滅を招く」, unrestrained「抑制されない」, rampant「はびこる」, diversify「~を多様化する」, stabilize「~を安定させる」, finite「限界のある」, ravage「~を荒らす, 破壊する」, replenish「~を補充する」, incessant「絶え間のない」, prudence「思慮分別」, well off「裕福な」

(38) －解答 ③

問題文の訳　何がチンチャ諸島のグアノについて言えたか。

選択肢の訳
1　その島々の地域の海流はグアノの山に大量の硝酸塩を運び, 島々の乾いた空気の影響に対する耐性をグアノの山に持たせた。
2　硝酸塩を最も多く含むグアノは, 形成された巨大な山の内側部分に閉じ込められていたので, 入手するのは困難だった。
3　肥料としてのそれの有効性は, 島々における特定の気候条件によるもので, その気候条件が主要成分の保存を可能にした。
4　その地域に住んでいた先住民族は, グアノを産出する海鳥が既に姿を消してしまうまで, グアノが肥料としての可能性を持つことに気付かなかった。

解説　第2段落第3, 4文から「冷たい海流と暖かい空気の組み合わせが乾燥した環境をつくったのでグアノの栄養分は流失せず保存された」,「グアノは窒素含有量が高いので理想的な肥料だ」とわかる。このことを言い換えた 3 が正解。3 の particular climatic conditions と key component はそれぞれ本文の exceedingly arid environment と nitrogen を指す。

(39) －解答 ④

問題文の訳　1800年代半ばの英国でのグアノに対する需要は, …の結果だった。

選択肢の訳　1　ペルーの企業がグアノのメリットについて誤ったうわさを流し，悪化している収穫量を押し上げようと必死である英国農場経営者をうまく利用したこと
　　　　　　2　処理する資源のない農村地域に蓄積した大量の人間の排せつ物によって損害を受けた農地を再生したいという望み
　　　　　　3　農村地域で行われる非常に無駄の多い農業のやり方のせいで発展した，都市農業に向かう傾向
　　　　　　4　都市化に付随して起こった廃棄物利用のやり方における大きな変化のせいで生じた，深刻な農業問題

解説　1800年代半ばの英国の状況は第3段落にある。①都市への人口移動により人間の排せつ物が肥料として使われなくなっていたが，グアノは②痩せた土壌（depleted [degraded] soil）に活力を与えるとわかり取引が本格化した，ことが述べられている。①を「都市化に伴う廃棄物利用法の大きな変化」，②の「痩せた土壌」を「深刻な農業問題」と言い換えた4が正解。

(40) – 解答　2

問題文の訳　なぜ英国の商人は，グアノの販売を遅らせたのか。

選択肢の訳　1　発送とマーケティングの問題に対処するための資金援助に関するペルーとの交渉が，当初予想していたよりも長くかかっていた。
　　　　　　2　ペルー政府がグアノの販売から得るお金を長く待たなければならないほど，商人は融資の利子からより多くの収入を得ることができた。
　　　　　　3　海外からの融資の受け取りに合わせた時にしかペルー政府が商人たちに手数料を支払おうとしないので，商人たちはうろたえた。
　　　　　　4　海外の買い手とグアノの販売価格を交渉する時間を取ることは商人にとって極めて重要で，彼らの利益を最大にすることができた。

解説　第4段落中ほどで，ペルー政府は英国商人から金を借りて，販売完了時に支払われるグアノの代金で返済していたことが述べられている。つまり，販売完了（即ち借金返済）までのプロセスが長ければ長いほど利子が膨れて商人の収入は増えるので2が正解。第4段落最終文で，商人がこのプロセスを長引かせる利点を理解してもうけていたことがわかる。

(41) – 解答　2

問題文の訳　ペルーが長期的にグアノ産業から経済的な利益を得なかった1つの理由は何か。

選択肢の訳　1　チンチャ諸島からグアノを取り出す高い費用のせいで，政府は予算の管理を誤って国内産業に損害を与えた。
　　　　　　2　外国との協力関係の結果として信用貸しを獲得する能力が上がったため，ペルーは過大な負債を負った。
　　　　　　3　1870年代にグアノ採取に対する規制が終わったので，裕福なペルー

人たちは海鳥の繁栄を気にせずに個人の利益のためにグアノの多くを持ち去った。
4 ペルーと英国の企業に相互協力を強いることの効率の悪さが原因で、その産業の利益は大幅に減少した。

解説 第8段落第3文から、「グアノのにわか景気後は以前より裕福にならなかった」(すなわち問題文の「グアノ産業から経済的な利益を得なかった」)理由は「ペルーの経済的思慮分別の欠如」だとわかる。その内容は第5、7段落で述べられている「英国との協力関係 (partnership) がペルーの信頼度を高めたので海外から融資を受けられたが、ペルーは無制限に借り入れるという破滅的習慣に陥った」ことだと考えられる。このことをまとめて言い換えた **2** が正解。

一次試験・筆記 4 問題編 p.104

解答例

There are numerous reasons why overpopulation threatens the future of humankind. But I believe the gravitas of the issue can be understood best by considering the impact unrestricted population growth has on economies, resources, and the environment.

Firstly, statistics indicate that population growth correlates negatively with economic performance. Experts attribute impressive economic growth to citizens' high level of savings and investments. However, people in countries with growing populations tend to have large families, and many of these households are unable to save money or make investments due to increased living costs, which impacts economic development.

Furthermore, the strain on resources from overpopulation can manifest itself in many ways. Food shortages, for example, still affect many poorer countries. Attempts to improve agricultural yield in answer to greater demands of larger populations are hampered by limited land space, and with the earth's finite capacity to produce such resources, the problem will likely worsen.

Finally, environmental degradation caused by overpopulation cannot be ignored. Humans' reliance on the planet has intensified in the wake of population booms over the last century, as evidenced by environmental issues such as climate change. While solutions are frantically being researched, many believe the damage to nature may be irreversible.

Clearly, without some measure of population restriction, the future appears bleak. Stagnated economies, resource exhaustion, and a withered earth are just some of the issues we must resolve if we are to leave a legacy of hope for later generations.

トピックの訳「賛成か反対か:世界的な人口過剰は人類の未来への深刻な脅威だ」

解説 解答例は,トピックに対して賛成の主張を「序論,理由①,理由②,理由③,結論」の5段落構成で述べている。

3つの理由とその根拠は,①経済への悪影響:著しい経済成長は市民の貯蓄と投資のおかげだが,人口が増える国では大家族で高い生活費のため貯蓄も投資もできない,②資源への負担:食糧不足を例にすると,需要は増えるが地球上の土地には限りがあり農業生産高を上げられない,③環境の劣化:過去の人口急増のため人間の地球への依存度が高まったが,損なわれた自然は元に戻せない(irreversible)かもしれない,というもの。経済,資源,環境という人類にとって極めて重要な3つの視点から理由を挙げているため説得力がある。

また,最終段落の結論で,3つそれぞれの視点からのショッキングな未来像となる,停滞した経済(stagnated economy),資源の枯渇(resource exhaustion),枯れた地球(withered earth)を提示することで,トピックの重大さをより強く印象づけているところは巧みだ。

語彙では manifest(~を明示する),finite(有限の),degradation((質などの)低下),frantically(必死に),bleak((見通しなどが)暗い)など難しい語が文を引き締めている。「人」を意味する humankind,citizen,people,humans の言い換えは,全体が単調になるのを防いでいることにも注目したい。

なお,トピックに反対の主張をする場合の理由は,ほかの惑星への移住を見据えた宇宙開発,遺伝子組み換え技術などでの食糧確保,ベーシックインカムでの生活保障,などであろう。

一次試験・リスニング Part 1

問題編 p.105～106 ▶MP3 ▶アプリ ▶CD 2 26～36

No.1 - 解答 ②

スクリプト
★: Julia, we're considering you for the regional sales director position. You'd still work here at the head office, but it'd mean having to travel more.
☆: Ah... that might be a problem. My kids are still young, and you know that I'm a single mother, so I can't be gone too much.
★: Right. We realize that, but there may be a way to cut down on the trips. We've been trying out video conferencing, and so far, so good.
☆: Then I'd certainly be interested.

Question: How does the man suggest solving the problem?

全文訳
★: ジュリア，君を地区の営業部長にどうだろうと考えているんだ。このまま本社勤務は変わらないが，もっと外回りをしなくちゃならなくなる。
☆: うーん，それは難しいかもしれません。子供たちがまだ小さいですし，ご存じのように私はシングルマザーですから，あまり家を空けるわけにはいきません。
★: そうだね。それはわかっているよ。ただ，出張を減らす方法があるかもしれない。試験的にビデオ会議を導入していて，今のところうまくいっている。
☆: それでしたら，もちろん興味があります。

質問：男性はどのように問題を解決することを提案しているか。

選択肢の訳
1 女性を地方の営業所へ異動させることによって。
2 女性が外回りをする必要を減らすことによって。
3 女性の子供の世話を手伝う人を雇うことによって。
4 女性に違う役職を提示することによって。

解説 女性の問題点は家をあまり空けられないこと。男性の提案は彼の2つ目の発言にある。ビデオ会議の導入によって，出張の回数を減らせるのではないかと述べている。

No.2 - 解答 ③

スクリプト
☆: Gary, it's me. I'm afraid I have to work late again.
★: Again? That's the third time this week! When do you think you'll get home?
☆: Probably around 9. Listen, Clive's baseball practice ends at 8:30. Can you pick him up?
★: Well, I'm supposed to be giving your mom a ride to the airport.

181

☆ : Ah, I forgot. Well, I guess he'll just have to wait for a bit until I get there.

★ : He'll understand. And I'll pick up some dinner for us on my way back.

Question: What will the woman do?

全文訳　☆：ゲイリー，私よ。悪いんだけど，また残業しなくちゃならないの。
★：またかい。今週3回目だよ！　何時に帰って来られそうなんだい。
☆：たぶん9時くらいね。それでね，クライブの野球の練習が8時半に終わるのよ。車で迎えに行ってもらえないかしら。
★：いや，僕は君のお母さんを空港まで送って行くことになっているんだよ。
☆：あっ，忘れてたわ。じゃあ，クライブは私が着くまでの間，少し待っているしかなさそうね。
★：わかってくれるさ。それから帰る途中でみんなの分の夕食を買って来るよ。

質問：女性は何をするか。

選択肢の訳　1　職場を早めに出て，クライブを迎えに行く。
2　母親を空港に送って行く。
3　仕事の後でクライブを車で迎えに行く。
4　帰る途中で夕食を買って来る。

解説　女性は2つ目の発言で夫に Can you pick him up? と頼んでいるが，断られて，自分でそうすることにしているので，**3**が正解。**2**と**4**は夫がすること。

No.3 – 解答 ③

スクリプト
☆ : Hey, Steve. Wasn't that board meeting really frustrating?
★ : Yes! Margaret dominated again. Her constant sniping at others and negativity about fresh ideas is hampering the organization.
☆ : Should we try talking to her?
★ : You think she'll listen? We only joined the board a few months ago.
☆ : True, but we can't just sit back and do nothing. Let's sound out the president and see if he can encourage her to step down.
★ : That's a bit drastic. We should rally the other board members around us first.
☆ : You're right. Then maybe we can push for her resignation!

Question: What do these two colleagues decide to do?

全文訳　☆：ちょっと，スティーブ。委員会はすごくフラストレーションがたまらなかった？
★：たまったよ！　またマーガレットの独り舞台だ。彼女がほかの人たちを

攻撃してばかりいることと新鮮なアイデアに否定的なことは，組織の邪魔になっているよ。
☆： 彼女と話してみるべきかしら。
★： 彼女が耳を貸すと思うかい？ 僕たちは数カ月前に委員会に入ったばかりなんだよ。
☆： 確かにそうだけど，何もせずに手をこまねいているわけにはいかない。会長の考えを探って，彼女が辞めるよう会長から促してもらえないか見てみましょうよ。
★： それはちょっと過激だな。まずはほかの委員を味方に付けて結集するべきだよ。
☆： そのとおりね。そうすれば，彼女の辞任を要求できるかもしれない！
質問：この2人の同僚は何をすることに決めているか。

選択肢の訳
1 委員会を辞任すると脅す。
2 会長に辞任するよう忠告する。
3 ほかの人たちの支持を集める。
4 マーガレットと彼女の態度について話す。

解説 女性は2つ目の発言で Should we try talking to her? と提案しているが，男性は却下している。男性の3つ目の発言の rally ... around us がわかるかどうかがポイント。「自分たちの周りに結集する」は「支持を得る」ことなので，**3** が正解となる。snipe at ～「～を（陰険な手段で）攻撃する」，sound out「～の意見を探る」。

No.4 – 解答 ③

スクリプト
★： Did you hear that Jason Lind is going to direct a new cable TV series?
☆： Isn't he a movie director?
★： Yes. And a very good one, too.
☆： I wonder why he decided to go into TV.
★： A lot of film actors have been successful in hit TV shows recently. I suppose it was just a matter of time before directors tried to make the same shift.
☆： Well, if his TV debut is anything like his movies, it'll be fantastic.
Question: What do we learn about Jason Lind?

全文訳
★： ジェイソン・リンドがケーブルテレビの新しいシリーズの監督をするって聞いた？
☆： 彼は映画監督じゃないの？
★： 映画監督だよ。それにとてもいい監督でもある。
☆： どうしてテレビに移ろうと決めたのかしらね。
★： 最近はたくさんの映画俳優がテレビのヒット番組で成功している。監督

が同じように移行しようとするのも時間の問題だったと思うよ。

☆：まあ，彼のテレビデビュー作が少しでも彼の映画に似ていたら，素晴らしいものになるでしょうね。

質問：ジェイソン・リンドについて何がわかるか。

選択肢の訳　1　映画を監督した経験がほとんどない。
　　　　　　2　最新の映画の評価は低かった。
　　　　　　3　これまでテレビで監督したことはない。
　　　　　　4　自分のテレビ番組でいい俳優を使うことができなかった。

解説　男性の最初の発言から，ジェイソン・リンドがこれからテレビで監督をすることがわかり，女性の最後の発言の his TV debut から，それが最初に監督するテレビ作品であることがわかる。したがって **3** が正解。

No.5 - 解答 ②

スクリプト
☆：Look at this TV ad, George. That vegetable cutter can cut, slice, and dice just about anything.
★：If it really worked, it would be selling well in regular stores.
☆：Why are you always such a cynic?
★：My father bought something like that once, but he could never get it to work.
☆：That was years ago. Things are more advanced now.
★：Only the promotion methods! But if you really want it, get it.
☆：No, because if it breaks, I'll never hear the end of it.

Question: What do we learn from this conversation?

全文訳
☆：このテレビ広告を見てよ，ジョージ。あの野菜カッターはほとんど何でも切ったりスライスしたりさいの目切りにしたりできるのよ。
★：本当に役に立つのなら，一般の店でもよく売れるだろうに。
☆：どうしてあなたはいつもそう嫌味なの？
★：父があんな感じのものを買ったことがあるんだけど，全然使い物にならなかったんだよ。
☆：昔のことでしょ。今は物事はもっと進歩しているのよ。
★：進歩したのは宣伝方法だけさ！　だけど本当に欲しいのなら買いなよ。
☆：やめるわ。だってもし壊れたら，いつまでもあなたの嫌味を聞かされるもの。

質問：この会話から何がわかるか。

選択肢の訳　1　男性は女性にその製品を買わせない。
　　　　　　2　男性は広告の主張内容を疑っている。
　　　　　　3　女性の父親が同じ製品を持っている。
　　　　　　4　女性は一般の店で買い物する方を好む。

解説　夫婦らしき2人の日常会話。男性・女性それぞれの考え，態度の違いを

184

聞き取ることがポイント。「本当に役に立つのなら…」や「進歩したのは宣伝方法だけさ」など，男性が商品に疑いを持っているのは明らかである。ただ，**1**の「買わせない」というレベルには至っていないので注意。

No.6 - 解答 ④

スクリプト
★: See you later, Kay. I'm off to the gym.
☆: Since when did you become Mr. Fitness?
★: I got this great deal at the new gym in the mall — a one-year membership for only 300 dollars.
☆: And you really think that's a good deal?
★: Well, yeah. All the equipment is state-of-the-art, and they have four Jacuzzis.
☆: You know the place across the street from my office? With the Olympic-sized swimming pool? I got two years there for that price.
★: Great. Now you tell me.

Question: What does the woman imply?

全文訳
★: じゃあまた，ケイ。今からジムに行くんだ。
☆: いつからミスター・フィットネスになったの？
★: ショッピングモールの新しいジムがすごくお得だったんだよ。1年間の会員資格がたった300ドルなんだ。
☆: それがお得だと本気で思っているの？
★: あー，うん。設備は全部最新鋭のものだし，ジャグジーが4つあるんだよ。
☆: 私のオフィスのある通りの向かい側のジムを知っているわよね。オリンピックサイズのプールがあるところ。そこは，その料金で2年間だったわよ。
★: 参ったな。今さら言われてもなあ。

質問：女性は暗に何と言っているか。

選択肢の訳
1 設備が旧式である。
2 男性はもっとお金をためる必要がある。
3 男性はそんなに運動するべきではない。
4 男性は会員資格にお金を払い過ぎた。

解説
女性は3つ目の発言で自分の行っているジムについて I got two years there for that price. と言い，男性の a one-year membership for only 300 dollars と比べている。同じ料金で女性のジムは期間が2倍だから，女性は男性のジムが高過ぎると言っていることになる。Now you tell me. は「今になってそんなことを言われても」という意味の決

まり文句。

No.7 - 解答 ②

スクリプト
★: Hey, Annie! Long time, no see. How's art school going?
☆: Pretty well, Mark. I switched my major from fine art to design, and I just got accepted as an intern at a furniture company.
★: Great! But I thought your real love was sculpture.
☆: It is, but I had to face reality. I can make a much better living following this career path.
★: Do you think it'll satisfy you enough to do it long term?
☆: I guess I'll see how the internship goes.

Question: Why did Annie decide to change her major?

全文訳
★: やあ，アニー！ 久しぶり。美術学校の調子はどう？
☆: まあまあ順調よ，マーク。専攻を芸術からデザインに変えて，家具会社にインターンとして雇ってもらったところなの。
★: すごいね！ だけど君が本当に好きなのは彫刻だと思っていたよ。
☆: そうだけど，現実を直視しなくちゃ。この職業の進路に従って行けば，はるかにいい暮らしをすることができるわ。
★: その仕事を長期間できるくらい十分満足できると思う？
☆: インターンシップがこの先どうなるかを見てみようと思うわ。

質問：アニーはなぜ専攻を変えることにしたのか。

選択肢の訳
1 彼女はずっと家具をデザインしたかった。
2 デザインの方がたくさん稼げる可能性がある。
3 彼女はもう彫刻に興味がない。
4 芸術は彼女が思うより難しかった。

解説 本当に好きなのは彫刻だろうと言う男性に対し，女性が2つ目の発言で It is と答えていることから，彫刻を諦めたのではないことがわかる。**2** が，女性の2つ目の発言の make a much better living を greater earning と言い換えている。

No.8 - 解答 ①

スクリプト
★: I'm finished studying. Let's grab lunch.
☆: But I still have to finish my psychology paper.
★: Come on, take a break. We've been at it all morning.
☆: It'll only take me another hour or so. I have to get it done today.
★: That's what happens when you put it off until the last minute!
☆: I know, I know. Will I see you later?
★: Yeah, as long as you're still planning to go to Jim's party tonight.
☆: Wouldn't miss it!

Question: What does the man imply?

全文訳
★：勉強が終わったよ。急いで昼ご飯にしよう。
☆：でも私はまだ心理学のレポートが終わっていないの。
★：おいおい，休憩にしようよ。朝からずっとやっているんだから。
☆：あと1時間かそこらしかかからないわ。今日中に終わらせないといけないの。
★：ぎりぎりまで先延ばしにするとそういうことになるんだよ！
☆：わかってるわよ。後で会える？
★：うん，今夜のジムのパーティーに行く気がまだあるんだったらね。
☆：絶対行くわ！
質問：男性は暗に何と言っているか。
選択肢の訳
1　女性はもっと早くレポートを書くべきだった。
2　彼は昼食を食べに行く時間がない。
3　女性はジムのパーティーに行くべきではない。
4　男性は後で女性と会うことができない。
解説　男性の3つ目の発言がポイント。put off は「〜を延期する，先延ばしにする」。That は提出期限ぎりぎりになってレポートに取り組む女性の状況を表している。つまり，この発言で男性は女性を批判している。

No.9 – 解答

スクリプト
☆：Lucas, don't forget Judy's expecting an answer to whether we're going to her daughter's dance recital.
★：I just can't see why we have to drive two hours each way to spend an entire Saturday doing that. We were at her son's birthday party just a couple of weeks ago.
☆：I'm with you, but that's just the way she is. You know she's really big on family and loves having us visit.
★：Well, we have to let her know somehow that we can't just drop everything whenever a nephew or niece has a birthday or soccer game.
☆：She only does it because she wants to include us in things.
★：I know, and I appreciate that. She's the best sister-in-law you could ask for. But we've got to draw the line somewhere.
☆：Fair enough. We just have to figure out how to wriggle out of this. Maybe I could remind her about my migraines and tell her they're forcing us to limit our trips.
★：Now, that's an idea. It's not an outright lie, either, although they haven't been that bad recently.
☆：Well, I'll send her an e-mail and let her know. But she won't be happy about it.

Question: What is the man's opinion?

☆：ルーカス，私たちがジュディの娘のダンス発表会に行くかどうかの返事をジュディが待っていることを忘れないでね。

★：なぜ土曜日丸1日をそうやって過ごすために片道2時間運転しなきゃいけないのか，どうもわからないよ。2，3週間前に彼女の息子の誕生日会に行ったばかりなのに。

☆：同感だけど，彼女はそういう人なの。彼女は本当に家族が大好きで私たちに来てもらいたいって知ってるでしょ。

★：うーん，おいやめいの誕生日やサッカーの試合があるたびに，すべて放り出せるものじゃないって何とか彼女に知らせないと。

☆：彼女は私たちをいろんなことの仲間に入れたいからそうしているだけよ。

★：わかってる，それはありがたく思うよ。彼女はこれ以上ない最高の義理の姉だ。だけど，どこかで線を引かないといけない。

☆：もっともだわ。これをうまく切り抜ける方法を見つけ出すしかないわね。もしかしたら彼女に私の片頭痛のことを思い出させて，そのせいで外出を制限せざるを得ないとでも彼女に言おうかしら。

★：まあ，それも1つの手だな。最近，片頭痛はそんなにひどくはないけど，まったくのうそでもないしね。

☆：さて，私が彼女にメールして知らせるわ。だけど，彼女はうれしくはないでしょうね。

質問：男性の意見は何か。

1　妻の姉は多くを望み過ぎだ。
2　妻は1人で出かけるべきだ。
3　妻の姉は時々うそをつく。
4　妻はジュディの気持ちを傷つけるかもしれない。

男性の2つ目の発言の nephew or niece と3つ目の発言の sister-in-law から，ジュディは女性の姉妹だとわかる。ジュディの家族のイベントのたびに呼び出されることに男性は不満で，女性はジュディを擁護しながらも，歯止めが必要だという男性の意見に同意している，という会話の流れは明快。家族のイベントに頻繁に参加してもらうことを expects too much と表した **1** が正解である。**4** の「ジュディの気持ちを傷つける」は女性の考え。migraine「片頭痛」。

No.10 解答 ④

★：Well, guys, we need to discuss how to shut down our Hong Kong office next year with minimal impact.

☆：That's going to be tough. Word has already leaked out, and employees there are beginning to panic.

188

● : That's the last thing we need. Morale will plummet.
★ : Well, the Japanese staff will be transferred to other offices, most to locations in Japan, but it's the local Hong Kong staff I'm worried about.
☆ : Agreed. If we just lay them off, our reputation could be irreparably damaged.
★ : Well, we can transfer a handful of them to our Shenzhen office. For those who aren't willing to go or have ties in Hong Kong, we need to compensate them if they leave the firm. That'll help us maintain our reputation as a fair employer.
● : We also have to meet with our local legal counsel to review any remaining contractual obligations to clients.
☆ : I don't foresee that as being a major concern, as our office in Shenzhen can handle clients in Hong Kong.
★ : It seems we agree company standing is our primary concern. Would the two of you draft a formal letter to announce our plans?
● : No problem. We'll include something about management meeting with each one of them to discuss their options.
★ : Great. Let's get ahead of this problem before it explodes in our faces.

Question: What do the speakers conclude is the main issue?

全文訳
★ : ではみんな，私たちはいかに影響を最小限に抑えながら来年香港支社を閉鎖するかを話し合う必要がある。
☆ : 厳しくなりそうね。情報はもう漏れてしまって，現地の従業員たちはパニックになり始めているわ。
● : それだけは絶対嫌だな。士気ががた落ちになる。
★ : ええと，日本人スタッフはほかの支社，ほとんどが日本の支社に転勤になるけど，心配なのは地元香港のスタッフだ。
☆ : 同感よ。もし彼らをただ解雇してしまうと，わが社の評判は修復できないほど傷つくかもしれない。
★ : うーん，彼らのうち少数なら深圳支社に転勤させられる。転勤を渋ったり香港につながりがあったりする人に対しては，退社するなら補償しないと。それが，公正な雇い主としてのわが社の評判を保つのに役立つ。
● : また，顧客に対する契約上の義務が何か残っていないか精査するために，現地の法律顧問と打ち合わせをしなければならないよ。
☆ : それは大きな心配事にはならないと思うわ。深圳支社が香港の顧客に対応できるから。

★：会社の評判が一番の心配事ということで意見が一致しているようだね。君たち2人でわが社の計画を発表する正式なレターの草稿を作ってくれるかな。
●：任せて。選択肢を話し合うために経営幹部が一人一人と面談することについて何か入れるよ。
★：それはいい。この問題が手に負えなくなる前に先んじよう。

質問：話者たちは主な問題は何だと結論を出しているか。

選択肢の訳
1 日本人スタッフが辞めるのを防ぐこと。
2 従業員が会社を訴えるのを防ぐこと。
3 現在の顧客を引き継ぐ現地企業を見つけること。
4 よい雇い主としての会社のイメージを守ること。

解説 1人目の男性の4つ目の発言に，皆が合意している主な問題は「会社の評判（company standing）」とある。また，辞職者への補償が「公正な雇い主（fair employer）」としての評判の保持に役立つ（同男性3つ目の発言）と述べているので **4** が正解。plummet「急落する」，explode in *a person's* face「（計画・もくろみが）突然つぶれて（人の）面目をつぶす」。

A

(スクリプト) **Youth-Apprenticeship Programs**

CareerWise is a large-scale youth-apprenticeship program in the US that allows high school students to learn a skill by working at a company. CareerWise is modeled after programs in Switzerland, where over two-thirds of students do apprenticeships. Thanks to such apprenticeships, Switzerland has extremely low student debt and high employment rates, whereas the US has over $1 trillion in student debt and large numbers of unemployed college graduates. CareerWise aims to prepare participants for a profession while challenging the assumption that earning a college degree is the only path to a successful career.

Critics say many apprenticeship programs direct low-income students into blue-collar jobs. They also question whether the specialized skills students learn will be applicable across jobs or industries, but supporters insist they are highly transferrable. What is more, CareerWise offers participants a broad range of industries to choose from, including healthcare and IT. Upon completion of the program, CareerWise apprentices receive their high school diploma, plus college credit and thousands of dollars in wages. They can choose to go on to college, continue at their current job, or seek other employment. Meanwhile, employers benefit by developing a skilled work force while reducing labor costs.

Questions

No.11 What do we learn about Switzerland's apprenticeship programs?
No.12 What is one criticism of apprenticeship programs?

(全文訳) **若者の見習いプログラム**

キャリアワイズは，企業で働くことで高校生が技術を学ぶことができる，米国の大規模な若者の見習いプログラムだ。キャリアワイズはスイスのプログラムを手本にしており，スイスでは3分の2を超える学生が見習いをする。そのような見習い制度のおかげで，スイスでは学生の借金が極めて少なく雇用率が高いが，それに対して米国では学生の借金は1兆ドルを超え，失業中の大学卒業生が大勢いる。キャリアワイズは，大学の学位を取ることが仕事で成功する唯一の道だという想定に異議を唱える一方で，参加者に職業に就く準備をさせることを目標とする。

多くの見習いプログラムは低所得の学生を肉体労働職へ向かわせる，と批判者たちは言う。彼らはまた，学生が学ぶ専門技能が仕事や業種にわたって適用できるかどうか疑問を呈するが，支持者たちは大いに転用できると主張する。その上，キャリアワイズは

参加者に，医療や情報技術を含む広範囲にわたる業種の選択肢を提示する。プログラムの修了時に，キャリアワイズの実習生は高校の卒業証書，それに大学の単位と賃金として数千ドルを受け取る。彼らは，大学に進むか，今の仕事を続けるか，ほかの勤め口を探すかを選べる。その一方で，雇用主は人件費を削減しながら熟練した労働力を養成することで利益を得る。

語句 apprenticeship「見習い［徒弟］（期間・制度）」，blue-collar「肉体労働（者）の」，transferrable「移転［転用］できる」，apprentice「見習い工，徒弟」

No.11 解答 ④

質問の訳 スイスの見習いプログラムについて何がわかるか。
選択肢の訳
1 少数の学生しか利用することができない。
2 給料が最も高い仕事に主に重点を置いている。
3 雇用率に影響を及ぼさない。
4 学生が多額の借金をするのを防ぐのに役立ってきた。

解説 第1段落中ほどで，見習い制度のおかげでスイスでは「学生の借金が極めて少ない（has extremely low student debt）」と述べている。このことを言い換えた**4**が正解。同じ文で高い雇用率も言及されているので**3**は誤り。

No.12 解答 ①

質問の訳 見習いプログラムに対する1つの批判は何か。
選択肢の訳
1 参加者の仕事の選択肢を制限するかもしれない。
2 雇用主が参加者を不当に利用する。
3 高校生が卒業するのをより困難にする。
4 高校生は職業を決めるには若過ぎる。

解説 批判者の意見は第2段落初めにあり，「学生を肉体労働職（blue-collar jobs）へ導く」，「学ぶ専門技能を広く適用できるか疑問」の2点。前者を「仕事の選択肢を制限する」と言い換えた**1**が正解。

B

スクリプト **Bioplastics**

Conventional plastics are made from petroleum, a nonrenewable resource. They are also hard to dispose of, as petroleum-based products do not break down easily. To address this, some environmentalists are promoting plastics that are mostly made using plant materials. Known as bioplastics, these require fewer fossil-fuel resources to produce. For proponents, the ability of bioplastics to break down into natural, mostly harmless materials is considered their biggest selling point.

Their biodegradability, however, often depends on high-temperature processes at specialized factories, which most places do not have. Consequently, after they can no longer be used, bioplastics are often buried in landfills, where they may release methane, a greenhouse gas that damages the ozone layer. Also, if bioplastics get mixed in with ordinary plastics during the recycling process, they can damage the recycling infrastructure and ruin entire batches of recycled plastic. Bioplastics require a separate recycling system in order to be reused, which is expensive and inconvenient. Another drawback is that chemical fertilizers and pesticides would be required to cultivate enough plants to make the bioplastics industry globally viable. Therefore, many people want to increase the recycling of regular plastics rather than expanding the use of bioplastics.

Questions
No.13 What is one advantage of bioplastics?
No.14 What is one problem with used bioplastics?

全文訳　バイオプラスチック

　従来のプラスチックは，再生不能な資源である石油から作られる。石油由来の製品は簡単には分解しないので，プラスチックは廃棄するのも難しい。これに対処するため，主に植物原料を使って作られるプラスチックを推進する環境保護主義者もいる。バイオプラスチックとして知られているもので，製造するために必要な化石燃料がより少ない。支持者には，自然でほぼ無害な物質に分解するバイオプラスチックの能力が最大のセールスポイントだと考えられている。

　しかし，生分解できるかどうかは，しばしば専門の工場での高温処理によって決まり，ほとんどの場所に専門の工場はない。その結果として，バイオプラスチックはもはや使えなくなるとしばしばごみ処理場に埋められ，そこでオゾン層にダメージを与える温室効果ガスであるメタンを放出する可能性がある。また，リサイクル過程でバイオプラスチックが普通のプラスチックと混ぜられると，リサイクルにかかわるインフラに損害を与え，一括処理された再生プラスチックを全部駄目にすることもあり得る。バイオプラスチックを再利用するためには独立したリサイクルシステムが必要だが，それは費用がかかり不便だ。もう1つの欠点は，バイオプラスチック産業を全世界で実現可能にするのに十分な植物を栽培するには，化学肥料と殺虫剤が必要となるだろうことだ。それ故，多くの人々は，バイオプラスチックの利用を拡大するよりも，普通のプラスチックの再利用を増やしたいと思っている。

語句 biodegradability「生（物）分解性」, methane「メタン」, drawback「欠点」, viable「実行可能な」

No.13 解答　③

質問の訳　バイオプラスチックの1つの利点は何か。
選択肢の訳　**1**　オゾン層に害を及ぼさない。

2 石油由来の古い製品を再利用することによって作られる。
3 化石燃料への依存度がより低い。
4 役立つ製品に，より変化しやすい。

解説 第1段落後半で，バイオプラスチックは「製造に必要な化石燃料がより少ない（require fewer fossil-fuel resources to produce）」と述べている。このことを「化石燃料への依存度がより低い（less reliant on fossil fuels）」と言い換えた **3** が正解。be reliant on 〜「〜に依存している」。

No.14 解答

質問の訳 使用済みのバイオプラスチックの1つの問題は何か。
選択肢の訳
1 1回しか再利用できない。
2 再利用されるのに特別な処理が必要だ。
3 それらが出すメタンがリサイクルシステムに害を及ぼす。
4 それらを作るのに利用される植物がなくなりつつある。

解説 第2段落中ほどで，普通のプラスチックと混ぜると損害が出るため，再利用するには「独立したリサイクルシステム（separate recycling system）」が必要だと述べている。これを「特別な処理（special processing）」が必要だと言い換えた **2** が正解。メタンが害するのはオゾン層なので **3** は誤り。

スクリプト Raye Montague

Raye Montague, an African-American engineer, started working for the US Navy in 1956 as a digital computer systems operator and later advanced to the position of computer systems analyst. One day, her boss, who Montague said held discriminatory attitudes toward black people, attempted to set her up for failure. He told her to create a computer program that could design ships, but he only gave her a six-month deadline and neglected to mention that his department had been struggling with the same task for six years. Montague was determined to succeed, and even worked alone at night until her boss finally granted her staff support.

Montague met the deadline, creating the first-ever computer-generated ship designs. US president Richard Nixon, who wanted to produce warships at a more rapid pace, was highly impressed. Montague was then commissioned to design an actual ship. She completed the design in less than 19 hours, and soon all naval ships and submarines came to be drawn up in this manner. Thanks to her remarkable achievements, she received numerous awards and became the US Navy's first female program manager of ships.

Questions

No.15 What did Raye Montague's boss likely assume about her?
No.16 What is Montague remembered for?

> 全文訳　**レイ・モンタギュー**

　レイ・モンタギューはアフリカ系アメリカ人の技術者で，デジタルコンピューターシステムのオペレーターとして1956年に米海軍で働き始め，後にコンピューターシステムの分析者の地位に昇進した。ある日，モンタギューによると黒人に対して差別的態度を取る上司が，失敗するように彼女を陥れようとした。彼は彼女に船を設計することができるコンピュータープログラムを作成するように言ったが，6カ月の期限を与えただけで，彼の部門が6年間その同じ任務に苦しんできたことを言わないでいた。モンタギューは成功させると堅く決心し，上司がようやくスタッフの支援を彼女に与えるまで，夜間に独りきりで働きさえもした。

　モンタギューは期限を守り，史上初のコンピューターが生成した船舶設計図を作った。もっと速いペースで軍艦を製造したかった米大統領リチャード・ニクソンは非常に感心した。モンタギューはその後，実際の船の設計を依頼された。彼女は19時間足らずで設計を完了し，間もなくすべての軍艦と潜水艦はこの方法で設計図が描かれるようになった。彼女の素晴らしい業績のおかげで，彼女は数多くの賞を受賞して米海軍の最初の女性船舶プログラムマネージャーになった。

> 語句　set up「～を陥れる，はめる」, commission「～に依頼[委託]する」, draw up「（文書など）を作成する」

No.15 解答　**②**

> 質問の訳　レイ・モンタギューの上司は彼女についておそらく何を想定したか。
> 選択肢の訳　**1** 彼女は抗議して米海軍を辞めるだろう。
> **2** 彼女は割り当てられた任務を完成することができないだろう。
> **3** 彼女はコンピューターシステムに損害を与えるだろう。
> **4** 彼女は期限の延長を求める必要はないだろう。
> 解説　第1段落によると，上司は失敗するように彼女を陥れようとして（attempted to set her up for failure），彼の部門が6年間苦しんだプログラムを半年で作るように彼女に指示したのだから，彼女がこの任務を完成できないと想定したのだ。

No.16 解答　**④**

> 質問の訳　モンタギューは何の理由で記憶されるか。
> 選択肢の訳　**1** 米政府に軍艦の数はもっと少なくていいと納得させたこと。
> **2** 潜水艦の操作においてより高い安全性を確保したこと。
> **3** 海戦の新しい方法を見いだしたこと。
> **4** 近代的な海軍艦艇が設計される方法を変えたこと。
> 解説　第2段落で，モンタギューが船の設計ができるプログラムを完成させた後，すべての軍艦と潜水艦の設計図がこの方法で描かれるようになり，

その業績で彼女が多くの賞を受けたことが述べられている。この業績を「近代海軍艦艇の設計方法を変えた」と言い換えた **4** が正解。

（スクリプト） **Salps and the Environment**

　Salps are small, transparent marine organisms that resemble jellyfish. Their unique life cycle and ability to change sex make them fascinating creatures. In their initial stage as females, they go through a reproductive process called budding, during which they produce exact copies of themselves without mating. These tiny clones are linked together in a chain, with each female clone containing a single egg. Later, when the chains have matured, they break apart. Meanwhile, the original female salp becomes male and fertilizes nearby eggs. The resulting female embryos eventually swim out and create their own chain of clones.

　Salps have been drawing the attention of scientists because of their potential to help fight climate change. Algae, which make up a significant portion of salps' diet, must absorb CO_2 in order to grow. Salps' consumption of algae means they also take in the associated carbon. This is then turned into a waste product that sinks to the bottom of the ocean floor, effectively preventing the carbon from returning to the atmosphere. Scientists hope it will one day be possible to utilize salps' enormous appetite to help manage atmospheric CO_2 levels.

Questions
No.17 What is one thing the speaker says about salps?
No.18 How might salps help fight climate change?

（全文訳）　サルパと環境

　サルパは小さくて透明なクラゲに似た海洋生物だ。それらは独特なライフサイクルと性別を変える能力があるので非常に興味深い生き物だ。雌としての初期段階に出芽と呼ばれる生殖過程を経るが，この過程で交尾なしに自分自身と完全に同じ複製を産む。これらのとても小さいクローンは鎖で互いに結合しており，雌のクローンはそれぞれ1つの卵子を持つ。後に，鎖は成熟するとばらばらになる。一方で元々の雌サルパは雄になり，近くの卵子を受精させる。その結果生じる雌の胚は最終的に泳ぎ出て，自分自身のクローンの鎖を作る。

　サルパは気候変動との闘いに役立つ可能性があるので，科学者たちの注目を集めてきた。サルパの食餌の大部分を占める藻は，成長するために二酸化炭素を吸収しなければならない。サルパによる藻の摂取は，関連した炭素を取り込むことも意味する。この炭素がその後，海底の最下層に沈む廃棄物に変えられ，炭素が大気に戻るのを効果的に防ぐ。科学者たちは，いつか，大気中の二酸化炭素量を管理するのを助けるために，サルパの旺盛な食欲が利用できるよう願っている。

語句 reproductive「生殖の」, mating「交尾」, mature「成熟する」, fertilize「〜を受精させる」, algae「藻」(algaの複数形)

No.17 解答 ③

質問の訳 サルパについて話者が言っている1つのことは何か。
選択肢の訳
1 ほかのどの海洋生物よりも多くの卵を産む。
2 雌は雄よりも大きい。
3 生殖を助けるために性別を変える。
4 雌は時々雄に食べられる。

解説 第1段落で,サルパは初期には雌で自己のクローンを作るが,後に「雄になって近くの卵子を受精させる (becomes male and fertilizes nearby eggs)」と述べている。このことを「生殖 (reproduction) を助けるために性別を変える」と言い換えた **3** が正解。

No.18 解答 ①

質問の訳 サルパはどのように気候変動との闘いに役立つかもしれないのか。
選択肢の訳
1 炭素を老廃物に変えることで。
2 空気から二酸化炭素を直接吸収することで。
3 藻がより速く繁殖するのを助けることで。
4 藻が沈むのを防ぐことで。

解説 気候変動との闘いは第2段落にある。サルパが藻を摂取すると,藻が吸収した二酸化炭素関連の炭素もサルパに取り込まれ,「この炭素が廃棄物に変えられ (This (= associated carbon) is then turned into a waste product)」海底に沈み大気に戻るのを防ぐ。is turned, waste product をそれぞれ converting, waste matter と言い換えた **1** が正解。

E

スクリプト **Ancient Egyptian Mummies**

In 2011, researcher Roger Montgomerie published some surprising findings regarding ancient Egyptian mummies. Montgomerie examined the lungs of 15 preserved bodies and found that the mummies' lungs all contained tiny particles known as microscopic particulates. Today, microscopic particulates are associated with various diseases, including lung cancer and pneumonia, and are thought to result from the burning of fossil fuels by modern industry. Montgomerie's research, however, showed that the particulate levels in the mummies were nearly as high as those found in modern humans, indicating that some forms of pollution also affected people in ancient times.

The mummies examined by Montgomerie came from all walks of life, and included laborers, priests, and upper-class city dwellers. In spite of the fact that these people came from different social and geographic backgrounds, their lungs all contained similar levels of particulates. Montgomerie therefore speculated that the particulates, probably produced by metalworking, mining, or even fires for cooking, could have been spread throughout the population by sandstorms, which are common to the region. The research suggests that the majority of ancient Egyptians suffered from the ill effects of having microscopic particulates in their lungs.

Questions
No.19 What was surprising about the Egyptian mummies?
No.20 What does the research indicate about microscopic particulates?

全文訳　**古代エジプトのミイラ**

　2011年，研究者のロジャー・モンゴメリーが古代エジプトのミイラに関していくつかの驚くべき調査結果を発表した。モンゴメリーが15の保存された死体の肺を調べると，ミイラの肺はすべて微細粒子として知られる微粒子を含むことがわかった。今日，微細粒子は，肺がんや肺炎などさまざまな病気と関連しており，近代産業による化石燃料の燃焼によって生じると考えられている。しかし，モンゴメリーの調査によれば，ミイラ内の微粒子量は現代人に見られるのとほぼ同じくらい多く，古代においてもある種の汚染が人々に影響を与えていたことを示した。

　モンゴメリーが調べたミイラはあらゆる職業および階層の人々で，労働者，聖職者，上流階級の都会人が含まれていた。これらの人々は異なる社会的そして地理的背景を持っていたという事実にもかかわらず，彼らの肺はすべて同じような量の微粒子を含んでいた。それ故モンゴメリーは，微粒子はおそらく金属加工や採鉱，料理の火によっても作られ，その地域でよく起こる砂嵐によって住民全体に広がったのかもしれない，と推測した。大多数の古代エジプト人は微細粒子が肺にある悪影響で苦しんだことを，調査は示唆している。

　語句　mummy「ミイラ」，particulate「微粒子」，pneumonia「肺炎」，all walks of life「あらゆる職業および階層」，dweller「居住者」，metalworking「金属加工」

No.19 解答

質問の訳　エジプトのミイラの何が驚くべきことだったか。
選択肢の訳　
1　彼らの肺はこれまで信じられていたよりも大きかった。
2　彼らはまれな種類のがんを患っていた。
3　彼らの肺は大気汚染の影響を受けていた。
4　彼らは，現在では一般的な病気の治療を受けていた。

解説　第1段落で示されている驚くべき発見は，調べたミイラの肺はすべて微細粒子を含み，その微粒子量が現代人と同程度なので「古代でも汚染が人々に影響を与えていた」（最終文）こと。このことを言い換えた**3**が正解。

198

No.20 解答 ④

質問の訳 この調査は微細粒子について何を示しているか。
選択肢の訳
1 裕福なエジプト人に特に影響を与えた。
2 ミイラの保存で重要な役割を果たした。
3 古代エジプト人によって初めて確認された。
4 古代エジプトで幅広い人々に影響を与えた。

解説 第2段落に，調べたミイラは「あらゆる職業および階層（all walks of life）」で「異なる社会的・地理的背景」を持つ人々だったので，調査が示すのは「大多数の古代エジプト人は微細粒子が肺にある悪影響で苦しんだこと」（最終文）とある。このことを「幅広い人々に影響を与えた」とまとめた**4**が正解。

一次試験・リスニング Part3　問題編 p.109～110　▶MP3 ▶アプリ ▶CD 2 43～48

F

スクリプト

You have 10 seconds to read the situation and Question No. 21.

You've asked about healthcare coverage during your stay. In the past, those enrolled full-time in university courses on a student visa were covered free of charge. However, new rules require the payment of a healthcare surcharge of $150 per year. This needs to be made when you apply for your student visa, and you must pay in advance for the total number of years you'll study here, not a year at a time. Once approved, you'll receive the same healthcare services as citizens and permanent residents do. Alternatively, some students opt for travel health insurance instead, which can offer certain benefits for private medical services that are not covered by the national healthcare system. However, the travel health insurance costs substantially more than the surcharge, especially if you'll be studying here for more than one year.

Now mark your answer on your answer sheet.

全文訳

滞在中の医療保障についてのお尋ねですね。以前は，学生ビザで大学の講座にフルタイムで登録した人は無料で保障されていました。しかし，新しい規則により年150ドルの医療追加料金の支払いが必要です。これは，学生ビザの申請時にする必要があり，一度に1年分ずつではなく，こちらで学ぶ総年数分を前納しなければなりません。いったん承認されれば，市民や永住者と同じ医療サービスを受けることになります。別の方法として，旅行医療保険を代わりに選ぶ学生もいます。旅行医療保険は国民医療制度では保障されない自己負担の医療サービスに対して一定の給付が出ます。しかし，旅行医

療保険は，特に1年を超える期間こちらで学ぶなら，追加料金よりもかなり費用がかかります。

No.21 解答 ②

状況の訳 あなたは日本に住んでいる。海外の大学で3年間フルタイムで学ぶ予定である。医療保障について尋ねるために大学の留学生担当アドバイザーに電話をかける。

質問の訳 一番安い医療の選択肢を確保するために，あなたは何をすべきか。

選択肢の訳
1 学生ビザを使って無料保障に申し込む。
2 学生ビザの申請時に料金を払う。
3 全滞在期間の旅行医療保険に加入する。
4 初年度は自己負担の医療サービスにだけ申し込む。

語句 surcharge「追加料金」，alternatively「別の方法として」

解説 アドバイザーが最初に言っている free of charge の保障は昔の話で，今は年150ドルの追加料金が必要。アドバイザーが提示しているもう1つの選択肢は旅行医療保険だが，1年以上の場合は追加料金より高額になると最後に言っている。したがって，前半で言っているように，学生ビザの申請時に追加料金をまとめて払う方が割安ということになる。

G

スクリプト

You have 10 seconds to read the situation and Question No. 22.

There are a couple of things to consider when choosing a mortgage. First, the term of the loan. You're quite young, so a 30-year loan would be reasonable. Of course, a 20-year loan would cost less overall. But if you currently have other debts, I'd recommend going with the lower monthly payments of the longer-term loan. Then you need to decide if you want your interest payments to be at a fixed or adjustable rate. With an adjustable rate, you'll pay less interest to start with, but it'll probably go up considerably after a few years. The fixed rate of interest is currently a little higher than the adjustable rate, but it won't change. Since you tend to get anxious about money, I think you'd be better off without the uncertainty of any changes.

Now mark your answer on your answer sheet.

全文訳

住宅ローンを選ぶときに考慮すべきことがいくつかある。まず，ローンの期間。君はかなり若いので，30年ローンが妥当だろう。もちろん，20年ローンの方が全体としてはかかる費用は少ない。しかし，現在ほかの借金があるなら，ローンの期間を長くして月々の支払いを低くする方がお勧めだ。それから，利払いを固定金利にしたいか変動金利にしたいかを決めなければならない。変動金利だと，最初は支払う利息が少ないけれ

ど，おそらく数年後にかなり上がる。固定金利は現在のところ変動金利よりも少し高いけれど，変わることがない。君はお金のことで気をもむ傾向があるから，変わる不確かさがない方がいいと思う。

No.22 解答 ①

状況の訳 あなたはマンションを購入するために銀行ローンを組みたい。あなたはまだ学生ローンを払っている。銀行勤務の友人があなたに助言する。

質問の訳 あなたはどの種類のローンを選ぶべきか。

選択肢の訳
1 30年固定金利ローン。
2 20年固定金利ローン。
3 30年変動金利ローン。
4 20年変動金利ローン。

語句 adjustable rate「変動金利」

解説 友人は，20年の方が総費用は少ないが，ほかの借金があるのなら支払う月額が少ない長期の方がいいと言っている。あなたには学生ローンがあるので長期の30年がよい。また金利について，お金を心配しがちなあなたには the uncertainty of any changes「変わる不確かさ」がない方を勧めている。よって選ぶべきは，30年固定金利だ。

H

スクリプト

You have 10 seconds to read the situation and Question No. 23.

First on the agenda: We have our new line of Organic Power Protein Bars coming out this fall. We need everyone on board to promote these new products. Obviously, the digital marketing team is responsible for building awareness and product promotion through paid media and social media channels. We're going to offer a 20% online discount and free shipping for customers who purchase the new products through our website, so you guys need to integrate that into the digital campaign. The customer marketing team will focus externally. We need exposure. We're making sample-sized products to give away in stores and at events over the next few months. As you know, the city marathon is coming up in August, so you'll need to ask around for volunteers to pass out samples during the race. You'll also need to identify further opportunities and locations, but that can be done once the marathon promotion is set.

Now mark your answer on your answer sheet.

全文訳

最初の議題ですが，わが社の新製品の有機栽培パワー・プロテインバーのシリーズがこの秋に販売されます。これらの新製品の販売促進のため，全員に協力してもらう必要

があります。言うまでもなく，デジタル・マーケティングのチームが，有料メディアとソーシャルメディアのルートを通して，知名度の構築と商品販売促進活動を担当します。わが社のウェブサイトで新製品を購入する顧客には，20%のオンライン割引を付けて送料を無料にするので，皆さんはそのことをデジタル・キャンペーンに織り込む必要があります。顧客マーケティングのチームは，対外面に重点的に取り組みます。当社には露出が必要です。今後数カ月の間に店とイベントで配るためのサンプル用サイズの製品を作っています。ご存じのように，市内マラソン大会が8月に迫っているので，皆さんはレースの間にサンプルを配るボランティアを依頼して回る必要があります。皆さんはまた，さらなる機会と場所を見いださなければなりませんが，それはマラソンでの販促の準備ができ次第やればいいでしょう。

No.23 解答 ④

状況の訳 あなたは健康食品会社の顧客マーケティング部長である。スタッフ会議で上司が会社の新製品について話すのを聞いている。

質問の訳 あなたはまず何をすべきか。

選択肢の訳
1 顧客に対して20%の割引を宣伝する。
2 デジタル・キャンペーンの準備をする。
3 販促できそうなイベントを特定する。
4 マラソンの間手伝いをしてくれる人々を募集する。

語句 on board「参加して」, externally「外面的に」, exposure「(メディアなどへの) 露出」

解説 議題は新製品の販促。digital marketing チームへの話に続いて，後半からが部長のあなたが率いる customer marketing チームの話。すべきことは①to ask around for volunteers to pass out samples during the race と②to identify further opportunities and locations だが，②はマラソンでの準備後でいいと最後に言っているので，最初にすべき①を言い換えた4が正解。3は②の言い換え。

スクリプト

You have 10 seconds to read the situation and Question No. 24.

Our smallest truck is 3 meters. Generally speaking, this is best for a studio or small one-bedroom apartment with minimal furniture. The charge for this would be $545. Our medium-sized truck is 4.5 meters. It's best for two-bedroom apartments or small homes with up to 100 square meters of living space. It's just $150 more than the smallest truck at $695. Our 6-meter truck is big enough for three-bedroom apartments, and costs $895 per day. Currently, our largest truck happens to be on special at $995. At 7 meters long, it moves a 200-square-meter property. Finally, if you'd prefer, we could offer a couple of professional movers for an extra $200. These guys are great at maximizing truck space and can squeeze in some extra items.

Now mark your answer on your answer sheet.

> 全文訳

当社の最小のトラックは3メートルです。一般的に言えば，ワンルーム・マンションや最低限の家具が付いた寝室が1つのマンションには，こちらが最適です。料金は545ドルです。当社の中型トラックは4.5メートルです。寝室が2つのマンションや居住部分が100平方メートルまでの小さい家に最適です。最小のトラックよりもちょうど150ドル高くて695ドルです。当社の6メートルのトラックは寝室が3つのマンションに十分な大きさで，1日当たり895ドルかかります。現在，当社の最大のトラックはたまたま特別価格で995ドルです。長さ7メートルで，200平方メートルの物件の荷物を運びます。最後に，よろしければ200ドルの追加料金で引っ越し専門業者を2人ご用意できます。この人たちはトラックのスペースを最大限に生かすのが得意で，いくつか追加の品を詰め込むことができます。

No.24 解答 ②

> 状況の訳

あなたは100平方メートルで寝室が2つのマンションから引っ越す。あなたは所有物を自分で移動させたくない。予算は900ドル。トラック・レンタル会社の担当者が，あなたに次のように言う。

> 質問の訳

あなたはどのトラックを選ぶべきか。

> 選択肢の訳

1 3メートルのトラックで引っ越し業者なし。
2 4.5メートルのトラックで引っ越し業者あり。
3 6メートルのトラックで引っ越し業者あり。
4 7メートルのトラックで引っ越し業者なし。

> 語句

mover「引っ越し業者」，squeeze in「~を押し込む」

> 解説

3メートルのトラックは狭いマンション向けなので小さ過ぎ，7メートルは予算オーバー。4.5メートルか6メートルを選ぶことになるが，自分で荷物を運びたくないのだから，作業員を頼む必要がある。引っ越し業者は追加で200ドルなので，4.5メートルならぎりぎり予算内に収まる。細かい数字が読まれるので，丁寧にメモを取って判断する必要がある。

J

> スクリプト

You have 10 seconds to read the situation and Question No. 25.

As you know, when you leave the country, you're entitled to claim back some of your compulsory pension payments. The refund process depends on how much is in your pension account. If it is less than $5,000, you can fill out the online form, and all the money you've paid will be transferred to your bank account within two weeks. If you've paid more, you'll need to download and print out the Certification of Immigration Status form and submit it by mail. To complete that form, you'll need your tax file number, your passport with your visa, and your bank account details. You should apply before you leave, as it can be difficult to certify the necessary documents once you're out of the country. Finally, bear in mind you won't receive any payments while your visa is still valid.

Now mark your answer on your answer sheet.

全文訳

　ご存じのとおり，出国する際には，義務付けられている年金納付金のいくらかを返還してもらう権利があります。払い戻し手続きは，年金口座にいくらあるかよって決まります。5,000ドル未満なら，オンラインのフォームに入力すればよく，払った全額が2週間以内に銀行口座に振り込まれます。もっと払ったのなら，在留資格証明の記入用紙をダウンロードして印刷し，郵送で提出する必要があります。その用紙に記入するには，納税申告番号，ビザ付きパスポート，銀行口座の詳細が必要です。いったん国外に出ると必要書類を認証するのが困難になることがあるので，出発する前に申請するべきです。最後に，ビザがまだ有効な間は何の支払いも受けないことを覚えておいてください。

No.25 解答 ④

状況の訳　あなたは海外での2年間のワーキング・ホリデーの後，帰国するところだ。あなたは年金納付金を返してもらうことについてアドバイザーに尋ねる。納付金の総額は6,000ドルである。

質問の訳　年金納付金を返還してもらうために，あなたはまず何をすべきか。

選択肢の訳
1　すぐにオンライン申請を完了する。
2　ビザの期限が切れた後にオンライン申請を完了する。
3　出国後に紙の申請書を提出する。
4　帰国する前に紙の申請書を提出する。

語句　refund「払い戻し」，certify「〜を証明する」

解説　返還手続きは，年金口座にある金額によって決まると最初に言っている。あなたが払った納付金は計6,000ドルなので，中ほどの If you've paid more, ... が当てはまる。記入用紙をダウンロード・印刷して郵送するので，申請書は紙である。最後の方で You should apply before you leave とアドバイスしているので，帰国前に提出することになる。

Part 4

スクリプト

This is an interview with Joseph Smith, a product manager at a solar panel manufacturer.

I (Interviewer): Thanks for tuning in to *Careers in Focus*. Today, we are talking with Joseph Smith. Welcome.

JS (Joseph Smith): Thanks for inviting me.

I: So, could you tell me what you do?

JS: I work for a manufacturing company that makes photovoltaic modules, more commonly known as "solar panels." My main role in the company is collaborating with an international organization called the IEC to develop standards for the industry.

I: How would you currently describe the state of the solar power industry in Japan?

JS: Well, it has changed dramatically. When I first joined the industry, Japan was the largest manufacturer and the largest installer of solar panels in the world. Today, China holds both of those titles. It has really been the force driving the dramatic drop in the cost of solar energy over the past few years. One of the reasons for the shift was due to the growth of the German solar market at the turn of the century. As German demand for solar energy grew rapidly due to aggressive government incentive programs, the country turned to China for support with manufacturing, providing capital, technology, and experts. Prior to this, Japan had already developed their own manufacturing base and was selling product internationally, but as China's manufacturing capacity grew, costs came down and quality improved. Eventually, Japan could no longer compete and many manufacturers either went out of business or scaled back to focus on the domestic market, where the average selling price was higher.

I: Interesting. Are there any challenges the industry faces in environmental terms?

JS: Many companies are still using fossil fuels to produce their panels, but as costs continue to fall and manufacturers place more emphasis on reducing their carbon footprint, I am seeing more companies commit to the use of renewable energy to run their factories. With that said, the "energy payback," which is the number of years it takes to produce the energy used to make the product, is only about one to four years. With an assumed service life of 30 years and zero emissions during that time, solar energy is still much cleaner than energy produced from fossil fuels.

I: So, do you think the solar power industry should be subsidized?

JS: All industries, including fossil fuel-based industries, are subsidized based on market conditions and influence from lobbyists. The solar industry is unique in that average consumers can purchase solar panels and have a power plant installed directly on their homes. This means that subsidies are more widely distributed than those in other industries, increasing the likelihood that the benefit actually reaches the end user.

I: Do you foresee the world weaning itself off of fossil fuels in our lifetimes?

JS: In the past, I think the idea was that renewable energy would replace fossil fuels only when the supply of fossil fuels ran out. However, the cost of renewable energy is dropping so dramatically that it is likely it will eventually surpass fossil fuels simply because it is the cheaper option. This year, one research organization reported that not only is renewable energy now cheaper than building a new coal- or gas-fired power plant, it will soon be cheaper than using existing fossil fuel power plants. That is an extraordinary finding.

I: Well, Joseph, time has got the better of us. Thank you. That was very interesting.

JS: My pleasure.

Questions

No.26 What is one way that Joseph says the solar power industry has changed?

No.27 What is one thing that Joseph thinks will affect the popularity of renewable energy in the future?

全文訳

これはソーラーパネル製造会社のプロダクトマネージャーであるジョセフ・スミスとのインタビューです。

聞き手（以下「聞」）:『注目の仕事』にダイヤルを合わせてくれてありがとうございます。今日はジョセフ・スミスさんとお話します。ようこそ。

ジョセフ・スミス（以下「ジ」）: 招いてくださってありがとう。

聞: それでは，お仕事について話してくださいますか。

ジ: 私は，一般的に「ソーラーパネル」として知られている太陽光電池モジュールを作る製造会社で働いています。会社での主な役割は，IECという国際機関と協力して，業界の基準を開発することです。

聞: 日本の太陽光発電業界の状況は現在どうですか。

ジ: そうですね，劇的に変わりました。私が最初に業界に入ったとき，日本は世界で最大のソーラーパネルの製造国であり最大の設置国でした。今日では，中国が両方のタイトルを保持しています。中国はここ数年にわたって太陽エネルギーのコストを劇的

に低下させる推進力となってきました。この変化の理由の1つは，世紀の変わり目にドイツの太陽光市場が成長したためです。政府の積極的な奨励プログラムのため，ドイツの太陽エネルギー需要が急増したので，国は製造，資金提供，科学技術，専門家の支援を求めて中国に頼りました。これ以前に日本は既に独自の製造拠点を開発しており，国際的に製品を販売していましたが，中国の製造能力が増大したのでコストが下がり品質が向上しました。結局，日本はもはや競争できず，多くの製造業者は廃業するか，規模を縮小して平均小売価格がより高い国内市場に焦点を合わせたのです。

聞：興味深いですね。環境という点で，業界が直面する課題は何かありますか。

ジ：多くの企業がパネルを製造するのに化石燃料をまだ使っていますが，コストが下がり続けるにつれ，そして製造業者が二酸化炭素排出量の削減をより重視するにつれ，より多くの企業が自社工場の稼働に再生可能エネルギーを使うことに尽力するのを私は見ています。そんな訳で，製品を作るのに使われるエネルギーを生み出すのにかかる年数である「エネルギー・ペイバック」は，ほんの1～4年ほどです。想定される耐用年数は30年で，その間の排出量がゼロなので，太陽エネルギーは化石燃料から作り出すエネルギーよりもやはりずっとクリーンです。

聞：それでは，太陽光発電業界は補助金を受けるべきだと思いますか。

ジ：化石燃料を基にした業界を含め，すべての業界が市場状況とロビイストからの影響に基づいて補助金を受けています。太陽光発電業界は，普通の消費者がソーラーパネルを購入して発電所を自分の家の上に直接設置してもらうという点で独特です。つまり，補助金がほかの業界よりももっと広く分配され，利益が実際にエンドユーザーに届く可能性が高いのです。

聞：私たちが生きているうちに，世界は化石燃料と縁を切るようになると思いますか。

ジ：昔は，化石燃料の供給が尽きたときにのみ再生可能エネルギーが化石燃料に取って代わるという考え方だったと思います。しかし，再生可能エネルギーのコストはとても急激に下がっているので，最終的には，単により安い選択肢であるという理由で化石燃料を上回りそうです。今年，1つの研究機関が，再生可能エネルギーは石炭やガスを燃料とする発電所を新しく建設するよりも今や安価であるばかりでなく，間もなく既存の化石燃料発電所を使用するよりも安価になるだろう，と報告しました。これは驚くべき研究結果です。

聞：ではジョセフさん，時間が来てしまいました。ありがとうございました。とても興味深かったです。

ジ：どういたしまして。

〔語句〕 photovoltaic「光起電の」，scale back「規模を縮小する」，carbon footprint「カーボン・フットプリント，二酸化炭素排出量」，with that said「そんな訳で，そうは言うものの」，payback「元回収」，service life「耐用年数」，subsidize「～に補助金を支給する」，lobbyist「ロビイスト，ロビー活動を行う人」，wean *A* off (of) *B*「AにBをやめさせる，AをBから引き離す」，get the better of ~「～より優勢になる，

～に勝つ」

No.26 解答 ①

質問の訳 1つには，どんなふうに太陽光発電業界が変わったとジョセフは言っているか。

選択肢の訳
1 ドイツの太陽光発電市場の成長が，中国が業界のリーダーになるのを助けた。
2 中国の太陽光発電の需要が，日本の輸出を増やすのを助けてきた。
3 日本の科学技術が中国とヨーロッパの競争相手に模倣されてきた。
4 中国は今，ドイツでビジネスを行いたい日本企業を支援している。

解説 ジョセフは3つ目の発言で，業界トップが日本から中国に変わったと述べ，その理由は「ドイツの太陽光市場の成長（growth of the German solar market）」と言っている。政策による需要増に伴いドイツが中国に支援を求めたので，中国の生産力増・低価格・品質向上につながった。このことを「中国が業界のリーダーになるのを助けた」とまとめたのが**1**。

No.27 解答 ③

質問の訳 将来，再生可能エネルギーの人気に影響を及ぼすだろうとジョセフが考える1つのことは何か。

選択肢の訳
1 発電所を建設する企業は，化石燃料の使用をやめたがらない。
2 環境に優しいエネルギーの需要が，企業に方針を変えるよう強いている。
3 再生可能エネルギーは費用効率の点で化石燃料を上回りそうだ。
4 企業は長期にわたって十分なソーラーパネルを供給できない。

解説 聞き手は最後の質問で将来に関連するジョセフの考えを尋ねている。ジョセフの考えは彼の6つ目の発言の it is likely it（＝ renewable energy）will eventually surpass fossil fuels simply because it is the cheaper option にある。この「より安い選択肢なので」を in terms of cost efficiency「費用効率の点で」と言い換えた**3**が正解。

二次試験・面接　トピックカード A日程　問題編 p.112

ここでは，A日程の5つのトピックをモデルスピーチとしました。
A日程

1. Should the government ultimately be responsible for the health of its citizens?

I believe the government should ultimately be responsible for the health of its citizens. Here are three reasons for my opinion. Firstly, the COVID-19 outbreak has shown the need for governments to take greater responsibility for public health. There have been considerable differences in the ways governments handled the situation, and when they were slow to act to prevent the virus's spread, the outbreak generally became far more severe. The significant number of deaths in some countries is clear evidence that it is absolutely essential for governments to take immediate action on public health issues. Another reason is that medical costs have increased so much in recent years. Treatments for serious diseases like cancer are so expensive that without some sort of government-provided health insurance, many low-income citizens' lives will be at risk. Finally, any government action that improves public health is beneficial to the economy. Studies have shown that universal healthcare systems help to improve the overall well-being of the workforce, decreasing absences from work and increasing workers' productivity. Therefore, healthcare is an investment that governments cannot afford not to make. In light of the recent pandemic, increasing medical costs, and the economic benefits of public health, I think it's clear that governments should do everything in their power to maintain the health of their citizens.

解説　「政府が最終的に国民の健康に責任を持つべきか」

トピックに対して，①コロナ禍のような状況においては政府の対策が重要，②高額の医療費は政府による負担が必要，③健康保険によって労働者の生産性が担保される，という3つの観点から賛成の意見だ。コロナ以降，健康・医療問題は以前にも増して重要なトピックになっているので，ぜひ自分の意見をしっかりとまとめておきたい。このように結論で要点を再度まとめると，より完成度の高いスピーチとなる。

2. Agree or disagree: The militarization of space is a threat to future generations

I believe the militarization of space is a grave threat to future generations. I'd like to give you three reasons explaining why I think so. First, weapons in space are likely to be much more dangerous than those based on Earth. Weapons such as lasers could be used to kill huge numbers of people anywhere in the world with no warning. Because a satellite with lasers could strike in just a few tenths of a second, there would be no way to prevent an attack by it. Another serious issue is the risk of accidents. It's likely that space weapons would be built into unmanned satellites. If one were to malfunction, there would be no one nearby to prevent it from accidentally killing innocent people. Finally, the militarization of space could start an entirely new arms race. The nuclear arms race between the US and the USSR in the 20th century nearly led to the world's end on more than one occasion. If a new arms race were to start, we would face huge risks all over again. For these reasons, I believe it is essential that treaties be created immediately to prevent the proliferation of weapons in space.

> **解説** 「賛成か反対か：宇宙の軍事化は未来の世代にとって脅威である」
> トピックに対して，grave threat（深刻な脅威）という言葉を使って賛成の立場を強調している。ここでは，①衛星からの攻撃は防ぎようがないこと，②無人衛星による事故，③新しい兵器競争の可能性，の3つから未来の世代への大きな脅威になるとしている。結論ではまとめではなく，I believe it is essential that ... と未来への提言をすることでスピーチを締めくくっている。内容を簡潔にまとめるのが難しい場合，このように「将来，未来」に言及することで上手にスピーチを終えることができるのでやってみよう。

3. Will there ever be a need for Japan to revise its firearms laws?

I don't believe that Japan should ever revise its firearms laws. I have three reasons, all of which are related to the situation in America. First, Japan is one of the safest countries in the world, and its strict gun laws are an important reason for this. If firearms laws were made as liberal as they are in the US, Japan could see a wave of mass shootings. When advanced firearms, such as semi-automatic rifles, are available to anyone, it creates a dangerous situation in which terrorists or mentally ill individuals can use them to kill dozens of innocent people. Secondly, it could lead to an increase in violent crimes. If criminals had easy access to firearms, as they do in the US, it would be much easier for them to commit crimes such as bank robberies. In addition, when people have access to firearms, there is a much higher chance that arguments or fistfights will escalate into someone using a gun. Finally, keeping firearms in one's home is extremely dangerous. In the US, thousands of people, including children, are killed or injured in accidents involving guns each year. Also, the majority of gun-related deaths in the US are from suicides, and firearms laws can easily prevent these tragedies. To keep Japan safe, I believe it is crucial that we maintain our strict gun laws.

> 解説 「日本は銃刀法を見直す必要があるか」
>
> トピックに対して反対の立場を取っているが，すべての理由がアメリカの現状との比較によるものだと最初に明言している。このように，自分が特に内情に詳しい国や地域があれば，具体的な比較の対象とするのはとても効果的だ。ここでは，①日本の世界でもまれな高い安全は厳しい銃刀法のおかげである，②銃が入手しやすくなれば犯罪が増加する，③個人が銃を持つことで自殺者を増やす，という3つの観点から，日本が銃刀法を見直す必要はないことを強く主張している。

4. Are concerns about the safety of genetically modified food warranted?

I don't believe that we should be very concerned about the safety of genetically modified foods. My reasons are as follows. First of all, every type of genetically modified food needs to be approved by the government. Rigorous safety assessments are done before any product can be sold in stores in Japan. Also, most countries where genetically modified crops are produced have strict regulations about how they are grown, so consumers are well protected. Another thing to think about is that genetically modified foods could actually improve food safety. Genetically modified foods are often modified to resist pests. This means that they can be grown without as many of the agricultural chemicals used to protect ordinary crops from insects and weeds. My final reason is that there has never been any evidence of harmful health effects from genetically modified foods. There have been numerous scientific studies, but none of them have produced evidence of genetically modified food causing allergies, digestion problems, or diseases, as far as I'm aware. Although it may take time for genetically modified foods to earn the trust of the general public, I think that people will soon begin to accept the strong evidence that they are just as safe as, or perhaps even safer than, ordinary foods.

> 解説 「遺伝子組み換え食品の安全性に対する懸念は当然か」
>
> トピックの Are concerns ... warranted? は「懸念は正当・妥当・当然か」という意味なので覚えておこう。ここでは，①政府の厳重な検査を

通っている，②遺伝子的に害虫などに強いので薬品散布の必要が少ない，③健康被害を起こしたという科学的な証拠がない，の3つの理由から，さほどの懸念はいらないという立場を取っている。具体性が高く，ある程度の知識がないと話せない内容だが，このような問題を扱った英語の記事から知識や表現を得て参考にするとよい。

5. Have humans done irreversible damage to the planet?

I believe that much of the damage done to the earth is irreversible. Please let me explain my thinking. First, scientists say global warming has become so severe that it may be impossible to stop it from causing catastrophic events like droughts, increased typhoon activity, and rising sea levels. Even if we completely stopped emitting carbon today, global warming would continue for many years. Another reason is that many plant and animal species have gone extinct as a result of human activity. Hunting, habitat destruction, and pollution have killed off some of the world's most incredible creatures, and many more are likely to disappear before the environmental crisis is solved. Lastly, the damage from pollution is also irreversible. Plastics in the oceans and landfills will last for hundreds of years, and nuclear waste will be with us for a hundred times longer. Leaks from landfills also do serious harm to surrounding ecosystems. We have produced such a massive volume of harmful waste that it will continue to be a problem. Since we have already done so much damage to our planet, humans must keep making efforts to develop clean energy and recycling to prevent more harm from being done in the future.

解説　「人類は地球（この惑星）に取り返しのつかないダメージを与えてしまったか」

トピックに対して肯定の立場からの解答。①深刻な温暖化による災害の発生，②人間の活動による多くの動植物の絶滅，③廃棄物などによる環境汚染，の3つを不可逆なダメージとして紹介している。結論部分を「だからこそ人間はこれ以上の被害を地球に与えないためにも努力を続ける必要がある」という前向きな主張で終えているのが印象的だ。環境問題のトピックを論じる際に，このような締めくくりを自分の言葉で言えるようにしておこう。

2020-1

一次試験
筆記解答・解説　　p.214〜232

一次試験
リスニング解答・解説　p.233〜260

二次試験
面接解答・解説　　p.261〜264

解 答 一 覧

一次試験・筆記

1
(1)	3	(10)	3	(19)	1
(2)	1	(11)	2	(20)	1
(3)	1	(12)	4	(21)	3
(4)	3	(13)	4	(22)	2
(5)	2	(14)	3	(23)	3
(6)	4	(15)	4	(24)	1
(7)	1	(16)	2	(25)	4
(8)	2	(17)	4		
(9)	4	(18)	1		

2
(26)	3	(29)	2	
(27)	4	(30)	1	
(28)	2	(31)	4	

3
(32)	3	(35)	4	(38)	2
(33)	2	(36)	1	(39)	1
(34)	1	(37)	2	(40)	4
				(41)	1

4　解答例は本文参照

一次試験・リスニング

Part 1　No. 1　4　No. 5　2　No. 9　2
　　　　No. 2　1　No. 6　2　No.10　1
　　　　No. 3　3　No. 7　4
　　　　No. 4　3　No. 8　1

Part 2　No.11　4　No.15　2　No.19　1
　　　　No.12　1　No.16　1　No.20　4
　　　　No.13　3　No.17　4
　　　　No.14　4　No.18　2

Part 3　No.21　2　No.23　2　No.25　3
　　　　No.22　3　No.24　4

Part 4　No.26　1　No.27　3

一次試験・筆記 1 問題編 p.114〜116

(1) ― 解答 **3**

訳 その男性は，長患いが原因で顔がやつれてきていた。規則正しく食べているのに，体重を増やすことがまったくできないようだった。

語句 1「人を見下すような」　2「耳障りな」
3「やつれた」　4「狂信的な」

解説 病気で体重が減っているのだから，男性は「やつれた」顔をしていたと考えられる。emaciated は，病気や栄養不足によって「やせ衰えた」状態を言う。

(2) ― 解答 **1**

訳 女性のキャリア機会は近年向上しているものの，男尊女卑はいまだに職場に存在する。女性は男性より能力が低いと考える男性上司もいる。

語句 1「男尊女卑」　2「言外の意味」　3「礼儀正しさ」　4「冒瀆(ぼうとく)」

解説 逆接の接続詞 Although と第 2 文の内容から，空所には女性のキャリア機会向上と対立する意味の語が入るとわかる。chauvinism には「狂信的愛国主義」と「男尊女卑」(= male chauvinism) の 2 つの意味がある。

(3) ― 解答 **1**

訳 議会で持っていた全議席を失う大敗を選挙で喫した後，その党は解党を決めた。

語句 1「大敗北」　2「潜水，浸水」　3「告発，弾劾」　4「一時的休止」

解説 全議席を失ったのだから，選挙はその党にとって debacle「大敗，大失敗」に終わったことになる。debacle の類義語 fiasco も覚えておきたい。

(4) ― 解答 **3**

訳 ケビンはとてもシャイなので，友人のスーザンは，ミランダをデートに誘うよう彼をけしかけなければならなかった。「ケビン，すぐに誘わないと，ほかの人が誘っちゃうよ」と彼女は言った。

語句 1「(人)を存分に楽しませる」　2「(試験など)に失敗する」
3「(人)をけしかける」　4「〜をくすねる」

解説 goad A into doing で「A (人) をけしかけて〜させる」という意味。類義語に urge, provoke などがあるが，goad には，うるさいくらいせき立てるというニュアンスがある。

(5) ― 解答 **2**

訳 A：1 人で外国に行かせてくれるよう，ご両親を説得できた？
B：いいえ。両親の不安を鎮めるよう全力を尽くしたんだけど，危険過ぎるとそれでも言い張るのよ。

語句　**1**「(権利など) を没収される」　　**2**「(恐れなど) を鎮める」
　　　3「〜を推論する」　　　　　　　**4**「(人) を混乱させる」

解説　両親は1人で外国に行くのは危険だと反対しているのだから，その fears を「鎮める，和らげる」ために全力を尽くしたと考えられる。allay の類義語は alleviate。

(6) ― 解答　**4**

訳　その家の外観は非常に美しかった。しかし，まったく対照的に，家の中は散らかり放題だった。

語句　**1**「薄っぺらい」　　　　　　　　**2**「非常に緊張した」
　　　3「人目を盗んでの」　　　　　　**4**「まったくの」

解説　extremely beautiful と a complete mess なのだから，外と中はまるで違うということになる。stark にはいくつか意味があるが，in stark contrast「まったく対照的に」は定型表現なのでこのまま覚えておきたい。

(7) ― 解答　**1**

訳　アイススケートのチャンピオンには，トーナメントでの勝利をゆっくり味わう時間はほとんどなかった。数日のうちに，彼女は既に次の競技会に向けたトレーニングをしていた。

語句　**1**「〜をゆっくり味わう」　　　　**2**「(計画など) を阻止する」
　　　3「〜をめった打ちにする」　　　**4**「〜をゆがめる」

解説　動詞 savor は「〜をゆっくり味わう」の意味だが，「食べ物，香り」などにとどまらず，「時間，記憶，感情」などの抽象的なことについても用いられる。

(8) ― 解答　**2**

訳　長期間の投獄の後，その犯罪者は再び社会に足を踏み入れることが許された。

語句　**1**「開始，加入」　**2**「投獄」　　**3**「増幅」　　**4**「要約」

解説　犯罪者が再び社会に出るのだから，刑期を終えたことになる。incarceration「投獄，監禁」は imprisonment と同義の堅い語。

(9) ― 解答　**4**

訳　政府はその自然災害後の鈍い対応について新聞各紙で酷評された。批判のすべてが，大統領の再選の可能性に打撃を与えている。

語句　**1**「愛撫された」　　　　　　　　**2**「じらされた」
　　　3「引き伸ばされた」　　　　　　**4**「厳しくとがめられた」

解説　空所には，第2文の All of the criticism に対応する動詞が入ると考えられる。lambaste (または lambast) は，「〜を厳しくとがめる，激しく批判する」という意味。

(10) ― 解答　**3**

訳　夫の体重が増えたことをさりげなく言っても夫が気付かなかった後，ク

リスティーンは，ダイエットする必要があるとはっきり言うことにした。
- 語句 1「曖昧に」 2「途方もなく」 3「はっきりと」 4「ひどく」
- 解説 ほのめかしに気付かなかった夫に対して，次は「はっきり」言うことにしたと考えられる。explicitly の反意語 implicitly「暗黙のうちに」も覚えておきたい。

(11) – 解答 ②

- 訳 その投資は名案だろうと CEO は思ったのだが，後から考えると，結果的に会社に数百万ドルの損害を与えた大きな間違いだった。
- 語句 1「慰め」 2「後知恵」 3「否認」 4「後退」
- 解説 in hindsight は，過去の失敗などについて「後から考えると」ほかにやりようがあった，といった場合に使う決まり文句。with hindsight とも言う。

(12) – 解答 ④

- 訳 その山火事の原因は，完全には消されなかった近くのキャンプファイアの残り火だと消防士たちは考えた。
- 語句 1「重罪」 2「切り込み」 3「ほのめかし」 4「残り火」
- 解説 キャンプファイアの不始末が山火事に拡大したと考えられる。ember は石炭・まきなどの「燃え残り，残り火」の意味で，普通複数形で用いられる。

(13) – 解答 ④

- 訳 その幼い男の子は泊まり客の前で汚らしい食べ方をした。後で母親は，夕食中に不作法な振る舞いをしたことで彼を叱った。
- 語句 1「陰気な」 2「口語体の」 3「昏睡状態の」 4「不作法な」
- 解説 uncouth は，人や言動が「粗野な，不作法な」という意味の形容詞。couth「洗練された」という対義語もあるが，uncouth ほど一般的には用いられない。

(14) – 解答 ③

- 訳 スキャンダルの後，記者たちが 1 週間以上そのスターの自宅を取り囲んだが，彼女は一切インタビューに応じようとしなかった。
- 語句 1「言い争った」 2「〜に押し寄せた」 3「〜を取り囲んだ」 4「〜を変形させた」
- 解説 名詞 siege「（軍隊・警察などによる）包囲」の動詞形 besiege「〜を包囲する，取り囲む」は，問題文のように，名詞より幅広い意味で用いられる。be besieged with 〜「（手紙・要請など）が殺到する」という意味もある。

(15) – 解答 ④

- 訳 安い給料に嫌気が差したイーサンは，今の仕事を辞めてもっと高収入の仕事を探すことにした。

語句　**1**「ぞっとする」　**2**「煩わしい」　**3**「必要な」　**4**「もうかる」
　　　解説　安い給料が嫌で仕事を辞めるのだから，次は給料の高い仕事を望んでいることになる。lucrative は「もうかる，利益の上がる」という意味。

(16) – 解答 ②

　　　訳　政府の報道官によると，政治難民には亡命が認められる。しかし，不法にその国にいる移民は自国に送られることになる。
　　　語句　**1**「頑迷」　**2**「亡命」　**3**「ロビー」　**4**「蜃気楼」
　　　解説　第2文の However から，政治難民は，自国に送還される不法滞在者とは対照的な扱いを受けることがわかる。それにふさわしいのは asylum「亡命」である。

(17) – 解答 ④

　　　訳　その国には最低賃金がないので，多くの労働者は悲惨な貧困のうちに暮らしており，毎日の必需品を買うお金すらない。
　　　語句　**1**「光り輝く」　　　　**2**「暗黙の」
　　　　　　3「とてもおいしい」　**4**「悲惨な」
　　　解説　生活必需品すら買えないのだから，人々はひどく貧しいと考えられる。abject は「絶望的な，悲惨な」という意味で，poverty や misery といったネガティブな語を修飾する。

(18) – 解答 ①

　　　訳　今そのテロリストグループは組織内部で送られるメールをすべて暗号化し，政府の機関がメールの内容にアクセスできないようにしている。
　　　語句　**1**「～を暗号化している」　**2**「～を不正に奪っている」
　　　　　　3「～を打ち破っている」　**4**「～をむやみに欲しがっている」
　　　解説　メールの内容を知られないための対策として考えられるのは，encrypt「～を暗号化する」。cipher, cryptogram「暗号」，decode, decipher「（暗号）を解読する」などの関連語もまとめて覚えておきたい。

(19) – 解答 ①

　　　訳　くぎはとても堅く木材に埋め込まれていたので，抜くのはほとんど不可能だった。
　　　語句　**1**「埋め込まれている」　　**2**「殴り書きされている」
　　　　　　3「変色している」　　　　**4**「分極化されている」
　　　解説　embed は「～を（動かないように）埋め込む，はめ込む」の意味で，受動態 be embedded in ～「～に埋め込まれている」で用いられることが多い。

(20) – 解答 ①

　　　訳　カスタマーコールセンターの管理者として，キムは激怒した客に対処する達人である。客がどれだけ取り乱していても，必ず落ち着かせることができる。

20年度第1回　筆記

217

- 語句　**1**「激怒した」　**2**「半透明の」　**3**「生ぬるい」　**4**「上品な物腰の」
- 解説　第2文の upset と calm them down から，空所には「怒った」といった語が入ると推測できる。irate は「かんかんに怒った，激怒した」の意味で，類義語は furious。

(21) — 解答 ③

- 訳　その彫刻は，美しく<u>のみで彫られた</u>細部と完璧な均整を称賛された。
- 語句　**1**「鎮静剤を与えられた」　**2**「理不尽な」
　　　3「のみで彫られた」　**4**「散発的な」
- 解説　chisel は，名詞は「(道具の) のみ」，動詞は「〜をのみで彫る」という意味。carving「彫刻 (術)」，mallet「木づち」などの関連語もまとめて覚えよう。

(22) — 解答 ②

- 訳　その政治家の新法への支持は汚職<u>の匂いがする</u>とその記者は思ったので，調査を始めた。案の定，政治家が賄賂を受け取っていたことがわかった。
- 語句　**1**「〜を思い焦がれた」　　　　**2**「〜の気味があった」
　　　3「〜をののしった」　　　　　**4**「(ろうそくなど) を消した」
- 解説　smack of 〜 は「(嫌なこと・不正など) の感じがする，匂いがする」という意味。名詞 smack にも a smack of 〜「〜の気味，感じ」という意味がある。

(23) — 解答 ③

- 訳　海外工場の労働者に1日数ドルの給料しか払っていないことがわかると，その会社は多くの批判<u>を受けた</u>。
- 語句　**1**「〜から立ち直った」　　　　**2**「〜に気付いた」
　　　3「(批判など) を受けた」　　　**4**「〜に帰着した」
- 解説　come in for 〜 は「(批判・称賛など) を受ける，浴びる」という意味。come, do, get などの基本動詞を用いた句動詞もしばしば出題されるので，確認しておこう。

(24) — 解答 ①

- 訳　その政治家が殺人の脅迫を受けた後，警察は彼女の屋敷の警備<u>を強化する</u>よう求められた。
- 語句　**1**「〜を増強する，強化する」
　　　2「(問題など) をはぐらかす」
　　　3「(魚) をリールを巻いて引き寄せる」
　　　4「〜を入念に調べる」
- 解説　名詞 beef には「筋肉，筋力」という意味があり，それを知っていれば beef up のニュアンスを推測できる。beef には「不満；不満を言う」の意味もある。

(25) – 解答 4

訳 ブライアンは，高価な宝飾品を買ってやったりぜいたくな休暇に連れて行ったりと，常に妻を溺愛している。

語句 1「(人) を (昇進などの) 対象から外す」
2「～を全体的に理解する」
3「(生産など) を増やす」
4「～を溺愛する」

解説 dote on [upon] ～ は「～を溺愛する」という意味の句動詞。形容詞 doting「溺愛している」も覚えておきたい。

一次試験・筆記 2 問題編 p.117～119

全文訳 畏怖の進化

　恐怖などの感情は人が身の危険を避けるのに役立つよう進化したのかもしれないことや，愛は人の生存の可能性を高める相互依存関係を促進することは容易に想像がつくが，一方，畏怖のような感情には進化論学者も頭を抱えたままのことがある。しかし，ここ数十年で，ペンシルベニア大学のデイビッド・ヤデンのような研究者は，畏怖が発達した理由として考え得る説明を見つけ出している。畏怖は，例えば壮大な風景や途方もない破壊の現場といった，肯定的または否定的な経験によって喚起され得る。ヤデンによると，これは，つながっているという感情を生み出す。ヤデンの研究は，畏怖と，社会的絆の形成といった事柄の間の相関関係の証拠を示すことで，この主張を裏付けている。したがって，この感情は人間の生存と関連するはずであり，集団の結束を促すよう進化した可能性もあると彼は示唆する。

　原始の昔，畏怖は安全を求める人間の欲求の反映でもあったかもしれないとヤデンは推測する。私たちが壮大な眺めを好むことは，私たちが周囲より高い台地やそびえ立つ崖といった風景に引き付けられることから明らかだが，私たちの原始の祖先がそうしたものを探し出したことには，ほかにも理由があったかもしれない。接近する捕食動物や敵の姿を捉えられること，そして周囲より高い位置が与えてくれる防御の可能性が，人間が壮麗な風景に引き付けられるようになった一因なのかもしれない。

　あるいはまた，アリゾナ州立大学の研究者ミシェル・シオタは，畏怖は違う理由で進化したのかもしれないと示唆する。シオタが指揮した研究で，研究者たちは参加者に，畏怖，または幸福のような肯定的な感情を経験したときの記憶を説明するよう求めた。この研究で参加者は，評判の悪い意見を支持する論争的な論文を読む課題を課され，これらの論文に賛成する参加者は論文の論拠にうまく説得されたはずだと研究者たちは想定した。論文のいくつかには薄弱な論拠が含まれる一方，ほかの論文は強い説得力を持つことになっていた。畏怖を説明した参加者は，ほかの感情を説明した参加者より，薄弱な論拠に潜む問題をはるかによく見抜けることがわかった。したがって，畏怖は人が

情報を批判的に処理する助けとなる，とシオタは結論付けた。この研究が正しいとするなら，畏怖の感覚を発達させることには日々の生活において明らかなメリットがあるのかもしれないと思える。

> 語句 awe「畏敬，畏怖」，interdependent「相互に依存する」，scratch one's head「(困って)頭を抱える」，bonding「絆の形成」，facilitate「～を促進する」，cohesion「結束(力)，団結」，fondness「愛好，好み」，elevated「(周囲より)高い」，plateau「台地，高原」，towering「そびえ立つ」，seek out「～を探し出す」，adversary「敵」，argumentative「論争的な」，feeble「弱い，不十分な」，demonstrable「証明可能な，明白な」

(26) ― 解答 ③

> 解説 空所の次の文の a correlation between awe and things like social bonding がポイント。これがヤデンの主張の裏付けになるのだから，空所前の this（畏怖の喚起）が「つながっているという感情を生み出す」と考えると文脈に合う。connectedness は social bonding の言い換えで，第1段落最終文の group cohesion も同じことを指している。

(27) ― 解答 ④

> 解説 空所の次の Our fondness から towering cliffs までは，第1段落に関連する記述。その後の for other reasons too が空所前の also に呼応しているので，続く記述を注意して読む。高い場所は捕食動物や敵を発見しやすく身を守ることもできる，という内容を「安全を求める人間の欲求」とまとめた④が適切である。

(28) ― 解答 ②

> 解説 空所にはシオタの結論が入る。シオタの研究では畏怖を説明した参加者とほかの感情を説明した参加者を比較し，前者の方が「薄弱な論拠に潜む問題をはるかによく見抜け」た。それを「情報を批判的に処理する」と言い換えた②が正解。

全文訳 **新無神論**

　無神論とは神の存在を信じないことで，西洋社会では過去100年の間により一般的になっている。しかし，2000年代初頭に，知的でおおむね科学に基づいた「新無神論」運動が西洋で勢力を増した。新無神論者は主に科学者と知識人で構成され，より対決的な姿勢を取った。過去の無神論者は，科学は神という概念に取り組むことはできないと考える傾向があり，科学と宗教は重なり合うことのない2つの別個の領域として扱われるべきだと一般に認めていた。だが新無神論者は，自然界のほかのどんなものとも同じく，神の存在は科学的に正当性を検証されるべきだと猛然と主張した。さらに，宗教的過激主義の高まりといった傾向によって，新無神論者は組織化された宗教を世界平和と科学の進歩の障害と見なすようになったため，彼らはその国際的影響を減らそうと積極

的に努めた。

　この目的のため新無神論者は断固とした手法を取り，批判者たちはこの運動を「戦闘的無神論」とまで呼んだ。実際，この運動は宗教的過激主義に著しく類似していると指摘されることもあった。例えば，新無神論の重鎮サム・ハリスは，「人間の一集団を別の集団から分断し，結局殺しくにおいて１つにするだけの理念は，一般に宗教に根源を持つ」といった発言をした。意見を異にする人たちへのこうした妥協を許さない糾弾は，過激な宗教的見解を持つ人たちを思わせるという印象を批判者たちに与えた。

　2001年9月11日のテロ攻撃に引き続く宗教的過激主義を巡る論争のおかげということもあるが，新無神論の重鎮たちは見たところあらゆるメディアに登場し，彼らの著書はさまざまなベストセラーリストで１位になった。そうは言っても，視野を広げて考えると，新無神論の影響を誇張すべきではない。人口統計学者エリック・コーフマンによると，発展途上国の若い世代は，新無神論者の影響を受けて西洋諸国で生じている，宗教から遠ざかろうとする傾向，そしてその傾向を形成したほかの力を拒否している。コーフマンの示唆によると，最も宗教色の弱い社会すら，宗教色の濃い地域からの移民の増加によって影響を受けると予想される。つまり，新無神論者は人々を無宗教に転向させることに成功したにもかかわらず，彼らの努力はほかの要因によって無に帰すかもしれない。

> 語句　atheism「無神論」, atheist「無神論の；無神論者」, nonoverlapping「重なり合わない」, strenuously「熱心に，猛烈に」, extremism「過激主義」, inflexible「柔軟性のない」, uncompromising「妥協しない」, condemnation「激しい非難，糾弾」, reminiscent of ～「～を思い出させる」, demographer「人口統計学者」, negate「～を否定する，打ち消す」, confrontational「対決的な」, overstate「～を誇張する」

(29) - 解答 **②**

> 解説　空所の後で，新旧の無神論者の違いが述べられている。昔の無神論者は科学は宗教に干渉しない立場だったが，新無神論者は神も科学の対象だと考え，積極的に宗教に反対する立場を取る。つまり，新無神論者は宗教への対決的な姿勢を強めたことになる。

(30) - 解答 **①**

> 解説　空所には，批判者から見た新無神論と宗教的過激主義の関係を表す語句が入る。新無神論者を代表する人物の発言の引用に続き，こうした容赦ない非難は過激な宗教的見解を思い起こさせる，と書かれている。つまり，批判者にとって，新無神論はその戦闘性において宗教的過激主義と大差ないことになる。なお，引用中の unite them in slaughter の unite は「統合する」ではなく，戦争という１つの場に集結させる，という意味合いで使われている。

(31) - 解答 **④**

> 解説　空所後で述べられているのは，西洋と違い発展途上国の若者は宗教的で

あり続けていること，そして，そうした地域からの移民が西洋に影響を与える可能性があること。新無神論者の努力が無に帰すかもしれないと最終文に書かれているように，新無神論者の影響は限定的で，過度に評価されるべきではないことになる。

一次試験・筆記 3　問題編 p.120〜128

全文訳　ハロルド・ピンター

　ハロルド・ピンターは1960年代と1970年代に，20世紀で最も重要な英国の劇作家の1人として名を上げた。彼の劇作で注目されるのは，ありふれた設定の中で起きる物語の一見事実に見えることに疑問を投げかけることで彼が伝える謎と脅威の雰囲気である。例えば，最初の長編劇『バースデー・パーティー』では，見知らぬ2人の他人がある下宿屋に入り込み，下宿人の1人スタンリーに恐怖を味わわせる。見知らぬ2人が誰で，目的が何で，彼らの犠牲になる人とどんなつながりがあるのかは一切説明されない。しかし，そうした演劇的仕掛けを利用する戯曲は，当初は批評家と観客を等しくいら立たせた。戯曲の意味と登場人物の行動の背後にある動機を彼らが理解できるようにする説明が，劇作の不可欠な部分だと考えられていたからである。『バースデー・パーティー』は当初商業的に失敗したものの，因習にとらわれないピンターのスタイルは，続くいくつかの戯曲で名を高めた。

　ピンターの登場人物は，心理操作を用いながら，手の込んだ覇権争いを互いに繰り広げ，優位に立とうと争い，支配権を握るための武器として言葉を用いる。単純な質問と応答とは対照的に，彼らの会話は，むしろ聞き手が時折口を挟むことのある個人的独白のように聞こえる傾向があり，情報を明快に伝えるという目的に資することはめったにない。実際，彼らの対話はしばしば考えていることと裏腹であり，彼らの考えは沈黙によって暗示されるにすぎないこともある。彼らは自分が誰なのかはっきりわからないことも多く，恐怖と不確実さが支配する世界に住んでいる。典型的には，優位に立つ侵入者が前触れなく到着し，そこにいる者たちに自分の意志を押し付けようとして現状を乱す。それに続くのは，見知らぬ2人の他人の間であろうと，夫婦の間であろうと，あるいは拷問者とその犠牲者の間であろうと，何らかの優位な立場を得ようとする交渉である。彼の伝記作家マイケル・ビリントンが「日常の言葉から演劇的な詩を創造する能力」と呼ぶものを用いて，ピンターは，めったに爆発はしないけれども，劇的で説得力があり時に暗いユーモアのある効果を生む緊張状態を高めていく。

　ピンターは革命的なストーリーテリングと対話で広く称賛されたものの，ほかの一部の劇作家が勝ち得た広範な敬愛を獲得することはなかった。1つの理由は，彼の作品は困惑で迎えられることが多く，それにいら立ちが続き，もったいぶっている上に難解だと多くの人に退けられたことである。しかし，ジャーナリストのポール・バレリーは，そうした反応は，「誰もが自分なりの現実の体現を投影できる真っ白なスクリーン」を

作り出すピンターの才知の帰結だと見なす。昔の作家，例えばチャールズ・ディケンズの作品では，登場人物は明白に善か悪いずれかの側にいたのだが，対照的に，ピンターの主要な題材は現代的存在の道徳的曖昧さだった。ピンターの「強みは，そうした感覚を言葉で表現するすべを持たないであろう人たちにすら，その感覚を伝える臨場性にある」とバレリーは論じる。ピンターの名声は幾分賛否が分かれるものの，彼の作品は定期的に上演され続けており，劇作家の大多数に共通の運命である，世間から忘却されるなどということはありそうにない。

> 語句　playwright「劇作家」，scriptwriting「劇作」，boarding house「下宿屋」，terrorize「～を怖がらせる」，exposition「説明，解説」，unconventional「因習にとらわれない」，monologue「独白」，intruder「侵入者」，status quo「現状」，torturer「拷問にかける人」，biographer「伝記作家」，adoration「敬愛」，brilliance「抜群の才能」，incarnation「化身，権化」，immediacy「直接（性），即時（性）」，divisive「対立を引き起こす」，thematic「主題の」，devalue「～の価値を減じる」

(32) – 解答 ③

問題文の訳　なぜハロルド・ピンターの戯曲は最初否定的な反応を招いたのか。

選択肢の訳
1. 互いに相いれないと一般に見なされる演劇ジャンルの混合の典型だと考えられた。
2. ありふれた設定と見たところ無意味な登場人物が，観劇しているまさにその人たちを批判していると見なされた。
3. そうした演目を理解するには演劇上必要と一般に見なされる情報と背景を伝えていなかった。
4. 主題の性質が，観客が自らより能動的に作品を解釈するよう強制し，したがってプロの劇評家の意見の価値を下げた。

解説　第1段落によると，ピンターの長編第1作の不評の理由は，下宿屋に入り込む見知らぬ2人についての説明がまったくないことだった。これは，第5文の since 以下に書かれているように，劇中で意味や動機を説明するのが演劇の常識だったからである。**3** がそれを failed to deliver information and context ... と言い換えている。

(33) – 解答 ②

問題文の訳　ピンターの戯曲の登場人物についてわかることの1つは何か。

選択肢の訳
1. 与えられた状況のよりよい理解を得ようと試みるのではなく，自分自身をもっと十分に知りたいという欲求に動かされる傾向がある。
2. より深い理解を築くのではなく，しばしば彼らの会話は彼らが実際に思っていることを隠す。
3. ある状況でひとたび侵入者が優勢になれば，彼らの攻撃的態度に抵抗するために犠牲者ができることはほとんどない，というピンターの考

えを反映している。

4 観客には明白だが彼らにはそうではないように書かれている，ほかの登場人物に関する事柄を誤解する傾向がある。

解説 第2段落前半で，登場人物について their conversations ... rarely serve the purpose of clearly conveying information，また their dialogue frequently contradicts their thoughts と書かれている部分が 2 と合致する。彼らは自分の identity すらよくわかっていないのだから 1 は誤り，侵入を受けた者も優位に立とうと交渉するのだから 3 は誤りである。4 に関する記述はない。

(34) – 解答 ①

問題文の訳 ポール・バレリーは以下の記述のどれに同意するだろう可能性が最も高いか。

選択肢の訳
1 ピンターには社会の善悪の不確実さを描写する才能があったが，そのせいで，得ていたかもしれないほどの人気を得ることはなかった。
2 ピンターの文章スタイルは多くの人を怒らせたものの，チャールズ・ディケンズのような作家も存命中は大いに議論を呼んだ。
3 ピンターの戯曲はとても不道徳だったので，ほかの偉大な劇作品と同列に考えることはできない。
4 ピンターの対話とストーリーテリングの才能のせいで，多くの人は彼の戯曲が実際より優れていると思った。

解説 第3段落の中ほどでピンターの主要な題材として挙げられている the moral ambiguities は，善人と悪人を明確に分けているディケンズと対比されていることからわかるように，善悪の境界が不分明なことを言う。1 がそれを the uncertainty about right and wrong と言い換えている。1 の but 以下は，第3段落第1文の Pinter failed to attain ... と最終文の Pinter's somewhat divisive reputation に対応している。

全文訳 記憶を発見する

人間の記憶の根底にあるメカニズムに関する近代の研究は，16世紀の顕微鏡の発明とともに可能になり，ついにはニューロンの発見と分類に至った。一層の進歩が見られたのは，スペインの神経科学者サンティアゴ・ラモン・イ・カハールのニューロン染色法によってであり，この技法によって，人間の神経系を構成するこの分化細胞の画像が得られた。彼の研究は，ニューロンは融合して継ぎ目のない網を作るのではなく実際は別個の構成単位だとする，いわゆるニューロン説が優位を確立する一助となった。これがひいては，ニューロンはシナプスというこぶ状の構造体を経由して可能になる電気信号の転送によって互いに情報伝達をする，という発見につながった。この研究が，記憶の形成はニューロン間のシナプス結合の強化に依存するという，現在一般に認められている考えの基礎になった。

しかし，カリフォルニア大学ロサンゼルス校の神経生物学者デイビッド・グランズマンが率いた最近の研究は，カタツムリを使った実験で，この支配的理論に疑問を呈している。カタツムリのグループに軽い電気ショックを加え，通常より長い時間にわたって体を収縮させるよう刺激を与えた。電気ショックを受けずに再び優しく触られると，やはりカタツムリは体の部位の一部を最長 1 分間引っ込め，ショックに対する防御行動を学習していることを証明した。次に，タンパク質合成の指令を運ぶ役目を担うリボ核酸（RNA）という分子がこれらのカタツムリから抽出され，まったく電気ショックを受けていない第 2 のカタツムリグループに注入された。すると，最初のグループのカタツムリ同様，第 2 グループのカタツムリが優しい非電気的な接触に反応して，通常より長い時間にわたって体を引っ込め始めたのである。この反応が示唆するのは，刺激に対する脳の神経反応の間に確かにシナプスの強化は生じるが，経験が実際に記録されるのはRNA 分子が作られる場所であるニューロン内部ということだ，とグランズマンは主張する。「記憶がシナプスに保存されたのなら，われわれの実験がうまくいくことは絶対になかっただろう」と彼は言う。

　しかし，伝統主義陣営の科学者は納得していない。RNA に基づく生物学的変化は分や時間という長さの単位で起きるものだと彼らは指摘し，それがほぼ瞬時に行われる記憶の想起のようなもののメカニズムの一部であり得るのか，と異議を唱えている。事態を一層複雑にしているのが，ジェイムズ・V・マコーネルが 1950 年代に行った，自身が「記憶 RNA」と呼ぶものの存在を証明しようとする悪名高い試みである。マコーネルは迷路を通り抜けられるよう扁形動物を訓練し，次いでその体を訓練されていない虫に餌として与えたところ，突如としてその虫は，訓練された虫の迷路を走る技能を見習うことができるようになるように見えたのである。この研究とそれを再現しようとするおびただしい試みは嘲笑の的となり，センセーショナルだが科学的に疑わしい研究によって耳目を集めようとする科学者に関する警告として話のネタにされている。このことは，記憶の形成を RNA と結び付けて考えるあらゆる理論に恥辱を加えている。しかし近年，マコーネルの研究の一部の側面の再現が成功したようである。したがって，グランズマンを支持する科学界のメンバーは，RNA が記憶の形成についての理解を深める鍵かもしれないという考えに，今や彼の研究が納得のいく証拠を加えたのではないかと示唆している。

> 語句　underlie「～の基礎をなす」，neuron「ニューロン，神経細胞」，neuroscientist「神経科学者」，specialize「分化する」，fuse together「融合する」，seamless「途切れのない」，knoblike「こぶ状の」，synapse「シナプス」，enhancement「向上，増加」，synaptic「シナプスの」，neurobiologist「神経生物学者」，prevailing「支配的な，優勢な」，recoil「後ずさりする」，ribonucleic acid「リボ核酸」，neural「神経（系）の」，traditionalist「伝統主義の」，timescale「時間的尺度」，flatworm「扁形動物」，emulate「～を見習う」，cautionary「警告となる」，stigma「汚名，恥辱」，disprove「～の誤りを証明する」，

uninterrupted「中断されない」, groundwork「基礎，土台」

(35) – 解答 ④

問題文の訳 サンティアゴ・ラモン・イ・カハールは記憶の理解にどのような貢献をしたか。

選択肢の訳
1 彼の染色法によって，後の科学者たちは，どのタイプのニューロンが電気信号を送ることができるのかを発見できた。
2 ニューロン網がどのように電気信号を用いて互いに情報伝達をするかを実証することによって，ニューロン説の誤りを証明した。
3 ニューロンが送り出す電気信号を表す彼の画像は，神経系が連続するニューロン網で構成されていることを証明した。
4 ニューロンは実際は分離した個々の細胞だという証拠を示し，シナプスの発見の基礎を作った。

解説 第1段落には，カハールの業績だけでなく，それに基づく後年の発見も書かれているので，区別しながら丁寧に読む必要がある。ニューロンの types の違いに関する記述はないので **1** は誤り。本文に His work helped establish the dominance of the so-called neuron doctrine とあるので，**2** は disproved が誤り。また，ニューロンの情報伝達を実証したのは後の科学者である。ニューロンは distinct units とあるので，**3** は uninterrupted が誤り。また，彼の画像は電気信号を表すものではない。その distinct units を separate, individual cells と言い換えた **4** が正解である。

(36) – 解答

問題文の訳 カタツムリ実験の結果は次のことを示している。

選択肢の訳
1 記憶はシナプス結合に保存されているというより，脳のニューロンそれ自体の中に保存されているように見える。
2 シナプスの強化は，ニューロン間の RNA 分子の流れによる，そこに残された情報への一時的な反応である。
3 記憶の形成は，脳がさらされる刺激よりも，刺激に対する脳の化学的な反応の仕方により多く依存する。
4 記憶の正確さは，脳が作ることのできる RNA 分子の量と直接の相関関係があり得る。

解説 第2段落によると，実験では，防御行動を学習したカタツムリの RNA を学習していないカタツムリに注入すると，後者も防御行動を示した（つまり，記憶が移植された）。記憶の形成にはシナプスが重要な働きをするという理論が現在の主流だが，この実験ではシナプスではなく，RNA を用いた。RNA はニューロンで作られるのだから，記憶がニューロンに保存される可能性を示唆したことになる。それに合致する選択肢は **1** である。

(37) – 解答 ②

問題文の訳 デイビッド・グランズマンの研究が受けている批判について考えられる説明の1つは何か。

選択肢の訳
1 カタツムリと扁形動物の違いは非常に大きいので，グランズマンの実験結果は両方には適用されそうにない。
2 グランズマンの考えは科学界のメンバーに，過去に見下された研究を思い起こさせる。
3 グランズマンが別の研究者の考えを借用しながら，その人の功績を十分に認めていない強い可能性がある。
4 RNAが効果を生むには長い時間がかかることをジェイムズ・V・マコーネルが証明したので，グランズマンが正しい可能性は低いように思える。

解説 グランズマンへの批判は第3段落に2つ書かれている。1つは，記憶の想起のような一瞬の出来事はRNAの性質に合わないこと。もう1つは，マコーネルの怪しげな研究のせいで，記憶の形成とRNAを関連させる理論一般がばかにされるようになった苦い経験である。つまり，グランズマンとマコーネルを同列に考える科学者たちがいることになる。マコーネルの研究を research that had been looked down on in the past と表した **2** が正解。

全文訳 **フォークランド戦争**

アルゼンチン沿岸から480キロメートル東に位置するフォークランド諸島の領有権は，1833年に英国が力ずくで占拠した後，アルゼンチンと英国の継続的な論争の源となった。しかし，ついに英国政府は，遠隔の植民地が重荷になりつつあるという結論を下し，現地の警備に投資するのをますますためらうようになった。

1982年，アルゼンチンの独裁者レオポルド・ガルチェリ将軍は，外交交渉を打ち切り実力で諸島を取り戻す決断を下した。これは主に，民衆の不満を和らげるためだった。経済的失敗と人権侵害が原因で彼の独裁政治はひどく嫌われるようになっており，ガルチェリは，国民の目を自身の政権の欠点からそらしてくれる愛国的熱狂に火をつけたいと考えたのである。4月2日にアルゼンチンの軍隊が諸島に上陸し，そこにいたわずかな英国軍を圧倒したことで，アルゼンチンでは広く歓喜の声が上がり，ガルチェリ政権への支持が急上昇した。この侵攻は完全に英国政府の意表を突くものだった。それどころか，侵攻の直前にマーガレット・サッチャー首相は，フォークランド近辺から英国の唯一の軍艦を予算の都合で撤退させていた。

アルゼンチンの地理的優位と比較的高度な軍隊を考えれば，諸島を力ずくで取り返すのは無理かもしれないと多くの英国司令官は考えた。それにもかかわらず，海軍の機動部隊が速やかに編成され，英国政府は諸島周囲370キロメートルの交戦区域を宣言した。そうすればガルチェリはひるんで外交的解決を受け入れるだろうというのが彼らの

当初の想定で，解決案には相当の譲歩を加え，より受け入れやすくしていた。

　機動部隊が南に航行する間，平和的決着を得るための懸命な外交活動が米国と国際連合双方により試みられたが，ガルチェリは，アルゼンチンが完全な領有権を持つこと以外の何もいらないと主張した。ヨーロッパのほとんどの国が英国への支持を表明したのに対して，ラテンアメリカ諸国の大多数はアルゼンチンを支持した。米国の中立を初めから当てにしていたアルゼンチンにとって，米国が英国を支持することで明らかに戦略的に不利な立場に置かれたのは大きな痛手だった。今や敵が，米国の高度な通信技術と極めて重要な軍事機密データを利用できるようになったからである。

　5月2日，正式な交戦区域の外にいたアルゼンチン軍艦，アルゼンチン共和国海軍ヘネラル・ベルグラーノを沈めるよう，議論の分かれる命令が英国の原子力潜水艦に下された。ベルグラーノが英国の機動部隊に向かって航行していたという根拠で英国側がこの攻撃を正当化する一方，アルゼンチンは，船は反対方向に向かっていたと主張した。この戦闘の結果，紛争中単独の戦闘では最多の死者である323人が死亡した。サッチャーは，意図的に紛争がエスカレートするよう挑発し外交的決着の望みを弱めるためにこの攻撃を命じた，と政敵から非難された。だが後にアルゼンチン海軍上層部が認めたところでは，交戦区域を縫うように出たり入ったりしていたベルグラーノは，実際に英国の機動部隊にとって進行中の脅威だった。さらに，その時点では両者とも，南大西洋が妥当な戦場だとおおむね考えていた。

　ベルグラーノを沈めたことは，力ずくで諸島を取り返そうという英国の決意の証明であり，アルゼンチンに明確なメッセージを送ったが，自国の船が魚雷攻撃に弱いと悟ったアルゼンチンは，船のほとんどを港に留め置いた。戦争の残りの期間，アルゼンチンの海軍は事実上出番がなくなったが，間違いなくそのおかげで，その後の海での死傷者が両者とも制限されることとなった。

　アルゼンチンの空軍力ははるかに劣っていたものの，パイロットは英国側への軍事行動において，技量もモチベーションもあることを実証してみせた。だが，フォークランド諸島は彼らの飛行機の戦闘範囲の末端にあったため，機動部隊に対して1回きりの攻撃しか行えなかった。5月21日に英国側が海から上陸するのをアルゼンチンは防げなかったが，彼らの内陸防衛は効果的で，数度の激しい戦闘になった。アルゼンチンの正規兵は手ごわい敵であることが証明されたが，部隊は意思に反して軍に徴兵された人が大半で，ろくに訓練を受けておらず，覚悟も足りず装備も不十分だった。「われわれは勝てるはずのない戦争で砲弾の餌食になった」と1人の退役軍人は後に主張した。

　英国側は約11,400人のアルゼンチン人を捕虜にし，6月14日，アルゼンチン軍は正式に降伏した。敗北はこの国の軍事政権の終わりを意味した。完全に信用を失った軍事政権に代わり，1983年に文民政権が成立した。反対に，英国側が最小限の死傷者——255人の英国人の命が失われた——で諸島を奪還したことはサッチャーの人気を大いに高め，次の選挙での彼女の勝利を助けた。しかし，この戦争で論争が決着したわけではない。アルゼンチンは，フォークランド諸島は自分のものだと言い続けているのである。皮肉なことに，無分別な軍事的企てに乗り出さなければ，アルゼンチンがフォークラン

ド諸島を手に入れていた可能性が高い。なぜなら，人口が減少していたので，結局英国の統治はそれ以上続かなかっただろうからである。その代わり，1982年以降，英国は諸島に対する軍事的関与と経済的関与を共に強化し，現状が変わらず維持されている。

> 語句　ongoing「継続している」，forcible「力ずくの」，hesitant「ちゅうちょする」，reclaim「〜を取り戻す」，mismanagement「誤った管理」，jubilation「歓喜」，unprepared「準備ができていない」，budgetary「予算の」，warship「軍艦」，retake「〜を取り戻す」，task force「機動部隊」，palatable「好ましい」，ARA「アルゼンチン共和国海軍」，escalation「段階的拡大」，curtail「〜を短縮する，削減する」，torpedo「魚雷」，sideline「〜を（仕事などから）外す」，outclass「〜よりはるかに優れている」，conscript「〜を徴兵する」，ill-equipped「装備が十分でない」，cannon fodder「砲弾の餌食」，discredit「〜の信用を傷つける」，conversely「逆に」，ill-advised「無分別な」，governance「統治」，status quo「現状」

(38) －解答　2

問題文の訳　レオポルド・ガルチェリ将軍が1982年にフォークランド諸島に侵攻することを決めたのは次の理由による。

選択肢の訳
1 諸島の将来に関する公式の議論に加わることを英国が拒否したので，軍事力に訴える以外の選択肢が彼にはなかった。
2 そうすれば自国の士気が高まり，その結果アルゼンチン国内の状況から国民の目をそらすことになると正確に見積もった。
3 英国の軍事的存在感が増しているのだから，勝利を得ようとするならアルゼンチンは素早く攻撃する必要がある，と配下の司令官たちが彼を説得した。
4 一般大衆からの侵攻への要求が，諸島を侵攻するリスクを冒したくない彼の気持ちに打ち勝った。

解説　第2段落第2文に This was chiefly to diminish popular discontent ... Galtieri hoped to spark a patriotic fever that would divert the public eye from his regime's shortcomings. とあるように，対外強硬策で国民をあおることで内政の失敗に対する不満の矛先をそらすという，為政者が古くから使うやり口をガルチェリも用いた。2 が patriotic fever を morale と，divert the public eye を distracting citizens と言い換えている。

(39) －解答　1

問題文の訳　戦争を回避しようとする外交努力はなぜ失敗したのか。

選択肢の訳
1 最終的解決に関して英国側がある程度の柔軟性を示したにもかかわらず，アルゼンチンが所有権に関して柔軟性のない姿勢を取った。
2 米国のような信頼していた同盟国の支持を突然失ったことで，軍事力

を用いる以外の選択肢は残されていないと英国が感じた。
3 国際社会が分裂していたので，国際連合は和平合意交渉のための地ならしを十分にすることができなかった。
4 国連の支持がひとたび自分たちの有利に傾くと，英国側は交渉という手段で目標を追求することを拒んだ。

解説 開戦直後の外交的動きは第3段落後半と第4段落前半に書かれている。英国は交戦の構えを見せつつも substantial concessions を行い，平和的解決を望む姿勢を示した。一方，米国と国連が和平を仲介しようとしたが，アルゼンチンはフォークランド諸島の complete sovereignty を要求して譲らなかった。sovereignty を ownership と言い換え，英国とアルゼンチンの姿勢をそれぞれ flexibility と inflexible という語を用いてまとめた **1** が正解である。

(40) – 解答 4

問題文の訳 アルゼンチン共和国海軍ヘネラル・ベルグラーノが沈められたことは，紛争を巡る状況をどのように変えたか。

選択肢の訳
1 アルゼンチンの司令官たちが海軍戦術を修正し，その結果彼らの軍艦は，英国の援軍が交戦区域に接近するのを防いだ。
2 マーガレット・サッチャー首相が自国の軍事司令官たちに耳を貸そうとしなかったことで，状況全体の深刻さがエスカレートした。
3 力を誇示して外交的に有利な立場を得ようという当初のアルゼンチンの意図が，軍事的勝利を勝ち取るという真剣な取り組みに変容した。
4 英国海軍がアルゼンチンの水上艦に対してあまりにも大きな脅威であることが自明だったため，それ以上の海軍の交戦はほとんど生じなかった。

解説 第6段落にベルグラーノ撃沈後の状況が書かれている。本気を見せた英国海軍に対して勝ち目がないと知ったアルゼンチンはその後海軍をほとんど動かさず，したがって両国とも海戦での死傷者は少なかった。**4** がその内容と一致する。ほかの選択肢に関する記述はない。

(41) – 解答

問題文の訳 この文章の筆者は，フォークランド戦争についてどのような結論を引き出しているか。

選択肢の訳
1 アルゼンチンにはフォークランド諸島を力ずくで永続的に奪う見込みはほとんどなかったが，英国が去るのを待っていればたぶん手に入れていただろう。
2 アルゼンチンの空軍が英国の上陸を防ぐことにもっと真剣に取り組んでいれば，紛争が違う結果になっていた可能性は大いにある。
3 英国はアルゼンチンの軍事政権を転覆させることができたが，新たな文民政権の方が多くの点でさらに悪かった。

4 フォークランド諸島を取り返すことをサッチャーが命じなければ、そこに住む人々はおそらく今ではもっと裕福になっているだろう。

解説 最終段落後半の Ironically, ... の文がポイント。まず、ill-advised という語は、最初からアルゼンチンに勝ち目はなかったという筆者の評価を表している。そして、it may well have gained possession of them 以下は、英国はいずれフォークランド諸島を放棄しただろうから、黙っていてもアルゼンチンのものになっていたはずだという筆者の推測を表す。これに合致する選択肢は **1** である。

一次試験・筆記 4 問題編 p.128

解答例 Many countries prosper from increased interconnectedness, and in the same way, Japan can benefit from improving its relations with other Asian nations. If the government prioritized this, it could help to stabilize the work force, stimulate the economy, and raise Japan's international standing.

Firstly, the population decline in Japan is well documented. While efforts have been made to help boost numbers, the possibility of labor shortages in the future is particularly worrying. By bettering connections with other Asian countries, Japan can attract more foreign workers and help offset a shrinking work force.

Additionally, Japan could encourage economic growth by looking to examples of successful trade agreements between nations. The EU has provided its members with benefits such as free market access. Japan should strive for a similar political and economic union with other Asian nations as a way to secure markets for its goods and services.

Finally, better international standing in Asia would be advantageous for Japan. In times of national crises, such as natural disasters, the support of neighboring countries is crucial. Fostering diplomatic solidarity through mutual respect is clearly a better option for the Japanese government than simply existing in solitude.

It is imperative that the Japanese government improves ties with other Asian nations given the clear benefits. Doing so would put Japan in a strong position to tackle a decreasing work force and economic stagnation, while also allowing it to prosper from a stronger international position.

トピックの訳　「賛成か反対か：ほかのアジア諸国との関係改善が日本政府にとって優先事項であるべきだ」

解説　このトピックで「反対」の立場を取るとしたら，「米国との同盟を中心とする西欧諸国との関係をこれまでどおり重視すべきだ」という結論になると思われる。解答例の第1段落で用いている If the government prioritized this, it could help ... という仮定法過去は，「政府はアジア諸国との関係より西欧諸国との関係を重視している」という現状認識を暗に示している。このように，agree か disagree かを選ぶ問題では，もう一方の立場も考慮した論述を心がけると内容に深みが生まれる。

　対外政策を考える場合，政治・経済・軍事・文化などいくつかのアプローチが可能だが，この解答例では主に経済面に焦点を当て，「労働力の安定」「経済の活性化」「国際的信望の向上」の3つを理由に挙げている。全体の構成は，自分の立場とその理由を示す導入の段落，理由について詳述する3つの段落，自分の立場を再確認する結論の段落，という基本的な5段落から成っている。理由を説明する段落の冒頭はそれぞれ Firstly, Additionally, Finally という副詞で始めており，極めて明快な構成である。

　最初の理由では，人口減少による労働者不足の解消には外国人労働者を増やす必要があり，そのためにはアジア諸国との良好な関係が必要だとしている。人口減少や少子高齢化はたびたび取り上げられるトピックなので，女性の社会進出や AI の活用など，関連する論点について普段から考えておく必要がある。2つ目の理由として，EU を手本とする広域自由貿易圏をアジアに形成することのメリットを論じている。3つ目には，アジアで日本の国際的信望が高まれば，自然災害などの際に協力を期待できるとしている。この解答例は全体に理念的な記述が多いので，時事的な視点を導入すると説得力が増すと思われる。例えば，外国人労働者の問題であれば，移民としての受け入れには賛否両論あること，貿易問題なら，東アジアの経済連携を目指す構想はあるが妥結に至っていない状況などを交え，そうした障壁を乗り越えなければならないという展開にすることもできる。

　表現面では，improving its relations → bettering connections → improves ties のように，同じ英語を何度も繰り返さずにできるだけ言い換える，という原則が徹底されている。記述の流れや文の構造に応じて多種多様な表現を駆使する力も問われるので，特に時事問題に関する英文の記事などを読むときは，言い換えがどのように用いられているかに注目することも大切である。

| 一次試験・リスニング | Part 1 | 問題編 p.129〜130 |  |

No.1 - 解答 ④

スクリプト
☆: I see you're reading Susan Horn's latest novel.
★: Actually, I just finished it. Have you read it?
☆: Yes, but I wasn't that impressed.
★: Really? I thought it was pretty good. I liked the interesting characters and the plot twists.
☆: Me, too. But the way she wrapped it up didn't make any sense to me.
★: Really? I enjoyed the way it turned out. I was surprised when I found out who the murderer was, but looking back, there were a lot of clues.
☆: I guess I should pay more attention to the details.
Question: What is the woman's opinion of the book?

全文訳
☆: スーザン・ホーンの新しい小説を読んでいるのね。
★: 実は、ちょうど読み終えたところなんだ。君は読んだ？
☆: うん、だけどそんなに感心しなかった。
★: 本当？　僕はなかなかいいと思ったよ。興味深い登場人物とプロットの意外な展開が気に入った。
☆: 私も。だけど、話の終わらせ方が私には訳がわからなかった。
★: 本当？　僕はこの結末が面白かったよ。誰が殺人犯かわかったときは驚いたけど、思い返すと手がかりはたくさんあったよね。
☆: 私は細かいところにもっと注意すべきなのね。
質問：その本についての女性の意見は何か。

選択肢の訳
1　登場人物が退屈だった。
2　手がかりが見え見えだった。
3　プロットが十分に複雑でなかった。
4　結末が魅力的でなかった。

解説 女性は3つ目の発言で the way she wrapped it up didn't make any sense to me と言っている。wrap up は「〜を（滞りなく）終わらせる」という意味なので、女性は **4** のように結末に不満を持っていることになる。登場人物とプロットを褒める男性に女性は同意しているので、**1** と **3** は誤り。

No.2 - 解答 ①

スクリプト
★: I think I really blew my presentation. I was so nervous I could hardly talk.

☆ : Well, you were a bit shaky at the start, but once you got going, everyone was really interested by what you said.

★ : You really think so? Public speaking is just not my forte.

☆ : But the examples you used to explain difficult scientific concepts were so clear. Even a dummy like me could get it.

★ : You're hardly a dummy, but thanks.

Question: What did the woman say about the presentation?

全文訳 ★：発表は全然うまくできなかったと思う。緊張してほとんどしゃべれなかったよ。

☆：うーん，最初は少しおぼつかなかったけど，始まってからはみんなあなたの言うことにすごく興味を持っていたわよ。

★：本当にそう思う？ 人前で話すのは全然得意じゃないんだ。

☆：だけど，難しい科学的概念を説明するのに使った例はすごくわかりやすかった。私みたいなばかでも理解できたもの。

★：君は全然ばかなんかじゃないよ，だけどありがとう。

質問：女性は発表についてどう言ったか。

選択肢の訳 1 男性の説明は理解しやすかった。
2 男性はもっと例を使うべきだった。
3 トピックが聞き手には難し過ぎた。
4 最初の部分が最も興味深かった。

解説 発表は失敗だったと思っている男性に対し，女性は，everyone was really interested や the examples ... were so clear などと言って発表を褒めている。女性の2つ目の発言の get は「～を理解する」という意味なので，**1** が正解。forte「得意なこと」，dummy「ばかな人」。

No.3 - 解答 ③

スクリプト ★ : Hi, Jane. This is Peter. I just flew in from L.A.

☆ : I've been expecting your call. I just got off the phone with your client in L.A.

★ : Is there a problem? They agreed to give us the contract.

☆ : Not for long, apparently. Two hours after you left, their chairman overruled the decision. It seems he's not convinced we're the right company to go with.

★ : You're kidding. A week of work wasted.

☆ : Not necessarily. I suggest you get right back on the plane and try again.

Question: What happened after Peter left L.A.?

全文訳 ★：もしもし，ジェーン。ピーターです。ロサンゼルスから今飛行機で着いたところ。

☆：ずっと電話を待っていたのよ。ロサンゼルスのあなたのクライアントとの電話を今切ったところなの。

★：何か問題でも？ 契約はうちにくれると了承してくれたよ。

☆：長い契約期間じゃなかったみたいね。あなたが帰った２時間後に，あちらの社長が決定を覆したのよ。取引相手としてうちがふさわしい会社だと社長は納得していないようなの。

★：うそだろ。１週間分の努力が無駄になったよ。

☆：そうとも限らない。すぐにまた飛行機に乗って，もう一度トライしてみたらどうかしら。

質問：ピーターがロサンゼルスを去った後に何があったか。

選択肢の訳
1 社長がジェーンにロサンゼルスを訪れるよう頼んだ。
2 ピーターの上司が契約を取り消す決定をした。
3 クライアントが決定を変更した。
4 ジェーンが契約に少し変更を加えた。

解説 女性は２つ目の発言で Two hours after you left, their chairman overruled the decision. と言っている。つまり，ピーターが契約をまとめた直後に，相手の会社の社長がその決定を取り消した（＝変更した）ことがわかる。

No.4 －解答 ③

スクリプト
☆：The Dawsons' summer house was gorgeous, wasn't it? What do you think of us doing something like that?

★：I don't know. We'd have to worry about maintaining another home, and we'd have less money to spend on traveling.

☆：Still, it might be a good investment. I've been doing a little research about it.

★：From what I've read, the second-home market is more volatile than first homes. And remember property taxes.

☆：Can you at least give it some thought? We don't really travel that much anyway, you know.

★：OK. I'll talk to some people at work and see what they think.

Question: What would the woman like the man to do?

全文訳
☆：ドーソン家の夏の別荘は豪華だったわよね。私たちも何かそういったことをしてみたらどうかしら。

★：どうかな。家をもう１軒管理する心配をしなければならないし，旅行に使えるお金も減るよ。

☆：それでも，いい投資かもしれない。そのことについてちょっと調べているの。

★：僕が読んだところでは，セカンドハウス市場はファーストハウスより不

安定だ。それに固定資産税を忘れちゃいけない。
☆：せめて少し考えてみてくれない？　どうせ私たちは実際はそんなに旅行しないんだから。
★：わかった。職場の連中と話して，どう思うか聞いてみるよ。

質問：女性は男性に何をしてもらいたいか。

選択肢の訳
1　旅行にもっとお金をかけることを考える。
2　投資にもっと慎重になる。
3　セカンドハウスを買うという考えを検討する。
4　セカンドハウスについてドーソン家に助言を求める。

解説　セカンドハウスの購入に積極的な女性に対し，男性は「管理が必要」「旅行費が減る」「市場が不安定」「固定資産税」とマイナス要素を並べて慎重な姿勢を見せている。その男性に対し女性は Can you at least give it some thought? と言っているので，正解は **3**。volatile「不安定な」。

No.5 – 解答 ②

スクリプト
★：Sue, remember when you and Ted built that fence around your house?
☆：Sure. What about it?
★：Well, I'm putting up my own fence this weekend. Do you know if it's OK to put it directly on the property line between my yard and my neighbor's?
☆：To be safe, you should put it an inch or so inside the line so you don't encroach on your neighbor's land. Otherwise, there may be big trouble when selling either property. You should check with the town office to make sure, though.
★：Great. Thanks.

Question: What does the woman tell the man to do?

全文訳
★：スー，君とテッドが家の周りに塀を造ったときのことを覚えている？
☆：もちろん。それがどうかしたの？
★：えー，僕も今週末，家に塀を建てるんだ。うちの庭と隣の家の土地の境界線に直接建てて構わないかどうかわかる？
☆：安全策としては，お隣の土地を侵害しないよう，境界線から1インチくらい内側に建てた方がいいわ。そうしないと，どちらかが土地を売るときに大問題になるかもしれない。間違いがないよう，役場に確認した方がいいけど。
★：助かるよ。ありがとう。

質問：女性は男性に何をするよう言っているか。

選択肢の訳
1　隣人について役場に苦情を言う。
2　塀は土地の境界線の内側にする。

236

3　その問題について彼女の夫と話し合う。
　　　4　塀について隣人から助言をもらう。
解説　女性は2つ目の発言で you should put it an inch or so inside the line と言っている。it は fence のことで，line は直前に男性が言っている property line を指す。**2**がこの助言と一致する。女性は役場に確認するようにとも助言しているが，苦情を言えという意味ではない。encroach on ～「～を侵害する」。

No.6 - 解答 ②

スクリプト
★：How's your daughter doing these days? Is she still working on her Ph.D. in astrophysics?
☆：Actually, she graduated last year and was offered a research position at the University of Arizona.
★：Very impressive! I've heard Arizona is at the forefront of planetary exploration.
☆：Yes. Now, she's part of a team searching for new planets and remapping the solar system.
★：Is that so? I've heard that the competition for those research posts is so tough.
☆：That's true, but as a graduate student, she discovered a new star.
★：Well, no wonder she got the position!

Question: What do we learn about the woman's daughter?

全文訳
★：お宅の娘さんは最近どうしているの？　まだ天文物理学の博士号に取り組んでいるの？
☆：実は去年卒業して，アリゾナ大学の研究職をオファーされたの。
★：すごいじゃないか！　アリゾナは惑星探査の最前線だと聞いたよ。
☆：そう。娘は今，新しい惑星を探して太陽系の地図を書き換えるチームの一員なの。
★：そうなの？　そうした研究職の競争はすごく厳しいと聞いたよ。
☆：そのとおりなんだけど，娘は大学院生のときに，新しい星を発見したのよ。
★：へえ，それならその職に就いたのも納得だね！
質問：女性の娘について何がわかるか。

選択肢の訳
1　博士号を終えるのを延期した。
2　新しい仕事に非常に適任だった。
3　新しい職に応募した。
4　大学からの仕事のオファーを断った。

解説　astrophysics, planetary exploration, remapping などの専門語に惑わされず，女性の娘が大学で天文関係の研究職に就いた，という話の流

れがわかればよい。娘が新しい星を発見したという女性の3つ目の発言と，no wonder she got the position! という男性の最後の発言から，娘はその研究職にふさわしい人材だと考えられる。職はオファーされたものだと女性が最初に言っているので，3 の applied for は誤り。

No.7 - 解答 ④

(スクリプト) ☆：What's wrong with your eye, Lewis?
★：I don't know, but it's really itchy. I don't have insurance, so I can't afford to go to a clinic.
☆：You should try Lens Makers. They specialize in glasses, but I went there for a prescription when I got an eye infection last year. The eye exam only cost about $25.
★：You're kidding!
☆：You'll have to pay full price for the medication, though.
★：Well, at least I'll save something.
Question: Why will the man go to Lens Makers?

(全文訳) ☆：目をどうかしたの，ルイス？
★：わからないけど，すごくかゆいんだ。保険に入っていないから，クリニックに行くお金の余裕はないよ。
☆：レンズメーカーズに行ってみるといいわ。眼鏡の専門店だけど，去年目の感染症にかかったとき，処方箋をもらいに行ったの。目の検査は25ドルくらいしかかからなかった。
★：冗談だろ！
☆：薬代は全部払わなければならないけど。
★：まあ，それでもいくらか節約にはなるよ。
質問：男性はなぜレンズメーカーズに行くのか。

(選択肢の訳) 1　彼が欲しい眼鏡を売っている。
2　彼の保険を受け付けてくれる。
3　クリニックより安い薬がある。
4　低料金で目の検査をしてくれる。

(解説) 目の検査料が25ドル，という女性の2つ目の発言に男性が驚いていることから，この料金が破格の安さだとわかる。薬代は full price を払う必要があるので 3 は誤り。

No.8 - 解答 ①

(スクリプト) ★：How are things working out with your new job?
☆：Not so well. It's a full-time position, but I just learned that contract workers from outside get paid more than I do for the same work.
★：That doesn't sound right. What are you going to do?

238

☆：I've only been working there for a few weeks, so I'll just hold off for now and bring it up with personnel when the time is right.
★：Well, I hope things work out.
☆：Me, too.

Question: What is the woman planning to do?

全文訳
★：新しい仕事の調子はどう？
☆：あまりよくないわね。フルタイムの職なんだけど，同じ仕事をしても，外部からの契約社員の方が私より給料がいいって知ったところなの。
★：それはおかしな話だな。どうするつもりなの？
☆：あの会社で働いてまだ2，3週間だから，今のところ行動は控えて，頃合いを見て人事課に話を持ち出してみる。
★：まあ，丸く収まるといいね。
☆：そうね。

質問：女性は何をする計画か。

選択肢の訳
1 行動を起こす前に待つ。
2 すぐに上司と話す。
3 別の職を探す。
4 契約社員になる。

解説　新しい仕事の給料に不満がある女性は，2つ目の発言でI'll just hold off for now and bring it up with personnel when the time is rightと言っている。hold off「行動を控える，先延ばしにする」をwaitと言い換え，bring以下をtaking actionと短くまとめた**1**が正解。

No.9 －解答

スクリプト
★：Did you see that article about how budget cuts are forcing school districts to slash services?
☆：I did. I knew things were bad in some districts, but charging extra for bus service at public schools seems a bit drastic. We're already paying taxes, so it's like being charged twice.
★：I know, but districts could bring in $1 million a year that way.
☆：I heard that another district has eliminated bus service completely for students who live within 2 miles of the school.
★：Well, kids nowadays could do with more exercise, so maybe that's not such a bad idea!
☆：True, but a lot of people, myself included, are also worried about the kids getting hit by a car or something. I'm more in favor of cutting back on custodial staff — one district did that.
★：Yeah, I saw that. Janitors only come in three times a week, and teachers clean classrooms, too.

☆ : Why not get the students to help out, too? They might take better care of the facilities if they had more responsibility for them.
★ : Interesting idea. And that'd help turn these negatives into something positive.

Question: What is one point the woman makes?

全文訳 ★：予算削減のせいで，学区がサービスをばっさり削らざるを得なくなっているというあの記事は見た？
☆：見たわよ。うまくいっていない学区もあることは知っていたけど，公立学校のスクールバスに追加料金を請求するのはちょっとやり過ぎに思える。既に税金を納めているんだから，2回請求されるみたいなものよね。
★：まあね，だけどそうすれば，学区には1年で100万ドル入るんだよ。
☆：別の学区は，学校から2マイル以内に住む生徒にはスクールバスを完全に廃止したって聞いたわ。
★：まあ，近ごろの子供はもっと運動が必要だろうから，それも悪い考えじゃないかもしれないね！
☆：それはそうだけど，私も含めたくさんの人が，子供が車にはねられたりすることも心配している。私は用務員を削減する方に賛成だわ——1つの学区はそうしたし。
★：うん，それは見た。用務員が出勤するのは週3回だけで，教師も教室の掃除をするんだよね。
☆：生徒にも手伝わせればいいんじゃない？ 施設に対する責任が増えれば，もっと大事にするかもしれない。
★：面白い考えだ。それにそうすれば，こうしたマイナス面をプラスに転じるのに役立つだろうし。

質問：女性が示している論点の1つは何か。

選択肢の訳　1　教師に教室の掃除をさせるべきではない。
　　　　　　2　スクールバスの廃止は生徒の安全に影響するかもしれない。
　　　　　　3　学校の費用を賄うために増税すべきだ。
　　　　　　4　設備の維持管理にもっとお金を使うべきだ。

解説　会話には，男女それぞれの意見と実際の動向が混在している。女性が述べている point「論点，意見」は，①スクールバスへの追加料金はやり過ぎだ，②バスに乗れない子供が車にひかれるのが心配だ，③用務員を減らすのがよい，④生徒にも教室を掃除させるべきだ，の4つ。このうち②が 2 と一致する。custodial staff は janitors と同じ「用務員」という意味。

No.10 解答 ①

スクリプト ★ : Sarah, let me introduce Paula, the new manager of the software development department.

☆ : Nice to meet you, Paula.
○ : You, too, Sarah.
★ : Paula has an idea she'd like to run by you.
○ : That's right. I've been wanting to ask you to help us develop new software applications. We need someone young and dynamic on our team to lend a different perspective. What do you think?
☆ : Wow. This is a bit sudden. Um . . . I don't have a lot of experience with software application development. I've only recently started to feel like I can keep up with my co-workers in the hardware section.
○ : Don't underestimate yourself. And you'd get a lot of training.
☆ : What about the project I'm working on now? Our team hasn't finished the design for the new tablet computer.
★ : Most of the important work has already been finished. That's why I think it'd be great timing for this new assignment.
☆ : It's flattering, but I've really been planning to build my career around hardware. May I have some time to think about it?
★ : Of course, but you know, Sarah, a willingness to broaden your horizons is one of the things the personnel department looks at when considering promotions. This could really work in your favor.
☆ : I understand. I'll give it my full consideration.

Question: What does the man imply?

全文訳
★ : サラ、ポーラを紹介するよ。ソフトウエア開発部の新部長だ。
☆ : 初めまして、ポーラ。
○ : こちらこそ、サラ。
★ : ポーラには、君に仕切ってほしいアイデアがあるんだ。
○ : そうなのよ。新しいアプリの開発を手伝ってくれるようあなたにお願いしたいとずっと思っていて。違う視点を与えてくれる若くて生きのいい人がうちのチームには必要なの。どう思う？
☆ : わあ。ちょっと急ですね。うーん……私はアプリ開発の経験は大してありません。ようやく最近、ハードウエア部の同僚に遅れずについていけると感じるようになったばかりで。
○ : 自分を過小評価しないで。それに、たくさん訓練を受けることになるし。
☆ : 今取り組んでいるプロジェクトはどうなります？ うちのチームは新型タブレットパソコンの設計図をまだ仕上げていないんです。
★ : 重要な作業はもうほとんど片付いている。だから、この新しい任務には絶好のタイミングだろうと思うんだ。

20年度第1回 リスニング

241

☆：ありがたいお話ですが，ハードウエア関連でキャリアを築いていこうと本気で思っているんです。考える時間を少し頂けますか。

★：いいとも，だけどいいかい，サラ，進んで視野を広げようとする気持ちは，人事部が昇進を検討する際に考慮することの1つだよ。これは大いに君の有利に働くかもしれない。

☆：わかりました。よくよく検討してみます。

質問：男性は暗に何と言っているか。

選択肢の訳
1　その職を受けることがサラのキャリアの助けになるかもしれない。
2　サラはアプリについて学ぶ必要はない。
3　サラはハードウエアのスキルに専心する方がいいだろう。
4　サラは現在のプロジェクトで成績がよくない。

解説　サラを自分の部署に誘う部長ポーラと，今の仕事でがんばりたいサラ，という構図は明快。サラの上司と思われる男性は，ポーラを援護する立場で後半に2度発言している。まず，サラの今のプロジェクトはほぼ終わりなので異動にはいいタイミングだと言い，そして，視野を広げようとする気持ちは昇進につながるかもしれないと言っている。broaden *one's* horizon「視野を広げる」はここでは，部署を移ることを指している。つまり**1**のように，異動の話を受ければ昇進に有利に働くかもしれないと言っていることになる。

 Part 2　問題編 p.131～132　

A

スクリプト **Mining in Cornwall**

　The history of copper and tin mining in the Cornwall region of southwest England dates back thousands of years. By the time of the Industrial Revolution, Cornwall was the world's leading producer of these metals. However, in the late nineteenth century, mining sources that were far more accessible were discovered in Australia and Malaysia. International demand for Cornish copper and tin collapsed, and thousands of miners emigrated to the Americas, where they found work in the iron industry. The last working mine in Cornwall closed in the 1990s.

　Now, Cornwall may be poised to return to its mining roots with a project to mine lithium, a highly conductive metal used in rechargeable batteries. Although lithium is relatively common, it is generally found at such low concentrations that extracting it is not economical. However, the underground hot springs that flow hundreds of meters beneath Cornwall contain high concentrations of lithium.

In other parts of the world, lithium in underground water is extracted by evaporating huge amounts of water in gigantic storage areas. Researchers in Cornwall, however, are working on a project that utilizes new, more environmentally friendly, processing technology. They believe it will eliminate the need for the evaporation process in storage areas and greatly improve the purity of the finished product.

Questions
No.11 What reason does the speaker give for the decline of mining in Cornwall?
No.12 What is one advantage of the project in Cornwall?

全文訳　コーンウォールの鉱業

　イングランド南西部コーンウォール地方の銅とスズ鉱業の歴史は，数千年の昔にさかのぼる。産業革命の時代には，コーンウォールはこれらの金属の世界最大の産地だった。しかし19世紀後半に，はるかに容易に入手できる採掘源がオーストラリアとマレーシアで発見された。コーンウォールの銅とスズの国際的需要は激減し，数千人の鉱山労働者が両アメリカに移住してそこで製鉄業の仕事を見つけた。コーンウォールで最後まで稼働していた鉱山は1990年代に閉鎖された。

　今コーンウォールは，充電式電池で用いられる高伝導性金属であるリチウムを採掘するプロジェクトで，鉱業という原点に立ち返る用意ができているかもしれない。リチウムは比較的ありふれたものだが，抽出するのが経済的に見合わないくらい低濃度で見られるのが一般的である。しかし，コーンウォールの下数百メートルを流れる地下温泉は，高濃度のリチウムを含んでいる。

　世界のほかの地域では，地下水のリチウムは巨大な貯蔵エリアで膨大な量の水を蒸発させることによって抽出される。しかし，コーンウォールの研究者は，より環境に優しい新しい加工処理技術を利用するプロジェクトに取り組んでいる。そうすれば貯蔵エリアの蒸発処理の必要はなくなり，完成した製品の純度は大幅に向上すると彼らは考えている。

語句　poised「用意ができている」，lithium「リチウム」，conductive「伝導性の」，gigantic「巨大な」

No.11 解答 ④

質問の訳　コーンウォールの鉱業が衰退した理由として話者は何を挙げているか。
選択肢の訳
1 銅とスズが少しずつ尽きた。
2 鉱山労働者の給料の要求が高過ぎた。
3 アメリカの鉱山がもっと優れた採掘技術を使い始めた。
4 ほかの場所で銅とスズがもっと手に入れやすくなった。

解説　コーンウォールの鉱業が隆盛を極めたという冒頭に続くHoweverの文で，mining sources that were far more accessible were discovered in Australia and Malaysia と言っている。これが理由で需要が減り，労働者は海外移住を選択した。**4** が more accessible を easier to obtain, Australia and Malaysia を elsewhere と言い換えている。

No.12 解答

質問の訳 コーンウォールのプロジェクトの利点の1つは何か。
選択肢の訳
1 環境への被害が減るだろう。
2 既存の貯蔵施設を使うだろう。
3 自然の熱を使うことでコスト削減になるだろう。
4 リチウムの精製に地表水を使うだろう。

解説 最後の段落で，コーンウォールで進行中のプロジェクトは more environmentally friendly だと言っているので，それを言い換えた **1** が正解。蒸発処理が不要になるので **2** は誤り，用いるのは地下の温泉水なので **4** は誤り。**3** については触れていない。

B

スクリプト **Push and Pull Marketing Methods**

The rise of social media and Internet search engines has altered how companies market their products. Until recently, most companies focused on "push" marketing, such as TV or print advertisements. Push marketing attempts to build awareness of a product among the general population. However, these strategies require significant financial resources and must reach a large audience frequently to be effective. Today, many firms rely less on push marketing because contemporary consumers tend to take little notice of traditional, broadly focused advertisements and instead seek out the items that they want online.

Now, companies, especially those without large advertising budgets, are increasingly relying on "pull" marketing. Pull marketing, rather than raising awareness of a product or service, assumes there is an existing demand for it. By using strategies such as search engine optimization, companies ensure that the content on their websites will be prominently displayed when consumers search for a relevant product online. Moreover, pull marketing actively involves consumers. For example, consumers are encouraged to write reviews on websites or share their favored products with others who have similar interests through social media. By doing so, they provide free advertising.

Questions
No.13 What is one thing the speaker says about "push" marketing?
No.14 According to the speaker, what is true of "pull" marketing?

全文訳 プッシュ型とプル型マーケティング手法

ソーシャルメディアとインターネット検索エンジンの台頭は，企業による商品のマー

ケティング方法を変えた。最近までほとんどの企業は，テレビ広告や印刷物広告などの「プッシュ型」マーケティングを中心に据えていた。プッシュ型マーケティングは，一般市民の間に商品に関する意識を形成しようと試みる。しかし，こうした戦略はかなりの資金を必要とし，効果を生むには頻繁に多くの受け手に届かなければならない。今日では，多くの企業がプッシュ型マーケティングへの依存を減らしている。なぜなら，現代の消費者は，幅広く焦点を当てる伝統的な広告にはほとんど注目せず，欲しい品物をオンラインで探し出す傾向があるからである。

　今では企業，特に多額の広告予算がない企業は，「プル型」マーケティングへの依存をますます高めている。プル型マーケティングは，商品やサービスに関する意識を高めるのではなく，商品やサービスには既存の需要があると想定する。企業は検索エンジン最適化などの戦略を用いて，消費者が関連商品をオンラインで検索する際，確実に自社ウェブサイトのコンテンツが目立つ位置に表示されるようにする。さらに，プル型マーケティングは積極的に消費者を関与させる。例えば，消費者はウェブサイトにレビューを書いたり，似たような関心を持つほかの人たちにソーシャルメディアを通じてお気に入りの商品を教えたりするよう促される。そうすることで，彼らは無料の広告を提供するのである。

　　　語句　optimization「最適化」

No.13 解答

　質問の訳　話者が「プッシュ型」マーケティングについて言っていることの1つは何か。
　選択肢の訳　1　特定のタイプの消費者をターゲットにする傾向がある。
　　　　　　2　ほかのタイプの広告より費用が安い。
　　　　　　3　近ごろは消費者に無視されることが多い。
　　　　　　4　テレビ広告や印刷物広告よりいい結果を出す。
　解説　前半でプッシュ型，後半でプル型が説明されている。プッシュ型は多くの人に届くようテレビや印刷物広告を用いる従来型のマーケティングで，お金がかかり，消費者から注目されなくなっているので利用する企業が減っている。consumers tend to take little notice を often ignored by consumers と言い換えた 3 が正解。

No.14 解答

　質問の訳　話者によると，「プル型」マーケティングに当てはまるのは何か。
　選択肢の訳　1　ソーシャルメディアサイトの利用を避ける。
　　　　　　2　消費者調査の結果に依存する。
　　　　　　3　ずっと長い広告キャンペーンを用いる。
　　　　　　4　既に欲しいと思っているものを探す人たちに依存する。
　解説　第1段落の最後で，今の消費者は「欲しい品物はオンラインで探し出す」と言っている。そうした傾向を利用するプル型の特徴を話者は2つ挙げ

ている。1つは，消費者が商品を検索するときに自社のサイトの表示を目立たせること。もう1つは，商品のレビューやSNSによる口コミを通じて，消費者に自発的に商品を宣伝してもらうこと。2つ目の特徴が4と一致する。

スクリプト **Cyrus the Great**

　Throughout much of history, the rise of civilizations and the spread of warfare have often proceeded hand in hand. One ancient ruler after another invaded his neighbors' lands, killed or enslaved the conquered peoples, and then forced his preferred religion and culture on those who remained. Following in this tradition, the ruler Cyrus the Great created an enormous empire by conquering several neighboring nations, including the powerful city of Babylon. However, it is said that Cyrus allowed people enslaved in those lands to return to their homelands and lifted various restrictions on religious practices.

　Although many scholars question the truth behind the stories of Cyrus, his policies inspired the writers of the US Constitution and other documents that emphasize individual human rights. Cyrus's famous declaration can be seen on an object known as the Cyrus Cylinder. According to one historian, the declaration is the first to say that when a society has people who use different languages and have different beliefs, it is not possible to impose one system on everyone. In addition, a statement by the United Nations says that Cyrus's empire was significant as a pioneering example of a multicultural, multifaith state.

Questions
No.15 What is one thing we learn about Cyrus the Great?
No.16 Why is the declaration on the Cyrus Cylinder important?

全文訳 **キュロス大王**

　歴史の多くを通じて，文明の台頭と戦争の拡大はしばしば密接にかかわり合いながら進行してきた。相次ぐ古代の支配者は，隣国の土地を侵略し，征服した民族を殺すか奴隷にし，そして，残された人々に自分が好む宗教と文化を強制した。この伝統に倣い，支配者キュロス大王は，強大な都市バビロンを含むいくつかの隣国を征服して巨大帝国を築いた。しかしキュロスは，そうした土地で奴隷となった人々が祖国に戻ることを許し，宗教的慣行に関するさまざまな制約を解除したと言われている。

　多くの学者はキュロスの物語に隠された真相に疑いを持っているものの，彼の政策は，米国憲法をはじめとする個人の人権を重視する文書の起草者に刺激を与えた。キュロスの有名な宣言が，キュロスの円筒として知られる物体に記されている。ある歴史家によると，この宣言は，異なる言語を使い異なる信仰を持つ人々がいる社会では全員に1つ

の制度を課すのは不可能だ、と初めて述べたものである。加えて、国際連合による声明は、キュロスの帝国は多文化・多宗教国家の先駆的事例として重要だったとしている。

語句 enslave「～を奴隷にする」，multifaith「多宗教の」

No.15 解答 ②

質問の訳 キュロス大王についてわかることの１つは何か。
選択肢の訳 1 神として崇拝されることを要求した。
2 奴隷だった人々を解放したと言われている。
3 自らの帝国をほかの支配者たちに分け与えた。
4 新しい宗教をつくったと言われている。

解説 冒頭で文明と戦争の関係，古代の支配者に関する一般論を述べた後，キュロス大王については，巨大帝国を築いたこと，そして However と続けて，it is said that Cyrus allowed people enslaved in those lands to return to their homelands と言っている。これを release を用いて短く言い換えた **2** が正解。

No.16 解答 ①

質問の訳 キュロスの円筒に記された宣言はなぜ重要なのか。
選択肢の訳 1 人権に関する近代の理念に影響を与えた。
2 古代の言語の翻訳を可能にした。
3 強大な帝国の没落につながった。
4 国際連合創設の契機となった。

解説 Cyrus Cylinder は第２段落中ほどに出てくるが，その前の his policies inspired the writers of the US Constitution and other documents that emphasize individual human rights がポイント。この his policies = declaration が Cyrus Cylinder に書かれているという話の流れを理解できれば，**1** が正解だとわかる。国際連合は声明でキュロスに言及しているだけなので **4** は誤り。

スクリプト **Doubting Science**

Surveys indicate that some Americans refuse to accept well-established scientific research. For example, there are people who do not believe in evolution or in the safety of vaccinations. These science skeptics exist at both ends of the political spectrum and at every socioeconomic level. In other words, such beliefs do not correspond to education or upbringing. However, there is one common factor that appears to unite the skeptics: they tend to place more faith in the beliefs of the people they associate with on a day-to-day basis than in conclusions arrived at by scientific methods.

According to geophysicist Marcia McNutt, the problem is a failure to grasp an important principle behind science. McNutt says people need to understand that science is not simply a collection of facts. Rather, it is fundamentally a method of inquiry — a way of determining whether a theory can be supported by experimental evidence. Results arrived at by this method sometimes challenge long-held beliefs and common sense, which makes those results hard to accept. However, when people refuse to get their children vaccinated, for example, human lives are at stake. Therefore, scientists need to make greater efforts to promote understanding and acceptance of how they work among the general public.

Questions

No.17 What is one thing that influences the beliefs of those who doubt science?

No.18 What is one thing Marcia McNutt says?

全文訳　科学を疑う

　一部のアメリカ人は確立した科学的研究を認めるのを拒むことを，意識調査が示している。例えば，進化やワクチン接種の安全性を信じない人たちがいる。これらの科学懐疑論者は，政治的スペクトルの両端に，そしてあらゆる社会経済的レベルに存在する。言い換えると，そうした信念は教育や育ちに対応しない。しかし，懐疑論者を結び付けるように見える共通の要素が1つある。彼らは，科学的手法によってたどり着いた結論よりも，日々付き合っている人たちの信念の方を信頼する傾向があるのだ。

　地球物理学者マーシャ・マクナットによると，問題は，科学を支える重要な原理を理解しないことである。科学が単に事実の集積ではないことを人は理解する必要がある，とマクナットは言う。むしろ科学は基本的に，問いかけの手法，つまり，理論が実験的証拠によって裏付けられ得るかどうかを決定する方法である。この手法によってたどり着いた結果は，長年信じられてきたことと常識に時に異を唱えるものであり，そうであればそうした結果を認めるのは難しくなる。しかし，例えば自分の子供へのワクチン接種を拒むなら，人の命が失われかねない。したがって科学者は，自分たちの仕事についての一般大衆の理解と受容を促進するよう，より努力する必要がある。

　語句　well-established「確立した，定着した」，vaccination「ワクチン接種」，skeptic「懐疑論者」，socioeconomic「社会経済的な」，upbringing「養育，しつけ」，geophysicist「地球物理学者」

No.17 解答　④

質問の訳　科学を疑う人たちの信念に影響を与えるものの1つは何か。

選択肢の訳
1　彼らの経済的地位。
2　彼らが持つ政治理念。
3　彼らの教育レベル。
4　周囲の人たちの意見。

解説 前半で，科学懐疑論者の共通項は，科学よりも the beliefs of the people they associate with on a day-to-day basis を信頼することだと言っている。**4** がこの部分を全体的に言い換えている。ほかの選択肢はすべて，科学を疑うこととは関係ないとされている。

No.18 解答 ②

質問の訳 マーシャ・マクナットが言っていることの1つは何か。
選択肢の訳
1 科学的実験を行うのが難しくなっている。
2 科学の仕組みを誤解する人たちがいる。
3 かつてないほど多くの子供がワクチン接種を受けている。
4 科学的研究は偏っていることがある。

解説 後半の According to geophysicist Marcia McNutt 以下によると，問題は「科学を支える重要な原理を理解しないこと」。続けてその原理とは何かが説明されているが，それを how science works と簡潔にまとめた **2** が正解である。

E

スクリプト **Oxidative Stress**

The retina is a layer of tissue at the back of the eye. It receives light and processes it into signals that are transmitted to the brain. The process requires oxygen, however, and can lead to an effect known as oxidative stress. This can damage cells and has been linked to a number of medical conditions, including cancer and blindness. The cells of the retina are especially vulnerable to oxidative stress, as a significant amount of oxygen is used in this tissue.

Researchers have discovered, however, that a compound found in raw coffee beans can prevent damage to the retina in mice. The effect primarily comes from chlorogenic acid, which protects cells. But in the experiment, the chlorogenic acid was injected directly into the retina, so it is not clear whether drinking it as a liquid would have the same effect. What is more, roasting coffee beans reduces the amount of chlorogenic acid they contain, so additional research is needed to see whether drinking brewed coffee can protect the retina from damage.

Questions
No.19 What is one thing we learn about oxidative stress?
No.20 What did the research show?

全文訳 **酸化ストレス**

網膜は目の後ろにある組織の層である。網膜は光を受容して信号に加工し，信号は脳に送られる。しかしこのプロセスには酸素が必要で，酸化ストレスという現象を起こすことがある。これは細胞に損傷を与えることもあり，がんと盲目を含むいくつかの疾患に関連があるとされてきた。網膜の組織では相当な量の酸素が使われるので，網膜の細

胞は特に酸化ストレスに弱い。

　しかし，生のコーヒー豆に含まれる化合物がマウスの網膜への損傷を防ぐことができると研究者が発見した。この効果は主にクロロゲン酸に由来するもので，クロロゲン酸は細胞を保護する。だが実験ではクロロゲン酸は直接網膜に注入されたので，液体として飲むことで同じ効果が得られるかどうかははっきりしない。さらに，コーヒー豆を焙煎すると含まれるクロロゲン酸の量が減るので，入れたコーヒーを飲むことで網膜を損傷から守れるかどうかがわかるには，追加の研究が必要である。

語句 oxidative「酸化（性）の」，retina「網膜」，chlorogenic acid「クロロゲン酸」

No.19 解答 ①

質問の訳 酸化ストレスについてわかることの1つは何か。

選択肢の訳
1 網膜に特によく見られる。
2 網膜が光を受容すると減る。
3 人の失明を防ぐのに役立つ。
4 脳で始まるプロセスである。

解説 oxidative stress がどんな現象なのかという説明はないが，細胞に損傷を与え，がんと盲目に関連し，網膜の細胞が特にやられやすいことが前半で述べられている。最後が**1**と合致する。

No.20 解答 ④

質問の訳 研究は何を明らかにしたか。

選択肢の訳
1 コーヒーは網膜の酸化ストレスを増やす。
2 クロロゲン酸はあるタイプの細胞に損傷を与えることがある。
3 コーヒーを飲むと網膜はより敏感になる。
4 クロロゲン酸は網膜を損傷から守ることができる。

解説 後半冒頭の a compound found in raw coffee beans can prevent damage to the retina in mice とそれに続く説明から，クロロゲン酸には網膜の損傷を防ぐ効果があることがわかる。液体として飲む場合の効果が不明，コーヒー豆を焙煎するとクロロゲン酸が減る，など今後研究すべき課題は残るが，クロロゲン酸の効果自体は否定されていないので，**4**が正解である。

一次試験・リスニング Part 3 問題編 p.133～134　MP3　アプリ　CD 3 18～23

F
スクリプト

You have 10 seconds to read the situation and Question No. 21.

I've checked your current usage, and you often exceed your allotted time by almost an hour. Adding the Plus Pack to your current plan will give you additional Internet data for just $10 more, but won't change your call time. As for new plans, the Value Extra Plan includes 120 minutes of call time, which is 60 minutes more than you have now, but your monthly allotted data would be cut a little. That one's $70 per month. There's also the Mega Mobile Plan, which includes 80 minutes of calls, but would give you twice as much Internet data as you have now. That's why it's a bit pricey at $100 per month. Finally, the Free Together Service costs $70 per month and allows unlimited calls to family members on our network — handy if you talk with them a lot.

Now mark your answer on your answer sheet.

全文訳

　現在のご利用状況を確認したところ，割り当て時間を1時間近く超過していることが多いです。現在のプランにプラスパックを追加すると，10ドル上乗せするだけでインターネットのデータが追加されますが，通話時間は変わりません。新しいプランですと，バリューエクストラプランには120分の通話時間が含まれ，今の通話時間より60分多いですが，月々の割り当てデータは少し減ることになります。これは月額70ドルです。メガモバイルプランというのもありまして，含まれる通話時間は80分ですが，インターネットデータは今の2倍になります。そういうわけで，月額100ドルと少々高くなっています。最後に，フリートゥゲザーサービスは料金が月額70ドルで，当社のネットワークでのご家族との通話は無制限になります——ご家族とたくさん話すのでしたらお得です。

No.21 解答 ②

状況の訳　あなたは料金を下げる話をするために携帯ショップに行く。現在は月額80ドル払っている。顧客にしばしば電話をかけるので，あなたには通話時間が最も重要である。

質問の訳　あなたはどのプランを選ぶべきか。

選択肢の訳
1 現在のプランに加えプラスパック。
2 バリューエクストラプラン。
3 メガモバイルプラン。
4 フリートゥゲザーサービス。

|語句| allot「~を割り当てる」

|解説| 通話時間が増えて料金が下がるプランは何かに注意して聞く。Plus Pack を追加しても通話時間は同じ。Value Extra Plan は通話時間が 2 倍になり，料金は 70 ドルに下がる。Mega Mobile Plan も通話時間が増えるが，料金は 100 ドルに上がる。Free Together Service は 70 ドルで料金は Value Extra Plan と同じだが，適用される無制限通話は家族限定なので，主に仕事で利用するあなたには不適。したがって Value Extra Plan を選ぶことになる。

G

|スクリプト|

You have 10 seconds to read the situation and Question No. 22.

Thank you, everyone. You have one more hour to set up your booth. If you haven't checked in yet, please do so at the welcome desk just inside the front entrance. At check-in, you'll receive your Welcome Pack containing nametags, booth number, event map, and lunch tickets. If you have any issues with reserved equipment at your booth, go to the information table on the west side of the hall and show the staff there your confirmation receipt. If you need additional electrical equipment, we have spare items available on a first-come, first-served basis. Please pay for these at the information table, then pick them up from the nearby inventory room. For other issues, the event organizer is available until lunchtime at the corporate services booth on the east side. Thank you, and we wish you a successful event.

Now mark your answer on your answer sheet.

|全文訳|

皆さま，ありがとうございます。ブースの設営時間は残り 1 時間です。まだ入場手続きを済ませていない方は，正面玄関を入った所のウェルカムデスクで手続きしてください。入場手続きの際に，名札とブースナンバーとイベントマップと昼食券が入ったウェルカムパックをお渡しします。ブースで予約した設備に何か問題があれば，ホール西側の案内カウンターに行って，支払い確認済の領収書をそこのスタッフに見せてください。電気設備が追加で必要な場合は，早い者勝ちでご利用いただける予備の品物があります。案内カウンターで支払いを済ませてから，近くの備品室で受け取ってください。ほかの問題については，イベントの主催者が東側の企業サービスブースでランチタイムまで待機しています。皆さまにとって実りあるイベントになることを願っています。ありがとうございました。

No.22 解答 ③

|状況の訳| あなたは会社を代表して就職説明会に出席する。既に入場手続きは済ませた。テーブル 2 つ分の料金を払ったが，ブースには 1 つしか見当たら

なかった。あなたは次のアナウンスを聞く。

質問の訳 あなたはまず何をすべきか。

選択肢の訳
1 備品室のスタッフと話す。
2 ウェルカムデスクで問い合わせる。
3 案内カウンターで領収書を提示する。
4 企業サービスブースに行く。

語句 nametag「名札」

解説 入場手続きは終わっているので，最初の If you haven't checked in yet に関する説明はあなたには関係ない。続く If you have any issues with reserved equipment at your booth が，テーブルが足りないという問題にかかわる。この場合は go to the information table ... and show ... your confirmation receipt と言っているので，**3** が正解。welcome desk と information table は別なので，混同しないように注意。

H

スクリプト

You have 10 seconds to read the situation and Question No. 23.

Thanks for your interest in volunteering. First, there's the Palz Program, where you can make a huge difference in a teenager's life. With the same teenager every week, you'd be doing on-campus activities or going to see movies or sports events together. Because building a strong bond takes time, this program requires a two-year commitment. Next, our LifeTrip Program volunteers take kids on weekend day-trips to parks and hiking trails. This can involve relatively heavy physical exercise but is fun if you're up for it. You could also become one of our Playground Associates. You'd supervise and participate in physical activities and games here at the center's play area on weekdays before school starts. If you can't make a weekly commitment, join our Handy Helpers. You'd come in one Monday a month to assist in the cafeteria, do small repairs, or help with cleaning.

Now mark your answer on your answer sheet.

全文訳

ボランティア活動に関心を持っていただき，ありがとうございます。まず，パルズ・プログラムというのがありまして，1人のティーンエージャーの生活に大きな変化をもたらすことができます。毎週同じティーンエージャーと一緒に，キャンパス内での活動をしたり，映画やスポーツイベントを見に行ったりします。強い絆を築くには時間がかかりますから，このプログラムには2年間取り組んでいただく必要があります。次に，ライフトリップ・プログラムのボランティアは，子供たちを公園とハイキングコースへの週末日帰り旅行に連れて行きます。これは比較的激しく体を動かす運動を伴うことも

ありますが，やる気がある人なら楽しいです。プレーグラウンド・アソシエーツの1人になることもできるでしょう。平日学校が始まる前に，ここ，センターの運動場で，体を動かす活動とゲームを監督し，自分も参加します。毎週取り組むことが無理なら，ハンディー・ヘルパーズに加わってください。月1回月曜日に来て，カフェテリアで手伝ったり，こまごました修理をしたり，掃除の手伝いをしたりすることになります。

No.23 解答 ②

状況の訳　あなたは1年間米国で勉強している。週末をボランティア活動に費やしたいので，ユースセンターでのオリエンテーションに参加する。あなたは体を動かす活動が好きである。

質問の訳　あなたはどのボランティアグループに加わるべきか。

選択肢の訳
1　パルズ・プログラム。
2　ライフトリップ・プログラム。
3　プレーグラウンド・アソシエーツ。
4　ハンディー・ヘルパーズ。

語句　on-campus「キャンパス内での」，up for ~「~に気が進んで」

解説　weekends と physical activities がポイントになる。Palz Program に運動はない。LifeTrip Program は take kids on weekend day-trips で involve relatively heavy physical exercise だから希望に合う。Playground Associates に運動はあるが on weekdays だと言っている。Handy Helpers も Monday なので外れる。したがって，条件に合うのは LifeTrip Program だけということになる。

スクリプト

You have 10 seconds to read the situation and Question No. 24.

Unfortunately, you don't have proof the apartment was damaged before you moved in. The rental agreement you originally signed didn't mention any problems. This means you're not in a strong position legally, so going to court is not really an option. You could ask the landlord to contact previous tenants, but this could take time, and it's very unlikely they would want to get involved. Another option is to try to fix the damage yourself, but you could easily make things worse, and then the landlord might demand more money from you. Getting quotes from local contractors to see if their repair charges are less than your deposit offers the best chance of walking away with some money. You could show the estimates to your landlord and ask him to refund the difference.

Now mark your answer on your answer sheet.

> 全文訳

　残念ながら，入居する前からアパートに傷があったという証拠をお持ちではありません。最初にサインなさった賃貸契約は，問題点には一切触れていませんでした。つまり，法的に強い立場ではないということですから，裁判に訴えるのはあまり選択肢にはなりません。以前の賃借人と連絡を取るよう家主に頼むこともできるでしょうが，時間がかかるかもしれませんし，かかわりたいと思う人がいないのは間違いないところです。別の選択肢は，ご自分で傷を補修してみることですが，おそらく事態をさらに悪化させてしまうでしょうし，そうなると家主はもっとお金を要求するかもしれません。地元の業者から見積もりを取って，その補修金額が敷金より安いかどうか見てみるのが，何がしかのお金を簡単に手に入れる一番の可能性と言えます。見積書を大家に見せて，差額を返金してほしいと頼めばいいでしょう。

No.24 解答 ④

> 状況の訳

あなたの大家は，あなたが引っ越して出て行くアパートに傷をつけたと主張している。彼は敷金を返すことを拒否している。賃借人情報局が次のことを告げる。

> 質問の訳

お金をいくらかでも返してもらうためにあなたはまず何をすべきか。

> 選択肢の訳

1　この件を裁判で争う。
2　自分で補修する。
3　以前の賃借人と直接話す。
4　プロに補修の見積もりを頼む。

> 語句

quote「見積もり」，walk away with ～「～を楽に手に入れる」

> 解説

話者は賃貸物件トラブルの専門家と考えられる。裁判で争うのは is not really an option と言っているので **1** は外れる。以前の賃借人は，大家経由で連絡を取れてもかかわり合いになるのは避けると思われるので **3** も外れる。自分で補修しても，傷を広げて請求額が増えるのが落ちなので **2** も外れる。業者の補修見積もりと敷金との差額を返してもらうのが現実的だと話者は助言しているので，**4** が正解となる。放送文の quotes がわからなくても，その後の話の流れと，estimates と言い直していることから意味を推測できる。

> スクリプト

You have 10 seconds to read the situation and Question No. 25.

　We'd be happy to have you all here for a tour of WTBT studios. We have several broadcasters who could make time for your students. Brad Quentin is the host of "Mornings Live," our daily morning news program. He's on the air from 6 to 8 a.m. and stays in the office until noon. Katie Ferris does our popular 10 a.m. political-interview segment. She's a great interviewer and obviously knows a lot about the subject. She sticks around until about 1 p.m. Valerie Ortiz is around from 3 p.m. She does our nightly news broadcast at 7 p.m., which is a roundup of the day's local and national stories. Station manager Lance Bridges is also available by advance appointment, as long as there's no urgent station business. He can offer your students insight into the day-to-day running of our station.

Now mark your answer on your answer sheet.

全文訳

　喜んで皆さんをWTBTのスタジオ見学にお招きしたいと思います。学生さんのために時間を作れそうなキャスターが何人かいます。ブラッド・クエンティンは当局で毎朝放送しているニュース番組「モーニングズ・ライブ」の司会者です。出演時間は午前6時から8時までで，正午までずっとオフィスにいます。ケイティー・フェリスは午前10時からの人気のある政治インタビューコーナーをやっています。素晴らしいインタビューアーで，言うまでもなくそのテーマに詳しいです。彼女は午後1時ごろまで待機しています。バレリー・オーティーズは午後3時からいます。彼女がやっているのは午後7時からの夜のニュース放送で，1日のローカルニュースと全国ニュースのまとめです。前もって予約していただければ，緊急の局の用事がない限り，局長のランス・ブリッジズも時間を取れます。彼は，当局の日々の運営を理解するための知識を学生さんにお教えできます。

No.25 解答 ③

状況の訳 あなたは大学でジャーナリズムを教えていて，学生をテレビのニュース番組の司会者に会わせたい。午後1時より前にはテレビ局を訪問できない。担当者が次のことを告げる。

質問の訳 あなたはどのキャスターと会う手配をすべきか。

選択肢の訳
1 ブラッド・クエンティン。
2 ケイティー・フェリス。
3 バレリー・オーティーズ。
4 ランス・ブリッジズ。

語句 stick around「帰らずにいる」，roundup「まとめ，総括」

解説 担当番組などに関する情報も話されるが，1 p.m. 以降という条件にポイントを絞って聞いていく。Brad Quentin は stays in the office until noon なので条件に合わない。Katie Ferris も sticks around until about 1 p.m. なので外れる。Valerie Ortiz は is around from 3 p.m. なので条件に合う。Lance Bridges も予約すれば available だが，制作畑の人であり，news host というもう1つの条件に合わない。したがって，Valerie Ortiz を選ぶことになる。

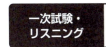 

> スクリプト

This is an interview with Nayalan Moodley, a filmmaker and photographer.

I (Interviewer): Hello, everybody! Today, we've got Nayalan in the studio. Welcome to the studio today.

NM (Nayalan Moodley): Thanks for inviting me.

I: So, could you briefly explain what you do?

NM: I am a freelance filmmaker and photographer. So, I basically do just that, I speak to whichever clients come my way, and I make movies or take photos for them.

I: Would you say there are any particular challenges of doing this kind of work, specifically in Japan?

NM: Japan isn't really a country that is friendly to the, the sort of lone wolf, the one-man-band producer. If you have a company name, it's a lot easier to find work. As an individual, many companies are reluctant to hire you. They rather work with another company, just because of the tradition of, "We're a company, we do business with companies." And so finding clients is actually really difficult. The sort of clients you find are either other individuals — and I've worked with rock stars, because they made a name for themselves the same way, they understand the hustle — and so finding sort of proper-paying work from regular clients is a bit of a challenge.

I: On the flip side, are there any benefits or advantages for working in Japan that you see more of here than elsewhere?

NM: Well, for me personally, I'm in Japan. I've gotten to travel the entire country through my work. I have been to everywhere except Hokkaido, through work, and I've been to some places in Japan that you wouldn't ordinarily go to, even if you were touring, you wouldn't go to some of these really small towns to try out some of these really local locations that many Japanese tourists know about but not many foreign tourists know about. But from a work standpoint, I'd say, the sort of look I can provide, the sort of — my attitude to filmmaking is sort of my own. And it's partially because I'm a foreigner and it's partially because of who I am and the sort of person I am. My clients who come back to me like my work, and for me, that's a really good thing, I like that. And they're doing it because they like my style and my look.

I: So, does that mean that you have complete flexibility and rein over your own work, or are you restricted in any way?

NM: It's really project dependent. My photography I am almost completely unrestricted. If I get a photography job, I have an outcome, but how I achieve that is completely up to me. With video, there are usually many moving parts, and coordinating between many other people. And you have other people in the production, sometimes you need other camera operators, sometimes you need to have a sound recording studio, etc. So, when there are other people involved, that also limits the amount of freedom I have, and very often your client does have the final say. And if you, you can be halfway through a project and if your client says, "Yeah, we really need to change this," and it's fully within the budget and the contract, then you say yes. And even if it isn't within the budget or the contract, you generally say yes. And you turn on a dime, and you have to change everything, but you do it.

I: Thanks so much, Nayalan, for talking to us. Good luck.

NM: Well, thank you for inviting me.

Questions

No.26 What is one thing Nayalan says about working in Japan?

No.27 What do we learn about the video projects Nayalan works on?

全文訳

これは映像作家で写真家であるナヤラン・ムードリーとのインタビューです。

聞き手（以下「聞」）：皆さん，こんにちは！　今日は，スタジオにナヤランに来てもらっています。本日はスタジオにようこそ。

ナヤラン・ムードリー（以下「ナ」）：呼んでいただきありがとうございます。

聞：さて，どんなお仕事をされているのか，簡単に説明していただけますか。

ナ：フリーランスの映像作家で写真家です。つまり，基本的に私がしているのは，偶然出会ったクライアント誰とでも話をして，彼らのために映画を撮ったり写真を撮影したりすることです。

聞：こうした仕事を特に日本ですることに，何かとりわけ難しい点はあるとお考えですか。

ナ：日本は，一匹狼，1人で活動するタイプの制作者に優しい国とは言えません。会社の名前を持っていれば，仕事を見つけるのはずっと簡単です。個人だと，多くの会社は雇いたがらないです。彼らは個人を雇うくらいなら別の会社と仕事をします。その理由は「自分たちは会社で，会社とビジネスをする」のが伝統だから，というだけのことです。なので，クライアントを見つけるのは，実際本当に難しいです。見つかるクライアントのタイプは，やはり個人でやっている人たちか——私はロックスターと仕事をしてきましたが，それは彼らも同じようにして名を成した人たちで，この悪戦苦闘を理解しているからですが——ですから，通常のクライアントからきちんと支払

いのあるような仕事を見つけるのはちょっと難題ですね。
聞：逆に，日本で仕事をすることの，ほかではあまり見ないような利点やメリットはあるでしょうか。
ナ：そうですね，私個人の話ですが，日本にいられることです。仕事を通して全国を回ることができました。北海道以外のあらゆる所に仕事で行きましたし，普通なら行かないような日本の土地にもいくつか行ったことがあります。旅行していたとしても，そうしたすごく小さい町のいくつかに行くことはないわけですよね，多くの日本人旅行者は知っているけれど外国人旅行者はあまり知らない，そうしたすごくローカルな土地のいくつかを実際に試してみようとはしません。ですが仕事という立場からだと，思うに，私が提供できるタイプの視点，映像制作に対する私の姿勢，そのタイプは，私ならではのものです。そしてそれは私が外国人だからでもあるし，私の人となり，私がどんなタイプの人間かということが理由でもあります。私のところに戻ってくるクライアントは私の作品を気に入っていて，私にとってそれはとてもいいことで，それがうれしいんです。それに彼らがそうするのは，私のスタイルと視点を気に入っているからです。
聞：すると，つまりあなたは完全に自由にすることができて，自分の作品を支配できるということなのでしょうか，それとも，何らかの形で制約はあるのでしょうか。
ナ：それは本当にプロジェクト次第です。写真撮影，これはほとんど完全に制約がありません。写真撮影の仕事を受ければ結果を出しますが，それをどのように成し遂げるかは完全に私次第です。動画については，たいてい動く部分がたくさんあって，ほかの大勢の人との調整があります。それに，制作にはほかの人たちもいて，ほかのカメラオペレーターが必要なこともあれば，音声録音スタジオを使う必要があることもあるなど，いろいろです。ですから，ほかの人たちがかかわっているときは，それは私が持っている自由の量を制限することでもあり，最終決定権はクライアントにあることが非常に多いです。そしてプロジェクトがやっと半分終わったところでクライアントが「うん，ここは変えなきゃならないな」と言ったとして，それが十分に予算内で契約内であれば，イエスと言うことになります。そしてそれが予算内でなかったり契約内でなかったりしたとしても，たいていイエスと言うわけです。そしてすぐさま方向転換して，全部変えなければならないけれどもやるんです。
聞：お話しいただきどうもありがとうございました，ナヤラン。がんばってください。
ナ：はい，呼んでいただきありがとうございました。

(語句) one-man-band「1人でやっている」, hustle「押し合い」, flip side「逆の面」, have the final say「最終決定権を持つ」, on a dime「すぐに」

No.26 解答 ①

質問の訳　日本で仕事をすることについてナヤランが言っていることの1つは何か。

259

選択肢の訳
1 彼が一緒に仕事をしてきたミュージシャンたちは，彼が直面する難題を理解している。
2 会社は1人で仕事をする人たちをしばしば都合よく利用する。
3 同じ仕事に対して，ミュージシャンはめったに会社と同じ金額を支払わない。
4 彼は日本人の好みに合うよう自分のスタイルを変えなければならなかった。

解説 ナヤランは3つ目の発言で，まず，日本は会社中心で動いているので，個人で働く人が仕事を見つけるのは難しいと指摘している。続いて，これまでのクライアントには，ロックスターなど自分と同じく個人で苦労している人が多く，彼らは the hustle を理解している，と言っている。話の流れから，この hustle は，会社中心社会の中で個人として働くことの大変さを指していると考えられるので，**1** が正解。**2** の take advantage of については述べていない。

No.27 解答

質問の訳 ナヤランが取り組む動画プロジェクトについて何がわかるか。

選択肢の訳
1 彼はたいてい自分が適切だと思うようにそれらを導くことができる。
2 ほかのクリエーターたちと働くとインスピレーションを得られるので，彼はその方が好きだ。
3 彼にはしばしばクライアントの要請を満たす以外の選択肢がない。
4 彼は予算内でそれらを完成させることを誇りにしている。

解説 ナヤランは5つ目の発言で，仕事で受ける制約について写真と動画を比較している。写真はほぼ制約がない。一方動画は集団作業なので自由が制限され，また，クライアントが途中で口を挟むことがある。クライアントからの変更要請についてナヤランは，予算と契約の範囲内ならイエスと言うが，範囲外であってもたいていイエスと言う，と話している。決定権を持つクライアントには逆らえず，**3** のように要請を満たす以外の選択肢はないと言っていることになる。**1** は写真についてなら該当すると考えられる。

二次試験・面接　トピックカード　**A** 日程　問題編 p.136

ここでは，A日程の5つのトピックをモデルスピーチとしました。

A日程

1. Should foreign policy be based on moral principles or national interest?

I believe that foreign policy should be based on moral principles. I'd like to tell you about my reasons for this opinion. First, acting on moral principles has long-term benefits. Japan has been donating money for foreign aid and supporting the United Nations for many years, and this has boosted our international reputation and helped our country to gain valuable allies. Nations need to cooperate because every country may, at one time or another, require assistance after natural disasters or other national crises. Furthermore, acting only in the national interest would likely cause problems domestically. Citizens today care greatly about issues like human rights. If their country's government is found to be supporting nations that violate these rights, it is likely to become less popular with voters. Finally, when thinking about foreign policy, it's important to remember that today's economy is globally interconnected. If every country acted only in its own interest, it would have serious economic consequences. For example, suppose the Japanese government imposes high tariffs on its rival countries' goods or stops providing foreign aid to developing countries. This would likely lead to an economic recession or seriously harm developing nations. Based on the three reasons I've given, I think it's clear that having a foreign policy based on moral principles is the best way to ensure a country's national interest.

解説　「外交政策は道徳的原則に則るべきか，それとも国家の利益に基づくべきか」

かなり高度な内容のトピックだ。ここでは典型的なイントロ＋3つの理由（①道徳的原則の長期的な価値，②国民の人権などへの関心の高まり，③経済的につながるグローバル世界）＋結論，の構成で，道徳的原則に則った外交政策が国益にもかなうとしている。理由の3つは内容が重複しないことが望ましいので，「3つの異なる視点」をまず決め，身近なものから外へ順番に広げていくと全体的にまとまりやすい。

2. Have modern societies become too focused on consumerism?

I strongly agree that modern societies have become too focused on consumerism, and I'd like to explain three of the reasons why I feel this way. Firstly, the most serious problem with consumerism is the harm it does to the environment. The production of large quantities of goods requires a lot of valuable resources and creates pollution. Also, modern consumers are constantly buying goods they don't need and throwing them away. These goods end up in landfills, which take up space, hurting the environment even more. Another serious problem is that people are losing sight of the important things in life. Many people are influenced by consumerism and feel the need to prioritize materialism over human relationships. As a result, they may become lonely or isolated in the long term. Finally, consumerism is having serious effects on people's health. Many companies market their products and services without considering the negative health effects they may have on consumers. In the case of fast food, huge numbers of people have become overweight or obese. On the other hand, in the area of health and fitness, many people are advised to use specialized products and services, but these are often ineffective or even counterproductive to the improvement of their health. Due to all the serious adverse effects that I've mentioned, I strongly feel that it's time for society to begin placing less emphasis on consumerism.

解説　「現代社会は消費主義に重点を置き過ぎるようになったか」

トピックを全面的に肯定する論調だ。消費主義のネガティブな面を，①環境破壊，②人間の精神への影響，③健康への影響，と3つの異なる視点から明確に説明している。精神面や身体面への影響は必ずしも常に真実とは限らないという認識から，they may become lonely ... / effects they may have ... のように助動詞を工夫して断定表現にせず，「事実」と「可能性」「推測」などを分けているのも印象がよい。

3. Should international child adoption be more strictly regulated?

I agree that international child adoption should be more strictly regulated. Here are the reasons that support my position. The first thing I'd like to mention is that it's essential to ensure that adopted children are going to live in a safe environment where they can receive all the love, education, and material things that are necessary for them to grow into healthy, happy adults. Without strict regulations, we can't be sure children won't be abused or neglected when they are adopted by parents in another country. Another serious issue is that there can be cultural gaps between children and their new parents. There should be regulations to ensure people who adopt older children get the necessary training so that they can be familiar with the children's culture. It's difficult for children to adapt to a new society, so parents need to do everything they can to help them. Another well-known problem, which is often broadcast in the media, is that there have been corrupt organizations paying parents who live in poverty to give up their children. More effective laws and strict monitoring are needed to ensure that this type of thing never happens again. So, in conclusion, although international adoption can be a wonderful thing for both parents and adopted children, it needs to be more strictly regulated to protect children's health and well-being.

> **解説**　「国際的養子縁組はより厳しく規制されるべきか」
> 国内での養子縁組自体も比較的少ない日本人にとってはハードルの高いトピックだ。だからこそ，このスピーチから国際養子縁組の持つ問題を学ぼう。ここでは「養子縁組された子供がきちんとした環境を与えられることを保証するべき」「養子縁組した親と養子がお互いの異なる文化背景を理解できるような研修システムを準備するべき」「養子縁組の目的が貧困家庭の搾取ではないことを確認するべき」といった非常に具体的な理由が挙げられている。The first thing, Another serious issue, Another well-known problem という理由の列挙の仕方も参考になる。

4. Agree or disagree: The work ethic of Japanese people has changed in recent years

I believe that the work ethic of Japanese people has changed in recent years. There are three main reasons for my opinion. Firstly, now that Japan is one of the world's largest economies, I think that people have realized we don't need to work as hard anymore. After World War II, Japan was poor, so people needed to make a considerable effort to catch up with other countries, but now we want to enjoy our prosperity. The second thing I'd like to discuss is work-life balance. There have been a lot of media stories about the harmful effects of overworking on people's physical and mental health lately, and they've made people realize that it's not a good idea to work unnecessarily long hours. These days, people understand that it's more important to have time for their families, friends, and themselves. Finally, there have been changes in government policy that have affected people's work ethic. The government has made various rules, such as limiting the number of overtime hours a person can perform per month, and they have helped to change workers' attitudes. I think that all these bottom-up and top-down changes are slowly altering people's attitudes and encouraging people to have a better work-life balance.

> **解説**　「賛成か反対か：日本人の労働倫理は近年変わった」
> 命題に対して賛成の立場で解答している。①日本が経済大国になった，②長時間労働の負の面がメディアなどによって周知された，③政府の規

制が人々の労働への考え方を変えた，という3点を理由としている。サポートが重複しないためと，複数の理由を具体的に引き出すために視点を変えるのは効果的だ。ここでは，①歴史的視点，②社会通念的視点，③政治的視点，の3つを組み合わせている。理由やサポートが思い付かないとき，視点を動かしてみよう。一般的にこのほかにも「一個人としての視点」「知人，友人の視点」「地域社会の視点」「国際社会の視点」「親の視点」「子供の視点」などがある。

5. Is capital punishment an effective deterrent to crime?

I don't believe capital punishment is an effective deterrent to crime. Let me tell you why. First, when it comes to the young people who commit serious crimes, the death penalty doesn't seem to be able to prevent them from doing so. Science has shown that young people's brains don't finish developing until about the age of 25, which may explain why young criminals have been capable of some of the most horrific murders. Since they might not yet be capable of thinking things through and controlling themselves, the death penalty is not an ideal solution. Second, a large percentage of murders are committed by people who suffer from severe mental illnesses. Many mass shootings in the United States, for example, have been carried out by mentally ill individuals. Such people are often incapable of thinking about the full consequences of their actions, so instead of the threat of a penalty, they need to be taken care of by their families or social services. Finally, it's clear from the situation in the world today that the death penalty does not stop crime. Countries like the United States have been using executions for hundreds of years. Still, they often have much higher rates of serious crimes than countries that do not use the death penalty, so it is hard to argue that executions are an effective deterrent. For these reasons, I disagree that capital punishment is an effective crime deterrent.

解説　「死刑は犯罪の効果的な抑止になるか」

とても重いトピックだが，1級ではよく出題されるので，一度考えをまとめてスピーチ練習をしておこう。ここでは，①若者による重犯罪と脳の発達の関係，②精神障害を持つ人による犯罪，③アメリカで抑止効果になっていない例，を挙げている。①と②は「死刑が抑止になりにくい特定の犯罪者」という視点では重複する部分もあるが，豊富な情報量と異なった結論付けでカバーしている。ほかに，現在の法律では実際の死刑執行までかなり長い年月を要することなども理由として考えられる。

2019-3

一次試験
筆記解答・解説　p.266〜284

一次試験
リスニング解答・解説　p.285〜312

二次試験
面接解答・解説　p.313〜316

解答一覧

一次試験・筆記

1
(1)	3	(10)	1	(19)	1
(2)	4	(11)	4	(20)	2
(3)	1	(12)	4	(21)	3
(4)	2	(13)	1	(22)	3
(5)	4	(14)	2	(23)	2
(6)	2	(15)	3	(24)	1
(7)	2	(16)	1	(25)	4
(8)	3	(17)	3		
(9)	4	(18)	4		

2
(26)	3	(29)	4	
(27)	3	(30)	4	
(28)	2	(31)	2	

3
(32)	2	(35)	2	(38)	4
(33)	4	(36)	1	(39)	2
(34)	4	(37)	4	(40)	1
				(41)	4

4　解答例は本文参照

一次試験・リスニング

Part 1
No. 1	3	No. 5	2	No. 9	3
No. 2	4	No. 6	4	No.10	2
No. 3	1	No. 7	3		
No. 4	4	No. 8	2		

Part 2
No.11	3	No.15	1	No.19	1
No.12	1	No.16	3	No.20	2
No.13	4	No.17	2		
No.14	4	No.18	4		

Part 3
No.21	2	No.23	4	No.25	2
No.22	4	No.24	3		

Part 4　No.26　1　｜　No.27　2

一次試験・筆記 問題編 p.138〜140

(1) ― 解答 **3**

訳　ベスがその課題を与えられたとき，克服できない任務のように思えた。だが自分でも驚いたことに，彼女は時間どおりに終わらせた。

語句　**1**「資格のない」　**2**「生命のない」　**3**「克服できない」　**4**「酔っ払った」

解説　時間どおりに終わらせたことに驚いたのだから，その課題は非常に難しいものだったことになる。insurmountable は，動詞 surmount「〜を克服する」に可能の接尾辞 -able と否定の接頭辞 in- が付いた語。

(2) ― 解答 **4**

訳　A：昨日の経済学の講義は理解できた？
　　B：いや，まったくわけがわからなかった。先生が外国語をしゃべっているみたいだったよ！

語句　**1**「綱でつながれた」　**2**「せっけんで泡立てた」　**3**「少しずつ削られた」　**4**「当惑させられた」

解説　外国語に聞こえたということは，内容を理解できなかったことを意味する。baffle は「〜をまごつかせる，当惑させる」で，confuse より意味が強い。

(3) ― 解答 **1**

訳　トレバーの病気は重いものだが，若くて疾患が早期に見つかったので，回復に関する予後は良好だ。

語句　**1**「予後」　**2**「威圧」　**3**「絶頂」　**4**「段階，等級」

解説　病状に関して医師が下す判断を diagnosis「診断」，病気がどのような経過をたどるかという見通しを prognosis「予後」と言う。

(4) ― 解答 **2**

訳　イーストフォード大学はかつて全国の学校の中で最上位の階層にいた。しかし，今ではごく普通だと見なされている。

語句　**1**「斉唱」　**2**「階層，階級」　**3**「典型，模範」　**4**「ツンドラ」

解説　空所には「ランク，レベル」に類する語が入ると推測できる。echelon は「（組織などの）階層，階級」という意味。類義語 tier も覚えておきたい。

(5) ― 解答 **4**

訳　その小説は書評家たちから酷評され，1人の書評家は，著者には文学の才能が完全に欠けているとまで言った。

語句　**1**「柔軟性に富む」　**2**「大胆な」　**3**「感情をあらわにした」　**4**「欠いている」

解説　be devoid of 〜 は「〜がない，〜を欠いている」という意味。de のな

い void も be void of ～ で同じ意味だが，多品詞・多義語の void と違い，devoid の用法はこのフレーズに限られる。

(6) ― 解答 ②

訳 先週，仕入部の社員の1人がリベートを受け取ったとして首になった。商品の質が低い供給業者に部品を注文してお金をもらっていたのだ。

語句 1「背景」　2「リベート」　3「短所」　4「抜け穴」

解説 英語の rebate は，払い過ぎた場合などに戻ってくる「還付金，払戻金」の意味。日本語の「リベート，賄賂」に相当する一般的な英語は kickback である。bribe は特に役人や政治家に渡す金品を指すことが多い。

(7) ― 解答 ②

訳 マーガレットは牛乳を入れたボウルで猫をおびき寄せて木から下ろそうとしたが，猫は動こうとしなかった。

語句 1「～を放り投げる」　　　2「～をなだめて…させる」
3「～に塗り付ける」　　　4「～をすっと動かす」

解説 persuade「～を説得する」の類義語はいろいろあるが，coax は優しく粘り強く説得するというニュアンス。ほかに，cajole はおだてたり甘言で釣ったりして説得するという意味合いである。

(8) ― 解答 ③

訳 販売員はそのスポーツカーの長所を長々と褒めそやしたが，客の方は，高い価格に見合う価値がその車にあると確信できなかった。

語句 1「～を記した」　　　2「～をとりこにした」
3「～を激賞した」　　4「～を要約した」

解説 客を前にした販売員が商品の長所についてすることだから，「説明する」「褒める」といった語が空所に入るはず。extol は praise の強意語。

(9) ― 解答 ④

訳 A：カナダでの妹の結婚式に行くための休暇願いを上司に拒否されたよ。
B：ティムに頼んで助けてもらうといい。彼は上司にかなりの影響力を持っている。彼ならきっと許可をもらってくれるんじゃないかな。

語句 1「仲間，同僚」　2「衝突」　3「空洞」　4「権力，影響力」

解説 ティムは上司を翻意させられる何らかの力を持つと考えられる。clout は power, influence の口語的な語で，政治やビジネスの場面で使われることが多い。

(10) ― 解答 ①

訳 自社のソフトウエアのまったく新しいバージョンを突然発売して顧客を混乱させるのを回避するため，その会社は2年間にわたる漸進的な変更を導入した。

語句 1「だんだん増える」　　2「挿入句の」
3「非常に裕福な」　　　4「回復力のある」

解説 会社は２年かけて少しずつソフトを変更したのだと考えられる。incremental は名詞 increment「増加（量），増大」の形容詞。increment は increase と同じ語源を持つ。

(11)－解答 ❹

訳 アマンダは企画の提出期限を変えてもらおうとしたが，上役は考えを変えようとしなかった。「締め切り厳守だ」と彼は言った。

語句 1「～と競争する」　　　　2「いやらしい目つきで見る」
3「～の隅々に広がる」　　　4「譲歩する」

解説 budge は問題文のように「譲歩しない，考えを変えない」という否定の文脈で使われることが多い動詞。not budge an inch「一歩も譲らない」というイディオムもある。

(12)－解答 ❹

訳 重罪で起訴されているにもかかわらず，被告は無表情のまま審理をずっと人ごとのように眺めていた。彼女の感情の欠如に多くの人が動揺した。

語句 1「悲しそうに」　　　　　2「とても優美に」
3「名目上は」　　　　　　4「無表情で」

解説 passively に否定の接頭辞 im- が付いた語と考えると，「無表情で」という意味は出てこない。impassive ＝ expressionless と単純に覚えておくのがよい。

(13)－解答 ❶

訳 休暇後，男性は旅行代理店に手紙を書き，無礼なホテルスタッフから粗末な食事に至るあらゆることに関する苦情を延々と並べ立てた。

語句 1「くどい説明」　　　　　2「放棄，棄権」
3「憂鬱」　　　　　　　　4「送金（額）」

解説 litany of ～ は「～を延々と述べたもの，くどくどと書き連ねたもの」という意味。of の後の名詞は，問題文の complaints のようにネガティブな内容が普通である。

(14)－解答 ❷

訳 ディランは失業して意気消沈した。だが２，３週間すると，より前向きな気持ちを持つようになり，職探しを始めようと決心した。

語句 1「扱いにくい」　　　　　2「落胆した」
3「身構えて」　　　　　　4「度量の大きい」

解説 逆接の副詞 though の後に前向きになったという内容が続くので，失業直後は落胆したのだと考えられる。despondent の類義語は dejected, dispirited, downcast など。

(15)－解答 ❸

訳 バスの運転手が突然急ブレーキをかけたとき，乗客全員が前によろめいた。幸い重傷者はいなかった。

語句　1「~を待ち伏せて急襲した」　2「~を厳しく叱った」
　　　3「よろめいた」　　　　　　4「怒鳴った」
解説　lurch は体の安定を失って「よろめく，よろける」こと。問題文の forward のように，方向や程度を表す副詞または副詞句を伴う。

(16) – 解答 ①

訳　歯科医は処置を始める前に，麻酔が効くまで待った。患者に一切痛みを感じてほしくなかったのだ。

語句　1「麻酔剤」　　　　　　　2「報酬，報奨」
　　　3「難儀，悩みの種」　　　4「(実業界の) 有力者」

解説　痛みを感じないようにするのは anesthetic「麻酔剤」である。第 1 文の the work は，患者の歯に対する直接の治療行為を指す。

(17) – 解答 ③

訳　よい作家は，心を揺さぶる物語を創作する才能を持つことが多い。彼らは選び抜かれたわずかな言葉で私たちの涙を誘うことができる。

語句　1「だまされやすい」　　　2「気難しい」
　　　3「感動的な」　　　　　　4「曖昧な」

解説　読者を泣かせる物語は，poignant「心を揺り動かす，感動的な」ものである。poignant は発音に注意。

(18) – 解答 ④

訳　エバは，子供たちをコンサートに連れて行き楽器を買い与えることによって，子供たちの音楽への関心をかき立てたいと願っていた。

語句　1「~を追い出す」　　　　2「~をいら立たせる」
　　　3「~をはねつける」　　　4「(関心など) をそそる」

解説　動詞 pique には「~を立腹させる，~の感情を害する」のほかに，pique a person's interest [curiosity]「(人) の関心 [好奇心] をかき立てる」という意味がある。

(19) – 解答 ①

訳　ジョナサンの仕事への態度は尊大だ。しばしば遅刻して出社するし，締め切りはめったに守らないし，決して上役に敬意を払わない。

語句　1「尊大な，横柄な」　　　2「人を魅了する」
　　　3「敬意を表する」　　　　4「つぼを心得た，利口な」

解説　大文字で始まる名詞 Cavalier は 17 世紀イングランドの「王党派の人」の意味だが，形容詞 cavalier はまったく違う意味なので注意が必要。

(20) – 解答 ②

訳　A：ビル，悪いけど，例の 100 ドルはやっぱり貸せない。
　　B：ええー！　今さら約束を破っちゃ駄目だよ。そのお金は家賃を払うのに必要なんだ。

語句　1「~をなだめる」　　　　2「(約束などを) 破る」

3「〜を困らせる」　　　　　　4「〜をなだめる」

解説 that $100 の that から，貸し借りに関する合意が既にあることがわかる。renege on 〜 で「(約束など) を破る，(合意など) に背く」という意味。

(21) —**解答** 3

訳 テントのロープが1本緩んでいたので，ぴんとなるようにポーラはテントのペグを動かした。

語句 1「牧歌的な」　　　　　　2「死去した」
3「緩んだ」　　　　　　　　4「もっともらしい」

解説 peg はテントのロープを地面に固定する道具。それを移動させてロープをぴんと張ったのだから，ロープは slack「緩んだ」状態だったことになる。

(22) —**解答** 3

訳 A：クリスマス休暇の間に何をするか決めた？
B：まだだけど，パリにいる兄を訪ねるのはどうかと検討しているところ。

語句 1「〜を得ようと画策している」　2「(罰など) を与えている」
3「〜をじっくり考えている」　4「〜を台無しにしている」

解説 mull over は「〜をじっくり考える，〜について熟考する」という意味。問題文のように，何かを決断する前によく考える，という場面で使われることが多い。

(23) —**解答** 2

訳 ブレンダは外国に住みたいとずっと思っていたので，会社がイスタンブールに支社を開設すると発表すると，直ちに異動を願い出た。

語句 1「〜と対戦した」　　　　　2「〜に応募した」
3「〜をどっさり買い込んだ」　4「(人) が汚した後を片付けた」

解説 put in for 〜 は「〜を (正式に) 申し込む，〜に応募する」という意味。イスタンブール支社に転勤したい，と正式に申し入れたことになる。

(24) —**解答** 1

訳 レジーには将来の野心的な計画などない。来る日来る日を楽しんで，惰性で生きていられれば幸せだ。

語句 1「気楽に行動する」　　　　2「忍び込む」
3「束になる」　　　　　　　4「質問を始める，話を始める」

解説 動詞 coast は，「(自転車・自動車などが) 惰力で進む」が原義。それが比喩的に用いられて，「(大して努力せずに) 楽々と成功する」または「だらだら過ごす」という意味になる。句動詞 coast along は後者と同じ。

(25) —**解答** 4

訳 テストでカンニングをしたことを白状しなければその生徒は停学だ，と校長は言った。カンニングを認めた後，彼は反省文を書かされた。

語句　1「(結局〜に) 終わる」　2「〜をしっかりとくぎで留める」
　　　3「目的もなく動き回る」　4「白状する」

解説　own up to 〜 は「(悪事・過ちなど) を潔く白状する，認める」という意味。to の後には名詞または動名詞が来る。

一次試験・筆記 2　問題編 p.140〜143

全文訳　**古代の労働力**

　多くの考古学者はエジプトの砂漠の下にミイラと金色に輝く財宝を探し求めるが，一方マーク・レーナーは，もっと俗なテーマの調査を追求している。ピラミッドを建設した労働者の生活というテーマである。レーナーの研究はきらびやかではないが，彼の考古学的発見物は，自身の言葉によると「ピラミッドがエジプトの建設にいかに役立ったか」を明らかにし始めている，と彼は主張する。長いキャリアの間にレーナーがした諸発見は，大規模な建設プロジェクトに要した数千人の労働者に食事を与え，組織化し，宿泊施設を提供するという総合的な事業管理の解明に手がかりを与えている。ピラミッドの近隣で労働者を住まわせた失われた都市を，彼は1つではなく2つ発掘した。この事業の壮大なスケールは国家的統一の発展に不可欠だった，とレーナーは論じる。なぜなら，この事業は巨大な王国の全域からやって来た労働者をまとめ上げ，それが，レーナーが特筆するように，事実上「これらのまったく異なる地域すべてを結び付けて……1つの全体にした」からである。

　レーナーの研究成果は，ピラミッド建設は奴隷労働力を用いて実行されたという通説と矛盾する。そもそもこの考えはギリシャの歴史家ヘロドトスの著作に由来するもので，ヘロドトスは，ピラミッドの完成後何世紀もたってから，自著『歴史』でこの主張を行った。しかし，レーナーが発掘した調理施設と作業員が収容された大規模な仮設住宅からは，食肉用に殺された牛の証拠と多数の宗教碑文が見つかっている。これらが示すのは，ピラミッドに取り組んだ建設作業員はむちで脅されて労働を強制されていたのではなく，むしろ，最高級牛肉のごちそうと，永遠の来世を手に入れる公算が大きくなることに動機付けられていたということである。

　熟練した主要労働力が常勤だった一方，肉体労働者の輪番制も利用された。奉仕は義務だったが，期間は一時的だったようで，これらの労働者は強い社会的義務感を持っていたことだろう。この考え方をレーナーは次のように説明する。「人々は，われわれが当然だと考えている政治的自由と経済的自由を持つアトム化したばらばらな個人ではなかった」。エジプトの階層制文明では，一人一人の個人が別の誰かに奉仕を提供する義務を持っていた——王国で最もエリートの官吏ですらそうだった。レーナーの研究が進むにつれ，エジプトのファラオはこれまで想像されていたよりずっと複雑で結束した文明を統率していたという証拠が蓄積されつつある。

語句　mummy「ミイラ」，mundane「日常の，ありきたりの」，logistics

「事業の詳細な計画・遂行」，unearth「～を発掘する」，vicinity「近隣，近辺」，epic「大規模の，壮大な」，undertaking「仕事，任務」，disparate「本質的に異なる」，barrack「仮設住宅」，inscription「碑文，銘」，afterlife「来世」，rotating「輪番の」，atomize「～を原子に分ける」，hierarchical「階級制の」，pharaoh「ファラオ」，cohesive「結合力のある」

(26) – 解答 ③

解説 第1段落後半には，労働者がピラミッド建設のために各地から集まることによって国家の統一が進んだというレーナーの主張が書かれている。つまり，レーナーの発見は，エジプトという統一国家の建設にピラミッドが果たした役割を明らかにするもの，ということになる。

(27) – 解答 ③

解説 空所前の common belief に該当する箇所を探すと，第2段落最終文の being forced to labor under the threat of whips がレーナーとは逆の考え，つまりヘロドトス以来の通説だとわかる。③の slave labor がこの部分に対応している。

(28) – 解答 ②

解説 空所後の this attitude とはどのようなものか。引用部からは，古代エジプトが自由を重んじる現代の個人主義社会とは違うことがわかる。次の文は，誰もが誰かに奉仕する義務を持つという社会システムを述べている。つまり，人々は強い社会的義務感に従ってピラミッド建設に奉仕した，と考えると文脈に合う。atomized は，共同体よりも個人が社会の基本単位として優先される状況を言う。

全文訳 **言語の多様性**

　人類は驚くほどの言語的多様性を示し，記録されている言語は今日7,500以上存在している。しかし，世界への言語の広がりになぜこれほどばらつきがあるのか，研究者は昔から頭を悩ませてきた。例えば，南太平洋の国パプアニューギニアが占める陸地面積は地球の0.5％以下なのに，この惑星の言語の約10％が用いられている。ロシアは，その広大さ――地球の陸地面積の何と11％を占めている――にもかかわらず，この惑星の言語の1.5％が用いられているだけである。最近，オーストラリア国立大学の生物学者シャ・ホアが行った地球規模の分析が，孤立と生態学的リスクという2つの有力な説を検証し，この現象を理解する糸口を与えている。

　ホアは，孤立説は彼女のデータからは十分に裏付けられないと結論する。川などの景観的特徴は昔から障壁と見なされ，その結果生じる孤立が，さまざまな集団間の言語の違いを生むと考えられていた。ホアの研究は，川の存在と地域における言語の数には確かに直接の関連があることを確認した。しかし，さらなる分析によって，川が多様性に寄与したのは，より人口の少ない集団の生存を川が容易にしたからにすぎないことが示

された。川は「人の交わりの障壁というよりも，生態学的資源として働くように思える」とホアは書いている。

　生態学的リスク仮説は，気候，資源の入手可能性などの要因が言語の多様性を決定する最も重要な要素だとするもので，ホアは，地域の気候条件が厳しいほど話される言語の数が少ない結果になることを発見した。言語の多様性は緯度と強い相関関係があり，赤道地域でははるかに多くの言語が話され，北方および南方地域では少ないことを彼女の研究は示した。絶えず暖かい気温と豊富な降雨量を誇る赤道付近の地域では，植物の生育シーズンがずっと長い。したがって，それほど協力が必要とされないと考えるのが理にかなっているように思える。そのため，自立したより小さな文化集団間での多種多様な言語の発達が可能になった。対照的に，冬が寒く不毛な地域では，遠く隔たった人々の集団間の情報交換が資源の獲得と生産力の最大化に不可欠となったので，異質な言語の発達は好まれなかった。生態学的リスク仮説は，世界中で観察される緯度による言語の多様性のパターンによって裏付けられている。

　語句　immensity「広大さ」，whopping「途方もなく大きい」，predominant「優勢な」，determiner「決定するもの」，correlate to ～「～と互いに関係がある」，equatorial「赤道の」，plentiful「豊富な」，barren「不毛の」，disparate「本質的に異なる」，latitudinal「緯度の」

(29) — 解答　4
　解説　空所後では，国土が狭いのに多数の言語を抱えるパプアニューギニアと，広大なのに言語の数が少ないロシアの例が挙げられている。つまり，言語の数は面積に比例せず，unevenly「不均等に」分布していることになる。

(30) — 解答　4
　解説　空所後の1文が孤立説の説明，それ以降がホアの研究結果の記述になっている。川が障壁となって，孤立した集団がそれぞれ異なる言語を発達させた，というのが孤立説。一方ホアは，川の存在と言語の数に相関関係があることは認めながらも，川はむしろ集団を守る役割を果たしていたという異論を唱える。つまり，ホアは孤立説を立証する証拠を見つけられなかったことになる。

(31) — 解答　2
　解説　この段落では，赤道付近の地域と赤道から遠い地域が対比されている。第6文の後者についての記述を見ると，寒く不毛な地域では情報交換が必須で，そのため諸集団の言語は類似したと書かれている。一方，前者の特色を述べる第3文の growing seasons are much longer は，これらの地域が農耕に適していることを示している。そうした自足した地域では後者ほど情報交換，すなわち協力関係が必要とされず，したがって多様な言語が発達した，というのがホアの考えである。

273

一次試験・筆記 3 　問題編 p.143～152

全文訳　ピノチェト治下のチリ

　1970年のチリ大統領選挙戦で，有権者は，鉱業の国有化と土地と所得の再配分という社会主義的綱領を掲げて出馬したマルクス主義者サルバドール・アジェンデを選んだ。わずか3年後，アウグスト・ピノチェト将軍率いるチリ軍部がアジェンデを打倒し，軍事独裁を敷いた。ピノチェトと支持者たちは，前政権は国を内戦寸前に導いたと確信していた。アジェンデは合法的に選ばれたのだが，彼の社会主義政府の政策と行動は国民の間に混乱を招いて商業を脅かし，国を分断する埋められない溝を作った。これらの分断は，政治的対抗手段としてチリへの援助を徹底的に削減した米国政府と，銅などの貴重な鉱物に利権を持つ外国企業によって助長された。いずれにせよ，ピノチェトのクーデターは1930年代にさかのぼるチリの民主制を終わらせ，国の歴史に類を見ない弾圧と残虐の時代の到来を告げた。ピノチェトは野党を禁止し，憲法を停止し，政治的異論を厳しく取り締まった。彼の政権は10万人以上の国民を逮捕させ，数万人を拷問し，およそ3千人の「国家の敵」を殺害した。多くのチリ人にとって，続く17年間は恐怖と弾圧の悪夢の時代だった。

　権力の奪取に続き，ピノチェトは米国で教育を受けたチリ人経済学者の一団を登用したが，アジェンデの国有化と中央集権的計画立案とはまったく対照的に，彼らは徹底的な自由市場経済政策を導入し，金融部門内における多数の失業と破産を招いた。賃金は下がり，福祉支出はばっさり削られ，社会の最下層に最も強い打撃を与えた。それでも，1982年の経済危機以降，チリのGDPは，ラテンアメリカ最速の平均5.9%という着実な率で伸び始めた。アジェンデ政府によって資産を没収された外国企業が再び招かれ，国有企業は民営化されたが，外貨の圧倒的な稼ぎ頭である銅産業は変わらず国の直接管理下に置かれた。輸出部門は繁栄し，貧困レベルは1984年の50%から1989年の34%に下落した。これらの業績はピノチェトの功績だとする世界の指導者もいたが，この国の豊富な鉱物資源が果たした決定的な役割を過小評価するわけにはいかない。

　独裁の後半期に，ピノチェトの強固な支配はやや緩やかになった。1980年の新憲法は国民投票への道を開き，国民は彼の支配の継続に関してアップ・オア・ダウン投票をすることができた。ピノチェトは，自らの経済的成功が権力の座の維持を可能にしてくれるという希望を持っていたが，1988年にチリ人は，賛成56%，反対44%の投票結果で民主制の復活を選んだ。1990年に辞職したピノチェトは，それにもかかわらず軍隊の指揮権を保持し，上院の終身議席の権利を要求した。彼が据えた経済的基盤を続く各政権が発展させた結果，チリは繁栄を続け，この国はラテンアメリカの成功者だと広く考えられている。だが，投資主導の好況が全般的な生活水準を向上させることになったのは，独裁の束縛が解かれてからにすぎない。彼はキューバ型の共産主義国になることから国を救ったと支持者が考える一方で，多くのチリ人にとって，ピノチェト治下で耐え忍んだ抑圧の前には，彼の経済的成功はいつまでもかすんでしまうことだろう。

語句 redistribute「~を再分配する」, dictatorship「独裁（政権）」, legitimately「合法的に」, turmoil「騒動，混乱」, unbridgeable「（溝が）埋められない」, drastically「徹底的に」, coup d'état「クーデター」, usher in ~「~の到来を告げる」, repression「抑圧」, brutality「残忍，野蛮」, unparalleled「前代未聞の」, crack down on ~「~を厳しく取り締まる」, dissent「不賛成，異議」, nationalization「国有化」, slash「~を大幅に削減する」, state-owned「国有の」, privatize「~を民営化する」, plebiscite「国民投票」, up-or-down vote「アップ・オア・ダウン投票（賛否のみを問う直接投票）」, shackle「束縛，拘束」, mold「タイプ，型」, overshadow「~を見劣りさせる」

(32) – 解答 ②

問題文の訳 この文章の筆者は第1段落で暗に何と言っているか。

選択肢の訳
1 サルバドール・アジェンデの政府は民主的に選ばれたのかという疑いが，政府の政治的目標に関する疑念を招いた。
2 アジェンデの排除は，チリの社会的安定と財政的安定を脅かしていた政治的決定を覆すために必要だと考えられた。
3 アウグスト・ピノチェトは，アジェンデを権力から排除しようと企てれば米国が支援してくれると誤って考えていた。
4 米国に親近感を持つ軍事指導者たちは，アジェンデを排除すれば米国人がチリの鉱物資源を管理できるようになると期待していた。

解説 Allende had been legitimately elected とあるので 1 は誤り。米国は支援を減らすことで既に反アジェンデ勢力を支援していたのだから，3 は mistakenly が誤り。4 に関する記述はない。第4文の caused turmoil among the people and threatened commerce を were threatening Chile's social and financial stability と言い換えた 2 が正解である。

(33) – 解答 ④

問題文の訳 ピノチェト政権の経済的業績に関してどのような結論を導くことができるか。

選択肢の訳
1 ピノチェトは自身の政策がアジェンデの政策より成功したと主張したが，実際は，長期的には多くの政策の成果は同じようなものだった。
2 業績のよくない金融企業に廃業を強制することが，1980年代初期に景気の回復を可能にした重要要因だった。
3 チリ経済の成長にもかかわらず，チリが鉱物資源に過度に依存していたため，外国はチリに投資したがらなかった。
4 政府が銅産業の管理を維持していなかったら，ピノチェトの経済政策は実際成功したほどは成功しなかったかもしれない。

解説 当初は失敗したピノチェトの経済政策だが，1982年以降チリ経済は大

きな成長を遂げた。それには，最大の外貨獲得源である銅産業を国の管理下に置き続けたことが大きく貢献した。第2段落最終文の mineral wealth は銅資源を指している。この事情を仮定法を用いてまとめた **4** が正解。

(34) — 解答 ④

問題文の訳 この文章の筆者は，何がチリの民主制への復帰に当てはまると考えているか。

選択肢の訳
1 国民投票の結果に構わず政府内の地位を維持するとピノチェトが言い張ったことが，最終的に，彼が権力を失う結果を招いた。
2 反ピノチェトに投票したにもかかわらず，チリ人の大半は，彼が権力の座にとどまることができれば経済の長期的改善の可能性が高くなるだろうと考えていた。
3 国の繁栄の拡大は，ピノチェトが確実に軍を掌握し続け政治的影響力を保つことで初めて可能になった。
4 ピノチェトは経済的繁栄の基礎を築いたが，政治的自由がなければ大きな経済成長は可能ではなかっただろう。

解説 第3段落後半に，民主制移行後のチリの経済的繁栄についての記述がある。Yet で始まる第6文がポイントで，独裁が終わって初めて広く行き渡る経済成長が可能になったという内容である。**4** の後半がそれを without political freedom という表現を用いて述べている。**4** の前半は第5文の the economic foundations he had put in place に対応している。

全文訳 **サイコパスの肯定的側面**

サイコパス（精神病質者）——ついでだが，ほとんどの場合男性である——は，人口のおよそ1％を占める。サイコパスを他と隔てるのは，他人の感情に共感する力を持たないことである。自己中心的で，うわべは魅力的で，人を説得するのがうまい彼らは，自分が必要と見なすどんな手段でも用いて，冷たい超然とした態度で目的を追求する。さらに，彼らは自分の行動が社会に与える結果をほとんど顧慮しない。精神病質の殺人者というハリウッドの通俗的な捉え方によって強化されるように，こうした特性は，額面どおりに受け取るなら非常に危険で有害に思えるだろう。しかし，「成功したサイコパス」という概念が昔から存在している。1940年代に，アメリカの心理学者ハービー・M・クレックリーはこの一見矛盾と思える点を明快に説明し，多くのサイコパスは社会の内部で正当な役割を果たすことを可能にするうわべの正常さを装うことができると仮定した。

2012年の著書『サイコパス 秘められた能力』で，心理学者ケビン・ダットンはクレックリーの論文をさらに押し進めた。ダットンは次のように主張し論争を呼んだ。ある特定の職業とプレッシャーのかかる状況においては，サイコパスの属性は彼らが正常

に役目を果たす助けとなるのみならず，彼らを秀でた地位に据える。感情面での超然さと恐れを知らないことが，ビジネス界での出世を助け，兵役においては名声をもたらす。ダットンは，一方の端に凶暴な犯罪者，他方の端にエリート軍人とCEOがいる幅広い精神病質があると仮定する。決定的な相違は，サイコパスが自らの特異な人格特性をどのように使う選択をするかだが，これらの特性はどれも「それ自体が本質的に悪い」のではなく，「柔軟性を欠いて有効活用されると」有害なのだ，と彼は言う。換言すると，サイコパスが自分の非情さをあまりに強く，あるいはあまりに不適切に適用すると，非情さが冷酷さに変容するのである。サイコパスは自分の行動を加減できるのだろうか。ダットンはできると考えている。「鍵は，特性の正しい組み合わせを，正しいレベルと正しい文脈で持つことだ」。彼は，サイコパスの貢献は長期的というより短期的な傾向があると考えるが，重要な地位を占めている少数のサイコパスは社会全般にとって純益に当たると結論付ける。

　『良心をもたない人たち』の著者である心理学者マーサ・スタウトは，精神病質の危険に対して人々の注意を喚起することに取り組んでおり，ダットンの主張に異を唱える。彼女は多くの度合いの精神病質が存在するという彼の考えに反論し，いわゆる穏やかなサイコパスはナルシシスト——エゴイストで共感力が欠如しているが，「それでもなお自分なりに愛することができる」人たち——と捉える方が正確だろうと指摘する。良心を持たないことがサイコパスのサイコパスたるゆえんであり，したがって，彼らは人を気遣ったり，彼らに備わっているとダットンが楽観的に考える「知恵」を示したりすることはできない。また，ダットンが主張の基盤にしている根拠はあやふやだとスタウトは考える。「彼が引用する科学の大半が，よく言っても曖昧，悪く言えばまったく誤解を与える関係を彼の論文と有している」と彼女は書いている。最近の諸研究による証拠は，スタウトの立場を支持している。研究者の調査結果によると，魅力があるにもかかわらず，経営陣の地位にあるサイコパスは，従業員間のいじめ，争い，福利の欠如によって損なわれる非生産的で混沌とした労働環境をしばしばつくり出す。さらに，デンバー大学が行ったヘッジファンドマネージャーの調査では，精神病質の傾向を持つファンドマネージャーが上げる収益は時間がたつと低くなることがわかった。そうした傾向は権力を手にする際には有効かもしれないが，いざその権威を建設的に用いる段になると，サイコパスは力不足に思える。

　　　語句　psychopath「サイコパス，精神病質者」, empathize with ~「～に共感する」, detachment「超然」, postulate「～と仮定する」, veneer「見せかけ，うわべ」, normalcy「正常」, high-pressure「重圧のかかる」, fearlessness「恐れを知らないこと」, posit「～を事実と仮定する」, psychopathy「精神病質」, detrimental「有害な」, deploy「～を有効に使う」, inflexibly「柔軟性を欠いて」, ruthlessness「非情，冷酷」, callousness「無感覚，無情」, modulate「～を調節する，加減する」, alert A to B「AをBに対して警戒させる」, empathy「感情移入，共感」, ascribe A to B「A（性質など）をBに属すると考える」,

equivocal「紛らわしい,曖昧な」,downright「まったく,徹底的に」,counterproductive「逆効果を生じる」,mar「〜を損なう」

(35) – 解答 ②

問題文の訳　「成功したサイコパス」に関するハービー・M・クレックリーの立場を最もよく特徴付けるのは何か。

選択肢の訳
1　ほとんどのサイコパスは男性なので,社会の性的偏見の結果,彼らが有する危険で好ましくない特性は見逃されるか許されることになる。
2　多数のサイコパスは世間通例の予想に適応でき,したがって,見たところ社会の通常の成員としての役割を務めることができる。
3　精神病質を犯罪性と結び付けて考える大衆の傾向に疑義が呈されるまで,サイコパスの治療における長期的進展はあり得ない。
4　サイコパスが自分の病気について感じる否定的感情に対処することが,彼らが他者と建設的にかかわり合うのを助けるための第一歩だ。

解説　第1段落最終文によると,クレックリーは,社会にとって危険とも思える特性を持ちながら成功したサイコパスもいるという矛盾を,彼らは正常さを装って真っ当な社会生活を営むことができるからだ,と説明した。それに対応するのは **2** である。選択肢の conventional expectations は,普通の人ならこう考えこう行動するだろうという社会通念のこと。なお,第1段落第5文は,ハリウッドが一連の映画でサイコパス＝殺人鬼という通俗的イメージを増幅させてきた事情を説明している。

(36) – 解答 ①

問題文の訳　ケビン・ダットンは,サイコパスには社会で果たすべき役割があるという自身の説をどのように正当化しているか。

選択肢の訳
1　正しく,適切な割合で適用されれば,彼らを定義する特徴は,彼らが同等の人たちより優れた成果を上げることができるように利用され得る。
2　彼らが得る短期的な成果は,普通の人々が仕事に就いている期間に得る小さく着実な利得よりも有益で広範囲にわたる。
3　社会に害を与える活動を行うサイコパスより,特定の属性に助けられて職業の頂点に上り詰めるサイコパスの数の方が多い。
4　根っからの悪人などいないのだから,サイコパスの行動がたとえ極端であっても,社会がそれを変える必要はない。

解説　第2段落全体がダットン説の記述になっている。犯罪者になるサイコパスと卓越した功績を上げるサイコパスの違いは,第7文と第8文にあるように,行動を調節して特性を適切に生かせるかどうかにある,というのがダットンの考え。**1** がそれを Applied correctly and in the proper proportions とまとめている。**3** のように両者の数を比較する記述はない。

(37) − 解答 ④

問題文の訳 この文章の筆者はダットンの主張について何を示唆しているか。

選択肢の訳
1 精神病質的行動の犠牲者と直接作業した経験がダットンにはないので，彼の主張はマーサ・スタウトの主張より説得力がない。
2 ダットンは証拠とデータを故意に変えたと思われるので，彼の主張が信頼できるとは考えられない。
3 ダットンの論文には欠陥があるものの，サイコパスは短期間しか職場でうまく職務を果たせない傾向がある，と考える点で彼は正しい。
4 経営陣の地位にあるサイコパスがたいてい長期的にはマイナスの全般的結果を生むことを考えると，ダットンの論文はおそらく間違っている。

解説 第3段落には，スタウトによるダットン批判とスタウトを支持する最近の研究結果が書かれている。サイコパスについて否定的な最終文から，筆者はダットン批判に同調していると考えられる。サイコパスの経営者が職場をめちゃくちゃにし（第7文）収益も下がる（第8文）ことを negative overall outcomes とまとめた **4** が正解。

全文訳 CRISPR 遺伝子編集

　1860年代のグレゴール・メンデルによる遺伝の原理の発見は，科学者が動植物の遺伝子を操作する道を開いた。しかし，遺伝子操作の初期には，突然変異誘発，すなわち遺伝子の変化の割合を選抜育種によって直接制御することはできなかったので，結果は予測できないことが多く，何世代もの試行錯誤を要した。放射線処理と化学処理を用いるといった後の進展は突然変異誘発の加速に成功したが，育種と同じ行き当たりばったりの結果を生むだけだった。

　外来 DNA の挿入による生物のゲノムの直接操作が1970年代についに可能になったが，開発された最初の技術はゲノムの特定の場所を標的にするのには適さなかった。人工タンパク質の合成により特定の遺伝子を標的にすることが現実になったときですら，デリバリーシステムを個々の遺伝子一つ一つに適合させるには入念で時間のかかるプロセスが必要だった。これは，この技術の応用可能性を極度に制限した。

　2012年にようやく科学者は一般に CRISPR（クリスパー）と称されるテクノロジーを開発したが，これは，遺伝子を操作する優れた技法として途方もない可能性を持っている。CRISPR は「クラスター化され規則的に間隔を置いた短い回文反復」の略である。本来 CRISPR は細菌がウイルスから自衛するために用いるもので，ウイルスの DNA の断片を保存することができる細菌の DNA 内部における DNA の構成要素，すなわちヌクレオチドの反復配列から成っている。細菌がウイルスに攻撃されその駆除に成功すると，細菌はそのウイルスの DNA を集める酵素を放出する。すると酵素はその DNA をさらに小さな部分に切断し，将来攻撃を受けた場合に使う照会先として細菌の CRISPR の間に保存する。細菌が同じウイルスに再度攻撃されると，以前敗北したウ

イルスから保存された DNA が分子にコピーされ，すると分子は捕食酵素がウイルスのゲノムの特定の場所まで進んでいくのを支援する。それからその酵素はウイルスの DNA の一部分を切り落とし，そうしてウイルスを無害化する。

　特定の DNA 配列を変えて遺伝物質を除去したり加えたり変えたりすることのできる自然のメカニズムが前から存在していたことの発見は，遺伝学者にとって思わぬ幸運となった。それ以来の年月で，科学者は CRISPR をだまして非ウイルス性 DNA を探し切断させる方法を編み出しただけでなく，所望の DNA 配列をその CRISPR の間の空間に挿入し，DNA が自然に持つ，切断された箇所を修繕する細胞修復機構を利用する方法も編み出した。CRISPR は，どんな生物の DNA のどんな断片でも標的とし，除去したり取り換えたりするのに利用することができる。加えて，CRISPR は自己完結型かつ自己決定型なので，以前の技術が何週間あるいは何カ月もかけて成し遂げたことを，数時間で，微々たる費用で達成することができる。

　数多くの産業が CRISPR に関心を寄せているが，直接の受益者は医療部門と農業部門である。このテクノロジーは，遺伝子の欠陥に由来する病気をなくす可能性だけでなく，有用な遺伝子の役割を拡大することによって，もしかすると医学を一変させる可能性ももたらす。がん性腫瘍と闘うよう免疫細胞に指図することや，移植可能な人間の臓器をブタの中で育てることを想像してみるといい——これは，研究者が楽観しているプロジェクトを2つ挙げただけである。農業科学者は，害虫と病気に抵抗力のある作物を作り出すことや，栄養が詰まった新品種の作物を開発するといった，長年抱いている目標の達成を思い描いている。CRISPR はとても正確に DNA を編集し，標的となる生物に外来遺伝子を包含させることなく遺伝子編集を可能にするので，遺伝子組み換え産物と結び付く遺伝子汚染の不安を鎮めることができ，CRISPR で作り出した作物は，遺伝子組み換え作物がさらされる批判と適用を受ける厳しい規制を回避できる，と農業部門の賛同者は考えている。

　遺伝の原理は，個々の遺伝子が有性生殖の間に次世代に受け継がれる可能性を 50% と予測する。理論上は，CRISPR はその確率を 100% 近くまで上げることができ，そうなれば科学者は，所望の変化をもたらすために，組み換えた遺伝子を種全体に広く行き渡らせる力を得るだろう。科学者は，人類最悪の災いを，遺伝子操作で絶滅させること——あるいは災いを広げる種を絶滅させること——によって撲滅するため，遺伝のルールを変更することを思い描いている。意図せざる結果を招く可能性があるにもかかわらず，このテクノロジーを用いて，マラリアとライム病と外来種は既に撲滅の標的とされている。

　しかし，そうした意図せざる結果が，CRISPR 遺伝子編集は特効薬などではないと批判者たちが言う1つの理由である。例えばマラリアをなくすために地上のすべてのハマダラカを殺すことの連鎖反応は，ほぼ間違いなく，誰も予想できないほど大きい。さらに，DNA の切断が起きるだろうと科学者が予期した以外の場所で CRISPR が DNA 配列を標的とした実例が，研究室の実験で起きている。加えて，CRISPR が編集した細胞ががんを誘発し得ることが，最近の研究で明らかになっている。現時点では，

CRISPR がどのように機能するのか,そして CRISPR による遺伝子の変化の継承が続く世代にどのような影響を与えるのかを巡るリスクと不確実さは極めて大きく,慎重なアプローチを取るしかない。

> 語句 mutagenesis「突然変異誘発」, selective breeding「選抜育種(人為的な品種改良)」, synthesis「合成」, delivery「デリバリー(外来 DNA を宿主細胞まで運ぶこと)」, cluster「~をクラスター化する(関連する機能を持つ遺伝子をひと固まりにすること)」, interspace「~の間に空間を置く」, palindromic「回文の」, nucleotide「ヌクレオチド」, predatory「捕食性の」, preexisting「前から存在する」, godsend「思いがけない幸運」, geneticist「遺伝学者」, non-viral「非ウイルスの」, cellular「細胞の」, self-contained「一式完備した,自足の」, self-directed「自分で決定する」, transplantable「移植可能な」, envision「~を思い描く」, long-cherished「昔から心に抱いている」, allay「(恐れなど)を鎮める」, circumvent「~を回避する」, sexual reproduction「有性生殖」, effect「~をもたらす」, Lyme disease「ライム病(ダニが媒介する感染症)」, unintended「意図的でない」, magic bullet「妙案,特効薬」, knock-on effect「連鎖反応」

(38) – 解答

問題文の訳 CRISPR 以前の遺伝子操作について当てはまるのは何か。

選択肢の訳
1 DNA を生物に挿入することが可能になって初めて,突然変異誘発は広く実用化され得るほど十分に加速された。
2 所望の遺伝子の変化は達成されるかもしれなかったが,数世代のうちに変化は逆転することを科学者は発見した。
3 放射線処理と化学処理は正確に変化を起こすことを可能にしたが,育種によって遺伝子を操作するのとせいぜい同じ速さだとわかった。
4 科学者が利用できた技術は,正確さを欠いているか,効率的なやり方で応用できないかのどちらかだった。

解説 CRISPR 以前の遺伝子操作は,結果が予測できず行き当たりばったり(第1段落)で,技術が発達しても個々の遺伝子に適応するのは難しかった(第2段落)。それに合致するのは **4** である。放射線処理と化学処理が正確に変化を起こすことを可能にしたとは書かれていないので **3** は誤り。**1** と **2** に関する記述はない。

(39) – 解答

問題文の訳 細菌の中で,CRISPR の間に保存された DNA は,

選択肢の訳
1 攻撃するウイルスの活動によって変えられた健康な DNA を酵素が誤って攻撃する原因となる。
2 ウイルスの DNA を切り離す力を持つ酵素を導く分子で用いられる。
3 健康な DNA を含む分子がウイルスに感染した酵素を確実に修復でき

281

るよう助ける。
4 酵素を，その細菌の DNA を含む分子を保存するのに理想的な空間に作り変えることができる。

解説 第3段落が CRISPR の仕組みを詳述している。第5文に，問題文に対応する store it (= the virus's DNA) between the bacterium's CRISPRs という箇所がある。以降の記述によると，再び攻撃された細菌は保存したウイルスの DNA を分子にコピーし，それを手がかりに酵素がウイルスの同じ部分を探し出して切り落とす。**2** がそれを，本文の assist ... in navigating を guide と，chops を cutting apart と言い換えてまとめている。

(40) — 解答 **1**

問題文の訳 農業界の人々は，CRISPR で遺伝子編集を行うことの主要なメリットは何だと考えているか。

選択肢の訳
1 外来の生物の遺伝子を挿入するリスクを冒すことなく，作物の遺伝子組み換えをすることができる。
2 適切な規制がひとたび実行されれば，CRISPR を用いた農作物の遺伝子編集は利用しやすくなり，効率的になる。
3 有害な生物の遺伝子を作物に移すことによって，作物に病気と虫に関係する被害に対する免疫を持たせることが可能になる。
4 CRISPR によって，科学者は，ブタなどの家畜の病気に対する免疫力を高め，それによって薬への依存を減らすことができるかもしれない。

解説 第5段落後半に，農業関係者が CRISPR に寄せる期待が書かれている。外来遺伝子を用いなくても DNA を編集できるので，通常の遺伝子組み換え作物が受ける批判や規制をかわすことができる。本文の instead of including alien genes in the target organism を without taking the risk of inserting genes from foreign organisms into them と言い換えた **1** が正解である。

(41) — 解答 **4**

問題文の訳 CRISPR を扱う際に慎重さを求める人たちもいる1つの理由は，

選択肢の訳
1 CRISPR の使用にはかなりの欠点があることが農業への応用の研究で明らかになっているので，がんの治療法になり得ると CRISPR を宣伝するのは誇張だ，ということである。
2 CRISPR は短期的にはメリットがあるものの，CRISPR が生物に引き起こす遺伝子の変化は長期的には受け継がれないかもしれない，ということである。
3 マラリアのような病気の根絶を1つだけのテクノロジーを用いて達成できると考えるのは非現実的だ，ということである。
4 種の DNA 編集の潜在的影響すべてを科学者が予知するには，

282

CRISPRの機能の仕方について科学者が持つ知識はあまりに限られている，ということである。

解説 CRISPRに対する批判的考えは最終段落に記述されている。1つの種を根絶したときの連鎖反応は予測を超えている，実験で想定外のことが起きている，がんの原因になり得る，といった例を挙げて，最終文で，CRISPRはリスクと不確実さが大き過ぎるので慎重なアプローチを取るしかない，とまとめている。これに合致するのは **4** である。

一次試験・筆記 4　問題編 p.152

解答例

Our reliance on finite resources is doing tremendous environmental harm, and I believe our desperation to find alternatives will result in renewable energy sources replacing fossil fuels. Moreover, the rapid advancement of technology and falling costs will ensure this happens in the not-too-distant future.

First, the greater focus on environmental issues like climate change has led to a shift in general sentiment regarding fossil fuels. This is where renewable energy sources can shine. The ability to generate energy from nature with minimal damage to it is attractive to an increasingly environmentally conscious population.

Additionally, the recent focus on renewable energies like solar and wind can be seen in cutting-edge technologies. Whereas these energy sources were once considered supplementary to fossil fuels, increased efficiency means they are now providing a genuine alternative. Solar panels, for example, have more than doubled in efficiency over the last half century and continue to be improved.

Finally, increasingly affordable prices are helping to foster wider adoption. As technology is refined, cost is reduced, which benefits consumers. For instance, many newly built houses now come with solar panels, allowing people to generate clean energy for themselves at a lower cost.

There is no doubt that renewable energy sources are the way forward. It is only a matter of time before so-called alternative energy becomes the norm, leading to a cleaner, safer future.

トピックの訳「再生可能エネルギー源は化石燃料に取って代わり得るか」

解説　再生可能エネルギー・化石燃料などのエネルギー問題は，一次試験英作文と二次試験面接では時事問題系トピックの定番であり，質問の表現を変えながら何度も出題されている。二酸化炭素排出削減などを目指す国際会議の話題はメディアで大きく取り上げられ，再生エネルギーに対する各国の取り組みが紹介されることも多い。こうしたニュースに普段から英語で接し，最新の知見を得ておくことが望ましい。

解答例は，環境問題を第1の理由，テクノロジーの発達とそれに伴うコスト低下を第2，第3の理由として冒頭の段落で挙げ，トピックに対してYesの立場を明らかにしている。再生可能エネルギー推進が世界的な潮流であるのは確かだが，あえてNoの立場から立論するとすれば，自然に左右される再生可能エネルギーは不安定なので化石燃料の需要はなくならない，再生可能エネルギーに投資する資金のない発展途上国では化石燃料が主要なエネルギー源であり続ける，二酸化炭素排出を抑えるクリーンな化石燃料利用技術の開発が期待される，といった理由が考えられる。また第3の道として，原子力への依存度を高めるエネルギー構成を提案することも可能だろう。

解答例の内容を見てみよう。1つ目の理由である環境問題については，気候変動などへの危機感から化石燃料への見方が変化し，再生可能エネルギーがより注目されるようになっている，という現状認識を述べている。2つ目の理由であるテクノロジーの発達では，過去50年で太陽光パネルの効率が2倍以上になったという例を挙げ，再生可能エネルギーが補助的な役割から主役へと移行しつつある状況を短くまとめている。最後の理由としてコスト低下を挙げ，太陽光パネルを備えた家が増えているという例とともに，再生可能エネルギーの一般への広がりを述べている。解答例が技術面の理由を2つ挙げているのは，トピックがCan ~? と可能性を問うているからである。これがWill ~? という問いであれば，化石燃料は将来枯渇するので再生可能エネルギー以外に代わるものはない，再生可能エネルギーは資源を巡る争いを減らすので世界平和にも貢献する，など違う視点から理由を考えることになる。トピックの質問形式に留意し，適切な理由を選ぶことも重要なポイントである。

解答例の構成は，序論，本論（3段落），結論の5段落で，本論はFirst, Additionally, Finallyで始めている。奇をてらった構成にする必要はなく，このように基本に忠実で，わかりやすく理由を提示する書き方を常に心がけるようにしたい。また，lead toばかりでなくresult inも使う，for exampleを使ったら次はfor instanceにするといった，表現のバリエーションにも注目したい。

一次試験・リスニング Part 1

問題編 p.153〜154

No.1 - 解答 3

スクリプト
☆: The election's a week away, honey, and I'm still undecided.
★: Well, both candidates are strong, but I'm voting for Jacobs.
☆: Jacobs has definitely been around a while.
★: Yeah, he has a long track record of achievements.
☆: Still, I'm impressed with Potter, even though she's young.
★: Quite frankly, I don't think she's ready to take on so much responsibility.
☆: Maybe, but her idealism is refreshing. We could use a change.
★: I agree that Potter would shake things up, but in politics, that's not always a good idea.

Question: What does the man say about the election?

全文訳
☆: 選挙まであと1週間だけど、まだ決めかねているの。
★: うーん、どちらの候補者も強力だけど、僕はジェイコブズに投票するよ。
☆: 確かにジェイコブズはしばらく前から活躍しているよね。
★: うん、彼にはいろんなことを成し遂げてきた実績がある。
☆: それでも、ポッターは若いけど、私は彼女にとてもいい印象を持っているの。
★: 率直に言って、そんな大きな責任を引き受ける準備が彼女にできているとは思えない。
☆: そうかもしれないけど、彼女の理想主義は清新だわ。私たちには変化が必要よ。
★: ポッターなら変革を起こすだろうという点では同意するけど、政治では、それは必ずしもいい考えではないよ。

質問: 男性は選挙について何と言っているか。

選択肢の訳
1 まだ選択肢を検討している。
2 女性の選択と同意見である。
3 経験のある候補者の方がいいと思っている。
4 今が新しい人の出番だと思っている。

解説 男性は実績のあるジェイコブズ支持だが、女性は理想主義を唱えるポッターに傾いている。変革がいいとは限らないと最後の発言で述べているように、男性のジェイコブズ支持は一貫している。男性の2つ目の発言の a long track record of achievements を experience とまとめた **3** が正解。

No.2 — 解答 ④

スクリプト
☆: Mark, I think it's time to fix that dent in the rear bumper.
★: But, honey, it's not even that noticeable.
☆: It looks awful! Anyway, our insurance will pay for the repairs.
★: True, but then our insurance premiums will go up.
☆: How do you know that?
★: That's what the company told me when I called to ask about it. I was responsible for the damage, remember? I backed into that parked car.
☆: Oh, that's right.

Question: Why is the man reluctant to fix the car?

全文訳
☆: マーク，そろそろ後ろのバンパーのあのへこみを修理したらどうなの。
★: だけどさ，そんなに目立つということもないよね。
☆: ひどいわよ！ いずれにせよ，修理には保険が下りるんだから。
★: それはそうだけど，そうすると保険料が上がるんだよ。
☆: どうしてわかるの？
★: この件について聞こうと電話したら，保険会社にそう言われたんだ。傷は僕の責任だったんだから。覚えてるよね。僕がバックしてあの駐車中の車にぶつけたんだよ。
☆: ああ，確かにそうね。

質問：なぜ男性は車を修理したがらないのか。

選択肢の訳
1 費用の件で妻が腹を立てると思っている。
2 事故は自分の責任ではなかったと思っている。
3 保険が修理をカバーしない。
4 保険料が上がる。

解説 男性の2つ目の発言の our insurance premiums will go up を言い換えた **4** が正解。女性が2つ目の発言で our insurance will pay for the repairs と言っているので，**3** は誤り。

No.3 — 解答 ①

スクリプト
☆: I hope you enjoyed your stay at our resort, Mr. Barker.
★: I sure did. My wife and I are thinking of returning in October. If we stayed for an entire week, would it be possible to get a better deal on our room rate?
☆: October is not our peak season, so it's probably not out of the question. Let me talk to the manager, and I'll get back to you before your airport limousine arrives.
★: Thanks, I'd appreciate anything you could do.

Question: What does the woman imply?

全文訳 ☆：当リゾートでのご滞在を楽しんでいただけたのならよかったのですが，バーカーさま。
★：もちろん楽しみましたよ。妻と私は，10月にまた来ようと思っています。丸1週間滞在するとしたら，部屋をもっとお得な料金にしていただくことは可能でしょうか。
☆：10月はピークシーズンではありませんから，たぶん問題なくそうできるでしょう。支配人と話させていただければ，空港のリムジンバスが到着する前に返事を持ってまいります。
★：ありがとう，どんなことでもしていただけるとありがたいです。
質問：女性は暗に何と言っているか。

選択肢の訳　1　値下げが可能かもしれない。
　　　　　　2　今日中には返答できない。
　　　　　　3　滞在が長いほど早い予約が必要になる。
　　　　　　4　10月はかなり忙しい時期だ。

解説　男性の最初の発言の get a better deal on our room rate は，宿泊料金を安くしてもらうこと。それに対して女性は，たぶん out of the question「不可能」ではない，と答えているのだから，支配人次第で値下げが可能ということになる。

No.4 - 解答 ④

スクリプト ★：How was the negotiating seminar you went to last month?
☆：I learned so much. Wish I hadn't wasted so many years trying to learn this stuff on my own. The trainers really knew what they were doing.
★：Have you had a chance to put your new skills into practice yet?
☆：As a matter of fact, I just closed a deal with a big electronics manufacturer. The stuff I learned at the seminar made a big difference.

Question: What does the woman imply?

全文訳 ★：先月行った交渉術セミナーはどうだった？
☆：すごく勉強になった。こうしたことを独力で学ぼうとして何年も無駄にするんじゃなかったわ。トレーナーたちは自分の分野にすごく精通していた。
★：新しいスキルを実践してみる機会はもうあった？
☆：実はね，ちょうど大手電子機器メーカーと契約を結んだところなの。セミナーで学んだことがあったから，大違いだった。
質問：女性は暗に何と言っているか。

選択肢の訳　1　出席したセミナーは時間の無駄だった。
　　　　　　2　その商取引をまとめることができなかった。

3　その電子機器会社は価格交渉をしない。
　　4　交渉能力が最近向上した。

解説　セミナーで多くのことを学んだと話す女性は，最後の発言で，大手メーカーと契約を結んだが The stuff I learned at the seminar made a big difference. と述べている。つまり，セミナーに参加して向上した交渉能力を早速発揮できたことになる。

No.5 - 解答 ②

スクリプト
☆：How's your studying going, Terry? Are you ready for the Spanish test?
★：It's tough, Kate. I'm really making an effort to get through the vocabulary list, but nothing seems to stick.
☆：It's not easy to memorize so many words, is it?
★：That's one way of putting it. I guess all I can do is keep at it.
☆：You might want to change your focus. Mr. Sharpe said the grammar section is worth more points.
★：Really? Maybe that's the way to go, then.
Question: What does the woman imply?

全文訳
☆：勉強の調子はどう，テリー？　スペイン語の試験の準備はできた？
★：厳しいよ，ケイト。語彙リストを終わらせようとすごく努力しているんだけど，全然頭に残らない感じなんだ。
☆：単語をそんなにたくさん暗記するのは簡単じゃないよね。
★：そういう言い方もできるね。とにかく根気よく続けるしかないよ。
☆：重点を置くところを変えるといいんじゃない？　文法セクションの方が配点が高いとシャープ先生が言っていたよ。
★：そうなの？　だったらそっちをやるべきなのかも。
質問：女性は暗に何と言っているか。

選択肢の訳
1　テリーは抱えている問題について先生と話し合うべきだ。
2　テリーは語彙の勉強に費やす時間を減らすべきだ。
3　テリーは単語を覚えるために違う方法を使うべきだ。
4　テリーは彼女に試験勉強を手伝ってもらうべきだ。

解説　女性の最後の発言の change your focus は，文法の方が配点が高いらしいという続く内容から，語彙から文法に勉強の焦点を移す，という意味だとわかる。したがって **2** が正解。

No.6 - 解答 ④

スクリプト
☆：Keith, I need your opinion.
★：Sure, Leila.
☆：I just got my annual evaluation. Lots of positive comments, but I was passed over for promotion again.

★: What about other staff who were hired at the same time as you?

☆: If they're still here, they've all moved up already. As it happens, they're all men.

★: I see. Well, if there aren't any complaints about your work, perhaps you need to be a bit more upfront about your expectations.

☆: I guess I can try.

Question: What does the man suggest the woman do?

全文訳 ☆: キース，意見を聞かせてほしいんだけど。

★: いいよ，レイラ。

☆: 年次評価をもらったところなの。いいコメントがたくさんあるのに，また昇進を見送られたのよ。

★: 君と同期のほかのスタッフはどうなの？

☆: まだここにいる人なら，みんなもう昇進している。何と，全員男性だけど。

★: なるほど。そうだね，君の仕事に何の苦情もないのなら，期待していることをもう少し率直に表す必要があるのかもしれない。

☆: 何とかやってみるわ。

質問：男性は女性が何をするよう提案しているか。

選択肢の訳 1 仕事の成績を上げる。
2 同僚にアドバイスを求める。
3 新しい仕事を探し始める。
4 仕事の野心をもっとはっきりさせる。

解説 また昇進できなかったと不満を漏らす女性に対し，男性は最後の発言で，expectations「期待」＝昇進したいという気持ちをもう少しはっきり示した方がいいと言っている。expectations を work ambitions と言い換えた **4** が正解。upfront「率直な，正直な」。

No.7 - 解答 ③

スクリプト ★: Sarah, Mr. Li is flying in from Singapore today. Have you made arrangements to pick him up?

☆: Yes. I'll drive to the airport to get him. We should be back at the office by 4.

★: Why don't you take him directly to his hotel so he can take it easy?

☆: But I scheduled a meeting for you both at 4:30, and dinner from 7. Should I cancel them?

★: Yes. It's a long flight. Besides, he'll be here until Friday. We can talk business later.

Question: What does the man suggest doing?

全文訳 ★: サラ，今日リさんがシンガポールから飛行機でお見えになる。迎えに行

く手配はできているかな？
☆：はい。私が車で空港まで迎えに行きます。4時には会社に戻れるでしょう。
★：ゆっくりしていただけるよう，直接ホテルにお連れしてはどうかな。
☆：ですが，お二人の会議を4時半，夕食を7時に予定しました。キャンセルした方がいいでしょうか。
★：うん。長いフライトだし。それに，彼は金曜日までこちらにいるわけだから，ビジネスの話は後でできる。
質問：男性は何をすることを提案しているか。

選択肢の訳
1　今日の午後に会議をすること。
2　7時にリさんを夕食の迎えに行くこと。
3　リさんに休む時間を与えること。
4　夕食を食べながらビジネスの話し合いをすること。

解説　空港へ迎えに行き，そのまま会社に戻ると話す女性に対し，男性は2つ目の発言で，ホテルに直行してのんびりしてもらうよう提案している。take it easy を 3 が rest と言い換えている。

No.8 — 解答 ②

スクリプト
★：Hey, Andrea. It's been a while. How's the family?
☆：Good, actually. You remember my rebellious son?
★：How could I forget!
☆：Well, he somehow managed to graduate from college and land a pretty good job.
★：Sounds like he's really changed.
☆：He has. In fact, he called last week to tell me that his boss is very pleased with his performance. If he plays his cards right, he could be promoted in the not-too-distant future.
★：That's great news.

Question: What do we learn about the woman's son?

全文訳
★：やあ，アンドレア。しばらくぶりだね。ご家族は元気？
☆：元気よ，本当。うちの反抗的な息子を覚えてる？
★：忘れられるもんか！
☆：でね，どうにかこうにか大学を卒業して，結構いい仕事に就いたのよ。
★：すっかり別人になったようだね。
☆：そうなのよ。何しろ先週電話をよこして言うには，息子の仕事ぶりに上司がとても満足しているんだって。抜かりなくやれば，そう遠くない将来に昇進するかもしれない。
★：それは素晴らしい知らせだ。
質問：女性の息子について何がわかるか。

選択肢の訳
1 最近職場で昇進した。
2 人生を立て直した。
3 大学に戻る決心をした。
4 上司と言い争いをした。

解説 以前は反抗的だった息子は，今ではまじめに働き，上司にも気に入られている。男性は3つ目の発言で he's really changed と言っているが，それを全体的に言い換えた **2** が正解。turn around は「（経済・会社など）を立て直す」が基本の意味。昇進は今後の可能性にすぎない。

No.9 - 解答 ③

スクリプト
★： Wouldn't it be nice to have a dog around the house?
☆： Yes, and walking it would help us stay fit. But one condition: I want it to be from a local animal shelter.
★： Really? I was hoping to get a puppy from a reputable breeder.
☆： But the prices can be outrageous, and there are already so many dogs without homes. You know that thousands of shelter dogs are put to sleep every year, right?
★： Yeah, I know, but I've heard nasty rumors about shelter dogs.
☆： Like what exactly?
★： Well, that they're temperamental and aggressive. And I heard of one guy who got a shelter dog, and it cost him 2,000 bucks to treat it for some kind of genetic illness.
☆： Look, I'm sure there are a few horror stories, but most shelters make sure their dogs all have medical exams and are observed for behavioral issues before being handed to new owners. And remember, the neighbors' Labrador and Uncle Jimmy's dog Charlie were both shelter dogs.
★： I get the point. I'm just a bit worried, that's all.
☆： Fair enough. We'll be very careful before we make a decision.
★： OK. Let's have a look online for more information, and then head to a local shelter this weekend.

Question: What is the woman's opinion?

全文訳
★： 家に犬がいるといいと思わない？
☆： うん，散歩させれば私たちの健康維持に役立つしね。だけど1つ条件がある。地元のアニマルシェルターの犬がいいわ。
★： そうなの？ 評判のいいブリーダーから子犬を買えればと思っていたんだけど。
☆： だけど値段がとんでもなく高いことがあるし，家のない犬が既にものすごくたくさんいるのよ。シェルターの犬が毎年何千匹も殺処分されてい

☆：ることは知っているよね。
★：うん，知っているけど，シェルターの犬については嫌なうわさを聞いている。
☆：正確にはどんなうわさ？
★：うーん，気性が荒くて攻撃的だとか。それに，シェルターの犬をもらったとある男のことを聞いたんだけど，ある種の遺伝病の治療に2千ドルかかったって。
☆：いいこと，ひどい体験談がいくつかあることはよく知っているけど，ほとんどのシェルターは，犬が新しい飼い主に引き渡される前に，間違いなくみんな健康診断を受けて，行動面での問題がないか観察されるようにしている。それに，覚えているよね，お隣のラブラドールとジミー叔父さんの犬チャーリーは，どっちもシェルターの犬だったのよ。
★：言いたいことはわかる。ちょっと心配なだけ，それだけのことだよ。
☆：まあいいわ。よくよく慎重に考えてから決めましょう。
★：わかった。ネットでもっと情報を探して，それから今週末に地元のシェルターに向かうことにしよう。

質問：女性の意見は何か。

選択肢の訳
1 犬のブリーダーが最も安全な選択肢だ。
2 彼らはこれ以上犬を引き取るべきではない。
3 慎重に選べばシェルターの犬で問題ない。
4 犬は若い方がしつけるのが簡単だ。

解説 アニマルシェルターに悪い印象を持っている男性と，シェルターの犬を積極的に引き取りたい女性の会話。女性はシェルターの犬なら何でもいいと思っているわけではなく，最後の発言で We'll be very careful before we make a decision. と条件を付けている。それを if you choose carefully と表した 3 が正解である。

No.10 解答 ②

スクリプト
★：I wish we had more support from Jack.
●：I know. After all, he's supposed to be the director of our department, but he's always off at some conference or entertaining clients. He doesn't seem to have a clue about what's going on here on a daily basis.
☆：That's true, guys, but that might not be a bad thing in the long run.
★：How so?
☆：Well, think about it. We're pretty much left to ourselves. It's given us the chance to develop some innovative strategies for improving our productivity without his interference.
★：Yes, but look at our budget. We're underfunded, and Jack's the

only one who can really do anything about that.
● : Well, the main problem I have is that he hires people who don't have any relevant experience for the actual position. Imagine what we could do with appropriate staffing!
☆ : Remember, though, he agreed to hire Cynthia. She's been a great asset.
★ : True, but Jack also takes all the credit for our successes.
☆ : Sure, that's frustrating, but he's not the first boss I've worked for who does that. The bottom line is that we know what needs to be done for clients, and we're doing a great job with that.

Question: What is one thing the woman says about the director?

全文訳
★ : ジャックがもっとサポートしてくれるといいんだけど。
● : そうだよね。何といっても彼は僕たちの部署の部長のはずなのに，会合だのクライアントの接待だので，いつもいない。日々ここで何が起きているのか，まったくわかっていないみたいだ。
☆ : そのとおりね，お二人さん，だけど長い目で見れば悪いことじゃないかもしれない。
★ : どうして？
☆ : うーん，考えてみて。私たちの好きにして構わないも同然なのよ。彼に干渉されずに，私たちの生産性を向上させる革新的な戦略を生み出すチャンスをもらったわけ。
★ : うん，だけど経費を考えて。お金が足りないんだし，それを実際に何とかできるのはジャックだけなんだから。
● : えー，僕が抱えている一番の問題は，実際のポジションに関連する経験が皆無の人を彼が雇うことだ。適切な人員配置をすれば何ができるか，想像してみてよ！
☆ : だけど覚えているよね，彼はシンシアを雇うことに合意したのよ。彼女はなくてはならない人材になっている。
★ : 確かにそうだけど，ジャックは僕たちの成功も全部自分の手柄にしてしまう。
☆ : そう，むしゃくしゃするよね，だけど私は，そういうことをする上司に仕えたのは彼が初めてじゃない。一番大事なのは，クライアントのために何をする必要があるか私たちが知っていること，そしてそれについて私たちが立派な仕事をしているということよ。

質問：女性が部長について言っていることの１つは何か。

選択肢の訳
1 彼の生産性重視は役に立っている。
2 彼の監督欠如は部下に自由を与える。
3 彼の過度の支出は彼らの経費にしわ寄せを与える。

4 彼の雇用のやり方は以前の上司のやり方よりよい。

解説 上司 Jack が director の責務を果たしていないことに不満を持つ部下3人の会話。批判に終始する男性2人と違い女性の考え方は前向きで，2つ目の発言では，上司に干渉されずに新しいことをするチャンスだと述べている。これを全体的に言い換えた **2** が正解。男性の1人が経費が少ないと言っているが，上司の乱費が原因だという発言はないので **3** は誤り。

A

スクリプト **Biochar**

Biochar is a type of agricultural fertilizer that looks like charcoal. It is produced by burning plants and agricultural waste under extremely low-oxygen conditions. Then, it is ground up and added to soil. Supporters say biochar also benefits the environment. This is because when biochar is produced, the carbon in the plants and waste becomes trapped in the biochar. Additionally, it is claimed that when added to soil, biochar absorbs more carbon. This prevents carbon, which contributes to the greenhouse effect, from being released into the atmosphere. Some people have therefore been calling for biochar to be produced on a massive scale to combat global warming.

However, the claims regarding biochar's agricultural and environmental benefits are mainly based on observations of small-scale traditional agricultural practices and lab experiments. Several large field trials came to a different conclusion. First, they showed that, in many cases, when biochar was buried, carbon levels in the soil were generally unchanged. Second, the field trials showed that biochar's effects on crop production were at best inconclusive. While more research is definitely needed, biochar may not be a magic solution for food security and climate change after all.

Questions

No.11 What do supporters believe about biochar?
No.12 What did the field trials suggest about biochar?

全文訳 **バイオ炭**

　バイオ炭は，石炭に見た目が似た農業用肥料の一種である。植物と農業廃棄物を極度の低酸素状態で燃やして生産される。次に細かく粉砕され，土に加えられる。推進者たちは，バイオ炭は環境にもメリットがあると言う。それは，バイオ炭が生産されるとき，植物と廃棄物の炭素がバイオ炭の中に閉じ込められるからである。さらに，土に加えるとバイオ炭はもっと炭素を吸収する，と主張されている。これは，温室効果の一因である炭素が大気中に放出されるのを防ぐ。したがって，地球温暖化と闘うため，バイオ炭を大規模に生産することを求める人たちもいる。

　しかし，バイオ炭の農業的メリットと環境的メリットに関する主張は，主に，小規模な伝統的農法と研究室での実験に基づいている。いくつかの大きな畑での試験では，違う結果が出た。第1に，これらの試験の結果では，多くの場合，バイオ炭が埋められたとき，土の炭素量はだいたい元のままだった。第2に，畑の試験の結果では，作物生産に対するバイオ炭の効果は，よく言っても判定不能だった。さらに研究が必要なのは間

違いないが，結局バイオ炭は，食料安全保障と気候変動の魔法の解決策ではないのかもしれない。

語句 inconclusive「結論に達しない」

No.11 解答 ③

質問の訳 推進者たちはバイオ炭についてどう考えているか。
選択肢の訳
1 有害な植物を殺すことができる。
2 土が酸素生産量を増やす助けとなる。
3 炭素の空気中への放出を防ぐことができる。
4 通常の肥料よりも速く炭素を放出する。

解説 バイオ炭の大きな環境的メリットとして，炭素を吸収することが挙げられている。第1段落後半のThis prevents carbon ... from being released into the atmosphere. と**3**が同じ内容である。

No.12 解答 ①

質問の訳 畑での試験はバイオ炭について何を示唆したか。
選択肢の訳
1 土に与える潜在的効果は誇張されているかもしれない。
2 使用すると作物の質と量を向上させることができる。
3 現代の農業に最も適している。
4 長期的な環境被害をもたらすかもしれない。

解説 畑での試験結果は2つ述べられている。1つは，バイオ炭を土に埋めても土の炭素量は変わらなかったこと。もう1つは，作物生産に効果が認められなかったことである。前者は推進派の主張を否定する結果なので，**1**が正解。at best inconclusive は，結論が出ないというより，むしろ悪い効果を与えたかもしれない，という含みを持たせた言い方。

B

スクリプト **A New Bandage**

A company has created a product that is faster and more efficient at stopping blood flow from serious wounds than ordinary gauze bandages are. The new bandage is manufactured with plant fibers that have been modified in the laboratory so they can hold large amounts of blood. When applied over a wound, the bandage turns into a gel that helps prevent blood from escaping. By holding blood in place, this gel improves the body's natural ability to form a clot — the mass of thickened blood that forms over a wound and halts bleeding. This new product, therefore, has enormous potential for preventing blood loss in patients.

Another remarkable feature of the bandage is that, as the wound heals, it dissolves and is absorbed by the body within a week or so. Ordinary gauze bandages also soak up blood and slow or stop bleeding, but they must be removed eventually. Taking them off can disturb the clot that has formed over the wound, which can cause bleeding to restart. The new bandage does not have this drawback.

Questions
No.13 What is one thing the new bandage does?
No.14 What is one special feature of the new bandage?

> 全文訳　**新しい包帯**

　ある会社が，通常のガーゼの包帯よりも，重傷からの血流を止めるのが速くて効率的な製品を開発した。新しい包帯は，大量の血をためておけるよう実験室で変更を加えられた植物繊維で製造される。傷に当てると，包帯は血が漏れるのを防ぐ助けとなるジェルに変わる。血をその場にとどめることによって，このジェルは，体が生まれながらに持つ，凝血——傷を覆って形成され出血を止める，濃縮された血の塊——を作る能力を高める。したがって，この新製品は患者の失血を防ぐ多大な可能性を持っている。

　この包帯のもう１つの注目すべき特徴は，傷が治癒するにつれて溶けていき，１週間かそこらのうちに体に吸収されることである。通常のガーゼの包帯も血を吸い取って出血を遅らせるか止めるかするが，最終的に外さなければならない。ガーゼの包帯を取り去ると，傷を覆って形成された凝血の邪魔になりかねず，再出血が始まる原因になることがある。新しい包帯にはこの欠点がない。

> 語句　gauze「ガーゼ」，clot「凝血」

No.13 解答 ④

質問の訳　新しい包帯がすることの１つは何か。
選択肢の訳　
1　傷の近くでの凝血の形成を防ぐ。
2　患者の血圧を下げる。
3　血液の組成を変化させる。
4　傷を塞ぐ体の能力を高める。

解説　前半と後半で１つずつ，新しい包帯の特徴が紹介されている。１つは冒頭で言っているように，faster and more efficient at stopping blood flow from serious wounds であること。続けてその原理を説明しているが，その中の improves the body's natural ability to form a clot と **4** が一致する。clot についての放送文の解説を，選択肢は close a wound とまとめている。

No.14 解答 ④

質問の訳　新しい包帯の特殊な特徴の１つは何か。
選択肢の訳　
1　何度か再利用できる。
2　有害な細菌を傷から除去する。
3　通常の包帯より安く作ることができる。
4　取り除かなくてもよい。

解説 もう1つの特徴は，it dissolves and is absorbed by the body であること。通常の包帯は they must be removed eventually で，それが再出血を引き起こすことがあるが，新しい包帯にはその欠点がない。つまり，新しい包帯は溶けて吸収されるので remove する必要がない，ということになる。

C

スクリプト **Planned Obsolescence**

For years, consumer-rights groups have claimed that some product manufacturers use what is called "planned obsolescence" to boost sales of their products. Planned obsolescence is a way of intentionally limiting the life span of products by, for example, manufacturing them so they are likely to break down after a few years. The rights groups say that another element of this strategy involves manufacturing companies creating obstacles which make it difficult to get items repaired. This can be done by not supplying repair manuals, by limiting repairs to licensed shops, or by making it difficult to obtain replacement parts. Faced with such obstacles, consumers often choose to simply replace older items with new models.

Recently, many people have been fighting back against what they see as unfair business practices. Some have created websites giving consumers tips on repair techniques, while others are lobbying for regulations that require manufacturers to provide repair information and replacement parts. Companies are starting to listen. In 2014, some car manufacturers agreed to make repair information available to independent garages, and advocates now hope other manufacturers will follow their example.

Questions
No.15 What do consumer-rights groups say some companies do?
No.16 What is one way people are trying to fight the problem?

全文訳 **計画的陳腐化**

　一部の製造業者は自社製品の売り上げを増やすために「計画的陳腐化」と呼ばれるものを用いている，と消費者権利団体は長年主張している。計画的陳腐化とは，例えば，数年後に壊れる可能性があるように製品を製造することによって，製品の寿命を意図的に制限する方法である。この戦略の別の要素は，商品の修理を困難にする障害を製造会社が作り出すことを眼目としている，と権利団体は言う。これは，修理マニュアルを供給しないこと，ライセンスを受けた店に修理を制限すること，あるいは交換部品の入手を困難にすることによってなされ得る。そうした障害に直面した消費者は，単に旧商品を新機種に買い替える選択をすることが多い。

　最近は多くの人が，不公正な商慣行と考えるものに反撃している。修理技術に関するヒントを消費者に与えるウェブサイトを作った人もいれば，修理情報と交換部品を提供

することを製造業者に命じる法令を作るようロビー活動をしている人もいる。企業も耳を傾け始めている。2014年に，一部の自動車製造会社が，独立系の自動車修理工場が修理情報を利用できるようにすることに合意し，ほかの製造業者がその例に倣うことを支持者たちは今期待している。

語句　obsolescence「廃れかけていること」

No.15 解答 ①

質問の訳　一部の企業は何をしていると消費者権利団体は言っているか。
選択肢の訳
1　長持ちするように設計されていない製品を売る。
2　旧製品を新製品と呼ぶ。
3　修理マニュアルを理解困難にする。
4　技術的スキルを持つ労働者の雇用数が少な過ぎる。

解説　第1段落の初めで，planned obsolescence とは，例えば壊れやすい製品を意図的に作ることだと説明されている。これを「長持ちするように設計されていない」と言い換えた1が正解。

No.16 解答 ③

質問の訳　人々がこの問題と闘おうとしている方法の1つは何か。
選択肢の訳
1　製造業者を訴えることによって。
2　中古の部品と製品を転売することによって。
3　情報の共有を奨励することによって。
4　オンラインで商品を購入することによって。

解説　第2段落で，計画的陳腐化と闘う方法が2つ挙げられている。1つは修理に関する情報をネットで提供すること，もう1つは企業が修理情報と交換部品を提供することを求めるロビー活動。3が前者と後者の「修理情報」を「情報の共有」とまとめている。

D

スクリプト　**The Gini Coefficient**

Statisticians who want to measure a country's prosperity tend to rely on gross domestic product, or GDP, but this measure is not perfect. While a country with a high GDP is considered affluent, that country's population may be composed of a small number of the super-rich and a large number of poor people. Another measure, which indicates the degree of social inequality within a country, has come into use. Known as the Gini coefficient, it is a number ranging from a low of 0 to a high of 1. Zero represents perfect equality of income and 1 indicates that all wealth is owned by a single person. By considering both the GDP figure *and* the Gini coefficient, it is possible to gain a more accurate measure of the true prosperity of a nation's citizens.

As well as indicating wealth distribution, the Gini coefficient is also a reliable indicator of social cohesion. Countries with greater income equality tend to have lower crime, and their citizens report greater levels of overall well-being. One way a country can lower its Gini coefficient is by taxing the rich and redistributing the income to poorer citizens.

Questions

No.17 Why can GDP be an imperfect measurement?

No.18 What is one thing we learn about countries with a low Gini coefficient?

全文訳 ジニ係数

　国の繁栄度を測りたい統計学者は国内総生産（GDP）に依拠する傾向があるが，この尺度は完璧なものではない。GDP が高い国は裕福だと見なされるが，その国の人口は少数の超金持ちと多数の貧民で構成されているかもしれない。国の中の社会的不平等の度合いを示す別の尺度が用いられるようになっている。これはジニ係数として知られるもので，最低値 0 から最高値 1 の範囲の数字である。0 は所得の完全な平等を表し，1 はすべての富がたった 1 人の人に所有されていることを示す。GDP の数値とジニ係数の両方を考慮することで，ある国の国民の真の繁栄のより正確な尺度を得ることが可能なのである。

　ジニ係数は富の分配を示すだけでなく，社会的結束の確かな指標でもある。所得の平等度が高い国ほど犯罪が少ない傾向があり，国民が報告する全般的幸福度は高くなる。国がジニ係数を下げることのできる 1 つの方法は，金持ちに課税し，より貧しい国民に所得を再分配することである。

語句 coefficient「係数」, statistician「統計学者」, cohesion「結合，結束力」, redistribute「～を再分配する」

No.17 解答 ②

質問の訳 なぜ GDP は不完全な尺度になり得るのか。

選択肢の訳
1. いくつかの種類の所得を含んでいない。
2. 国の富の分配を測定しない。
3. 測定される方法が時を経て変化した。
4. 計算の仕方について経済学者の考えが一致していない。

解説 冒頭の this measure（= GDP）is not perfect に続いて，その理由が説明されている。GDP が高くても，超富裕層が富を独占しているかもしれない。つまり，2 のように，GDP からは国の内部における富の分配がわからないことになる。

No.18 解答 ④

質問の訳 ジニ係数が低い国についてわかることの 1 つは何か。

選択肢の訳
1. 国民が高い犯罪率に苦しんでいる。
2. 国民がジェンダー平等を享受していない。
3. 国民にもっと課税すべきだ。

4 国民が満ち足りている可能性がより高い。

解説 後半の Countries with greater income equality は，ジニ係数が低い国のこと。そうした国は犯罪率が低く，国民は greater levels of overall well-being を得ている。それを content と短く表した **4** が正解である。

スクリプト **Clothing Matters**

It is well known that the clothes people wear can influence the way others react to them. But psychologist Adam Galinsky believes clothes can have an even more profound effect on the wearer. To determine if clothes can affect an individual's psychological processes, he conducted an experiment in which subjects were split into two groups. All the subjects wore identical white coats, but the symbolic meaning of the coats was different for each group. One group was told the coats they were wearing were used by doctors, while the other group was told the coats were used by painters. When the subjects were given cognitive tests requiring skills which are associated with physicians' work, those who thought they were wearing doctors' coats performed substantially better.

Real-world data seems to support Galinsky's beliefs. For example, female prisoners at Utah Department of Corrections facilities were frequently disruptive and disobedient. Prison administrators believed the dull, plain-looking prison clothing was part of the problem, so they gave the women attractive new uniforms. Inmate discipline improved significantly after this rule change. Observers theorize that the original uniforms, intended as punishment, identified the women as "prisoners," and they acted accordingly. However, when the inmates could present themselves differently, their self-perception was transformed.

Questions
No.19 What does Adam Galinsky's study suggest?
No.20 What was one result of the prison administrators' decision?

全文訳 **着る物が大事**

着ている衣服が，その人に対する他者の反応の仕方に影響し得ることはよく知られている。しかし心理学者アダム・ガリンスキーは，衣服は着る人によりいっそう深い影響を与え得ると考えている。衣服が個人の心理的プロセスに影響を与え得るかを突き止めるため，彼は，被験者を2つのグループに分けて実験を行った。被験者全員がまったく同じ白衣を着たが，白衣の象徴的意味はそれぞれのグループで異なっていた。1つのグループは，彼らが着ている白衣は医者が用いるものだと告げられ，もう1つのグループは，白衣は画家が用いるものだと告げられた。医師の仕事と関連するスキルを必要とす

る認知テストを課されると，医者の白衣を着ていると思った被験者の成績の方がかなりよかった。

　現実社会のデータはガリンスキーの考えを裏付けているように思える。例えば，ユタ州矯正局の施設の女性囚人はしばしば問題を起こし反抗的だった。さえない地味な囚人服が問題の一部だと刑務官たちは考えたので，魅力的な新しい制服を女性たちに与えた。このルール変更後，収容者の規律は著しく向上した。評論家の説によると，罰として意図された元の制服は女性たちに「囚人」というアイデンティティーを与えるもので，彼女たちはそれに応じて行動した。しかし，違う自分を見せられるようになると，彼女たちの自己認識は一変したのである。

> 語句　real-world「現実社会の」，disruptive「混乱をもたらす」，disobedient「服従しない」，inmate「（刑務所などの）収容者」，theorize「〜という理論を立てる」

No.19 解答 ①

質問の訳　アダム・ガリンスキーの研究は何を示唆しているか。
選択肢の訳
1　人が着ている衣服は成績に影響することがある。
2　同じような服装をすると人間関係が向上する。
3　人の衣服は他者がその人をどう判断するかにめったに影響しない。
4　衣服の色は認知パフォーマンスにほとんど影響を与えない。

解説　ガリンスキーの研究では，医者の白衣を着ていると思ったグループと画家の白衣を着ていると思ったグループを比較した。医師の仕事に関連するテストでは前者が performed substantially better だったのだから，衣服が成績に影響したことになる。

No.20 解答 ②

質問の訳　刑務官の決定の結果の1つは何だったか。
選択肢の訳
1　収容者数が急速に減った。
2　収容者の行動の問題が減った。
3　収容者がより頻繁に罰せられた。
4　収容者が新しい制服を着るのを拒んだ。

解説　女性囚人が荒れる理由の1つが地味な囚人服だと考えた刑務官は，魅力的な制服に変えた。すると Inmate discipline improved significantly という結果になった。これを「行動の問題が減った」と言い換えた 2 が正解。

| 一次試験・リスニング | Part 3 | 問題編 p.157〜158 | ▶MP3 ▶アプリ ▶CD 3 43〜48 |

F

スクリプト

You have 10 seconds to read the situation and Question No. 21.

To be honest, you're a bit late getting started. You should already be doing some detailed research on your topic or working on the grant application paperwork, but since you're unsure about your research focus, you need to choose a professor as an adviser and then work it out. A topic that you choose after simply reading journal articles might not satisfy the grant organizations. A good professor in your field will know what areas are currently in demand, and they should support you throughout the program. Be careful, though. Some professors may be too busy to give you guidance, so don't automatically go to one you already know. You should talk to current students first and get some details about each professor before approaching them. Once you've done that, I'd recommend contacting the local government just to confirm what the grant requirements are.

Now mark your answer on your answer sheet.

全文訳

正直言って，君は始めるのがちょっと遅いね。既に自分のトピックに関して何か詳しい研究をしているか，助成金の申請書類に取り組んでいるべきだけど，研究の中心テーマがはっきりしないんだから，教授を1人アドバイザーに選んで，それからテーマを練る必要がある。単に専門誌の記事を読んでから選んだトピックでは，助成団体を納得させられないかもしれない。君の分野のいい教授なら，どんな領域が現在求められているか知っているだろうし，課程の間ずっと君を支えてくれるはずだ。だけど，注意して。教授の中には指導するには忙し過ぎる人もいるから，知り合いの教授のところに機械的に行っては駄目だ。まず今の学生たちと話して，教授に話を持ち込む前にそれぞれの教授について少し詳しい情報を聞くべさだ。それが済んでしまえば，助成金の要件を確認するために地方自治体に連絡を取ることを勧めるよ。

No.21 解答

状況の訳 あなたは工学の博士課程に入る予定で，研究助成金が必要である。研究の中心テーマはまだ決めていない。最近卒業した人が次のアドバイスをする。

質問の訳 あなたはまず何をすべきか。

選択肢の訳 1 以前あなたに教えたことのある教授に頼む。
2 工学の教授について聞いて回る。

3 あなたの全般的研究分野に関する専門誌の記事を読む。
4 助成金の申請について地方自治体に連絡を取る。

語句 automatically「無意識に，機械的に」

解説 you need to choose a professor as an adviser and then work it（＝ your research focus）out なので，まずは指導してくれる教授を選ぶ必要がある。ただし，その際は talk to current students first and get some details about each professor とアドバイスしている。これを Make inquiries ... と言い換えた **2** が正解。何も考えずに知り合いの教授に頼むのは駄目と言っているので，**1** は誤り。

G

スクリプト

You have 10 seconds to read the situation and Question No. 22.

The hospital's maternity ward is the most popular option, and your insurance would cover everything. You'd visit your baby for feedings several times a day, but she would have to remain in the nursery. Your insurance would also cover the next option, which is the in-hospital birth center. It's staffed by midwives and offers natural childbirth, and there is quick access to hospital facilities in case of emergency. The baby would be moved to the hospital nursery for monitoring after the birth, but you would be able to visit several times a day. Now, a private birthing center would offer on-site physicians, and you could keep your baby with you. However, your insurance only covers 50 percent of the cost, which is $5,000. Since you're in good health, having a midwife help you give birth at home is another option. That would cost $3,000, but insurance would cover half, and of course, you get to stay with your baby.

Now mark your answer on your answer sheet.

全文訳

病院の産科病棟が一番人気の選択肢で，お持ちの保険で全部カバーできるでしょう。1日に何回か授乳で赤ちゃんを訪ねることになりますが，赤ちゃんは新生児室にずっといなければならないでしょう。次の選択肢は病院内の出産センターですが，これも保険でカバーできるでしょう。助産師が配属されていて自然分娩ができますし，緊急の際は病院の施設をすぐに利用できます。出産後赤ちゃんは観察のため病院の新生児室に移されますが，1日に何回か訪ねることができるでしょう。さて，個人経営の出産センターにはその場に医師がいて，赤ちゃんとずっと一緒にいられるでしょう。ですが，費用が5,000ドルで，お持ちの保険ではこの5割しかカバーできません。健康状態は良好ですから，助産師に助けてもらって自宅で出産するのも1つの選択肢です。それには3,000ドルかかるでしょうが，保険で半分カバーできるでしょうし，もちろん赤ちゃんと一緒にいることができます。

No.22 解答 ④

状況の訳 あなたの担当医師が出産の選択肢を説明している。あなたはいっときも赤ん坊から離れたくない。保険でカバーされない費用があれば支払えるよう，1,500 ドル持っている。

質問の訳 あなたはどこで出産すべきか。

選択肢の訳
1 病院の産科病棟で。
2 病院内の出産センターで。
3 個人経営の出産センターで。
4 自宅で。

語句 midwife「助産師」，childbirth「出産，分娩」，on-site「現場の」

解説 産科病棟と病院内の出産センターだと赤ん坊は新生児室にいることになるので，条件に合わない。個人経営の出産センターについて $5,000，自宅出産について $3,000 という数字が出てくるが，どちらも保険が半額カバーする。自己負担が 1,500 ドルで済む自宅出産なら，手持ちのお金で賄えることになる。

H

スクリプト

You have 10 seconds to read the situation and Question No. 23.

We'll be short a marketing manager once you leave for Japan. I'd been considering Victoria from sales as your replacement. However, I just learned she'll be moving into a sales manager position in a month. As you know, Alberto's next in line in our department, but I haven't been impressed with his organizational skills. Another option is to use a recruitment agency to locate an outside candidate, but that process would take at least three months. Coincidentally, Evelyn Sutherland, your predecessor, contacted me out of the blue last week. She'd consider returning to our company if we can meet her salary and benefit requirements. It's a stretch, but I think it's doable. I'd like you to follow up on this with personnel. Remember that we need someone in place at least a month before you leave so you can get them up to speed.

Now mark your answer on your answer sheet.

全文訳

君が日本へ去ってしまうと，マーケティング部長が不在になる。君の後任には営業のビクトリアを考えていた。しかし，彼女が1カ月後に営業部長職に昇進することがついさっきわかったんだ。知ってのとおり，うちの部署ではアルベルトが次の候補だが，私は彼の組織運営力にいい印象を持っていない。別の選択肢は人材紹介会社を使って外部の候補者を探し当てることだが，その手続きには最低3カ月かかるだろう。偶然だが，君の前任者のエブリン・サザーランドが先週思いがけず連絡してきたんだ。給料と手当について彼女の要求を満たせれば，会社に戻ることを検討してくれるだろう。無茶な話

だが，できると思う。この件について人事部と引き続き対処してほしいんだ。必要な情報に精通してもらえるよう，君が去る最低1カ月前には誰かを就けておく必要があることを忘れないで。

No.23 解答 ④

状況の訳 あなたはカナダの会社の部長である。8週間後に日本に転勤することになっている。上司が次のことを告げる。

質問の訳 あなたはまず何をすべきか。

選択肢の訳
1 営業部長に助けを求める。
2 その役職に備えてアルベルトの訓練を始める。
3 人材紹介会社に相談する。
4 エブリンについて人事部に連絡する。

語句 in line「見込みがあって」, coincidentally「偶然にも」, stretch「困難な仕事」, doable「実行可能な」, up to speed「最新情報を持って」

解説 ビクトリアは営業部長になるので後任候補から外れる。上司はアルベルトを気に入っていない。人材紹介会社だと3カ月かかるので遅過ぎる。エブリンは，She'd consider returning to our company から，この会社を辞めた人だとわかる。It's a stretch, but I think it's doable. がポイント。エブリンに戻ってもらうのは大変だができないことはない，というのが上司の考え。彼女が望む給与などについて人事部とさらに検討してほしい，という上司の希望に沿うのが当面はベストと考えられる。

スクリプト

You have 10 seconds to read the situation and Question No. 24.

OK, here's your custom-fitted mouthpiece. Put a small amount of this whitening gel in the mouthpiece. Initially, keep the mouthpiece in for only 30 minutes at a time, as your teeth will be sensitive. After a week, you can use it for 60 minutes. After each session, rinse your mouth with water. In about a month, Dr. Parkinson will want to see how it's going. I see you've already scheduled that appointment. If you have implants, keep an eye on your progress. The gel does not affect the color of implants, so if you go too far with the whitening, your natural teeth won't match them anymore. You can decrease the time you use the mouthpiece or stop if you are concerned about this. Finally, we've included some desensitizing cream. Apply it to your teeth if you have any discomfort.

Now mark your answer on your answer sheet.

全文訳
さて，こちらがオーダーメードのマウスピースです。マウスピースにこのホワイトニ

ングジェルを少量入れます。初めのうちは,マウスピースを入れておくのは一度に30分だけにしてください。歯が知覚過敏になりますから。1週間たったら,60分使用して構いません。使用が終わるたびに,水で口をすすいでください。1カ月後くらいに,パーキンソン先生はどんな具合か見てみたいでしょう。その予約はもうお取りになっていますね。インプラントが入っている場合は,経過によく注意してください。ジェルはインプラントの色に作用しませんから,あまりホワイトニングをやり過ぎると,天然の歯ともう色が合わなくなってしまいます。それが心配でしたら,マウスピースを使う時間を減らしてもいいですし,使うのをやめてもいいです。最後ですが,知覚過敏を抑えるクリームを一緒に入れておきました。痛みを感じたら歯に塗ってください。

No.24 解答 ③

状況の訳 歯科医院の助手が,自宅で歯をホワイトニングするキットの使い方を説明している。あなたは歯の2本を去年インプラントで取り換えた。

質問の訳 最良の結果を得るにはあなたは何をすべきか。

選択肢の訳
1 早めに経過観察の診察予約を入れる。
2 ホワイトニングする時間は最初は長くする。
3 歯の色の変化を注意してチェックする。
4 ホワイトニングのたびに,その前に知覚過敏を抑えるクリームを使う。

語句 desensitize「~の敏感性を減ずる」

解説 状況の Two of your teeth were replaced by implants がポイントになると考えられる。中ほどの If you have implants 以降で,インプラントの色は変わらないからホワイトニングをやり過ぎるとほかの歯と色が合わなくなるので注意が必要,といった説明がされている。それを動詞 monitor を使って表した 3 が正解。

スクリプト

You have 10 seconds to read the situation and Question No. 25.

The Australian government encourages investment by nonresidents and foreigners in various types of real estate, including undeveloped land, newly built residences, and properties requiring redevelopment. Regardless, you must acquire approval from the Foreign Investment Review Board beforehand. You can do this through the Board's website by clicking on the link and then filling out the online application form. Prior to that, however, you need to know what kind of investment you'll make. My recommendation would be to make an "off-the-plan purchase," which is a contract to buy a property before the house has actually been built. Once you've identified a property, you'll need to list it on the application for Board approval that I mentioned. When you actually make the purchase, you're required to obtain an Australian tax file number, which you'll need in order to fulfill tax obligations.

Now mark your answer on your answer sheet.

全文訳

オーストラリア政府は非居住者と外国人によるさまざまなタイプの不動産への投資を奨励しており，未開発の土地，新築住宅，再開発が必要な不動産物件もその中に含まれます。いずれにせよ，あらかじめ外国投資審査委員会の認可を得なければなりません。これは，委員会のウェブサイトを通して，リンクをクリックしてからオンライン申請書に記入することでできます。ですが，その前に，自分がどういった種類の投資をするのか知っておく必要があります。私がお勧めしたいのは「オフ・ザ・プラン購入」をすることで，家が実際に建つ前に物件を買う契約です。物件を特定したらすぐ，先ほど言った委員会の認可を求める申請書に記載する必要があります。実際に購入すると，オーストラリアの納税者番号を取得することが求められますが，これは納税義務を果たすために必要になります。

No.25 解答 ②

状況の訳 あなたは日本に住む日本国民である。投資としてオーストラリアに家を買いたいと思っている。不動産業者が次の話をする。

質問の訳 あなたはまず何をすべきか。

選択肢の訳
1 オーストラリアの住民になる申請をする。
2 購入する物件を見つける。
3 認可書類を提出する。
4 オーストラリアの納税者番号を取得する。

語句 nonresident「非居住者」

解説 不動産業者は必要な手順を順不同に説明している。役所の認可を得なければならないが，Prior to that「その前に」投資物件を決める必要がある。具体的な物件を申請書に記載し，購入が済んだら納税者番号を取得する。選択肢では2→3→4の順に進むことになる。外国人による投資を奨励していると最初に言っているので，1をする必要はない。

スクリプト

This is an interview with Rob Russel, a mental health counselor and emotional-support coach.

I (Interviewer): Rob, thanks for joining us on Careers in Focus.

RR (Rob Russel): Yeah, thanks for having me. It's my pleasure.

I: So, some people may feel that, by seeing a coach, they've failed in some way. How would you respond to that?

RR: I think that this is something that hopefully, quite soon, but at some point in the future will become a non-question. So you take somebody like who is working really hard, right? They're working too many hours, and they don't see their family as much as they'd like to, they've probably developed a few unhealthy lifestyle habits, like drinking or smoking, whatever. And they start to get stomach pains, right? A stomach ulcer or whatever. Go to the doctor, like, diagnosed with a stomach ulcer. That person does not feel like they've failed in any way, like they're not made to feel that. And in fact it can be almost a kind of badge of honor, like, I've been working so hard that I got a stomach ulcer, right. So why somebody who, for example, gets depressed, or just develops some kind of, psychological challenge, should be made to feel like they've failed because, for something which probably happened through no fault of their own. I think is, at some point soon, when attitudes evolve, and prejudices kind of lift, it will be ridiculous to make that distinction, basically.

I: So society needs to be educated about this, then.

RR: I think that's really important, yeah.

I: OK. Do most companies, or schools or colleges, do enough to provide emotional support to their employees or their students?

RR: Most organizations that I have had contact with, they don't pay enough attention to the emotional side. So, technically, you go into a company, there's computers for everyone and the Internet's all set up, there's some training about how to use that, there's tech support if you get in real trouble, right? Whereas the emotional side of things — which is very stressful for people, I mean, just dealing with relationships at work, dealing with a difficult colleague, dealing with your own kind of challenges on a day-to-day basis — I think is probably the main stress for the majority of people. To parallel the technical support that people get, you need emotionally intelligent managers who can create a basic, kind of healthy and emotional workplace.

I: Right. What kind of person makes a good coach in your experience?

RR: I think some people who are naturally just very emotionally intelligent don't make the best coaches, 'cause it's just too easy for them. They can't understand why other people struggle. So I don't — you certainly need to be, I think, to be emotionally intelligent, and to be aware of what it means to be emotionally intelligent. You don't necessarily have to be the most kind of skilled person at human relationships. Because it's actually important to, so empathy, I think, is one of the key skills, basically. And in order to empathize, it kind of helps not to have been perfect yourself, and to have had your own struggles, I think. So, some experience, I think, of overcoming difficulties is important.

I: This has really been interesting. I think your work is so important. Thank you very much.

RR: Thanks. Thank you very much.

Questions

No.26 What is Rob's opinion about people with psychological challenges?
No.27 What is one thing Rob says about being an emotional-support coach?

全文訳

これはメンタルヘルスカウンセラーでエモーショナルサポートコーチであるロブ・ラッセルとのインタビューです。

聞き手（以下「聞」）：ロブ，「注目の仕事」にお越しいただきありがとうございます。

ロブ・ラッセル（以下「ロ」）：はい，呼んでいただきありがとうございます。光栄です。

聞：さて，コーチに見てもらうことで，自分が何か失敗したんだという気持ちになる人もいるかもしれません。それにはどのように対応なさいますか。

ロ：これは，願わくばすぐにでも，でなければ将来のいつか，聞くだけ無駄な質問になってほしいものだと思います。では，すごくがんばっている人を取り上げてみましょう，いいですか？　そういう人たちは長時間働き過ぎで，会いたいと思うほどには家族に会えず，たぶんいくつか不健康な生活習慣がついているんです，飲酒とか喫煙とか，何でもいいですが。そして胃が痛くなり出すわけですよね？　胃潰瘍とか何か。医者に行って胃潰瘍と診断される，とか。そういう人は，自分が失敗したような気持ちには決してなりません，そういう気持ちにさせられることはない，というか。そして実際それがほとんどある種の名誉の印であることもあります，これだけがんばってきたので胃潰瘍になってしまった，うんそうだ，みたいな。では，例えばうつになる人，あるいは何らかの心理的困難を抱えるようになる人でもいいですが，なぜそういう人は，たぶん自分の責任でなく起きたことのせいで，自分が失敗したような気持ちにさせられるべきなのでしょうか。思うに，近いうちに考え方が進化して，偏見が少

し消えれば，そんな区別をするのはばかばかしくなります，基本的に。
聞：ということは，社会がこれについて教育される必要がある，と。
ロ：それはとても重要なことだと思います，はい。
聞：わかりました。ほとんどの企業は，あるいは学校や大学は，従業員や学生に感情サポートを提供するために十分なことをしていますか。
ロ：私が接触したことのあるほとんどの組織は，感情面に十分な注意を払っていません。ですから，形の上では，入社すると全員にパソコンがあってインターネットはすっかりセットアップしてあり，その使い方に関する指導が少しあり，本当に困った状況になれば技術サポートがある，そうですよね？　一方，物事の感情面――それは人にとってとてもストレスになります，つまり，ただ職場の人間関係に対処すること，厄介な同僚に対処すること，自分なりの困難に日々対処すること――大多数の人にはそれがたぶん主なストレスだと思います。人々が得る技術サポートと並行して，基本的な，いわば健康的で感情のある職場を作ることのできる，感情的知性の高い管理職が必要です。
聞：そうですね。ご経験では，どんな人がいいコーチになるでしょうか。
ロ：生まれつき感情的知性の高い人もいますが，そういう人は最高のコーチにはならないと思います。そういう人には簡単過ぎるからです。他人がなぜもがき苦しむのか，彼らは理解できないんです。なので，私は――思うに，感情的知性が高くて，感情的知性が高いことが何を意味するかを認識している必要は間違いなくあります。必ずしも，人間関係のスキルが最も高いような人でなくても構いません。なぜなら実際に重要なのは，共感力ですね，これが必須のスキルの1つだと思います，基本的に。そして共感するためには，自分自身が完璧ではなかったこと，自分自身がもがき苦しんできたことが，少し役に立つと思います。ですから，困難を乗り越えた多少の経験が重要だと思います。
聞：とても興味深いお話でした。とても重要なお仕事をされていると思います。どうもありがとうございました。
ロ：どうも。どうもありがとうございました。

(語句) non-question「（答えが自明なので）聞くだけ無駄な質問」，ulcer「潰瘍」

質問の訳　心理的困難を抱える人たちに関するロブの意見は何か。
選択肢の訳　1　彼らは自分が失敗したという気持ちにさせられるべきではない。
　　　　　　2　もっと精神的に強くなるのに役立つよう，彼らは運動をすべきだ。
　　　　　　3　似たような病気を持つ人たちと時間を過ごすべきだ。
　　　　　　4　家族からもっと支援を得るべきだ。
解説　冒頭で言っている emotional-support coach は，感情面で人を支援し目標達成に導くカウンセリングを行う専門職の人。そういうコーチに向

かい合うだけで自分が失敗を犯したのではないかと感じる人への対応策を聞かれたロブは，2つ目の発言で，失敗したとは感じない人の話から始めている。そういう人は，病気になっても，がんばったことの名誉の印だと考える。一方，psychological challenge を持つ人については，why ... should be made to feel like they've failed と言っている。これは反語的意味だと考えられるので，**1** が正解。

No.27 解答 ②

質問の訳 感情サポートコーチであることについてロブが言っていることの1つは何か。

選択肢の訳
1 自分のストレスレベルを注意してチェックすることが重要だ。
2 よいコーチはたいてい自ら感情的困難に直面したことがある。
3 実業界で働いた経験があると役に立つ。
4 その仕事は自身の個人的人間関係に深い影響を与えることがある。

解説 どんな人がいいコーチになるか問われたロブは，5つ目の発言の後半で，empathy ... is one of the key skills と述べ，続けて，完璧な人ではなく，苦労して困難を克服した経験のある人がいいと言っている。**2** がロブの発言の have had your own struggles と overcoming difficulties を faced emotional challenges とまとめている。

二次試験・面接　トピックカード A 日程　問題編 p.160

ここでは，A日程の5つのトピックをモデルスピーチとしました。

A日程

1. Will artificial intelligence transform the world economy for the better?

I believe artificial intelligence will transform the world economy for the better. There are three reasons which support my position. Firstly, AI has already created a lot of wealth around the world. For example, banks and insurance companies use AI to help them make investments and provide personalized service to customers. As AI becomes more sophisticated, it will be able to prevent stock market crashes. Stock markets will use algorithms that analyze investment patterns to help governments and regulators find warning signs of a potential crash or fraud. Secondly, when AI becomes more advanced, it will be able to minimize damage from natural disasters. The algorithms will provide earlier warning of things like typhoons and earthquakes so that steps can be taken to make them less destructive. AI will not only save lives, but protect the economy. Finally, I predict that AI will positively reform the job market. While AI cost-effectively improves and automates tasks for industries, human workers can start to do more work in the highly-skilled fields of IT. Also, many people will do more creative and innovative jobs, ranging from producing music to designing products. All of these activities will stimulate the economy. Although some people worry that AI may behave dangerously in some cases, I think that because of the points I mentioned, it will transform the world economy for the better.

解説　「人工知能は世界経済をよりよいものに作り替えるか」

トピックに対して全面的に賛同する解答例。①AIは富を作り出し株価暴落を防げる，②自然災害による被害を最小限にできる，③雇用市場を好意的に改革する，という3つの理由を挙げている。①と②はどちらもAIのアルゴリズムを用いた予測能力の活用についてだが，フィンテックと環境問題という異なる視点を取り入れている。単にAIの利点を述べるのではなく，「経済にプラスになるか」という論点を捉えられるよう注意しよう。

2. Is it ever acceptable for companies to monitor employees' social media use?

　I believe that it's acceptable for companies to monitor employees' social media use for the following three reasons. First of all, many employees deal with confidential information in their jobs. If there is a leak of this information on social media, it can be extremely harmful to the company's reputation. Therefore, companies have the right to protect themselves by monitoring workers' social media usage. Secondly, using social media during working hours can be a big temptation for staff members. If employees are posting or reading things online instead of doing their jobs properly, it can lead to considerable productivity losses that will affect the company's profits. Therefore, companies have to monitor their workers' computer usage during working hours, including social media. Finally, businesses must protect their computer networks from hackers and online attacks. If employees use their work computers to access social media sites or use the same passwords on social media as they do at work, hackers may find a way to access the company's computer network. Such attacks are becoming increasingly common and are a significant threat to companies these days. Based on these arguments, I think it's clear that companies need to monitor their employees' social media use.

>　**解説**　「会社が従業員のSNS利用を監視することは許されるか」
>　トピックに対して企業の立場からその必要性を，①機密情報の漏えい，②生産性の低下，③サイバーアタックによる脅威，という3つの観点から主張している。どの問題も近年話題になっているものばかりだ。構造はシンプルに3つの理由をFirst of all, Secondly, Finallyで始めているが，企業側がさらされる危険性について聞き手がその状況をかなり具体的にイメージできるところまで落とし込んでいる。このサンプルのように丁寧な展開で説得力のあるスピーチを心がけよう。

3. Is reducing poverty the key to reducing crime?

　I believe reducing poverty is the key to reducing crime. I'll present three reasons explaining why I believe this is true. First, one factor that can lead to high crime rates is a lack of education. If people had higher incomes and could afford better education, they would be less likely to commit crimes. Education would provide more opportunities for people to live stable and comfortable lives, and as a result, people would follow their moral values and be good citizens. Secondly, many crimes are committed by people suffering from drug and alcohol addiction or mental illness. Many of them cannot afford to get treatment for their problems. If poverty were reduced, more people would be able to get the addiction or psychological treatment they need to live productive lives. Finally, crime tends to happen in areas where there is a lot of poverty. When there are many unemployed people and low-income families in an area, the residents have little hope that they'll ever be able to live comfortable lives by working at ordinary jobs. So there is more temptation to turn to crime. However, if more people had jobs and higher incomes, this would be much less likely to happen. In conclusion, if we want to reduce crime, fighting poverty would be the best way to do it.

> **解説** 「貧困を減らすことは犯罪を減らす鍵となるか」
>
> トピックに対して賛成の立場からのスピーチ。理由として貧困がもたらす以下の3点，①教育の不足，②薬やアルコールへの依存，③不安定で希望の見いだせない環境，について言及している。このように，前半により明瞭な理由を述べ，後半に主観的な理由＋未来への希望などで前向きにスピーチを終えることができれば，説得力のあるものになるだろう。

4. Should violent sports, such as boxing, be banned from the Olympics?

I don't believe that violent sports should be banned from the Olympics. I have three reasons to support my belief. First, although some people say violent sports are hazardous for athletes, I don't think those people realize how safe these sports really are. Athletes use high-quality equipment, and there are strict rules that enforce the practice of safety. In addition, there are always trained medical personnel at competition sites in the case of injury. Another reason is that violent sports can actually make society less dangerous. Some people are naturally aggressive, and sports allow them to release their aggression in a controlled situation. Similarly, watching violent sports in the Olympics can also help people to relieve stress and aggression. Finally, combat sports are significant in various world cultures. The sport of judo, for example, has become a symbol of Japan and its culture. It's taught worldwide, and its emphasis on health and self-defense has helped millions of people. The Olympics is an excellent chance for people to watch the highest level of judo competition, so it would be a shame if it were banned. To sum up, because they are safe, can reduce violence, and contribute to world culture, it would be a huge mistake to ban violent sports from the Olympics.

> **解説** 「ボクシングのような暴力的なスポーツはオリンピックで禁止されるべきか」
>
> トピックに対し，①危険そうに見えるだけで実は安全，②暴力的な世間の欲求のガス抜きに役立っている，③格闘技は文化的にも重要な意味が

ある，の3つの理由から禁止すべきではないと主張している。最初にAlthough some people say ... と世の中には正反対の見方もあることを示すことで，逆に自分の主張の客観性を強調している。効果的なアプローチだが，しっかり練習しておかないとこの部分に余計な時間をかけてしまいかねない。表現などを十分に練習してからスピーチに組み込もう。

5. Agree or disagree: More resources should be spent on pushing the frontiers of science

I agree that we should spend more resources on pushing the frontiers of science. Some governments are actually cutting scientific funding these days, but I think they should do the opposite and increase it. My first reason is the environment. Global warming has become an urgent crisis, and science is the best way to solve the problem. We urgently need to develop green technologies, such as efficient solar energy. If we fail to do so, global warming will lead to water shortages, natural disasters, and animal and plant extinction. Secondly, advancements in science bring economic benefits. Technologies such as computers, for example, have increased prosperity around the world. If we wish to do things like eliminating poverty and ensuring further economic growth, we need to increase science investments. Finally, I'd like to talk about healthcare. Although many groundbreaking medical treatments have been developed recently, we need to devote even more healthcare resources to save more lives. Deadly diseases, such as cancer, are becoming more common, so we need to increase the effort to develop treatments for them, no matter how expensive it is. All things considered, it is essential that we spend more resources on promoting the progress of science.

解説　「賛成か反対か：科学の最先端を切り開いていくためにより多くの投資がされるべきだ」

最近増えている Agree or disagree タイプの設問だが，普通の Yes / No 問題と同じ対応だ。このスピーチでは最初に I agree that ... と命題の内容を再度繰り返しているが，話したいことにより時間を割きたければ I agree with the statement. だけでもよいだろう。ここでは，①環境問題解決，②継続的経済成長，③医療・健康促進，の3つの視点から科学技術へのより積極的な投資が不可欠であると主張している。

MEMO

旺文社の英検®書

☆ 一発合格したいなら「全問＋パス単」！
旺文社が自信を持っておすすめする王道の組み合わせです。

☆ **過去問集** 過去問で出題傾向をしっかりつかむ！
英検® 過去6回全問題集 1〜5級
[音声アプリ対応] [音声ダウンロード] [別売CDあり]

☆ **単熟語集** 過去問を徹底分析した「でる順」！
英検® でる順パス単 1〜5級
[音声アプリ対応] [音声ダウンロード]

模試 本番形式の予想問題で総仕上げ！
7日間完成 英検® 予想問題ドリル 1〜5級
[CD付] [音声アプリ対応]

参考書 申し込みから面接まで英検のすべてがわかる！
英検® 総合対策教本 1〜5級
[CD付]

問題集 大問ごとに一次試験を集中攻略！
DAILY英検® 集中ゼミ 1〜5級
[CD付]

二次対策 動画で面接をリアルに体験！
英検® 二次試験・面接完全予想問題 1〜3級
[DVD+CD付] [音声アプリ対応]

このほかにも多数のラインナップを揃えております。

旺文社の英検® 合格ナビゲーター https://eiken.obunsha.co.jp/
英検合格を目指す方のためのウェブサイト。
試験情報や級別学習法、おすすめの英検書を紹介しています。

※英検®は、公益財団法人 日本英語検定協会の登録商標です。

株式会社 旺文社 〒162-8680 東京都新宿区横寺町55
https://www.obunsha.co.jp/